The Brahmo Samaj
AND THE SHAPING OF THE
Modern Indian Mind

The Brahmo Samaj
AND THE SHAPING OF THE
Modern Indian Mind

David Kopf

PRINCETON UNIVERSITY PRESS

PRINCETON, NEW JERSEY

0721987

Publication of this book has been aided by a grant from
The Andrew W. Mellon Foundation

This book has been composed in V.I.P. Baskerville
Clothbound editions of Princeton University Press books
are printed on acid-free paper, and binding materials are
chosen for strength and durability

Printed in the United States of America by Princeton
University Press, Princeton, New Jersey

To Calcutta
EX ORIENTE LUX

To have paced out the whole circumference of modern consciousness, to have explored every one of its recesses—this is my ambition, my torture, my bliss.

NIETZSCHE

Contents

List of Tables   ix

List of Illustrations   ix

Abbreviations   xi

Preface   xiii

Chronology   xxi

Part I. *Reformist Modernism*

1. Unitarian Social Gospel and the Foundations of Hindu
   Modernism
                                                                    3
2. The Deification of Science, Humanity, and Reason:
   Brahmo Secularism
                                                                    42
3. Identity, Achievement, Conscience: The Human
   Development of the Bhadralok Reformer   86
4. Family, Faction, and the Dilemmas of Political Reform
   under Colonialism
                                                                    129

Part II. *Nationalist Ambivalence*

5. The Confrontation between Trinitarian Christianity and
   Reformed Hinduism
                                                                    157
6. The Issue of Brahmo National Identity and the Rise of
   Cultural Nationalism
                                                                    176
7. The Frustration of the Bhadralok and the Making of a
   Revolutionary Nationalist: The West Desanctified   187

Part III. *Synthesis*

8. Western-Inspired Brahmo Evangelism and the Vaishnav
   Spirit in the Mofussil
                                                                    217
9. World Crisis and the Quest for an Ideology of Salvation:
   Keshub, Prophet of Harmony
                                                                    249
10. Rabindranath Tagore as Reformer: Hindu Brahmoism
    and Universal Humanism
                                                                    287

Part IV. *Conclusion*

11. The Brahmo Reformation Diffused: Bengal's Legacy to   313
    Twentieth-Century India

    Notes   336
    Bibliography   357
    Index   387

List of Tables

1. Principal Members of the Progressive Faction of the   28
   Brahmo Samaj Who Were Founders of the Sadharan Samaj
2. Most Outstanding Brahmos in Arts, Sciences, and   115
   Professions circa 1900
3. Principal Ascetic Missionaries of the Sri Durbar   230
4. Report of Brahmo Samajes in India by 1872   325

List of Illustrations

1. Keshub Chandra Sen and his wife   256
2. P. C. Majumdar, 1917   285
3. Maharani Suniti Devi of Cooch Behar (eldest   328
   daughter of Keshub Chandra Sen)
4. Maharaja Nripendra Narain Bhupa Bahadur of   328
   Cooch Behar

Abbreviations

BI	Bose Institute, Calcutta, D. M. Bose Collection
BSPA	Bangiya Sahitya-Parisat, Archives, Calcutta
BSP-PCRP	Bangiya Sahitya-Parisat, Calcutta, Prafulla Chandra Ray Papers
DACB	District Archives, Cooch Behar
GLA-UC	Goethels Library and Archives, St. Xavier's College, Calcutta, Upadhyay Collection
KL	Sati Kumar Collection, Calcutta, J. Koar Letters
RBM	Rabindra Bharati Museum, Calcutta
RBMA	Rabindra Bhaban Museum and Archives, Santiniketan, West Bengal
RBMA-TFP	Rabindra Bhaban Museum, Santiniketan, Tagore Family Papers
RBM-KTC	Rabindra Bharati Museum, Calcutta, Khitindranath Tagore Collection
SBSL-ARSBS	Sadharan Brahmo Samaj Library, *Annual Report of the Sadharan Brahmo Samaj*
SBSL-BSC	Sadharan Brahmo Samaj Library, Calcutta, *Brahmo Samaj Chronicles*
SBSL-SDCC	Sadharan Brahmo Samaj Library, Calcutta, Sophia Dobson Collet Collection
SCAC-GRC	Sanskrit College Archives, Calcutta, General Records and Correspondence of Sanskrit College

Preface

This book is a detailed history of the Bengali forerunners of Indian modernization. It is an analysis of the lives, the consciousness, and the ideas of early rebels against the Hindu tradition whose community has come to be known as the Brahmo Samaj. Originally the Calcutta Unitarian Committee in 1823, the Brahmo Sabha in 1829, and finally the Brahmo Samaj in 1843, this community played a crucial role in the genesis and development of every major religious, social, and political movement in India from 1820 to 1930. Brahmos were the first Hindus to defy the taboo about crossing the seas to the West. They were the first social reformers, and the first to extend full equality to their women. Brahmos were the pioneers of liberal political consciousness and Indian nationalism, and they introduced ethical and professional standards into Indian law, medicine, natural sciences, teaching, journalism, and civil administration. Significantly, the man often known as the "Father of Modern India," Rammohun Roy, was also the founder of the Brahmo Samaj.

My study of individual Brahmos, out of whose minds the ideas of modernization emerged, has convinced me of the critical need to study their ideas in relation to their consciousness, and their consciousness in relation to their life. Within the ideological framework of most chapters, then, I have included relevant biographical data to establish causal relationships between the ideas and the actual life situations of the men who conceived them.

When one examines such ideas as Rabindranath's Hindu Brahmoism, or Keshub Sen's New Dispensation, or Brahmobandhab Upadhyay's desanctification of the West against the consciousness and life style of each of these individuals, then one is struck immediately with the intricate problem of identity that underlies the human participation in the process of modernization. From a variety of biographical sources, many in Bengali and never before used in research, I have been able to trace the question of identity to the preadult lives of the intelligentsia. The data reveal patterns of what Erik Erikson has called identity crisis. Though I have made use of Erikson's basic notions of identity in human development, I have restrained myself from trespassing into the mysterious land of psychiatric research. Also, whereas Erikson worked with well-documented, well-researched charismatic heroes from Martin Luther to Thomas Jefferson, I had often to work with scanty sources of lesser-known persons; but my own objective as a historian has been to illuminate the special problem of identity among the Bengali intelligentsia from a great number of cases, and to arrange these subsequent patterns in appropriate categories. I do not believe that identity crisis among the modernizing Brahmo intelligentsia can be understood deeply through a study of only one of its conspicuous leaders, even Keshub Sen or Rabindranath Tagore. Not only should the historian study the group portrait, but he must study the problem over generations, to achieve the advantage of diachronic perspective. Finally, the shifting identities of the Bengali intelligentsia were so integral a part of India's encounter with the West that identity crisis appears to be as much a social as a psychological process.

I do not want to leave the reader with the impression that I have given undue emphasis to the psychohistory of ideas at the expense of the social history of the Brahmo Samaj. My focus on the Brahmo community has given me the opportunity to pursue further the origins and growth of the bhadralok, or new urban Hindu elite of Bengal. John Broomfield's study of this class in the twentieth century and his concept of bhadralok have been well appreciated among Bengali historians. As Broomfield himself intimated, the Brahmos were so characteristically bhadralok that they represented the group as its ideal type.[1] The new material I have collected on Brahmo factionalism opens up new vistas on the relationship between the movement as a whole and the pragmatic conflict resolution of social interests and ideological issues among the various factions. Brahmo factionalism also raises questions about the relative importance of dominant families in bhadralok society, and about common origins in caste, religious orientation (Shakto or Vaishnava), and birthplace (village, district, and whether from East or West Bengal).

My framework is explicit in the divisions of the book. Part I deals with the relatively modernist or reformist intelligentsia, who were favorably disposed to the progressive ideas and values of the West. Part II presents the counter group of Brahmos, whose ambivalence to reform stemmed from their sensitivity to Western dominance and their own idea of nationalism. Part III discusses three attempts to bring together modernistic reform and national identity without the one violating the other. Then Part IV explores the Brahmo

missionary movement and offers some generalizations on how
Brahmoism expanded over the whole of India and on its impact
upon the twentieth-century Hindu middle class.

In Chapter 1, the fundamental question is how the rational faith
and social gospel of nineteenth-century British and American Unitarianism affected the modernizing process in Bengal. I should
make it very clear that my concern here is with the history of Bengali Unitarianism, and not with its history in the West. The reason I
selected certain sources on Unitarianism in the West is because they
were meaningful to individual Bengalis, who appropriated them
and adapted them to their own conditions. For those interested in
the image of India among American Unitarians, I would suggest
they read the work of Professor Spencer Lavan, a historian and
himself a Unitarian minister.[2]

In Chapter 2, the ideas of humanism, scientism, and rationalism
are explored in the milieu of Bengal and as values among the modernizing intelligentsia. Again, the reader will learn nothing new
about such ideas in the West, but he will learn precisely what they
meant in an Asian situation. In Chapter 3, I address myself to the
problem of identity among the modernizing wing of the intelligentsia by analyzing the cycle of human development in the bhadralok reformer. Starting with an idea suggested by Erikson, I try to
show how a liberalized Brahmo functional equivalent of the Puritan ethic resolved a youthful identity crisis and led to an adult consciousness of achievement and the responsibility of social reform.
Chapter 4, entitled "Family, Faction, and the Dilemmas of Political
Reform under Colonialism," addresses the question of political
consciousness among the modernizers, and raises some doubts
about current interpretations of the so-called moderate nationalists
who founded the Indian National Congress. Cases of constitutional
agitation within the Brahmo Samaj are intended to deepen our
understanding of how the idea of liberalism actually worked in the
Bengali context.

Chapter 5 traces nationalism in Bengal to the confrontation between Trinitarian Christianity and reformed Hinduism. Chapter 6
demonstrates how the second stage in the development of nationalism resulted from the issue of national identity during the Brahmo
schism of 1866. This chapter analyses the ideology of cultural nationalism and places "National" Mitra, the *National Paper*, and the
Hindu Mela in their proper context. In Chapter 7, I return to identity crisis, but this time from the vantage point of the nationalist.
From a close study of the making of a revolutionary nationalist, I

seek to dramatize the contrast between the problem of identity in the nationalist and that of the modernizer. What I suggest in the nationalist pattern is an identity crisis based on "them and us" rather than on tradition and modernity, a saintly ethic in place of the Puritan ethic, and a persisting tendency throughout life to leap radically from one identity to another.

My treatment of Brahmo synthesis in Chapter 8 begins with a history of neo-Vaishnavism in Bengal, to establish exactly how and when progressive Western values were fused with Hindu religious inspiration. This chapter also investigates the modernizing consciousness of the non-English-knowing, non-Westernized intelligentsia, and that of the Western-educated who best expressed their reformism through the emotionalism of the indigenous faith. Chapter 9 is perhaps the most ambitious in tracing the complex ideological development of Keshub Chandra Sen, prophet of universal religion or the New Dispensation. Sen is so pivotal to the book that questions of identity, consciousness, and modernization are arranged in this chapter around the thesis that history is shaped largely by the thoughts of great men, even though I do not subscribe in any way to the "great man" approach to history. I find it remarkable that every single Brahmo discussed in this book who joined the movement after 1860 was personally converted to the new faith and community by Keshub Sen. But, ironically, his supreme religious synthesis, probably the greatest intellectual adventure of nineteenth-century Bengal, had the least influence of any of his ideas in his own time. Section III, on synthesis, ends with Chapter 10, which represents my own particular interpretation of Rabindranath Tagore and his ideological contribution in the proper setting of Brahmo history. I have tried to see Rabindranath as a historical man and human being with an ambiguity of identity which he resolved by reinterpreting the Brahmo heritage, and by developing his two most influential ideas of universal humanism and Hindu Brahmoism. The latter idea is especially important as an introduction to Chapter 11, "The Brahmo Reformation Diffused: Bengal's Legacy to Twentieth-Century India."

I have chosen a method of transliteration from Bengali to English that is becoming increasingly common in Bangladesh; it was, in fact, conceived in consultation with linguists there. Instead of using diacritical marks in the manner of Sanskritized Bengali, the tendency now is to drop literary formalities and conventions for a straightforward, though not always accurate, form of transliteration. One main point of departure from earlier attempts to do this is that nineteenth-century Anglicized distortions of Bengali words have been largely eliminated. Thus "Chunder" now becomes "Chandra" and "Chatterji" becomes "Chattopadhyay." Second, commonly or universally accepted spellings of Bengali names and expressions now take precedence over transliteration into esoteric spellings. Though "Tagore" is "Thakur" in Bengali, "Tagore" is preferred because it is commonly accepted by those who know and use the name. Though I was influenced by several Bangladeshi scholars, I take full responsibility for the choice of method.

This book would hardly have been possible—certainly not in its present form—without the sources, without libraries and archives and the people who maintain them, without cooperative, friendly, and informative persons, and without financial support for travel and local maintenance while doing research.

I am thankful that Sivanath Sastri, spiritual leader of the Sadharan Brahmo Samaj, published *A History of the Brahmo Samaj* in 1912. Though he wrote it from the partisan point of view of a true believer, it is a monumental descriptive work of the highest quality. I suppose that my own justification in rewriting that history from a fresh perspective is in answer to Sastri's own reservation as expressed in the preface to the first edition: "I was deterred by the thought that, having been one of those who had a leading hand in the organisation of a schismatic Brahmo movement, I was not the proper person to write a history of the Brahmo Samaj, and that it should be left to outside observers."[3]

I appreciate the help that Dilip Biswas, Professor of History at Sanskrit College, and Archarya of the Sadharan Brahmo Samaj, gave me in finding many useful sources in the library and archives of the Sadharan Samaj. I was very fortunate to have gone through the Sophia Dobson Collet Collection at the Sadharan library before Naxal threats to destroy nineteenth-century collections forced the Samaj to remove it.

Without the help of Sati Kumar Chatterji, the world's foremost specialist on the history of the Keshubite Brahmo organization, I could not possibly have written the chapters dealing with Keshub Chandra Sen, the ascetic Vaishnavas, Protap Chandra Majumdar, and the New Dispensation. His personal warmth, his devotion to nineteenth-century studies, his intellectual companionship, and his hospitality I shall never forget. To Chatterji I also owe a recommendation to the West Bengal Government to allow me to visit the archives of the former Maharaja of Cooch Behar. Chatterji wanted me to find out the truth about the aftermath of the controversial marriage of Keshub Sen's eldest daughter to the prince of Cooch Behar in 1878.

My information on the Adi Brahmo Samaj, from Debendranath to Rabindranath Tagore, comes chiefly from the archival sections of Rabindra Bharati Museum in Calcutta and Rabindra Bhaban Museum in Santiniketan. I am most thankful to Subhendu Mukherji, then an archivist at the Rabindra Bhaban, who let me see the "Tagore Family Papers" at a time when Visva Bharati University was closed because of political assassinations and the threat of a campus war between the local CPM and the Naxalites. I am deeply indebted, also, to the hospitality and cooperation of my old friend and colleague, Protul Chandra Gupta, who was then Vice Chancellor of Santiniketan. I shall not forget his "Bengali James Bond" who accompanied us on our evening strolls across the campus.

In January 1971, I crossed over into East Pakistan to do research on the spread of Brahmoism into the rural towns of East Bengal. I want to thank my host in Dacca, Manik Ghose, whose financial help and guidance sustained me in a strange land during a period of political unrest. The Maghutshab festival at the Brahmo mandir, Dacca, was one of the most interesting religious festivals I ever attended in South Asia. Manik Ghose was later tortured by the Pakistan army, but fortunately he survived and lives on in Dacca as head of the Brahmo community of Bangladesh. I might add that the Rammohun Roy library, contiguous to the Brahmo mandir in Dacca, which provided me so much useful material on the lives of East Bengali Brahmos, was completely looted by the Pakistan army in 1971.

Most of the basic books on Brahmo leaders, institutions, and activities were available at the British Museum, the India Office Library in London, and the National Library, Bangiya Sahitya Library in Calcutta. The staff at these places were always helpful and courteous to me. Data on the Christian missionary reaction to Brahmoism came from the London Mission Society, to whom I also extend my heartfelt thanks. I wish I could mention the dozens and dozens of Brahmos who showed me family records and other materials that proved valuable as building blocks in fabricating the grand design. In particular, I should like to single out Miss Sujata Bose, whose anecdotes on the life and times of her grandfather, Ananda Mohun Bose, were invaluable in recreating the social atmosphere of late nineteenth-century Calcutta. I want to thank

Shyamasree Devi, who helped me to locate sources on her grand-father, Ramananda Chatterji. I hope her husband, Professor P. Lal, forgives me for having visited the famous Lake Gardens residence not in hot pursuit of Writers Workshop publications, but rather to discuss Brahmo history with his wife.

I thank my assistant, Amalendu Chakrabarti, a very sincere, hard-working young man who shared many an adventure with me in North Calcutta, when the burning of a tram would halt all public transportation, or when we went to Cooch Behar and Santiniketan together. I want to express my amazement at, as well as my thanks to, Tarun Mitra, executive officer of the American Institute, Calcutta, for his enormous capacity to tolerate my excessive enthusiasm for Brahmo history. His caustic wit, eclectic reading habits, efficiency, and love of small children made the lives of me and my family a beautiful experience.

I am also profoundly grateful to the Office of International Programs, University of Minnesota, for a grant to London (summer 1969), the Department of Health, Education, and Welfare for a Hays Fulbright grant to India (1969-1970), and to the American Institute of Indian Studies who appointed me a senior fellow in Calcutta (1970-1971). Without the enthusiastic support of these agencies, I could not have carried out my research to its conclusion. Finally, I want to express my appreciation to those who have read the manuscript at different stages of its development and offered me advice on how I could improve the book. I am especially indebted to John Broomfield of the University of Michigan, Blair Kling of Illinois University, Spencer Lavan of Tufts University, V. C. Joshi of Jawaharlal Nehru Museum and Archives, Pradip Sinha of Rabindra Bharati University, Gholam Murshid of Rajshahi University, Margaret Case of Princeton University Press, and Joanna Kirkpatrick of Bennington College. Above all, I should like to extend my love to the most maligned but greatest city in the world, Calcutta.

Chronology

1823   Establishment of the Calcutta Unitarian Committee by Rammohun Roy, Dwarkanath Tagore, and William Adam.

1828   Rammohun Roy founds the Brahmo Sabha, a universalist theistic society.

1839   Tattvabodhini Sabha, or truth-teaching society, started by Debendranath Tagore to arrest trinitarian Christian conversions in Bengal.

1843   Birth of Brahmo Samaj when Debendranath institutionalizes Rammohun's ideology of Hindu reform. Vedanta accepted as the authentic scriptural source of Hinduism.

1851   Akkhoy Kumar Dutt convinces Debendranath to give up Vedanta as the "book" of the Hindus.

1855   Renewal of Unitarian influence on Brahmoism when Charles Dall, American Unitarian missionary arrives in Calcutta. Dall, only non-Indian member of the Brahmo Samaj, to remain in Calcutta to his death in 1885.

1857   Keshub Chandra Sen, charismatic theistic reformer, joins the Brahmo Samaj as disciple of Debendranath.

1859   Tattvabodhini Sabha abolished after Vidyasagar, its famous secularist reformer and secretary, resigns in protest against Keshub.

1861   Keshub and the younger Brahmos try to convince older Brahmos of the need for practical social reforms and a mission society.

1866   Formal schism between liberal younger Brahmos and conservative older Brahmos leads to creation of the Brahmo Samaj of India under Keshub.

1867   Brahmo missionaries first propagate the Hindu reformation across the subcontinent, making use of the railway system.

1867   Bijoy Krishna Goswami persuades Keshub to use Vaishnavism in the service of Brahmoism.

1870   Keshub visits England as a spokesman for the Hindu reformation.

1870   After returning from England, Keshub establishes the Indian Reform Association, primarily to publish cheap literature for the poor and to educate women.

1872   Marital reform among the Brahmo community finally wins approval of the government with the enactment of Act III, the Brahmo Marriage Act.

1872   The new tradition of reformed Hinduism is forcefully articulated before orthodox Hindu leaders of Calcutta by Adi Brahmo Samaj president, Rajnarian Bose, in a lecture entitled "The Superiority of Hinduism."

1874   Liberal faction within Brahmo Samaj of India organizes the Samadarshi party to counter Keshub's growing conservatism.

1875   Keshub abandons Unitarian gospel of social reform, turning instead to the intellectual study of all major Eurasian religions. He and his disciples begin a series of elaborate seminars known as "Pilgrimages to the Saints."

1876   Political-minded members of the Samadarshi party found the Indian Association in support of the moderate nationalist ideology of Surendranath Banerji. The movement leads a decade later to the formation of the Indian National Congress.

1878   Marriage of Keshub's eldest daughter to the Cooch Behar maharaja in violation of the Brahmo Marriage Act of 1872, becomes exciting cause for a second major schism in Brahmo history. Samadarshi party reconstitutes itself as the Sadharan Brahmo Samaj.

1879   Keshub and his loyal followers inaugurate the Nava Vidhan, or New Dispensation Church, with Keshub as prophet of a universal religion.

1884   Death of Keshub followed by renewed factionalism within the New Dispensation between the Vaishnava-dominated

Durbar and the Christian Unitarian group headed by Protap Chandra Majumdar.

1886   Resignation of Bijoy Krishna Goswami as Missionary, indicative of factional struggle within the Sadharan Samaj between devout Vaishnava theists and the rationalist Vedantists led by Sitanath Tattvabhusan. Differences are reconciled, however, by Sivanath Sastri, Sadharan spiritual leader.

1891   Brahmo philanthropy among Bengal's urban and rural poor considerably extended with the creation of the Das Ashram under the direction of Ramananda Chatterji.

1893   Protap Chandra Majumdar invited by American Unitarians to help organize the first world Parliament of Religions in Chicago.

1907   Bengali Brahmos start the Society for the Improvement of Backward Classes, which is the earliest pioneering movement in India dedicated to ameliorating the conditions of Hindu untouchables.

1911   Rabindranath Tagore assumes leadership of the Adi Brahmo Samaj, and becomes charismatic hero of younger generation of Brahmos. His action arrests growing tendency of Brahmos to defect to revolutionary nationalism.

1912   According to Sivanath Sastri, the peak of Brahmo expansion is reached by this year, when 232 Samajes were reportedly active throughout the subcontinent.

1921   Rabindranath Tagore formally inaugurates *Visva Bharati University* at Santineketan as an expression of Brahmo universalism.

1941   Death of Rabindranath this year signifies end of an era and the decline of the Brahmo Samaj per se. But his philosophic program of fusing Hinduism with Brahmo ideas and ideals lives on among the progressive middle-class Hindus of contemporary India.

PART I

Reformist Modernism

I've been in India, Pyle, and I know the harm liberals do. We haven't a liberal party any more—liberalism's infected all other parties. We are all either liberal conservatives or liberal socialists; we all have a good conscience.

GRAHAM GREENE

CHAPTER ONE

Unitarian Social Gospel and the Foundations of Hindu Modernism

ON September 28, 1833, a funeral sermon was delivered for a Bengali by a prominent British Unitarian in the port city of Bristol on the west coast of England. Rammohun Roy had died a day earlier while visiting the Carpenter estate in Stapleton Grove. The Reverend Lant Carpenter, who had known of Rammohun and his work for fifteen years, spoke with great depth of feeling about the career of the "enlightened Brahmin from the British capital of Hindustan" who was "undoubtedly a Unitarian." "My heart is with the Unitarians," the Bengali had told Carpenter often.[1]

The Unitarianism that in Carpenter's mind linked Rammohun to his British counterparts represented a new and radical approach to religion, society, and ethics. It was a pioneering faith that emerged out of the changing conditions of the nineteenth-century world. It challenged many of the religious presuppositions of the traditional societies of Eurasian civilizations. Though Unitarianism was never a mass movement, the implications of its protest had far-reaching effects among the modernizing intelligentsia in India. Three simple though radical ideas for the time (1815 to 1835) provided the link between the enlightened few in Calcutta and the enlightened few in England and the United States.

The first was liberal religion, or the substitution of a rational faith for the prevailing popular religions of the world, which, they thought, increasingly curtailed the freedom of human beings by enslaving them to mechanical rituals, irrational myths, meaningless superstitions, and other-worldly beliefs and values. The second was the idea of social reform, or emancipation in which all known penalized classes and groupings such as workers, peasants, and women were to be elevated through education and the extension of civil rights to participate fully in the benefits of modern civilization. Finally, there was the idea of universal theistic progress, or the notion that the perfectability of mankind could be achieved by joining social reform to rational religion.

"Though dead," said Lant Carpenter of Rammohun Roy, "he yet speaketh and the voice will be heard impressively from the tomb." That voice, which still can be "heard by his intelligent Hindoo friends," will continue to express the Unitarian credo:

> It may excite them to renewed and increased effort to carry on the work of intellectual and moral improvement among their countrymen: to diffuse the pure light of religion which his writings contain, among those who are yet debased and superstitious; to give the advantages of a wise education to the young and uninformed to rise themselves and teach others to rise, above the narrow prejudices of caste and sex; and thereby weaken that thraldom which so much intercepts the progress of truth and virtue; and elevate by knowledge . . . those who may thus be the friends and companions of the present generation and whose early instruction and training will so much promote the welfare of the next.[2]

One tragic aspect of Rammohun's death was that it precluded a meeting with American Unitarians whom he admired, and with whom he had hoped to establish closer ties for coordinated Unitarian programs on an international scale. One, William Ellery Channing, whom a Unitarian later called the "Rammohun Roy of America,"[3] was, since the revolt of 1815, a leading spokesman of liberal Unitarianism in the United States. According to Lucy Aiken, who corresponded with Channing from England, and who had met Rammohun at various social gatherings in London, Rammohun had spoken to her on September 6, 1831, "of ending his days in America." "I have just seen the excellent Rammohan Ray," she wrote, "and he speaks of visiting your country . . . and to know you would be one of his first objects." After Rammohun's death (October 23, 1833), she recorded sadly to Channing that "Ray has been frustrated of one of his cherished hopes, that of seeing you face to face, either in this or the other hemisphere."[4]

The second American Unitarian with whom Rammohun evidently had long years of correspondence was Joseph Tuckerman.[5] Indeed, the reason why Rammohun came to Stapleton Grove as the house guest of Lant Carpenter was to discuss preliminary matters in anticipation of Tuckerman's visit to England in 1833, when the Unitarian representatives of three cultures were to meet and discuss a common program of social action.

The ideology of liberal Unitarianism was slowly emerging from the parallel experiences of like-minded individuals in Boston, Bristol, and Calcutta. Channing, who was Rammohun's equal as an inventive and versatile genius, did not begin his revolt against the established church until 1815, when he was thirty-five years old.[6] The main target within orthodoxy for the Harvard-trained Unitarian liberals such as Channing, Emerson, and Parker was Calvinist religion and ethics, with its stress on man's damnation and God's vengeance through the eternal fires of hell, as well as the notion of the predestined election of a privileged few. In orthodox Christianity generally, Channing and others repudiated all forms of religious revelation, the doctrine of Trinity, and those aspects of popular religious behavior that prohibited the human being from achieving that "sense of unity with God" experienced only by those dedicated "to a life of reason."[7]

Most probably, however, the most radical departure in the thought of Channing and other Unitarians was not on the level of theology and religion. Though it is true that the abandonment of revelation for intuition led Unitarians into the mystical realms of monism and transcendentalism, when modified by reason and a constructive social philosophy this led not to other-worldliness but to intellectual emancipation. In fact, the general Unitarian outlook was itself a reflection of a new social conscience and consciousness.

According to one biographer, Channing was "not content to preach an arid religion from the moral isolation of the pulpit, but sought to realize his Christian ideals in the market place of daily living."[8] In an important sermon entitled "Religion, a Social Principle," he referred to "progressive religion," which purifies men's minds by stressing "good done to others." "Religion was no private affair, between man and his maker," he said, "nor was it a secret to be locked up in our hearts." Rather, religion is to be "communicated, shared, strengthened by sympathy and enjoyed in common with all."[9]

The underlying assumption of the new social gospel of Unitarianism is contained in a simple sentence by Channing, which was radical for the time he lived in: "every human being has a right to all the means of improvement which society can afford." Like most Unitarians, Channing was a staunch abolitionist, and believed that "never will man be honored till every chain is broken."[10] He expressed a strong sympathy with those oppressed by colonialism,[11] and in 1840 he viewed his own work in establishing night schools for workers as the start of a "social revolution." As he put it, "I see in it a repeal of the sentence of degradation passed by ages on the mass of mankind. I see in it the dawn of a new era, in which it will be understood that the first object of society is to give incitements and means of progress to all its members.[12]

Joseph Tuckerman, with the same Bostonian upbringing and Harvard degree as Channing, was equally affected by the misery of the poor and underprivileged. In 1826 he left a well-to-do congregation to whom he ministered in order to work and live among the urban poor of Boston. Soon a chapel was constructed for his use, which was not only a religious center but a social welfare center designed to find ways and means of alleviating the agonies of poverty.[13]

In 1839 a tract of Tuckerman's was published describing his philosophy of religion as a social gospel, and his method for coping with the problem of the poor. As was common with pre-Marxist reformers, he attributed poverty to intemperate habits, and rebuked those who profited from the small pay of poor workingmen—earnings that were diverted from family savings to gin mills. He was dismayed with the callous indifference of nominal Christians who "ignored the masses in the city" and made no allowance for the fact that these people would increase in proportion to the increase of urban areas. After describing the grim life of the poor, he advocated a program of moral training and attending to physical wants "as a means of inculcating the desire for self-improvement."[14]

When Tuckerman came to England, in 1833, he immediately lectured in the new industrial cities of the Industrial Revolution, where he found cesspools of humanity living in conditions that defied description. Lant Carpenter's daughter, Mary, was so taken with Tuckerman's humanitarian spirit and practical efforts to help the poor that she turned to social work as a career. When in 1835 Tuckerman returned to America, he left behind him in Bristol a Society for Visiting the Homes of the Poor of the Congregation. The Carpenters could now gain entrance into the families of the poverty-stricken to render assistance to them directly. Mary Carpenter was its secretary for twenty years.[15]

Lant Carpenter had himself come to the same conclusions as had the Americans about the need for religious leaders to help the poor. In 1817 he had first come to Bristol to take over the congregation at Lewin's Mead, a notorious slum neighborhood in the port city. There, like Tuckerman in Boston, this well-educated elitist could so modify his sermons as to be appreciated by the common man, and he was certainly the first minister at the Unitarian chapel to attract a mass following. Again like his American counterparts, he stressed education and moral training for the purpose of self-strengthening. Until his death in 1840, the same year Tuckerman died, Carpenter remained consistently liberal both socially and politically. Carpenter joined the antislavery agitation in 1824, he worked to alleviate the deplorable conditions in British prisons, and in 1831 he joined the great struggle for the passage of the Reform Bill.[16]

Equally interesting are Carpenter's theological expositions on the new Unitarianism, which not unlikely influenced Rammohun Roy in Calcutta. In a discourse published as early as 1810, which Carpenter entitled *On the Importance and Dissemination of the Doctrine of the Proper Unity of God*, there is a brief but illuminating summary of the pillars of modern Unitarianism as it later came to be known after its formal inauguration in England and America in 1825. There was, for example, an eloquent defense of what may be termed the pivot of Unitarianism, or the belief in God without second, which is so reminiscent of Rammohun Roy in his own writings. There was the stress on Christ as the ethical teacher, which again recalls Rammohun's approach in his *Precepts of Jesus* written a decade later. There was Carpenter's defense of the Unitarian doctrine of atonement, which not only denied all the mystery and metaphysics surrounding the crucifixion, as well as the Calvinist view of sin and damnation, but also reestablished the image of a merciful God full of justice and compassion for mankind.[17]

Besides rational theology and the social gospel, there appeared a third integral part of liberal Unitarian ideology, which not only set off Unitarians from the more orthodox Christians in their own culture, but contributed greatly to bridging the differences between themselves and the more enlightened portion of contemporary Calcutta society. That same liberal religious and social spirit which Unitarians attributed to their imitation of the true ethical Christ, they gradually extended tolerantly to peoples of all cultures. If most religious institutions of the time were moving away from the universal humanism and rationalism of the eighteenth century toward the romanticism and nationalist self-glorification of the nineteenth, Unitarians maintained an outgoing cosmopolitanism, which ultimately became the most significant pillar of the Unitarian faith.

On June 8, 1826, Joseph Tuckerman, in response to an appeal from Rammohun's Calcutta Unitarian Committee, printed and circulated a public letter addressed to American Unitarians asking for their support in missionary enterprises. Rammohun Roy, the Unitarian "spokesman of the East," began Tuckerman, has "solicited our assistance in establishing there in Calcutta a perpetual Unitarian mission." Tuckerman then went on to say that: "Native gentlemen in India have contributed largely to the cause of establishing Christian worship upon Unitarian principles, in their country; and they with their English associates, are earnestly requesting the aid of Unitarians in England and America for the accomplishment of their object."[18]

Especially noteworthy about Tuckerman's letter was his commentary on the principles of missionary enterprise, which he appears to have shared with another sympathetic American Unitarian named Henry Ware (the same Henry Ware who had corresponded with Rammohun from as early as 1821).[19] On the surface, Tuckerman's conviction that the Christian gospel was superior to anything indigenous in Asia for the purpose of effecting religious and social reform may seem to differ little from the attitude of the orthodox Christian missionary. But a closer examination of Tuckerman's position reveals that what he meant by Christianity was not the institutional trappings that followed Christ's death, but simply Christ's acknowledged teachings, which could be readily adapted anywhere. Rather than equate Christianity with Western civilization, he demonstrated how the benevolence of Christianity "modified and improved civil government and public morals [in the West]" itself.

Moreover, Tuckerman rejected the most common beliefs by orthodox missionaries that all non-Christians were heathens consigned for all time to damnation. Tuckerman could not accuse "God of partiality in conferring the benefit of revelation upon so small a portion of the human race." To him, it was a shockingly false idea "that the actual knowledge of revelation is necessary to salvation." His conclusion was that Christianity ought not to come to India to save souls, but to improve the human condition and society: "from what it has done, bad as Christianity is, we can demonstrate its adoption to the condition and to the wants of all men, and its tendency to an indefinite improvement of the human mind and character."[20]

Channing's *Remarks on Creeds, Intolerance, and Exclusion* is equally revealing in the context of a developing Unitarian universal humanism. Christianity, he argued, was a spirit rather than a fixed creed, dogma, institution, or theological system. "Christian truth is infinite," he wrote, "it is a spirit . . . of boundless love and cannot be reduced to a system." Thus, the spirit of Christ's teachings can transcend human diversity or "the immense variety of opinion and sentiment in the world."[21] His conclusion directly applicable to Unitarian missionary principles is contained elsewhere, but is meaningful only when set against his liberal interpretation of the Christian spirit, which to him was not an integral part of any cultural system but was free, tolerant, and adaptable.[22]

Precisely how and when Unitarianism reached Calcutta—if indeed it reached there at all by diffusion in its earliest stage—it is impossible to say. It may be argued that Bengali Unitarianism was a movement parallel to the Unitarian movements in the West, but some caution must be exercised in this judgment for the reason that the conditions which gave rise to it in Bengal were not akin historically to those of England and America. Nor when viewed as a functional equivalent can it be said that the ideological developments in Bengal and the West served the same purpose. An alien ideology, whether Marxism today in Bengal, or Unitarianism over a century ago, should be seen essentially in terms of historical and cultural relevance. It should be analyzed in the manner it stimulates change or in the manner it is adapted by the receiving culture for its own purposes.

A hasty generalization might also be drawn from the remarkable coincidence of events in the early history of modern Unitarianism both in the East and in the West. We have already seen how Channing, Tuckerman, and Carpenter led their revolt against orthodoxy from approximately 1815, and that their revolt became formally accepted with the establishment of the Unitarian Association in 1825. In Bengal, Rammohun Roy began his leadership in the Hindu reformation in 1815, after he settled permanently in Calcutta. His revolt against the orthodox Hinduism of his day occurred between 1815 and 1820. By 1822 he had helped form a Calcutta Unitarian Committee and by 1825/26, his scattered writings in their cumulative effect already contained a kind of syllabus for activists dedicated to Hindu reform.[23]

No doubt, there is a connecting link between Calcutta and the West which helps to explain the simultaneous happening of overtly similar acts. Certainly the progressive part of the world of the time was on the eve of momentous economic, social, and political revolutions; and certainly, as far as the religious community was concerned, Unitarians were among the most articulate early advocates of the varieties of social emancipation that would ultimately result from the revolution.

But between India and the West there was a great elementary difference with reference to these momentous changes. No Industrial Revolution, no universal suffrage, no universal compulsory education swept through India in the nineteenth century, as it swept through England and the United States. Thus, the "Bengali Unitarian" operating from the British capital of India could only participate intellectually in the modernization that was radically altering European cultures in the last century. So long as the fundamental material aspects of modernization were arrested in their own country, the corresponding reformation of Hinduism was bound to be limited because only a comparative handful could be educated as moderns. It was also bound to be exotic, not in a cultural sense but socio-economically, because the technological environment remained primitive.

This leads to a second vital area of difference between Bengali Unitarians and their Western counterparts. The very presence of alien rule in India created a rather delicate psycho-cultural relationship between the native intelligentsia and the British officials. There were two basic cultural attitudes of concerned British officials to Bengalis and their society: the Orientalist and the Westernizer. The well-meaning Orientalist type tended to be sympathetic to Indian traditions, and went so far as to engage himself in academic research geared to rediscovering the Hindu past or to systematizing available knowledge of Indian civilization. As a social reformer he started many projects designed to update Indian traditions and institutions by fusing them with modern values from the contemporary West. He fashioned himself as a syncretistic modernizer of the Hindu traditions. The well-meaning Westernizer, on the other hand, who tended to downgrade Indian traditions as dead and useless, urged instead complete assimilation to Western cultural traditions, which were in his mind increasingly equated with modernization.

This conflict of modernizing alternatives between Westernizers and Orientalists, known in history as the Anglicist-Orientalist controversy, is of considerable significance in our present context because it provides a frame of reference for the development of Bengali intellectuals, including Unitarians such as Rammohun Roy. Rammohun, who learned English well and was close to a number of Europeans in Calcutta, was greatly influenced by the cultural attitudes of foreigners to whom he related, and whom he used as windows to the West. As I have shown elsewhere, Rammohun lived during the Orientalist period of policy formulation, and it was Orientalist scholarship that provided him with the building blocks necessary for his ideological reconstruction of Hindu society and faith.

In comparison to Western Unitarianism, therefore, the Bengali variety was a far more complex phenomenon, in that the problems faced by a Rammohun Roy were always magnified by the perspective of cross-cultural contact. Unlike Channing in America or Carpenter in England, who sought to convince their countrymen to liberalize their religion and care for the underprivileged among them, Rammohun was continually challenged by the question Europeans in India invariably raised: do you improve the lot of Hindus from within the system or must you undermine it by assimilation to a foreign system? As for the specific content of religious Unitarianism, for example, Rammohun was confronted by the central question as to whether India should follow Christ (however denuded of later excrescences), or whether India should follow some Christ-like figure in her own tradition who seemingly represented the same principles.

Thus, it should come as no surprise that Rammohun's ideological development and career as a Hindu reformer reveals many twists and turns, contradictions and inconsistencies. But on balance, I would argue that his preoccupation with an authentic Hindu tradition or golden age which he sharply set off against a dark age of popularized religion and social abuses stamped him as a figure in the camp of the Orientalist modernizers.[24]

As a leading pioneer of the reformation, his non-Westernizing sympathies were equally apparent in the way he adapted Christian Unitarianism to Indian circumstances. To be sure, Rammohun's *Precepts of Jesus* was so thoroughly Unitarian in a European sense, and so sophisticated in theological erudition and subtlety, that one could easily be misled about the author's identity. Indeed, one has only to compare the *Precepts* by Rammohun published in 1820 with a tract by Lant Carpenter that appeared at approximately the same time, entitled *An Examination of the Charges Made against Unitarians and Unitarianism*, to understand the remarkable ideological kinship between the Bengali intellectual and Western Unitarians.

M. M. Thomas, in his recent analysis of the debate between Rammohun and Marshman calls it "the first Christian intellectual encounter of a serious theological nature in modern India."[25] Thomas, who has written the best book to date on the impact of Christianity on the Indian renaissance, has unfortunately in this debate understressed the Unitarian-Trinitarian aspect and perhaps overstressed the nationalist polemic aspect whereby an Indian intellectual takes European Christianity to task. My own impression is that the *Precepts of Jesus* was largely an extension of the debate in the West between Unitarianism and orthodox Christianity. Rammohun's primary concern was to maintain the unity of God against all the false ideas and techniques devised by man to adulterate the purity of monotheistic faith. Thus, he repudiated all myths, mysteries, miracles, and images, which made a mockery of the unity of the Godhead. Rammohun here resembled the familiar liberal and rationalist Unitarian upholding the historic, ethical Christ, while rejecting vicarious atonement, the Trinity, and other "fabricated fables."[26] Rammohun's view that justice and mercy were more acceptable to God than sacrifice was equally Unitarian in spirit, as was his scriptural reliance on the "Synoptic Gospels with the emphasis on Jesus' teachings rather than the Gospel of St. John with its meditation of Jesus."[27]

Joshua Marshman's argument was entirely a defense of orthodox Trinitarian Christianity, and the crux of his defense, as Thomas has ably shown, was "to criticize Rammohun for teaching doctrines opposed to those held by the mass of real Christians of any age."[28] The rational, critical approach to Scripture was, in terms of a wider appeal, actually a chief weakness not only in Rammohun but in Unitarians generally. The Unitarian attack on orthodoxy was, in fact, an attack on the religion of the masses, where the unity of God was most grossly humiliated and violated. Unitarianism provided Rammohun and his successors with a thinking man's reformation, and the attempt to transmit the new religion to the unintellectual, uncritical masses left the Bengali reformers in a great dilemma.

Shortly after the debate, Rammohun and a former Baptist named William Adam formed the Calcutta Unitarian Committee. By 1823, Adam, Rammohun, and Dwarkanath Tagore seem also to have established a Unitarian Press in north Calcutta.[29] In that same year, Rammohun, under the pseudonym of Ram Doss, conducted another debate in the local press with an orthodox Christian physician named Tytler. Remarks by Tytler make it evident that Rammohun was considered by Europeans to have become a Unitarian—a term of disrepute to the orthodox. But the debate was no mere theological conflict, as in the case of Marshman. Faced with narrow, bigoted attacks on Hinduism in particular and Asians in general by a member of the ruling foreign elite, Rammohun was forced into a defensively nationalist position. But because Rammohun was a modernizer and not a revivalist, he faced his opponent as an Orientalist would a Westernizer.

This is well elucidated in Rammohun's "Reply to Certain Queries Directed against the Vedanta," printed in the *Brahmmunical Maga-*

zine on November 15, 1823. Dr. Tytler had accused Rammohun of reading into the Vedanta the sublime message of Christ. Since only the Christian Scriptures were revealed, Rammohun's interpretation was a fraud. In reply, Rammohun, with his customary analytical approach, proceeded to prove that the message of the Vedanta not only contained the unity of God, but did so in a way superior to the Judeo-Christian Bible. Unlike the Bible, the Vedanta did not attempt to categorize the attributes of the Almighty—a gesture that Rammohun found both anthropomorphic and futile. That Rammohun was now using Unitarianism in an Indian way was evidenced by his attack on the Trinity. He argued that whereas Christianity required a blood sacrifice to expiate the sins of man, the Vedanta taught that the "only means of attaining victory over sin is sincere repentence and solemn meditation." In the following quotation, it is clear that the Bengali reformer had made a kind of cultural transference from the Synoptic Gospels to Sankaracharya: "The sin which mankind contracts against God by the practice of wickedness is believed by us to be expiated by these penances, and not as supposed by the Querist, by the blood of a son of man or son of God, who never participated in our transgressions."

Equally interesting was Rammohun's use of the comparative religious approach, which constituted another marked difference between himself and his Western Unitarian counterparts. Channing and Tuckerman maneuvered primarily in one religious tradition and aimed to reform it, whereas Rammohun was challenged by the need to reconcile at least two major faiths. In the process Rammohun was compelled to think comparatively, with the result that his vision sharpened in a refreshingly expansive manner, leaving a narrow sectarian view of the universe behind forever. He could, for example, in the same reply to Tytler, rebuff his opponent for attacking popular Hinduism by pointing to the comparable malpractices in popular Christianity: "A Hindoo would also be justified in taking a standard of Christianity the system of religion which almost universally prevailed in Europe previous to the fifteenth century . . . and which is still followed by the majority of Christians with all its idols, crucifixes, saints, miracles, pecuniary absolutions from sin, trinity, transubstantiation, relics, holy water, and other idolatrous machinery." Rammohun could argue that as the authentic Christian tradition was submerged and corrupted, so the authentic Hindu tradition was likewise submerged and corrupted. He willingly admitted that "our holy Vedanta and our ancient religion has been disregarded by the generality of moderns."[30] This approach, infused with a modernist outlook, placed the Hindu reformation movement on an Orientalist foundation. Indigenous traditions could be defended at the same time as they were modified according to progressive values in contemporary Western societies. Though the foundation was a precarious one, it saved the Hindu reformation repeatedly from the snare of militant nationalism.

It is in this context that we ought to assess the social aspect of the Hindu reformation. There is little doubt that Rammohun was as much inspired by the social gospel of Unitarianism as he was by its rational religion. But it is well to be reminded of the differences between historical circumstances in Bengal and in the West. We have already noted that Unitarians in England were among the first to point an accusing finger at nominal Christians for ignoring the plight of the proletariat in the new urban industrial centers. But in India in the early nineteenth century, there was no fundamental change in technology, no Industrial Revolution, no industrial urban centers, and no industrial proletariat. Moreover, foreign rule in India placed social reform in the context of cultural encounter. The question of social reform, therefore, was less the need to cope with the consequences of a changing social, economic, and political order as it was a question of British attitudes to Indian culture and Indian responses to those attitudes. Because of the profound influences of the Orientalist heritage, social reform entailed an internal revitalization aimed at bringing India up to the level of the other progressive nations of the world.

Thus, the inventive Rammohun Roy used the building blocks provided by Orientalist scholarship, and adapted Unitarian social reform to Bengali circumstances. In so doing, it is important to point out, he was no more traditionalist or revivalist than were Western Unitarians who referred back to the historic Christ of the ethical teachings to promote modernist ends. With a Puritan fervor quite possibly reinforced by his Islamic background, Rammohun attributed social evils in Hindu religion and society to the poisonous effect of "idolatrous notions" which, by the middle period of Indian history, had completely undermined the pure Upanishadic belief in the "unity of the Supreme Being as sole Ruler of the Universe."[31]

Of more interest, perhaps, in terms of social action is the way Rammohun altered the object of Unitarian compassion in the West to suit the special historical circumstances in Bengal. If Unitarians increasingly worked to alleviate the sufferings of the industrial proletariat, Rammohun chose the Bengali Hindu woman as his "proletariat." With extremely important implications for his successors, he saw in her depressed condition the root cause of social immobility in India. The new social conscience and consciousness of Unitarianism was in Rammohun almost entirely directed to the miserable state of Hindu women. He found them uneducated and illiterate, deprived of property rights, married before puberty, imprisoned in purdah, and murdered at widowhood by a barbaric custom of immolation known as sati. One has only to read Rammohun's works on social reform to realize that most of it deals with one aspect or another of man's inhumanity to women in Bengal. The conclusion is that only by freeing women and by treating them as human beings could Indian society free itself from social stagnation.

By 1829, it appears that Rammohun had abandoned the Unitarian Committee and had helped to form a new kind of organization known as the Brahmo Sabha. The only relevant document that might have suggested what Rammohun intended to accomplish through the Sabha is the Trust Deed for the new "church," if one could call it that, signed by Rammohun and his friends on January 23, 1830.[32] Unfortunately, except for a few general universalist Unitarian principles contained in the document, it is impossible to say whether Rammohun hoped the Brahmo Sabha to be a domesticated form of the Unitarian church or a general meeting place for people of all faiths to congregate and pray. What makes it even more difficult to ascertain Rammohun's purpose is the fact that ten months after signing the deed, he left for England, never to return.

Between Rammohun's death in 1833 and the arrival in Calcutta of the American Unitarian missionary, C.H.A. Dall, in 1855, Western Unitarianism seems to have had no appreciable effect on the modernizing Bengali intelligentsia. In fact, until the 1840s the movement advanced little, ideologically or institutionally. Ram Chandra Vidyabagish was the intellectual leader or spiritual preceptor of the Brahmo Sabha during that decade.[33] Vidyabagish, however, extremely limited in his knowledge and appreciation of Western Unitarianism, could not continue the momentous work started by Rammohun, and for all practical purposes the Sabha became just another Hindu sect with a Vedantic bias.

In 1843, Debendranath Tagore changed the name of the Brahmo Sabha to Brahmo Samaj (society) and revitalized the movement considerably, but there is no evidence that he was motivated in doing so by Unitarian considerations. We do know that when

Charles Dall arrived in Calcutta to start his mission in November 1855, he immediately established contact with Debendranath and other Brahmos.[34] Apparently, Debendranath's "suspicion of foreigners" alienated Dall, who was not made to feel welcome at Brahmo meetings and functions, and Dall later accused Tagore of denying "free speech and discussion" at Brahmo meetings.[35]

On the other hand, Dall seems to have developed a long and enduring relationship with Debendranath's arch critic and rival, Keshub Chandra Sen. We can only speculate how much influence the Reverend Dall had on Keshub and his followers, who broke with the Adi (original) Brahmo Samaj in 1866 to form an association of their own. Dall had come to Calcutta believing that Rammohun Roy, author of the *Precepts of Jesus*, had been a Unitarian Christian like himself. Dall seemed convinced that Keshub's new Brahmo association would ultimately move in the same direction, and that Keshub was Rammohun's true successor. Not only had he come to look upon Keshub as his own son, but after years of "cheering him, instructing him and helping him," Keshub's theism in its last "distillation," was the "theism of Jesus."[36] Keshub so admired Dall that he welcomed the American missionary into the Brahmo Samaj as its only non-Indian member, allowed him to sign the Brahmo covenant, and gave him every opportunity to spread Unitarian literature and ideas among Brahmos in Bengal and elsewhere.[37] Through Dall's efforts, thousands of copies of the complete works of Channing, Emerson, and Parker were circulated among Brahmos.[38]

We can surmise that Dall influenced Keshub about the validity of the Unitarian social gospel as well, and his activism was also respected by the more radical wing of the Calcutta intelligentsia. He started schools for boys in Calcutta, supported female education and emancipation generally, and helped the urban poor in various ways.[39] In this context, of some consequence was the visit to Calcutta by Lant Carpenter's daughter, Mary, in 1866, to promote the Unitarian social gospel in India. She visited Vidyasagar and many of the younger Brahmo radicals. Her warmest admirer and friend was Monomohun Ghose, the "Bengali Unitarian," while her first visitor upon arriving in Calcutta was Keshub Sen, whom she viewed at the time as the truest follower of her father's friend, Rammohun Roy.[40]

Between 1866 and 1872, Keshub Sen was deeply enthusiastic about the Unitarian social gospel, which he observed first hand during a trip to Great Britain in 1870. He seemed convinced that

British reform efforts could be duplicated in India. Thus, under his direction the Indian Reform Association was established in November 1870 to promote "the social and moral reformation of the Natives of India." To accomplish this end, "it is proposed to avoid as far as possible mere theories and speculation," and to aim "chiefly at action."[41] Five sections of the association were set up: charity, temperance, women's improvement, mass education, and cheap literature.

For charity Keshub set up a social service committee that stood ready to help the distressed during times of natural catastrophe. Predating the Ramakrishna mission by at least two decades, Keshub sent volunteers to Behala in 1871 to help fight the crippling effects of a malaria epidemic.[42]

Keshub placed temperance high among his social reforms, and joined the Temperance Society in its effort to reduce the import of whiskey from England and to penalize its distributors in India; in the West, reformers now looked upon extreme alcohol consumption as a root cause of poverty. The magnitude of the problem, especially among the industrial proletariat, was immense. At the time Keshub visited London, it was reported that if

> London's 100,000 pubs were laid end to end, they would have stretched a full thirty miles. In East London alone, . . . every fifth shop was a gin shop; most kept special steps to help even tiny mites reach the counter. The pubs featured penny glasses of gin for children; too often child alcoholics needed the stomach pump. Children less than five years old knew the raging agonies of delirium tremens or died from cirrhosis of the liver . . . all the products of a £100 million a year trade.[43]

In Bengal it was the Western-educated who appear to have suffered most from excessive drinking habits and the subsequent physiological, psychological, and sociological effects. A general perusal of biographical sources conveys the impression that almost every Calcutta elite family had cases of young men who died directly from the disease, or who committed suicide as a result.[44] Peary Charan Sarkar, who started the Temperance Society in Calcutta, saw his own brother die of the disease. Keshub organized Bands of Hope among the young all over Bengal to prevent the habit from materializing among the college students who, from Rajnarian's time, imbibed liquor as a badge of Western civilization.

To improve the condition of women, Keshub sought to "promote the intellectual, moral, and social development by means of girls' schools, adult schools, and moral schools; the publication of books and periodicals; and communicational meetings."[45] As shown previously, this was considered by Rammohun Roy the crucial area of reform.

It was in the fields of mass education and cheap literature that Keshub made his most radical departures as a social reformer. For the first time, a Bengali reformer acknowledged in a practical program that the peasants and workers must be reached for a full-scale improvement of Indian society. Whether, as some Indian Marxists have suggested, Keshub met Karl Marx in Europe is irrelevant, since the program he established was influenced more by the Salvation Army and Unitarians than by socialist groups. Nevertheless, Keshub was a pioneer in his attempt to shift, at least partially, the target of social reform in Bengal away from the underprivileged female to the underprivileged masses.

He set up an industrial arts school in Calcutta to teach laborers such crafts as tailoring, clock repair, printing, lithography, and engraving.[46] He established a night school, the first of its kind among Brahmo Samajes in South Asia. Perhaps most important in the long run was Keshub's achievement in awakening mass consciousness by printing a paper known as *Sulabh Samachar*, which was designed not for the bhadralok or scholars, but for "the people who do not have much time, but must labor day and night. We want to offer them news of their country, of the world, instruct them in morality, entertain them with stories, inform them of their history, inspire them with the tales of great men, and teach them about the differences between superstition and science."[47]

Salvation through class struggle was not the message of *Sulabh Samachar* for the working man. Rather, as with most liberal publications of the nineteenth century, hope for the poor lay in cultivation of moral discipline, self-reliance, and a good basic education. The function of the newspaper was clearly to convey current events, classroom knowledge, and moral instruction in simple, lucid Bengali prose to those who could afford a single pice per issue. And far more than any other paper of the period, it was immensely popular. After fourteen months of publication from its first appearance on November 15, 1870, it had sold 281,149 copies. Even as late as 1879, one year after the split of Keshub's Samaj, the *Sulabh Samachar* still sold 190,000 copies.[48]

On the spiritual side of Unitarianism, Dall's most important conquest in the Keshubite organization was Protap Chandra Majumdar. Majumdar and Dall were for years Brahmo missionaries to non-Bengali Indian urban elites on the subcontinent. Dall, in fact, saw himself as duel emissary of the American Unitarian Church and of Keshub's Brahmo Samaj of India. In South India, Majumdar propagated the faith in Madras, while Dall lectured in Bangalore. Majumdar's career as a dedicated missionary may well have been inspired by Dall's example. Dall urged Brahmos to preach the new rational religion with "apostolic faith, self-denial and trust."[49] Dall's sermons and lectures, which aimed at wedding Christian Unitarianism with Indian Brahmoism, proved remarkably similar to Majumdar's own.[50] Though, for obvious reasons, Protap Chandra never referred to Christ in his mission tours, it was the image of the ethical Jesus, which Rammohun Roy had beautifully articulated and which Dall stressed in his lectures, that appealed to him more and more in his later years.[51] The critical issue on which Majumdar ultimately supported Dall as against most other Brahmos, including Keshub, was whether Christ was indeed the last word among universal reformers. Most Brahmos argued that he was one among equals, like Buddha, Confucius, and Mohammed, but Majumdar favored the idea that all reformers were most perfectly personified in Christ.

In 1874, Majumdar's passion for extended mission tours took him to England and America for the first time. Among Westerners, Protap Chandra spoke freely in support of Dall's Christian Unitarianism. No Brahmo up to his time, and certainly no Bengali before Vivekananda, spoke so often to so many different kinds of people and with such effectiveness as did Majumdar. Under trying travel conditions, and with short intervals of rest between talks, Majumdar later recalled, he gave seventy speeches in three months, in fifty Unitarian chapels to a total audience of forty thousand people.[52]

By 1882, Protap Chandra had dedicated a book to Rammohun Roy as a pioneer of Christian Unitarianism, "who lighted the holy lamp of eclectic theism."[53] The title was *Faith and Progress of the Brahmo Samaj*, and the book established strong parallels between Rammohun's spiritual universalism and Keshub's. Majumdar found no need of reconciling the ethical Christ of the Unitarians with eclectic theism, a position identical to Rammohun's. And like Rammohun, Majumdar believed that the challenge came not from Unitarians but from Trinitarian Christians.

In 1883, Protap Majumdar published the *Oriental Christ*, probably his most important book, and among Unitarians in America assuredly his most popular.[54] The idea that motivated him to compose the work is contained in his letters to Max Müller. Written at the same time as the book, these letters demonstrate his sympathy to Keshub's task of building a church around a "science of comparative theology." He told Müller that "what you are doing as a philosopher and as a philologist we are trying to do as men of devotion and faith." Were not Brahmos waging the "same war against exclusiveness and bigotry"? In defense of the comparative method, he concluded that "the Fatherhood of God is a meaningless abstraction unless the unity of truth in all lands and nations is admitted. And the brotherhood of man is impossible if there is no recognition of the services which the great peoples of earth have rendered unto each other."[55]

There was at least one crucial difference, however, between Keshub's universal ideal as expressed in the New Dispensation and P. C. Majumdar's universal ideal as expressed in the *Oriental Christ*. Superficially, the *Oriental Christ* may be viewed as a nationalist polemic, much as Keshub's famous lecture of 1866 on "Christ, Asia, and Europe." On this level, the book is an effective attack on the Eurocentric notion of Jesus, which according to Majumdar has been taken "completely out of historical and cultural context." Like Rammohun Roy, Majumdar argued that Christ was an "Oriental," and it was his task to make the prophet's image conform as much to the "original" authentic atmosphere and circumstances as was possible. The result is to offer the objective reader the true Oriental Christ as opposed to the "erroneous European conception of Christ."

But a closer analysis of the book reveals it as an enriched conception of the Unitarian Christ, which was started early in the century by Rammohun Roy in his *Precepts of Jesus*. It is no accident that the image of Majumdar's Oriental Christ was similar to the image of the Unitarian Christ—both devoid of superstition, miracle, and mystery. Dall's influence is clear enough in Majumdar's Christian Unitarian conception of the prophet of Judea embodying the most perfect form of cosmopolitan religion. Unlike Keshub, Majumdar placed Christ above all other reformers because "His doctrines are the simple utterances about a fatherhood which embraces all the children of men, and a brotherhood which makes all the races of the world one great family."[56]

It is interesting that the Unitarian view of a century ago on Christ's role among the ethical and religious reformers, which Majumdar boldly affirmed, has recently been rediscovered and freshly appreciated by Indian Trinitarian Christians. M. M. Thomas, for one, has perceptively isolated this belief as constituting the real issue dividing Keshub Sen from Protap Majumdar during the period of inaugurating the New Dispensation Church. According to Thomas, Majumdar came finally to see prophets other than Christ as "isolated principles of God's nature" limited by the times and cultures they lived in. Thus, "Socrates is for the Greeks, Moses is for the Hebrews, Confucius for the Chinese, Krishna for the Hindus." But there is a need for a "central figure, a universal model, one who includes in himself, all these various embodiments of God's self-manifestations." Majumdar assigned to Christ this function: "He is the type of all Humanity. Humanity broken up before and after is bound up in him, so that he is the human centre and bond of union in the religious organizations of mankind."[57]

In September 1893, the American Unitarians sponsored a Parliament of Religions in Chicago. "For the first time in history," said one of their later reports, "the leading representatives of the great Historic Religions of the World were brought together." It was an important event, the conveners believed, "for it would promote and deepen the spirit of . . . brotherhood among the religious representatives of diverse faiths." It would help ascertain what religions "held and taught in common" and the "important distinctive truths taught by each religion."[58]

On the Advisory Council and Selection Committee of the Parliament of Religions was Protap Chandra Majumdar, whose trip to Chicago was his second visit to the United States. The Unitarians thought so well of Majumdar that after the Parliament closed, they invited him to deliver the prestigious Lowell lectures in Boston. They evidently saw in this elegantly dressed and highly Westernized Bengali Brahmo their own perfect counterpart in Hindu society.

Protap Chandra's own speech to the Parliament, "The World's Religious Debt to Asia," was an extremely able one emphasizing the need to understand and accept equally the varying spiritual impulses and higher moral purpose in all the major religions of all the great traditions throughout the world. No doubt appealing to the liberal theologians present at the august gathering was Majumdar's conviction that social progress must be fulfilled in the name of religion. "Nature is spiritual still," he said, "but man has become material; Asia calls upon the world to once more enthrone God in his creation."

It was an intellectual's lecture: formal in structure, precise in vocabulary, and deliberately elevated in tone and style to attract the cultivated mind. His easy comparative approach to "Asian religious principles," which was totally antinationalist in sentiment, was characteristic of the universalist-inspired Brahmos. To be sure, he used expressions such as "the Asian Religion" and the "genius of Asiatic spirituality," while equating Asian spirituality with the model of the Hindu great tradition.[59] But in the absence of cultural defiance, aggressiveness, and apology, one can only conclude that his phraseology was intended more as terms to fit a conceptual scheme than as nationalist propaganda. Though it is difficult today to assess the overall impression made by Majumdar on the Americans at the meetings, we do have one comment by a prominent Unitarian, who said that Majumdar's was the best talk given at the Parliament. The reason was that he knew "all religious systems" and is the "prophet of the new dispensation of faith, hope, and love—the apostle of the Oriental Christ."[60]

It was Majumdar's notion of an Oriental Christ rather than his broad universalist leanings that explains his popularity among American Unitarians during the latter decades of the nineteenth century. This is evident in letters to the Bengali from American well-wishers.[61] In a letter of December 30, 1899, the Unitarian president of Harvard University, Samuel A. Eliot, officially offered to pay Majumdar's way to Boston (his fourth and final visit to the United States) to attend the seventy-fifth anniversary of the American Unitarian Association.[62]

On the night of December 5, 1893, Majumdar had given his last talk to Unitarians at the Arlington Street Church in Boston. Addressing the congregation as friends, he emotionally proposed taking them all back with him to Calcutta. "Your Emerson is there," he said, "your Theodore Parker is there and have done for the Brahmo Samaj greater good than you know." "And some of our great men are here too," he continued, "Rammohun Roy and Keshub Sen." On Keshub, he commented that: "If today, Keshub Chandra Sen had been living, he would have stood here before you a glorious figure, a transcendent spirit, a true child of God, a true benefactor of his race. It seems to me that the great men of your land and the illustrious departed of my land are here from the bosom of God, calling us all into greater friendship, into greater sympathy, into greater identity, than there ever has been yet."[63] However maudlin these sentiments may appear today, they were important in generating affection for Majumdar from Boston Unitarians, whose warm feeling won for the Bengali Brahmo a grant of $1,000 a year, which was paid to him annually until his death in May 1905.

Unitarian American friends occasionally visited Calcutta, as in December 1896, when Dr. John Henry Barrows, the prime mover behind the Parliament of Religions, came to India as a Unitarian representative to the Brahmo Samaj. Majumdar not only welcomed him but arranged at his Peace Cottage one of the largest receptions ever given by a Brahmo in Calcutta. This event rekindled memories of the now vacant Lilly Cottage next door, where two decades earlier Keshub had held receptions and soirees that he and Reverend Dall had attended regularly.

In 1900, Protap Chandra found himself in America for the third time. In his diary entry of May 23, he referred enthusiastically to the beginnings of a new era in the history of comparative religion. During that very day in Boston, there was founded the "International Council of Unitarian and other Liberal Religious Thinkers and Workers." Majumdar was invited to its first congress, held in Amsterdam in 1903, where he read a paper on "What Is Lacking in Liberal Religion?"[64]

During his last years in Calcutta, Majumdar openly expressed his predilections for Christianity, but he consistently refused to join any established Christian sect, carefully preserving his integrity as a Brahmo with a Unitarian conception of Christ's mission and character. In 1899, his friend Max Müller had urged him to declare himself a Christian because Brahmos like himself were so indebted spiritually to Jesus. Majumdar replied: "that we are disciples of Christ but we shall not call ourselves Christians because in so doing we shall add another petty sect to the innumerable petty sects into which Christians had divided themselves."[65]

Nevertheless, in the later years Majumdar and his coterie had become Christian in all but name. In 1901, Majumdar's Brahmos observed Good Friday. In 1903, in Bankipur, Bihar, Protap celebrated "Christmas Utsab," which featured two days of "services, sermons and readings on the personal experiences of Jesus." Majumdar's final public lecture was on the "Meaning and Message of Good Friday." It contained a defense of the celebration and another eloquent testimony to "Jesus Christ who was no mere prophet among prophets but was the universal man, the universal prophet."[66]

In 1873, it appeared to Trinitarian missionaries that Dall's influence on Keshub Sen was so profound that the Brahmo Samaj of India had become Unitarian in all but name. Members were exposed to Unitarian pamphlet literature, which was being translated into Bengali. At their Allahabad conference in 1873, missionaries reported that Brahmos had decided in favor of Unitarianism. The Reverend Jardine revealed to his colleagues that Dall was an active member of the Brahmo Samaj and intimated that the Samaj had become a virtual branch of the American Unitarian Association by means of financial and moral support.[67] Curiously enough, Jardine left out of his report the fact that in February 1873, the Brahmos had accepted Dall's proposal to establish a theological school in Calcutta along Unitarian lines. Such a school would "improve the powers of logic and clear thinking," Dall had argued in a neutral vein, without reference to the issue of Christ's status among prophets.[68]

By 1875, however, the Christian missionaries were aware of a profound change in Keshub, whom the Reverend Dyson viewed as succumbing to an "exorbitant oriental imagination." According to him, Keshub had invented an "empty synthesis of religious thought that would fail because it failed to satisfy the deep and powerful cravings of the human heart."[69]

Most of the Christians believed that beneath the rational facade of Keshub's experiment was emotionalism, idolatry, and mysticism. Even worse to the missionaries was the apparent neglect of ethics in Keshub's recent religious development. In the 1878 intelligence report from Calcutta to the Church Mission Office in London, there is an interesting reference along these lines:

> In recent years a marked growth of devotional fervor, solitary contemplation, ascetic austerities, and sweetness of prayer is evident among the more advanced Brahmos. But unfortunately there is no corresponding elevation of moral character. [Amid] the development of the softer emotions, the sterner virtues seem to have been neglected, such as frankness, justice, forgiveness, veracity, justice and self-surrender. On the other hand, there has been an increase of mutual jealousy, pride, vanity and selfishness among even the best members.[70]

Keshub added fuel to the fire of his critics' wrath by defending his new path with customary brilliance, sophistication, and wit. In March 1877, for instance, his lecture at the Town Hall, Calcutta, which he entitled, "Philosophy and Madness in Religion," seemed to anger not merely Westerners (including Charles Dall) but Bengali Westernizers, as well. The most significant aspect of the lecture was the total absence of any faith in social improvement or the idea of progress. What Keshub argued throughout was contained in the following dichotomy between two prevailing forms of madness:

"The men of the world are mad for riches, outward refinement and the pleasures of the senses. For material wealth and natural prosperity, for selfish enjoyments and selfish honors they are running mad. In matter and self they are wholly immersed. The question naturally suggests itself—why should not men be equally mad for God?"[71]

In 1877, Keshub decided to break publically with Dall and to disavow Christian Unitarianism. In an editorial of the *Indian Mirror*, dated April 8, 1877, presumably written by Keshub's brother Krishna Behari Sen, Dall was attacked for misrepresenting himself as a Brahmo. "Mr. Dall is accustomed to call himself a Brahmo," wrote Krishna Behari, "when he has to deal with Brahmos," and a Christian missionary when "he is in the company of Christians." He is "always pleased to combine the two functions in his person." The editor then proceeded to give public notice of the split: "We have never been able to persuade Mr. Dall that he cannot be a Brahmo and a Christian at the same time, and that his views of Christ, Christianity, and the Christian Church, are very different from what the Brahmo Samaj holds. . . . All Brahmos in whatever Presidency, ought to know that Mr. Dall is a Unitarian Christian missionary, pure and simple, and we dispute his right to preach Christianity under the cover of the Brahmo name."[72] Evidently, it was Dall's earlier criticism of Keshub as a would-be modernizer turning his back on social reform that sparked the angry outburst by Krishna Behari Sen. On January 22 of that year, Keshub had delivered a public lecture on "The Disease and the Remedy," in which he placed great emphasis on "the terrible curse . . . and loathsome disease of sin that has it roots in the depths of man's being." We have been "only cutting off branches of the tree," said Keshub, "while the root of corruption lies intact below."[73]

In Dall's eyes, Keshub was backsliding into a form of Calvinism. He singled out the jargon of the lecture, which included expressions such as "natural depravity," "sinful human nature," and even "original sin." These were all false issues to the ardent theistic reformer, who had little sympathy with Keshub's diagnosis for the disease of sin afflicting mankind and the spiritual therapy recommended.[74] Keshub had advocated moral discipline, meditation, asceticism—all leading to the birth of a new type of spiritual man who presents himself "before the world as a child." This notion of Keshub's, which would evolve in years to come as an ingredient of the New Dispensation, aroused the wrath of Dall. Keshub's exact words enunciating the doctrine were: "He has become an altered man. Behold this transformation of age into spiritual childhood. The deceit of the world, the pride of the age is dissolved into thin air, and innocence, joy and child-like simplicity come pouring into the heart of this infant from Heaven."[75]

Dall was convinced that Keshub had surrendered his modernism and was drifting back to a nonprogressive, asocial preoccupation with personal spiritual realization. He warned Keshub not to cut himself off from "the world's progress" and "be run down and run over." To be sure, the "past has good in it," but "mind you don't lose sight of the fact that the future has good in it." "Keshub Babu," continued Dall, "eloquently defended the conservative side of theistic life," but on the "worship of work and progress," he said nothing of "positive value." Is sin the only disease? There are other diseases that require different remedies, "as in the case of a mother in poverty with a large family of children taking for herself time and attention that belong to her family. My work for years as a minister to the poor clearly showed me that since a mother can have contemplation only on her pillow, with her little ones sleeping around her on her bosom, so we pray and think of the Lord only in society or while at work. Retirement for solitary contemplation is not her 'remedy.' "[76]

The full debate need not concern us here, since the only real issue was, from Dall's point of view, between the religion of individual salvation and the social gospel of Unitarianism. The rupture between them, therefore, went well beyond the issue of Christ as chief among prophets, to a recognition of fundamental differences that led to a parting of the ways. By 1877, to Dall, Keshub appeared to have put all his eggs in the basket of the sacred against the profane, of faith against reason, and of individual salvation above social improvement.

The spiritual leader of the revolt against Keshub Sen in 1878 was Sivanath Sastri, who possessed a remarkably gifted intellect. Sastri was a learned scholar and prolific writer of fiction and nonfiction. In the annals of nineteenth-century Brahmo history, there is not another more dedicated to fundamental Brahmo principles sustained over three generations than Sastri. He considered Brahmoism from Rammohun's time to his own a rational this-worldly faith, humanitarian in sympathy, and humanist in the way religious belief was reconciled with the belief in the idea of progress. In short, the Unitarian social gospel that Keshub abandoned in the 1870s Sastri continued to defend and develop as an essential ingredient of his own Brahmo ideology.

Sastri represented a generation of Brahmos profoundly influenced by British and American Unitarianism. But is was not so much the Jesus-centered Unitarian gospel, with its stress on the ethical and historic Christ that moved Sastri and his friends, as it was the social reformist programs of Unitarianism, which championed the oppressed and provided material means to alleviate their poverty and degradation. This is the line that separates Sastri and the Sadharans from both Rammohun Roy and his *Precepts of Jesus* and Protap Majumdar and his *Oriental Christ*, as well as from Keshub Sen himself, who never ceased to admire the exalted image of Christ as prophet.

During the 1870s, Sivanath moved from liberalism to radicalism in his social and political views. From the start, he affiliated himself with the progressive wing of the Keshubite movement, which included Durga Mohun Das, Ananda Mohun Bose, Monomohun Ghose, Shib Chandra Deb, Umesh Chandra Dutt, Sasipada Bannerji, and others. They were mostly Western-educated, some actually having lived and studied in England; they were all fairly well placed professionally in positions where contact with the British in the English language was common; and they had strong ties with foreign Unitarians (see Table 1).

Sastri's Brahmo career and identity were from the early 1870s conducted on two levels. Keshub gave young progressives such as Sastri a sense of identity through a new community and even a home, the Bharat Ashram, where Sivanath lived. But on a different, more intimate level, Sastri's true sense of belonging was invariably with the smaller group or faction of progressives. These Brahmo progressives were held together not by caste, or locality, or Hindu religious background, or even by being of the same generation. Their common denominator was the ideology of nineteenth-century liberal religion transmitted, oddly enough, through the works of Theodore Parker. It was the discovery of Parker by Brahmos—his collected works in Bengali translation in the 1860s—which provided them with a vital and powerful bond of common values and ideals. What was the image of Parker that so moved the progressive Brahmos? Theodore Parker had felt the sudden influence of Emerson in 1840, turned to socially activist Unitarianism in the 1840s, and became its most outspoken and dynamic leader.[77] It was his combination of a superb oratorical style and political reformism in the name of Jesus that endeared him to religious progressives the world over.

Not only Bengali Brahmos but Unitarian progressives in England felt inspired by Parker's tracts, sermons, and essays. There

TABLE 1

**Principal Members of the Progressive Faction of the
Brahmo Samaj Who Were Founders of the Sadharan Samaj**

Name	Birth, birthplace	Caste	Religious orientation	Profession, occupation	First exposure to Brahmoism or Unitarianism
Svanath Sastri	1847, 24 Pargannas	Brahman	Sakto	Preceptor, Sanskrit professor	Liberal pundit. Family knew Tagore. Knew writings of Theodore Parker.
Sib. C. Deb	1811, Calcutta suburb	Kayastha	Sakto	Civil servant	Exposed to Parker's writings in 1850s. Influenced by A. K. Dutt.
Monomohun Ghose	1844, Vikrampur, Bangladesh	Kayastha	Unknown	Barrister	Met Keshub Sen at Krishnagar College; met Mary Carpenter in England.
Durga M. Das	Vikrampur, Bangladesh	Kayastha	Sakto	Barrister	To avert conversion to Christianity, brother recommends works of Parker.
Dwarkanath Ganguli	1844, Vikrampur, Bangladesh	Brahman	Sakto	Journalist, educator	First exposed to Brahmoism in Calcutta. Durga M. Das earliest *pati*.
Umesh C. Dutt	1840, 24 Pargannas	Kayastha	Unknown	Educator	At school, exposed to writings of Rajnarian Bose. Follower of Parker.
Ananda M. Bose	1847, Myminsingh, Bangladesh	Kayastha	Sakto	Barrister	Influenced by Bhagaban C. Bose, future father-in-law, while at Mym. High School. Unitarian exposure in England.
Nagendranath Chatterji	1843, Barisal, Bangladesh	Brahman	Sakto	Missionary	Father knew Deb. Tagore. Wrote biography of Theodore Parker in Bengali.

SOURCE: Compiled from biographical and autobiographical material in contemporary books, tracts, newspapers, and periodicals.

was no other minister of any church in the world at that time as actively committed to the equality of all men, to women's rights, and to the idea of man's perfectability.[78] His candor amazed and angered the English when, in 1849 during a trip to Great Britain,

he criticized their government for "neglect of the common people's education." He openly attacked aristocratic privilege in British society, including the almost sacred notion of the "Gentleman as the type of the State." In Britain, unlike the United States, said he, "all effort is directed to producing the Gentleman whereas the people require education enough to become the servants of the Gentleman." In the following passage, one of hundreds like it, the voice of the righteously indignant reformer carried as far as Bengal: "The Parliament which voted £100,000 of the nation's money for the Queen's horses and hounds, had but £30,000 to spare for the education of her people. . . . You wonder at the Colleges and Collegiate churches of Oxford and Cambridge, at the magnificence of public edifices—the House of Parliament, the Bank, the palaces of royal and noble men, the splendor of the churches—but you ask, where are the school houses for the people?"[79]

In 1858 during a famous sermon against the wave of fundamental revivalism sweeping America, Parker blasted the movement for "being opposed to social reform." He had been to their prayer meetings, but where in their prayers had he heard a single reference to temperance, to education, to the emancipation of slaves, or to the elevation of women? Said he: "I do not hear a prayer for honesty, for industry, for brotherly love, any prayers against envy, malice, bigotry. . . . The Revival may spread all over the land. It will make church members—not good husbands, wives. . . . It will not oppose the rum trade, nor the trade in coolies, nor the trade in African or American slaves."[80]

One link in the chain of humanitarian concern from Parker in America to Sivanath Sastri in Bengal was the famed Englishwoman, Mary Carpenter. No Unitarian in England, male or female, defended Parker's social gospel with more ardor than she did. In a letter to Miss Carpenter in 1859 shortly before his death, Parker expressed profound admiration for Unitarian social improvement schemes in Bristol. He, she, and her father shared a common liberal Unitarian faith. "Many things are called Christianity," he wrote, "sometimes it means burning men alive; in half the U.S.A. it means kidnapping, enslaving men and women." But there was another kind of Christianity, Parker went on, "which your admirable father loved and thought and lived. . . . Piety, Morality, Love to God, Love to Man." He was proud of Mary Carpenter because she had carried on her father's work. "It is this which I honor and love in you," he wrote, "especially as it takes the form of humanity and loves the Unlovely." Both Parker and Carpenter shared the belief that "the greatest heroism of our day spends itself in lanes and alleys, in the haunts of poverty and crime seeking to bless such as the institution of the age can only curse. If Jesus of Nazareth were to come back and be the Jesus of London, I think I know what work he would set about. He would be a new Revolution of Institutions, applying his universal justice to the causes of the ill. . . . You are doing this work—the work of humanity."[81]

Probably the earliest recorded evidence of Parker's influence in Bengal can be found in a letter written to the American Unitarian by the Brahmo Rakhal Das Haldar, dated October 6, 1856.[82] The letter suggests that the Brahmo defense of intuition against revealed scriptural sources, an important theological issue in the 1850s, was in part derived from Parker's influence. The letter also intimates that little if any direct communication had taken place between Bengali Brahmos and American Unitarians. Parker expressed surprise that Asians were so familiar with works by him and other American Unitarians, and he promised to arrange for more of his volumes to be sent to Calcutta.

In 1858, Keshub Sen used Parker and Emerson as the basis of his own sermons.[83] Sivanath Sastri has also written that Parker was a very important influence on the younger Keshub.[84] In his autobiography, the East Bengali Keshubite Banga Chandra Roy reported that by 1863 Parker was being read widely among the Western-educated Brahmos of Dacca,[85] who also read English Unitarians such as Cobbe and Martineau.

One of the more interesting cases of Parker's influence in East Bengal was that of Durga Mohun Das of Barisal. In the early 1860s, Das was a student at Presidency College, Calcutta, and under the influence of Professor E. B. Cowell he decided to convert to Trinitarian Christianity. His brother, a pleader, interceded before baptism, and sent Durga Mohun back to Barisal, urging him to read the complete works of Parker. The reading of Parker in 1864/65 not only turned Durga Mohun away from Christianity, but made him incline in favor of the Brahmo faith. Thus, when Bijoy Krishna came to Barisal in 1865 as Keshub's missionary to East Bengal, Das was already receptive to Brahmoism.[86]

Dwijidas Datta, a founder of the Sadharan Samaj and himself from Comilla, East Bengal, has written that by the mid-1860s, "the name of Theodore Parker was familiar to every Brahmo."[87] By the time Sivanath Sastri turned to Parker to resolve his feelings of remorse and guilt, Parker's works had evidently been translated into Bengali, and was circulating widely through town and country.

The very sermons by Parker that Sastri read had been translated by the Brahmo Girish Chandra Majumdar of Barisal in 1866. As these sermons dealt with social issues in a religious context, Bengalis were particularly receptive to them, as they were to Parker's equation of intimate love for God with love of all humanity.[88]

According to Sastri, so widespread was Parker's influence by the late 1860s that Debendranath Tagore feared a whole new generation would become "contaminated" by Parker's philosophy.[89] Bipin Chandra Pal has also placed emphasis on Parker's enormous impact on Brahmo progressives. What precisely was the nature of the impact? Pal wrote: "Sivanath Sastri and his generation imbibed the indomitable spirit of freedom, liberalism and the love of universal humanity from Theodore Parker. It was doubtful whether they were in the least inspired by Parker's theology."[90]

Thus, early in the 1870s a faction of social progressives had formed, within Keshub's larger Brahmo organization, a group held together ideologically by the Parker social gospel. In that year, Keshub favored the group, and when he returned from England he started the Indian Reform Association. There was little in his behavior to suggest that he would ultimately abandon the social gospel for comparative religion and the New Dispensation, turning then for support to the ascetic Brahmo faction. In the 1870s, Keshub's views coincided nicely with those of Sastri, Deb, Das, and other progressives.

In fact, just about the time Keshub announced formation of the Indian Reform Association, Sastri wrote an interesting tract articulating what he saw as the major principles of the Brahmo Samaj of India. He supported Keshub and the organization fully. His tract was a declaration of faith in the community of Brahmo brethren and sisters under Keshub's leadership, who were seeking to propagate the "progressive religion" of Brahmoism. Progressive religion was a cosmopolitan faith in the "whole human race," in the "growth and development of the human personality," and in social improvement through emancipation. The last item was, in light of subsequent events, most significant of all: "We look upon every form of denial of social and individual rights by individuals or classes, as impietous and reprehensible, and as such a proper field of increasing warfare for all true lovers of God."[91]

By 1872, however, the honeymoon between the progressives and Keshub seemed over. The one key issue that separated them, the most burning issue of the day, was female emancipation. Besides Parker, whose influence was less direct on this issue, the two British

Unitarian ladies—Mary Carpenter and Annette Akroyd—had a profound impact on Brahmo thinking in Calcutta.

Mary Carpenter, whom we have noted to have been a British follower of Theodore Parker, was born in 1807, the daughter of Rammohun Roy's Unitarian friend and associate, Lant Carpenter. Much of her mature life from 1831 on was spent as a leading social worker among the urban poor in England, as the economy industrialized. At first she helped the poverty-stricken people of Bristol, but later she extended her concern to the Oliver Twist variety of ragged youth among the industrial proletariat. As a champion of Parker's radical views on universal education, Carpenter was among the first social activists in Great Britian to provide reliable statistical information to Parliament on behalf of free compulsory education.[92]

One of Mary Carpenter's chief concerns was achieving equal rights for those of her own sex. In Victorian England, however advanced technologically and industrially, the majority of people still lived outside the pale of cultivated society as nonparticipants in modern civilization and as nonconsumers of its fruits and benefits. Numerically, most conspicious among the outsiders were the industrial proletariat and among these, women were least protected by the law or by political power. Lacking education or special training, and being barred from most respectable jobs before the invention of the typewriter, the Englishwoman without means in the job market had the choice of being exploited in factories, along with children, as part of the proletariat, or prostitution in order to survive. The Industrial Revolution in nineteenth-century England had not changed the traditionally callous disregard for women.

But on the more positive side, modernization also awakened an awareness of inhumanity among an increasing number of liberal-minded people in good families and in high positions. Their combined efforts and shocking disclosures led, for instance, to the first enactment of an Age of Consent Bill in 1885. The following facts, which the liberals brought to light to win support for the bill, demonstrate not only how deplorable the situation was but how pervasive the new humanitarian consciousness had become: "Girls over 13 lacked any legal protection whereas no policeman could enter a brothel to search for girls under 13. . . . Most of the girls were drugged . . . 8 million pounds a year traffic in selling young girls . . . ⅓ of the girls were seduced before 16. In London, there were 80,000 prostitutes. The right square mile round Charing Cross harboured over 2,000 pimps. One in every 50 Englishwomen was a streetwalker . . . it cost 100 pounds to have a virgin seduced. . . ."[93]

Many of these women ended up in prison, where conditions were evidently so bad as to defy the imagination. Prison reform was in fact one of Mary Carpenter's concerns, and it was in the jails that she encountered the lower depths of female degradation and dedicated herself to rescuing and rehabilitating these women. Carpenter was also among the earliest reformers to bring documented evidence to parliament dramatizing the urgent need for prison improvement.[94] It is in this activist context that her trip to India in 1875 can be framed. She was simply extending her reformist activities on prisons and other humanitarian concerns to a wider area that included South Asia. The prisons she left behind her in England were bad enough, as was the fate of any Englishwoman unfortunate enough to be trapped behind those walls. Perhaps in India prisons were worse.

The disabilities of women were not limited to the poor. Even the well-known and well-respected Mary Carpenter was discriminated against professionally. In 1836, she wanted to give a paper at the British Scientific Association, which was to meet in her native city of Bristol on aspects of social welfare and sociology. The Association replied that they "did not permit ladies even to be present at the meetings of the sections." It was not until 1860 that she was permitted to give a paper at the yearly session.[95]

Unitarian ladies like Mary Carpenter and Frances P. Cobbe worked hard to improve the lot of women through education and legislation. It was the combined efforts of such women and the sympathy of liberal men that got parliament to pass a Married Women's Properties Act in 1858.[96] As educated persons, one of their primary objectives was to break the monopoly of men in institutions of higher learning that awarded degrees. Thus, it was no accident that the first modern college for women in England was the Bedford College of Manchester, conducted by Unitarians. Not until 1878 did Oxford establish a college for women, the first degree-awarding institution of its kind in the British Isles.[97] Indeed, the problem of extending equal rights to women was a world-wide phenomenon in the nineteenth century, and not restricted to traditional societies in Asia. During Mary Carpenter's first two trips to India, she met with Brahmos and urged them to help extend American and English efforts at women's emancipation to India.

Among her most devoted stalwarts in Bengal were the progressives in Keshub Sen's Brahmo organization, and among these, the most active was Keshub's former youthful enthusiast from Krishnagar, Monomohun Ghose. Ghose and Miss Carpenter had become warm friends in England from 1862 to 1866, where Ghose and Satyendranath Tagore had gone together to compete for the Indian Civil Service. Monomohun had failed, but later turned to law and became a successful barrister in Calcutta.

When Mary Carpenter visited Calcutta in 1869 with a definite scheme for promoting women's education, Ghose was among her most ardent supporters. She proposed the establishment of a Brahmo normal school to train women teachers for girls' schools, and she urged them to expand the usual domestic arts program by offering additional subjects that would stimulate the women's curiosity and develop their minds.[98] Keshub, with the backing of Ghose, Sastri, Deb, and others, did start a normal school for women as part of his Indian Reform Association, and most of the progressive Brahmos offered their services as teachers in the school.[99]

At that time, there was only one educational institution for young women in Calcutta—Bethune School—which Vidyasagar, Sastri's uncle Vidyabhusan, and other liberals had supported solidly for twenty years. Despite the conservative curriculum of the school, which taught women domestic arts and a modicum of liberal education to make them better wives, the institution never received wide public support. In 1868, Miss Piggot, the headmistress, was forced to resign because she had brought Christianity into the teaching program, thus exposing the girls to the dreaded alien faith.[100]

By 1870, especially among Brahmo men, the issue was sharply drawn between those who viewed female education as preparatory for the domestic bliss of the enlightened housewife, and those who wanted women educated on the same basis and to the same levels as men. Bengali reformers, Brahmo and otherwise, still held the notion first promulgated by Rammohun Roy that Hindu social reform in Bengal must start with the emancipation of women, because women played such a crucial role in shaping the character and thought of children. Yet nothing concrete had been done so far to accomplish that purpose.

At this point there entered the Calcutta scene a second British Unitarian lady, Annette Akroyd. Her father had been a liberal Unitarian industrialist from Birmingham who in 1849 supported the establishment of Bedford College, which was among the earliest institutions providing higher learning for women.[101] Annette received her degree from Bedford in 1863, devoted herself to social work, and in 1865 she helped establish a school for women of the industrial proletariat. Like Mary Carpenter, she saw herself as a follower of Theodore Parker's program of social action as an integral part of Unitarian religion.

Sometime in the early 1860s, she met Monomohun Ghose, with whom she formed a deep friendship. Thus, by the time Keshub Sen visited England in 1870, Annette Akroyd had already formed a favorable impression of Brahmo social reform, which made her one of his most inspired listeners. She was especially receptive to one of Keshub's lectures in which he urged educated Englishwomen to come to India and help free Indian women from their chains of ignorance and superstition. She recalled later that his lecture of August 14 had an "electrifying effect on us Victorian ladies."

No doubt important to her state of mind at the time was the fact that her father had died in 1869, leaving her with a "blankness and dreariness inexpressible." She reconsidered life in England, which she thought a "boring life of moral classes, ragged school collections, balls, social engagements, visits, journeys to London and yearly trips to the seaside," and so she came forward to answer Keshub's appeal. Arriving in Calcutta on October 25, 1872, she was the house guest of Monomohun Ghose and his wife. Mrs. Ghose, incidentally, who had been an uneducated bride, spent the first several years of her married life as a student at Loreto School and College in Calcutta. Monomohun had insisted upon it after returning from England.

The Brahmo progressives welcomed Annette as an ally within the community in their effort to achieve more equality for Brahmo women. In this endeavor, Keshub proved far more conservative than the progressives anticipated, with the result that women's emancipation became the hot issue that divided the Brahmo organization. One of the first incidents took place in February 1872, when Durga Mohun Das insisted that ladies be permitted to sit with their families during services at the mandir. Because Keshub insisted that ladies sit behind screens, Das, Ghose, Sastri, and the other progressives accused him of enforcing purdah. Joined by another fiery young Brahmo enthusiast named Dwarkanath Ganguli, the progressives demanded an end to the purdah system. Keshub stood firm at first, arguing that women seated in the congregation would distract the men from their spiritual purpose, but finally he relented and provided seats outside the screen for "advanced" families.[102]

The problem of what girls should learn in school was not solved so easily. Miss Akroyd played a leading part in this debate, sarcastically distinguishing Keshub, the rhetorician of women's liberation in England, from Keshub, the typical Hindu male keeping knowledge from the minds of women. Nowhere in the Indian Reform Association did Keshub allow women to study such male-monopolized subjects as geometry, logic, natural science, or history.[103] In fact, in the normal school, Keshub's executive committee and a majority of faculty were of the nonprogressive ascetic faction. Of the three-man executive committee, only one, Umesh Chandra Dutt, the secretary, was progressive. As for the faculty, Keshub carefully selected men who were non-Westernized and traditionally Hindu in educational background—men like Bijoy Krishna Goswami, Aghore Nath Gupta, and Gour Govinda Ray.[104]

Keshub tried to convince Miss Akroyd, Ghose, and Sastri that he was progressive, but at the same time wary of radical change. To be sure, they all wanted women to be emancipated, but it should be a gradual process and carried out chiefly by liberal Brahmo husbands. Keshub implored them to imagine the disastrous consequences of women so quickly released from the purdah-like situation in the Bengali household. "Go slow," he told the progressives, and give women the inner strength with which to protect themselves.

In 1872, however, Miss Akroyd decided to start a new school based on her own ideas and those of the progressives. Keshub was invited to join the committee, which he did at first, but then he withdrew his support, arguing the need to move gradually in the area of female emancipation. Miss Akroyd disagreed both publicly and privately. She had no patience with Keshub's gradualist methods which she openly labeled hypocritical. "I lost faith in Keshub Chandra Sen," said Miss Akroyd indignantly, "because of the contrast in him between preaching and personal practice." Lord Beveridge, her future husband and a civil servant in Bengal for many years, explained Keshub's dismal failure as a reformer in terms of a presumed defect in the Bengali character: "The besetting sin of the Bengalees is that they will think and talk, talk and think, but that they will not act . . . that is the very reason we are here for if Bengalees could act half as well as they talk, there would be no reason for us Westerners to rule over them. We must, therefore, take them as we find them and do our best for them."[105]

But Annette Akroyd remained furious with Keshub, whom she soon held to be hardly distinguishable from an orthodox Hindu, since both sought to keep their women steeped in ignorance and child-like innocence. Her description of Keshub Sen's wife, for example, which was hardly a flattering profile for the wife of India's most reputed social reformer, was a devastating public exposure of an unemancipated Hindu woman. Miss Akroyd was "shocked" when she finally met Sen's wife. She had expected to meet someone as well-educated and sophisticated as Monomohun Ghose's wife, but instead found "that the wife of the great apostle of women's emancipation in India was ignorant of England." But worse, she found her "covered by a barbaric display of jewels, playing with them like a foolish petted child in place of attempting rational conversation."

Keshub countered with two arguments: a continued defence of his "go slow" policy, and a warning about "denationalized" female education in Bengal. In April 1873, at a prize-awarding ceremony in his own normal school for women, Keshub warned "how delicate and difficult is the work of female emancipation and if sufficient care is not taken, the experiment might prove harmful and dangerous." He reiterated his own dismay with the bad effects of keeping women in "ignorance and seclusion," while at the same time justifying his gradualism not as conservatism but as good sense. "Before they share the privileges of society," he said, "they must have sufficient moral training and intellectual capacity." Keshub pointed to the grim image of "Indian males, even the educated classes who do not possess right notions about the other sex and do not know how to protect women in society."[106]

Keshub's second line of attack dealt with Annette Akroyd's Anglicized curriculum and her suggested personal habits for Bengali girls, which he attributed to her ignorance of Bengali culture. Whatever good she intended to accomplish in her school, the end result would be to denationalize Indian women. Miss Akroyd had proposed "the adoption of petticoats with the preservation of the remaining upper part of the dress." Thus she reasoned, "a compromise would be reached between indecency and denationalization—and both secured against."[107] Progressives like Monomohun Ghose had supported her, but Keshub treated her proposal with contempt. For Keshub, Miss Akroyd did not care in the least for indigenous customs nor for the "Bengali modes of thinking."[108] In his mind, all this bother about clothing only proved that Miss Akroyd confused female emancipation with Westernized habits and customs.

Miss Akroyd's school opened on September 18, 1873, as the Hindu Mahila Vidyalay (school for Hindu women), with Dwarkanath Ganguli as headmaster.[109] The move represented the first serious rupture between the progressives and Keshub, a decisive step toward ultimate schism. Two months before classes opened in the new school, Lord Beveridge had written to Annette that "I see you have broken with Keshub Chandra Sen. I expect he is too fluent a speaker to be a greater doer."[110]

Sivanath Sastri has implied in his *History of the Brahmo Samaj* that, with the establishment of the Vidyalaya, the progressive or "liberal" Brahmos formed themselves into a semi-autonomous group. These same Brahmos paid most of the school's expenses, although the greater portion of that came out of the pockets of three fairly well-to-do East Bengali liberals: Ananda Mohun Bose, Durga Mohun Das, and Dwarkanath Ganguli. In November 1874, the progressives formally constituted themselves the "Samadarshi (liberal) party" and started a journal of their own called by that name, with Sivanath Sastri as editor.[111]

The female emancipation issue so angered conservative Brahmos that by 1874 Keshub found himself forcing liberals out of his educational institutions or accepting letters of protest and resignation. Sastri himself resigned his teaching position at the girls' school to become headmaster of the South Suburban School in Bhawanipur. The same issue created bad feelings in the Brahmo living quarters (Bharat Ashram), which resulted in Keshub's decision to expel a liberal family.[112]

In April 1875, Miss Akroyd became Mrs. Beveridge, which meant that she had to give up the school. For diplomatic reasons, perhaps, her husband urged her to reconcile differences with Keshub Sen, whom he "believed to be a good man." He also warned his wife not to become "too much identified with the Anglicized Bengalees." In this category, Beveridge included Monomohun Ghose and his wife: "I have nothing to say against Mr. and Mrs. Ghose, who were kind to me, but I do not believe that they represent the best section of Young Bengal or that Bengal will eventually follow in the track they are going."[113]

The arrival of Mary Carpenter on her third and last visit to India not only saved Annette Akroyd's school, but prompted the adoption of a more ambitious scheme to train Indian women for higher education. With the active backing of the Samadarshi party of Brahmos, the first women's liberal arts college in India was established on June 1, 1876, the Banga Mahila Vidyalay (Bengali women's college).[114] Two years later, on August 1, 1878, this institution was merged with Bethune to become Bethune College, and immediately it won the recognition and financial support of the government.

The year 1878 was indeed a bad year for Keshub. At the same time the government decided to back the liberals and Bethune College, they withdrew financial support from his own female normal school, which had continued to restrict its curriculum to the domestic arts.[115] This was also the year in which the liberals finally brought on the long-awaited schism in Brahmo ranks, leading to the formation of the Sadharan Samaj. Considering the fact that women's emancipation was the major issue of the 1870s, it should come as no surprise that the immediate cause for this schism was Keshub's marriage of his eldest daughter to the Hindu Maharaja of Cooch Behar.

Despite his growing unpopularity with liberal social reformers, Keshub continued to voice his opinion against "alien Unitarian" ideas about advanced education for Indian women. In opposition to the Bethune College merger, he charged that its objective was to "Europeanize the girls." Keshub wrote in an editorial of February 25, 1878, that a distinction should be made, but was not being made by the founders of Bethune College, between Anglicizing Indian women and emancipating them. At Bethune College, the women would learn "to wear European costumes and to adopt European habits in eating and drinking." "This may be progress in the estimation of a few go-ahead reformers," wrote Keshub, "but it is a progress of a very doubtful character." It certainly "has no value in the eyes of the true well-wishers of the country." Keshub concluded that "we have no desire to make Europeans of our ladies. . . . To denationalize them will be grievous misfortune to our country. . . . The Lt. Governor should consult the parents of the Hindu community. . . . To Europeanize ourselves in our external habits and manners is one thing, and to regenerate ourselves is another thing."[116]

The Sadharan Samajists replied to Keshub in their own newly formed journal, *Brahmo Public Opinion*. In an editorial of July 4, 1878, presumably written collectively, the opening observation was made that Keshub had joined the growing legion of Hindu revivalists and militants who had nothing but contempt for things Western. Keshub was identified with a "sort of mania at present raging among our countrymen on the question of nationality." Everything "European is looked upon with perfect horror." The real issue was whether Indian women were to achieve freedom or not. In "ancient times our women enjoyed the highest liberality but lost that privilege with the Mohammedan conquest." The Sadharan Brahmos went on to argue that if India wanted again to raise the status of its women, it should follow the lead of Western nations. They denied aping Western customs. Keshub was wrong about the purpose of having their girls use English dress, for "all we have done at the *Vidyalay* is adopted a dress for the girls that combines the elegance of the national dress with the decency of the European."

This was an interesting editorial, not only in the reply to Keshub, but as a document expressing the practical difficulty of distinguishing "modernization" from "Westernization" in this kind of institutional operation. Even Keshub's charge about food or the means of taking food had to be rationalized by the Sadharan Brahmos in these terms. "No doubt that our girls dine on tables and use spoons and forks," the editorial went on, "but it is because they find it convenient and decent to do so." Then, as a counter blast against Keshub's own eating habits: "so do several of our own pseudo reformers when they go to the Great Eastern Hotel on the sly." Has that made them "Europeanized"? Finally, the vital concern about meat was brought up in the editorial, and defended not as a food that would denationalize the girls but as one that "makes them healthy and civilized members of society." The final passage is most significant for its plea against cultural sectarianism directed against Keshub Sen, the leading contemporary spokesman for eclecticism and universalism: "Why should we not take what we find good and socially and morally acceptable in the Western nations? We say it is blind perverse nationality which despises what is good and of steady merit in any other nationality. Truth is truth in all nationalities, religions and creeds."[117]

Keshub's opposition fell on the deaf ears of the government, which applauded the official opening of the Bethune College in 1879. The Sadharan progressives also petitioned the government to affiliate Bethune with Calcutta University so that the girls could be awarded B.A. degrees.[118] The first two recipients of that degree in 1882 were Miss Kadambini Bose, a Brahmo, and Miss Chandra Mukhi Bose, a Christian.[119] Interestingly enough, Oxford University first awarded bachelor's degrees to women in 1878/79, at about the same time that Bethune College became an accredited affiliate of Calcutta University. Thus, when the two Bengali women received their degrees in 1882, they became the first women graduates in the entire British empire.[120]

The triumph of the Sadharan Brahmos over the Keshubites on the issue of women's emancipation clearly represents the impact of Unitarian social philosophy on Hindu society and culture. As the facts disclose, Unitarian impact was not merely intellectual or ideological. Through the advocacy and work of Carpenter and Akroyd, its impact was intrusively practical. In the immediate context of the Hindu reformation seen in historical perspective, however, the Sadharan victory represents the culmination of a century of struggle to realize Rammohun Roy's central belief that only by freeing women and by treating them as human beings could Indian society free itself from social stagnation. To be sure, the higher education of Indian women did not immediately revolutionize Hindu society, but it proved an important stage in the process of achieving the ultimate goal of equal rights. Certainly, the relatively emancipated professional Indian women of today owe a considerable debt of gratitude to the Brahmo pioneers of the nineteenth century.

CHAPTER TWO

The Deification of Science, Humanity, and Reason: Brahmo Secularism

IF Unitarianism appealed exclusively to the religious-minded liberal reformers, other modern ideas from the West had a wider appeal among nontheistic as well as theistic reformers. In the first place, varieties of Western ideas seemed to flow easily into the port of Calcutta, which was the capital of British India and a veritable laboratory of intercivilizational encounter between the East and the West. Radical ideas that challenged the bases of the traditional world order in Europe and America were a form of intellectual cargo unloaded on the docks of the great metropolis, along with the other industrial and commercial products. Moreover, under British Orientalist cultural policy in Calcutta between 1772 and 1830, a congenial atmosphere had been created for the dissemination of European thought, along with an institutional structure and technological means to facilitate this dissemination. By serving as avenues linking the regional elite with the dynamic civilization of contemporary Europe, the Orientalists contributed to the formation of a new Indian middle class and assisted in the professionalization of the Bengali Hindu intelligentsia.

Thus, at a period that roughly approximates Rammohun Roy's lifetime, Calcutta had entered the orbit of London's intellectual climate and boasted an intelligentsia sophisticated about the ways of the West. By 1830, Calcutta had Hindu College, the only Western-styled institution of higher learning to be found anywhere in what is presently known as the third world.[1] It had several printing and publishing establishments, turning out thousands of copies of Western scientific and other textbook sources in Indian-language translations;[2] it had three colleges with modern scientific laboratories, each with a full curriculum of science courses.[3] Calcutta had a free public library as early as 1816.[4] By 1830, Calcutta had three major Bengali newspapers that carried foreign and local news.[5] Suffice it to say that through the efforts of British officials, missionaries, and free lance humanitarians, organizations and associations proliferated together with a network of communication media that functioned to expose the nascent intelligentsia to the currents of progressive thought in the West.

Between 1826 and 1831, a young teacher at Hindu College named Henry Vivian Louis Derozio inspired a whole generation of Westernizing radical intellectuals known historically as Young Bengal.[6] Under him, students read John Locke on civil liberty and natural rights; Rousseau on the justification of a representative democracy; David Hume on the bankruptcy of metaphysics; Voltaire on the supremacy of reason, enlightenment, and good taste; Bentham on the reformation of the legal system to achieve the most happiness for the largest number; and last but hardly least, Tom Paine on liberty and the flowering of the human spirit.[7] Derozio was a pioneer among a distinguished coterie of nineteenth-century Calcutta academicians who, however distant from the shores of England, championed the fashionable ideas of progress while they shared with the Western humanist enthusiasts an optimistic vision of mankind's future.

It should be stressed that humanism or the deification of man in place of God, and not the idea of progress, sharply divided the secular intelligentsia from the Unitarians. Unitarians and Brahmos with a Unitarian bias, though they attacked the orthodox tradition, advocated social improvement, and struggled for progress, did so as theists in the name of God. As we shall see, many of these liberal theists and some deists glorified science and reason. Is this a contradiction? I think not. In the first place, before Darwinism challenged the fundamentalist Christian concept of genesis, science and religion were neatly compartmentalized in the world view of many progressive Christians. In the second place, we in the twentieth century are inclined to misread secularism into the methodology of science, the philosophy of science, and even into the psychohistory of the scientific mind and personality. Too infrequently are we reminded that the paradigms of history are relative, that science may have metaphysical roots, and that scientific geniuses such as Newton and Einstein were religious men.

Though Unitarianism can claim no monopoly on the flow of thought into the ranks of the Brahmo Samaj, few Brahmos until the 1930s accepted an unqualified humanism or a materialist conception of life and society. (The same may be said for the Unitarian movement itself, which is today divided into liberal theist and humanist camps.) Nevertheless, Brahmos not only appropriated science and reason in a very special and positive way, but deified them. Brahmo scientists were among the first modern scientists in contemporary India; Brahmo philosophers waged a relentless struggle to denude Hinduism of its "excesses" at the same time as they reconstructed the "authentic" Hindu tradition by endowing it with an intellectual respectability on a par with other major religious traditions.

This is not to say that a secular humanist intelligentsia played an insignificant role in the process of reform or modernization in Bengal. There were two types of secularists: the Westernized man aping his European counterparts, and the indigenous humanist who repudiated the tyranny of religion from sources within his own tradition. Both formed coalitions with the Brahmos to promote social reform against conservative opposition. These humanists maintained their distance from Brahmoism primarily on theistic grounds. Indeed, the sharp cleavage that exists today among the Indian middle-class intelligentsia between secular and religious reformers has its roots in the nineteenth-century cleavage between humanists and Brahmos.

The Westernized Bengali humanist of the nineteenth century imbibed the identical antireligious bias of his European counterparts, not simply because such literature was readily available in Calcutta, but because he was conditioned by his educational background to do so. It was no accident, for example, that Derozio should profess secularism and the philosophy of man's perfectability to students at Hindu College. From the beginning, when the college charter was drafted, the Calcutta *nouveaux riches* founders insisted that the college not teach Hindu theology and metaphysics but concern itself primarily with "the cultivation of European literature and European science." According to the official account in the *Presidency College Centenary Volume*, "the most striking feature of the Hindu College was its determined effort to impart secular education."[8]

But even before the sons of Calcutta's new elite entered Hindu College, they went to a preparatory school known as Hare's School. David Hare, the principal, was a Scottish philanthropist who had settled permanently in Calcutta and involved himself in various educational experiments. Hare was an outspoken atheist and secular rationalist. When Lal Behari De, later a Christian convert, sought admission to Hare's School after having spent some time in a mission school, he was told quite candidly by Mr. Hare that boys who had studied in a Christian institution were never allowed into his school for fear that the new arrivals would contaminate the other students.[9] Not until the Brahmo Samaj started its own schools in the 1840s did a single educational institution in Bengal offer students a rational and systematic exposition of their own faith.

The Christian religion was, of course, taught in mission schools. But again the actual historical situation does not necessarily follow what may logically be believed to have taken place. The best mission school in Calcutta after 1830 was Duff's School, named after the fiery, controversial, Presbyterian missionary Alexander Duff.[10] To be sure, Duff converted many Bengali intellectuals from good families. But at his school he did not stress either Christianity or religion. By offering Western education free of cost, he made his school popular, and by introducing an effective Socratic mode of teaching he liberated the minds of his students, and hoping to prepare them to accept an alien faith.

It would be a gross injustice to Duff if we pictured him as surreptitiously using the educational process to seduce impressionable minds away from Krishna to Christ. His was a subtle technique to inspire thinking, and it was precisely in this role of missionary educator that he achieved his remarkable success as a religious Westernizer. Lal Behari De, one of his converts, has described the Duff method of instruction in some detail. Duff aimed first to bring out what was in the mind of the pupil by interrogation, with the hope that logical error and misinformation could be "purified" through self-awareness. "We were taught," wrote De, "the clear conception of an idea and secondly, the expression of that conception in words." No notes were encouraged in class "under the apprehension that they might lead to cramming." De's contrast between Duff's method and the subsequent method of Calcutta University after 1857 is significant: "Today it is different. The students of the present day never open their mouths in the classroom—unless, indeed, it is to make a noise. They take down the professor's words, commit them to memory—often without understanding them— and reproduce them in the examination hall. A copying-machine could do the same."[11]

I am suggesting two important things about Duff's method of education that had tremendous influence on Bengali intellectual life throughout the century. First, by wedding Trinitarian Christianity to a scientific attitude and rationalism, he became an effective opponent of Unitarians and Brahmos, while also converting many former disciples of Derozio. Second, by stressing science and reason at his school and at his Scottish Church College, he unwittingly produced secularists. The intellectual atmosphere in Calcutta was at first more conducive to secular reformism than to religious reformism. When Duff first arrived in Calcutta in 1830, Rammohun Roy welcomed him. Rammohun's greatest foe was the "godless atmosphere of the intellectual life" in Calcutta. The younger generation learned to despise not only Hinduism, but Christianity as well. Theism was on the defensive. To emancipated intellectuals of nineteenth-century Europe, Christianity had become as odious a stumbling block to reform as capitalism among twentieth-century intellectuals. Such antireligious movements as Benthamite Utilitarianism and early Comptean Positivism were not long in crossing the seas to Calcutta, where a segment of the intelligentsia readily consumed the new ideas.

The irrelevance of God (in agnosticism and atheism) and humanism were not in themselves new ideas in the West. Momentous historical changes, accompanied by a radical transformation of the physical environment through technological and industrial innovations, brought these ideas into predominance. The potentialities of man's progress in this world through the incredible achievements of science accelerated the process of this-worldly asceticism begun centuries before with the Protestant reformation, and gradually secularized it. Indeed, in this sense, and from a twentieth-century perspective, Unitarianism itself may be viewed as a half-way house between Christ and Marx.

It is important in this context to reiterate a point made earlier in relation to Rammohun Roy's adaptation of rational and social Unitarianism in Bengal. His environment never underwent the changes that Europeans experienced in the wake of the Industrial Revolution. The significant fact about Roy and other Bengali intellectuals was that they were ruled by foreigners and were compelled to maneuver in a colonialist situation. Therefore, as must be stressed once more, the Bengali intelligentsia was able to participate only intellectually in the modern movements of the time, because however much British imperialism disrupted the old traditional order, it did not propel the society forward along the lines of material and social development.

On the other hand, as should be most apparent in this book, this did not mean that the intelligentsia operated in a vacuum or that their ideology was academic and socially useless. It meant that they had a far more difficult challenge than their European counterparts trying to implement new currents of thought in a novel way to produce positive change. How and what they accomplished is a study of historical importance, for it was their ideological contribution, as a result of their own peculiar situation in history, that later provided independent India with its fundamental cultural presuppositions and guidelines.

But it is often overlooked that while secular humanism in nineteenth-century Bengal was stimulated by Western contact, its most effective proponents were indigenous modernizers rather than Westernizers. It cannot be stressed enough that though Calcutta was exposed to the same modernistic ideas as London, its situation was completely different from London's. In short, such radical notions as secularism, humanism, and rationalism had to be reinterpreted to fit the Indian situation. It is precisely in this context that Vidyasagar's life and career can be understood, and the apparent paradoxical nature of his role and the ambivalence of his reformist thought made plausible. As we shall see later, Vidyasagar was Bengal's most learned Sanskrit scholar, but also her most successful social reformer; he was an ardent rationalist, but spent most of his time justifying that rationalism from Hindu texts; and he considered himself a good Hindu—dressed, ate, and acted accordingly—yet was known to be a dedicated humanist and a professed atheist.

To trace the chief source of indigenous secularism as against the Westernized variety, we must once more refer back to the early nineteenth-century Orientalist legacy, which contributed so much to the making of the modern Bengali mind. In 1823, the British Orientalists founded Sanskrit College, not as a means of perpetuating the Hindu tradition, but as an educational experiment in cultural fusion. To appreciate Vidyasagar and other humanist pundits like him who were students of Sanskrit College, and their intellectual syncretism, one should read the twofold aim of the institution written by its founder, H. H. Wilson: "to preserve from decay and degradation a system of science and literature held in pious veneration by the great body of its subjects, deeply interwoven with their domestic habits and religious faith . . . but . . . to combine with this the still more important one of opening new sources of intellectual and moral improvements by the gradual admission of . . . European science and learning."[12]

Contrary to its image in the historiography of modern Bengal, Sanskrit College proved to be a fascinating experiment. Together with the traditional Sanskritic studies of rhetoric, sacred literature, law, and grammar, Wilson initiated a science curriculum of mechanics, hydrostatics, optics, astronomy, chemistry, mathematics, anatomy, and medicine.[13] In 1828, Dr. Tytler, the anatomy professor, introduced anatomical dissection to his class, and before long the "students not only handled the bones of the human skeleton without reluctance, but in some instances themselves performed the dissection of the softer parts of animals."[14] It should be added that almost half of the student body chose to study English and the sciences, even though these were not required subjects. Among them was Vidyasagar.

Besides social reform and the idea of progress, it was scientism and rationalism that brought indigenous modernizers like Vidyasagar and Vidyabhusan together with theistic Brahmo progressives. Faith in science and in reason were so crucial to all Bengali liberals until well into the twentieth century that I think we are justified in looking upon these leading ideas as the most fundamental and characteristic features of Hindu modernist ideology. To the Bengali intelligentsia, science connoted certain values: unity over diversity; the compilation and successful application of useful knowledge about man, society, and the universe; the search for natural laws; optimism about the role of science in progress. Rationalism in Bengal connoted the supremacy of reason in every area of human endeavor, including religion. We have already observed how rational religion was a pillar of the Unitarian faith. But a tendency was manifested late in the nineteenth century through which certain philosophical and theological Brahmos mercilessly subjected faith and the spirit to analytical scrutiny and system building. These rationalists were charged with having lost their theism along with their Unitarian faith, and were disparingly referred to as "Brahmo Scholastics."

As the Hindu reformation drifted into the twentieth century, deep factional cleavages had formed within the ranks of the progressive intelligentsia. Even before the shocks of World War I, the Great Depression, fascism, and other forms of totalitarianism, liberals in the West and in Bengal found themselves increasingly polarized from within. Humanism versus theism, reason versus faith, collective harmony versus individualism—these were some of the major issues that cried out for reconciliation and synthesis.

As intimated, straightforward secular humanism did not exist in the Brahmo Samaj. Rammohun Roy's Unitarian paradigm of rational theism, however domesticated, had never been seriously challenged within the Samaj. Nevertheless, a qualified humanism did emerge that was deeply influenced by Western positivism and deism, as well as by science and rationalism. The earliest figure to combine these ideas meaningfully as an ideology of salvation for an ailing Bengali society and culture was Akkhoy Kumar Dutt (1820-1886).

Dutt's educational background is noteworthy. He learned his English first from a missionary school outside of Calcutta. His father's fear about missionary influence, and the happy coincidence of the establishment of a cheap but good school in Calcutta backed solely by prominent elitist Hindus, prompted him to shift the boy to the metropolis. The Oriental Seminary started in March 1829 by the educator Gour Mohun Addy[15] was the earliest privately run, first-rate, Hindu-supported modern school in Calcutta open to all castes. It offered Western mathematics, the sciences, English language and literature, and most of the other eagerly sought-after foreign subjects.

Interesting with reference to the later intellectual development of Dutt was his favorable reaction to science and the scientific method, which he first acquired in college. This is clearly seen in his choice of subjects as a student at the Calcutta Medical College, which he appears to have attended just after the inception of the institution in 1835. There he studied chemistry, geology, geography, and other natural sciences.

In 1839, Dutt had emerged from the life of an anonymous squalor-beset intellectual by joining Debendranath Tagore's newly formed Tattvabodhini Sabha. It is a credit to Debendranath's broad sympathies as a leader of the reformation movement that he could recognize and support a young intellectual whose openly proclaimed rationalism, deism, and scientism were so alien to his own highly mystical and intimate theistic faith. In 1840, Tagore gave Dutt a teaching position in the recently established Brahmo school, where he taught the natural sciences and translated textbooks on physics and geography into Bengali.

In 1843, Debendranath chose Akkhoy Kumar to be editor of the *Tattvabodhini Patrika*, a position in the Brahmo Samaj that the young man filled with considerable distinction until 1855. It was the perfect vehicle for the searching intellectual who refused to stop learning. Though the paper served primarily to keep the increasingly far-flung Brahmo members abreast of Samaj news in Calcutta, under Dutt it served equally as an education gazette informing the reading public of happenings in the arts and sciences. The *Patrika* also helped elevate the language by widening it to accommodate a vast range of new knowledge and information.

To Akkhoy Kumar, the *Patrika* was important for helping him to clarify his thinking and to evolve an ideology. His editorials represent the intellectual strivings of a thoroughly emancipated thinker, groping for ways and means of applying European secular ideas to his immediate historical situation in Bengal. The fact that Dutt, a Brahmo, was engaged in such a quest indicates that the reform movement was not restricted to theists.[16]

To understand Dutt's thought, it is important to note that he was not, as often alleged, an atheist. In general, his concept of God resembled that of the eighteenth-century deists who saw the Almighty as the supreme watchmaker. Only an Absolute Being could possibly conceive something as intricately complex in its interrelationship between parts and whole as the clock-like earth.[17] The world was therefore neither accidental in its creation nor purposeless in its operation. One can understand God's plan by discovering the laws of nature, which show how all things are harmoniously interrelated, and this knowledge can be used to improve human relationships and bring the kingdom of God on earth.

In the application of this philosophy to conditions around him, Dutt stressed three points in particular: that the approach to God was not through prayer or monistic union, but through the study of the sciences and natural laws upon which they were based; that a complete understanding of these natural laws or "God's scripture" would reveal the total harmonious interrelatedness of the universal elements; and that in terms of social improvement, the interdependence of classes and groupings was analogous to physical interrelatedness, whereas the goal was to discover those ethical principles that would bring about the most perfect organic relationship between social units and the total society.

The first proposition led Akkhoy Kumar to disown the Vedanta as the revealed source of the Brahmo Samaj. The second proposition led to an article of faith in unity over diversity, which he continually confirmed and which led him farther and farther away from nationalism, toward internationalism.

As early as 1843, about the time of the Brahmo oath-taking ceremony, Akkhoy Kumar was trying to convince Debendranath that if the Samaj were effectively to reform Hindu society, it had to abandon the supporting prop of Vedantism and supplant the worship of God per se with a scientific understanding of His wonderful creation. "We were poles asunder," Debendranath would recall in 1858, "as I was seeking to know my relations with God while Dutt was seeking to know the relations of man with material objects."[18] The best Dutt could do at the time was to cast doubt in the mind of

Debendranath whether the Vedanta or any other classical Hindu source did actually contain a message of pure monotheism. According to Satis Chakrabarty, Akkhoy Kumar consistently opposed the notion that any Vedic source was revealed, until 1850, when Debendranath finally concurred with his judgment.[19]

Dutt's scientific bias and insistence that there were natural laws of universal applicability drove him into a position of advocating that the Brahmo Samaj put less stress on national character and more stress on "the religious impulses common to all men." Brahmoism, if it would emancipate itself from the artificial barriers imposed between peoples by "religious fanaticism" and other factors, could offer itself to the modern world as a scientifically constructed "natural religion." The quest for a universal science of religion through the Brahmo faith, which became a leading idea throughout the century, finds its origin in Akkhoy Kumar Dutt.

In 1848, Dutt's principles of a natural religion were as yet rudimentary, but they were certainly powerful enough to persuade Tagore of their validity, thus changing the course of Brahmo history. According to Akkhoy Kumar in 1854, natural religion was first and foremost for the people of all races because "all human beings are the children of God and the worshipper of God considers this earth to be his home and all human beings to be his brothers." Second, a natural religion was based on the need to understand God through His design in nature, and not by sectarian worship in mosque, temple, or church. In his third principle, Dutt interposed the ethical ingredient within the universalist context by urging that there were no revealed scriptures as such, because the true religious impulse was "expressed universally as a moral doctrine urging that good be done to others." His fourth, fifth, and sixth principles were exceedingly important, for they clearly reflected the genesis of a Brahmo ethic: "The asceticism of self-inflicted torture is a perverted and crude practice. . . . There is no injunction of the Brahmo religion to renounce the world. God desires all of us to live together. He has given us qualities like friendship, kindness, love and affection. . . . Religion has no connection with ostentation. All true worshippers of God practice meditation, devotion, acquire knowledge and do good deeds."[20]

In 1855, the very year Akkhoy Kumar suffered a mental breakdown and physical paralysis from which he never recovered, there appeared in print his *Dharma Niti*. The book was not so much a manual of ethical precepts and aphorisms as it was the culmination of an ideological quest to apply his notion of natural law to ethics, with the end of harmonizing social relationships and promoting progress. His main points were: the reaffirmation of his deistic faith that the word of God lies in His creation; the discovery of ethical principles governing that creation, which God intended as the real determinant for social improvement; and the responsibility of man to apply these ethical principles to politics, economics, and other aspects of society for the progress of the human race.

The contradictory interpretations of Dutt's rationalism stem largely from his view of a God who after creation left the affairs of men to themselves. Thus, Dutt has given later writers the impression of atheism by virtue of the fact that in his scheme of things man plays such an important role in shaping his own destiny. Actually, as Professor Pronob Ranjan Ghose has correctly asserted, Dutt never surrendered God's majesty to man's usurping power, but argued instead that "happiness" lay only in the intellectual path of discovering the natural laws of God and in the moral path of applying those laws.[21] To Dutt, therefore—and this point cannot be stressed enough—science and morality were not playthings for man's disposal but were part of the divine plan, design, or "riddle of existence."

What is especially significant about the *Dharma Niti* from the outset is the author's unqualified universalism. Though Dutt made ample use of Bengali examples throughout, he was really talking about one God, one divine plan, one human race. "All human nature is the same," he said, "in the Nature of Morality." Akkhoy Kumar felt no apparent need to assert his cultural integrity by coloring his philosophy with nationalist agitation.

Indeed, it is precisely here that Dutt was able to make his most important impact—on none other than his close associate in the Tattvabodhini Sabha, Vidyasagar. Having discovered the natural laws of morality (with the acknowledged assistance of Coombes, Comte, and other Western intellectuals), Dutt was next faced with the problem of using them to improve society. As an ethical determinist, he tackled the much larger problem of social reform through political and economic change. The social body was an organism, not in the classical sense of cyclical history with its pattern of birth, growth, and decay, but in the biological sense of homeostasis. Consequently, Dutt reduced the social organism to its most characteristic unit, the family, arguing that it was from this vantage point that change must be initiated.

For Dutt, the proper education of all family members was the means to achieve social reform, and the aim of that education was the fully developed "well-rounded human being." Through education, he wrote, "we learn the physical and mental rules of God," and that education "molds our behavior, enlightening us as to our moral responsibility to one another." Ultimately, by "behaving well with others and creating conditions for their happiness, we beautify human society."

The educational system he recommended was one that aroused scientific curiosity, above all, so that when the student "fixes his eyes to the sky he remains engaged in studying the wonders of the endless universe." History, geography, and the anthropological study of peoples will arouse such "intellectual curiosity."

"Human society," wrote Dutt, "is like a machine and its pluralistic sub-units or sub-cultures are the wheels." If humans pull away individualistically from the social organism by refusing to acknowledge their dependence on others, then society will resemble a malfunctioning machine. But if humans develop their own potential, while at the same time assisting others in society to help themselves, then their society will progress. Said Dutt, "it is far better for the human being to live in society than alone," and within the basic family unit "marital love and companionship must prevail for all to all."

It is at this point in Dutt's argument that the immediate Bengali situation was offered as an example of a social organism functioning contrary to natural law. The social ends in Bengali society are derived from a lack of true moral education in the family. Child marriage is a moral violation of the child by the father. It is a "great sin," said Dutt, while the "punishment for disregarding God's principles" was clearly evident in "the decadence of our society." The harsh treatment of widows and the exploitive institution of Kulin polygamy were gross violations of natural law, which destroyed "family harmony" and undermined any attempt at social improvement.

Without belaboring the point, there emerges from the author of *Dharma Niti*, far more than from any other previous Bengali writer, the rational justification for making female education and emancipation the central issue of Hindu social reform. As Akkhoy Kumar reviewed the social evils in the Bengali family, he found that almost all were derived from the servile and oppressive condition of the women in the household. Here then must social reform begin, and it must begin through education. The Hindu husband may be learned, but if he is truly moral, how can he tolerate her present degenerate state of illiteracy? He may "value knowledge," but "if his wife remains illiterate she can neither satisfy him nor relate harmoniously to him." An illiterate mother, instead of transmitting "enlightenment to her children," perpetuates superstition. All subsequent social evils thus stem from a lack of moral consciousness by the husband, and all subsequent reform will take place when the husband realizes the need for true equality between himself and his wife in "the meeting of minds and in friendship."[22]

Vidyasagar was born in September 1820, two months after Akkhoy Kumar Dutt. It is remarkable that these two giants of the Hindu reformation and Bengal Renaissance, who were the most outspoken humanists of their generation, differed so widely in their caste background, education, profession, and cultural self-image. Dutt, who was more profoundly influenced by Western secular philosophy, managed to accommodate himself to Brahmo theism. Vidyasagar, who immersed himself in the study of classical Hindu civilization, remained a devout atheist, rationalist, and humanist throughout his life.

Both Dutt and Vidyasagar started their formal schooling at nine years of age, the former in a mission school at Kiddapur and the latter at Sanskrit College, Calcutta. On the surface, it would appear that the two young men were moving in totally different directions. The Calcutta Sanskrit College, however, noted earlier as being originally an Orientalist institution, was not intended to promote traditional learning, but to fuse modern education from the West with Sanskrit learning in the hope of producing something new that was both indigenous and progressive. Both Vidyasagar and Dutt were excellent students, hard working, and avidly curious about the world. It was at the Oriental Seminary that Dutt first displayed that "insatiable thirst for knowledge" which became a characteristic feature of his mature life. He was later remembered as the student who "eagerly grasped every kind of information within reach."[23] This was no less true of Vidyasagar at Sanskrit College; he was an excellent student and voracious reader. These qualities are documented in a letter by G. F. Marshall, secretary of Sanskrit College, dated January 4, 1841, praising the young man for his twelve years of "great success" as a student and certifying his qualifications for a degree.[24]

As for Vidyasagar's scientific orientation, a search through the Sanskrit College records has turned up two relevant documents for the year 1839. The first is a letter of July 13 by the lecturer in "natural philosophy" to the secretary discussing the teaching of natural sciences at the college.[25] The second is a letter to Marshall, dated

November 21, announcing the prize-winning essay of the year by an Ishwar Chandra Sarma (Vidyasagar) on the topic of comparative science. Though I have not been able to find the essay itself, an outline is enclosed in the letter. With the title "On Natural Philosophy," Vidyasagar compared a "correct account of the several theories of Geography and Astronomy in the puranas with the Copernican System."[26]

Vidyasagar represents the ideal result of the union between traditional culture and the Western learning, which Sanskrit College only realized partially in a handful of graduates whom Amales Tripathi has aptly called "traditional modernisers."[27] In 1851, when appointed principal of Sanskrit College, Vidyasagar began his first serious effort at reforming the tradition according to Western rational precepts. In this case, it was the college curriculum, which he altered after a hard, critical, and pragmatic review. Courses in language, literature, law, and philosophy had been taught mechanically; students were made to memorize passages verbatim; the content was always inflexibly the same, the duration of the study invariably unaltered. Vidyasagar ruthlessly accomplished what no Orientalist had dared to try—he transformed the ritualistic corpus of Sanskrit learning into an updated and rational scheme of Sanskrit education. He reintroduced English, which the Bentinck administration had dropped in 1835, and introduced Bengali, the living language of the people. He cut out what he considered "false" content, or traditional sources that conflicted with the truth. For example, Sanskrit treatises on mathematics, science, and philosophy were dropped. Simultaneously, he deleted "useless" Sanskritic sources or methods of learning, substituting such things as essay writing for rote learning, and English texts for certain dead wood from higher Sanskrit courses.

Vidyasagar's object was clearly to use rationalism to modernize the Sanskritic tradition. After making English a compulsory subject for eight years, and introducing Western philosophy into the *Darsana* (Indian philosophy) course, he said, "students wishing to transfer the Philosophy of the West into a native dress will possess a stock of technical words already to some degree familiar to intelligent natives." He also contended that "young men thus educated will be better able to expose the errors of ancient Hindu philosophy than if they were to derive their knowledge of Philosophy simply from European sources."

Vidyasagar's was a nineteenth-century view of objective truth. He was positive he would find it if the means he employed to pursue truth were sound and rational. He favored the modern learning of the West not because it was Western, but because the West had broken away from an uncritical, unthinking reverence for tradition. And he sought to use the Western achievement to revitalize his own civilization. He was never a nationalist, but always a rationalist.

In 1852, Dr. J. R. Ballantyne of Benares Sanskrit College visited Vidyasagar in Calcutta. His aim was to convince Vidyasagar that teaching the truth of India and the truth of Europe separately, leaving the student "to determine for himself whether the principles inculcated in these correspond to one another, or altogether conflict, or correspond partly," often frustrated the purpose of reconciling the two major traditions. Ballantyne seems to have been less concerned with truth as it is, and more concerned with presenting truth in such a way as not to offend the sensibility of the Indian students. Thus he had prepared his own books, which he called *Synopsis of Sciences*, or commentaries designed to "bridge the chasm" between Indian and European cultural attitudes and "to interpret the mind of Europe to that of India."

Vidyasagar's reaction was interesting, in that he refused to concede the priority of cultural deference as an integral part of the educational process. Ballantyne had juxtaposed Vedanta with Berkeley's *Inquiry* to show similarities in idealist philosophy. Vidyasagar's response was that the Vedanta was bad enough without reinforcing its false assertions and spurious reasoning with the help of Berkeley. If Vedanta were to be retained at all in the Darsana course, it would be only to have its life-negational presuppositions demolished by the philosophy of the modern empiricists. Nor would he budge from his own method of placing the two philosophic and scientific systems side by side. His own words show clearly that not Westernization but rationalism was the underlying purpose in his choice of method: "Truth is truth if properly perceived. To believe that 'truth is double' is but the imperfect perception of truth itself—an effect which I am sure to see removed by the improved courses of studies we have adopted at this institution."

In the 1850s, Vidyasagar also launched his campaign to emancipate the Hindu woman from her basic disabilities and traditionally imposed slavery. He accepted Rammohun Roy's conclusion that only by freeing women and by treating them as human beings could Indian society free itself from social stagnation. Vidyasagar's contemporary, Akkhoy Kumar Dutt, had done likewise. But if Rammohun argued from the vantage point of the Unitarian social gospel, and Dutt from that of the positivist ethic, Vidyasagar approached the problem as an indigenous modernizer. To be sure, Vidyasagar deplored inhumanity as a rationalist and humanist, but winning over other pandits to his way of thinking meant proving it from the classical sources. Rammohun had also gone to the sources, but he had reinterpreted them by refashioning the Vedanta in the mold of the Unitarian rational faith, asserting that monotheism was the central factor in the authentic Hindu tradition and golden age. Vidyasagar's pragmatism and atheism not only set him apart from Rammohun, but explains his lifelong ambivalence to the Brahmo Samaj.

In 1853, Vidyasagar discovered a sloka or verse from the *Parashara Samhita*, an ancient legal text in Sanskrit, which favored widow remarriage. Parashara had stated three alternatives for the widow—remarriage, sati, and an ascetic life. Since sati had been abolished by law in 1830 and the rigors of asceticism were no longer feasible, remarriage was the only suitable alternative. This was only part of Vidyasagar's technique for changing social values from within the system. He knew that to the pundits, the earlier the scriptural source, the more authority it commanded. But he also sought to demonstrate on ethical grounds that it was inhuman to prohibit child widows from remarrying. Vidyasagar was extremely effective. His ideas were incorporated into a Widow Remarriage Bill that became law on July 26, 1856. In the same way, Vidyasagar attacked the evils of Kulin polygamy, the denial of female education, and child marriage. Throughout he implied that evil and unscrupulous Brahmans had probably falsified the ancient texts to satisfy their own brutal inclinations.

Like Akkhoy Kumar Dutt, Vidyasagar formed an alliance with the Brahmo Samaj through its associative organization, the Tattvabodhini Sabha. An enlightened attitude to reform was the basis of the alliance. The Sabha had been formed by Debendranath Tagore in 1839 to combat Trinitarian missionary influence and to provide an umbrella society for alienated young intellectuals, both humanist and theist. Evidence suggests that Vidyasagar and Dutt attracted to the Sabha a number of secular-minded members of Young Bengal.

Kali Prosanna Singh, the fiery young zamindar whose Calcutta palace was a stone's throw from Debendranath Tagore's, in Jorasanko, has realistically described the factionalism in the Tattvabodhini Sabha. He has explained how "as young people we had to make a name for ourselves and so we began to cast about for a means of becoming famous." To "achieve this end" we began to "write, to edit papers, establish clubs"—and "become Brahmos." Soon "we would be invited to attend meetings of the Tattvabodhini Sabha and to take part in the discussions." The position taken on issues such as widow remarriage put us "in factional disputes," and before long we found ourselves "waiting on famous leaders of the factions like Debendranath Tagore, Ishwar Chandra Vidyasagar, and Akkhoy Kumar Dutt."

Sociologically, Kali Prosanna represented a class of zamindars whom Debendranath, for one, greatly prized as recruits to the Brahmo movement. Obviously, zamindars brought wealth and status into any organization of the period, nor must it be forgotten that Rammohun Roy and Debendranath Tagore were also zamindars. These facts about class interest are no doubt important, but they in no way explain why a landholding intellectual such as Kali Prosanna Singh drifted into one camp and not into another. Kali Prosanna was also a member of Young Bengal, educated at Hindu College, who reacted against "imitation of foreign manners" and subsequent "denationalization." In many ways, he moved along the same path as Rajnarian Bose into cultural nationalism, which he best expressed in his ardent defense of Bengali language and literature.[28]

But in terms of factional affiliation in the Tattvabodhini Sabha, it was not Rajnarian that young Kali Prosanna hailed as his *dolpati* (faction leader) but Dutt and Vidyasagar, neither of whom, interestingly enough, was a landholder or blessed, in the early 1850s, with much wealth or privilege. Rather, both were at the time noted for their "Brahmo puritanism" based on "plain living and high thinking." Moreover, the young people who clustered about these two towering intellects were equally attracted by their rationalism, their scientific curiosity, and their passion for reform. Former members of Young Bengal, in particular, were influenced by the curious fact that these two "Brahmos" were conspicuously indifferent to matters of religious faith.

Though I have no evidence to prove it, my impression is that the humanist faction began to dominate the Sabha sometime after 1855, under Vidyasagar's leadership. It was then that Debendranath the theist confronted Vidyasagar the atheist. Not social reform but religion became the key issue between them. It was then that Debendranath befriended the young liberal theist, Keshub Chandra Sen, who became Vidyasagar's most serious rival among the younger generation. One source contends that the reason Debendranath dismantled the Tattvabodhini Sabha in 1859 was that he felt the "atheists" had taken over and were acting in a way detrimental to Brahmo interests.[29] We do know that in 1858 Vidyasagar had become secretary of the Sabha and editor of the *Tattvabodhini Patrika*.[30] In 1859, Debendranath abolished the Sabha, and transferred to the Brahmo Samaj the printing press, the newspaper, and other properties of the defunct organization. At the same time (1860), Debendranath and Keshub Chandra became joint secretaries of the Brahmo Samaj.[31]

After the incident, Vidyasagar seems to have drawn closer to other liberal pandits who, like himself, were graduates of Sanskrit College. One such was Dwarkanath Vidyabhusan, a professor of literature at the college and its assistant secretary. The circle of little-known pandit reformers also included Taranath Tarkabachaspati, Modan Mohun Tarkalankar, and Sirish Chandra Vidyaratna.[32] Sivanath Sastri, a later graduate of Sanskrit College, first imbibed his liberalism from this group of humanists before exposure to Unitarian ideas. Sastri's uncle was the above Vidyabhusan, who was among Vidyasagar's closest friends. From 1855 on, Vidyabhusan actively assisted Vidyasagar's female reform campaign—especially in the area of widow remarriage. But when, in 1866, the young Sastri announced that he would follow Keshub Sen, Vidyabhusan exploded. "He tried to reason with me," Sivanath said later on, "and told me I was suffering from monomania or religious madness." Vidyabhusan's dislike of Keshub's intense religiosity was evidently so extreme that he continually ridiculed the reformer and his disciples. He predicted that under Keshub's leadership, Brahmoism would "reduce itself into a sectarian cult."[33]

Though most of the other pandits managed to accommodate themselves to the revival of orthodoxy and conservatism later in the century, Vidyasagar lived out his remaining years as "the lonely Prometheus,"[34] forever challenging God for the sake of improving man's condition. According to Tripathi, he grew weary "of the pundits who sold their souls for a mess of pottage." He continued to distrust the Westernized intelligentsia who acculturated themselves adequately to the trappings of European civilization, but who lacked the convictions of a truly rational and modernist mentality. As for religion, he distrusted all theists to the very end. And as Tripathi has, I think, rightly pointed out, "if he had any religion, it was the religion of humanity." In brief, "his ceaseless activity to alleviate human suffering or to improve the human condition was rooted in a belief in the perfectibility of man and man's responsibility for his neighbour."

Vidyasagar, who was essentially an educationist and reformer, never systematized his humanism as a philosophy. This was done by a Brahmo, curiously enough, in the twentieth century, Brajendranath Seal, who represented a shift from liberal theism to secular humanism. Seal, who died in 1938, was like Vidyasagar an educator, a devotee of science and rationalism, a student of comparative studies, and a very convincing advocate of the religion of humanity. And like Vidyasagar, he spent most of his mature life evolving intellectually as a result of his eternal quest for truth. Only infirmity and disease shortly before his death brought to a close Seal's indefatigable pursuit of systematic knowledge and a synthetic view of unity and diversity in the world.

In view of the fact that Brajendranath gave up his Brahmo religiosity for scientific positivism, it is noteworthy that his father, Mohendranath Seal, was one of the earliest disciples of Comte in Bengal.[35] It is regrettable that available biographical data on Brajendranath neither suggest how this influence affected the young man nor reveal why he originally turned to Brahmoism as a college student.

When Brajendranath studied at the General Assembly Institution, his teachers were amazed at his mathematical aptitude.[36] In 1878, he was admitted into the college department of the same institution. Here among his classmates and friends was Narendra Nath Dutt, the future Vivekananda. Both of them evidently attended Sadharan Brahmo meetings, but whereas Brajendranath stayed with that community as an initiated member, Naren Dutt went on to Keshub's New Dispensation, and later beyond that to found his own movement. According to Seal, a bond between himself and Vivekananda as college students was their interest in European philosophers. They read Mill, Comte, Spencer, and Hegel not out of idle curiosity or for course requirements, but to gain understanding and insight into problems of faith, evil, and progress.[37]

In 1884, Brajendranath secured his M.A. in philosophy and was appointed assistant professor at City College, Calcutta. His first major work, which took him twenty-four years to complete (1883 to 1907), was a book, *New Essays in Criticism*, in which he expressed partiality for English romantic literature. But he was not so much interested in the creative side as he was in applying Hegelian philosophy to literary criticism. Between 1884 and 1896, Seal shifted from college to college, restlessly in pursuit of academic responsibility and a secure financial position commensurate with his potential genius.[38] During that period he published virtually nothing.

Then in 1896, the Maharaja of Cooch Behar, notorious son-in-law of Keshub Sen, invited Seal to become principal of the recently established Victoria College. And here, finally, Seal attained stability, peace of mind, and time for studious reflection. It was in Cooch Behar that Brajendranath was able to finish his *New Criticism* and was able to begin his first cantos of the *Quest Eternal*, a philosophic epic that traced his own intellectual development. At Cooch Behar he began exploration of the "positive sciences of the ancient Hindus," which led ultimately to his contributing a chapter on that subject in Prafulla Chandra Ray's *History of Chemistry in Ancient India*.[39] It was from Cooch Behar that Seal first acquired a reputation abroad, and in 1902 he was first considered seriously for a post as professor of philosophy at Cambridge University, England.

One good reason for Brajendranath's growing reputation was that by means of liberal support authorized by the Maharaja in the form of travel grants he was able to go to Europe in 1899, 1906, and 1911. In 1906, for example, he attended the International Congress of Orientalists in Rome, and in 1911 the Maharaja arranged a handsome grant to take Professor Seal to London to give the inaugural paper for the First Universal Race Congress.

When, in September 1911, Brajendranath heard that the Maharaja had died suddenly while also visiting England, it seemed as if the world had collapsed around him. A letter to the Diwan's Office of Cooch Behar State dated March 22, 1912, indicates that without the Maharaja's patronage, his financial situation had suddenly worsened.[40] On December 20, 1912, Seal tendered a letter of resignation from Victoria College, in which he blamed bad health for his decision. What is revealing in this long letter justifying his termination of service is the prevailing mood of despair about his future career and about the completion of "research projects." He seemed pessimistic about his chances of finding a post at London, Cambridge, or Calcutta Universities. What most dismayed him was whether he would ever again find a position that would afford him the time to carry out his research on cultural history, on developing a "philosophical system of the universe," and on perfecting a "synthesis of all the modern advances in Science."[41]

This was a critical period in his life, which some believe to have been resolved by his alleged repudiation of the Brahmo faith and by his conversion to "Godness humanism."[42] A manuscript copy of a later book by Brajendranath published as *Comparative Studies in Vaishnavism and Christianity*, and written just at this time (1912), reveals less a lack of religious feeling and more a groping for a comparative methodology free of the stranglehold imposed by Westerncentric academic scholarship. Here, in the brilliant introduction, Seal exposed the excesses of Western imperialism, which he combated not as a militant nationalist but as a cool man of reason.

In contrast to most of the Sadharan Brahmo philosophers, by 1911 Seal had rejected Hegel largely because of the German's unilinear philosophy of history, which traced "a single flow of progress" through time from East to West. To Seal, Hegelianism was typical of the Westerncentric notion that "all other races and cultures have been a preparation for the Greco-Roman-Gothic type," which is now the "Epitome of Mankind, the representation of Universal Humanity, the heir of all the ages." Therefore, any comparison between Christianity, Vaishnavism, or any other religion by a Western scholar would necessarily be one "between a rudimentary and a developed organism." For Seal, this attitude "seems to be a mischievous error due to an essentially wrong conception of the philosophy of history and the evolution of culture and an essentially perverse use of the historico-comparative method."

What Seal proposed instead as an antidote for imperialist comparative studies is based on the proposition that "historical comparison implies that the objects compared are of co-ordinate rank and belong more or less to the same stage in the development of known culture." Moving in the direction of cultural and historical relativity, in which traditions evolve in parallel patterns, Brajendranath argued that "every code, language, myth or system, has its own history—its origin, growth and development—a study of which is essential to a proper understanding of its function in society, its place, meaning and worth."

His concern was with the different types of cultures that appeared to develop in similar patterns of historical development. In opposition to the Hegelian view, Seal maintained that Chinese and Hindu cultures have "passed through most of the stages observable in the growth of the Hebraic-Greco-Roman-Gothic civilization." The same may be said for Islamic civilization. Thus humanity is "a circle of which the center is everywhere and the circumference nowhere." To be sure, each culture is "diversely embodied, reflected in specific modes and forms." But "in spite of multiformity and in spite of the diverse ethnic developments all very real, all very special, there has been a general history of human culture and progress, the unfolding of a single ideal, plan, or pattern, a universal movement."

The task of the comparative historian was to take the different departments of the major cultures and work out their histories "in the same general historic plan and in obedience to the same general law of progress." His own work on Vaishnavism and Christianity was a step in that direction, in which two comparable religions in diverse cultures underwent similar historical development. Though Christianity has been treated historically and has undergone considerable change and continuity over its long span of history, Vaishnavism, which is an equally complex phenomenon with over two thousand years of history, has yet to be studied intensively using the same objective modes of historical inquiry.[43]

In such a manuscript, Brajendranath Seal explored unity and diversity. According to D. M. Bose, this interest in comparative history ran side by side with a growing appreciation of the positive sciences; the belief being that they were far better equipped than religion to guide mankind into a higher level of human relationships.[44] Bose argues that from 1911, Seal had elevated humanity into "a modern hero," an attitude attributed to Comte's influence.

In 1913, fortunately for Seal, the worst fears reflected in his letter of resignation from Victoria College never materialized; he was given the post of King George V professorship of philosophy at Calcutta University. For the next eight years he taught, traveled, labored on his projects, published from time to time, and always absorbed new funds of knowledge and theory from a countless array of sources. He was so knowledgeable about so many different things that he was described as a walking encyclopedia.

In 1921, he was appointed vice chancellor of Mysore University, a position he held until 1930, when he was compelled to retire due to bad health. In 1926, he was knighted.[45] With the exception of a classical syllabus of Indian philosophy for student use in 1924, and his slim volume on *Rammohun Roy: the Universal Man*, there was little during his Mysore period to trace his ideological development. The most significant aspect of the Rammohun Roy study was Seal's strong attachment to the great men throughout history who have sought ways of reconciling cultural encounters by synthesis. As Seal himself put it: "This indeed is the meaning of progress in history. For history is a confluence of many streams, bringing together conflicting cultures, conflicting national values and ideals, and those who can find peaceful solutions of these conflicts are the true heroes of latter-day Humanity."[46]

In the 1930s, while living in a state of forced retirement due to his failing eyesight and general physical deterioration, Brajen-dranath finally had the opportunity of bringing his research proj-ects to a conclusion—though under the condition of decreasing mental effectiveness. In 1936, bedridden and blind, he appears to have completed his *Quest Eternal* at last, one of the few modern In-dian epics of the Faustian man in search of the meaning of exist-ence. The book is so rich in symbolism taken from the literary tra-ditions of both East and West that only a highly sophisticated analysis in a cross-cultural perspective would do justice to the full meaning and import of Brajendranath's poem.

What Brajendranath has done in this poem is to divide man's eternal quest for understanding into two dimensions. The first or historical dimension delineates how a world view is shaped by an ancient, medieval, and modern ethos. The second or cultural di-mension suggests how a world view is shaped by the specific forms and values of human configurations. Therefore, in a far more world-encompassing and challenging arena of conflicting forces than Goethe's *Faust*, the book it most resembles, Brajendranath created as his hero the prototype of cosmopolitan man in quest of unity through a pluralistic universe.

The ancient ideal is of the "birth of the Godhead" and of the "Maid Eternal," quite possibly representing the male and female principles in all archaic religions. Brajendranath did not take his illustrations from any one tradition of early mythology, but from major ones in both East and West. The universal religious impulse predominates in the ancient ideal, while historical consciousness remains dim in an outlook of historical drift and cyclical reoccur-rence:

> The human mysteries,
> They dance of Love,
> They dance of Death,
> Thy Graces, Pities, Charities,
> Are as the desert Sphinx impressive
> Implacable as Fate!
> O World-drift cyclical!

From man's humble position in ancient society, where he re-mains prisoner of his fate, Brajendranath moved into the more ag-

gressive quest of the wizard knight seeking truth in the medieval cultural context. The medieval ideal here is not to be confused with a figure in the actual chronological period of the middle ages. In fact, his Wizard knight resembled modern man in search of scientific rationalism in the world of nature. He conducted his search in the name of the "Magician Commonwealth of Reason" and won the "Zodiac shield of the Sun for his victories over Untruth." After meanderings for truth, and maintaining himself as a pure devotee of the Commonwealth of Reason, the Wizard knight's quest ended in failure. The pursuit through reason had led to mere reason and not to the truth of self:

> But all quest of knowledge blest,
> Himself it cannot save!
> O mercy! from illusion free
> This knowledge loses life!
> For Beauty and Love, Pity and Alone,
> Are Still with illusion rife.

This led Brajendranath into a quest for wisdom which he called "modern," and which featured the hero in the role of the "homeless wanderer . . . in search of a Wisdom that is able to master Death." But death here is not "death in a physical sense" so much as "that dark power in life who frustrates our goals and strivings." The hero wandered through the "realms of Soul, of Nature, and of Man in History," but found everywhere "the leaguered powers of brute Matter and blind Sense." In complete despair he heard voices in colloquy:

> Is this Man's kingdom?
> Man, bound, manacled.
> Sold in the mart
> And fattened for the yoke.

This modern section of the epic is most fascinating because it seems to suggest that Brajendranath Seal had abandoned rationalism, scientism, Marxism, or any other salvation ideology of the "coming kingdom of man," which he also depicted as the "Finale of the evolution of the Spirit." All "isms" of this sort are but "a vain dream." His hero learned ultimately how "the Forces of the prime" in "conspiracy with the stars" humbled man continually, so that "on Earth's soil, an increasing barrenness." Thus said the hero, "I urged no pygmy proletariat war," nor "cursed a tyrant Punch upon the puppet stage."

> Before the Lord; the hunt resounds,
> Death chases Life
> Life, Death.

The hero then changed his perspective until the "dimensions of the original problem are now enlarged." From an individual's quest of life and wisdom he passed to the "problem of redemption of Humanity as a whole." He questioned his despair by asking, "is the darkest hour born before the dawn?" The great man of the future he believed is a "new Prometheus" or universal man whose dream is to "redeem Humanity from the bondage of the gods." The hero called to the universal redeemer:

> Oh come, Prometheus, come out of the shadow
> Of ages, out of the Deep,
> The dark, dark Deep!
> Arise and lead from Darkness to Light,
> Arise and lead from Death to Deathlessness!
> Arise and lead from Untruth's snares to truth.

But the faith in a charismatic hero to save humanity also proved a futile hope. The hero internalized the question to find spiritual strength in the victory over death. Much agony had passed with time between Vidyasagar's unfettered optimism and Seal's restrained faith in the religion of humanity. Seal's epic ended, disappointingly to some, on a note of hope through collective suffering. Perhaps Seal had returned to God in his final years. His hope was shrouded in a mysticism illuminated only by what he called the "One Suffering God." After enduring world war, totalitarianism, and genocide, Seal thought of the nineteenth-century religion of humanity as a oneness with the human race, achieved by "universal sympathy and compassion for the drama of divine suffering."

> Ottoman, Ottoman
> Unbound thyself, and rise!
> Learn:
> Psyche's curse is annulled,
> And Prometheus has unbound himself.[47]

If the alliance between secular humanism and science was always a delicate one in Bengal, that between liberal theism and science flourished. In fact, among scientists themselves, as we shall see—at least those within the Brahmo community—science seemed to justify and intensify their religiosity. The exceptions began to appear in the twentieth century, in the 1930s, when Marxism rather than theism satisfied a younger generation in quest of a secularized ideology of salvation for India. It should also be pointed out that many of the humanists before them who championed science— Dutt, Vidyasagar, and Seal—were themselves not scientists as such.

So pervasive were certain aspects of scientism in nineteenth-century Bengal that Brahmos often justified their rational religion in the name of science. The "science of religion" was not an uncommon expression in Brahmo writings. What they meant was the discovery of natural laws about religion from the comparative study of religions carried on without sectarian bias, and leading to a unified concept of the religion of man. And as good scientists, in the spirit of positivist sociology, they could apply what they learned either to the reformation of existing religions or to the creation of a new faith. Since Brahmos were influenced by Unitarian cosmopolitanism, there is an overlap in their writings between religious universalism and scientistic unity.

In an important work by Rajnarian Bose of the Adi Brahmo Samaj (1863), the science of religion, Unitarian universalism, and the importance of national identity were all interwoven to prove that Brahmoism was the most advanced and rational religion of all in the nineteenth century. It is also revealing as a document in reply to a Christian critic.

Rajnarian began with a defense of intuition, placing himself in the position of accepting from whatever culture all genuine theistic impulses as equal. If that be the case, he asked, then why must we insist so much "on the acceptance of a book of revelation as necessary for salvation?" On the other hand, Brahmos have not ignored religious diversity or the particular aspects of each national faith. Indeed, the Brahmo policy of accepting all faiths as diverse expressions of a universal need for religion was done in response to modern times, while the alteration of Brahmo doctrine put their religion well ahead of Christianity as a progressive faith. Brahmoism was, in fact, the prototype for the next stage of religious evolution in the world. Therefore Brahmos, far from playing intellectual games, were performing God's work in the nineteenth century, and it is their faith that would certainly supercede narrow sectarian Christianity. Why were Brahmos superior to Christians in the quest for a "modern" religion? Rajnarian's reply was that Brahmos now had the key to the "science of religion." This science was predicated on the belief in "unity in essentials, variety in non-essentials and toleration for all."

Rajnarian the nationalist hardly ignored the diversity of the Hindu tradition, and at one point said candidly that "Rammohun's catholicity had to be corrected by a more Hindu aspect." Nevertheless, it was the universal, scientific, and unifying aspect of natural religion that was paramount. In India it had expressed itself through Brahmoism, which sought to reform Hinduism. The natural religious characteristic of Brahmoism could do the same for other creeds. Natural religion, Rajnarian wrote, "by which the Jew applying it to his Bible, the Hindu to his Sastra, the Greek to his Plato, the modern European to the New Testament, the Muhammedan to the Koran, and so forth, mankind might gradually become more united in a brotherly eclectic feeling of piety and reverence, mutually allowing variety of customs, and consenting out of former creeds to reject the weeds and keep the flowers."[48]

If Rajnarian Bose used science in the sense of religious reformation, Keshub Chandra Sen went so far as to justify his new synthetic ideology of salvation or New Dispensation in the name of "science of religion." His argument is interesting in light of his differences with Vidyasagar, who was also an advocate of science. It suggests once more the fact that religion and science were as natural together as humanism and science.

In a public lecture on "God Vision in the Nineteenth Century" given in 1880 to defend his new religious system, Keshub distinguished between his own rational and scientific religion and the dark age of misguided religion, which "shrouded the world in superstition." It has been a long night for the world, which "has slept for long ages dreaming dreams and seeing visions." Night was the time when "the magician waves his mysterious wand and fascinates and enthralls the senses, and when 'priests' . . . hold the human soul in hopeless intellectual bondage and spiritual servitude."

"Thank goodness," said Keshub, "the hideous night of superstition and priestcraft has gone by." We are now living in "the age of science." Does that mean disregarding God? No, because "God cannot be banished from your minds." There is a science of religion just as there are other sciences. But it is neither the "painted fiction of ancient mythology nor the polished abstraction of modern metaphysics." Science is "complete unity" and the science of religion is "religious unity." Keshub concluded that: "It is our task to apply the unity of science to God because that is all science is but reduction to unity and order. God is all around us . . . all that you are required to do is to take off the huge dial from its face. Then you will see the secret spring of the machinery which keeps the universe in working order."[49]

If Brahmo religious leaders found it necessary to defend their religion along scientific lines, Brahmo scientists found it equally necessary to defend their scientific careers as being in no way contradictory to the faith they shared with other members of the Brahmo community. The common factor among them all was their acute rational outlook, always inseparable from their devotion to progress. Thus, to understand the birth of science in modern India, it is perhaps necessary to trace their lives as individual people trying to develop as scientists in the Indian colonial situation.

As the pioneer of modern science in India, probably no other name has been so well remembered as that of Jagadish or "Jessie" Bose. Bose was born in 1858 in that birthplace of Brahmo heroes, Vikrampur, near Dacca, East Bengal. He enjoyed a privileged boyhood as the son of the remarkable Bhagaban Chandra Bose, one of those early members of the Western-educated Brahmo society of Dacca. As headmaster of the Mymensingh Zillah School, the elder Bose inspired and indoctrinated many an East Bengali youth with the tenets of the Brahmo faith.[50] He is perhaps best recalled for his distinguished career as a civil servant. He was also an entrepreneur who invested money in various ventures ranging from tea plantations in Assam to an industrial weaving concern in Bombay.

In 1863, Bhagaban sent his son Jessie to a vernacular school because he believed that a boy should learn Bengali before English.[51] Four years later, Jessie was admitted to Hare School in Calcutta, where his English education began in earnest. Then in 1874, while his father served as personal assistant to the commissioner of Burdwan, Jessie entered St. Xavier's College. While there, and under the guidance of Father LaFont, professor of physics, Jessie received his first impulse to become a scientist. In 1880, at twenty-two years of age, Bose received his B.A. and the blessings of Father LaFont, who urged him to pursue science as a career.[52]

Upon graduation, Jessie's parents were inclined to send their boy to England for medical training. Finally, they agreed to support his own desire to continue his studies in the natural sciences. Significant at this stage in his life was the enlightened attitude of his Brahmo parents. In contrast to many a Hindu young man in similar circumstances, young Jessie experienced no grief resulting from a broken-hearted superstitious mother worried about crossing the forbidden seas, or an angry father concerned primarily with the prospect of losing caste. In fact, his mother willingly offered the sale of her jewelry to send the young man to England.[53]

Jessie was fortunate and bright enough to win a national science fellowship to Christ's College, Cambridge, in 1881. Rather like his brother-in-law, Ananda Mohun Bose, Jessie Bose left behind him at Cambridge a brilliant record.[54] Like Ananda Mohun, also, Jessie was a diligent worker with good study habits and a burning desire to succeed.

Back in Bengal, Jessie entered the Government Educational Service and was appointed as officiating professor of physics at Presidency College. The fact that Jessie Bose was placed in the Class IV bracket of the service, at a salary grade two-thirds of that received by a European in a similar position, gave him his earliest humiliating experience at the hands of British imperialism.[55] He was unwilling, however, to be discriminated against for his race, and courageously refused to accept his salary for three years. Finally, the government reversed their policy and accepted him as an equal.[56] When we consider that at this very time Jessie was responsible for paying off his father's debts incurred by investment failures, the young man's heroic character and stature seems remarkable indeed. Moreover, during the same time, Jessie was a target for the racist director of public instruction, Sir Alfred Croft, who once declared that "no native was fit to teach the exact sciences."[57]

In 1887, Jessie married Abala Das, the very talented and well-educated daughter of Durga Mohun Das.[58] It was a critical year for Jessie; he had wanted to begin serious investigation of electric radiation, but had discovered no laboratory in Presidency College to carry on his research. Nor were there mechanical facilities at his disposal.[59] The system, which had relegated Calcutta University to the status of bureaucratic clearing house for examinations and degrees, thwarted the young man who desperately wanted to do original research.

By 1892, Bose managed through his own efforts to carry on limited observation of electric waves. Two years later his perseverance began to show results. The government finally agreed to give him an annual grant of 2,500 rupees to defray his expenses as a research scholar. On November 30, 1894, Professor Bose, who taught twenty-six hours every week, dramatically announced that he had now "dedicated himself to pure knowledge."[60] In 1895, he gave his first scientific paper before the Asiatic Society of Bengal on the "Polarization of Electric Waves."

The paper is of enormous consequence, since it revealed the findings of his research on wireless transmission, establishing the later claim of his friends that he and not Marconi had laid the groundwork for the breakthrough in radio transmission. From one source, back in 1894, Bose "operated his transmitter in Dr. Roy's lecture room sending energy through closed doors guarded by Father LaFont across the next room to Professor Pedlar's classroom." Bose met Marconi in September 1896, and the two were in regular contact with one another.[61]

In 1896, the government of India dispatched Bose to England to give papers to learned societies. Bose availed himself of the opportunity to acquiring an M.A. from Cambridge and a D.S.C. from the University of London. Bose's papers on such topics as "On the Determination of the Indices of Electric Refraction" and "On the Determination of the Wave Length of Electric Radiation" won him support from the physicist Lord Kelvin of the Royal Society, who arranged for their publication in journals. Of immense importance to others was Bose's work on the detection of molecular change in matter under electrical stimulation. Such research led to the invention of highly sensitive electrical receivers used on ships and lighthouses for communication and transmission of danger signals at sea.

When, in 1900, Jessie Bose was selected by the Government of India to be a delegate to the International Scientific Congress in Paris, he had already achieved considerable success and fame. Because he was such an unusual phenomenon in the India of his time, Bose could easily have settled back comfortably and rested on his laurels. But as a this-worldly ascetic deeply committed to hard work and the need to achieve, Bose now entered a totally new field of research as if he were a young graduate student enthusiastically tackling his first experiment.

In Paris, and then in London, he developed a thesis about the similarity of the effect of electrical stimuli on inorganic and living substances, and like a graduate student he found it necessary to defend each idea against the weighty criticism of his senior colleagues.[62] More disturbing to him was the anger of many physiologists who did not respond favorably to a trained physicist shifting into their area of speculation. Another problem was that Professor Bose had begun to address himself to the differences between living and inanimate beings, which to the scientific materialist was suggestive of Hindu mysticism.

According to those who knew Bose well, such as Rabindranath

Tagore, the scientist's new line of inquiry was as much prompted by Brahmo religious sentiment as by anything else.[63] Ramananda Chatterji, a fellow Brahmo and close friend of Bose's, has written that questions were now being directed at the nature of life itself. "How do lifeless atoms combine to form living matter?" Chatterji reported Bose as asking himself at the time. Another question was whether there was "anything really without even a primal form of life?" Chatterji concluded that such questions were asked by a "theistic Vedantist demonstrating religious conviction through inductive scientific methods."[64]

Bose, on a prolonged leave of absence in Europe, did not return to Calcutta until October 1902. As much a technologist as a scientist, he went beyond inductive methods to prove that so-called inanimate objects such as plants responded as much to pleasure and pain as did animate creatures. He coined his current research interest "differential sensibilities,"[65] and he was determined to prove his contentions through delicate mechanical instruments designed for the purpose. In Calcutta, at his laboratory in Presidency College, the indefatigable Professor Bose labored to produce the technology necessary to demonstrate the divine spark in everything that exists on earth. It is reported that by the time of his death, Bose had invented fifty machines to carry out his purpose.[66] Some of his instruments could actually record the growth of plants, and one such, the balanced crescograph, was adopted by the American government for agricultural research. One of his machines, which he named the morograph, could record the "critical point of death of a plant."

In 1907, after bringing out a volume on comparative electrophysiology, Bose was sent by the Government of India once again on a scientific deputation to England and America. In February 1908, Bose stood before members of the United States Department of Agriculture in Washington and summed up his work on "The Growth Response of Plants." He also delivered lectures to science faculties in major American universities. He was less flamboyant than Vivekananda, but his return to India in July 1909 was every bit the return of a national hero. Even to the militant Tilak, for instance, Bose's moderate nationalist stance was overlooked in favor of the image of the national hero who had redeemed India's unfavorable image as scientifically backward in the family of nations.

Between 1909 and 1914, when Bose went on his fourth scientific deputation to England and America, he continued to work furiously, inventing new machines and refining his theory.[67] One instrument, called the Resonant and Oscillating Recorder, actually induced nervous paralysis in a plant. Americans were extremely interested in these remarkably sensitive machines. Bose's books were adopted as physiology texts in some places, while his lectures formed the basis for new courses.

Bose retired from his professional duties at Presidency College shortly after returning to Calcutta. He was then fifty-seven years old, and in the eyes of his contemporaries, perhaps, ready at last to diminish the pace of diligent application he had set for himself. Patrick Geddes believed he was summing up Bose's achievement in "exploring the border region between physics and physiology . . . to find boundary lines vanishing and points of contact emerge between the reaches of the Living and Non-living."[68]

But Jessie was hardly prepared to retire from his calling as a research scientist. In fact, the government awarded him a grant of 150,000 rupees to be paid annually for continuing his work. In 1917, when the British conferred knighthood upon him,[69] Jessie also built an institute named after himself at a cost of five lakhs of rupees in order to pursue the questions that suited him best.

His wife has reported that throughout his active life, which ended only with his death in November 1937, Jessie was a pious Brahmo who began each day with a prayer and lived strictly according to the ethical precepts of his religion.[70] During the last years, he spent much time at his second home in Darjeeling, where he had established a branch of the Bose Institute.[71] In Darjeeling, also, he formed a circle of Brahmo compatriots who discussed intellectual, aesthetic, and spiritual matters with him; the *adda* included Rabindranath, Nilratan Sarcar, Ramananda Chatterji, and Brajendranath Seal.[72]

Bose's speeches and lectures throughout the 1920s stressed Brahmo universalism and scientific unity. In 1924, while summing up the achievements of the institute since its inception, he said that the reason he had turned to bridging the gap between organic and inorganic life since 1900 was to realize in scientific terms the underlying unity of life.[73] Though a national figure and hero to many, Bose was hardly a nationalist. Unity and not diversity seemed to be his predominant theme, as in a lecture of 1925, when he spoke movingly of the unity of scientific achievement through the interdependence of peoples and cultures. His Brahmo-inspired universalism was clearly expressed in the following:

Nothing could be more vulgar or more untrue than the ignorant assertion that the world owes its progress of knowledge to
any one particular race. The whole world is interdependent and
a constant stream of thought has throughout the ages enriched
the common heritage of mankind. It is the realization of virtual
dependence that has kept the mighty human fabric bound together and ensured the continuity and permanence of civilization. . . . Science is neither of the East nor of the West but international.[74]

A somewhat different kind of response by another Brahmo scientist is that of Prafulla Chandra Ray. Ray was also an East Bengali,
born in a Jessore village on August 2, 1861.[75] Like Bose, Ray had a
Western-educated father who, back in 1846 while a student in
Krishnagar College, sat at the feet of Ramtanu Lahiri, the famous
Brahmo sympathizer. Moreover, P. C. Ray's father was an enlightened zamindar, owning an enormous library filled with
Brahmo books and other progressive literature to which the boy
was exposed at a tender age.

In 1870, after four days of travel by rail and steamer from Jessore, the nine-year-old Prafulla Chandra arrived in the metropolis
of Calcutta for the first time. Like Bose and most sons of the
privileged Westernized elite, Ray was sent to Hare's School for his
English education.

He was fond of the Unitarians, whom he first read in his father's
study back in Jessore. Like most of the better-known Sadharan
progressives, he, too, revered Theodore Parker and for the same
reason, that rational religion and social reform were inseparable. It
was the acceptance of the Unitarian social gospel by Brahmos that
attracted him to the community in the first place. And as he himself
revealed, "it was the social aspect of the Brahmo Samaj that specially appealed to me."

As in the case of Jessie Bose, one looks for P. C. Ray's Brahmoism
not in church activities as such, but in his professional calling. Ray's
first exposure to his future career as a scientist came as a result of
attending lectures in chemistry at Presidency College as an external
student. In 1881, Ray successfully competed for a Gilchrist
Scholarship, which paid his way to London University. When he
reached London in 1882, he was warmly received by a Bengali delegation led by Jessie Bose. We might add that, as in the case of Jessie's mother, Prafulla Chandra's mother was also enlightened
enough not to raise any objection to her son going abroad.

After six years at London and Edinburgh, P. C. Ray returned to Calcutta with a doctorate in inorganic chemistry. And like Bose years earlier, he encountered racism and other features of the British colonialist attitude. Indeed, Ray had no job at first, and only through Professor Bose's help could he find a temporary assistant professorship at Presidency College that paid 250 rupees a month. Later, as a Gandhian nationalist, he would recount with extreme bitterness the blatant forms of discrimination against Indians— mostly Bengalis—within the Educational Service. In 1888, for example, he recalled that within the Departments of Geology, Trigonometrical Survey, Meteorology, and the Forest Service-Telegraph, out of 211 top appointments, only three were held by Indians.[76] He would also relate that after seven years of service he received the same salary of 250 rupees, and that nine years later he was drawing a salary of 400 rupees per month.[77]

In the next few years, Prafulla "threw himself heart and soul into Brahmo activities," serving on various committees.[78] It was a difficult time for him both professionally, as he tried to achieve something as a scientist, and physically, as his health broke down. Chronic indigestion ultimately drove him out of Calcutta and Bengal to hilly Deoghar, in Bihar, where he met the old Brahmo Rajnarian Bose, who then was enjoying his last years in retirement.

In the 1890s, Ray decided to extend his interest and zeal beyond the confines of the classroom into the world of business. He bought an acid factory in 1893 for 800 rupees, which he paid off in installments. There, with the cooperation of Brahmo medical practitioners such as Nilratan Sirkar, he prepared prescriptions for druggists "from indigenous drugs whose active principles were extracted according to up-to-date scientific methods." After considerable ups and downs, including the death of his partner from the plague in 1898, P. C. Ray persevered until he was able to establish the successful firm known as the Bengal Chemical and Pharmaceutical Works. An inventive chemist, he prepared a new mercury compound in 1896, and as a devoted and gifted teacher, he left behind him a coterie of brilliant students. Ray's scholarship was seldom free of profit-making considerations or the political exigencies of nationalism. In 1900, for example, it was Ray who first used China clay to produce fine pottery, and the same Ray who displayed courage as a Gandhian against the protestations of his own bhadralok Brahmo colleagues.

Intellectually, he left behind him a monumental *History of Chemistry in Ancient India*, which took fifteen years to complete and which has not yet been surpassed for its careful scholarship and technical virtuosity. He dismissed the notion that he wrote the book to supply ammunition for national glorification, but said he intended to supplement the scholarship of "Orientalists who have worked on all departments of Hindus of old but for one branch, chemistry."

As someone deeply religious and openly antimaterialist, Ray was as much a Brahmo scientist as Jessie Bose. Religion and science were not incompatible, but on the contrary, Ray looked upon them as two sides of the same philosophic quest for truth. Science is a discovery of operational laws and not the search for natural causation. In one article, Ray argued that there was "a limit of scientific research," and that men of science often forget that "the discovery of law is not an adequate solution to the problem of causes." "When all the motions of the heavenly bodies have been reduced to the dominion of gravitation," said he, "gravitation itself remains an insoluble problem." His contention was that

> The mind of man which can track the course of the comet, and measure the velocity of light, has hitherto proved incapable of explaining the existence of the minutest insect or the growth of the most humble plant. . . . An impenetrable mystery lies at the root of every existing thing. . . . We know nothing or next to nothing of the relations of mind to matter, either in our own persons or in the world around us; and to suppose that the progress of natural science eliminates the conception of a first cause from creation by supplying natural explanations, is completely to ignore the sphere and limits to which it is confined.[79]

One of the principal reasons why Brahmo scientists could defend religion, and Brahmo religious leaders could justify science, is that Brahmo religion had become so free from superstition, so amenable to rational reform, and so intellectually appealing to liberal theologians that the more emotional Brahmo enthusiasts began to complain that Brahmo religion had everything—except the religious impulse. Before long, the Sadharan Brahmo leader, Sivanath Sastri, himself no stranger to the rational spirit, felt the need to single out for attack the "philosophy cult" within the Samaj, which had reduced theism to dry rationalism and theology.[80]

The "philosophy cult" of radical rationalists was one of the fruits of Rammohun's attack on the excesses and abuses of popular Hinduism. The worship of images, the absence of congregational worship, caste rigidity in the performance of Hindu rituals, and above all, erotic "indecency" coupled with primitive outbursts of medieval

Vaishnavism—all these aspects of popular religion were judged by Brahmos to be excrescences on the true Hindu faith (Brahmoism). If Brahmos found it hard to change Hindus, they found it comparatively easy to perform the necessary reformist surgery in the religious practices of their own community.

The more Hindus clung to their "primitive" ways, the more sophisticated Brahmo rationalists jeered at their backwardness. In 1883, P. C. Majumdar sailed around the world, everywhere faithfully recording his daily impressions in a diary which he then published upon his return to India. Probably no Asian up to that time had left such a sophisticated account of life in the West. Majumdar commented on a variety of observations, including urban life in Chicago, the female emancipation movement in America, "pluralist society" in America, and the "modernization" of Japan. On occasion his comparative assessments betrayed feelings about popular Hinduism. As for example, his attitude to American Negroes: "In the absence of intellectual culture they break forth into visions, trances, shouts, and violent bodily movements." In fact, they reminded him of the Vaishnavas in his own country: "It will be at once perceived how closely allied all this is to the Hindu Vaishnavas. The negroes have both the virtues and vices of the Vaishnavas. And for that reason they are very much looked down upon by the other more intellectually organized sects."[81]

One interesting letter written in 1910 by Rabindranath Tagore on the theme of the true Brahmoism is further evidence of this attitude. In an unusually derisive tone, Tagore defended the older rational and classical form of Brahmo worship against the emotional Brahmoism introduced into the movement by Bijoy Krishna Goswami. "Emotionalism is not Brahmo spiritualism," wrote Tagore. In a manner reminiscent of Protap Chandra Majumdar, Tagore said that he saw "little difference between the activities of African witchcraft and our own emotionalism." He refused to believe that Bijoy Krishna's neo-Vaishnavism ever led to any significant truth. In fact, the contrary may be true, since Goswami attained not "spiritual stability" but "madness." Rabindranath condemned Shaktism in the same breath with Vaishnavism: "The last goal of Shaktism and Vaishnavism is emotionalism. . . . We can achieve nothing lasting by drinking wine or playing on the *khol* or by smoking *ganja*. When we try to create an excitement in ourselves by disregarding the outer world completely, then we can imagine ourselves anything or anyone such as Krishna. To avoid the rightful protest of the outer world, we declare such religious outbursts as meaningless. . . . Instead we should try our best to spiritualize the outer world."[82]

In 1897, when Sivanath Sastri was elected Samaj president, he drew up a set of institutional reforms that he felt were necessary to recapture the old Brahmo religious inspiration. But the same congregation that voted him into office rejected his recommendations, forcing him to resign the presidency and leave Calcutta. The congregation invited him back in 1900 by making him president, but in 1903 internal ideological divisiveness and increased tension compelled Sastri to resign again.[83] The problem lay with the faction of radical rationalists who had banded together to form a neo-Vedantist circle. They had become most articulate and influential in Samaj affairs, and saw the problem of Brahmo religious identity in a totally different light from Sastri. The Vedantist intellectuals, who could be found in both the Sadharan and Keshubite branches of the Samaj, were largely professional philosophers holding university positions. P. K. Roy, Sitanath Tattvabhusan, Hiralal Haldar were the most famous within the Sadharan Samaj, whereas the three Sens—Benoyendra Nath Sen, Mohit Chandra Sen, and Promathalal Sen—were most conspicuous among the younger generation of New Dispensation philosophers.

As highly Westernized professional intellectuals, these men saw the hope of Brahmoism in theology, and worked to produce a distinctive Brahmo philosophy. Most of them were advocates of neo-Vedantism, which they equated with neo-Hegelianism as two contemporary philosophies that could be used effectively against the countervailing contemporary scientific materialism. As trained scholars and technical philosophers with an extremely rational bent of mind, they distrusted the religions of feeling manifested in neo-Vaishnava cults.

Perhaps the most distinguished of all was Dacca-born Prosanna Kumar Roy, who in the 1870s established for himself one of the most brilliant records of any Indian studying in a British university.[84] In 1876, he was the first Indian to receive a D.S.C. from London University. He had also been a student at the University of Edinburgh and the Royal School of Mines.

In 1877, he returned to India and entered the Government Educational Service. Despite the usual discrimination against Indians in the predominantly white European faculties of Indian universities, Roy advanced himself from assistant professor of philosophy at Patna College to full professor at Calcutta University. Roy was by reputation a superb teacher, and an active Brahmo who in scores of lectures and seminars at City College, and at the Students Weekly Service, sought to convey to the young a high regard for rational religion, moral discipline, and intellectual achievement. Roy championed more "thought and reflection" among Brahmos, which could help arrest the tendency to emotionalize religion. He was an advocate of formal theological training for Brahmo ministers, which would "induce habits of deeper and more scientific metaphysical study," "join the older and younger Brahmos through intellectual pursuits," and lead to "an understanding of common interest."[85]

A Brahmo theology was one of those persisting ideas among many well-intentioned Brahmo leaders that had never gained full acceptance among the congregation, nor was ever institutionalized. In 1859, Debendranath Tagore and Keshub Sen had started a theological school, but without reconciling among themselves and their followers the conflict between individual religious experience and systematic knowledge. The scheme thus collapsed. Writing about the incident in 1907, the Brahmo neo-Vedantist, Benoyendra Nath Sen, said that had the theological school been continued with the full support of all, the schism of 1866 would surely have been avoided.[86] Keshub had made two further attempts at founding a theological school—one in 1867 and the other in 1871—but both failed for ostensibly the same reason as the earlier failure.[87]

By 1876, Keshub and his ascetic followers had retreated almost full circle to an antitheological position, preferring instead to construct a serious study of comparative religion in the atmosphere of ecstatic devotion and deep religious conviction. Gour Govinda Ray, who was Keshub's most outstanding intellectual luminary in the circle of ascetics, candidly disavowed theology as greatly inferior to religious inspiration.[88] But to a neo-Vedantist like P. K. Roy, recently returned from England, the contrary was true. In a lecture on "Philosophy and Theology," Roy argued that no major religion had ever been sustained without a systematic theology. Theology was the philosophy of a religion which gave the community a sense of awareness and the faith a durable structure, enabling it to survive the vicissitudes of emotional religiosity.[89]

Charles Dall, the American Unitarian missionary who was a member of Keshub's Brahmo Samaj in the 1870s, also argued that a theological school was urgently needed to "avert emotionalism and mysticism among Brahmos." "Don't kill reason to save faith," he warned Keshub in 1877, "because a serious religion requires that its preachers and missionaries be exposed to sound and effective thought by hard, systematized and protracted study."[90]

Of all the proponents of the theological position among the Sadharans after the schism of 1878, none was more effective a spokesman and prolific a writer than Sitanath Tattvabhusan. Born in a Sylhet village in 1856, Sitanath later endured persecution and loss of ancestral property when he chose to become a Brahmo. Arriving in Calcutta for the first time in 1871, he immediately joined the other young students who sat at the feet of Keshub Sen in the Brahmo Niketan. It was in 1873 as a scholarship student in Keshub's theological institute that he first developed an interest in the philosophy of religion.

He recorded in his diary that despite lack of formal training in philosophy before joining the theological institute, "his mind was irresistibly drawn towards philosophy . . . having become inwardly entangled in the meshes of reasonings and argumentation." It was contact with the "saintly Keshub" that stirred up this "abiding inspiration." When Keshub's school failed, Sitanath went to the General Assembly's Institution in 1875.

By 1879, when Ananda Mohun Bose gave him a teaching job at the City School, Tattvabhusan had already formed what he called a "philosophical position." He had transcended his intellectual struggle between theism and skepticism by placing the Brahmo faith squarely in the tradition of the Upanishads and the Vedanta. In his diary, he wrote that the Brahmo Samaj should now make a "systematic study of the scriptures," which are philosophically so "similar to neo-Hegelianism."

In 1883, when the Sadharan Samaj established an Institute of Theology, Tattvabhusan was chosen its secretary. He recalled later that only his own Herculean efforts kept the school alive as long as twelve years. Lectures, even among other philosophers, reflected individual interpretations, whereas the attempt to construct a systematic philosophy or theology of Brahmoism failed completely. Though the faculty was distinguished, a good library was accessible, and the school never lacked financial support, a consensus was never reached as to what Brahmoism was.

This did not prevent Sitanath from carrying on the task by himself. During these years, he labored strenuously to transform Brahmoism into a fixed and formal theology. He reviewed the writings of previous Brahmo thinkers, but however much he admired their "high ideals of spiritual life," he could find "no knowledge in them properly so-called." Gradually, it dawned upon him why "so many well educated people in my country did not join the Brahmo Samaj": Brahmos "ignored philosophy" and preferred the dogmatic assertions resulting from "divine inspiration and dispensations." The only solution to the problem was to "build religious faith on philosophy."[91]

From 1888, when he wrote his *Brahmo Jijnasa* (Inquiry into the Philosophic Basis of Theism), to 1909, with the appearance of his *Philosophy of Brahmoism*, Sitanath worked out his theological system for the Brahmo religion. Natural religion or intuition, which had characterized national Brahmoism since 1850, Sitanath repudiated for its useless spontaneity, which "amounts to saying I believe because I believe." Nor did the argument from self-evidence appeal to him, because "what seems self-evident to you does not appear so to me." For Tattvabhusan, the key to the "metaphysics of theism is self-knowledge," and the most perfect philosophy for spiritual progress toward self-knowledge was the Vedanta, with its foundation in the profound Upanishads.

The Vedanta allowed for individual separation and realization, and at the same time it demonstrated the need for an individual to merge into a larger whole, unity, or Divine Nature. Thus, it reconciled the apparent dichotomies between monism and dualism, polytheism and monotheism. "You must see that the consciousness of God," wrote Tattvabhusan, "reveals your difference from as well as your unity with Him." He added: "With all your unity with the Light Eternal, you are unfortunately a small spark of it and that your relation with the Father of spirits is not merely a natural relation, but a moral one and spiritual one, making it possible for you to feel the sweetness and tenderest emotion for Him."

Brahmo morality ought to be based on Vedantic notions of the hierarchy of unities. Tattvabhusan argued that the more narrow the moral identity—as, for example, the individual to himself—the lower "the stage of ethical development." Ethical development is an idea of expanding conscience and consciousness. The individual develops by extending his morality to include "domestic life," tribe and nation, humanity (universal brotherhood), and beyond humanity the "Universal Father or Universal Source of which humanity itself is a partial manifestation." This concept was, according to Tattvabhusan, the basis of the Upanishads, which he quoted from freely to prove that this scriptural source of the Hindus contained as sublime a moral code as did the scripture of any other major religion.[92]

In 1912, Tattvabhusan attacked Vaishnavism quite openly, to the point of arguing that "Krishna, the great idol of the country—idol alike of the ignorant and the learned must be broken." It is "the greatest obstacle to the promotion of the true religion." He was convinced that "no intellectual light is to be expected from Indian philosophical waters of medieval times." Elsewhere, he concluded about Vaishnavism that "far from teaching anything beyond what the Upanishads teach, it has led the natural religion in a quite wrong direction." What were the shortcomings of the Vaishnava faith? According to Tattvabhusan, "it reveals in imagination and makes it, instead of insight into the divine nature, the basis of religion. When it shakes off the imaginative drapery . . . it has nothing better to give than monism pure and simple. It does not see the philosophical basis of *bhakti*—the true nature of God. Its *bhakti* is based primarily on imagination and therefore never reaches any notable depth . . . the most repulsive feature of this religion—very prominent in the *Bhagavata*—is its sensuality and disregard of ethical distinctions."

This anti-Vaishnavism was written by one born and brought up in a Vaishnava family who was carefully instructed in its tenets by an uncle, Debiprasad Datta, a pious Vaishnava of the Ramayat sect. When Sitanath abandoned the Krishna-Chaitanya faith, he evidently remained consistently unshaken in his Vedantic outlook until his death. To the end, he believed that Debendranath Tagore, "by discarding Vedantism . . . which in the primary sense is what I understand and accept as Brahmoism . . . had made a great mistake . . . one which had done and was doing a good deal of harm to the Brahmo Samaj." That damage, which Tattvabhusan had dedicated his intellectual and spiritual life to undoing, was that "it had led to a neglect on the part of Brahmos of our ancient scriptures, and was thus discouraging scholarship and causing spiritual sterility. It has also created an unnecessary gulf between the old and the new society, leading many Brahmos to call themselves non-Hindus and to cease from taking a just pride in the glorious literary and spiritual achievements of the Hindu race."[93]

The bitterness of failure and frustration which underlies much of Tattvabhusan's autobiography seems to suggest a certain prevailing resistance by Brahmos to the intellectualization of their faith and the crystallization of its main ideas into a commonly held theology. Back in 1896, Tattvabhusan had been elated when the foreign Unitarian, Sunderlund, visited Calcutta and recommended to Brahmos that they seriously contemplate theological training. Encountering resistance, Sunderlund offered the Brahmos scholarships for qualified young men to study systematic theology in the Unitarian colleges of England and America.[94] Several Brahmos from all over India did receive scholarships and were trained abroad. Enough support for theology was generated by members of the three Brahmo groups in Calcutta to prompt the establishment of a theological seminary in 1907, but once more the project failed.[95]

Tattvabhusan's crusade made him the target of abuse from religiously inspired Brahmos, who began to accuse him of representing "the rise of scholasticism in the Brahmo Samaj." According to one such writer, Tattvabhusan would have the Samaj give up "justification of faith, right of private judgment, priesthood of every believer, and all other achievements of the reformation." "Formalism will never surpass spontaneity of the Spirit," the writer argued, but will only lead to "scholasticism among a few." Sitanath was singled out as the philosopher wishing to replace "our regeneration of faith with the solid rock of logic." Through him and those like him, "dry intellectualism" has crept into the Brahmo ideal.[96]

Much of this criticism seems to have come from the New Dispensation branch of Brahmos, who were quick to point out that sterile intellectualism differed little from secular humanism. But, in fact, the younger generation of Keshubite Brahmos did support Tattvabhusan because they too saw the need for a Brahmo theology. Though the Keshubite philosophers were more inclined to use theology to find a compromise between "faith and reason," their approach to the problem was philosophic, and the end they sought was not that different from Tattvabhusan's. Benoyendra Nath Sen, in particular, who was a much younger man than Tattvabhusan, struggled throughout his comparatively short life to wed the Brahmo's passion for inspiration with the obvious need to structure Brahmo thought into a distinct theology.

Born in Calcutta in 1868, Benoyendra Nath received an excellent Western education under the encouragement of his enlightened Brahmo father, who had not only been initiated into Brahmoism by Debendranath Tagore, but had married Keshub Sen's sister. Benoyendra was a brilliant student who stood first in his class throughout his educational career. His English was superb, and he soon started mastering the intricacies of European philosophy.

Sen received his B.A. from the General Assembly's Institution in 1888, with honors in English and philosophy. In 1890, he received his M.A. from Presidency College, and immediately began his teaching career at Behrampur College under the tutelage of the famous Brahmo philosopher, Brajendranath Seal. In 1893, he moved to Presidency College as a lecturer in history, establishing there a favorable reputation for himself as a devoted teacher.[97]

In the Brahmo Samaj, Benoyendra Nath allied himself with the two other famous New Dispensation philosophers, Promothalal Sen[98] and Mohit Chandra Sen,[99] to update the church's organization and doctrine as well as to promote unity with the other Brahmo groups. Benoyendra Nath's generation saw no conflict between science and reason on the one side and faith on the other. Religion had to be purified through reason to rid it of emotional excess, superstition, and dogma. On the other hand, the basis of Brahmoism was its unyielding faith in the divine nature of reality, against the opposite position held by fanatic advocates of "godless materialism." The answer lay in a humanism framed in a religious context. Benoyendra Nath's position was therefore somewhere between Sivanath Sastri's and Sitanath Tattvabhusan's.

What separated Sen from Sastri was his professional philosopher's orientation; and from Tattvabhusan, his reluctance to reduce the rich diversity of the Hindu philosophic tradition to a single reverence for the Vedanta. In 1905, Benoyendra Nath went to Geneva to attend a world conference of liberal religions organized by the Unitarians. His paper dealt with the problem of religion in modern India. While arguing the need for more theology, he warned against "dry rationalism" that would stifle the spiritual impulse. Ever since 1895, he had wrestled with the problem of how not to divorce the abstract idea and symbol from the spiritual experience. Could the Vedantic or any other philosophic system capture the meaning of a vital spiritual act? According to Benoyendra Nath, "symbols are valuable as representing a spiritual fact." The danger of dry intellectualism was real when "facts became simply facts of the intellect without being also facts of the heart." The only justification for theory in religion was: "the presence of some exalted emotion, some deep, mystic, spiritual experience which transcends the ordinary methods of embodiment in simple prose."[100]

Rather than reject the Vedanta, Benoyendra Nath chose it as the most perfect Indian embodiment of the intellectual ideal. His lectures on the Vedanta that he gave in 1900 appeared to support Tattvabhusan on the validity of the Upanishadic tradition.[101] Sen's argument was that the Vedanta represented the very highest "intellectual ideal" because it was such a successful attempt to synthesize the central truths of the Upanishads. But without the essential religious experience, even the Vedanta was simply a dry and sterile intellectual exercise. Brahmoism was not a philosophy or theology but a faith that conformed to reason—a rational faith.

Benoyendra Nath's attempt to heal the breach between religious enthusiasm and philosophy in order to preserve a common Brahmo identity did not succeed. Perhaps it would have been different had Benoyendra Nath lived longer—he died in 1913 at the age of forty-five. Ultimately, neither the Vedanta nor a rational faith could sustain itself against the inroads of secular humanism. Like Unitarianism in the twentieth century, Brahmoism lost theism and then its rational faith.

CHAPTER THREE

Identity, Achievement, Conscience: The Human Development of the Bhadralok Reformer

IF the progressive wing of the Bengali intelligentsia responded favorably to such alien intellectual imports as the Unitarian social gospel, humanism, positivism, scientism, and rationalism, it would seem to suggest that they identified positively with many of the hopes and aspirations of nineteenth-century European liberals. It might also suggest that throughout most of the nineteenth century, Bengali progressives believed so much in the triumph of British liberalism that they were unable to view the presence of the British in India as a colonial system. In fact, it was not uncommon for Bengali political moderates and social reformers to look upon British rule as being so beneficial for India that it was providential. Despite the fact that the British had deliberately arrested industrial urbanization in India, had monopolized the administration for their own elite, had denied the principle of legislative and municipal representation for Indians, and had drained India of its wealth to pay for Britain's wars abroad, Bengali liberals identified closely with the modern progressive West, adapting their ideas and programs to the Bengali context.

Why did the Bengalis in the "modernist" camp ignore the negative features of British rule in India? Surely, intellectuals sophisticated enough to understand Bentham, Comte, Parker, J. S. Mill, and others, could fathom the debilitating effects of British colonialism. Or could they? Or did they wish to? If they knew and were sincerely concerned about India, why did they not become nationalists? Were they simply guided by self-interest? What indeed were the psycho-sociological dynamics underlying the Bengali liberals as a group?

It is remarkable that within a single generation or two, men from rural areas—Jessie Bose, Akkhoy Kumar Dutt, and Vidyasagar—mastered English, received an excellent liberal arts education, became competent, efficient professionals, were creative thinkers, prolific writers, inventive scientists, and labored long and hard as social and cultural reformers. They were, in short, the equals of any comparable Westerner. They called themselves and were called by others, bhadralok,[1] a term that can be defined as the Bengali equivalent of the comprador class that served Western colonialism as native intermediaries and agents. Compradores were brokers either in the commercial sense or in the intellectual sense of interpreting the West to their own countrymen. In the Bengali example, the bhadralok were composed of members of the three upper Hindu castes of Brahmans, Vaidyas, and Kayasthas who availed themselves of the opportunities provided by British colonial and imperial rule.[2]

This class or grouping, which in a qualified sense was the closest thing to a "middle class" under British colonialism in India, was perhaps best represented by the Brahmo Samaj. Side by side with the image of Brahmo liberal theism and reformism in present-day Bengali society, is the image of Brahmo elitism characterized by hard work, achievement, financial success, and social esteem *vis-à-vis* the Western world. To the cynical, they constituted a colonialist elite concerned only with their own self-interest and material comfort. But to other Bengalis of today more sympathetic to the values and virtues of the achievement-oriented style of life, Brahmo professionalism in the generations of their grandfathers and fathers was a proud episode in the modern history of the region.

The poet, Sudhindranath Datta, for example, has written in his provocative autobiographical sketch *The World of Twilight* that, though Brahmos of his own generation "seem to resemble their hum-drum neighbors in all except name," the Brahmo "forefathers three-quarters of a century ago formed a dedicated community surprisingly rich in talent and character." That talent and character, according to Datta, which made the Brahmos one of the most achievement-oriented communities in nineteenth-century India, was derived from a simple but unyielding faith in "the identification of virtue and knowledge which freed Brahmos quickly from the caste system."

Datta associated the ethic of early Brahmos with the "new prestige attached to professional men who rose in the world without any obvious favor from the British." This class realized "that their success depended on their personal qualifications and not on their family connections." Datta goes on to explain that many of them: "learnt their trade abroad; and if incidentally, they had returned with esoteric affectations that provoked the unmitigated to rude laughter, they received at the same time, homage as national heroes because they claimed absolute equality with the European."[3]

Datta's nostalgia for a lost generation of Brahmo-inspired morality, which is strikingly similar to that held by another famous Bengali autobiographer named Nirad Chaudhuri, represents also an hypothesis about the decline of Bengal in the twentieth century. Nirad Chaudhuri, one of India's greatest living journalists, has interpreted the failure and decline of the Brahmo spirit as the failure and decline of the nineteenth-century Bengal Renaissance. Chaudhuri, a colorful fellow traveler of the Brahmo movement, looked back in dismay on the rise of Hindu revivalism and militant nationalism, which in his estimation constituted a "virtual counter-reformation against Brahmo Protestantism." "By the time the nationalist agitation over the partition of Bengal had reached its climax in 1907," he wrote, "Hindu conservatism may be said to have definitely won the battle."

To Chaudhuri, the triumph of "atavistic nationalism" was modern Bengal's worst calamity, for it crushed the only movement that contained within itself the potential for a full-scale modernization of Indian society and culture. The mainspring of that Brahmo movement was the "ethical value" or Puritan ethic. He argued that instead of being a preliminary stage in the Renaissance of India, the Brahmo epoch came and went, until by mid-twentieth century it was simply a historical curiosity piece. In one of the strongest passages of the revealing *Autobiography of an Unknown Indian*, Chaudhuri concluded that: "Perhaps there never was any period in the last 200 years of the history of the Hindu middle class in which it showed greater probity in public and private affairs, attained greater happiness in family and personal life, saw greater fulfill-ment of cultural aspirations, and put forth greater creativeness in every field, than the fifty years between 1860-1910—dominated by the moral ideals of Brahmoism and the new Hindu Puritanism."[4]

Of all the self-critical Brahmos in search of an explanation for the failure of the Bengali "middle class" and the decline of Bengal, none grew more bitter in his indictment of the Bengali character than Prafulla Chandra Ray. To P. C. Ray, it was not Hindu revivalism of militant nationalism that broke the back of the progressive movement, but the lack of entrepreneurial spirit, which he came to view as endemic to the "Bengali race." No Bengali Brahmo ever condemned his people as fiercely as did P. C. Ray for allowing Marwaris, Gujaratis, and other non-Bengalis to control the trade and commerce of Bengal. To Ray, who had succeeded admirably well in business during Swadeshi, the efforts of most Bengalis to do the same proved as ludicrous as it did tragic. When, for example, Bengalis stopped smoking English cigarettes and used the *biri* instead, it was the Gujaratis who saw the commercial possibilities and established an industry around its production.

Significantly, the image of the middle class that evolved out of the elaborate detailed analysis of Bengal's decline in P. C. Ray's autobiography directly contradicted Nirad Chaudhuri's glorious image. In fact, to Ray, Bengal produced no modernized middle class but only an "intellectual proletariat." Bengalis of the upper three castes simply pursued the university degree for limited service-related occupations and professions, which only a comparative few could achieve. The majority of them settled for much less, ending their careers as pencil-pushing clerks. Thus, between the upper crust of parasitic zamindars and lawyers and the mass of people stood no middle class as such, but a legion of modestly paid clerical help lacking drive and ambition. Progressive movements come and go, reported Ray, but the fundamental elitist caste structure remained the same: 2,500,000 Brahmans, Kayasthas, and Vaidyas, or 5 percent of the total Bengali population, maintaining its social dominance over fifty million people.[5]

The unwillingness or inability of Bengalis to face the problem of their own identity *vis-à-vis* the West is one explanation for the confusing historiographical image of Bengali Brahmos and other progressives. Before one can discuss the achievement ethic of the liberals and the knotty problem of social reform, however, it seems essential that an analysis be made of the quest for identity by an intelligentsia faced with alternative values.

Erik Erikson's notion of an identity crisis, which he attributes to unresolved tensions in the development between adolescence and maturity, is, I believe, useful in the context of a modernizing Bengali intelligentsia seeking to justify their new status, position, and self-image. The bhadralok were, as I have written elsewhere, "a distinctively new social grouping in India . . . composed of an elite and an intelligentsia. The class was urban, not rural; it was literate and sophisticated; its status was founded more on wealth than on caste; it was a professional, not a literati group; it was receptive to new knowledge, ideas, and values; it absorbed new attitudes and its intellectuals created a syncretic cultural tradition; and perhaps most important, it mentally transcended kin and caste and thought in broader social terms."[6] Though increasingly alienated from fellow nationals with contrary characteristics, the bhadralok were never accepted as Europeans in European society. Erikson has traced identity conflict or crisis to adolescence where dependence, insecurity about the future, and a general instability accentuate tension and pain in the emerging adult consciousness.[7] Through intensive studies of charismatic religious and political figures—mostly within the Western orbit of cultures—who have had a crucial impact on history, Erikson has demonstrated that behind momentous ideologies and earth-shaking events lies a persisting identity crisis, traceable in the first flaunting of a negative identity in the formative stages of a person's development. On the other hand, the resolution of the identity crisis and the achievement of a positive identity in adulthood and maturity has contributed its share of charismatic leaders who have shaped history. Concluding a series of lectures on Thomas Jefferson, Erikson wrote:

> From the point of view of development, I would say: in youth you find out what you *care to do* and what you *care to be*—even in changing roles. In young adulthood you learn whom you *care to be with*—at work and in private life, not only exchanging intimacies, but sharing intimacy. In adulthood, however, you learn to know what and whom you can *take care of* . . . as a principle it corresponds to what in Hinduism is called the maintenance of the world, that middle period of the life cycle when existence permits you and demands you to consider death as peripheral and to balance its certainty with the only happiness that is lasting: to increase, by whatever is yours to give, the good will and the higher order in your sector of the world. That, to me, can be the only adult meaning of the strange word *happiness* as a political principle. What Jefferson said about the limit of the debts that should be inherited by the living generation—as well as other quotations we underscored—could well include the hope that adults will learn to help each other and not to burden the next generation with the immaturities which they themselves inherited from previous generations.[8]

This is precisely where Erikson offers us a meaningful insight that I think can be applied fruitfully to our understanding of the liberal Bengali intelligentsia—especially the Brahmos. To be sure, there are limitations in applying the full Eriksonian model to studies of third-world intelligentsia, and caution must be exercised. In the first place, Erikson, a psychoanalyst, seems to net his best results from intensive studies of profoundly important individuals. Second, the sources on these individuals are voluminous. Third, depsite a brilliant book on *Gandhi's Truth*, and evidence of an acutely sensitive eclectic mind, Erikson has not yet produced anything in depth on transcultural psychoanalysis in historical perspective. In studying a movement such as the Brahmo Samaj, the identity of the leadership infrastructure is more revealing than psychohistories of conspicuous figures. But where are the sources? What Brahmo leader's life, including that of Rabindranath Tagore, has been so thoroughly documented as the lives of Martin Luther, Adolf Hitler, or Thomas Jefferson? Moreover, where has Erikson paid serious attention to the psychohistory of intermediaries in the East-West encounter whom the historian Toynbee conceptualized as "intelligentsia,"[9] and the anthropologist Redfield termed "culture broker"?[10]

The best way to proceed is to interpret what is relevant in Erikson against the available data on the lives of the intelligentsia. Since the data on identity crisis is scanty, what follows is intended not as conclusive evidence to support a theory, but as valuable new data suggestive of new hypotheses. My questions, then, must be reformulated on the basis of the data. Is there evidence of an identity crisis in the lives of Bengali liberals whose mature consciousness was so favorably disposed to progressive Western values, attitudes, and ideas? If so, what was the nature of this crisis? Specifically, from available evidence, what kinds of social and cultural stress challenged and unsettled the adolescent's accepted view of the traditional order, disrupted his life, and brought on that form of cognitive dissonance conveniently labled as identity crisis? What means were at his disposal in alleviating the distress? What were the immediate results?

One recurring theme in the data is the impact of a big sinful city on the sensitive rural boy. In the case of Akkhoy Kumar Dutt, of whom we know pitifully little before adulthood, agonizing years as a youth in Calcutta seem to have made him critical of urbanized Bengalis whom the city ruined. Death in the family and poverty often led to a disrupted orientation and a heightened sense of self-awareness. Dutt's father died about the time he was in Medical College, leaving him entirely on his own. It may be that his father's death occurred while Akkhoy Kumar was still at the Oriental Seminary. Whatever the facts, it is quite certain that for some time he lived with his mother in Calcutta under the most degrading conditions of poverty.[11] The experience appears to have moved him deeply and may help to explain his later compassion for the poor and underprivileged.

In 1846, while he was editing the *Tattvabodhini Patrika*, Dutt could recall the agony of being down and out in a heartless city like Calcutta. It was the indictment of a morally indignant man on the bottomless sea of sin and corruption that was his view of the metropolis. He singled out the aristocratic elite as a class who "cared only for accumulating wealth" and had not the slightest concern for "social welfare" or uplifting the mass through "social reform." These zamindars would "spend 50,000 rupees to marry off a son," he charged, but "only 5 rupees for his education."

Dutt blamed all urban elitists for hypocrisy and lack of social conscience. The Western-educated, both secular and those "that followed Christ," were for the most part too denationalized to do "Mother India" much good. The traditional Brahman pundits of Calcutta were useless, backward, and as addicted to making money on the sly as were any other group. The Vaishnava gurus were a decadent bunch, Dutt charged, consumed by their own licentiousness while engaged in debauching female disciples in the name of Lord Krishna. As for the whole nasty brutish urban situation, Dutt pitied primarily the women "enslaved by barbaric customs," imprisoned by their husbands so that they never knew "the joy of knowledge and fulfillment," and sold off into prostitution, which was spreading in Calcutta like a plague.[12]

This response to Calcutta was shared by young men who experienced neither the death of their fathers nor sudden poverty. Sivanath Sastri is a case in point. When Sastri reached nine years of age, his liberal uncle, Vidyabhusan, and his father decided it was time he learn English while also studying Sanskrit at Sanskrit College. And so they got Sastri admitted into Hare's School. Thus in 1856, young Sastri left a village in the Twenty-four Pargannas to live in Calcutta, an event which he recalled much later in life with considerable dismay. Like Akkhoy Kumar Dutt, Sivanath Sastri saw the great metropolis not as a super bazaar where enormous fortunes could be made, but as a bottomless pit of misfortune and suffering, poverty, and degradation.[13] Such accounts of poverty, prostitution, drunkenness, and dope addiction suggest a growing sense of humanitarian conscience and consciousness among sensitive young Bengalis, preparing them emotionally for conversion to the Brahmo faith.

Sastri's identity problem, about which we know considerably more than Dutt's, seems to suggest that however negative was their image of Calcutta, it was Calcutta with its new intellectual atmosphere and reform movements that introduced them to Western thought. Sastri's new mental outlook and new feeling of compassion, which he derived from his Calcutta educational background and related experiences, set up a potential conflict with his family between reason and conscience on the one hand and the established values on the other. This was apparent in 1859, when the twelve-year-old Sastri was compelled to marry against his will. Evidently, his father found nothing immoral, indecent, or inhuman about the act.

Sivanath's earliest institutional exposure to the Brahmos Samaj was probably in 1862, when he attended meetings and services with his friends.[14] It is probably not insignificant that in 1866, when Keshub Sen led the younger Brahmos out of the parent body in direct opposition to Debendranath's policies, the nineteen-year-old Sivanath, who followed Keshub, underwent his first serious "mental crisis." This was an important year, he recalled in his autobiography. Besides the crisis as a result of Brahmo conflict, he experienced another great personal agony. After passing his college entrance exam, he was forced by his father, displeased with his daughter-in-law, to discard her and marry a second time.[15]

Sivanath objected violently at first, out of compassion and love for his wife. In the end, however, his father's threats of physical harm to him and his wife made him change his mind and marry a second time. The event so tortured Sastri that he thought he would lose his mind.[16] He became engrossed with a sense of sin and started questioning everything, including his very identity as a human being.

To transcend this critical juncture of his life, Sivanath turned to Unitarian and Brahmo literature. Umesh Chandra Dutt, Sastri's close Brahmo friend from his own village, gave him a copy of Theodore Parker's sermons. Sastri read the American's sermons each night before retiring, and later adapted them to his own cultural and personal needs by composing prayers of his own. In this way, he found God and through God found the courage to "choose the only right path open."[17]

The year 1866 was painful also because by drawing close to Keshub, he necessarily offended and alienated others in the family circle whom he had loved deeply over the years. The rivalry between Keshub and Vidyasagar since 1858 had turned the family against the Brahmo Samaj. This was certainly an important factor explaining Vidyabhusan's anti-Brahmo and anti-Keshub editorials in the *Samprakash*. As far as Sivanath's father was concerned, it was Keshub's Vaishnava leanings that greatly perturbed the old Shakto. As Sivanath himself felt at one time: "Born in a Shakto family accustomed to shakti worship from childhood, I had an inborn repugnance to the Vaishnava khol and kirtan."[18]

The years 1868 and 1869 were a kind of turning point in Sastri's life. In the former year, he identified himself with the Keshubites by joining them openly in their Vaishnava-inspired sankirtan procession. There he sang the Sanyal sangit, which proclaimed the equal rights of men and women while repudiating caste. On this occasion, Bijoy Krishna Goswami, the Vaishnava saint, "heartily welcomed him with an embrace." In August 1869, Sastri was officially initiated as a Keshubite Brahmo at an impressive ceremony at the mandir. At the same time, under Brahmo influence, he decided to take back his first wife, while trying to get his second wife married to someone else. And in the midst of all these developments, Sastri passed his F.A. examination at Sanskrit College, standing at the head of his class. As a result, he was given a scholarship worth fifty rupees a month.[19]

Naturally, under the circumstances, relations between Sivanath and his father went from bad to worse. Then when the young man renounced his sacred thread to the great satisfaction of the Brahmo community, his father grew furious and vindictive.[20] One day at home, he asked Sivanath to bow before the family image, threatening to beat him if he refused. Sivanath's answer was "that he might beat me to death, but could not make me worship the idol against my conscience."[21] Finally, Sivanath broke off relations with his "tyrannical father," who drove his son out of the house and for the next nineteen years refused to see him.[22]

Another relatively well-documented case of identity crisis is that of Protap Chandra Majumdar. Like Dutt and Sastri, he came from a West Bengal village (in Hugly District), moved to Calcutta, experienced inner turmoil and change, became a respected pro-Western bhadralok liberal. Majumdar was a relative of Keshub Chandra Sen. His grandfather, Tara Chandra Majumdar, had married a niece of Ram Camul Sen, Keshub's grandfather. Protap Chandra was born on October 20, 1840, and spent his youth at his paternal village of Garifa, which was also Keshub's paternal village.[23]

Majumdar's father, a senior bank clerk, died when the boy was only nine years old. That experience, plus the treatment of his mother as a widow in the paternal household, deeply affected the sensitive boy. He himself recorded much later how his mother was considered "excess baggage," and when in 1858 she was seriously ill from cholera, the family did nothing for her, but let her die alone and unattended.

Everything about Majumdar's upbringing he later recalled as brutal and lacking in compassion or reason. To get ahead, for example, required a good knowledge of English. Thus, at six years of age the boy was compelled to start learning the alien language whether he wished to or not. Because he was beaten for resisting, Protap Chandra applied himself to the mastery of English and succeeded admirably at a tender age. As a member of the Westernized elite, the family was able to get Protap Chandra admitted into Hare School, followed in 1857 by his admission into Hindu College— then already called Presidency College. Also as was the practice, Protap, like Sivanath, was compelled to marry while in college, a custom that often had disastrous results for a student.

The most critical year for the adolescent Majumdar was 1859. His mother having died in July of the preceding year, he found himself "adrift" in the streets of Calcutta. He described himself then as a spirited young man with much "intelligence, sentiment and power of language," but without much "force of character."

The nineteen-year-old young man in search of an identity took himself and his child bride to Keshub Sen, who convinced him to become a Brahmo. Like Keshub, who had lost his own father early, Protap Chandra viewed Debendranath as a father-substitute, guide, and preceptor. Without much hesitation, Majumdar signed the Brahmo covenant even though, in his own words, "it meant personal sacrifice, alienation from friends, bitter sorrows as well as grand aspirations, uplifting experiences and glorious truths."[24]

Protap's family turned against him when they learned that he and his wife had dined at the Brahmo house of Debendranath Tagore, and took steps that led ultimately to his excommunication.[25] To Protap and his wife it meant that "no cook would prepare their meals. No servant would touch their clothes. Even the people of the neighborhood would not talk to them. . . . The experience was powerful and humiliating."[26]

Protap Chandra's agonizing youthful experiences with Hindu society and his subsequent excommunication seems to have had a profound impact on his ideological commitment to Brahmoism. He became a foe of the injustices attributed by many Brahmos to decadent popular Hinduism. Until 1872, when he moved into the Bharat Ashram, he lived with his wife in the office of the *Indian Mirror*, the Brahmo newspaper that he himself edited.

Not until 1862, when his family and friends drove him out of society, did his full commitment to Brahmoism begin. He recalled later how for the first time, "I was given a purpose in life, a definite direction." Through the Brahmo Samaj, and responding to the "impulse of a high, loving merciful spirit," he could rise above his deplorable situation and find at last his life-long identity: "The Brahmo Samaj gave me that. Brahmo Religion furnished the key to all that I am, to all that I know."

According to Majumdar, he was possessed and read "everything that I could lay my hands on." He read the modern theologians in general, the Unitarians in particular, and a variety of other books in his endless "path of knowledge." Said he in his autobiographical notes: "My thirst for knowledge was insatiable. I cannot say I understood all I read but it did me one good: it concentrated my powers, and gave compactness to my character, and continuity to my faith and devotion."[27]

Another form of alienation that deserves serious study is that of the young Bengali abroad. The first two who went to London in 1862 to prepare themselves for a civil service career were Satyendranath Tagore and Monomohun Ghose—both Brahmos. The letters from Monomohun to friends in Calcutta are interesting in what they reveal about the feelings of a young man who later earned the reputation of being among the most Anglicized liberals of his generation. His language, dress, food, and habits were thoroughly Westernized. This is a curious fact about his generation of moderate nationalists, when one considers his feelings of alienation from England while studying there, and the fact that the British discriminated against him for his "race" during the examination. Until the late 1870s and early 1880s, one can explain this apparent contradictory behavior in terms of a common rationalization among the liberal bhadralok that Providence dictated British rule of India. In a letter to Calcutta from London dated February 9, 1863, Monomohun wrote that "we should thank God for being placed under so powerful and civilized a nation."[28]

There are probably no more revealing letters in existence about the alienated feelings of a Bengali abroad in London in the nineteenth century than those written by Monomohun Ghose. Ghose, who was initially Miss Carpenter's most radical exponent of female emancipation in India, and was equally radical in his ac-

ceptance of British cultural values, wrote home in 1862 how wasteful it was to work so unbelievably hard mastering a wide range of
subjects befitting members of the English elite. "We have no other
enjoyment or occupation but our studies," he wrote on August 18,
1862.[29] It was a grueling experience, having to memorize every
significant parcel of information on English language, literature,
and history—all so alien to him. Moreover, he was sick and tired of
the regular "English diet of cold beef and ham." In several places,
the nostalgic Bengali yearned for the food of his own culture: "Oh!
if only we could get *macher jhal* and *bhat*" (fish curry with rice) was
the refrain of a man who would, on his return to Bengal, gain the
reputation for being Anglicized.

Once, after having visited a Tagore who had converted to Christianity and then fled to England where he lived as an expatriate,
Ghose wrote home his dismay at having spent the day with a denationalized "caricature." "Tagore," wrote Ghose, "is vain-glorious
and regards himself more an Englishman than an Indian."[30] "He
has gone so far as to ask Satyendranath and I to give up our Indian
costumes and call ourselves Mr.," wrote the indignant Monomohun. In these letters, Ghose expressed a wide range of discontent
living in that alien land. Even the climate bothered him, as he complained of bad health and long periods of mental anxiety. During
the winter of 1862, he wrote home a letter that seems to have
summed up his general despondent state of mind: "I shall never be
happy until I return home and see you all. Several reasons have
conspired to make me unhappy in this country. It will please God
to take me back to my native country so I may then enjoy peace of
mind. The recollections of past days only extracts tears from my
eyes. I am no longer the same in body and mind. If the task we
have willingly undertaken had not been imposed upon us by the
interests of a nation, I should not have thought it worth while to
sacrifice my body and mind."[31]

Nevertheless, when Monomohun returned to Bengal in 1866, he
promptly took on all the characteristics of an Anglicized Bengali
babu in defiance of family and Hindu society. In future years,
whenever the local press sought to ridicule the denationalized
Bengali, invariably the primary target they chose was Monomohun
Ghose. Meanwhile, he remained a steadfast progressive as a
Brahmo, choosing Keshub in the schism of 1866 and Sastri in that
of 1878.

It was the boys from rural East Bengal who seem to have suffered
the most in their struggle to emancipate themselves from the

diehard conservatism of parents, relatives, and neighbors. With the spread of Western education and Brahmo reformist ideology into mofussil towns—especially in the late 1850s and 1860s—many students renounced the religious abuses and deficiencies of orthodox Hinduism, and became Brahmos. The defenders of orthodox Hinduism, which included members of the Western-educated, struck back, making the lives of the youthful Brahmo recruits a living hell. This appears to have led to an exodus of excommunicated, outcasted Brahmo youths into Calcutta. Their arrival in the city compelled Keshub Chandra Sen to establish the Brahmo Niketan in 1871 as a sanctuary for boys who in most cases had been cut off from family, caste, and village society. Here sixty-six students were admitted at any given time for a nominal fee, and were subjected to rigorous moral discipline, common prayer, and informal talks by Keshub. Here Sitanath Tattvabhusan, for one, future theologian and philosopher, was first given a home after leaving behind him his family in Sylhet. It was at the Niketan where boys like Tattvabhusan overcame their identity crises and were made to feel part of a new community. As Tattvabhusan wrote many years later: "I had been denied the right to inherit my father's property because I had given up the ancestral religion. I had no money in Calcutta. Finally, my family arranged for my excommunication. I need hardly to say that I remained excommunicated and still remain so. . . . Instead of feeling sorry for being excommunicated I rather felt proud of having been the first excommunicated Brahmo in my native district."

When Sitanath's father died, he performed the funeral according to Brahmo rites, exacerbating the estrangement between himself and family. For a while he was a penniless drifter in Calcutta. Before joining the Brahmo Niketan, he experienced only the ugly side of metropolitan life. It was a hopeless period of extreme poverty, intermittent physical illness, and unendurable mental agony. When in 1877, at twenty-one years of age, he failed to pass his examinations at college, the tormented young Sitanath contemplated suicide.

According to his own account, the pure study of philosophy sustained him amid fits of "vertigo" and chronic malnutrition. In his autobiography, he expressed enormous satisfaction in having read Spencer, John Stuart Mill, and Berkeley during those dark years. The study of European philosophers reaffirmed his faith in faith, which "when disavowed brings disaster." After reading Mill's *Three Essays in Religion*, he wrote, "it clearly shows what an undesirable turn a man's life takes when he is given a purely intellectual education devoid of religious faith and emotional culture."

Sitanath repudiated agnosticism either of the Comptean or Spencerian types, which "reigned supreme among the educated classes of India in the 1870s and 1880s," and became a confirmed liberal Brahmo theist.[32]

Crucial for understanding the formative stages in the development of the bhadralok progressives, these cases of repression of young Brahmos in East Bengal indicate something about the price in psychic pain that every young man groping for a new identity had to pay. The new identity through Brahmoism divided the most respected families, even those that had valued Western education. The case of the famous Chattopadhyay family of Vikrampur provides an excellent illustration of how families were split as a result of the new Brahmo consciousness and intrusion. The Chattopadhyays were Kulin Brahmans, whose oppression of women was a primary target of East Bengali Brahmo reformers. Naba Kanta, the eldest son, was evidently won over to Brahmoism and converted personally by Keshub Sen during a visit by the latter to Dacca in 1869.[33] The father, Kali Kanta, who was a pleader in the Dacca court, immediately dispossessed his son and founded the local society called Dharma Rakhini Sabha against Brahmo reformers.[34]

The persecution of Brahmos seems to have been extreme in East Bengal. Buikunthanath Ghose, who was directly influenced by Brahmo ideas in 1868 while a student at the Mymensingh Government High School, has in his autobiography reported vividly on the persecution of himself and other young Brahmos. In December 1869, Bijoy Krishna of Calcutta came to Mymensingh to open the new Brahmo mandir, and it was at that ceremony that Ghose and other young men took the oath as Brahmos. The ususal persecution followed: his mother threatened suicide, while his father imprisoned him at the family home in their native village. Ghose managed to escape to Calcutta, but when he returned he was continually harassed and beaten, his property burned or otherwise destroyed. Ghose also relates an interesting experience in Tangail. After a Brahmo prayer hall was consecrated by a Brahmo missionary, the villagers came secretly at night, desecrated the building, and stole the benches. Before leaving, they urinated and defecated in the prayer hall. The sweeper who agreed to clean it all up for the Brahmos was promptly excommunicated by the villagers, and several nights later his house was burned to the ground.

Ghose has also related another type of experience that Brahmos commonly encountered during their travel to East Bengal villages. East Bengal being a highly riverine country, the only way to visit some villages at times was by boat. Boatmen, however, had been instructed by villagers not to convey Brahmos. If they managed somehow to reach such a village, the only place they could stay would be along the riverside. Often that space would become the new village defecation ground in an effort to force the Brahmos to move on elsewhere.[35]

Ananda Mohun Bose, himself from Mymensingh, in a letter to Sophia Dobson Collet, recalled the disabilities of becoming a Brahmo in East Bengal. His earliest exposure to Brahmoism had come at the Mymensingh school, where the headmaster, Bhagaban Chandra Bose, his future father-in-law, helped indoctrinate him with the tenets of the new faith. Because his elder brother had become a Brahmo before him, Ananda Mohun's mother resigned herself as gracefully as possible to what seemed inevitable. In the letter to Sophia Dobson Collet, Bose referred to the persecution of his family when his elder brother had become a Brahmo: "My brother became a gentleman of very reduced circumstances and whose poverty and distress are principally owing to his unpopularity as a Brahmo. . . . Brahmans pronounced sentence of excommunication on the whole family . . . as all our neighbors cut off every kind of intercourse and all the servants came as a body to give up their service. . . . Our home was filled with wailing and mourning. They willed for my mother and aunt to spend the last days of their ebbing life as outcastes; their funeral rites will not be performed; and the girls, the grandchildren of my aunt, will not be married."[36]

Thus, when Bose became a successful lawyer in Calcutta in the late 1870s, he established a Purba Bangla Sabha (East Bengal Society) for East Bengal boys in Calcutta colleges or for those simply adrift in the big city.

Most representative of the East Bengal student whom Bose helped was Krishna Kumar Mitra, born in a Mymensingh village in 1852. Like Bose, Mitra imbibed his Western education at Harding vernacular school and at Mymensingh zillah school. He first heard Keshub Sen when he was in Mymensingh as a boy of thirteen. Evidently, it was Girish Chandra Sen and other Brahmo teachers at the zillah school who indoctrinated him with the new faith and morality. A contributing factor leading to his conversion was that many Brahmos whom he met were from his ancestral home.

When Krishna Kumar openly declared his Brahmoism, he was

persecuted, and when his family supported his convictions, they were excommunicated. In 1870, Dacca College admitted him with a scholarship that paid ten rupees a month. But shortly thereafter, an uncongenial atmosphere drove him to Presidency College in Calcutta. As a student there, he experienced a new type of persecution. He was jeered at by West Bengal boys for being a rustic "Bangal" from the East. "Students from Calcutta used to torment us," he himself wrote later on,[37] an experience reminiscent of others in Calcutta experienced by Bipin Chandra Pal, Prafulla Chandra Ray, and Nirad Chaudhuri—all from East Bengal.

The explosive impact of Brahmoism in the 1860s cannot be minimized. And always it was the young who responded favorably to Brahmo ideas and acted defiantly against established norms and practices. One event in the important nineteenth-century river port of Barisal is significant, as it was typical of what was happening everywhere. Durga Mohun Das, a Brahmo youth of Barisal fired up by the ideal of female emancipation, married off his widowed stepmother to a local medical practitioner. It was a love marriage. What were the consequences? Sivanath Sastri has written that "the doctor's clients deserted him and he had to give up his practice. About Durga Mohun, men threw dust at him and abused him on the streets. Dirty stories were told about his stepmother. The Hindus would never hear the name of Durga Mohun uttered, but spit on the ground as a mark of their abhorrence."[38]

In Mymensingh in 1870, a solemn ritual was held in the Brahmo mandir in which six high-caste young men removed their sacred threads and placed them on the pulpit as "a mark of public renunciation of caste."[39] The Hindu forces went on a rampage and cut off all services to Brahmo families. Not a single house-servant came forward to offer himself to the Brahmo community.

The evidence is clear: adolescence and young adulthood for the bhadralok progressives was in the great majority of cases—where evidence is available—full of storm and stress. The formation of a new identity in the young between tradition and modernity, between Bengali cultural values and the challenging values of the West was hardly ever a smooth transition and was never afforded the luxury, by the irate orthodox, of becoming compartmentalized. The humiliation of persecution polarized differences with their antagonists. Perhaps it was different elsewhere in India, but in Bengal the facts are plain enough.

The question then arises, how could these young people sustain a new identity, which favored progressive Western values, in the midst of so much aggressive hostility? Not all Brahmos could emigrate to Calcutta, where tolerance and pluralism followed naturally in the wake of British institutional innovations. Was it not easier after a burst of youthful rebellion to accommodate one's differences with family, relatives, and neighbors? I would argue that because these young people chose to maintain their new identity in adulthood, they became the forerunners of modern India. Had these boys succumbed to social pressures, the names of Sivanath Sastri, Protap Chandra Majumdar, Sitanath Tattvabhusan, Ananda Mohun Bose, Durga Mohun Das, Jessie Bose, Profulla Chandra Ray, and many others would not be famous, as they still are today.

What sustained these young people into forming a "Protestant movement" was their Brahmo ethic which, though purtannical, was liberal as a result of nineteenth-century European reform movements such as Unitarianism. The ethic of Brahmoism, more than its religion, made heroes of the bhadralok progressives in the face of a persecuting majority, and encouraged them to work hard to achieve great things while living simple and austere lives. The fact that the Brahmo Samaj, which was the pivot of the Hindu reformation, was so successful in the achievement process seems to hint at the validity in Bengal of Max Weber's central thesis on the relationship between Puritan ethic of reformed religion and achievement-oriented entrepreneurship.[40]

We have already demonstrated how the Brahmo Samaj offered itself as a refuge to young people experiencing identity crises and persecution. One of the most effective and practical ways early Brahmo leaders offered protection was to organize, institutionalize, and legalize community solidarity. The process took many forms. It was of vital importance, because it buttressed the individual Brahmo's religious fervor and ethical determination by uniting otherwise isolated outcasts into cooperative endeavors and coordinated activities. In time, Brahmos saw themselves as a minority of the elect manifested by hard work, achievement, and success.

Brahmos in East Bengal settled in neighborhoods of their own, maintaining themselves without servants. The Brahmo neighborhood, or Brahmo Basha, as it was called, became the prototype for other such neighborhoods in East Bengal. Wari, in the old town of Dacca, was a famous Brahmo ghetto. In Mymensingh, living as virtual outcasts, Brahmos became self-reliant and self-sufficient. In 1872, Sarat Chandra Ray pioneered a joint-stock company for Mymensingh Brahmos, which provided the community with commodities, profit, and pride.[41]

In the 1850s, Calcutta Brahmos began to articulate their insecurity amid the great majority of Hindus. This was expressed by Debendranath Tagore, who said that "we Brahmos are situated amidst a community which views us with no friendly feelings" since "we ourselves attack their Puranic and Tantric systems." He went on to say that Brahmos show "practical hostility" to Anglicized "secularists" and to other "denationalized" sorts such as the Christian converts. In short, the Brahmo community was in a precarious and delicate position: "that is, so long as our numbers are so small, our resources so limited and our enemies so powerful as they now are."[42]

When the new mandir of the Brahmo Samaj of India was opened, Keshub initiated twenty-one young men into what he tried to make them believe was not merely a religion or ideology or a social gospel, but a full-fledged community. Three things, in particular, were painfully obvious to Keshub at the time. First, that most of the young people coming to him were excommunicated from their caste and ostracized from their families. Second, the reason they had been cut off from Hindu society was that they were *anusthanic* Brahmos (a Brahmo term meaning those who practiced what they preached). These two together added up to the third realization that his Brahmo community was already *de facto* separated from the Hindu samaj, but lacked *de jure* recognition of its existence. Even the Christian families were protected legally as to inheritance and the validity of their marriages.

In fact, a year before the Keshubite mandir was completed and the new community came into existence publicly, the advocate general of India had ruled that Brahmo marriages, which conformed neither to Muslim nor to Hindu rites, "were invalid and the offspring of them were to be considered illegitimate."[43] The Keshubites, however, found themselves in the most unfortunate position of being penalized by a Western government for adopting Western reform measures. Keshub was forced to pressure the government to give legal recognition to the Brahmo marriage and family, a formidable task when it is considered how tiny a minority the new Brahmo community was against any organized opposition by the vast majority of Hindus.

Between 1869 and 1872, the controversy over the proposed Brahmo Marriage Act was so violently abusive and so interlaced with other issues, that it led to a final and irrevocable split between Hinduized Brahmos and radical Keshubites. Adi Brahmos, in particular, lashed out against the Marriage Act proposals from the pulpit of their church, through the *National Paper*, and at public meetings. They hoped that powerful Hindu opposition to the proposed act might neutralize Keshub's influence with the government.

What appears to have disturbed the Adi Brahmos most was the familiar fear of total estrangement from the Hindu samaj. Most of their articles, editorials, and speeches added up to one conclusion—by no means unfounded—that it would arrest the course of "healthy and spontaneous reformation" by legally defining the "Brahmos as a body distinct from the general body of Hindus." Said Rajnarian Bose in an official memoir against the Marriage Proposal on April 12, 1871: "The Brahmos now in fact form an integral part of Hindu Society. The law will dissociate the former from the latter—a contingency to be highly dreaded as it will injure the course of religious reformation in India."[44]

During the last stage of the controversy, P. C. Majumdar on Keshub's behalf wrote a revealing article on the problem of identity in an effort to arrive at a new perspective. Who were the Brahmos? Majumdar asked whether, as people charged, Keshubites were Christians. "We do not believe in the divinity of Christ," or in the infallibility of the Bible, or in "miracles," or in prophecies of sacraments, he wrote. Brahmos are certainly not Muslims. Are they Hindus? Majumdar's answer was, "Yes, nationally and socially we are. The Brahmos take pride in calling themselves Hindus so far as the name of their country goes, so far as their ancestry and the society of their countrymen among whom they live are concerned."

But then Majumdar went on to declare that in ideology, ethics, and social practice "we Brahmos are not Hindus." Brahmos do not accept the Vedas and Puranas as infallible, nor do they believe in "the sacred wisdom of the Rishis," nor do they accept the "Incarnation of Vishnu." To round out his argument, Majumdar said that "if again by Hinduism is meant idolatry, caste . . . incantations and all the false superstitions, then we are certainly not Hindus."[45]

When the Brahmo Marriage Bill was enacted by the government on March 19, 1872, the Brahmos who adhered to it were legally separate from the Hindu samaj. The fact was momentarily ignored by the jubilant progressives all over India who hailed Keshub as a miracle worker. They pointed not to the provision on Brahmo identity, but to the provisions allowing for such reforms as inter-caste and widow marriage, or prohibiting such social evils as child marriage and polygamy. Keshub had by means of memorials, letters, visits to bureaucrats in Simla, and by publicized consultations with doctors as to the proper marital age for young adults, convinced Lord Lawrence to sign into law a virtual social reform act.

The only problem was that in the wording of Sir Henry Maine, who wrote the act, the reforms applied to "those marrying parties who declared that they did not profess the Hindu, Mohammedan, Christian, Parsee, Buddhist, Sikh, or Jaina religion."[46] Thus at the stroke of a pen, in the eyes of the government, Brahmoism was no longer reformed Hinduism but a separate religion with a distinct legal identity.

Meanwhile, realizing that he was indeed leader of a distinct community, Keshub decided to lay the foundation of a Brahmo neighborhood where families professing the new faith could live together as a model community. Thus was born the Bharat Ashram.[47] At first located in a single home, one hundred people lived together as a joint family, working at assigned tasks for the good of the group, praying, dining, and sharing expenses.[48] It was at this time (1872) that the influx of outcasted boys from East Bengal convinced Keshub of the need for founding a Brahmo Niketan. These and other similar bodies established later by the Sadharan Brahmo Samaj (1880 to 1890) were vital for the survival of the community and for the liberal spirit of the intelligentsia. Moreover, as already intimated, they helped reinforce the Brahmo ethic, which resembled Puritanism, on the one hand, insofar as self-discipline, hard work, and the need to achieve were emphasized. On the other hand, the ethic was liberal in the nineteenth-century sense of fusing individual responsibility to the greater responsibility of helping the underprivileged.

Discipline was important, since without regular and moderate habits in matters of food, drink, sex, and material consumption in one's total life style, nothing of tangible success could be accomplished. In fact, I would suggest, in light of the question raised by Sudhindranath Datta and Nirad Chaudhuri on the twentieth-century decline of the Brahmo spirit in Bengal, that one should examine the difference in life style between first-generation Brahmos who acquired fame and fortune and the second-generation Brahmos who reaped the harvest.

In 1916, Sasibhusan Datta, then president of the Sadharan Samaj, delivered the annual anniversary address around the theme of the declining Brahmo spirit. He carefully noted the gradual disappearance of the "early Puritan vitality" with its "spiritual fervor, strict love of truth and strict purity in conduct." The younger generation, according to Datta, had lost the older reverence for plain living and accomplishing God's work but instead had grown "morally lethargic."[49]

The earliest attempt by a Brahmo leader to codify a Brahmo

ethic (dharma) in the context of the reformed Hindu faith, was that of Debendranath Tagore, who first published the *Brahmo Dharma* in 1850. Evidently, it was occasioned by the Brahmo decision to disown the Vedanta as the revealed scripture of the Brahmos. Akkhoy Kumar Dutt was elated and "hailed it as a great achievement."[50] Most likely, then, the first creative attempt to conceive a Brahmo ethic was the necessary consequence of the momentous act announced by Debendranath at the annual seventh of Pous festival in December of 1850 that the "Vedantic element of Sankara had been eliminated from the Brahmo covenant."[51] It was clearly a victory for Akkhoy Kumar, but even more, as Satis Chakrabarti has intimated, it represented also Debendranath's willingness to respond to pressure from many Brahmos and sympathizers who had come to the same conclusion.[52] In actual fact, Debendranath's *Brahmo Dharma*, which did supplant the Vedanta, was a compromise between his own Hindu bias and Akkhoy Kumar's rationalism.

Debendranath divided his work into two parts, theological and ethical. The theological portion, though original in its selection of sources to prove the basic tenets of Brahmoism, was nevertheless entirely drawn from Hindu sources, principally from the Upanishads. The exclusion of sources from other major religions could hardly be interpreted as a triumph of natural religion over national religion. But this portion was reasonable and rather ingeniously integrated. Besides, there was not a single sentence condemning Christianity. On the contrary, from the very first page, mutual tolerance and universalism was the intended message: "To be a theist or a professor of theism it is not necessary to belong to a particular country, age or nationality. The theists of all countries have the right to teach about God."

It is in the ethical portion of the *Brahmo Dharma* that one finds evidence of Akkhoy Kumar's influence on Debendranath. These "moral precepts" constitute the earliest of a series of Brahmo codes of "practical morality" for the guidance and edification of the theistic householder. Here in the second portion of Debendranath's book can be found, in clear unequivocal language, the official birth of the Brahmo Puritan ethic. However, the sources justifying the ethic are not from Calvin reinterpreting Moses, but from Debendranath reinterpreting Manu.

The "Precepts" begin with family dharma, delineating very carefully the duties of husband to wife, wife to husband, both to children, and children to parents. The spirit is Dutt's rationalism, and the objective is his stress on harmonizing the basic social unit. It was a nineteenth-century puritanism that underlay the emphasis on the social good that is derived from sincerity, devotion, purity, forgiveness, and gentleness, and that castigated the social evils derived from their opposites, including "trivial talk and gossiping" by the wife. And what fascinates is that this perspective was allegedly sanctioned by Manu thousands of years ago.

Debendranath stressed the importance of self-reliance, perseverance of effort, and the utility of hard work. "God has endowed man with wonderful faculties," he wrote, but they must be developed by "self-respect and self-improvement." "Laboring in the path of righteousness" will help to overcome the "miseries of poverty" and to "know yourself as competent to acquire riches throughout life." And as Manu said: "As far as possible one should do his own work. . . . One should gratefully accept help from others, but should not lack in self-exertion and as far as possible one should not be dependent on another and should never stoop to begging."

The aphoristic quality of the work is typical of this genre of literature. Said Debendranath, "acquire knowledge, religion and the habit of industry early in life," or "when old age will come," the body will become feeble "and there will be no hope of peace and rest." Debendranath declared, "do not be enchanted with earthly things in forgetfulness of the transitory character of life," nor should one "despair and neglect this life in looking after the next." There are aphorisms on "earning money to do God's work on earth" as against loving money for its own sake, and on one's profession and occupation as a calling of God, "remembering that one cannot advance a single step without the favor of God." In summation, then, as Manu said: "patience, forgiveness, control of mind, honesty, purity of body and mind, control of the senses, knowledge of scriptures, knowledge of god, truthfulness and control of anger—these are the ten characteristics of religious morality."[53] From that time onwards, Puritan virtues were continually underscored as a fundamental aspect of the Brahmo creed. In Keshub Sen's *Sulabh Samachar*, for example, which was intended as a journal for peasants and workers, the stress in articles week after week was clearly on self-improvement through Puritan practices.

In the very first issue of the *Sulabh Samachar*, dated November 15, 1870, an article appeared against begging. "Giving alms to beggars is not an act of kindness," the article proclaimed, "because it is wrong to live on another's charity." Rather, incapacitated beggars ought to be trained to do "useful things for society."[54] On February 18, 1871, the journal carried an essay on the proper use of time, recommending seven hours of sleep as a good moderate habit for the industrious man.[55] A month later there appeared an article on the need for "high ambition to rise in life." Games as harmless as card playing were frowned upon as time-consuming occupations. Instead, the Brahmos recommended that all our activities show "honest thinking and good works."[56]

Keshub Sen's *Nava Samhita* or Code of the New Dispensation served since 1884 as the main set of moral precepts for the community. Intended to update and partly to supplant the *Brahmo Dharma* of the Adi Samaj, Keshub's *Samhita* represents another piece of evidence in support of the contention that the Brahmo ethic was fundamentally Puritan. Indeed, on matters of personal habits and the desire for self-perfection and success, Keshub sounds much like Benjamin Franklin prescribing his oft-quoted formulae for attaining health, wealth, and wisdom. But even in a Weberian Protestant sense, the following admonition from Keshub reveals the puritanical spirit: "Whether at home or in a shop, in the bank or in the merchant's office, in the manufacturary or in the observatory, in the council chamber or in the field of survey, remember that it is a sacred place where you are employed, and that you are doing sacred work under the eye of the Heavenly Master who is before thee."

Also in the Puritan tradition was Keshub's unequivocal position on the value of work. "Be not slothful," he said, "but active and diligent and persevering, doing the full measure of the work appointed by the Master." Keshub was adamant about the belief that the professional man is no free agent pursuing a secular goal but an instrument of God's will. He wrote, not only is "the place where one works holy, and the work holy, but the very tools with which you work shall you consider sacred."[57]

The evidence from Brahmo biographical materials demonstrates the immense power of the new ethic to reinforce progressive values against the possible negative effects of an earlier identity crisis. In reviewing the following cases of Brahmo puritanism, it should be made clear that this ethic was intended for a comprador class of professional intelligentsia, and not for Max Weber's early modern European class of merchant capitalists.

Ananda Mohun Bose, whom we noted earlier to have suffered persecution in Mymensingh when one of his brothers became a Brahmo, transcended his fears and insecurities and became one of the most ideal types of liberal Brahmo Puritans in the history of the Sadharan Samaj. Born a Kayastha at a Mymensingh village in 1847 (the same year as his friend Sivanath Sastri), Bose grew up as the son of a local zamindar who served the government as an officer in the district court. Ananda Mohun was one of three brothers who were all well educated from the proceeds of the family estate. His eldest brother, Hara Mohun Bose, became a munsif in government service, whereas his youngest brother, Mohin Mohun Bose, studied homeopathic medicine at New York University and returned to Calcutta to enjoy a lucrative medical practice. All three were fortunate in having a mother who, following her husband's death in 1862, was able to manage the zamindari with considerable ability.

In 1863, Ananda Mohun passed his entrance exam for Presidency College and left for Calcutta, where he spent four brilliant years as a student. His self-discipline was as robust as his memory. Bose would shut himself up in a room with his books at six o'clock in the evening and not leave the room until six the next morning. When he got his B.A. in 1867, he was commended for excellence in most subjects, especially mathematics. In 1869, at twenty-two years of age, this intellectual prodigy "was hired by Presidency College to profess mathematics in the Engineering Department."[58]

It was in the same year that Ananda Mohun Bose appeared before Keshub Sen at the opening ceremony of the Brahmo mandir and offered himself publicly for initiation.[59] At that important event, he met Sivanath Sastri for the first time, and the two of them immediately developed a warm and lasting friendship. Also in the same year, a momentous one of good fortune for Bose, he was awarded the Premchand-Raychand fellowship of 100,000 rupees to study in England at a college of his own choice.

According to Hem Chandra Sarkar, his biographer, even at this stage of his life Ananda Mohun was already the perfect image of a Brahmo Puritan. When on August 22, 1869, he accepted the moral and religious principles of Brahmoism, "henceforth his life was one of incessant endeavor to live out the ideal which he had solemnly accepted that day: worship and work became the motto of his life."[60]

In February 1870, Bose accompanied Keshub Sen to England, where he then proceeded to Christ's Church, Cambridge. There he continued his hard work and established a superb record over the next four years. Bose continued to excel in math, but he had now become a proficient debater as well. Law is what he had decided upon, and on April 30, 1874, he was called to the bar. In 1874 he returned to Calcutta, and by 1875 was already a successful barrister.

When Prafulla Chandra Ray, the Brahmo chemist, first came to Calcutta from East Bengal in 1870, he was placed in Hare School as the first stage in the process of preparing him for a successful career. Though Prafulla was the son of a liberal father with an excellent zamindari library, and was encouraged by him to imbibe progressive Western values, the West Bengal boys heckled him for being a rustic "Bangal." But his early Brahmo affiliation and the comradeshjp at Keshub's Niketan sustained his ethical fervor. As a student, he exhibited regular habits and industry that would characterize him for the remainder of his life. Prafulla Chandra has recalled how "voracious a devourer of books" he was. "When I was barely twelve years old," he wrote, "I sometimes used to get up at three or four o'clock in the morning so that I might pour over the contents of a favorite author without disturbance."

In point of fact, when one considers that to Max Weber, Benjamin Franklin was the ideal type of Protestant Puritan, then it is most interesting to find Franklin as P. C. Ray's lifelong mentor and model of moral strength. Prafulla Chandra acknowledged this in his *Autobiography*, when he said that "Benjamin Franklin has been my special favorite ever since my boyhood and in 1905 while on my second visit to England I procured a copy of his *Autobiography* which I have read and reread any number of times." With his usual candor, Ray explained that "the career' of this great Pennsylvanian—how he began his life as an ill-paid compositor, and by sheer perseverance and indomitable energy rose to be leading man in his country—has ever been an object lession to me."[61]

As illustrated by the case of Satyendra Prasanna Sinha, better known as Lord Sinha, the ferocious dedication to hard work and the unquenchable desire to achieve were conspicuous puritanical traits too often concealed by the later lordly manner of a Bengali bhadralok emulating the English aristocrat. The same Lord Sinha who sat in the House of Peers was once the young Bengali Brahmo boy from Birbhum district, who learned English for the first time at the local zillah school. But Sinha started life with the advantage of being a child prodigy, as attested by the fact that he began his undergraduate career at the age of thirteen.

In 1881, after four years at Presidency College, he went off to England to study medicine, shifted to law, and at twenty-one years of age was called to the bar. In 1887, we find him in the Calcutta

High Court as a brilliant advocate. But it was only the start of a career. No other lawyer, Brahmo or otherwise, was so courted by the British bureaucracy, and no other lawyer achieved so much in the space of a single lifetime. It might be mentioned that Sinha was given a professorship at City College in law, and might have been satisfied with the position had it not been for a driving ambition to achieve a much higher status.

Sinha's career was so outstanding that he became the first Indian to hold at least a half-dozen positions of great importance that were traditionally the monopoly of the most privileged British officials. In 1907, he became the first Indian advocate general of Bengal; in 1909 he was made first Indian member of the Viceroy's Executive Council; in 1917 he represented the Government of India in the Imperial War Conference; a year later he was the first Indian to serve on the King's Council; in 1919 not only was he knighted, but he became the first Indian member of the English peerage; that same year, also, he became the first Indian appointed as undersecretary of state; and in 1920 Sinha was made first Indian governor of a province, Bihar.[62] In terms of esteem by the British ruling class in England and India, Lord Sinha was undoubtedly the most famous Brahmo of the Calcutta Sadharan congregation. And he was a good lay Brahmo, who regularly supported his church both morally and philanthropically.[63]

A glance at fragments of his diary should help convince us that aside from his sharp intelligence, it was the Puritan ethic that most typified his sensational climb up the ladder of social success in a foriegn-imposed system. We learn from his diary of 1902 and 1906 that Sinha scheduled his daily events with utmost care and that he put in an extraordinarily long working day.[64] Like most Brahmo Puritans, he scorned idleness and believed in the utility of hard productive work. Sinha kept meticulous accounts of income and expenditure, including his investments in numerous commercial enterprises. Later in life, Lord Sinha became more aristocratic, but in the early stages he was essentially the young Brahmo Puritan making government service his entrepreneurial activity.

Another prominent group of Brahmo professionals who both excelled in their fields and proved good businessmen on occasion were the medical practitioners. Next to law, medicine seems to have been the most lucrative profession. Many doctors in the late nineteenth century went abroad to study homeopathy, which was an esteemed course of study in the medical colleges of America and the

British Isles. One of the earliest Brahmos to go abroad to study homeopathy was Mohini Mohun Bose, brother of Ananda Mohun, who left for Glasgow in 1876 to qualify himself as a homeopath.[65]

The successful career of Dwarkanath Roy, the lesser known brother of P. K. Roy, Brahmo philosopher and professor, was another somewhat later case in point. Born in Dacca on November 6, 1855, he enjoyed the benefits of an excellent English-style education. As fits the pattern, his earliest exposure to doctrinal Brahmoism was at Dacca Collegiate School, under the influence of Brahmo teachers. In 1876, Roy passed his entrance examination for Presidency College, but two years later was compelled to drop out as a result of bad marks. Then came a period of uncertainty in his life as he wavered between starting once more as an engineering student or going into business.

By 1879, he had decided to try medicine and in that same year entered Calcutta Medical College, subsisting largely on funds made available by Ananda Mohun Bose's association for East Bengali students. Three years later, on the advice and support of his sister-in-law, he left for England to study advanced medicine. While there he developed a friendship with Jessie Bose and Prafulla Chandra Ray. Ultimately, Dwarkanath Roy chose homeopathy and went on to America, where he enrolled in the New York Homeopathic College. He did a thesis on cholera and stood first in his graduating class. He seems to have returned to India by 1886 and to have spent some time in Bombay, where among other medical activities he was the personal physician of Dadabhai Naoroji, the Parsi businessman and nationalist. Then, in 1888, he came back to Calcutta, married the youngest daughter of Durga Mohun Das and settled down as a highly successful medical practitioner.[66]

Dr. Dwarkanath Roy's career was typical enough of the Brahmos in the secular profession of medicine who persevered despite limited resources and early failures, who advantageously studied abroad to improve their reputation, and who finally came back to Calcutta in triumph, ready and able to carve out small fortunes for themselves as respected physicians.

Nilratan Sircar, another Kayastha from an East Bengali family, who migrated from Jessore to Diamond Harbor (West Bengal), represented a different type of Brahmo physician with considerable drive and enterprise. He was born in Diamond Harbor on October 1, 1861, the second son in an immense family of brothers and sisters. According to a reliable source who knew Sircar well, his mother's death when he was fourteen years old had a profound effect on his future career. "He resolved at her death bed to take up the study of medicine," reported D. M. Bose, "and to devote his life to the alleviation of human suffering." Thus, in 1876, when he departed for Calcutta to seek fame and fortune, it was to Campbell Medical School that he applied successfully and from which he received a diploma in 1879. After some years in Mayo Hospital, Nilratan went on to medical college; and then to Calcutta University, where he was awarded his M.A. and M.D. in 1889. D. M. Bose has written that Nilratan Sircar was sustained all these formative years by a fervent Brahmo faith imbibed for the most part from Keshub Sen and from disciples of Keshub who were of "spotless moral character." Sircar was known to his friends as a humble, diligent, humanitarian, and exceedingly unpretentious man. Like the "true" Brahmos he selected as friends, his life was "characterized by simplicity of living and uprighteousness of character."

Far more than Dr. Dwarkanath Roy, Dr. Sircar prided himself as a professional and worked hard to elevate and modernize the medical profession in India. As a doctor, Sircar was competent and famous enough to attend Rabindranath Tagore on his death bed.[67] Professionally, no other doctor in India worked so devotedly to establish a code of medical ethics for Indian physicians, or to free his profession from dominance by the British Medical Association.[68] Sircar helped establish much-needed institutions such as the Calcutta Medical School, the School of Physicians and Surgeons, and the Jadavpur Tubercular Hospital. He was also for some time the editor-in-chief of the *Journal of the Indian Medical Association*.

As a Brahmo Puritan of the P. C. Ray variety, Nilratan Sircar was an ardent believer in self-help or Swadeshi, and advocated entrepreneurship among Bengalis as the only effective means of achieving "industrial regeneration." He himself turned to business enterprise by investing in a tea garden at Jalpaiguri, which later became the Eastern Tea Company. In 1905, as part of the Swadeshi movement, he started the National Soap Factory and a year later established a National Tannery. His medical practice, which was extremely lucrative, enabled him also to purchase a coal field.

To his death in 1943, Dr. Sircar was a hard-working, self-sacrificial Brahmo professional who more than any other single individual "helped to bring the countryside of Bengal under organized scientific medical and health services." In 1918, he was knighted by the British. In 1919, Dr. Sircar served simultaneously as vice chancellor of Calcutta University, dean of the Faculty of Medicine and Science, trustee of Rabindranath Tagore's Visva

Bharati University, and member of the Executive Committee of the Bose Institute. Then between 1933 and 1941, he served as president of the Indian Association for the Cultivation of Science.[69]

The record of Brahmo achievement, representing as it did—and still does—such a small minority of the Indian population, was phenomenal. A complete list of Brahmo achievements during this generation alone as pioneering efforts in Indian modernization in all elitist fields of endeavor would take a volume in itself. The yearly membership roll of the Calcutta Brahmo Samaj a half century ago would never show more than nine hundred names, but one has only to glance at them to grasp immediately the power and influence of its civil servants, lawyers, judges, scientists, professors, doctors, and journalists (see Table 2).

A Brahmo public official like Lord Sinha, a Brahmo educator like Heramba Chandra Moitra, or a Brahmo scientist like Jessie Bose, a Brahmo physician like Nilratan Sircar, a Brahmo journalist like Ramananda Chatterji, and a Brahmo writer like Rabindranath Tagore were no mere professionals, but inspired men with an inexhaustible supply of energy and a ferocious passion to work hard and produce. Their Brahmo piety and Puritan ethic helped transform them into creative giants; but unfortunately the net impact of their work was diminished, living as they did in a nation long subjected to foreign rule and among a mass of people incapable of appreciating such achievement and unmindful of their own right and potentiality to fulfill themselves in precisely the same manner.

The Brahmo Puritan ethic, and the nineteenth-century liberalism that sustained it, was no less committed to social conscience than it was dedicated to achievement. It was precisely in their compassion for the poor and the underprivileged, in their self-sacrificial acts of heroism to improve society, and in their legacy to future generations of Indians, that they best represent Erik Erikson's ideal type of adult personality. Here, not unlikely, lies the most enduring contribution of the Brahmo Samaj to the progressive spirit of modern India. More than religion as such, it was Brahmo puritanism that permeated the ranks of the bhadralok and Brahmoized the Hindu middle class. Even Vidyasagar, one of the earliest and most effective bhadralok reformers, though a secular humanist and no lover of Brahmo theism, shared with his Brahmo contemporaries a common ethic based on "plain living, high principles, industry and perseverance."[70]

The conscience and compassion of the bhadralok for the less for-

TABLE 2

Most Outstanding Brahmos in the Arts, Sciences, and Professions circa 1900

Name	Birth, birthplace	Higher education	Profession	Major achievements	Awards, distinctions
Bose, A. M.	1847, Mymensingh	Presidency, Cambridge	Barrister	Founder, City College, Indian Association	President, National Congress, Premchand-Raychand Fellowship
Bose, J. C.	1858, Vikrampur	St. Xavier's, Cambridge	Professor of physics	With Marconi, breakthrough in radio telepathy; study of life in inorganic substances	International recognition as scientist, knighted
Chatterji, R.	1865, Bankura	Presidency, City College	Journalist	Editor of *Prabasi* & *Modern Review*	National recognition as first journalist of India
Majumdar, P. C.	1840, Hugly	Presidency	Author, scholar, missionary	Author, *Oriental Christ*, helped initiate first Parliament of Religions	Lifetime fellowship by United States Unitarians
Pal, B. C.	1858, Sylhet	Presidency, Manchester College	Journalist, missionary	Modernizer of Vaishnava tradition; all-India Swadeshi leader	Unitarian fellowship to England
Ray, P. C.	1861, Jessore	London Univ., Edinburgh	Professor of chemistry	Started Bengal Chemical Pharmaceutical Works; *History of Chemistry in Ancient India*	International recognition as scientist; knighted
Roy, P. K.	Unknown	London. Univ., Edinburgh	Professor of philosophy	Brilliant exponent of neo-Vedantism & neo-Hegelianism	Fellowship, London Univ.

TABLE 2 (*cont.*)

Most Outstanding Brahmos in the Arts, Sciences, and Professions circa 1900

Name	Birth, birthplace	Higher education	Profession	Major achievements	Awards, distinctions
Seal, B.	1864, Calcutta	Scottish Church College	Professor of philosophy	Works in comparative religion; pioneer in philosophy of science; wrote epic *Quest Eternal*	Hailed as greatest of Brahmo thinkers
Sinha, S. P.	1864, Birbhum	Presidency	Law, administration	Calcutta High Court, first Indian governor; advocate general of Bengal	Knighted, made Lord Sinha
Sircar, N.	1861, Diamond Harbor	Calcutta Medcal School; Calcutta Univ.	Medical practitioner	Started tubercular hospital & school for surgeons; editor of *Journal of Indian Medical Association*	Knighted
Tagore, R.	1861, Calcutta	Irregular	Poet, philosopher, educator	Most prolific Indian writer of poetry, plays, novels, music, essays; started Vishva-Bharati Univ. at Santineketan	Nobel Prize in literature (first Asian recipient); knighted
Tattvabhusan, S.	1856, Sylhet	Scottish Church College; City College	Philosopher, theologian	Systematized Brahmo religion into theology; *Philosophy of Brahmoism*	Official philosopher, Sadharan Samaj

SOURCE: Compiled principally from biographical and autobiographical materials found in the footnotes and bibliography of this book.

tunate, which in Bengal historiography is called "social reform," can be traced back to the efforts of Akkhoy Kumar Dutt and Vidyasagar on behalf of female education and emancipation. We have noticed elsewhere the common belief by Bengali social reformers, which was first developed ideologically by the rationalist Akkhoy Kumar Dutt and rendered into an effective program of social action by Vidyasagar, that the oppression of women in Hindu society was the most serious obstacle to regeneration and modernism. The family was the basic unit of society, and unless the women were liberated from purdah, no progress was possible. To the sensitive humanitarian Bengalis, women were the proletariat of their society, a not unnatural supposition in light of contemporary exploitation of women, and in view of the fact that there was no industrial proletariat in India as such, since there was no industrial revolution.

This is not to say that Akkhoy Kumar Dutt, who was a most progressive man for his time, did not show compassion for other underprivileged classes of the population. His articles and editorials in the *Tattvabodhini Patrika* throughout the early 1850s do indicate awareness of the exploitation of peasants by zamindars and foreign planters. He was one of the first writers in the Bengali language to expose the "distressing conditions of the village people,"[71] exploited through such devices as obnoxious taxes and free labor while unprotected by British administrators concerned only with the collection of taxes and maintaining law and order.

In 1855, Dutt wrote a damning article about the total disregard of the educated class and British officials for the "poor and oppressed in Bengal."[72] In that year also, Dutt wrote *Dharma Niti*, which besides strongly advocating the emancipation of women as the key to social progress, also endorsed mass education in the vernacular as the only realistic path to enlightenment.[73] In the midfifties, it might be pointed out, only a handful of Brahmos, missionaries, and Christian converts championed mass education in the popular language.[74] It was the remarkable Reverend James Long who first appealed to the Church Mission Society for support of mass education, citing the dismal statistic in 1857 that out of every one hundred persons in Bengal, only one could read and write, and that out of 66,290 boys in his own district of the Twenty-four Parganas who should be in school, only 565 actually were.[75]

It comes as no surprise that during the famous Indigo Rebellion of Bengal in 1859, the same coteries of Brahmos and Christians with other compassionate sorts came forward to condemn the planters and to demand legal protection for the workers. Among the Brahmos who assisted Reverend Long during the *Nil Darpan* controversy were Akkhoy Kumar Dutt, Harish Chandra Mukherji, and Kali Prosanna Singh.[76] It should be pointed out that the Indigo Rebellion has been appropriated by nationalists as an opening skirmish in Bengal against foreign tyranny. But the question too rarely asked is whether native planters and zamindars treated their employees any more mercifully than did the Europeans. Landowners and planters, whether European or Indian, represented a class whose common economic interest far exceeded racial and national differences.

In 1870, as already noted, when Keshub Chandra Sen returned from England, he started the Indian Reform Association which, among other objectives, aimed to improve the lot of Indian peasants and workers. It may be recalled that he opened workingmen's schools and night schools for peasants in rural areas, published a journal called the *Sulabh Samachar* to educate the masses by means of a simple Bengali prose style, and wrote a series of public letters to the government advocating free compulsory education for the Indian masses as the only effective means of modernizing India. The Indian Association, as suggested, was the first such ambitious plan of social action in India designed to raise the level of the underprivileged, and it is of no small importance that it started from religious devotion within the Brahmo Samaj.

The *Sulabh Samachar*, which is modern India's earliest journalistic enterprise devoted solely to uplifting and enlightening the mass of people, is a fascinating document delineating the aspects of social consciousness within the strict moral requirements of the Brahmo Puritan ethic. Here was a journal that openly identified with "the lamentations of the poor"[77] or the chotolok (the masses), whose grievances were aired in every issue and whose interests were defended against their exploiters. In one early issue dated November 23, 1870, there is an interesting article on the "Distress of the Tenants," which is seemingly Marxist in its depiction of a virtual class war between bhadralok zamindars and chotolok cultivators. Take, for example, the following passage: "The bhadralok in the countryside enjoy the fruits of the chotolok's toil as a cultivator. While the chotolok's children starve, the bhadralok looks on callously and takes everything for himself and his family. Even the police and other government officials instead of performing their functions, join the zamindars in exploiting the poor. The reason the bhadralok opposes education is that he wants to keep the chotolok ignorant forever as his das or slave."[78]

Such articles and editorials could easily be taken out of context and made to appear as if Keshub Sen, the Brahmo leader, brought back with him from Europe not merely the warm greetings of Queen Victoria but the germs of socialist thought from Karl Marx. On the other hand, if we read through most of the issues and examine carefully what is intended in this Brahmo journal, it is not Marxism but puritanism that is being advocated. On November 30, 1870, for example, the *Samachar* strongly endorsed compulsory mass education against the narrow self-interest of the bhadralok, so that the "poor people will gain knowledge to combat ignorance and superstition, and gain a moral sense."[79] On December 21, 1870, in an article on "The Sufferings of Calcutta's Workers" the point was made that poverty in many cases was a result of working irregularly, going into debt for nonproductive reasons, lack of systematic budgeting, and self-defeating habits such as smoking *ganja* and excess drinking, which not only consumed most of the salary but led to the worker's physical and mental debilitation.[80]

A week later, in the issue of December 28, poverty was again deplored but without attacking the system that condoned this social evil, and without any recommendation to workers that they band together collectively to defend their self-interest. Rather, the *Samachar* editorial staff offered as a solution to the problem of poverty a formula based on cultivating habits of self-discipline and other moral virtues through education. There was also the tendency on the part of the writer to reduce the problem to the meaning contained in pithy moral aphorisms such as: "Those who are virtuous and yet poor, attain heaven. This is the essence of all truth."[81]

We have already indicated that a chief source for Brahmo inspiration on religious and social matters throughout the nineteenth century was the modern Unitarian movement in England and America. The social gospel of Theodore Parker in America and Mary Carpenter in England profoundly influenced the younger generation of radical Bengali Brahmos desirous of merging social reform with rational religion. When in 1867 Mary Carpenter visited the Brahmo Samaj in Baranagar at the heart of the developing jute industry of Bengal, she recommended to workers that they give up drinking and other vices to transcend their poverty-stricken condition. As for a practical immediate measure to improve their financial situation, she referred to the Penny Banks recently started in England to give workers the opportunity to put away a few pence each week as "medical insurance and social security." The Brahmo Samaj immediately started such banks in its capacity as a voluntary association. On April 8, 1871, the *Sulabh Samachar* ran an editorial asking the government to sponsor a scheme whereby savings banks for the common people would be established in every district of Bengal.[82]

The Brahmo leader most inspired by Keshub Sen's idea of mass awakening and the one who invited Mary Carpenter to Baranagar was Sasipada Bannerji. It was Bannerji who started the first Brahmo Samaj among India's new class of industrial proletariat. Probably no other Bengali was so beautifully in the image of the Brahmo social reformer of the period than Sasipada. He was born in Baranagar in 1840, long before the town developed as an industrial center specializing in jute production. Sasipada was a well-educated Kulin Brahmin from a tightly knit joint family. In 1860, the family married him off to an illiterate girl of thirteen. As with many other sensitive Kulin young men in both East and West Bengal imbued with Brahmo ideals, Sasipada underwent a period of anti-Hindu rebellion which led to psychological uncertainty about his identity and a break with his family. As was also common under these circumstances, Sasipada was excommunicated and lost his share in the jointly held ancestral property.[83]

According to Sivanath Sastri, Bannerji's identity crisis and rebellion against family and system were largely inspired by Keshub Sen. It was Keshub who convinced Sasipada to remove his sacred thread and to convert to the Brahmo faith. Presumably this took place in 1865, when Sasipada was twenty-five years old, placing him in a different category from most of his contemporaries, who underwent their crises of identity and Brahmo conversion between the ages of seventeen and twenty. From 1865 to 1867, we find Sasipada under Keshub's direct inspiration and guidance, starting a Brahmo Samaj in Baranagar followed by a girls' school and an informal reading club for workingmen.[84]

In 1868, Sasipada experienced his first severe persecution by the local townspeople. His widowed niece, whom Sasipada married off to a widower, was dragged out into the street and humiliated physically while he himself endured insults and beatings. But such experiences seem only to have intensified his determination to help improve the lot of women and workers. With the limited resources of his Samaj, he enlarged his workingmen's reading club by adding to it a circulating library and a lecture room where he and other

Brahmos from Calcutta discussed the value of moral discipline on family well-being. Like the Unitarian social reformers in the West who attributed poverty to intemperate habits, Bannerji launched a campaign against the whiskey shops in the vicinity of the jute mills. All this time, we might add, Bannerji supported himself and his family as a schoolteacher and as a superintendent of the local post office.

In 1871, Sasipada shocked the established Hindu society by taking his wife to England with him. Ever since Rammohun Roy had crossed the forbidden seas to Europe in 1830, Brahmo young men had increasingly followed suit for educational reasons or for competing in the civil service. Not until the late 1860s did enlightened Hindu young men begin to defy the taboo. Then, in 1871, Mrs. Bannerji became one of the first Indian ladies to travel abroad. In a single decade, Sasipada had transformed his wife from an illiterate girl to a comparatively well-educated and liberated woman. While in England, the Bannerjis resided at the Red Lodge Estate of Mary Carpenter.

There, Sasipada was given ample opportunity to express his ideas in a series of lectures to Unitarians, workingmen, and teetotalers. Some of these talks are revealing not only of Bannerji's views on social reform, but of Brahmo objectives in conducting social work among the laboring class. In one lecture, particularly, given on September 23, 1871, Sasipada spelled out the nature of Brahmo involvement among the workers. The lecture supports the argument that the early Brahmos who pioneered public concern for the underprivileged were less motivated by socialism than they were by puritanism. In Bannerji's own words: "I have opened a night school for the working class . . . but a loud cry is opened against me that I am disturbing society—setting class against class. Let them cry; I shall go on. The greatest drawback I have is that the working classes do not think labour is honorable. This makes a miserable state of society little better than the brutes of creation. I have been trying to teach them that labour is honorable, not to bring disorder and confusion amongst us, but to bring class with class in sympathy with each other."[85]

The night school referred to by Bannerji had been established the year before in response to Keshub Sen's Indian Reform Association, which had underscored the need for such instruction in all Brahmo Samajes throughout South Asia. The night school in Baranagar had been started with the assistance of two members of the progressive faction of the Samaj in Calcutta, Dwarkanath Ganguli and Krishna Kumar Mitra. When he returned to India, Sasipada naturally drew closer to the progressives because of their common interest in promoting social reform.

Throughout the 1870s Bannerji worked hard expanding existing facilities in Baranagar to accommodate jute workers. By 1871, his library included over one thousand volumes, which circulated freely among the laborers.[86] Another project that consumed his attention was the Workingman's Savings Bank, which he was able to establish in February 1871 with a total deposit of 390 rupees. The idea was originally Mary Carpenter's, but the initiative for enlisting the support of government officials and local capitalists came from Brahmo leaders in Calcutta and Baranagar. Bannerji evidently turned more and more to capitalists for help in social work, particularly in the area of education. He has himself related how he was able to persuade a Mr. William Alexander of the Borneo Jute Company, who owned several factories, to start a night school for workers on the Brahmo model.

Bannerji's technique of enlisting capitalist cooperation to aid workers by means of savings banks, reading rooms, libraries, night schools, and lectures on moral discipline and responsibility, only supplies further evidence to support the contention that the most radical of Brahmo reformers aimed to help workers transcend their miserable state by means of the Puritan ethic rather than by class conflict. This is well illustrated by still another of Sasipada's projects, the Workingman's Club, which might well have become the nucleus of a socialist cell or a trade union. But according to Sasipada's son, writing much later about the Workingman's Club of the 1870s, the contrary seems to have been intended: "The Club exercised a healthy influence on the workers with a view to ending the use of the strike weapon. . . . Bannerji urged them to practice thrift, self-help with the result that several of them were able to put all their savings to carry on a small business in cloths (*dhotis*)— several of them weaving cloths on Sundays."[87]

In 1874, Sasipada brought out a periodical in Bengali which he called the *Bharat Sramjibi* or in its English subtitle, *The Illustrated Indian Workingman's Journal*. It was the first periodical in India devoted exclusively to the concerns of the industrial laborer, although precisely how this was carried on we cannot say, since all the 15,000 copies published during its few years of existence have apparently disappeared. We can only surmise that it was an illustrated version of the *Sulabh Samachar* with a didactic purpose rather than promoting class warfare. And if the journal were at all like a later edition under the same title but under different management, then the illustrations were mostly diagrams explaining to workers the elements of modern science and technology.

Among the hundreds of East Bengal boys who in the 1860s renounced their caste, fled from their homes, and drifted about as defiant rebels, none has captured the imagination of later generations of reformers as much as Dwarkanath Ganguli. He was the most popular of the middle-class reformers. Like Sasipada Bannerji, Dwarkanath Ganguli was a Kulin Brahmin, though from Vikrampur, East Bengal, where he was born in April 1844. At seven, he went to a pathsala and later learned English in a school at a neighboring village. One significant fact about his early influences while at school is that he was first influenced as a social reformer by reading Akkhoy Kumar Dutt's *Dharma Niti*. We can only surmise that from this source he became aroused about the plight of the Bengali woman, and was influenced by Dutt's main thesis that the vital first step to social regeneration was liberating woman from her bondage.

We know little for certain about Ganguli's later education or earliest occupation. In the 1860s, he was evidently moving about from village to village in East Bengal living from day to day doing odd jobs, mostly "teaching here and there." It seems evident that long before this he had left his family and had broken with the Kulin system.

By 1869, he had gained a reputation as a social reformer among East Bengalis, for he had become a dedicated foe of the Kulin system of female oppression. He started a journal that year known as *Abolabandul* ("Friend of Women") which recorded in great detail, among other things, the murders and suicides of Kulin women as a consequence of the system. This journal, which is perhaps the first in the world devoted solely to the "liberation of women," represented clearly what we have described elsewhere as the compassion for the Bengali woman as proletariat. Ganguli played the role of humanitarian muckraking journalist bringing to light concrete cases of the exploitation and extreme suffering of women, as, for example, the sensation he created when he featured the story of one East Bengal village where "in a single year thirty-three Kulin women committed suicide or were murdered." According to Ganguli, every one of them was the victim of premarital or extramarital conception as a result of rape or seduction.

Not until 1870, when Dwarkanath came to Calcutta, did Ganguli become a Brahmo officially, and as one might expect, his views on female emancipation drew him into the progressive camp. He also lived in Keshub's experimental Bharat Ashram. Dwarkanath at first acknowledged Durga Mohun Das as pati, and in 1872 supported him against Keshub on the issue of whether wives should sit with their husbands during religious services.

We may recall also that during the subsequent women's education controversy between Keshub and the progressives, Sivanath Sastri, Monomohun Ghose, Durga Mohun Das, and Dwarkanath Ganguli were strongly opposed to what they referred to as a double standard of education for males and females. It may be recalled also that the progressives, spurred on by the Unitarian Annette Akroyd, finally established their own school, the Hindu Mohila Vidyalaya. Dwarkanath Ganguli served that school simultaneously as headmaster, teacher, dietician, darwan, and maintenance man. When the school later became known as the Bangiya Mohila Vidyalaya, Ganguli was responsible for so many of the jobs around the school that this egalitarian Brahmo even swept up daily after class.[88]

In 1876, two years before the official split with Keshub and the formation of the Sadharan Samaj, Dwarkanath and other Brahmo progressives started the Indian Association.[89] It was through this purely political organization and the National Congress that was derived from it, that Dwarkanath and his Sadharan Brahmo associates were able to champion the cause of the underprivileged through what they believed to be the most effective means at their disposal. Their technique in general was to include social issues in political platforms, to publicize those issues from a humanitarian point of view, and to pressure the government into rectifying the abuses underlying the issues. In 1885, for example, Dwarkanath was a prime mover through the Indian Association to win government support for an improved tenancy act designed to protect peasant proprietorship. He and K. K. Mitra, another politicized progressive Brahmo, actually went into rural areas mobilizing peasants to agitate for the bill.[90]

In 1886/87, Dwarkanath went to the backwaters again—this time to Assam—for a closer look at what Brahmo missionaries had reported as slave conditions in the tea plantations.[91] Ram Kumar Vidyaratna, who may have been the earliest of Brahmo missionaries to visit Assam, had brought back a dismal report on the deplorable state of agriculture, on the effects of opium addiction, and on coolie exploitation by tea planters. It was the latter group whom Vidyaratna accused of "reaping in the major share of profit leaving little for the natives as wages and virtually nothing to build up the state of Assam."[92]

In 1887, Dwarkanath's articles on the "Slave Trade of Assam" began to appear regularly in K. K. Mitra's nationalist paper, the *Sanjibani*. All the grim details of illegal contracts for indentured labor were brought to light, as were cases of coolies being flogged to death for trivial reasons and the general slave-like conditions that characterized plantation life. All the time Dwarkanath traveled about the countryside incognito. Later Ganguli and another politicized Brahmo named Bipin Chandra Pal brought these facts before the National Congress in hope of winning resolution support in condemnation of the conditions in Assam.

There was so much opposition by conservative Congressites to the Bengali "sedition mongers," that Ganguli and Pal had to go from the authorized committee for discussing and drafting resolutions to the open session itself. Even so, as a result of the cautious mentality of the Congress leadership, Ganguli's resolution on labor problems in Assam was tabled until 1896, when the twelfth session accepted it for action.[93] Dwarkanath's reputation as a Bengali sedition-monger also stemmed from his radical behavior in 1889 in forcing the admission of six women delegates to the annual session in Bombay, the first time women were admitted to a Congress convention.[94] Dwarkanath's wife was among the delegates.

Ganguli's wife, Kadambini, was appropriately enough the most accomplished and liberated Brahmo woman of her time. From all accounts, their relationship was most unusual in being founded on mutual love, sensitivity, and intelligence. Mrs. Ganguli had been a graduate of her husband's Banga Mohila Vidyalaya, which she attended after receiving her first English education at the Brahmo Eden Female School in Dacca.[95] She was one of the first two female B.A.s in India, and among the first in the British empire. She entered the Calcutta Medical College in 1883 and later completed her course of study in Edinburgh, becoming the first fully qualified woman physician in India.[96]

Mrs. Ganguli's case was hardly typical even among the more emancipated Brahmo and Christian women in contemporary Bengali society. Her ability to rise above circumstances and to realize her potential as a human being made her a prize attraction to Sadharan Brahmos dedicated ideologically to the liberation of Bengal's women. But for this very reason, as Nirad Chaudhuri has pointed out, such women as she were looked upon "as legitimate prey" by Hindus, not merely for seduction but as objects of hate, scorn, and defamation.[97] In 1891, the orthodox Hindu journal *Bangabasi* lashed out at Mrs. Ganguli as a despised symbol of modern Brahmo womanhood and accused her, a mother of five children, of being a whore.[98] Immediately, Sivanath Sastri, Nilratan Sircar, and her husband Dwarkanath instituted legal action against the journal and its editor. On May 3, 1891, the *India Messenger* said the following about the social issue underlying the continued persecution of Brahmos: "The logic is that maintenance of female virtues is incompatible with their social liberty. Every woman may enjoy freedom. Therefore a vast majority of them are unchaste. Farces are written against us and performed in theaters that continually ridicule and heckle . . . our work of female emancipation. Newspapers cast foul aspersions. . . ."[99]

Ganguli fought bitterly, as he did always, not only to defend his wife but to support the principle of liberating women against what he considered the forces of narrow privilege. On July 12, the *Brahmo Public Opinion* announced jubilantly that the libel case had been settled and that the accused was found guilty. Mohesh Chandra Pal, the *Bangabasi* editor, was sentenced to six months' imprisonment and made to pay a fine of one hundred rupees.[100]

The progressive Brahmo conscience was not overwhelmed by the Hindu revivalism of the 1880s and 1890s. The fervor of the Brahmo ethic kept compassion for the underprivileged burning during the enveloping darkness of the extremist period. In 1891, the Brahmos established the *Das Ashram* (Sanctuary for Servants of Society), which was the most ambitious Brahmo social welfare institution up to that time.[101] Under the leadership of Ramananda Chatterji, ashram members founded bands, charitable associations, small hospitals in the rural areas, a leper asylum in Deoghar, Bihar, and places of refuge for orphans and dying destitutes. They offered legal aid to oppressed women and rented a building in Calcutta's red-light district for the purpose of rehabilitating the daughters of prostitutes. The *Das Ashram* also conducted a Medical Hall in North Calcutta for the poor, which was under the supervision of Dr. Nilratan Sircar and other Brahmo physicians.

Included among the activities of the ashram was the attempt to help the blind. Ramananda Chatterji turned his efforts to this task, and with remarkable ingenuity and patience, he studied the English Braille system, adopted it, and converted it into a Bengali system in 1892.[102]

In the early 1890s, the fight for female emancipation intensified suddenly as a result of the Age of Consent controversy, and at the forefront of the struggle in Calcutta stood the three formerly Kulin Brahmins, now Brahmo reformers: Sasipada Bannerji, Dwarkanath Ganguli, and Ramananda Chatterji. Ramananda, the journalist among them, was especially active in his editorial role of interpreting the facts in support of the government bill. When, in 1890, for example, a ten-year-old girl died as a result of sexual intercourse, Chatterji called it murder in an editorial of a Brahmo newspaper condemning early marriage among Hindus.[103] In March 1891, the Sadharan progressives launched an organized campaign against the orthodox Hindu opposition to the bill and for a year afterwards they carried on a tireless debate with conservatives and revivalists. Chatterji himself wanted the age of consent raised to sixteen, but ultimately age twelve was accepted in the final passage of the act.

The controversy over age of consent produced a host of other issues centering about the degradation of women and their unequal social position. By the 1890s, Sadharan Brahmos, continually prodded by the more radical members such as Ganguli and Chatterji, came gradually to accept a very modern outlook on the general problem of female equality. Proud of the academic and professional achievements of several of their women, they began to favor higher education not merely as an aid to intelligent companionship or motherhood at home but as preparatory for a career in the outside world.[104] Brahmos were particularly proud of the superior education they provided to women from elementary school through college. Pride came as a result of official recognition, as in 1891 when the Brahmo Girls School was considered by the government as the "best boarding girls' high school in the Bengal Presidency."[105] Sadharan Brahmos were also exceedingly proud of their record in higher education, at that time in Bethune College. In 1895, of a total of forty-four girls boarding at Bethune, twenty-nine were progressive Brahmos and only four were from the predominant Hindu population.[106] The other two branches of the Brahmo Samaj, however, did not share this liberal attitude on female education. The Keshubite Victoria Girls' School followed the domestic arts curriculum set up by its founder until 1911, when it was transformed into Victoria College for Women with an egalitarian course of study. As for the Adi Samaj, its leader K. N. Tagore busied himself writing long essays in support of education for intelligent wifely companionship and motherhood.[107]

The degradation and humiliation of women, another aspect of the same problem, was equally the concern of the progressives. In the latter part of 1893, ashramites, along with liberal government officials, gave a series of well-attended lectures at the Calcutta Town Hall on dope addiction and prostitution.[108]

Even in 1906, at a time when the partition of Bengal embittered the bhadralok and precipitated the Swadeshi movement, Brahmo progressives continued to crusade on behalf of their less fortunate countrymen in the face of extremist opposition. In that year, Sadharan Brahmos under Sivanath Sastri founded what came to be known as the Society for the Improvement of Backward Classes in Bengal and Assam. Brahmo missionaries were dispatched to rural areas where they lived in Sudra villages and started schools. Under dedicated missionaries such as Hemchandra Sarkar, the work was carried on with great efficiency and gusto. By 1916, the Society for the Improvement of Backward Classes, which was entirely Brahmo in administration, had established sixty-two schools among the Harijans of Bengal and Assam. The number increased to 441 schools by 1932, the year that the organization was stopped for lack of funds. According to the last report of 1932, 17,809 children—13,106 boys and 4,703 girls—were in the 441 schools that were distributed in 384 villages. The report claimed that in twenty-three years the Brahmo missionaries had brought literacy to or "reclaimed 45,000 boys and girls."[109]

What the Brahmos achieved was certainly no immediate social revolution, but the routinization of a reformist ideal sustained by moral conviction and compassion. This was no mean accomplishment when understood against the context of British imperialism and Indian nationalism. Through their voluntary associations, newspapers, and journals, they left future generations a legacy: the new consciousness of the liberal adult.

CHAPTER FOUR

Family, Faction, and the Dilemmas of Political Reform under Colonialism

THE rise of a political consciousness, or the "politicization of the Bengal renaissance," is a familiar theme in the historiography of modern Bengal.[1] The context is generally seen as the freedom movement, which presumably began in the 1870s when the professional intelligentsia turned increasingly to political activities as a means of advancing their common interest. Crucial was the birth of the Indian National Congress in 1885, an event always subsumed under "nationalism." In the first generation of Congress history, the "moderates" prevailed, whereas in the first decade of the twentieth century the "extremists" or swarajists (independence fighters) predominated.[2]

This was the earlier interpretation, rooted in India's actual struggle for independence. It was predicated on a monolithic nationalist movement represented by the Congress, and a monolithic imperialism represented by British bureaucratic authority. In this atmosphere, Indian nationalist historians viewed their struggle as a confrontation between good and evil. Gradually, out of a logic dictated by the polemical nature of the struggle, Britain and the West came to be thought of as totally evil. The intensification of xenophobia during the height of the nationalist struggle erased the difference between the good in the West (liberalism) and the bad (imperialism). When the leadership of the Congress passed into the hands of Gandhi, his central idea of truth force was coupled with his condemnation of the West as an unmitigated source of horrors.[3] I contend that the pervasiveness of xenophobic nationalist ideology has so distorted the place of liberalism in the recent history of India that it has become almost impossible to assess the contribution of the progressive bhadralok to shaping a modern political consciousness. Nationalist historiography prompts us to assume that the "early" liberals were "moderate nationalists," and that the later generations were the true nationalists or freedom fighters. One of the important questions with which this chapter deals is whether the liberals were nationalists at all. I question the assertion that moderate and extremist were two phases in the nationalist movement. Rather, as the chapter and subsequent chapters should make clear, these groups were antithetical to one another. Liberals were reformers who tended toward xenophilia; nationalists were cultural apologists who leaned toward xenophobia.

The monolithic interpretation of Indian nationalism has been challenged in recent years from the varying points of view: Marxist theory, the sociology of elites, the psychohistory of nationalist leaders, and the cultural factors in the making of a nationalist.[4] Most of these new approaches have undermined the older interest in mass movements against foreign oppression. Instead, they have introduced a new, more sober image of nationalists as regional elites, engaged in competition with the British ruling elite for positions of status, privilege, and wealth. A culturally more relevant view of the nationalists would also include internal factional issues over questions of family, caste, and religion. And because the new literature reflects the brutally realistic, sometimes cynical conception of material self-interest in human affairs, the Bengali bhadralok of the last century have been resurrected in all their comprador splendor to support a picture of nationalism akin to revolution by circulating elites.[5]

Though accurate enough in depicting the bhadralok as products of the British system, the new concept of elites seems to be reductionist—politically, socially, economically, and culturally— because it treats of the bhadralok in a one-dimensional analytical framework. Thus, a purely political analysis of the bhadralok in their function as collaborator to the British would make it appear that a liberal such as Ananda Mohun Bose was simply a Bengali version of Machiavellian man. But in fact, as already depicted in this book, the bhadralok were liberal theists, humanists, rationalists, or scientists; we have observed their human development from identity crisis in youth to adult preoccupation with the ethic of achievement, and their compassionate concern for fellow countrymen and women. They were surely liberal, however much we modify the term in either the colonialist or the Bengali cultural context.

My own approach in the chapter is to view the progressive bhadralok's political consciousness and action as an extension of their thought and behavior as reformers. From data on the Brahmo liberals, many of whom we have already discussed in other roles and functions, I hope to give an integrated picture of political liberalism both from the inside view of issues within the Brahmo Samaj, and from the outside view of issues generated by encounter with British imperialism and Indian nationalism. In this manner, and by exploring the relevant data on such issues as national identity and universalism, swaraj and creative nationalism, I hope to demonstrate the distinctive qualities of the liberal as a political reformer.

On the other hand, as we shall see, even the most liberal Brahmos were not without a blemish in compromising their Puritan ethic for rational self interest. My purpose is not to redeem the moderates as men more worthy than nationalists, but to paint complete and honest portraits of human beings in history, which include the blemishes as well as the nobler aspects of their appearance. There is considerable evidence on how Brahmos modified the Puritan ethic and political liberalism as a result of family and factional considerations. Such distasteful incidents always seemed to emerge within the Brahmo Samaj during periods of factional dissension, erupting finally into schisms. But it is important to note that such exposures of hypocrisy and other forms of deceit were garbed in positive liberal values and ideas. In the two major Brahmo schisms of 1866 and 1878, nasty disclosures about family-centered corruption were expressed as justification for constitutional procedures and representative government against the arbitrary decisions of authoritarian rule.

The liberals faced British authoritarian rule rather as they faced paternalism within the Samaj. Thus, they aimed at liberalizing autocratic British rule in India with ideas learned from their rulers. If we can grasp the reformist role of the bhadralok as constitutionalists, then we can begin to understand their distinctive pioneering contribution to the political process in modern India. Not nationalism, but the parliamentary system—representation and the accommodation of conflicting interests—was India's legacy from the liberals. The Indian National Congress, which nationalists used as a forum to agitate for independence, was originally established by the liberal bhadralok to achieve equality and justice through the agency of a representative body. No doubt, the political activity of the liberals and the political agitation of the nationalists were both activated by the rising tide of British imperialism.[6] But the responses from the two groups were totally different. For the liberals, especially, imperialism threatened their role as reformers of Hindu society. Imbued with Unitarian, positivist, and progressive ideas, their quarrel had not been with British rule as such but with Hindu conservatism and reaction. The dilemmas of their delicate position as interpreters of the West increased as their situation grew more precarious. If they chose to desanctify the West (nationalism), then they could no longer function as reformers of their own tradition (modernism). If they persisted as liberals defending Western values in an imperialist atmosphere, they would lose both popular support to the nationalists and their own self respect as denationalized caricatures aping the manners of the alien overlord.

In 1865, the Brahmo Samaj under Debendranath Tagore's leadership went through a severe crisis in which the movement became seriously divided between liberals and conservatives. Reviewing the positions of the two factions is valuable because it will delineate an integrated view of the ideological differences between conservative and liberal in contemporary bhadralok society. Noteworthy is the genesis of a nationalist-universalist dialectic within the Brahmo Samaj, which is so similar to the later nationalist-liberal dialectic at the turn of the century. Also significant is the age difference between the liberal faction and the conservatives. The liberals who rallied behind Keshub Chandra Sen were the same young men we encountered in Chapter 3, experiencing the identity crisis of their adolescent years in the 1860s. The conservatives were of an older generation, who were more inclined to compromise their own youthful zeal for reform in an effort to heal psychic wounds and to narrow the gulf between themselves and the Hindu community.

Keshub Sen, increasingly surrounded by new recruits who joined the Brahmo Samaj in response to his appeal and promises, soon found himself as their champion against the established practices of the older generation. The younger people, like younger people always, revolted against the older people's hypocritical behavior in not living up to the Brahmo code or dharma. Here was the first evidence of a generational clash in the history of the Brahmo Samaj.

The younger generation wanted two types of reforms.[7] The first was internal, the implementation of measures to compel Brahmos to live according to the spirit of their liberal, rational religion and ethics. They insisted that ministers remove both their sacred threads and caste marks; that the ministry be earned by merit rather than be awarded for caste; that intercaste marriage be encouraged and child marriage discouraged; that Bengali and not Sanskrit be used in worship; and that in every way so-called Brahmos were to be dissuaded from the hypocritical course of paying lip service to rational religion at Brahmo meetings, while continuing to practice Hindu rites in the privacy of their homes.

The second program of the younger generation Brahmos was external: the demand that the Samaj join other progressive groups in promoting social reform. It was an extension of an idea germinated by Rammohun, developed by Akkhoy Kumar Dutt, and embodied in a practical reform program by Vidyasagar: that the true victims of society, enslaved by an oppressive Hindu social system, were the women. With the exception of supporting the temperance movement and relief for the victims of famine, flood, and disease, the younger Brahmos concerned themselves exclusively with female emancipation. Widow remarriage, which had by the 1860s become virtually synonymous with the name of Vidyasagar; Kulin polygamy, which Vidyasagar again had made a central issue; support for the Bethune School for Hindu Girls, of which Vidyasagar had been first native secretary—these were typical of what they considered liberal social reform.

Keshub had thrown himself into the struggle for change as spokesman of the young, and he had endorsed both their internal and external demands. Since, constitutionally, Debendranath was the sole source of authority to decide on such matters, Keshub appealed directly to him to institute the reforms. But a letter of Tagore's dated January 23, 1863, on sacred thread wearing and caste distinction, made it clear how far he was willing to go. He wrote that "I disapprove also of Brahmos continuing to wear the sacred thread and I am also opposed to caste distinction . . . but I want these things to happen by individual choice and slowly."[8]

Part of the problem was Debendranath's ambivalence about the issue of female emancipation. Though the Tagores were well known for educating their own women privately at home, there was a line drawn by Debendranath between the home and the outside world. One of the best sources for understanding this rather delicate situation is through his son, Satyendranath, who was critical of his father's social conservatism. Satyendranath was a member of the young liberal Brahmos who rallied around Keshub, and so he opposed his father on purdah. There is the revealing incident about his father's violent reaction to his inviting his wife to see him off to England at the steamer station. When Debendranath heard that his daughter-in-law went to the station by open carriage rather than by palanquin, he exploded in fury, shouting that "the faces of women must never be exposed to the glances of the public."[9]

There were other issues equally important, which by 1865 prompted Debendranath to drive Keshub and his faction out of the Brahmo Samaj. The exchange of letters between them that year is most revealing about key issues that divided the generations. In a letter by Keshub on August 1, a plea was made that Debendranath join the "tide of progress" before it was too late. "You have given us leadership these past thirty years," wrote Keshub, and "we have accomplished much in the moral improvement of our character," in the "propagation of religion," and in the "reformation of society." But the present disagreement, he continued, "has sprung from the very tide of progress. It is indeed true that such a controversy is to be regretted but it is by no means a matter of astonishment. Such disputes and controversies happen . . . in the time of transition . . . when old and new ideas run against each other. . . . For unless the Brahmo Samaj keeps pace in the progressive spirit of the age, and is modified so as to suit the new ideas and new wants of society, it will suffer in estrangement, from the sympathy of progressive men and fail to accomplish its higher objectives."[10]

Debendranath's reply may have been conservative from Keshub's vantage point, but it introduced a note of warning which, considering the extremely delicate and complex framework of pursuing a national identity under foreign rule, was perspicacious and almost prophetic. Debendranath started by saying that the impending rupture did not surprise him at all, but "only speaks of the progress of the Samaj." He was perfectly aware that in the course of time men's circumstances change. Otherwise how could there be progress? But Debendranath felt that the real issue was possibly one of Hindu identity, and that the older generation of Brahmos were being penalized for being Hindus. Thus, he felt it his duty "to avoid a clash between the older men who helped make the Brahmo Samaj what it is (yourselves are but the fruits of their zeal, agitation and patience). . . . If you can with the spirit of charity, tolerate them . . . and like elder brothers consent to take them with you as you go forward, there shall be greater progress."[11]

But it was the question of identity and community that seemed most to perturb Debendranath. Sivanath Sastri, who was there at the time as a follower of Keshub but still sympathetic to Debendranath, said that Tagore "feared setting up an impossible gulf" between Brahmos and the Hindu Samaj. Most of the recommended reforms were in effect anti-Hindu, and their acceptance would not only infuriate the Brahmo congregation, but "would violate the long cherished dream of Debendranath's to preach Brahmoism in a national and acceptable form."[12]

It is against the greater problem of identity and reform that we must understand the political issue of constitutionalism within the Samaj. Debendranath was greatly disturbed at the results of a general meeting held on February 26, 1865, in which thirty-two Brahmos signed a petition demanding democratic proceedings to determine Brahmo policy and the election of all officers including ministers. The petition by the liberals referred to a "Brahmo public" that could not be excluded from the decision-making process. There was a key sentence from Keshub's petition, which read: "The Brahmo Samaj, whatever they believe, is not a piece of property or a building but a community of which we are members and were therefore fully entitled to manage our own affairs."[13]

As for determining the most critical issue leading to the schism of 1866, Max Müller, the German Orientalist, who had played musical duets with Debendranath's father, Dwarkanath, and who corresponded regularly with both Debendranath and Keshub, saw the problem of national identity as paramount. "So far as I can judge," he wrote, "Debendranath and his friends were afraid of anything likely to wound the national feelings of the great mass of people." Said Müller: "They wanted above all to retain the national character of their religion. A so-called universal form would make their religion appear grotesque and ridiculous to the nation. They pleaded for toleration of Hindu usages and customs which appeared to them innocent."[14]

I have discovered one letter by Keshub to Rajnarian Bose dated February 6, 1865, in which, as one might expect, there was contained an urgent appeal for support. "My blood dries up," wrote Keshub, "when I think of the way I am being driven out of the Samaj." In anguish, Keshub reminded Rajnarian that "the Samaj is my whole life, and everything—my honor, my wealth—has been bartered for the good of the Samaj."[15]

At a general meeting of Brahmos on November 15, 1866, the formal break between generations finally occured. The birth of the Brahmo Samaj of India at that meeting was anticlimactic, but the resolutions passed by the Keshubites and subsequent debates are important for sharply defining the increasingly vital issue of nationalism and universalism between the two camps. One resolution in particular should be singled out in this regard, proposed by the Vaishnava Brahmo Bijoy Krishna Goswami, on behalf of the Keshubites. It read: "Men and women of every nation and caste who believe in the fundamental doctrines of Brahmo Dharma, shall be eligible as members of the Brahmo Samaj of India."

Actually, Bijoy Krishna was not referring to Debendranath's book *Brahmo Dharma*, because he immediately called for a new "compilation of theistic texts to be taken from all the Scriptures of the world." It was in reply to Bijoy Krishna that Nabagopal Mitra, personal friend of the Tagores and ardent Brahmo nationalist, raised his voice. The same Nabagopal Mitra, whose many activities of a patriotic nature earned him the title "National Mitra," argued at the meeting that "if there was truth sufficient near home, why should we go abroad. There was all the truth which we require in the Hindu Scriptures and we need not therefore borrow anything from other Scriptures."[16]

Bijoy Krishna's proposal for a compilation of scriptures from all the major religious sources led to the *Sloka Sangraho*, which was used in Brahmo service. The opening of the Keshubite mandir on August 22, 1869, boldly proclaimed the universalism and reformist intent of the newly formed Brahmo Samaj of India. Keshub's declaration of principles was obviously an elaboration of Rammohun Roy's principles in the trust deed. "This building," Keshub declared, "is established with the object of paying reverence to all truths that exist in the world . . . that all quarrels, all misunderstanding, all pride of caste may be destroyed, and all brotherly feeling may be perpetuated." No idols were to be worshiped and no scripture was to be considered infallible. Furthermore, "no sect shall be vilified, ridiculed, or hated. No prayer, no hymn, sermon, or discourse to be delivered or used here, shall countenance or encourage any manner of idolatry, sectarianism or sin. Divine service shall be conducted here in such a spirit and manner as may enable men and women, irrespective of distinctions of caste, colour, and condition, to unite in one family, eschew all manner of error and sin, and advance in wisdom, faith, and righteousness."[17]

Even the architecture of the mandir reflected Keshub's universalism. It was a blend of Hindu temple, Christian church, and Muslim mosque. In 1870, when an expanded edition of the *Sloka Sangraho* was published for the congregation, the motto beautifully inscribed on the title page was "The Wide Universe Is the Temple of God."[18]

In the 1870s, the constitutional aspect of the liberal reformer's ideology was considerably developed as a consequence of legal training and the study of political processes in Great Britain. I would argue that this educational experience abroad was a major factor in developing a new political consciousness. At first, only Brahmos and Christians went overseas, either to study law or to compete for the I.C.S. (Indian Civil Service). We have already referred to two Brahmos, Satyendranath Tagore and Monomohun

Ghose, who went to England as early as 1862. Many others followed over the next decades, including emancipated Hindus such as W. C. Bonnerji, who returned from London in 1874.[19]

Returning to Bengal with Bonnerji was a young Brahmo, Ananda Mohun Bose, who had established a brilliant record for himself as a "wrangler" at Cambridge.[20] In England, Bose first met Surendra Nath Banerji, who was then preparing himself for the I.C.S. exam. The attraction and subsequent relationship between these two was to be vitally important in the history of the "nationalist" movement. Banerji, a Kulin Brahman son of a successful Western-trained medical practioner, was born in 1847, the same year as Ananda Mohun and Sivanath Sastri. After four years at Calcutta University, he, Bihari Lal Gupta, and Romesh Chandra Dutt went to England together (1868) for the common purpose of qualifying themselves for upper-echelon service positions in India. Though Banerji was neither a Brahmo nor especially religious, he greatly admired Keshub Sen, who in 1870 was the charismatic hero for most young Bengali progressives, secular or religious. It was Keshub who organized the welcome party for Banerji's return to Calcutta in 1871 at the Howrah Railway Station.

Bose himself returned from England in 1874 to find the progressive faction of the Brahmo Samaj estranged from Keshub, largely on the issue of women's rights. As for Banerji, he had become a famous issue in his own right when, shortly after being hired as assistant magistrate in Sylhet in November 1871, he encountered difficulty with his superior, H. C. Sutherland, over a minor matter, and was dismissed from service. Just as Ananda Mohun was returning from England, Surendra Nath Banerji had started back for England to plead his case. Trying to salvage his career, Banerji was called to the Bar, but was rejected by the Middle Temple for having been dismissed from the civil service.[21]

In 1875, Bose, already immensely successful as a barrister, found himself the leading participant in two related constitutional-type movements aimed at achieving justice and equality through legal agitation. In the first, he offered himself as chief legal adviser for the Samadarshi (liberal) faction against Keshub's paternalistic rule of the Samaj. Both Bose and Durga Mohun Das, as lawyers, were instrumental in leading the struggle for representative government within the Samaj. Second, Bose, who greatly admired Banerji and was fully aware of the undemocratic system that had led to his friend's dismissal, organized constitutional agitation against the excesses of imperial bureaucratic rule. Both these ends were pursued simultaneously, and were backed chiefly by the Brahmo progressives.

Though Vidyasagar came forward to give Banerji employment as an English professor at his Metropolitan College, the real organization behind the frustrated young bhadralok was composed largely of the progressive Brahmos under Ananda Bose. As for student support of Banerji, very important was the Purba Bangla Sabha (East Bengal Society), the organization of East Bengali boys in Calcutta colleges founded by Bose as a refuge and recruiting ground for the Brahmo Samaj. At the same time that they supported Banerji against British paternalism, they supported the Samadarshi faction against Keshubite paternalism.

In 1875, Keshub Sen, who ten years earlier had championed constitutionalism and liberal reform against Debendranath, now found himself opposing liberalism within his own Samaj. The Samadarshi faction felt they must challenge Keshub's authority because he had betrayed the reformation. In 1876, with Ananda Mohun Bose taking the lead, the constitutional issue within the Samaj between progressives and Keshub came to a head. Sivanath Sastri, then a Sanskrit teacher at Hare's School, as spiritual leader of the progressives also took a leading part in the agitation. Keshub was now being attacked as an advocate of the divine right of kings, in which his support of Queen Victoria was linked to his absolutist rule over the Brahmo Samaj.[22] Bose pointed to the failure by Keshub since the meeting of October 22, 1867, to provide for a constitution that would allow decisions by representative council. In the same breath, Keshub was ridiculed for his belief in "despotism." It was said that with "the eternal God as President, Keshub would be secretary eternally."

In April 1877, as a consequence of a "letter of requisition" signed by thirty-five Brahmos pointing out the need for a church representative assembly, Keshub agreed to the creation of a provisional committee to draw up a scheme for organizing such an assembly. The committee was predominantly progressive in composition: Keshub, Protap Majumdar, Shib Chandra Deb, Durga Mohun Das, Sivanath Sastri, Nagendra Nath Chatterji, P. K. Ray, and Ananda Mohun Bose.[23]

On May 19, a public meeting was held among all Brahmos to consider the report of the provisional committee. Keshub, refusing to be swept away by what he considered the sudden craze for representation, and obviously determined to save his own position, was absent. But the constitutionalists were not that easily set aside. On

September 23, another pratinidhi sabha or general assembly was convened—this time with representatives of twenty-seven provincial samajes who supported the progressive cause. Well-organized pressure and carefully prepared briefs on Keshub's authoritarian rule were starting to have their effect of undermining the leader's basis of support.

Keshub was accused of making decisions justified as adesh or direct messages from God through divine inspiration. In 1876, Keshub was no longer interested in active social reform but had turned instead to meditation and the comparative study of major religions. The progressives maintained that the majority of Brahmos were opposed to Keshub's latest policy. Sivanath Sastri argued that this radical departure from social reform alienated the younger generation from Brahmoism. He predicted that the movement would lose the college students.

Another charge was leveled against Keshub with sinister implications—that of hypocrisy. After February 1878, when the Cooch Behar marriage was announced publicly, the indictment seemed to gain widespread belief and became extremely damaging to Keshub's reputation. To the constitutionalists, Keshub simply ignored the wishes of the majority. Keshub's rejoinder was that the "Samadarshi party were secularists, infidels, radicals and men of little faith."

The progressives became more and more open in their disapproval of Keshub's motives and behavior. Sastri charged that Keshub bought Lilly Cottage, "a large mansion with spacious compound furnished in a rich style," because he required a "fitting abode" for reception of the Cooch Behar party who wanted to "come and see his daughter previous to the engagement."[24] A second even more damaging accusation against Keshub was that all the time he mouthed pious statements about Brahmo religion and universalism, he was secretly building up an empire through his family. The reason Keshub did not want to throw open Brahmo affairs to the will of the majority of members was because that would mean surrendering private property to the Brahmo community.

When Keshub denied these charges, the constitutionalists, now the Sadharan Samaj, actually went to the Office of the Calcutta Collectorate and located the Trust Deed of the Brahmo mandir, dated January 23, 1868. They then disclosed to the Calcutta press that "there was not a word in the Deed denoting that Mr. Sen had purchased the property on behalf of or in trust for, the Brahmo Samaj of India." Rather, the mandir property was a virtual "zamindari" made over to the Sen family exclusively for "his and their use."[25] There followed the claim that all the Brahmo institutions were suspiciously managed by other members of the Sen family. Thus Keshub, who had attacked Debendranath Tagore back in 1866 for treating the Brahmo Samaj as a family monopoly, had himself violated "the moral right of the community" with the "same deplorable results." The question therefore was "how sincere is Mr. Sen."[26]

To round off the case of the indignant Brahmo majority against Keshub, two additional accusations were brought before the public. In March 1878, the constitutionalists charged that Keshub had taken 10,000 rupees to sell his daughter to the jungly prince of Cooch Behar.[27] Second, Keshub's worldly life was sharply contrasted with his lip service to asceticism. As one critic charged,

> Let us see what physical enjoyments the ascetic Keshub has abstained from and what pains and penalties he has inflicted upon his person. He has always lived in splendid houses. The house he lives in at present is a palatial building with a noble garden round it, though he is pleased to call it a cottage. . . . On the Railway he travels but in first class carriages, nor is he ever seen on foot except on rare occasions. . . . Sen lives amid the luxuries of a lord. He eats choice edibles, wears rich dresses, uses all sorts of perfumes, and keeps half-a-dozen servants.[28]

The organizing genius who led the opposition against Keshub was clearly Ananda Mohun Bose, by 1879 one of the most successful lawyers in Bengal, who had never lost a case.[29] It was Bose who presided over the May 19 Brahmo public meeting at Town Hall, where the provisional committee report was submitted to the general body for consideration. It was Bose who in February 1878 organized protest meetings against the intended marriage. Gangs of anti-Keshub college students, presumably invited there by Bose, shouted slogans and turned orderly meetings into noisy tempestuous affairs. After one of these meetings, the pro-Keshubite *Indian Mirror* reported the following: "Students have taken the liberty to protest against the marriage. For their own good these students ought to be silenced. Already our colleges are impertinent enough in the absence of any kind of moral education. If they are allowed with impunity to say anything with regard to any gentleman, they are sure in after life to suffer great trouble for their insolent behavior."[30]

Sivanath Sastri recalled the crisis period in his autobiography. He and Bose would hold long sessions in the house of Ananda Mohun, the two of them discussing the impending split and a future course of action. Sastri would invariably lie on a couch, with "arms crossed on my bosom and with eyes closed, lost in deep thought, while my friend all the time walking by my side . . . lost in the same thought." Then after long intervals Bose would "bend over my prostrate figure and ask, 'Sivanath Babu, what should we do? A great responsibility rests upon us.' "[31]

Letters were sent to Keshub, but apparently none was answered. More protest meetings were held. Protap Majumdar, as a close friend of Keshub, was asked to intercede, but to no avail. When the marriage did take place, the constitutionalists brought out the first issue of their new journal, the *Brahmo Public Opinion*, on March 21, 1878. The formal split was now inevitable, as the journal viciously attacked Keshub for ignoring the wishes of "fifty Samajes from different parts of the country who have with one unequivocal and unmistakable voice condemned the marriage as inconsistent with the recognized and accepted principles of the Brahmo Samaj."[32] On March 24, a meeting was scheduled at the mandir to win congregational approval for deposing Keshub from his position of authority and leadership in the Samaj. The mandir, however, had been placed under lock and key by the Sen family, and a policeman was ordered to protect the property from damage.[33] The Samaj had now ceased to be a unified community, and the schism between the two major factions seemed irreparable.

On May 9, Bijoy Krishna Goswami, who by then had deserted Keshub, called for the "organization of a new Samaj" to be conducted on a "constitutional basis."[34] He submitted a set of guiding principles for the proposed Samaj, which included an acceptance of the electoral principle for executive officers, and representative principles by which only anusthanic or practicing Brahmos had the right to decide policy. On May 15, the creation of a Sadharan Samaj was openly declared at a meeting in Town Hall, Calcutta. The declaration stated that the main issue was one between authoritarian government and representative government: "Every individual Brahmo and every individual Samaj should feel that they have something to do, something to contribute towards the great future of their movement. The work of governing a Samaj was not his work or my work but it is the common work of us all."[35]

The presiding chairman for the meeting of May 15 was Ananda Mohun Bose.[36] The main task of the gathering was to draft a constitution. Naturally, as Sivanath Sastri reported, this too was Ananda Bose's task because none "had his experience in Constitution-making." "We worked at his home," wrote Sastri, "and sat at his dining table after the table cloth had been removed, day after day, till an early hour in the morning, deliberating upon the constitution of the new Samaj."[37] The Sadharan constitution submitted for approval in October 1878 was elaborately conceived, and revolutionary because it brought definite rules and procedures into the Brahmo church organization for the first time in its history. Through a system of checks and balances, it was hoped to prevent a single individual or family from dominating the affairs of the organization and community.

There were four separate "governing" bodies, whose proper coordination ensured the realization of the representative principle. First, on the highest level, there were four officers: a president, secretary, assistant secretary, and treasurer. Below was an executive committee of twelve elected by a General Committee yearly. The General Committee was composed of forty persons, elected annually by the Calcutta Samaj and the provincial samajes, and which met quarterly to "keep active control over the work of the Executive Committee." Finally, the constitution provided for a General Body that met once a year to review the annual report and to elect the office bearers of the General Committee. Only anusthantic Brahmos could hold office, and for the first time strict rules on accepting new members were articulated. One had to be eighteen years of age, willing to sign a covenant; and be of "pure and moral character." Only eight annas were required as a yearly fee for members, surprisingly low dues to carry on the ambitious program of the Samaj. Again, for the first time, a definite system of training, appointment, and support of missionaries was provided. Theoretically, every missionary had to undergo training for two years before being considered as a candidate. Even when the candidate was given a certificate to preach, he was on probation before being voted upon by the General Body.

These objectives of the Sadharan Samaj reflected a religious-oriented ideology as liberal in its social aspects as any in the world at the time. On matters of religion, the Sadharans expressed their faith in a personal God, their belief in the utility of congregational prayer, and their condemnation of "mysticism and sentimentalism," which "diverted religious enthusiasm" away from "channels of practical usefulness." The fourth principle stressed a faith in "the brotherhood of man," which included the denial of caste distinction, the "tyranny of class over class," and the oppression of

women. The fifth principle was a declaration of freedom of conscience, and the sixth was a renaissance type of goal by which
"moral energy, born of faith and earnest work" would be expended
for the moral and spiritual regeneration of the race."[38]

The philanthropic or social reformist aspect of Sadharan Samaj
activities was given a more permanent place in a Brahmo organization than ever before in the history of the movement. The solid institutional growth of Sadharan-backed schools and associations far
exceeded the brilliant (on paper) but ephemeral Indian Reform
Association of Keshub Sen. The earliest institutions, with the exception of the mandir (constructed in 1881), were all managed and
financed by the wealthy but liberal barristers from East Bengal,
Durga Mohun Das and Ananda Mohun Bose.

It is worth noting additionally that the Brahmo Press, *Tattva
Kaumudi* and *Brahmo Public Opinion*, the Bengali and English or-
gans respectively, were financed at first by both these barristers.
The foundation of the library was a donation of books made by
Durga Mohun Das. The City College, which started modestly in
January 1879 as a secondary school for boys, was entirely financed
by Ananda Mohun. The girls' school, Bangiya Mohila Vidyalaya,
which as noted elsewhere was merged with the Bethune School,
had been jointly financed by Bose, Das, and Dwarkanath Ganguli.[39]

Ananda Mohun was elected the first president of the Sadharan
Samaj, a position he would hold thirteen times before his death in
1906.[40] Professor Dwijadas Datta, who was a follower of Bose during the early years of the Sadharan Samaj but later returned to the
Keshubite fold, has in his memoirs testified to Bose's political effectiveness and power in Samaj affairs. According to Datta, Bose had
politicized Brahmoism in the name of constitutionalism. His purpose was to "capture the congregations in Calcutta and elsewhere."
Datta maintains that "politics was Mr. Bose's forte and the rebellion
against Keshub was conducted like a 'political campaign.' "

According to Datta, Bose's constitutionalism was a facade behind
which he and his faction manipulated the Sadharan Samaj to their
own advantage. He was, for example, able to maintain control by
the simple expedient of denying the General Body the freedom to
select members of the Executive Committee. The procedure was
for the outgoing Executive Committee to prepare a list of candidates from which the membership at large could choose their successors. Thus, said Datta, who was then part of Bose's faction, the
Executive Committee dominated by Bose's clique "really and directly controlled the Samaj."

To Datta, the Sadharan Samaj during its first two decades was ruled on the British model. Bose was king, Sivanath Sastri was prime minister, and the faction members were the cabinet. The Bose faction included his brother, M. M. Bose, and personal friends such as Shib Chandra Deb, Durga Mohun Das, Sivanath Sastri, and Dwarkanath Ganguli. There were also Bose's "salaried dependents" at the City College, such as Krishna Kumar Mitra, Kali Shankar Sukul, Umesh Chandra Dutt, Heramba Chandra Moitra, and Nagendra Nath Chatterji.[41]

Datta's indictment of Bose as a master politician is certainly not without foundation when one considers that until the early 1900s the posts of president and secretary were invariably held by loyal members of the Bose faction. Thus, constitutional guarantees did not necessarily end one-man rule of the Samaj. The real difference between Keshub's organization and the new one was ideological, in that the Sadharan Samaj was liberal in its outlook on social change, rational religion, and political reform. In perspective, its most important role under Bose's leadership was to fuse socio-religious reform with a liberal political consciousness.

The faction that seemed to control the Sadharan Samaj were the very same people who served on the managing committee of the Indian Association, which was founded on July 26, 1876. According to Sivanath Sastri, it was designed as a "mouth piece for the educated middle class of the country."[42] For Bengal, this referred to the majority of Calcutta University graduates since 1861, who were no longer gentry or aristocracy but who worked for their living in government service, law, medicine, civil engineering, education, or journalism. Most of them earned their income exclusively from their professions.

The Brahmo-dominated Indian Association made every effort to distinguish its middle-class character and program from the upper-class zamindari mouthpiece known, since 1851, as the British Indian Association.[43] The Indian Association represented a new generalized political consciousness in India, which went beyond begging or petitioning favors from the Queen but fell short of a direct confrontation with British authority and a declaration of independence. In the same way that they sought to rid the Hindu society of abuses, Brahmo liberals sought to rid the imperial order of injustice and inequality. "Stop draining India of its wealth," and "Throw out the racist bureaucrats and throw open all levels of the service to qualified Indians," were typical slogans. Ideologically, the Bose generation of the Indian Association and the National Congress aimed not for a free India but for the rights of British citizenship. Their attack on bureaucratic attempts to gag free speech and the press was framed in the broader appeal to the British nation for an extension of their liberal reforms to India.

This is the proper context for understanding the rise of Surendra Nath Banerji as the first important all-Indian moderate nationalist. Though not a Brahmo, Banerji was one of their most ardent sympathizers. With Banerji as the Indian Association's president, Samadarshi Brahmos managed the organization's affairs and carried out most of its activities. Ananda Mohun Bose, the association's first secretary, was prime mover and chief financier of its operations. Ananda Mohun's City School and College, which gave employment to a host of his Brahmo "salaried dependents," also gave employment to Surendranath Banerji.[44] One of Banerji's most ardent supporters in the association was a fellow City School employee named Krishna Kumar Mitra from Bose's own district of Mymensingh. Mitra was both devout Brahmo and political activist.

Brahmo missionary activity and zeal were important influences on the Indian Association. From 1877, Banerji accompanied Brahmo missionaries on their yearly tours of India, or would journey by himself along the same route. His objective was to set up Indian Association branches, largely in places where there were already Brahmo Samajes. Banerji sought to reach the same people as did Brahmo missionaries in such places as Lahore, Madras, Bombay, and elsewhere. In 1878, for example, Banerji visited Bombay as the Brahmo Ranade's house guest.[45] But unlike the Brahmos, Banerji minimized religion in his speeches, as he did social reform, stressing instead the need for organization to achieve political reform. Banerji simply secularized the Brahmo theme of national regeneration, demonstrating how political methods would achieve a similar purpose, but more effectively.

The Brahmo emissaries of the Indian Association treated the same theme from a somewhat different point of view. They were, after all, apostles who saw no conflict between politics and the sacred. As the Brahmo missionary and nationalist Bipin Chandra Pal rightfully observed, Banerji never referred to God in his lectures, nor to religion.[46] Krishna Kumar Mitra, who visited Lahore, Allahabad, and other cities of the north in 1878 as an emissary of the Indian Association, never forgot that he was a Brahmo.[47] The fiery speeches of Nagendra Nath Chatterji is another case in point. When he accompanied Banerji on his first tour in 1877 or when he traveled on his own, his speeches always integrated religious piety, social reform, and service to country, in the manner of the Brahmo preacher.[48]

Here, perhaps, lies the key to our final assessment of bhadralok of the type of Ananda Mohun Bose, whose Brahmoism not only distinguished him from the generation of Keshub Sen, but distinguished him also from the secularized Hindu reformers represented so admirably by Banerji, Bonnerji, and Romesh Chandra Dutt. To Professor Datta, as we have seen, Bose was at heart a political man in quest of power. Brahmo religion was a means to an end; contitutionalism was a facade. But to Sivanath Sastri, the reverse was true. Bose used politics to achieve a spiritual and moral end. Bose's speeches were never devoid of the Brahmo ideal. To Sastri, "Bose's heart was not in law or politics but in the service of God and his country."[49] Hem Chandra Sarkar, another Sadharan, makes the same point and quotes from a diary entry by Bose dated December 9, 1883, to support his contention. It is a revealing passage about the conflict that was most vital in the mind of a successful bhadralok who was also a devoted Brahmo:

> Having been thinking a good deal as to my future course, I feel myself between two forces. On the one hand, I feel an almost overpowering desire to give up all my secular work and devote myself entirely to the service of my God and country. . . . On the other hand, I see practical difficulties in realizing this. . . . If it pleases God, I will work for two, not more than three years more in the drudgery of my profession and then entirely devote myself to the nobler work of my country's spiritual, political and intellectual advancement.[50]

Such intimate disclosures by Brahmos suggest that the process of politicization, of which they were obvious agents, was accompanied by the process of sanctifying their service to country as pious Brahmos. Both these processes occurred simultaneously, but the fact that the Indian Association was inseparable from the Sadharan Brahmo association manifests a union of natural religion and liberal politics. Thus, the close association of religion with politics did not erupt suddenly with the rise of the next generation of militant nationalists, but was already an accomplished fact with the emergence of the moderates under the impetus of the Brahmos. The difference was in the religion: moderates advocated a reformist creed to match their political attitudes; extremists advocated an apologetic Hindu faith to match their political nativism.

If political liberalism intruded itself into the very core of the Brahmo institutional structure, it had the contrary effect of pulling religiously minded Brahmos away from Samaj affairs into the political arena, where they defended their liberal creed against Indian nationalists on the one hand and British imperialists on the other. Brahmo spiritual leaders found no conflict between their religious and moral duties in the Samaj and their political activism on behalf of the liberal moderates. To the Brahmos, and presumably to their counterparts elsewhere in India, their participation in Congress represented an alliance between liberal rational religion and liberal rational politics. Both were derived from the source of progressive Western values; both were expressive of the aspirations of the newly educated professional middle class; both moved along the treacherous path of exposing the shortcomings of British bureaucratic rule at the same time that they defended the utility and positive good of Western influences. The worst danger, possibly, for both was their reformist zeal, which brought them into direct confrontation with the nationalists who could tolerate no public exposure of cultural abuses at the very time they aimed to close Hindu ranks against the evil West. And when nationalists defended popular Hinduism in their own union of religion and politics as a means of mobilizing mass support, the Brahmos and political moderates found themselves increasingly alienated from their own society.

Brahmos themselves evidently did not see lack of support among the mass of people as a sign of weakness or failure. In fact, their leaders appeared jubilant at their success in linking up with likeminded emancipated intelligentsia willing to join organized efforts on an all-India basis. Speeches at the annual theistic conferences or at Social Reform Association meetings held at Congress conventions were full of optimism about the future, when the Brahmo faith and identity would be widely accepted as the basis ·of reformed Hinduism. In 1887, for example, Sivanath Sastri, then probably the most respected Brahmo in all India, gave a powerful talk on the need of merging Brahmo rational religion with the political aspirations of moderates. In the speech, Sastri established a close relationship between Brahmoism and nineteenth-century European liberalism. The enemies of Brahmo modernists were not merely militant Hindu revivalists and nationalists, but positivists, nihilists, materialists, and socialists. It was the mission of the Brahmos and the Congress to "advocate liberty of conscience—to establish the supremacy of human conscience—on the one hand and to bring men and women to God and to righteousness on the other—to lay the basis of all reforms whether social, educational or political in the spiritual life of the race."[51]

In 1888, Sastri went to England for six months and kept a diary of his impressions. The experience seemed to convince him more than ever that "service to humanity must be wedded to religion." The extremes of godless materialism so evident to him in the West, and otherworldly religion still predominant among Indians were both obstacles to the progress of mankind. Sastri identified Brahmoism with "British Liberalism," represented by the virtuous middle-class English family, and the way Christian societies were now engaged in humanitarian concerns.[52]

One has only to read Sivanath Sastri's *Jati Bhed* (Caste Distinction), which was so popular among liberals in the 1880s, to appreciate how the most reverend spiritual leader in the Sadharan Samaj was equally an ardent spokesman of British-style political liberalism. In this essay, his repudiation of caste is less that of a morally indignant Brahmo, and more along the lines of a nineteenth-century liberal worried about unity and social democracy. Caste distinction, he wrote, "is like a cancer that makes the freedom of India impossible." Caste is wrong because it divides Indians into separate units, creating antagonism and conflict in direct opposition to India's present need for unity and solidarity. Caste also impedes liberal democratic values in the self-development of all individuals as free men.[53]

The politicized aspect of social reform was also evident in Sastri's powerfully worded article in the *Modern Review* of 1910, entitled "The Duties of the Educated Classes to the Masses." Sastri argued that the Congress movement should take upon itself the duty of elevating the masses. He suggested that positive social change was more appropriate for the political objectives of the Congress than negative anti-Westernism, and that political behavior directed to larger social ends was the only purpose in having a Congress movement. In fact, Sastri in the article denied that India had developed a truely progressive political leadership because its elite looked upon the majority of its people as "a flock of sheep." "Look at England itself," he wrote, "where mass education has effected a revolution." In England, political behavior had become more democratic, diffusing "a spirit of self-help and cooperation into the minds of the mass." Sastri concluded that "unless educated men in our country ask for mass education—then in all their agitation for political privileges, they are principally concerned in securing political power for themselves and that their talk about the good of the country is a mere pretext."[54]

In the wake of the extremist challenge of the 1890s, the Partition agitation of 1905, and the consequent swadeshi movement, the temperature of bhadralok politics grew feverishly anti-Western and nationalist. Even leading Brahmos such as P. K. Ray, C. R. Das, and Rabindranath Tagore either temporarily or permanently defected from Brahmo liberalism at this time and became violently anti-Western. The magnet of Swaraj (independence), coupled with the pervasive desanctification of the West prompted some Brahmo liberals to advocate accommodation to nationalists, hoping that the nationalists would reciprocate by liberalizing their extreme nativism and xenophobia. Probably no one better characterizes this process among the liberals than Ramananda Chatterji, the most famous Brahmo journalist of his time.

Chatterji was born in 1865 in a Bankura village of West Bengal. Though his father had a modest position as local jailkeeper, Ramananda was the son of a Brahmin; he studied Sanskrit in his uncle's *tol* and received his sacred thread early in life. Ramananda was sent to the district zillah or high school, where he studied English for the first time. It was there that he came under the influence of a mathematics teacher who also happened to be a Brahmo. In the familiar pattern, young Chatterji and his class friends attended Brahmo services and lectures, surreptitiously coming under Brahmo moral and religious influence at a tender age. Another significant fact about this early exposure was the importance to Ramananda of Keshub Sen's journal for the masses, *Sulabh Samachar*, which apparently sold extremely well in Bankura district.

In 1883, at age eighteen, Ramananda matriculated at St. Xavier's College in Calcutta. Two years later, after standing fourth in the F.A. examination, he received a scholarship of 25 rupees a month to attend Presidency College. In 1886, in the midst of his college career, Chatterji was compelled to marry a girl of twelve. He was evidently still adhering to familial and caste obligations. But suddenly, though a good student in science and mathematics, Ramananda went to pieces physically and mentally, with the result that he never got his B.A. from Presidency. Instead, quite probably at the insistence of Brahmo professors at Presidency such as Jessie Bose, Ramananda shifted to Ananda Mohun Bose's City College, where he received his B.A. in 1888.[55]

He had not only shifted colleges, but subjects as well; from science and mathematics he now found himself a student of English composition and literature under the guidance of the venerable Brahmo Heramba Chandra Maitra. Professor Maitra, who succeeded Umesh Chandra Dutt as principal of City College, and who served in that capacity for the next thirty years, was perhaps the best known Brahmo Puritan of his generation. His "spotless character," his inability to tell a lie, his rigid honesty, and his humorless aphoristic tendency, made him a famous caricature in the Bengali society of the period.[56] His influence on young men such as Chatterji at the college was immense. His love for and superb mastery of English prose, coupled with a high level of intellectuality, which was reminiscent of Emerson, had a profound effect on students. But even more important was Maitra's dedicated political liberalism, which prompted him to be a founding member of the Indian Association and contributor to K. K. Mitra's *Sanjibani*.

Professor Maitra was so impressed with young Chatterji that he offered him a post as assistant professor of English at the College, and as his own assistant editor of the Brahmo organ, *Indian Messenger*. Maitra introduced the young man to Sadharan progressive leaders such as Sastri, Ganguli, and Bipin Pal, who were for the most part progressives deeply involved in the Congress movement. From this circle Ramananda acquired his orientation as a politicized Brahmo reformer.[57]

In 1895, primarily for financial reasons, Chatterji left Calcutta for Allahabad to become principal of the Kayastha College. Here a new stage opened in his life, important ideologically for the development of creative nationalism and important professionally for pioneering achievements in journalism. The possibilities and potentialities of journalism fascinated Chatterji. In April 1901, he started *Prabasi*, a journal for Bengalis living outside Bengal, which was not only creative intellectually but was technically interesting for embodying a new concept in that field of literature.

The first issue of *Prabasi* featured two improvements, which in the long run made Ramananda Chatterji not only famous but wealthy. The first was a superior form of half-tone reproductions of paintings that beautified the periodical without raising its cost. Second, the articles and poetry appealed to patriotic sentiments among Bengalis in a very sensible and sophisticated manner. Besides a poem by Rabindranath Tagore in the first issue, Chatterji also offered the reader some sixteen color reproductions of the Ajanta paintings in an article that combined low-cost aesthetic pleasure with collective pride in a national monument.[58]

But Chatterji, as an earnest Hindu reformer, could no longer feel comfortable as a Brahmo "minority sectarian" alienated from the greater Hindu society. Groping for avenues of accommodation, he coupled his new emphasis on the art treasures of the Indian people with a drive to reintroduce the aesthetic aspects of Hindu festivals into the Brahmo Samaj. His justification was to prevent the minds of Brahmo children from drying up as a consequence of the iconoclastic ardor of their elders.[59] Chatterji's self-acknowledged Brahmo Hinduism, which he shared in part with Rabindranath Tagore, endeared him to a wide range of modernized Hindus who were ordinarily repelled by Brahmo indifference to beauty.

In 1906, Chatterji resigned his principalship in Allahabad and returned to Calcutta, where he took up residence at the Sadharan Brahmo mission quarters. It was in this period of his life that his ideology of "creative nationalism" came to fruition. The appearance in January 1907 of his new English journal, *The Modern Review*, gave him the vehicle for articulating his new ideas, and the rise of militant nationalism during swadeshi offered him the situational context through which his philosophical appeal could be made. However, throughout this period of drawing closer to the greater Hindu society, Chatterji retained his spiritual and community identity as a Brahmo. He was not only active in Brahmo church affairs, but served on the executive committee of the Sadharan Samaj every year from 1909 to 1921, when he was offered the presidency.[60]

The immediate background for *The Modern Review* and Chatterji's creative nationalism was the extremist-moderate controversy in the Congress movement. In 1906, the Brahmo-style liberals of the Indian Association loosely connected with the National Congress issued a public indictment of the party of extremists for politicizing mass consciousness without first making the attempt to spread general enlightenment.[61] Are "we really trying to lift the masses from their present level of ignorance," asked the moderates, "or are we using them as pawns?" The moderates concluded that the extremists were simply "trading on the superstitions of the ignorant masses" in a bid to achieve power for themselves.[62]

This position is of great importance in understanding Ramananda's own nationalist ideology, because it represented, as it were, a bridge between the older moderate style of liberalism of the constitutionalists and the requirements of the new and more radical need to assert Indian autonomy or independence. Chatterji had for years been struggling for a way of reconciling the Brahmo moderate faith in internal regeneration or social reform with the extremist insistence upon freedom from foreign rule. The extremist party repudiated social reform as being self-defeating and devisive at the very time unity was necessary against alien tyranny.

Chatterji sought a way of supporting the freedom movement without falling into the extremist trap of despising all things Western. His solution was thoroughly Brahmo, and rather like Prafulla Chandra Ray's reconciliation of swadeshi or self-help with swaraj or self-rule. Chatterji denuded militant nationalism of its negative aspect of being antimodernist and anti-Western, and put all stress on the positive goal of achieving internal regeneration through nation building.

In 1907, Ramananda spelled out his own concept of swadeshi, which he saw as differing little from the Brahmo ideal of "modernizing Indian trade, industry and agriculture leading to economic self-sufficiency and an improved standard of living." Swadeshi was not to be confused with the expression of "verbal discontent with foreign rule," but was rather the internalized "discontent with the self—never to feel that we know enough, never to feel that we can do enough, or be perfect enough." This was clearly the Brahmo Puritan ideal dressed anew, reinterpreted and reintegrated by Ramananda. "The thirst after perfection for the sake of others," he wrote in the midst of swadeshi agitation, "this is nationality."[63]

In 1908, Chatterji openly deplored terrorism and the use of murder as a nationalist weapon.[64] Like Rabindranath at roughly the same time, Chatterji spoke out against the rising temper of antiforeign sentiment, which took the form of boycott, burning foreign goods, and doing injury to foreigners. Chatterji was at a loss to understand how the destruction of foreign commodities could possibly lead to internal growth and development. Then he reiterated the theme that not destruction but self-sufficiency was the key to nation building.

By 1910, the lines were clearly drawn between militant foreign-hating nationalists and creative nationalists who, like Ramananda, supported freedom, but not at the cost of xenophobia. In that year, Hiralal Haldar, the Brahmo neo-Hegelian philosopher, wrote his antixenophobic piece in Ramananda's *Modern Review*, which he called "Western Civilization." He accused aggressive nationalists of having interjected "race feeling" into their ideology. He wished to raise his "feeble voice" against the suicidal folly of hating everything Western. He saw nothing wrong with the "healthy type" of nationalism; but the "thing which we see all around us," said Haldar, is a "noxious poison" destroying the "vigorous genius of our national life." It is "race hatred pure and undiluted." Professor Haldar's conclusion was a powerful plea for Brahmo-inspired creative nationalism: "beware of the monster of race-hatred. Fear it, shun it, drown it. . . . By all means, stick firmly to what is best in your own civilization, but adopt the splendid virtues of the West, and adapt them to your conditions and environment. Above all, do not be puffed up with conceit and imagine that you are the chosen people of God, while the rest of the world are utter barbarians. That way damnation lies."[65] Ramananda treated the same theme but with more deference to nationalism in a *Modern Review* article of January 1925 with the title "Nation Building and the Critical Spirit." Beginning with a nationalist bias, he quickly shifted his attention and warned that "faith must not degenerate into bigotry and fanaticism." On the contrary, he argued, "as the welfare of every nation really depends on that of other nations, it is both foolish and unrighteous to seek to promote the interests of one's own nation at the expense of any other nation or nations. In fact, if Humanity is as it ought to be, be thought of as a grand and beautiful edifice, nations are the bricks of which it is to be built. And these bricks should be sound and well-made."

Of course, the well-made nation was to Chatterji a dynamic and progressive civilization—hardly fitting the militant nationalist image in defense of Hindu society, with its caste inequality, untouchability, and religious excess. Chatterji opposed Hindu orthodoxy, declaring that "we shall never have a liberal national and international mentality unless we can shake off the authority of priests, dogmatists and theologians." "We can never achieve dynamic national growth in India," he continued, by adhering to "sectarian orthodoxy," but only through "a liberal national education" for all. Untouchability and caste distinction should be destroyed. Untouchability in particular, Chatterji argued, was the curse of the Hindu social order and had to be uprooted.[66]

Ramananda's stress on untouchability in 1925 was probably a reflection of a deep concern over the years by Brahmo progressives in tackling the problem. In fact, the assault on untouchability constituted the last major social reform effort by Brahmo progressives in the twentieth century. Started in 1906 by Prarthana Samajists (Brahmins) in Maharashtra, the Depressed Class Mission, which aimed to reach and uplift primarily outcastes, was the pioneering movement of its kind in South Asia.[67] A year later, an all-Indian Brahmo Untouchability Conference was held with Satyendra Nath Tagore as president.[68]

Creative nationalists like Ramananda Chatterji were early convinced that social problems such as untouchability must be brought before the Indian National Congress, the political instrument of nationality, for endorsement and action by the delegates. Thus, at the 1917 Congress meeting, Ramananda and a Prarthana Samajist named V. R. Shinde finally got the delegates to support a resolution against untouchability.[69] It might also be pointed out that at the thirteenth annual untouchability conference in 1920, originated by Brahmos, a nationalist leader named Gandhi agreed to accept the presidency.[70]

Mass education was still another progressive component of building the Indian nation advocated by Ramananda Chatterji. He was, of course, not the first. In 1879, the Sadharan-dominated managing committee of the Indian Association supported mass education.[71] When Brahmos such as Benoyendra Nath Sen visited America, they brought back favorable reports on the effects of free mass education for all in developing "responsible citizenship."[72]

At the Benares session of the Indian National Congress in 1905, it was Ramananda Chatterji who helped muster support for a resolution advocating mass compulsory education in India.[73] His *Modern Review* continually dramatized the dire need of it. He courageously attacked the British for ignoring mass education in India while having extended it in their own country since 1871. In 1907, Chatterji printed the results of a comparative study on the educational progress of India and Japan. Japan, as a fellow Asian nation that had taken great strides in the modernization process, favorably impressed many Bengali intellectuals. Chatterji himself reported with amazement that by 1902, 96 percent of the Japanese boys and 87 percent of the girls could read and write. Naturally, in the comparison British efforts in India were looked upon as extremely feeble; for example, Japan with a population of 47,000,000 spent £5,000,000 for education, whereas the British in India with a population five times as great spent merely £1,500,000.[74]

The failure of Ramananada Chatterji to win wide support for Brahmo puritanism and modernism in the guise of creative nationalism, either from his fellow Indians or from the British, greatly contributed to the decline of the nineteenth-century progressive Brahmo spirit in Bengal. It was becoming increasingly obvious that without massive assistance from official sources, preferably from one's government rather than from a foreigner with little interest in the country he governed, nothing fundamental would be altered. Voluntary associations led by well-intentioned bhadralok proved simply Utopian schemes through which heroic figures emerged, fertile with ideas and burning with enthusiasm, who ended by beating their heads against the rock of the colonial system.

ical arena, where they defended their liberal creed against Indian nationalists on the one hand and British imperialists on the other. Brahmo spiritual leaders found no conflict between their religious and moral duties in the Samaj and their political activism on behalf of the liberal moderates. To the Brahmos, and presumably to their counterparts elsewhere in India, their participation in Congress represented an alliance between liberal rational religion and liberal rational politics. Both were derived from the source of progressive Western values; both were expressive of the aspirations of the newly educated professional middle class; both moved along the treacherous path of exposing the shortcomings of British bureaucratic rule at the same time that they defended the utility and positive good of Western influences. The worst danger, possibly, for both was their reformist zeal, which brought them into direct confrontation with the nationalists who could tolerate no public exposure of cultural abuses at the very time they aimed to close Hindu ranks against the evil West. And when nationalists defended popular Hinduism in their own union of religion and politics as a means of mobilizing mass support, the Brahmos and political moderates found themselves increasingly alienated from their own society.

Brahmos themselves evidently did not see lack of support among the mass of people as a sign of weakness or failure. In fact, their leaders appeared jubilant at their success in linking up with likeminded emancipated intelligentsia willing to join organized efforts on an all-India basis. Speeches at the annual theistic conferences or at Social Reform Association meetings held at Congress conventions were full of optimism about the future, when the Brahmo faith and identity would be widely accepted as the basis of reformed Hinduism. In 1887, for example, Sivanath Sastri, then probably the most respected Brahmo in all India, gave a powerful talk on the need of merging Brahmo rational religion with the political aspirations of moderates. In the speech, Sastri established a close relationship between Brahmoism and nineteenth-century European liberalism. The enemies of Brahmo modernists were not merely militant Hindu revivalists and nationalists, but positivists, nihilists, materialists, and socialists. It was the mission of the Brahmos and the Congress to "advocate liberty of conscience—to establish the supremacy of human conscience—on the one hand and to bring men and women to God and to righteousness on the other—to lay the basis of all reforms whether social, educational or political in the spiritual life of the race."[51]

In 1888, Sastri went to England for six months and kept a diary of his impressions. The experience seemed to convince him more than ever that "service to humanity must be wedded to religion." The extremes of godless materialism so evident to him in the West, and otherworldly religion still predominant among Indians were both obstacles to the progress of mankind. Sastri identified Brahmoism with "British Liberalism," represented by the virtuous middle-class English family, and the way Christian societies were now engaged in humanitarian concerns.[52]

One has only to read Sivanath Sastri's *Jati Bhed* (Caste Distinction), which was so popular among liberals in the 1880s, to appreciate how the most reverend spiritual leader in the Sadharan Samaj was equally an ardent spokesman of British-style political liberalism. In this essay, his repudiation of caste is less that of a morally indignant Brahmo, and more along the lines of a nineteenth-century liberal worried about unity and social democracy. Caste distinction, he wrote, "is like a cancer that makes the freedom of India impossible." Caste is wrong because it divides Indians into separate units, creating antagonism and conflict in direct opposition to India's present need for unity and solidarity. Caste also impedes liberal democratic values in the self-development of all individuals as free men.[53]

The politicized aspect of social reform was also evident in Sastri's powerfully worded article in the *Modern Review* of 1910, entitled "The Duties of the Educated Classes to the Masses." Sastri argued that the Congress movement should take upon itself the duty of elevating the masses. He suggested that positive social change was more appropriate for the political objectives of the Congress than negative anti-Westernism, and that political behavior directed to larger social ends was the only purpose in having a Congress movement. In fact, Sastri in the article denied that India had developed a truely progressive political leadership because its elite looked upon the majority of its people as "a flock of sheep." "Look at England itself," he wrote, "where mass education has effected a revolution." In England, political behavior had become more democratic, diffusing "a spirit of self-help and cooperation into the minds of the mass." Sastri concluded that "unless educated men in our country ask for mass education—then in all their agitation for political privileges, they are principally concerned in securing political power for themselves and that their talk about the good of the country is a mere pretext."[54]

In the wake of the extremist challenge of the 1890s, the Partition

PART II

Nationalist Ambivalence

That process of creating mythological entities which I spoke of as pseudospecies—that is, tribes and nations, creeds and classes, . . . has offered youth, in its ideological hunger, causes to live and to die for, and has attracted its heroism and self-sacrifice in periodical wars with other pseudospecies, foreign or domestic.

ERIK ERIKSON

CHAPTER FIVE

The Confrontation between Trinitarian Christianity and Reformed Hinduism

IF liberal Brahmos looked upon Unitarianism as a positive force that they freely accepted and adapted as a religion, ethic, and social gospel, they responded negatively to Trinitarianism, which they distrusted as alien and culturally destructive. Though Christian missionaries did much positive good in education and social welfare, their cultural values and ethnocentric view of Christ so alienated the intelligentsia that they negated whatever constructive work the church accomplished. The heavy-handed hard sell of the missionaries stamped them indelibly with the odious stigma of cultural imperialism; their blatant arrogance as agents of Western supremacy earned them incomparable animosity.

What the missionaries seemed to achieve, unwittingly for the most part, was not the conversion of Hindus into Christians but the conversion of "heathens" into reformed Hindus. The challenge of orthodox Christianity in India stimulated the Hindu intelligentsia to rediscover the sources of their own religious tradition and to reform their religion according to their new image of the remote past. In this process, the bhadralok intelligentsia of the Tattvabodhini Sabha and Brahmo Samaj were guided by the historical reinterpretation of the Age of Upanishads by Rammohun Roy, whose works were reprinted in the 1840s. Then the Vedanta, updated and revitalized by contemporary progressive values from the West, served as the Bible of the Hindu reformers. The Brahmos also borrowed freely from the missionaries, but as cultural apologists who adapted Protestant conceptions at the same time as they argued the superiority of Hinduism to Christianity.

Much of this chapter centers around a great debate between the Brahmo Vedantist Rajnarian Bose and the Bengali Christian convert Krishna Mohun Bannerji, on whether Christianity should become the religion of the Hindu reformation. A meticulous examination of the two positions is important not only to understand the issues that divided the two camps, but because in Rajnarian's skillful rebuttal was contained the seeds of modern Hindu cultural nationalism. Rajnarian went well beyond Rammohun in his articulate defense of the authentic Hindu faith against the Christian apology. Thus long before the creation of the Arya Samaj in the 1870s and the Ramakrishna Mission in the early 1900s, the Brahmo Samaj had already developed a standard defense of systematic and rational Hindu religion within the framework of a devastating critique of Christianity.

In 1835, with the triumph of Thomas Babington Macaulay's Westernizing alternative to Indian modernization, the official British Orientalist movement died in Bengal, along with many of their experiments in changing Hinduism from within by updating Hindu traditions.[1] Macaulay, as generally known, penned a *Minute on Education* that contained one of the most perfect expressions ever recorded of what may be called the philosophy of secular Westernization. The gist of what he advocated was that all cultural traditions except Macaulay's own Victorian English one were decadent and useless, and that the only true passport to modernity for a culture like India's was the complete assimilation to British manners, customs, and language. Macaulay's attitude was no mere academic argument without practical importance; he was supported fully by the governor general, Lord Bentinck (1829-1835).

During these very years, as I have shown more elaborately elsewhere, a polarization of cultural attitudes materialized among the Bengali intelligentsia in response to the Westernizing cultural policy of the government.[2] It was no accident that during this period the Young Bengal movement arose, which responded favorably to Macaulayism but at the price of alienation. The older generation of intellectuals, who had been reared by Orientalist contact, shifted to a "nativist" position and by means of the sati abolition issue organized India's first protonationalist movement, the Dharma Sabha, against foreign intrusion in the internal affairs of Hindus. Rammohun's Brahmo Sabha stood somewhere between Young Bengal and the Dharma Sabha, although it should be pointed out that Rammohun's successor, Vidyabagish, joined the Dharma Sabha against Bentinck on the issue as to whether or not the government had the right to abolish sati.[3]

Secular Macaulayism remained a dream, however, mere wishful thinking in a colonialist atmosphere where modernism for India was never really seriously entertained, either by the East India Company or by the British crown. The only fragment of Macaulay's Westernizing program that was retained was the stress on the English language, which itself became the passport not to modernity but to available positions in the administration. If secular Westernization proved a pipe dream (except among Indian voluntary associations dedicated to Western learning), religious Westernization did not.

Well-financed and well-organized mission societies in England, imbued with the same inflated national pride as Macaulay, sent out their legions of inspired men to save the heathen from eternal fire and damnation. Like Macaulay, they were convinced that Victorian England represented the apex of human development, but unlike Macaulay, they believed that their own Western-centered orthodox Trinitarian Christianity was the mainspring of that greatness.

Those who came to Bengal came mostly to Calcutta, where they aimed to persuade the newly emerging Western-educated to embrace the revealed truth of Christian dogma. Being fairly well educated themselves, they employed a method and philosophy of infiltration into elite circles, with the strategy of ultimately converting the mass after first converting the intelligentsia. Being Westernizers, in distinct opposition to the earlier generation of Serampore missionaries, who were Orientalists, they saw no need of learning Indian languages.[4] On the contrary, they carried on their debates entirely in their own native tongue.

From the point of view of mission history in Bengal, the era from 1830 to 1857 can properly be called the Age of Alexander Duff.[5] Not only was he one of the most intellectually gifted missionaries to serve in India, but he was certainly among the most effective in winning the minds of Western-educated people for Christ. As his name suggests, he was a Presbyterian from Scotland, as well intentioned as Macaulay and equally inflammatory, but as a spokesman of the sacred rather than the profane. Theologically, he was exactly the stereotyped Calvinist whom Unitarians in the West struggled to depose from their exalted position, but in terms of impact on the Western-educated in Calcutta, Duff was a rationalist and modernist, a rare combination that made him a formidable foe for non-Christian progressive Bengali intellectuals.

On July 13, 1830, shortly after arriving in Calcutta, Duff opened the General Assembly's Institution, which became one of the best boys' schools in India. He also launched the famed Scottish Church College on Cornwallis Square, an equally high-powered institution destined to play a critical role in the educational history of Bengal.

Duff, who had originally been asked to found his schools outside Calcutta, aimed as his strategy "to kill Hinduism by striking at its brain, Calcutta."

Duff was immensely successful in awakening the minds of Bengali youth, and moderately successful in his attempts to convince them of the validity of Christian gospel. Krishna Mohun Bannerji, a former Derozian, was his earliest major convert in November 1832. Then there followed the gifted Mohesh Chandra Ghose, who unfortunately died prematurely in 1837. Kailas Chandra Mukherji was another brilliant convert, but he died suddenly in 1845. There was Peary Mohun Rudra, who like Krishna Mohun Bannerji later left the Presbyterians for the established church, and carved out a distinguished career as an Anglican. The same may be said for A. C. Majumdar, who became highly Westernized after five years in England. In 1843, Lal Behari De and Michael Madhusudan Dutt, the famous poet, were converted through Duff's influence. In 1844/45, Prosana Chandra Bannerji and Tara Charan Bannerji, two brilliant Kulin Brahmin students at General Assembly's Institution, created a sensation when they were baptized by Duff. One has only to consult the pages of Lal Behari De's *Recollections of Alexander Duff* to determine how impressive was the list of Bengali intellectuals won over by the Scottish missionary directly or indirectly between 1832 and 1855.[6]

Nor were the families of liberal intelligentsia immune from the ideological appeal of the missionary. P. K. Tagore, an associate of Rammohun Roy from the early 1820s and a trustee of the Brahmo Sabha, watched with utter dismay his son's conversion in 1851, which came after five years of agonizing struggle in his mind between Unitarianism and Trinitarianism. Ganendra Mohun Tagore had himself baptized and hurriedly left for England, where he lived the rest of his days as an exile.[7]

On another level no less threatening in its consequences, Duff, his fellow missionaries, and their converts launched a massive ideological attack on Hinduism. Since the Christians sought to win over the intelligentsia primarily, they conducted the verbal skirmishes and battles on a high intellectual plane. There were two important results of this maneuver. In the first place, because there were so few Western-educated Bengalis, the missionaries found themselves in a limited arena of encounter, shut off from communication with the true spokesmen of contemporary Hinduism. The orthodox pundits had neither the sophistication, the linguistic capacity, nor apparently the inclination to defend their system.

Second, it became more and more evident to missionaries that among the few available intellectuals willing and able to defend Hinduism, most were groping not for an alien ideology whose acceptance meant certain excommunication from family and community, but for a reformist faith rooted in the indigenous soil.

Thus throughout the 1830s, though Rammohun Roy was only dimly recalled and imperfectly understood, he was not forgotten. Indeed the stage was set, once the Hindus produced a leader and institution to continue Rammohun's unfinished task, for a sociologically interesting religious encounter. Two forces—the Brahmos (or the Vedantists, as they were then called) against the Christians—both dedicated to the eradication of the evils of popular Hinduism, and both conducting this struggle outside the pale of the numerically populous Hindu society of a rural peasantry and their priests, who were ignorant of the esoteric happenings in Calcutta.

In 1833, Krishna Mohun Bannerji, most likely under Duff's guidance, published an attack on Rammohun Roy's "misinterpretation" of the Upanishads. Though immature and not at all representative of his later position, it is nonetheless important as setting a certain precedent in the manner of the debate for the next decade or so. "Much clamor has been raised about pure Hindooism as against popular Hindooism," Bannerji wrote, "as if they were capable of restoring it to holiness." Rammohun Roy has deluded us into believing in "the divine origin of the Upanishads."

Bannerji was frankly amazed how Rammohun could choose the "Vedic tradition" as containing monotheism and morality on a par with Christian revelation. Are not the Vedas saturated with idolatry? His most serious challenge to Rammohun and the Vedantists was his assertion that monism and not monotheism was the culmination of the Vedic tradition and wisdom: "The God of the Vedant . . . is an infinite something but that something is neither a Creator nor a Moral Benefactor. He is not a moral Being at all and cannot therefore, be regarded with moral feeling. We may wonder at his immensity, and omnipotence and eternity, and invincibility, but we cannot thank, or love, or reverence him, because there is nothing in his nature, or in his acts that is fitted to excite these feelings."[8]

It is hardly surprising that organized resistance against the missionaries on behalf of Rammohun Roy's ideology came from the emancipated Tagore family at Jorasanko. On October 6, 1839, six years after Rammohun's death in England, Debendranath Tagore established the Tattvabodhini Sabha precisely to mobilize intelligentsia support against missionary inroads. Debendranath was then the twenty-two-year-old son of Rammohun's famous contemporary, Dwarkanath Tagore. Often called India's first modern-style entrepreneur, Dwarkanath was not only an intimate friend of Rammohun Roy's, but a joint participant in the latter's Calcutta Unitarian Committee and Brahmo Sabha. It was his family, a collateral Tagore family, and the Roy family who made up the Board of Trustees for the Brahmo Sabha property on Chitpur Road, Calcutta.[9] For a Bengali of the early nineteenth century, he was a most unusual man, displaying almost a romantic's zest for life combined with an amazing success in commercial ventures.[10] He was the equal of any Englishman in business acumen and was enormously sophisticated, as demonstrated in his meticulous choice of Western wine, music, and food.[11] Like Rammohun, he defied the Hindu taboo about crossing the sea to England, and like Rammohun he died there, during a second trip in 1846.[12]

Unlike his father, Debendranath decided to carry on Rammohun's ideal through an independent association rather than immediately affiliating with the Brahmo Sabha. Even when he did become a Brahmo in 1843, the Tattvabodhini Sabha continued to expand numerically and to function effectively as an autonomous body. Not until 1859 was it discontinued and amalgamated with the Brahmo Samaj. It seems likely that in the early period Debendranath preferred to interpret Rammohun's legacy in a culturally apologetic manner, without becoming encumbered with the universalist Unitarian aspects of the Brahmo Sabha. At the time Debendranath started the Sabha, the Christians had taken K. M. Bannerji's lead and had shifted their verbal artillery from popular Hinduism to reformed Hinduism or Vedantism. The objectives of the Tattvabodhini Sabha leave little doubt as to the reason why it was created. First, the Sabha gave expression to "grave concern about the terribly rapid progress of Christianity due to the ignorance of our countrymen about our old religion." Second, to "bar this development" the Sabha would perform the worship of God "according to the doctrines of the Vedant" and would publish Vedantic books.[13]

Over the next few years Debendranath built his Sabha into a highly effective organization, functioning in a variety of ways to combat the missionaries. In 1840, a Tattvabodhini School was set up to combat Duff's own school, teaching in the Bengali medium rather than in English. Bengali textbooks in all subjects were pub-

lished immediately to assist in instruction. A Tattvabodhini Press was established, which had as its earliest main task the reprinting of all Rammohun's works. Then in 1843 a newspaper was started called the *Tattvabodhini Patrika*, which had the negative task of combating missionary propaganda and the positive function of educating fellow Bengalis.[14]

Meanwhile, since its inception, the Sabha had called weekly meetings to discuss religious and theological questions in an effort to clarify issues, resolve conflicts within the membership, and to arrive at conclusions about the "true sastra" of Hinduism. That Debendranath intended to combine the cultural defense of Hinduism with the rational faith of Brahmoism seems evident from a statement made by him in 1843 on why he had started the Sabha: "It was to counteract influences like these [missionary] and inculcate on the Hindu religious enquirer's mind doctrines at once consonant to reason and human nature, for which he has to explore his own sacred resources, the Vedanta, that the Society was originally established."[15] On December 21, 1843, Debendranath took an oath that bound him and twenty others to the tenets and practices of the Brahmo religion. The preceptor, Vidyabagish, administered the oath.[16] This covenant is of critical importance in the history of the Hindu reformation. By officially and intimately associating the Tattvabodhini Sabha with Rammohun's Brahmo Sabha, Debendranath revived the latter, and opened its membership to the most progressive forces of the day. The rather slim and ambiguous ideological content of the Brahmo Sabha trust deed was elaborated upon to accommodate the ideas of Debendranath and his followers. In fact, it may well be argued that the Brahmo Samaj as we have known it since began with the covenant ceremony in 1843 and not earlier. This very act of taking an oath and affixing one's signature to a document during a sacred ceremony constituted the beginnings of a distinctly new sense of Brahmo community.

The principles of the covenant, though still ambiguous about the nature of the new religion and morality, nevertheless represented a development of Rammohun's rudimentary ideas and a departure from existing forms of Hinduism then current in Bengal. New principles were defended as the real Hinduism against the corrupt contemporary form.

Following Rammohun's lead, the Vedanta was singled out as the true source of the Hindu religion. Second, while denying the validity of images in a divine service, the covenant explicitly repudiated the worship of idols. Third, there was a principle which, however mildly stated, questioned the need for Hindu rituals in the worship of the one true God. Fourth, several principles articulated, in rudimentary manner, the formulation of a new ethical code that said nothing of caste duties but spoke instead of the importance of doing good over evil. Finally, of enormous social significance for the future was the principle that expressed the solidarity of Brahmos and urged that one community member help the other in times of adversity.

These events did not go unnoticed by their Christian adversaries who, after 1843 and the formal acceptance by Brahmos of the Vedanta as a revealed source, redoubled their efforts to expose what Duff called a dangerous form of "self-delusion." Duff's attacks in the *Calcutta Christian Observer* and the newly formed *Calcutta Review* during the period were restatements of K. M. Bannerji's arguments of 1833, that the Vedas were idolatrous and ritualistic, while the Upanishads taught monism and not monotheism. The Reverend William Morton of the Church Mission Society warned Vedantists that there was no compromise with a system which through the ages has "debased the minds of men, deadened their consciousness, clouded their understanding, corrupted their hearts and countenanced every species of vice and immorality."[17] Lal Behari De, in a more conciliatory tone, introduced a personal note on morality that missionaries would use to their advantage in later decades. De admitted that "I myself was a Brahmo though not in name yet in reality but I enjoyed no peace of mind . . . I could not be sure He would pardon my sins."[18]

Private letters and reports to the home office in London by missionaries reveal a somewhat respectful attitude to the Vedantists. There is, for example, a letter from the Reverend James Long dated January 1846, in which he referred to the growing influence of Vedantism as evidenced by his "frequent and interesting conversations with educated Natives in Calcutta," leading him to conclude that "a momentous change has taken place in Bengal." He wrote: "A few years ago an educated Native repudiated Hinduism and admitted the truth of Christiantiy, now I find that they resort to Vedantism as a kind of half way house in which they lay outside the gross errors of Hinduism without admitting the Divine Origin of Christianity."[19]

There is another interesting letter in the same report of the Calcutta Corresponding Committee (1846) by an itinerant missionary named De Rozario who, on his most recent tour, was amazed at growing Vedantic influence in mofusil towns. The Brahmo news-paper was circulating widely, he reported, while Brahmo preachers were now appearing more regularly and making Christian-like speeches in the name of Vedantism. In the latter part of his letter, De Rozario recounted how in visiting a zamindar whom he knew well, he was shocked to learn that his friend's son called his father a "bigoted idolator" and Hinduism a "damnable system." But this was done not in the name of the Bible but the Vedanta. The son had subsequently "helped establish a Vedantic Sabha."[20]

Debendranath's apparent success was ignored by some of the missionaries, who in public and private utterances always seemed preoccupied with the intricacies of their religion and theology. As Debendranath's *Autobiography* shows all too clearly, theological de-bates were not of paramount concern to a man whose religious piety was derived from long years of soul searching and whose de-fense of Vedanta stemmed from a sense of patriotism. In the final analysis, the genius of Debendranath was far less intellectual than organizational.

It is a credit to Debendranath's leadership and organizational ability that however theistically inclined he himself may have been, and regardless of the religious reformist aspect of his movement, he was able to attract the most progressive members of the Bengali intelligentsia, including deists, agnostics, and atheists.[21] Men as in-different to the notion of a personal god as Akkhoy Kumar Dutt, or as hostile to religion as Ishwar Chandra Vidyasagar, joined Tagore in the Tattvabodhini Sabha and completely identified with its ob-jectives. The fact is that Debendranath, viewing himself as leader of an all-embracing Hindu reformation, enlisted progressives of whatever caste, class, or creed to join him in the endeavor. He aimed to defend and improve Hindu society, but in the early years he wisely interpreted Hindu society broadly without compelling his followers to embrace the Brahmo path. Around Tagore and ac-tively in support of his general principles were zamindars such as Sirish Chandra, the Burdwan raja, and Kali Prosanna Singha, edu-cators such as Ramtanu Lahiri, journalists such as Harish Chandra Mukerji, and scholars such as Rajendra Lal Mitra. The mem-bership of Tagore's Sabha soared from nine in 1839 to seven hun-dred in 1856.[22] According to Professor Muhamed Ali, who has studied the Sabha closely during this period, the real breakthrough numerically took place in 1845/46, when the membership in-creased from 145 to 500, largely as a result of an influx of young college students.[23] For at least two decades, the Sabha and the Samaj together became the most important single reformist movement in all Bengal.

The remarkable Debendranath worked miracles. With his movement the period of ideological stagnation that had followed in the wake of Macaulayism ended. Young Bengal's effervescence as rebellious Anglicized adolescents soon subsided, and their movement could produce nothing creative to sustain their emotional predilection for things Western. The Dharma Sabha, at the other extreme, like many nationalist associations formed to protest alien intrusion under the banner of cultural integrity, found that the very process of doing so dulled their passion for internal reform and rendered them impotent for the important task of building a new society.

By 1845, Debendranath had not only the remnants of Rammohun Roy's Brahmo Sabha in his control, but the influx of college students into his association suggested that Young Bengal preferred his middle path to Christianity or to the temporary solution of the brandy bottle. In that same year, as Debendranath related in his *Autobiography*, even Radhakant Deb, factional leader of the Dharma Sabha and head of the family that was traditionally arch foe of Rammohun Roy and the Tagore family of Jorasanko itself, joined forces with the Tattvabodhini Sabha. "The disagreement between the *Dharma Sabha* and the Brahmos disappeared," wrote Debendranath, "in an effort to establish a free school for children against the missionaries." The act is important for the partial acknowledgment by Radhakant Deb that the leadership of the reformation had passed into the capable hands of Debendranath. Together the two major Calcutta elite families could muster one thousand people, who attended a general meeting to establish the Hindu Charitable Association. They were able to get others to subscribe forty thousand rupees to be used for the new association. The president selected for the executive board was Radhakant, while the secretary was Debendranath.[24]

In September 1899, the venerable Rajnarian Bose died, six years before the death of Debendranath Tagore, the man whom he had succeeded as president of the Adi Brahmo Samaj. In 1909, Rajnarian's autobiography appeared in print with a dedication by his famous grandson, Aurobindo Ghose, the nationalist. That same year Jadunath Sarkar, the eminent historian, assessed both the book and the man in a *Modern Review* article that he entitled "Raj Narian Bose, the Grandfather of Nationalism in India."[25]

Rajnarian Bose was born in a village of the Twenty-four Pargannas on September 7, 1826. Among the first generation of Brahmo disciples he was the only important leader who was not a Brahmin, but a Kayastha. (Rammohun Roy was a Kulin Brahmin and Debendranath Tagore was a Perali Brahmin.) More significant is the fact that his father, Nanda Kishore Bose, who did clerical jobs of various sorts, was among the earliest followers of Rammohun Roy. This evidently applied to his father's brother as well, indicating that not all of Rammohun's backers were powerful zamindars. Equally important is the fact that his father knew English well and placed great stress on gaining proficiency in it. One might add that Nanda Kishore was among the first students of Rammohun's Vedantic Academy, that he accepted Vedantism as his religious orientation, and that he served for some time as Rammohun's secretary.[26]

Actually, however, his son Rajnarian did not become a Brahmo until 1846, when he signed the covenant. At twenty, the young man was groping for a new meaning in life to help him overcome the sterility of his Anglicized student days in Calcutta, when he became a drug and alcohol addict. He had been so culturally alienated that he had forgotten his own Bengali language. Later, he wrote that although Debendranath Tagore appreciated his knowledge of English and its usefulness for the Brahmo Samaj, Rajnarian regretted that his fluency in his native tongue was so weak that he "was actually coached in learning good Bengali."[27] The whole experience made him a bitter critic of the excessively Westernized intelligentsia, whom he considered "third rate Eurasians." The following sample of Rajnarian's wit against his denationalized contemporaries, who confused cultural trappings for national regeneration, was equally aimed at their progenitor in India, Thomas Babington Macaulay: "I can speak in English, write in English, think in English, and shall be supremely happy when I can dream in English."[28]

In one of Rajnarian's earliest sermons of December 15, 1847, there appeared an interesting reference under the general theme of the transitoriness of human existence. Rajnarian, after speaking of the rise and fall of empires generally, referred specifically to the present British raj in India. "The British kings have spread their dominion in our country," he began, "and they are so powerful that every other nation in the world fears them." Why were they so powerful? Because technology gave them an advantage over others, with the result that "their flag is flying almost everywhere." What follows may well be the earliest prophecy of Indian independence recorded by a Bengali: "But even the power and glory of this nation which may seem invincible today will also see eventual ruin. The high mansions that beautify their metropolises will crumble to dust and upon the ruins will be constructed a new civilization by a new people who will sing the praises of eternal humanism."[29]

To be sure, this was a mild statement in a church sermon where the realm of the sacred was being defended against the profane, and certainly Rajnarian concluded nowhere that Indians should actively assist in the process of dismembering the British empire. But less than a year later, in a sermon of July 6, 1848, there is no doubt at all that Rajnarian had infused his Brahmo religion with nationalist sentiments. "I tell you," he said, "that the pleasure of service to one's country is above every other pleasure." "What a great feeling of joy a patriot experiences," he went on to say, "when he can beautify his mother tongue and compose in that tongue such as promotes the cause of religion, knowledge and truth." Of what did service to the motherland consist? The answer suggests Rajnarian's nationalism was at this time liberal. He hoped that "the minds of his compatriots will one day be beautified by learning and liberated from ignorance, superstition and evil deeds. That someday they will perform the *real* religious performances [of their tradition] in such a cultural and reformed way that they will be respected as an equal among the other nations of the world. What a great delight to the patriot who devotes his whole life in the accomplishment of this noble ideal."[30]

Especially noteworthy was Rajnarian's continual references to the Bengali language as the basic ingredient of the true patriot. Since he himself increasingly chose Bengali to express himself in sermons, lectures, essays, and virtually everything else he said and wrote, his linguistic convictions were part of a personal transformation and natural development. The use of language to express symbolically a new sense of cultural identity reminds one of Madhusudan Dutt, the poet, who experienced a similar linguistic conversion from English to Bengali. Just as Dutt's turning away from his Anglicized Christian past actually enhanced his aesthetic sensiblity and led to poetic innovations in Bengali, Bose's return to the cultural fold through the Brahmo Samaj led to an admirable prose style.[31]

As for the genesis of an idea of nationalism in Rajnarian, one must go back to 1845 or even earlier, before he was initiated as a Brahmo. After a long silence in the war of cultural and religious polemics, Rajnarian and Debendranath collaborated in a tract against the missionaries called *Vedantic Doctrines Vindicated*. Though couched in religious and theological issues, the argument represents an early manifestation of an emerging ideology of cultural nationalism.

Alexander Duff and K. M. Bannerji had both questioned whether there was in the Vedic and Vedantic tradition a notion of a personal God analogous to Jehovah. The missionaries contended that even in the Upanishads the concept of God was so abstract as to be without analogy. This was the monotheistic-monistic issue. Duff's concept of Brahma, which Tagore and Bose were now prepared to refute, was of a Being who "unencumbered by the cares of empire or the functions of a superintending providence, effectuates no good, inflicts no evil, suffers no pain, experiences no emotion; his beatitude is represented as consisting in a languid, monotonous and uninterrupted sleep—a sleep so very deep as never to be disturbed by the visitation of a dream."

The Brahmo reply in *Vedantic Doctrines Vindicated* reveals the debating talent of Rajnarian, who had first acquired the skill at Hare's School, developed it in subsequent encounters with Christians, and brought it to perfection later in life as a nationalist critic of Keshub Sen's universalism. In this tract of 1845, which was his first recorded encounter with the missionaries, he took a phrase like "cares of empire" and asked Duff whether God was a king or an emperor. Rajnarian made capital of this ill-chosen expression, charging that the Christian god was an "Oriental despot" unacceptable to freedom-loving Asians.

Rajnarian's second point was directed at Duff's depiction of Brahmo as a god who "effectuates no good and inflicts no evil." "What kind of God is this," he replied, "who is the author of evil?" How can we possibly ascribe "the indiscriminate murder of millions" through "religious fanaticism or political hostility" to "our immaculate Creator?"

The third point seems reminiscent of Rammohun Roy's debate with Tytler in 1823 which, significantly, was reprinted in 1845, the year of Bose's tract. Rajnarian took Duff to task for characterizing God as a being who "suffers pain and experiences emotion." He accused Duff of "rushing headlong into the hideous errors of a reckless anthropomorphism." Can there be a worse doctrine than that which denudes and degrades God by bringing the "Almighty Creator" to the level of a man?

The nationalist import of *Vedantic Doctrines Vindicated* lies in its point-by-point defense of a Hindu tradition against the pretensions of religious revelation and superiority in an alien faith. If in Rammohun's writings cultural nationalism never went beyond the point of proving that Hinduism was equal to Christianity, in Rajnarian's earliest polemical tracts there was already the germ of a more defiant attitude, that Hinduism was superior to Christianity. Of course, by Hinduism he did not mean the popular form as much as he did long-lost traditions like the Vedantic: "The Vedanta, while it utterly rejects and condemns such degrading notions of the deity, conveys to our minds a far loftier, a more adequate, consistent, and ennobling idea of His attributes, by prescribing His worship as the Supreme Regulator of this boundless universe and as the glorious and beneficent originator of all earthly good."[32]

In this kind of religious encounter, superiority depended on the validity of one's defense of Vedanta or Bible as a revealed source. After years of soul searching on the part of Debendranath and other Brahmos, the issue was dropped and a momentous decision was reached denying revelation for any scriptural source, Hindu or otherwise. Rajnarian, who had in the meantime sharpened his wit in defense of classical Hindu superiority, accepted the decision of 1850 against the Vedanta as the word of God with great reluctance. He enjoyed his debates with the Christians—especially with one, the convert Krishna Mohun Bannerji, who was perhaps his most capable adversary.

Krishna Mohun Bannerji, though intellectually indebted to Duff, left the Presbyterian movement in the early 1830s for the Church of England. In 1836, he was given a scholarship to study theology at the Anglican Bishop's College and a year later, on June 24, 1837, he was made a deacon.[33] From then on, his abilities were recognized and he was given the most responsible positions available in the establishment for a non-European. Though clearly a bhadralok in his concern about wealth, property, and status,[34] Bannerji remained very much an intellectual, continually clarifying his thinking in an endless stream of publications.[35]

In a series of articles, sermons, and lectures throughout the 1840s and 1850s, Bannerji sought to convince Brahmos of their folly and to take the plunge into Christendom, as he had done. Bannerji argued four things, essentially: that Christianity was not a foreign religion but the fulfillment of ancient Hinduism; that only

Christianity represented an advanced stage of religious evolution that freed it from superstition, mystery, and obscurity; that only Christianity, because of its advanced stage in the process of development, had a history; and that Christianity was the mainspring of modern progressive civilization.

The first proposition (which he never full elaborated in print until the 1870s) he described as a theory on the relationship between "Aryan religions and Semitic Christianity." Believing that Aryans were migrants to India originally from somewhere in the West, who subsequently moved slowly across the Middle East to Iran, he was able to establish a link between comparable religious ideas from Moses and Zoroaster to the Vedic *rishis*. For example, he found a remarkable similarity in the creation myths of these apparently disparate cultures, and in the story of a great flood; and, most intriguing to him, in the sacrificial offering and ritual. These similarities were explained by Aryan contact with the cultures of the Euphrates and the modification of certain practices as they were diffused eastward.

Bannerji concluded that whereas in the Middle East religious development continued until it reached its highest point in Christianity, the Aryans remained arrested at a rudimentary level, awaiting a new diffusion of enlightenment from the West.[36] His passionate concern about the sacrificial ritual drew him into further study, until in 1882 he believed he had proved his point in a published essay on *The Relationship between Christianity and Hinduism*. The essay was mostly on an analysis of the death of Prajapati and the death of Christ, in which the one represented the height of the Vedic tradition, whereas the other represented the height of religious development. Somehow—Bannerji could not say exactly how—these two coalesced in history. Stemming from the same Middle Eastern source, the later *rishis* and early Christians arrived at the most sublime of all religious conceptions: that of "salvation from sin by the death of a Savior, who was God and man himself" and through whose act "vanquished death and brought life and immortality." Bannerji's final point:

> You may conclude that Jesus is the true Prajapati, true Savior of the world. . . . Thus can the Indian enter the Church of Christ, the true ark of salvation. This can bridge the gulf which now separates West from East. The Vedas forshew the Epiphany of Christ. The Vedas shed a peculiar light upon that dispensation of Providence which brought Eastern sages to worship Christ

long before the Westerners had heard of Him. . . . On what grounds then can a Hindu advocate demand the ostracism of those, who by accepting Christianity, are only accepting a Vedic doctrine in its legitimately developed form?[37]

Thus had Krishna Bannerji put the finishing touches to his ideological quest of forty years to prove that Christians were not denationalized Hindus but that Hindus had denationalized themselves from their own tradition. If the *rishis* were to be reborn, he said, they would find the "orthodox Hindoo himself the greatest foe to the system they had bequeathed to their descendants."[38]

Against the Brahmo charge of Christian denationalization, Bannerji countercharged them with being the ones truly denationalized. They say "we Christians have no feeling for our country or race" and that the adoption of Christianity is "an act of treachery to India." To Bannerji, "Brahmoism was a vague term," a mere fertile and ingenious composite of selected ingredients from this religion and that, creatively integrated in such a way as to constitute a "bar to the great mass of mankind . . . intended only for the contemplation of the initiated few." Brahmoism, by its eclecticism, by its intellectualism, by its elitism was doomed to remain exotic and "denationalized" in India.[39]

In his *Lectures to Educated Native Young Men on Vedantism*, Bannerji made a special plea to the intelligentsia that they not be misled by the Brahmos. Though Rammohun Roy was motivated by the sincere desire of "improving his country," it was to be regretted that he "adopted so inefficient a means for encompassing his patriotic end." There was no comparison between Christianity, which was the revealed word of God, and Vedantism, which was the word of men whose interpretation of Indian theism was a fraud.[40]

Though in his later life Bannerji became somewhat sympathetic to Indian "scriptures and philosophy," he never abandoned his belief that Western Christianity did indeed constitute a superior religion. It was difficult for him to disguise an intense love and admiration for all things "Western." Thus, in Krishna Mohun's most ambitious scholarly work, a twelve-volume bilingual compilation of existing knowledge in the West for the use of Bengali students (1848-1850),[41] he betrayed a sad lack of pride in Asian achievements as against those European. Here, under history, geography, natural sciences, and other disciplines that had little to do with his own professed Christianity, he adopted a posture of unabashed Macaulayism in which the progress of humanity was somehow inseparable from or intrinsic to the innate superiority of Western man.

The religious Macaulayism that he derived initially from Duff prevented Bannerji throughout his lifetime from ever improving or elaborating upon the foundations of the Christian faith for Indian domestic consumption. Bannerji simply argued the accepted version. Every word in Christian scripture was clear and without the slightest possibility of misrepresentation, because it was the word of God. Christianity was the only religion supported by historical fact. Finally, he argued that the only religion not incompatible with progress was Christianity, and he promised that when accepted in India, it would mean "mental emancipation" and the triumph of "physical science and history" over the "works of idolatrous untruth."[42]

It was precisely in the area where Bannerji was weakest—in his uncritical acceptance of fundamental Biblical history and Christology—that Rajnarian launched his earliest attack. Have Christian converts seriously examined the religion that they treat with so much reverence? If they did rationally, they would be surprised to learn about a faith built around a distorted, horrendous concept of God. Have converts bothered to examine the twistings and turnings of Christian theological disputes, conferences, and decisions? If they would bother to read the history of Christianity itself, they would become bewildered by endless inconsistencies. Wrote Rajnarian: "to leave man to his free thought, then to disable him from perceiving the face of a truth and yet to oblige him to hold a certain conviction for which he is quite incapacitated, and this under the pain of eternal damnation, does not seem to us to be the mark of Divine Mercy."[43]

Rajnarian made able use of Rammohun's Unitarian legacy in attacking orthodox Christianity. How, for example, could Bannerji claim that Christianity represented the most advanced stage of religious evolution when it was still so full of superstition, mystery, and miracles? Christianity had yet to be reformed or purified of these excrescences by critical judgment and reason. A list of the many conspicuous illustrations of Christian "irrationality" appeared in Rajnarian's tract of 1851 entitled *Remarks on K. M. Bannerji's Lectures on Vedantism.*

Rajnarian first pointed to the inconsistency between the all-merciful God and the "Warrior-God Jehovah marching in person before the Army of a primitive nation and sparing not in his whirlwind fury the little suckling babies." No "rational Hindu" could believe in a God blasting "the beauty of his own creation" and "walking everywhere like a roaring lion seeing whom he may devour among the sons of God." He could not believe that "God accepted the innocent as a sacrifice for the guilty." Nor could the rational Hindu believe in the blasphemous doctrine "that God changed his own nature which is an utter impossibility in the nature of things" to become flesh. Nor could he believe "in the absurd notion of a triune Godhead."

But Rajnarian's most spirited prose against Bannerji's "superior religion" was directed at the "melo-drama" of the Last Judgment and the "revolting doctrine of eternal punishment." The Brahmo depicted the scene vividly with "trumpets blowing, angelic heralds rushing through the air, the dead rising from the deep and profound slumber of the ages, and a tribunal erected for judging them like an ordinary earthly one." As for hell: "that doctrine of perpetual gnashing of teeth amid the worm that dieth not and the fire that ceaseth not to burn. . . . Now these are what the rational Hindu cannot believe."[44]

As for the claim that only Christianity was founded upon the facts of history and that Hinduism was built upon a quicksand of mythology, Rajnarian claimed to have had little trouble exposing the weakness in such a dogmatic position. One line of argument used by Bose was that if the works of Herodotus, written centuries after the Pentateuch, "confessedly contain a mixture of truth and falsehood why may not the same be said of the Bible?" The Bible is filled with dubious, unconfirmed anecdotes and allegorical tales. Taking as an instance the story of the ten commandments, Bose wrote, "the commandments are said to have been written on two slabs of marble. By whom? By God or by Moses? How have they been so long preserved? And where are they now to be seen?"[45]

As for the exalted claim by Duff, Bannerji, and others that Christianity was the motivating force behind modern progress, Rajnarian's reply showed considerable knowledge to prove the contrary. Here Rajnarian assumed a most rational and humanistic approach to the history of modernism in Europe. If Christianity was such a progressive force, then "what of the centuries of darkness and ignorance which followed the introduction of the Christian faith, and of the ages of abbeys and nunneries?" The following analysis of the rise of progress in Europe indicates an amazing sophistication and equally amazing secularism for a theist: "Surely the present state of things in the West was not brought about by Christianity but by the philosophy of Bacon and his followers, by the expansion of commerce, by the invention of printing, by the spread of education, and by other similar causes, that Europe owes its present civilization. Christianity is itself indebted to those very causes for all the seeds of reformation which it has since secured in its bosom."[46]

The Bannerji indictment of Brahmoism as being the exotic plant of an intellectually contrived religion was perhaps Rajnarian's most vulnerable area to defend. Rajnarian believed in Vedanta as superior to the Bible, and when Debendranath discarded the Hindu scripture as the "Book of Brahmos" and turned instead to natural religion or intuitionalism, Rajnarian was hardly pleased with the decision. It was approximately at this time that Bose left Tagore's employ (1848), spent a brief time as an instructor at Sanskrit College, then went off to Midnapur in February 1851 as headmaster of the Government School, where he stayed until 1868.[47]

In conclusion, the Trinitarians therefore not only failed to displace the indigenous content of the Hindu reformation, but they unwittingly contributed to the birth of a new religious identity among progressive Hindus—an identity whose conception emerged in an atmosphere of acrimonious debate. I would argue that the preconditioning stage of nationalism took place in Bengal as a consequence of Brahmo defense against attacks by missionaries such as Alexander Duff and Christopher Dyson, and converts such as K. M. Bannerji and Lal Behari De. Nationalism proved to be antithetical to liberalism, because the close association between the reformed Hindu identity and its defense against the Christians diverted many Brahmos from their liberal reformism. The task seemed completed by the 1860s, preparing the way for the second stage of nationalism, which occurred when a faction of Brahmos challenged the proposition that Brahmoism was tantamount to reformed Hinduism.

CHAPTER SIX

The Issue of Brahmo National Identity and the Rise of Cultural Nationalism

IF Macaulayism stimulated the rise of protonationalism in the formation of the Dharma Sabha, and the missionaries provoked the Brahmo Samaj into a reconstruction of Hinduism along national lines, the crisis of national identity within Brahmo ranks in the schism of 1866 led to the earliest expression in Bengal of a nationalist spirit and ideology. We have already examined the schism and the establishment of a new Brahmo Samaj of India from the point of view of the liberals under the leadership of Keshub Chandra Sen. But from the point of view of the conservatives who remained behind in what came to be known as the Adi (original) Brahmo Samaj, the liberals had betrayed Hindu reform for a diluted and meaningless eclecticism, or for one or another variety of Christianity.

The schism of 1866 not only divided Brahmos into younger men and older men, or radical social reformers and gradualists, but it also divided universalists from nationalists. Was Brahmoism a universal ideology of salvation or was it Hindu reform? Was it intended to deliver the world from the crisis of nineteenth-century civilization, or was it intended to purify the Hindu tradition and regenerate Hindu society? To Adi Brahmos, the Keshubite challenge not only violated the fundamental purpose and direction of the Hindu reformation but threatened the cultural integrity of Hinduism itself. The most immediate and profound reaction by Adi Brahmo leaders to Keshub was therefore one of militant defense of one's own culture or civilization (nationalism) against alien-inspired ideologies. It was believed that all such movements subverted Hindu society because they served to denationalize the intelligentsia, thus weakening their will to revitalize India within the framework of its own traditions, institutions, and values.

On January 23, 1866, at the Maghutsab festival, Keshub gave his last sermon from the pulpit of the Adi Samaj. Most interesting about the sermon was Keshub's stress on universalism as against Debendranath's continual references to Brahmoism as Hindu reform. In some ways, whether intended or not, Keshub had assumed Akkhoy Kumar Dutt's role as exponent of the universal religious ideal against the forces of national religion. For the first time, Brahmo theism divided itself along lines of unity and diversity. Instead of Brahmoism serving narrowly to reform Hinduism alone, Keshub argued that "the Brahmo Samaj was established to bring together the peoples of the world, irrespective of caste, creed, and country, at the feet of the One Eternal God."[1]

On May 5, 1866, Keshub Chandra Sen gave what was probably his most controversial lecture at Medical College Hall in Calcutta. The title, which later perturbed Debendranath and his friends no end, was "Jesus Christ: Europe and Asia."[2] On the surface, as many missionaries and Debendranath himself interpreted it, the lecture constituted a defense of Christ's teachings and early Christianity. Ignored for the most part was Keshub's careful distinction between "Christ's message of universal harmony" and the institutional Christianity of the nineteenth century with its Europeanized, sectarian, and "muscular" view of Christ. Also missed was his sophisticated challenge to British cultural imperialism, not as a militant but as a creative nationalist who attacked foreign imposition, without the expression of xenophobia. The lecture was also in part an essay on comparative religion which, saturated with Keshub's own spirit of Universal Unitarianism, expressed an objective and scientific attitude remarkable for the time he lived in.

Keshub's Jesus, whom P. C. Majumdar later popularized as the "Oriental Christ," was inspired by God to offer to "humanity groaning under a deadly malady and on the verge of death, a remedy to save it." Christ's remedy, a gift from the East to the West, was ethical and spiritual, as characteristic of Asian religions. The passage that shocked Debendranath as much as it pleased the missionaries was Keshub's apparent acceptance of the crucifixion. What Keshub accepted, as should be clear from the following quotation, was the ethical value of the symbol: "He laid down his life that God might be glorified. I have always regarded the cross as a beautiful emblem of self-sacrifice unto the glory of God . . . one which is calculated to quicken the higher feelings and aspirations of the heart, and to purify the soul, and I believe there is not a heart, how callous and hard soever it may be, that can look with cold indifference at that grand and significant symbol."

Most effective was Keshub's contrast between the noble self-sacrificing Christ of the Orient and the missionaries of Christ sent out from churches in the West. It is curious that passages which were anti-imperialist completely escaped the notice of Adi Brahmos and others who were quick to point to Keshub's alleged surrender to Westernized Christianity. After reporting that since the early part of the century only 154,000 converts were won over to Christ in South Asia, and that presently, 519 missionaries representing 32 societies, with an annual combined budget of £250,000, were combing the subcontinent for potential candidates to the new faith, Keshub asked why they had accomplished so little. The reason was that many of the missionaries not only "hate the natives with their whole heart but seem to take pleasure in doing so." Said Keshub: "They regard the natives as one of the vilest nations on earth hopelessly immersed in all the vices which can degrade humanity. . . . They think it mean to associate with native ideas and tastes, native customs and manners, which seem to them odious and contemptible; while native character is considered to represent the lowest type of lying and wickedness."

But Keshub's response was not that of the militant Hindu nationalist in a blind nativist defense of one's heritage. Like Akkhoy Kumar Dutt, Keshub Chandra Sen placed universalism above a glorification of national character. It is again curious how the following passage, so clear and unmistakable, has been ignored by those who have fashioned the reformer as an unqualified Christian apologist. Said Keshub: "The fact is, human nature is the same everywhere—in all latitudes and climes, but circumstances modify it, and religion and usages mould it in different forms. Educate the native mind, and you will find it susceptible of as much improvement and elevation as that of the European."

Indeed, Keshub was one of the first Bengalis to refer to cultural stereotypes, which he termed "caricatures." It was not "national character which keeps the Indian nation in darkness but circumstances." The trouble is, he said, "that we are a subject race and have been for centuries." In such passionate phraseology we find the very same indignant mood and mode of expression against imperialism as in Vivekananda later on. In contrast to Vivekananda, however, Keshub in 1866 attacked the excesses of imperialism in the name of the exalted image of the "true" Christ: "Christ . . . do Europeans follow him? I regard Europeans in India as missionaries of Christ and I have a right to demand that they should always remember and act up to his high responsibilities. . . . But I find pseudo-Christians with reckless conduct. . . . Yea their muscular Christianity has led many a native to identify the religion of Jesus with the power and privilege of inflicting blows and kicks with impunity. Had it not been for them, the name of Jesus . . . would have been ten times more glorified."

It may be difficult to see how a detached comparative religious attitude could possibly emerge from Keshub's angry mood, but it did. His underlying belief in unity over diversity made the comparative approach possible. In fact, though a theist and not a deist, Keshub in 1866 reminds one of Akkhoy Kumar Dutt in the way he was groping for the universal principles of religion. Even Keshub's identification with Christ may be misleading. There are a few revealing passages in the talk which suggest that it was not Christ as such that was crucial but what He represented universally in history: "It is my firm conviction that his teachings find a response in the universal consciousness of humanity, and are no more European than Asiatic, and that in His ethics there is neither Greek nor Jew, circumcised nor uncircumcised, barbarian, Scythian, bound or free."[3]

The period between 1866 and 1872 witnessed a great debate between Adi Brahmos and Keshubites on the issue of Brahmoism and cultural identity. Faced with the problem of survival, Adi Brahmo leadership passed from the hands of Debendranath to his successor as president, Rajnarian Bose. The period between 1866 and 1871 was a critical one for Rajnarian partly because of a nervous disorder that first appeared in 1866 and compelled him to leave his job in Midnapur two years later, and partly as a result of his profound reaction to Keshub's schism. In a letter of January 28, 1869, he seemed determined not to return to Calcutta but to spend the remainder of his life in Allahabad preaching Brahmoism.[4] But in 1870 he was invited back to Calcutta as Debendranath's successor, and was made president of the Adi Brahmo Samaj.[5]

Rajnarian was perhaps the earliest of all the Adi leaders to respond to Keshub's challenge with a bold nationalist plan aimed at rehabilitating the younger generation of Bengali Hindu intelligentsia. In April 1866, Rajnarian issued a prospectus to start a society for the promotion of national feeling among the educated natives of Bengal. It was conceivably the most radical proposal of its kind by any Indian nationalist up to that time.

Though the association never got off the ground, and was replaced by the more ambitious Tagore-supported Hindu Mela, it was a powerfully worded document in defiance of Keshub's universalism. Rajnarian was unimpressed by Keshub's desire to look abroad for inspiration. More important was the realization of Bengal's degradation. How shameful, for example, that "Hindu youth" had not only "severed themselves from Hindu society but had renounced even the Hindu name." A program of regenerating Hindu youth was necessary, which included physical training to "restore the manliness of Bengali youth and their long-lost military prowess"; the establishment of a school of Hindu music with the "composition of songs for moral, patriotic and martial enthusiasm"; the founding of a school of Hindu medicine to revive "our own medical sciences"; and the encouragement of "Indian antiquities" to illuminate the "glory of ancient India."

Along with the program of general Sanskritic revival, Rajnarian offered proposals for building up Bengal as a society and culture. He was most adamant about cultivating the Bengali language. "We must learn to communicate in our language," he wrote. Do the English communicate with one another in French or German? He recommended that Bengali boys learn Bengali before learning English in school. He urged giving up English food, dress, and even "dramatic entertainment." But in the last analysis Rajnarian was a Brahmo and not a Hindu militant. His method was "cultural adaptation" and not the total rejection of things foreign: "No reform is accepted by a nation unless it comes in a national shape. The Nationality Promotion Society will not take an active part in social reformation—as such reformation is not its principle end . . . but will aid it by rousing national feelings in its favor. Men naturally look to the past for sanction for their acts and nothing aids reformation so much as a former national precedent. We shall therefore publish tracts in Bengali containing proofs of the existence of liberal and enlightened customs in ancient India."[6]

In 1870, Rajnarian published a tract subordinating the universal to the national, unity to diversity. Though still paying lip service to the science (unity) of religion, his stress now was on the national form of religion. "Although Brahmoism is universal religion," he wrote, "it is impossible to consecrate a universal form of it." Attacking Keshub Sen rather than the missionaries and their converts, Rajnarian went on to say that "a so-called universal form would make it appear grotesque and ridiculous to the native . . . among whom it is intended . . . and would not command their veneration."

First, Rajnarian admitted that Hindu scripture and "innocent" Hindu usages and customs had been adopted by the Adi Samaj in a "Hindu form to propagate theism among Hindus." Second, Rajnarian nowhere defended those older, radical Unitarian tenets of the Brahmo faith. Indeed, it was fairly obvious that he was trying to close the gap of differences between Adi Brahmos and other Hindus. The following passage is revealing: "It is that Theism can be proved to be true Hinduism according to a right interpretation of the Hindu Shastra and that the orthodox Hindus, the opponents of the Brahmos, themselves admit Brahmo Dharma to be the *Sar Dharma* or the purest form of their own religion although they think it to be too high for their acceptance."

The tract revealed a hardening conservative attitude that compromised social reform and universalism for the sake of Hindu unity. There was one sentence in particular that betrayed Rajnarian's departure from his own liberal past and from the earlier spirit of Brahmo liberalism. "If it be asked," said Rajnarian, "why should such social distinctions of caste be observed at all, the reply is that the world is not yet prepared for the practical adoption of levellers and socialists."[7]

What Rajnarian felt the Hindu world of Calcutta was prepared for he gave them two years later in a crowded meeting room on 13 Cornwallis Street, with Debendranath presiding. Before an immense gathering including scores of orthodox Hindus, many of whom stood outside the packed hall on the street to listen, Rajnarian delivered his most famous lecture on the superiority of Hinduism to all other religions.

There was nothing especially new in the speech, since it was a restatement of Rajnarian's time-worn theme that Brahmoism was the true reformed Hinduism. What was new was the absence of any reference to the prospects of Brahmoism, and the unusual stress on the grandeur of the classical Hindu tradition. His full endorsement of the original purpose of Hindu institutions and complete defiance of Christianity as inferior to his nation's faith marked the beginning of a new stage in his development as a cultural nationalist. Moreover, when it is considered that Keshub Sen had taken with him most of the younger generation of Brahmos, Rajnarian's speech was a brilliant maneuver to rescue the faltering Adi Samaj from decline and extinction.

The result was that, with the speech, he reached the apex not of his ideological development but of his reputation as a Hindu nationalist. Any fine distinction between reformed Hinduism and Brahmoism was lost in the emotional outbursts he received and in the thunderous applause that followed his talk. In his autobiography, Rajnarian later wrote how embarrassed he was to have the leaders of orthodox Hindu society come to him one by one after his speech and "take his feet dust." The archconservative and revivalist

Shib Chandra Guha proclaimed that a statue should be erected for Rajnarian, whereas a journalist wrote that "Hinduism was dying but Rajnarian saved it."[8] When in 1879 Rajnarian resigned his post as president of the Adi Brahmo Samaj to retire to Deoghar in Bihar, he had become in the eyes of his generation a national hero. To the scores of Hindus who visited his home regularly for the next two decades as if on pilgrimage, Rajnarian was revered as the "Hindu Brahmo."

The *National Paper*, which Debendranath commissioned Nabagopal Mitra to start in 1865, proved from 1867 on to be the most effective means of propagating Hindu Brahmo nationalism against Keshubite universalism among the Western-educated in Bengal.[9] The articles that appeared in the newspaper during its first several years of existence, mostly written by Dwijendranath Tagore, were brilliant expositions in defense of both the Adi Samaj and of the national culture. More precisely, Dwijendranath took an Orientalist position, arguing that modernizers had first to identify with their culture and then work within it to revitalize it.

As a philosopher by inclination and personal choice, rather than by profession, Dwijendranath was one of Keshub's most formidable intellectual opponents. In contrast to his younger brother, Rabindranath, who experienced prolonged periods of identity crisis, continually shifting between universalism and nationalism, Dwijendranath remained steadfastly nationalist—even much later in life, when he debated his brother in support of Gandhi's non-cooperation movement. As early as 1867, Dwijendranath was convinced that the only way the Adi Samaj could survive Keshub's schism was to identify itself more closely than ever with the Hindu samaj. If Keshub could command the loyalty of the progressive theistic youth on the grounds of universalism, then Adi Brahmos could command the support of the theists in the much greater Hindu society—to which at long last they would emerge as leaders.

The underlying assumption of Dwijendranath's nationalist ideology was the familiar notion that the Westernizing model was a dead end to nation building and modernism. In an article of September 25, 1867, called "The European Model," he blasted those misguided progressives who "have mistaken views of progressive civilization." These people have sold themselves to "an exotic civilization" as if "there were only one civilization in the world, viz. English civilization." The more sensible alternative would be to work within that which was "genuine and national in the manners, customs, and habits of this country." Certainly, he argued, "English civilization deserves our esteem" but only because it is the "natural offshoot of the energies of the English nation and of no other people." Thus argued Dwijendranath: "Each nation holds a distinct nationality and for so holding it, is the more entitled to the appellation of a civilized nation. . . . But our countrymen rush madly to their own degradation by acting under the supposition that to imitate English civilization . . . is synonymous with making progress . . . and instead of making national institutions the bases of all progress, import a foreign air in all actions of reform."[10]

On October 2, Dwijendranath continued his exploration of the problem and added the contention that a well-intentioned foreign import could under certain circumstances "destroy the inner vitality and integrity of our native character."[11] In an earlier article on how "Hinduism Is Not Hostile to Brahmoism," he sought to define progress in terms of national identity. He discovered it to mean "what is harmonious in the fusion of past and present standards of a culture." Progress was assuredly not the substitution of something foreign for something national, but the "consolidation of institutions defunct as well as those fast growing up" for the benefit of a given culture.[12]

It was in the very depths of the psychology of cultural encounter under colonialism that Dwijendranath waxed most eloquent in his defense of nationalism. An article on "Nationality and Universality," dated February 24, 1869, was aimed specifically at Keshub. "That the Hindoos and the Europeans should have everything in common, is no doubt a desirable end," he began, but before that, "we must have a footing of equality with the Europeans." "Under present circumstances," he warned, "an adoption of European habits would be like wearing a badge of slavery."[13] On May 5, in an article dealing with the same subject, Dwijendranath made a striking comparison between Anglicized Bengalis and American Negroes:

> With all our present inferiority and infirmities we are little better respected by the world than the Christian Negro of North America who speaks English, dresses himself with the jacket and pantaloon, and whose habits of life and fact are mostly borrowed from the European settlers there. And why so? Simply because his civilization is nothing more than an image of European manners and habits, and he is no more like the true European than the monkey in the red-coat riding on the she-goat is like a human being. By means of mere imitation we can be just so much like the Europeans as slaves are like their masters.[14]

In another kind of article Dwijendranath openly attacked Keshub. In one called "Spurious Brahmoism," he tried to expose Keshub's universalism as a masquerade for European Christianity, his natural religion as "sectarian" in its Western-derived bigotry against Hinduism, and his "great man" theory as completely alien and blasphemous to Brahmo monotheism because it compelled mankind to seek God not through God directly but through other men partaking in God's divinity.[15]

Dwijendranath was not beyond attributing slyness and duplicity to Keshub in the latter's alleged campaign for influence and power. When Keshub stressed the equality of prophets, Dwijendranath interpreted the maneuver as political craftiness. Keshub was accused of shrewdly associating Nanak with Brahmoism while in the Punjab, Chaitanya with Brahmoism while visiting East Bengal, and "Jesus Christ as the founder of Brahmoism when lecturing to Christians."[16]

The Tagore family responded to Keshub's universalism by beautifying and popularizing their yearly national festival, which came later to be known as the Hindu Mela. Started in April 1867 by the combined efforts of Rajnarian Bose, Dwijendranath Tagore, and Nabagopal Mitra, it aimed at carrying out the principles articulated in Rajnarian's prospectus. Actually, by encouraging local industry, it went farther than Rajnarian had ever anticipated and may in this sense be looked upon as the precursor of the Swadeshi movement of the early 1900s. Fervent nationalist poems and songs were composed for the occasion, wrestling matches were arranged between Bengali and Punjabi students with the hope that the former would somehow defeat the latter. If and when it happened, as in 1868, it was well publicized. There were also exhibitions of every sort testifying to the abilities of Hindus in general, but Bengali Hindus in particular.

In 1869, the year of Keshub's new mandir, the Tagores invested more money and talent in the festival, thereby enlarging the program and drawing more people. The management was pleased to report that seven thousand people had attended the Mela that year. Three themes were promoted in the songs, poems, and speeches: "progress, unity, and self-reliance." Progress to the Adi Brahmo backers of the Mela meant progress of Hindus, whereas unity meant burying regional and caste differences for the sake of Hindu unity, and self-reliance meant the promotion of entrepreneurship, principally among Bengali Hindu youths.

It was not until 1870 that it was decided to change the date of the

Mela from April to February, and to designate it as a "National Gathering." In 1871, immense stress seems to have been placed on physical training, largely through the efforts of Nabagopal Mitra, who had in the same year started a National Society to sustain nationalist enthusiasm during the months between the Melas.[17] Mitra's influence is fairly apparent until 1875, when he mysteriously passed out of the Mela scene and Brahmo affairs generally. Rajnarian became Mela president that year, but the only sensation created was when he refused to eat with the governor general because that would mean dining with Christians and Muslims.[18] A year later Dwijendranath took over the gathering and stressed modern manufacturing and technology,[19] especially in the production of paper goods. The last Hindu Mela was evidently held in 1880.

The earliest form of nationalism, therefore, as articulated by leaders of the Adi Brahmo Samaj, defended Hindu national identity at the same time that it supported constructive programs of self-help and development. The ideological stress on the modernist spirit saved them repeatedly from the snare of militant nationalism and Hindu revivalism. Dwijendranath Tagore was probably the Adi Brahmo Samaj's most convincing advocate of this position. He argued in the late 1860s that in India assimilation to Western forms was neither necessarily equal to modernism, nor was it the most effective and desirable means for modernizing the society. Indeed, as a nationalist, Dwijendranath argued that the adoption of Anglicized habits only intensified India's bondage to British colonialism. India must change but without violating her cultural integrity.

Superficially, there seems little difference between this position and that of the neo-Hindus some thirty years later. But, if we take as an example the series of articles Dwijendranath wrote between 1884 and 1890 during the revivalist period on this very problem, then the subtle difference between Hindu Brahmoism and Hindu revivalism will become apparent. What he said again and again throughout the essays was that the task of the modernizer was to study his own culture deeply in light of Western experience, to learn how to change it from within. Instead, modernizers chose the easy but dangerous path of blending their superficial knowledge of their own culture with an equally superficial knowledge of England, to produce a hodgepodge of diverse elements that could never be accepted for the people they were intended because they were unrealistic and incomprehensible. In one very interesting essay on the stick of silver and the stick of gold, Dwijendranath discussed two alternatives to modernization. The stick of gold, which represents Hindu modernization, will bring life to the dead body (popular Hinduism), whereas the silver stick of Westernization will "cause death to the body which has life." Westernizers were "lotus eaters who put the silver stick on their own cultural forms instead of taking pride in them and seeking to make them work effectively and well."

Dwijendranath neither hated the British nor repudiated their modernist spirit. In a subtle essay written in 1890, he very perceptively distinguished between the characteristics of modern civilization in the nineteenth century, to which he subscribed, and cultural forms that were easily imitated but had little to do with change and progress. If only Bengalis would stop confusing the two; if only they first investigated their own cultural roots, studied the processes of modern civilization, and then learned how to infuse modernism into the cultural pattern, Hinduism would begin to undergo a remarkable transformation. In his own words, "if the Bengalis without caring for European style and form only accept the nineteenth-century civilization from the English, and model it in their own style, and adapt it to the country, then they will be cured of imitating the Sahib and become a nation in their own right."[20]

CHAPTER SEVEN

The Frustration of the Bhadralok
and the Making of a Revolutionary Nationalist:
The West Desanctified

IT should by now be apparent that the image of the West among the bhadralok intelligentsia differed appreciably between those favorably disposed to progressive values and those sensitive to blatant forms of ethnocentricism. Liberals defended the right to apply modern values from the West to reform their own society; nationalists defended the right to preserve their own cultural integrity against the arrogant claims of Western superiority. This cleavage occurred within the same comprador class of bhadralok, composed of the same upper castes and the same elitist families, and at the heart of the same Brahmo movement and community. Thus, neither the vested interest of the native middle class nor loyalty to caste, family, faction, or religion seems to have been able to avert this crucial division within their ranks.

How do we explain the sharp and persisting split between the liberals and nationalists? I have already suggested how a youthful identity crisis was resolved in the making of the Brahmo Puritan and liberal reformer. I argued that a sense of community, and an achievement ethic tempered by nineteenth-century liberal values, preserved both a favorable image of the West and the spirit of Indian reform and modernism. I also noted how the rise of imperialism did not diminish the faith of the mature liberal personality, who struggled heroically to keep open the gates of India's cultural frontier.

But the nationalist represents a different psychological type, predisposed from his earliest manifestation of an identity conflict to shape his dialectic between "them and us" rather than, as with the liberal, between tradition and modernity. Even among Brahmo youths and young adults socialized by the same liberal paradigm of Rammohun Roy, one group established cultural integrity as the cornerstone of their new identity, whereas the other dedicated their new self-image to social reform. It seems as if the nationalist Brahmo was from youth preoccupied with national identity, while paying lip service to reform; the liberal was preoccupied with reform, while paying lip service to matters of national identity. To be sure, historical events and processes such as those subsumed under late nineteenth-century British imperialism can and do favor the spread of nationalism as a consequence of bhadralok frustration. But I think the evidence is abundantly clear that bhadralok nationalist consciousness did not arise from the objective reality of their material condition so much as from their response to these aspects of the historical situation.

I am suggesting that the human development of the nationalist, or lack of it, from the earliest record of identity crisis through the subsequent stages of his intellectual and professional life, is strikingly dissimilar from that of the liberal. The distinction between the two patterns of development accounts for the diametrically opposed responses by liberals and nationalists to imperialism. Based on data about early Brahmo nationalists and later Brahmo defectors to nationalism, my guess is that among nationalists, the identity crisis between "them and us" never subsided. On the contrary, the tortuous trek in quest of identity seems to go on indefinitely. Nationalists were rarely totally committed to patriotic values. In fact, if one probes deeply enough, one finds radical leaps between one identity and another. When historians type-caste Indians as nationalists, I believe that they have frozen a stage in a person's journey in search of identity. Therefore, what makes the nationalist, beyond certain common factors in the composition of the type, is the perennial identity crisis that inhibits the further development of what Erik Erikson refers to as the adult personality.

In the case of the two principal Adi Brahmo leaders, Debendranath Tagore and Rajnarian Bose, neither of whom was a radical nationalist in the twentieth-century sense, the identity crisis was quite different from that of the liberals who clustered around Keshub Chandra Sen in the 1860s. The identity problems of Dwarkanath Ganguli, Durga Mohun Das, or Sivanath Sastri were characterized chiefly by their burning desire to reform their society according to Unitarian and other progressive Western ideas. As youths, they rebelled against a society that lacked the awareness and compassion to rid itself of such customs as Kulin polygamy and child marriage. Such feelings drove them closer to the West and to an international brotherhood of liberals dedicated to similar kinds of reform in their own societies. At the same time, they increased the social distance between themselves and their own society, which continued to remain unresponsive to the protestations of the reformers.

But in Debendranath and Rajnarian, the spirit of social reform was conspicuously absent from their identity crises. For Debendranath, the religious impulse and a profound humiliation from the missionary attack on Hinduism seems to have been at the core of his identity problem. With Rajnarian, it was in reaction against Western values or his anglicized background, and was resolved, for the moment, in the psychological process of returning to the fold. Of course, being a member of the Western-educated bhadralok, he could never actually return to the fold. Rather, he and Debendranath reformed the Hindu fold, built a community around it, and defended its new rational form against the missionaries. Whereas Debendranath was the forerunner of those who supported Hinduism as the basis of national identity, Rajnarian, "the Grandfather of Indian Nationalism," was the prototype of such nationalists as Aurobindo Ghose and Jawahalal Nehru—those who rediscovered India from a state of disenchanted Westernization.[1]

Born in 1817 at the Tagore *bari* in Jorasanko, Debendranath was brought up precisely as one might expect by a father who was a zamindari Brahman with Western contacts and eclectic taste. He was pampered in luxury, tutored at home in both English and Bengali, introduced to Kali worship by his mother, and to Vaishnavism through family association with the Goswamis of Khardah. Indeed, one is hard put to discover just what effect Unitarianism had on the private affairs of Dwarkanath in the light of his son's upbringing, except that the boy was sent to Rammohun Roy's Vedantic Academy.[2]

Also as was customary, he was married early, at twelve years of age, to a girl of six; rather much as his father before him married a girl of six while he himself was fifteen. In 1830, Debendranath was sent to Hindu College, the only Western-style institution of higher learning in Calcutta at the time, but during his five years there it can hardly be said that he distinguished himself in any way as a student. He was neither a rebel against Hindu society, as were the famed followers of the Eurasian Professor Derozio, nor was he an ardent defender of Hinduism in any way. All this time Debendranath, with his father, took meat prepared by a Muslim cook outside the house, and wine, a habit evidently introduced by Rammohun.[3]

In 1835, Debendranath's grandmother died, and the event affected him deeply. While his father went off on a pilgrimage to Vaishnava centers in northern India, the eighteen-year-old Debendranath underwent a transformation of character and mental outlook. According to Debendranath himself, two changes occurred immediately: he sought the truth about the enigma of human existence, and he sought to free himself of his addiction to material wants and comforts.

Subsequently, he developed a God intoxication which made some of his relations believe he had gone mad. Meanwhile he gave up meat, wine, and most of the luxurious tastes acquired from his father. Indeed, he seems to have undergone a rebellious hatred of his father at this time, which manifested itself in three ways. First, by studying the ancient Hindu scriptures under Ram Chandra Vidyabagish, he rediscovered Rammohun's reform ideology, which exposed to him his father's inconsistencies of behavior. Debendranath was now shocked by the hypocrisy between the religious ideal of the Brahmo faith and the fact that idols were still being worshiped in the Tagore household, that Durga Puja was celebrated yearly, and that after dining with Europeans members of the household purified themselves by bathing in the Ganges.

Second, Debendranath repudiated his father's worldliness with all his pompous display, status in the eyes of the foreigners, and lavish expenditure of wealth. Third, Debendranath became increasingly apathetic about administering the family landholding and business properties, with the inevitable result that his father was infuriated, and the gulf between them widened.[4]

Debendranath's crisis of identity, as it were, precipitated by his grandmother's death, certainly predisposed him to a career of religious reformer, but it does not explain why he chose a particular path to follow. He did not turn to Rammohun's Hindu reform overnight, because he did not officially embrace Brahmoism until eight years after this dramatic turning point in his life. It was the challenge of orthodox Christian missionaries, bent on conquering the minds of young Bengali intellectuals for Jesus, that provides the answer to why Debendranath ultimately reawakened Rammohun's Brahmo ideal and developed it ideologically and institutionally.

Debendranath's father was not pleased at the new developments, and in a letter to his son from London dated May 19, 1841, he made his displeasure perfectly clear. "It is only a source of wonder to me," he began, "that all my estates are not ruined." Instead of protecting Tagore interests, Dwarkanath accused Debendranath of consuming his time "fighting missionaries." "If I were strong enough to bear the heat and climate of India," threatened Dwarkanath, "I should immediately have left London."[5]

Evidence accumulated by Satis Chandra Chakrabarti indicates that Dwarkanath held Ram Chandra Vidyabagish guilty of diverting his son from material to intellectual and spiritual concerns. In August 1843, Dwarkanath not only denounced the pandit, but made an effort to "extricate his son from his clutches." There is another interesting letter dated May 22, 1846, during Dwarkanath's final trip to England, in which he rebuked his son, perhaps for the last time, for misguided values and neglecting property affairs.[6]

But Debendranath had chosen his life's work, and there was no way his father could alter that decision. What Debendranath did alter repeatedly was his commitment to nationalism, which he periodically disavowed for universalism. In the 1840s, he defended Vedanta as the book of reformed Hinduism; but in 1850, under Akkhoy Kumar Dutt's influence, he rejected not only Vedanta but the book of any national religion as a revealed source. In 1859, he supported Keshub Sen's liberal theism and universalism; but in 1865, as we have seen, he took a hard line against the Keshubites as a nationalist. In 1881, commenting from the Himalayas in a letter on Keshub's New Dispensation, Debendranath wrote that "Keshub inspired with a love catholic and extraordinary, has prepared himself to bring about a reconciliation between the monotheists of India with those of Arabia and Palestine. This is a difficult undertaking. The disputes and discussions which this has produced have no end. . . . That clamor has even reached me here in my solitary mountain retreat. . . . If only that desire of wisdom in him could have been satisfied by what our own Rishis have taught."[7]

In 1833, Rajnarian Bose was sent to Calcutta for education, and was fortunate enough to gain admission into David Hare's School. As we have seen, this institution was considered the best primary and secondary school in the metropolis and a preparatory school for Hindu College, India's premier institution of higher learning. Contrary to the idealized reports on the school, however, Rajnarian's own candid accounts of the institution were brutally realistic about David Hare's training method. Boys were beaten if their hands or fingernails were dirty, or if they violated any rule in the slightest degree, or even if, in learning English penmanship, the letters were not written in the same size and style. Rajnarian tried desperately to keep one step ahead of Hare in order not to be beaten. Though he succeeded in doing so, he lived in constant fear, and at eleven years of age wrote an essay designed to persuade Hare to give up his sadistic activity. Apparently one of Bose's friends committed suicide as a result of harsh treatment.

In 1840, at age fourteen, he left Hare's School and recalled later that what he learned best of all while there was the ability to express himself well in English. He was quite good in debating and cultivated a deep love for English literature. Like many Bengali boys since his time, Rajnarian developed a fascination for the school hand-driven printing press, which he and others operated to bring out the school newspaper every Monday. It should be added that since David Hare was an outspoken atheist, religion was totally ignored in the school curriculum.

Like Debendranath and other members of the Calcutta elite, Rajnarian went on to Hindu College. But unlike Debendranath, Rajnarian distinguished himself as a student. He read voraciously in the Western classics, and showed fondness for English historians like Gibbon and Macaulay. He won prizes annually, and was one of Principal Richardson's best students of Shakespeare. Indeed, it would be interesting to contrast Rajnarian the later nationalist with Rajnarian the college student acquiring remarkable proficiency in a language, literature, and history entirely alien to his own. As a member of Young Bengal, being nurtured totally on things foreign and without any religious or moral training, he began to drift, like most of his peers, into a life pattern based largely on observation of the English. He started drinking, and joined steamer parties "to hunt birds and eat their flesh."

By 1844, Rajnarian had become so addicted to wine, and was drunk so often—because "drink was a sign of civilization" to Young Bengal—that he was compelled to leave college. Then, on December 7, 1845, his father died, and like Debendranath ten years earlier, Rajnarian experienced an extreme personality crisis. His reading habits changed radically in the direction of religious literature. For the first time, he read Rammohun Roy's *Precepts of Jesus* and the available works of the American W. E. Channing. "I became a Unitarian Christian," he wrote in his autobiography. Then the "most important event of my life took place" when "at the age of nineteen I came in contact with Debendranath Tagore and became a Brahmo."

Though there was nothing in the Brahmo oath compelling members to abstain from drinking and other vices, it seems likely that by the time Rajnarian signed the covenant, he had already given up drinking, smoking *ganja*, and all the other "Young Bengal habits" acquired as a student. By 1846, he was also regularly employed by Debendranath doing English translations of the principal Upanishads.[8] Rajnarian repudiated his Young Bengal background not for its Western intellectual orientation, but for its denationalizing impact and for the injurious habits imbibed from the foreigners. He was among the first to condemn Young Bengal precisely in these negative terms of cultural alienation. But like Debendranath, he never fully disowned the universalist legacy of Rammohun, nor did he ever resolve his identity crisis. He shaped reformed Hinduism in the Unitarian mold, attempted to "construct a science of religion" as late as 1878, and so greatly did he admire Keshub Sen until the schism of 1866 that he said "the Brahmo Samaj owes everything to him."[9] Nevertheless, by persistently framing his ideological development around questions of Hinduism and the world, Rajnarian, no less than Debendranath, wrote his most inspiring prose and left his most indelible imprint on history as a nationalist.

There is a world of difference between the Brahmo nationalism of Rajnarian Bose or Debendranath Tagore and the Hindu nationalism of Brahmo defectors such as Brahmobandhab Upadhyay and Aurobindo Ghose. The earlier nationalists confronted missionaries and their own Brahmo coreligionists; the later nationalists took on the British empire. But the greatest difference between the two generations was a matter of time; the grim decades between 1870 and 1890 witnessed an unparalleled crisis of expectations among the bhadralok in an atmosphere of mounting hate for the British. The frustration of the middle-class young, in particular, accelerated the process of desanctifying the West—the ideological pivot for all subsequent varieties of militant nationalism.

Liberal Brahmos viewed bhadralok discontent unsympathetically for some time because of their puritanism. The socio-political implications of the Brahmo Puritan ethic are not without considerable interest in the present context. To the Keshubite Brahmo, for example, nationalism proved to be as bewildering an experience at first as it was ambivalent. The peculiar stress on self-discipline and morality diminished Brahmo indignation over the obvious harmful effects of British imperial policy. It was puritanism that led the *Indian Mirror*, Keshub's English daily newspaper, to view India's poverty not as a consequence of foreign exploitation but as a result of the moral bankruptcy of the Indian people. "No doubt India is a poor country," ran one such article, but "poor not on account of its lack of natural blessings and [development] . . . but on account of the moral condition of the people, which prevents them from availing themselves of the opportunities within their reach." The *Mirror* wanted no "Imperial grant of money which would soon be spent and leave India as poor as ever." What was needed instead was "moral strength, intellectual enlightenment, public spirit, and patriotic energy. Let individual selfishness give place to a broadminded patriotism—let energy take the place of the general apathy too characteristic of India,—let light both intellectual and moral, disperse the prevailing darkness,—Imperial grants will be neither needed nor asked."[10]

This attitude, often dismissed simplistically as political conservatism, was actually derived from the same Puritan ethic that considered popular Hinduism to be the chief obstacle to modernism in South Asia. Even the earliest Brahmo-supported programs of industrialization for India were treated within the context of a moral problem.[11] Only with intensification of British racism or cultural imperialism in the 1880s, and largely through the initiative of Sadharan Brahmos, did a shift take place from a sole faith in internal regeneration to a censuring attitude against the British for their debilitating social and economic policies in India.

But to the Brahmo nationalist, as distinguished from the later militant nationalist, condemnation of the foreigner was invariably accompanied by the basic moral need to regenerate the Indian people as a prior condition for positive change. This is clearly observed in the alleged lack of entrepreneurial spirit in Bengal. Brahmos were among the first to take the lead in exposing this as a social defect, and recommending ways and means of remedying it. Not surprising is the fact that one of the earliest voices raised against this failing in the Bengali character was that of Akkhoy Kumar Dutt, ideological father of Brahmo puritanism. In 1855, he had written an editorial in the *Tattvabodhini Patrika* on the deplorable condition of Bengal. He blamed that condition on the insistence of Bengalis in competing for government service rather than preparing themselves for industrial occupations.[12] He found this condition deplorable indeed in light of the fact that traditional crafts had declined under the British.

The *Indian Mirror* ran many articles and editorials developing the theme. On February 12, 1879, for example, the paper claimed that the young men of Bengal, "not being attracted to the mercantile field prefer the bare pittance to be earned in a subordinate sphere of the public service or in the close competition of over-crowded professions."[13] On May 14 of the same year, there appeared another article on "Why Our Young Men Should Learn Arts and Manufactures." In an extremely indignant tone, they traced the lack of entrepreneurship among their countrymen to "easy and indolent habits and above all, to our extreme hatred of manual labor of any kind." The *Mirror* urged the immediate establishment of a training program to "initiate middle class young men in the several branches of manufacture such as the production of cutlery, of hardware, cloth, sugar, and paper." If this were done, "in a few years we will have better carpenters, wealthy millowners, rich manufacturers, and the idea of removing the miseries of our middle class men may then be expected to have been fully realized."

Two other articles in the *Mirror* put the finishing touches on the dismal portrait of the Bengali lack of entrepreneurial spirit. On July 15, 1880, the average middle-class young man was seen as nothing more than a clerk characterized by "timidity and want of self-reliance." Wrote the irate editor of an editorial on September 22, 1881: "After a century of British rule, we have succeeded in imitating almost every quality of our British masters but their spirit of enterprise." With typically Keshubite antinationalist sentiment, the editor saw the solution not in blaming the British but in developing a proper moral outlook from within. "God helps those who help themselves," was the editor's defiant reply both to nationalists and babus.[14]

But even among Brahmo liberals, the earlier stress on lack of entrepreneurship as being responsible for India's backwardness gradually gave way to a sympathetic depiction of the middle class in distress. In Brahmo newspapers of the 1870s, the high hopes of their own achievement ethic seemed to be swamped in reports of educated unemployment among young bhadralok. This is not to say that the Puritan ethic ceased to have beneficial effects on Brahmo youth; on the contrary, as seen earlier, the imperialist era was a golden age of achievement for the Brahmo community. But for the bhadralok in general, the situation had grown desperate.

In the first place, there were too many Western-educated for the limited number of government and professional positions available. Between 1865 and 1885, some 700 Bengalis had gone abroad to England, largely to compete for civil-service positions.[15] Concurrently, from the establishment of the university system in 1857 to

1882, some 1,589 Bengalis had received degrees from Calcutta University. Whether trained at home or abroad, the majority of Western-educated found themselves frustrated from being unemployed, underemployed, or in positions far beneath their competence and expectations.[16]

Thus the plight of the Western-educated, which also found its way into the Brahmo press, must be viewed alongside the theme of lack of entrepreneurship. In an *Indian Mirror* article of February 12, 1878, on "High Education in India," the harsh tone of the Puritan was softened as sympathy was extended to the college graduate with limited opportunities for employment. "A political career is not open for him," ran the article, while "the military service and for all practical purposes, the covenanted civil service also is closed to him; agriculture does not offer a tempting field." It is precisely when we put such articles on the frustration of the bhadralok against articles on lack of enterprise that the ambivalence of Brahmos becomes apparent, as, for example, when the above article refers to the inability of the graduate to turn to manufacturing and commerce because of "deficiency of skill, dearth of capital and the inequality of the terms on which it has to compete with European industry."[17]

In such articles dealing with what the newspapers called the "distress of the middle-class natives," the theme of lack of opportunity and the lack of equality in capital resources for investment was coupled with the rising cost of living, which was looked upon as a cross the young bhadralok must bear. How on earth could a professional live respectably on a salary of 100 rupees per month?[18] In the decade of the 1880s, when escalating British imperialism manifested itself in highly publicized cases of individual discrimination, even the Brahmo press turned to nationalist agitation. When in 1884 an Act of Parliament reduced the maximum age of candidates for the Civil Service from 21 to 19, the *Indian Mirror* responded not by urging their readers to moral regeneration, but by condemning the British for their injustice. Nationalist and not puritanical wrath underlay the following: "the young people have a hard enough time as it is but now by this single act, the British have made it impossible for Natives to compete for the Service in England."[19]

One may conclude that the deep-rooted problem of bhadralok frustration neutralized the Puritan attitude about lack of enterprise among Bengalis, and drove the more concerned Brahmos into the lap of the nationalist movement. It should be stressed, however, that Brahmo nationalists, as against militants and freedom fighters, refused to drop the notion of puritanical hard work and self-help (Swadeshi) in favor of complete independence (Swaraj) as a panacea for India's ills. But from the 1880s, intensified British imperialism and an expanding political consciousness convinced the Brahmos that the Puritan ethic in itself could never work unless the foreign-imposed colonial system were considerably modified.

Broadly speaking, there were two categories of imperialism that contributed to the rise of nationalism during the late nineteenth century: the impersonal variety expressed in British policy, and the personal variety expressed in relationships between Englishmen and Bengalis. The record of imperialism in the first category is quite well known to students of Indian history. Famines, foreign military adventures at India's expense, the wasteful expenditure of railway construction, the general drain of wealth to England were some of the more notorious results of British imperial rule in India.[20] There were also the legal enactments that in the eyes of the Western-educated deprived Indians of their basic rights. The little-known Dramatic Performances Act of 1876, which gave police commissioners the power to stop any performance they considered objectionable, was one of a series of acts that infringed upon their subjects' civil rights. The better-known Vernacular Press Act of 1878 was another example of putting curbs on civil rights and denying the right of free expression. The *Samprakash* was actually closed under the act's provisions in 1879.

In the first category also were sensational, well-publicized issues such as Surendranath Bannerji's dismissal from service, and the Ilbert Bill controversy. Both these issues were related, in that well-qualified Bengali civil servants were discriminated against for the color of their skin or for the alleged inferiority of their cultural background. In 1880, Bahari L. Gupta, a police magistrate of Calcutta, was disqualified on the basis of his race for trying British subjects under the law.[21] The Ilbert Bill was prepared to end such obvious discrimination, and to put Indian and British members of the covenanted service on an equal basis. But the nonofficial British community in India raised such an outcry and exerted so much pressure on the government that the final Act of 1884 proved an extremely watered-down version of the original bill.[22] The public insults to Bengalis by imperialist Britishers, meanwhile, led to hard feelings, counter charges, and explosive incidents such as Surendranath's imprisonment for contempt in 1883.[23]

Feelings of inferiority in Bengalis, in response to feelings of

superiority on the part of the British in India, was a crucial factor
in the impact of imperialism. British values at the time were saturated by an imperialist ethos. Allen J. Greenberger, who has carefully studied the literature of British imperialism, has concluded
that between 1880 and 1910 the British saw themselves as possess-
ing "the right and obligation to rule" as a result of their superior
qualities, which they saw "in terms of race." Leadership and power
made them as partial to "India's martial races" as it made them hostile to those with intellectual pretensions. According to Greenberger, it was for this very reason that English writers of the period
singled out the urbanized Bengali babu as a caricatured object of
ridicule and distaste.[24]

Another factor of cultural and political importance in the rise of
extremism in Bengal was the futility of the liberals' attempt to arrest the escalation of British imperial policy. Amales Tripathi has
prepared a list of imperialist acts that moderates, with all their legal
know-how and constitutional agitation, were powerless to prevent.
On occasion, as with the passage of the Simultaneous Civil Service
Act of June 1893, moderates congratulated themselves; but immediately the British "disallowed" the legislative enactment as it
"might imperil the predominance of the European element."
When it came to using Indian money to fight imperialist wars
abroad, British politicians simply ignored pleas from Indian liberals to curtail such expenditures. Another vital area of British self-
interest was the economic sphere, which continued to disfavor the
birth of industry in India. The Tariff Acts of 1894 and 1896, as well
as the cotton duties that discriminated against Indian mill-made
goods, "was another important ingredient in the growth of extremism."[25]

Imperialism can perhaps best be gauged in the unmitigated discontent and frustration of the Bengali bhadralok between 1880
and 1910. I have collected a number of cases of attempts by the
British in this period to block Bengalis from achieving qualification
and recognition in service-connected professions. In February
1884, a cry was raised by Calcutta University that the British had so
manipulated the Lower Grade Pleadership Examination that almost all of the 312 candidates had failed. Students charged that
questions were not taken from textbooks, as was normally done,
and that admission fees for the examination were unusually high.
One newspaper editorial concluded that the new policy was geared
to "pass as few candidates as possible on the grounds that the Bar in
the Mofussil Courts was overcrowded."[26]

Also that year the *Indian Mirror* published "Grievances of the Native Engineers in Bengal." They reported that from 1872, of all the students who passed the I.C.E. or B.C.E. examinations from the Engineering Department of Presidency College, "not a single one had been taken into the P.W.D. Department for no other reason than that they are poor natives of Bengal." The engineers themselves bemoaned the fact that "after spending three years in college at great expense, and being subjected to examinations, they are then left to drift for themselves and to struggle for mere existence." "The greatest anomaly in British rule," they said, "is that there is no responsible head to whom to appeal."[27]

In July of that year, the Bengalis in the Indian Medical Service complained openly that "insidious race distinction . . . in the distribution of appointments and stations" was completely frustrating their professional careers. They claimed that "out of twenty appointments in the staff of the Medical College and the General Hospital of Calcutta, not one has been given to a native officer under the present regime." They then went on to show how the first and second-class positions in the service were monopolized by European doctors.[28]

When in that same year of 1884, a Parliamentary Act reduced the maximum age of candidates to the convenanted service from twenty-one to nineteen, the Calcutta newspapers complained bitterly at the injustice of "practically closing the Covenanted Service to the Natives." The *Indian Mirror* charged that this was directed primarily at Bengalis, who could compete successfully with the English.[29] In 1884, such incidents so hardened the relationship between babus and overlords that the cultural encounter came directly to the surface and, not infrequently, as the object of sardonic humor. A typical example was the article in the *Mirror* dated May 22, entitled "The Term Babu." Worth quoting is the following: "The word 'Babu' is synonymous with ape or baboon, as used by Anglo Indians in a spirit of contempt and derision from an association of ideas. We shall meet derision with derision. Once in the presence of four or five other English gentlemen [I was the only Native], I was asked, 'what is the difference between a Babu and a Baboon?' My reply was: 'the difference of only a letter, sir, as between a sot and a Scot.' "[30]

The hatred by the British for the Bengali intellectual was, according to Sudhindranath Datta, the most potent psychological component of the new imperialism of the 1880s and 1890s. According to Datta, who was referring to his grandfather's generation, babu came to mean "cowardly by birth, unruly by upbringing and polysyllabic by education." Bengali intellectuals or babus "could not gain admission into the Indian Army even as privates." What was it like for Datta's grandfather, a sensitive, moral, and well-educated Bengali, to live under British imperialism? Wrote his grandson: "When summoned on urgent business, Bengalis entered European clubs only through the back door reserved for servants; they lost their railway berths to light-skinned commercial travellers in the middle of the night. Most hotels denied them accommodation. They remained segregated in public gardens made out of their own land; and the worst insult of all, every paleface appeared to take pleasure in calling them babu."[31]

If one considers that by 1887, after so much agitation and protest conducted along constitutional lines, only 16 Indians were among 890 members of the covenanted civil service, then one can begin to grasp the desperation of the bhadralok. There is an obvious correlation between the mounting desperation and the rise of "nativist" expression.[32] One might consider also the growing unemployment situation among graduates of Calcutta University. Amales Tripathi reports that in the 1890s, Calcutta was filled with hundreds of students "averaging 30 or 40 rupees a month to live on," whereas the educated unemployed had risen to 40,000 men who "brooded, silent and aloof."[33]

But from the early 1880s on, the British establishment was not the only source of frustration for the increasingly depressed legion of Bengali bhadralok. In 1880, there was trouble in the North West Provinces as local elites began to organize themselves against the virtual monopoly by Bengalis of subordinate service-related jobs. In response to local pressures, the government changed the qualifying language examination to Persian and Urdu, thus making it difficult for Bengali intellectuals, whose sole linguistic competence was in English.[34] In October 1882, riots erupted in Bihar for the same reason as local elites clashed with the despised alien Bengalis.

The *Indian Mirror*, most moderate Brahmo paper of the time, blamed the Biharis for the trouble, and accused them of envy and lack of gratitude. As the irate editor, Krishna Bihari Sen expressed it, "can Biharis deny that it is through the agency of a few Bengalis among them that they have achieved what little social and political progress they have as yet attained?" These editorials defending Bengalis against the rising host of enemies saw intellectual capacity and achievement as the common denominator of bhadralok society. As Bihari Sen said, "could Bengalis help it if they had become India's aristocracy of intellect?"[35]

Here then was the historical situation that helps us to understand Brahmo defections to Hindu revivalism and militant nationalism. In traditional nationalist historiography, the British imperial monolith was the arch villain; but, in fact, the Bengali Hindu bhadralok found themselves cornered not only by arrogant Englishmen, but by non-Bengalis who were beginning to assert themselves throughout South Asia in the twentieth century. In Bengal itself, in the very bhadralok citadel of Calcutta, non-Bengalis were rapidly taking over in the commercial and financial spheres. And with the partition of Bengal in 1905, a Bengali Muslim bhadralok emerged defiantly from the eastern districts of the province.

In this dismal atmosphere for the Bengal intelligentsia, nineteenth-century Brahmoism was virtually crushed beneath the three-headed juggernaut of imperialism, regionalism, and communalism. For the Brahmo defector and others, revivalism and nationalism represented an escape. As the short and tormented life of Brahmobandhab Upadhyay will demonstrate, the search for an identity was a very real and earnest pursuit during the golden age of imperialism, when primordial loyalties were first manipulated for political ends. With the study of Brahmobandhab, who started life as a Keshubite universalist and ended as a militant nationalist, we have the ideal portrait of a Brahmo defector in a perpetual state of identity crisis. He was born as Bhawani Charan Bannerji on February 11, 1861, in a Hugly village thirty-six miles north of Calcutta. As the name suggests, he was born into a Kulin Brahmin family, which during his grandfather's generation underwent a radical transformation in disavowing the nefarious polygamous practices associated with the caste throughout the nineteenth century. Bhawani Charan's great-grandfather was, in fact, one of those lusty villains of Brahmo literature who apparently married some fifty wives.[36] His father, two generations later, had only one wife. Both father and mother died when he was a youth, leaving the responsibility of his upbringing to others in the family.

One important formative influence in the family was his uncle, Kali Charan Bannerji, the famous Bengali Christian lawyer and nationalist.[37] When Bhawani Charan was born, Kali Charan was fifteen years old and a student at Alexander Duff's missionary school. His uncle, who greatly valued an English education, presumably had Bhawani Charan shifted from the Hindu School at Chinsura to the English school in Hugly. When the boy proved an apt pupil, his uncle had him admitted at Duff's. But apparently the boy reacted unfavorably to the "denationalizing" tendencies in the missionary school curriculum. In 1873, when Bhawani Charan received his sacred thread and took a vow never to eat meat, he announced his desire to study Sanskrit language and literature at the Batpara Academy.[38] There he not only developed intellectually, but excelled in physical education by performing feats of strength. His physical prowess was to become an important characteristic of his nationalist image in later years. The fact that he excelled in gymnastics, wrestling, stick fighting, and cricket gave him an inflated pride as a Bengali who did not fit the British caricature of the cowardly babu.

This association of physical strength with nation building was already integrated into Rajnarian Bose's ideology of nationalism as early as 1867. Since wrestling was a valued manly art among Bengalis and other Indians, Bose underscored its importance in physical education. Nabagopal Mitra, the Adi Brahmo founder of the Hindu Mela, was himself an excellent wrestler and well-rounded athlete. It was he who made sports and games a regular part of the yearly melas.[39] Even the Keshubite *Indian Mirror* applauded the victory of a Bengali over a Punjabi in wrestling at the twelfth annual Hindu Mela in 1878.[40]

According to a manuscript biography of Bhawani Charan written twenty-six years after his death, the nationalist saw physical development as the crucial factor in promoting morality and discipline in the education of a Bengali Hindu youth. There is the anecdote about some Armenians who pestered Hindu women at the Ganges near Chinsura while they performed their daily ablutions. One day, young Bhawani Charan and his friends decided to intervene and teach the Armenian "bullies" a lesson. In a matter of moments, as Bhawani Charan proudly recollected, "the Armenian stalwarts lay prostrate on the ground, and they never troubled the Hindu women again."[41] Bhawani Charan also boasted of regularly swimming across the Ganges to cultivate endurance and discipline. In this connection, while a college student, he actually led a group of his closest friends on a wild escapade to Gwalior, trudging seventy miles over the desert "to drive out the English by learning the art of fighting." From his own account, he took with him "ten rupees, my college fee for two months, and a little *pan*."

Another significant feature of the younger Brahmobandhab's militant nationalist temperament was the fact that even as a college student attracted to Brahmoism, he felt uncomfortable with Surendranath Bannerji's constitutional methods of agitation in the Indian Association. At a time when most Bengali students looked up to Surendranath and Ananda Mohun Bose as charismatic heroes, Bhawani Charan had already repudiated their ends and methods. He was seventeen years old when his uncle Kali Charan introduced him to Ananda Mohun Bose. "I plucked up my courage," Bhawani Charan later recalled, "and told Bose that the pen was of no use to us but it was the sword that must be flashed to save India." Bose laughed and replied that, "mankind were no longer barbarians, that they had reached a very high peak of civilization and that the English especially were the apostles of liberty." He continued after a pause saying that "consequently, constitutional agitation was quite enough." Bhawani Charan recollected that: "Having heard this I became rather impatient and taking leave of him as soon as I could, I returned home saying again and again, 'What shall we do? Where shall we turn?' "

Another component of the young revolutionary's personality was his apparent stress on chastity. As a dedicated idealist in the service of his motherland, he continually referred to the importance of being pure and free of worldly entanglements—especially women. A politicized sannyasi and celibate role is what he envisioned from adolesence as the basis of a revolutionary organization. In 1891, when he left Protestantism for Catholicism, Bhawani Charan condemned Luther for having broken his vow of chastity by taking a wife. In his mind, Luther had committed an "unpardonable sin."

In 1877, the young man was a restless student at Vidyasagar's Metropolitan Institution. He had become too distracted by extraneous matters to pay too much attention to his studies. Unlike the young puritanical Sadharan Brahmos who were among his classmates, Bhawani Charan did not worry himself about marks and achievement. As for the popular English literature professor, Surendranath Bannerji, Bhawani Charan found him "a bore" as a lecturer. Bhawani Charan, restless and arrogant, had become very much the rebel against authority and was known to have come under the influence of drugs.[42]

His rejection of Surendranath Bannerji, Ananda Mohun Bose, and other Sadharan Brahmos in the late 1870s did not represent a repudiation of Brahmoism per se, although he did not accept the Westernized habits of establishment Sadharan Brahmos. A nationalist in temperament and identity, he was nevertheless much attracted to Keshub Sen's experiments with comparative religion. Thus, a year or so after the schism, Bhawani Charan offered himself as a recruit to Keshub's *Nava Vidhan*, proclaiming his devotion to the task of constructing a universal religion. Curiously enough, the young nationalist seemed most attracted to the new rituals designed to integrate comparable sets of religious functions and behavior from discrete cultures under a single harmonious umbrella of symbols. Bhawani Charan apparently felt no difficulty in accepting Keshub's universalist idea behind the pilgrimage to the saints, in which Hindu reformers were placed on the same level of inspired prophets of God as were those of the Buddhist, Christian, and Islamic worlds. He and Keshub began to develop a warm relationship that was both intellectual and personal.[43]

In fact, by 1881, much of Bhawani Charan's restlessness and insecurity, and perhaps adolescent identity crisis, seemed resolved. He had a fairly steady job teaching at the Free Church Institution; he had found in Keshub a charismatic leader in whom he had absolute faith and trust; and he was a member of a community of Brahmo ascetics, which appealed to his own asceticism. He had identified with a program of religious regeneration and social service, which appealed to him ideologically and helped resolve any conflict in his mind between nationalism and universalism.

It was just at this time that he met Narendra Dutt, later known as Vivekananda, and formed a close friendship with this man who had also seemingly found a home and refuge as an ascetic follower of Keshub. Bhawani Charan recalled years later how, in Keshub's play *Nava Virindaban* [New Jerusalem], "Narendra Dutt acted the role of Yogi while I busied myself selling tickets."[44] It is not without considerable irony that we find the future Vivekananda, pioneer Hindu revivalist, and the future Brahmobandhab Upadhyay, pioneer revolutionary nationalist, both originally enjoying peace of mind and inspiration at the feet of Keshub Sen, the supreme universalist of his time.

Narendra Nath Dutt, a Kshatriya by caste, was born in Calcutta on July 12, 1863. Like Bhawani Charan, as a youth he was a skilled wrestler and swimmer. They also had in common the need to lead others, and Narendra Nath was as much a *dolpati* or faction leader as was Bhawani Charan. In 1879, Narendra Dutt went to Presidency College, but a year later shifted to Duff's School.[45] Brajendranath Seal, future Sadharan Brahmo philosopher, who was then a friend and classmate of Narendra Nath, has recalled the latter's bitter intellectual cynicism, his restlessness, and sardonic wit. Two philosophical problems plagued him deeply: the existence of God and the problem of evil.[46] During his late adolescence, again like Bhawani Charan, "he flatly refused to marry but preferred to remain celibate." According to Christopher Isherwood, the neo-Vedantist biographer of Ramkrishna, Vivekananda did join Keshub's Brahmo Samaj in 1880; through Keshub's initiative he first met Ramkrishna.[47] Though future events built on Vivekananda's alleged discipleship under Ramkrishna have obscured the actual influences in his early development, contemporary evidence points clearly to the formative importance of Keshub and Brahmoism. K. K. Mitra, who also knew Vivekananda in the early 1880s, has stated that the latter engaged in Brahmo activities, attended Brahmo meetings, lived among Brahmo students, and loved to sing Brahmo songs.[48]

With Brahmobandhab the situation was somewhat different. He left no successful organization like the Ramkrishna Mission behind him continually to reinterpret history to suit institutional requirements. Even after Keshub's death in 1884, when factionalism destroyed the New Dispensation Church, Brahmobandhab continued his Brahmo activities, sharing his loyalty between Krishna Behari Sen's faction and the Christian Unitarian faction led by Protap Majumdar.[49] Vivekananda, on the other hand, quit the Brahmo Samaj and went through a difficult period in his life. His father died, leaving the family in abject poverty. His sister committed suicide.[50] In 1884, Vivekananda was twenty-one years old and as far as career and purpose in life was concerned, he found himself a bhadralok among the intellectual proletariat.

Vivekananda and Brahmobandhab parted, each moving in different directions. Vivekananda defected from the Brahmo Samaj, carrying with him into neo-Hinduism much of the ideological baggage of Brahmoism imbibed from Keshub. Brahmobandhab not only remained a Brahmo, but had himself initiated as an ascetic on January 6, 1887.[51] Vivekananda forgot Keshub and turned instead to the sannyasi Ramakrishna as patron saint of the new movement he founded in the 1890s. Brahmobandhab continued to admire Keshub and to acknowledge the departed leader's influence on him:

> Keshub had the spirit of fire . . . when he spoke, the world listened. When he prayed, the congregation sobbed like children. When he acted on the stage the spectators were in tears. . . . Keshub must surely be the greatest man that modern India pro-

duced. . . . He took up the seeds of Ram Mohan Roy and developed the seeds of eclecticism. Debendranath tried to revive them but his work was confined to the Upanishads. The eclecticism which he lacked was to be found in Keshub and it was under this new leadership that the New Dispensation becomes the harmony of all scriptures and prophets and dispensations.[52]

In a manuscript of reminiscences by one of the lesser known Keshubite ascetics, Priya Nath Mallick, there are numerous references to both Narendra Nath Dutt and Bhawani Charan Bann'erji. One interesting claim by Mallick is that he himself was instrumental in leading Vivekananda away from the Sadharan Samaj to Keshub. Both young men were, according to Mallick, attracted to Keshub because they were strongly motivated by spiritual concerns and because they wanted very earnestly to save themselves and their country. And according to Mallick, they received considerable inspiration and guidance from Keshub: "My age is now seventy-three years and of the men that I brought within the fold of Navabidhan, Bhawani and Naren became famous and even world-famous as speakers and leaders and have passed away and I am left here as insignificant as ever. But I can bear witness boldly that both these men, especially Vivekananda, owed their beginnings of their spiritual culture to the pattern set by Keshub Chandra."[53]

In 1881, Bhawani Charan went to Sind as a Brahmo missionary and to assist his friend Haranand conduct a newly founded Brahmo school in Hyderabad. These were evidently agonizing years for Bhawani Charan, who was undergoing a renewed crisis. A friend reported that while in Sind, "his heart was in a ferment and the constant object of his study was the personality of Christ." In 1889, after a lecture on Christ by an Anglican missionary that explored the problem of sin, Bhawani Charan began to attend bible class at a nearby church mission school.

In May 1890, he officially resigned as a Brahmo missionary before a community of his Sindhi friends, who wept bitterly when they heard the news. Postponing his baptism for six months, he started to study Christ with a savage determination to "reconcile and harmonize pure Hinduism with pure Christianity. He even began editing a journal that he called *Harmony*, certain that he had found peace at last: "What a consolation it is to be a Christian and believe in Jesus the Redeemer of fallen humanity and the source of all righteousness." Did this mean that "he had abjured Brahmoism?" He replied, "We believed that God raised up Keshub

Chandra Sen to preach the harmony of all religions in spirit and in truth. We believe also that it is our humble mission to preach and establish the principle of unity of religions as laid down by Keshub."

But if Bhawani Charan could reconcile the Christianity of the imperialist church with Keshubite universalism in his own mind, his fellow Protestants could not. In 1891, he underwent another identity crisis, as it were, and by September of that year he was converted to Roman Catholicism. Again, it was the problem of sin that "had tremendous power leading men to darkness and death." He took the Christian name Theophilos (the first Christian writer to use the word trinity). Later he would Indianize Theophilos to Brahmobandhab.[54]

In the early 1890s, Bhawani Charan began to develop his own thinking in a systematic way. Ideologically, he was still in the universalist camp, adapting Keshub's Brahmoism to his immediate intellectual and religious position as an Indian Roman Catholic. In 1894, the church gave him permission to edit a journal that he called *Sophia*, and through which for five years he was able to crystallize his thinking on comparative religion. He was clearly still following Keshub's task of "facilitating the comparative study of different religions . . . thus helping the seekers after truth to arrive at the true knowledge of the true religion."

Curiously enough, only one of the five objectives of the journal, as stated in the first issue, was "to expound the doctrines of the Roman Catholic Church." He also intended to explore the "fundamental problem of what is the end of man and how to attain it," while vowing that he would "represent faithfully to the Indian public the essential teachings" of all the Hindu scriptures.[55] It is surprising that it took the Roman authorities so long to realize that Theophilos was no ordinary convert to the faith, but was in quest of something far beyond dogma and church. He was using Catholicism in its original context of universalism, which he then found far more satisfying than Brahmoism. In an early article of *Sophia*, Bhawani Charan defended the Brahmo Samaj against the growing legions of revivalists and nationalists with characteristically masterful irony:

> The fate of the Brahmo Samaj is a sad warning to those who venture to deal in foreign creeds. Her leaders have rummaged the entire range of Hindu Scriptures to find out texts in support of their novel creed and have left no stone unturned to dress it

up in Hindu garb, but all in vain. The Brahmo Samaj is guilty of believing in God the Creator . . . scornfully rejected by Hindu philosophy; she is guilty of opposing transmigration; she is guilty of placing Jesus on the highest pedestal of honor. . . . She has committed sacrilege and she must pay the penalty which is death or surrender. There was a time when Brahmoism was very popular—and what is its fate now?—it is on the way of being engulfed in the historic past.

Why was the Brahmo Samaj in decline? In 1894, the future Brahmobandhab blamed it on "nationalism which is the ruling principle of the day." This nationalism, he went on to declare, was "a narrow bigoted patriotic sentiment." Revivalism and nationalism would lead to bankruptcy because they were based on a "dogged resistance against the importation of foreign truths, as if, there was such a thing as Indian truth or European truth." The following indignant indictment of nationalism uttered by one of the earliest martyrs in the cause of militant nationalism only suggests how hard it was for defectors to disown the Brahmo heritage: "We protest against the narrow spirit of nationalism. Truth is truth not because it has been first taught in this country or that country but because it resides in God and has proceeded from Him."[56]

Then, in 1895, he underwent a fresh crisis of groping once more for truth and loyalty. He suddenly changed his name from Theophilos to Brahmobandhab and began to shed everything European about his clothes and manner. He took on the saffron sannyasi garb—without first consulting his superiors—at the same time he accentuated his Brahman caste and Hindu appearance. Soon only an ebony cross worn around his neck could distinguish him from a Hindu ascetic.[57] By 1897, he was a prized lecturer in Calcutta on Vedantism and neo-Hegelianism. The Brahmo philosophers in the Sadharan group in particular seemed to respect his mind and passion for truth. He and Vivekananda were both looked upon as modern commentators on the Vedanta.[58] At the same time, Brahmobandhab was attempting to resolve a rather peculiar identity problem. He began to speak of a divided loyalty between his "Hindu identity which simply included his physical and mental constitution" and a "Catholic identity which claimed his faith, morality and mortal soul." Also that year, like Keshub much earlier and Vivekananda at approximately the same time, he began to organize a band of devoted ascetics who would give up worldly entanglements to regenerate India. But unlike Vivekananda, he clung to the idea that India's path to regeneration was through Christ.

By 1898, articles in *Sophia* indicate that he had raised the Vedanta to a virtual Hindu New Testament. A year later, to materialize his idea of an Indianized Catholic order, he and two others went to Jubulpore in the center of India to establish the Kasthalik Math, or monastery. Here the three Indian Catholics with shaven heads walked barefoot through the streets of Jubulpore, "each one begging, each one cooking his own meal, and each one observing the customs of his caste." During Lent of 1899, Brahmobandhab "retired to a hill and passed for forty days in imitation of his Master."

At this point, Brahmobandhab confronted imperialism directly. The Catholic hierarchy finally decided they would curb his excesses in domesticated experiments by squelching his infant order and monastery. Brahmobandhab journeyed all the way to Rome to appeal his case, but for unknown reasons he was denied an audience with Pope Leo XIII. Brahmobandhab naturally resented the way he was treated, grew embittered, and though remaining a Catholic, he turned sharply against "Euro-centric Christianity" for its racism and imperialism. In 1901, the church killed *Sophia*,[59] thus giving Brahmobandhab his pretext for starting the strongly pro-Hindu *Twentieth Century*, a journal that helped launch him on his career as a revolutionary nationalist. Whereas in *Sophia* he had refrained from politics, Brahmobandhab now made politics the cornerstone of his attack on imperialism. Ideologically, however, or theologically—as judged by his articles—he was using universalism to wage his intellectual war against European imperialism. In a brilliant essay on "Europeanism versus Christianity," he made his position extremely clear, arguing lucidly that "Christianity is generally confounded with Europeanism," whereas in fact "Christianity is distinct and transcends the racial genius of Europeans." The confusion arises from "not being able to sift the spirit from the form, to distinguish the temporal embodiment from the unchangeable essence." Because Brahmobandhab was not yet prepared to surrender his loyalty to Christ, while at the same time having become defiantly nationalistic, these writings during this stage of his development represent a creative contribution to the pioneering efforts at establishing indigenous Christianity in India. Like Keshub back in 1866, he argued in 1901 that the failure of Christianity in India may be attributed to imperialist missionaries who believed that "the European frame of society is alone compatible with the religion of

Christ, while the Hindu fabric has scarcely any sanction of reason."[60]

In an article published in *Twentieth Century* on "Christianity in India," Brahmobandhab lashed out at the dismal failure of European missionary effort in India after three hundred years of effort: "not a single flower of a saint has blossomed in India to adorn the altar of God." Under European missionary influence, India produced not a single theologian, not one philosopher, not a statesman, "nor historian, nor thinker worth the name to raise the status of the Indian Christian community." "Strange to say," he continued, "it is among non-Christians that we find a Keshub or a Ranade." How do we explain this "Christian stagnation in India?" By one word that characterizes the attitude of the missionary: "It is *contempt*. It is the contempt of the European missionary for the caste system . . . which he considers to be diabolical in its very conception. It is contempt for the Indian philosophical thought which is to him a heterogeneous mass of contradictions. It is his contempt for the political aspirations of the people which he dubs as sedition."[61]

As the months went by, and then the years, Brahmobandhab gradually ignored Christianity as he defended Hinduism. He was accelerating the pace of his nationalist development, leaving not only Christ behind him, but the Brahmo orientation that had sustained him for years. One might argue that with his defense of caste inequality, and his growing impatience with social reformers, whom he saw as dividing Hindu society from its true enemy—the British imperialist—his defection from Brahmoism became an established fact. His justification was the need for Hindus to preserve their integrity. Like a true revivalist and militant nationalist, he now equated all European influence (even beneficent) with imperialist penetration. In the end, "if we do not watch out, they will make bastards of us."[62] He now reasoned that "the nationality of a people was based upon self-respect. We should learn how to respect ourselves before we can rise in the scale of nations. Self-respect can be effectively engendered by dwelling upon the glories of the past."[63]

During this final militant phase in Brahmobandhab's life, the encounter between Europe and Asia, in the context of the imperialist experience, became the focal point for all his intellectual endeavor. The equation of all forms of Westernization with imperialist penetration produced in his thought an entirely different critique of imperialism from that of the Brahmo moderates who dominated the early Congress. No intellectual of the time in Bengal probed imperialism as deeply as Upadhyay. He studied it historically in the decline of the Roman empire; he studied contemporary examples of European empires in their political and military aspects; he studied the missionary organization as an agency of imperialism; and he studied the effects of capitalism on imperial policy.[64] Significantly, the new radical nationalist, Brahmobandhab, deplored capitalism, setting him off from many of the Brahmo-type nationalists whose Puritan ethic and material success made them advocates of capitalist entrepreneurship as a panacea for India's ills.

The case of Brahmobandhab illustrates the conflict within Brahmo ranks between ascetic types who pitted their belief in renunciation, self-sacrifice and poverty against the this-worldly asceticism of the establishment Brahmos. Vivekananda and Brahmobandhab were, as we have seen, attracted to the ascetic tradition in Brahmoism. The Brahmo ascetics looked suspiciously on their Puritan brethren's activities, which led so often to materialism and elitism. Because ascetics cherished poverty as a virtue and favored spiritual and social improvement of the rural masses, they repudiated capitalism. Dietmar Rothmund has viewed this anticapitalist attitude, when fused with a compassion for the masses, as a form of "ascriptive socialism."[65] Though ambiguous, the term is apt for a reformer like Vivekananda and other Brahmo ascetics. But for Brahmobandhab, the militant nationalist, capitalism was repudiated, to be sure; not for its crippling effect on spiritual regeneration or on peasant society, but for its violation of Hindu cultural integrity.

In a volume entitled *Samaj* (Society), Brahmobandhab evolved his social philosophy of nationalism. When he dwelled on the evils of capitalism, it is surprising how little he stressed the economic consequences. True, he was shrewd enough to identify modern Europe with the capitalist system and to recognize its economic side, but his serious objection to capitalism was that it would destroy the basic Hindu value system which, in his mind, was far more valuable than the capitalist. Among Hindus, Brahmobandhab contended, neither the soldier nor the merchant, the two chief agents of imperialism, ever achieved supreme power or status. Hindu administration in the classical age was conducted by a class distinguished for its "wisdom and poverty." They were the scholarly Brahmans, whom Brahmobandhab had by now raised to the status of heroes in the history of Hindu civilization.

He charged that Western scholars, strangely fascinated by and partial to their own merchant-militarist societies, had singled out the Brahman as the scapegoat for the decline of classical Hinduism. This, in his opinion, represented a "deliberate distortion of historical facts." He himself had two explanations. In the first place, time and not Brahmans or Brahmanic religion destroyed the wonder that was India. "However great be a society," wrote Brahmobandhab, "it will weaken and decay in the course of time." The other factor was race. The decay of the Hindus "was the mixture of blood between Aryans and non-Aryans, between the Brahmans and the Sudras and the growth of a new society as a result of the pejorative mixture."[66]

Underlying Brahmobandhab's militant ideology was a belief in an integral Hindu system that had to be kept undefiled from Western penetration at all costs. Unlike Vivekananda, who defended caste as the result of a universal need in all cultures to stratify their own societies, but nevertheless susceptible to reform in India, Brahmobandhab defended the institution purely and simply as an integral part of the Hindu system. During this militant period in his life, he violently attacked Brahmos as misguided reformers who unwittingly assisted the forces of imperialism by destroying caste, the very institution that held Hindu society together.[67]

In 1901, because Rabindranath Tagore was also undergoing a militant phase, he found much to admire about Brahmobandhab. The latter's spirit of intellectual and cultural integrity so moved the poet that he invited Brahmobandhab to be headmaster of the new boys' school at Santineketan. Rabindranath also sympathized with Brahmobandhab's inflated view of classical India, and hoped that the nationalist would implant the virtues of the golden age in the minds of the students. According to Rabindranath's son, Rathindranath, however, who was at Santineketan at the time, "Upadhyay's virulent nationalism" ultimately alienated the founder of the school. Rathindranath reported that Brahmobandhab could not divorce his aggressive nationalism from the "purely educational experience at Santineketan." Brahmobandhab laid great stress on physical strength and courage, which from an anecdote indicates that Rathindranath was not without some admiration for the nationalists. One day the schoolmaster challenged a professional wrestler from the Punjab, who happened to be a guest at Santineketan. "Upadhyay came running in tights," Rathindranath recalled, "and with loud slaps on the biceps, as was the custom, challenged the Punjabi." "And didn't the Bengali intellectual give a good time to the professional wrestler," wrote Rathindranath. In the final analysis, however, he assessed Upadhyay as a "Hitlerian type" who was compelled to leave Santineketan, and whose political editorials in *Sandhya* were venomous with hatred for everything foreign.[68]

Brahmobandhab started *Sandhya* (evening) in 1904 while deeply involved in political action. In 1905, he joined Bipin Chandra Pal and Aurobindo Ghose in their antipartition agitation, using his journal to proclaim *swaraj* or self-determination as the goal of India. One source maintains that *Sandhya*'s daily circulation averaged 15,000 copies. Tilak's influence seems apparent at the time, as evidenced by the fact that Brahmobandhab was in charge of the 1906 Sivaji festival in Calcutta, and was head of the delegation of several thousand Bengalis who greeted the Maharashtrian nationalist at Howrah Station.[69] At this time also, Brahmobandhab allegedly reconverted to Hinduism by eating cow dung, publicly declaring that "we must preserve the integrity and distinctiveness of Hindu society at any cost."[70]

In 1907, Brahmobandhab began to make frequent use of the Sakto symbolism for nationalist purposes in the manner of other contemporary Bengali revolutionaries. He had long ago turned his back on Keshub and Brahmoism, now joining the other revolutionaries in "praising Ramkrishna and Vivekananda who brought Bengalis back to the religious traditions of the true India." In October of that year, the police arrested him, closed down the *Sandhya* office, and destroyed his "revolutionary propaganda." The police burned everything they found in a secret warehouse, including a lively correspondence between Upadhyay and Rabindranath Tagore.[71] It might be interesting to note in passing that Brahmobandhab was defended in the *Sandhya* Sedition Case by C. R. Das, another famous Brahmo turned nationalist.[72] On October 27, Brahmobandhab Upadhyay died suddenly in prison from tetanus.

Brahmobandhab's repudiation of Brahmoism as a nationalist was representative of an increasing hostility by the younger generation of intelligentsia to universalism, Westernism, modernism, and constitutionalism. As Aurobindo put it, "the future lies not with the Indian Un-national Congress nor with the Sadharan Brahmo Samaj."[73] And yet, as the case of Bipin Chandra Pal well illustrates, defection from Brahmoism was not always clear cut, particularly for the ascetics like Brahmobandhab, Vivekananda, and Aurobindo. Bipin Chandra, however else he changed, could not disavow that fundamental Brahmo passion for exposing Hindu social abuses and calling for their reform. In fact, in Bipin Chandra's character sketch of Brahmobandhab, he pointed to this very "self-defeating" attitude in the zealous Hindu nationalist who, while wanting to free his country from the chains of external bondage, was unwilling to free it from the social tyranny of internal bondage.[74]

PART III

Synthesis

If you know the leading principles of my life and character, you will no doubt admit that I am pledged to reconciliation and harmony. If I live for any purpose it is for this, that I will preach the union of Eastern and Western theism, the reconciliation of Europe and Asia. The idea may seem absurd to many in the present age. It may provoke ridicule and angry reviling. But posterity will prove the better judge.

KESHUB CHANDRA SEN to MAX MÜLLER

Through the Visva Bharati as a whole we seek to establish a living relationship between East and West, to promote intercultural and international activity and understanding and to fulfill the highest mission of the present age—the unification of mankind.

RABINDRANATH TAGORE

CHAPTER EIGHT

Western-Inspired Brahmo Evangelism and the Vaishnav Spirit in the Mofussil

ON the basis of the biographies of Brahmo leaders thus far presented, one might well conclude that Hindu reformers were virtually all members of the Western-educated intelligentsia. Whether nationalist or universalist, conservative or liberal, they shared a common exposure to an Anglicized education and the English language, while most of them were sophisticated about Western efforts at social reform. The building blocks of the Hindu reformation thus far seem to have been designed on Western models. Whether liberal or nationalist, the class of bhadralok was elitist not so much because the participants belonged to the upper three castes of the regional Hindu society, but because they had done relatively well in the colonial system imposed by the British. Wherever they came from, most of them ultimately settled in Calcutta where, if successful, they lived in affluent or comfortable circumstances, and they socialized with Europeans as well as with enlightened members of their own society.

But sooner or later, the Hindu reformation would have to reach down below the thin layer of Western-educated persons to people in rural towns and villages, to the lower middle class, to those with little or no English-language background. It would have to alter its ideological appeal, since Unitarian-inspired rationalism and the reinterpretation of the Upanishads were far too exotic and abstract for Bengalis outside the reach of Calcutta intellectual circles.

The process of recruiting potential Hindu reformers in the far corners of rural Bengal was initiated by Keshub Chandra Sen in the 1860s as part of a new Brahmo missionary strategy. By casting widely into north and east Bengal, the Calcutta Brahmos netted two types of recruits: those discussed earlier who mastered English, attended a leading college or university, and became modern professionals; and those who, despite their lack of English, took on the new social consciousness without participating in comprador ac-

tivities. The first group included men such as P. C. Roy, Ananda
Mohun Bose, Durga Mohun Das, Sitanath Tattvabhusan—all of
whom joined the ranks of the bhadralok intelligentsia by virtue of
their superior knowledge of English and their positive attraction to
Western learning. Even a nationalist like Rajnarian Bose, who
turned to Bengali with a vengeance, had been a brilliant student of
English language and history at Hare School and Hindu College.
Brahmobandhab Upadhyay wrote some of his best nationalist
tracts in flawless English prose. Thus, the liberal thesis and nationalist antithesis represent a dialectic within the same community
of Western-educated bhadralok intelligentsia.

It is among the second group of non-Westernized intelligentsia
that the first major synthesis took place between progressive Western values and the Hindu tradition. The earliest important leader
of reformed Vaishnavism was Bijoy Krishna Goswami, the best-
loved and most effective Brahmo missionary in Bengal during the
nineteenth century. This is not to argue that all major attempts at
synthesis in Bengal were the creations of non-Westernized bhadralok. His was, simply, the first. There were also later attempts by
Westernized intellectuals like Keshub Sen and Rabindranath Tagore, who worked out their own synthetical formulae.

It might also be argued that of the three types of synthesis discussed in this book, Bijoy Krishna's was the most meaningful from
the point of view of subsequent efforts by Hindu reformers to
translate Brahmo modernism into Hindu forms and usages to
reach broad sections of the population. The Arya Samaj and Ramkrishna Mission, which were both the results of modernism and of
the requirements of a national identity, were among the more conspicuous examples of a process inaugurated by Bijoy Krishna while
he was a missionary of Keshub Sen's Brahmo organization. Why
were these movements so successful in reaching wider numbers of
Hindus? Was it indigenous modernization? Were not the Adi
Brahmos—men such as Debendranath, Rajnarian, and Dwijendranath Tagore—also indigenous modernizers of the Vedantic
tradition? But they failed to produce a mass movement. Was not
Vidyasagar, humanist and atheist, an indigenous modernizer? He
had enormous influence on the progressive intelligentsia and on
liberal pundits, but he left behind him no mass movement. The key
is, I believe, in communicating modernist values through the idiom
of postclassical Hindu devotionalism or bhakti. The Vedanta, as we
have seen, remained circumscribed among Brahmo intellectuals
and philosophers as a thinking man's religion, whereas the liberal

tenets of the new Vaishnavism could be grasped emotionally in songs and processions without the need of books or abstract reasoning. Finally, just as the Upanishadic golden age conceived by Rammohun Roy was characterized by egalitarianism and other modern values, so Vaishnavism had had a golden age in sixteenth-century Bengal, when the reformer Chaitanya, had preached brotherhood and other democratic values in the modern spirit.

Early disruptions in the lives of synthesizers such as Bijoy Krishna show similarities to the lives of the nationalists. One similarity was the persisting problem of identity. Like the nationalists, also, they attempted to substitute a saintly ethic for the Puritan ethic of the liberals. The difference was that Bijoy Krishna was a liberal also, though a highly indigenous one, who had little use for the virtues of chastity and physical strength. Nevertheless, through reevaluation and synthesis, Bijoy Krishna's saintly ideal represents a modified form of asceticism.

The circumstances of his birth, early development, and education indicate that Bijoy Krishna Goswami was, among all the Brahmos discussed so far, the least Westernized. Born in 1841 in Santipur, Nadia, in the vicinity of the sixteenth-century Vaishnava reformation, he was descended from an *advaita* preceptor in Chaitanya's movement.[1] His father was a devout Vaishnava priest, his uncle a scholar who traveled through north Bengal offering Vaishnava mantras and collecting donations for the local Goswami temple dedicated to Lord Krishna.[2]

How is it that this Goswami, brought up strictly within a specialized religious tradition, came to accept the Brahmo faith? One account of his conversion is typical of the legends that invariably proliferate around the lives of saints and mystics; take, for example, this tale of an incident that supposedly prepared him for the truth of Brahmo: "One day he fell into a trance and a voice came to him asking that he think of after-life. Later he asked himself fearfully where this voice could possibly come from. So deeply did the experience move him, that he became bedridden with fever. When Vaishnava devotees came to worship at his feet he turned them away for he suddenly realized that he could not help them since he himself required help. How could he help others salvage themselves when he himself did not know the correct path to salvation?"[3]

Shortly after, precisely when is not known, he chanced to be in Bogra (now in Bangladesh), where he heard three Brahmos preaching. He was so taken by their "regard for truth," that he went to Calcutta to meet their leader, Debendranath Tagore.[4] On arrival in Calcutta, he was robbed by a gambler and dispossessed of the little he owned,[5] so that when he finally met Debendranath, he was a poverty-stricken youth who slept nights on the Sanskrit College veranda. With characteristic honesty, Bijoy wrote that he first came to the Brahmo leader as much for economic assistance as for spiritual guidance, but the rustic boy was not impressed with the Brahmos of Calcutta. They "only filled their bellies with wine and tried to get him drunk too." Debendranath honored his application for monetary assistance, and the young man began to attend the Maharshi's sermons, which were so pure and so filled with the love of God that Bijoy would "shed tears throughout." Thus did Bijoy Krishna, a Goswami, come to sit at the feet of Debendranath, who sometime in the late 1850s, most likely, "became his preceptor." Bijoy was put on Debendranath's payroll, and the Brahmo leader even paid his way through a few courses at Calcutta Medical College. The training he received there proved invaluable later on when, on mission tours, he was able to help the victims of epidemics.

The earliest recorded impact of Brahmoism on Bijoy was the time he questioned wearing the sacred thread. He went to Debendranath and told him that the sacred thread was causing him "mental agony" because he no longer believed in caste. Debendranath's answer was neither radical nor reassuring: "The sacred thread is essential. It will harm society if you give it up. Have I not kept my sacred thread?"

Bijoy was also disturbed about eating meat and fish. Debendranath told him that if he could "kill bedbugs and misquitoes, why not eat meat and fish?" The young man was hardly satisfied with these "conservative replies" to questions that were "burning him up internally." He would discuss these matters with his closest friends at Medical College, youths who like himself were mostly East Bengalis, and rustic Vaishnavas, people out of place in the large metropolis.[6]

Doubts about the sacred thread so plagued Bijoy that he decided to leave the city and return to his family at Santipur. What followed was most probably the most serious crisis of his youth. Perhaps seventeen years old at the time he returned home, Bijoy Krishna sought to win family approval for removing the sacred thread. He tried to explain to them that Vaishnavism did not favor a "separation between Brahman and Sudra," but in fact advocated the contrary position, for Chaitanya preached against caste barriers. Bijoy's reasoning fell upon the deaf ears of the Goswamis, who simply performed their religious functions mechanically without the slightest urge to question underlying presuppositions or critically to evaluate Chaitanya's real intent. As for the sacred thread, there was no question but that wearing it was a sacred duty. Bijoy took off the thread, knowing that the act meant certain excommunication. In a moment, he deposed himself socially into the rank of the Sudras. He realized "that from then on neither Kayasthas nor Vaidyas could touch him or take water from his hands."

His mother "literally fell at his feet and threatened to kill herself unless he put on the sacred thread." This he did for her sake, but no sooner had he done it than his conscience drove him to despair. He simply had no peace. One biographer wrote that "the sacred thread literally stung him like a scorpion," and he wailed to his mother that "unless he could pull off the cursed thing forever, he would himself die." She gave in finally, and Bijoy was outcasted. No barber would cut his hair, no cook would prepare his food, no washerman would clean his clothes. Bijoy returned to Calcutta, signed the Brahmo covenant, and was ordained a minister of the church by Debendranath.

One might ask why Bijoy Krishna defied caste, and as a profoundly feeling Vaishnava elect to join the rationalistic and Westernized Brahmo Samaj as his new religious identity? Indeed, the rupture between himself and his community at Santipur was hardly peaceful. He has related how "rocks were thrown at him by some irate Vaishnava neighbors," while others were satisfied with "jeering and ridiculing him." Only his sister and brother-in-law supported him, and when Bijoy went to Calcutta they accompanied him, and even became Brahmos.

It was Bijoy's special talent to have developed a style of Brahmoism that made him appealing to many people whom the Brahmos of the time could not possibly hope to reach. First, though not Westernized, he too was a rational theist, a social reformer, and a liberal. It was not until the 1880s that he began to soften his harsh Brahmo attitude to icons. He had a clear, analytical mind, which however clothed in the traditional garb of Vaishnavism was still as emancipated as the most thoroughly rational Brahmo. This attitude was clearly present in 1868, as we shall soon see, when Bijoy attacked Keshub for "avatarism," or for having been seduced by followers to believe himself a "savior," directly partaking in God's divinity.

As for reformism, Goswami was ideologically akin to the most progressive Brahmos of the time. His sermons and lectures during trips to East Bengal were intensely liberal in spirit. He consistently supported the progressive faction of Sivanath Sastri against Keshub in the 1870s on the issue of female rights, then broke decisively with Keshub over Cooch Behar. His universalism, though often proclaimed in the name of Chaitanya, rather than of Channing or Emerson, was nevertheless predicated on faith in the "unity of God and the brotherhood of all men."

Despite his numerous shifts of identity, Bijoy Krishna never became a practitioner of other-worldly asceticism. Rather, if his wife's autobiography is evidence, Goswami appears as the householder to whom Debendranath addressed his *Brahmo Dharma*. Bipin Chandra Pal, a younger contemporary of Bijoy who wished to make him more attractive to modernists, contrasted precisely this feature of Goswami's sexual attitude to that of the neo-medieval saint, Ramakrishna, who "used to get public prostitutes from the bazaar and set them in the complete nakedness of their flesh before him with a noose placed around his neck and the moment he felt the least quickening of desire for carnal gratification, he used to tighten the noose and fall in a swoon groaning with mortal pain. By these means he acquired mastery over flesh and mind. . . . Bijoy was different and never suppressed his desire. Rather than advocating celibacy he worked to idealize and spiritualize his desires."[7]

Keshub Sen was the other major influence on Bijoy's Brahmo conversion. Goswami himself has related how, unlike Debendranath, who told him not to give up the sacred thread, Keshub instructed him to do so; and Bijoy joined the organization of youthful Keshubites known as the Sangat Sabha, with whom he found a second home.

When Satyendranath Tagore and Monomohun Ghose left for England in 1862, Bijoy Krishna and Protap Chandra Majumdar replaced them as Keshub's most ardent supporters within the Samaj. In those days, Bijoy was the listener, absorbing what he could from Keshub and other Brahmos. He applied his fresh insights about man, God, and the universe to Vaishnavism. Bijoy, who hardly knew English, became one of the more articulate members of the younger generation, and as already noted, was a prime mover in the resolutions of 1865/66 that led to the break with Debendranath and to the formation of the Brahmo Samaj of India.

It was after 1866, when Keshub was on his own and groping for guidelines as a reformation leader, that Bijoy Krishna's influence began to become apparent. He began to push Keshub in the direction of Vaishnavism, and suggested that Keshub model himself after Chaitanya by introducing into Brahmoism Vaishnava music and processions. The idea was to compose Vaishnava-type songs with Brahmo messages. In this way, he believed, Brahmo ideas, ideals, and sentiments could be conveyed to a much larger mass of Bengalis, not in the alien Christian way but in the native Bengali way.

By 1867, Keshub had been won by Bijoy Krishna's ideas. In that year he inaugurated his long flirtation with the image of Chaitanya and the possibility of following in the footsteps of the sixteenth-century reformer. But more than that, there was a change of personality in Keshub. In September of that year he was described as "no longer being stern, ethical and full of intellectual bitterness, but thawed into someone tender and full of humility, and . . . trusting dependence which dissolved every heart it touched into kindred tears. The didactic devotions of the older Jorasanko pulpit were by an unseen process transformed into an all-piercing pathos, an inseparable sympathy with every form of sin, suffering and desertion that made our daily services the veritable service of sorrow."[8]

By November 1867, the bhakti tradition had clearly won its way into the new Brahmo church. The sankirtan or Vaishnava devotional hymn was introduced, along with street processions characterized by "ecstatic devotion, rapture of the heart . . . zeal and emotional fervor." In the midst of the excitement, Keshub sang for the first time in public. Protap Majumdar has described it in the following way: "He loudly sang, a thing which his natural shyness had never permitted him to do before; he had never been seen to weep, but now streams of tears ran down his handsome face. He was turned into a new man." Majumdar perhaps reluctantly attributed this amazing personal transformation to Bijoy Krishna Goswami, "the greatest leader of Vaishnavism in Bengal."[9] Protap Chandra, who spent much of his life weathering the storms of Keshub's "religious aberrations," asked in one book "why did Brahmos borrow the old-fashioned plebeian forms of Vaishnava music and musical appurtenances?" Though Majumdar never answered the question, his comments are revealing. After all, he tells us, Vaishnavas were "neither high socially," nor "distinguished by modern education." Moreover, they "were noted for grotesque personal habits, intense wild devotional excitement leading sometimes to inconveniences." Then on January 24, 1868, at the mandir consecration ceremony,

Majumdar reported that "Keshub held his Nagar Sankirtan with great flags inscribed with theistic mottoes. . . . Vaishnava kirtans had degenerated into mobbish assemblies and it required great moral courage and deep religious compulsion to be able to borrow and reform them."[10]

Two events, before and after the introduction of Vaishnavism into the Brahmo Samaj, are important in assessing Bijoy Krishna's influence over Keshub Sen. In early 1866, with the formation of the new Brahmo Samaj, Keshub, Bijoy Krishna, and Aghore Nath Gupta toured parts of East Bengal as missionaries of their Brahmo church. They went principally to Dacca, Faridpur (outside of Dacca), and Mymensingh. Their impact was instantaneous. When Keshub and Bijoy Krishna arrived in Dacca in late 1866, their presence led to a veritable explosion. Sivanath Sastri, for one, has described the sudden impact of the Keshubites in Dacca: "They set the district [Dacca] ablaze and young men were drawn to the movement dedicating themselves to reform. The Dacca Keshubites had abandoned idolatry, abolished caste, rescued young Hindu widows, and other young women from misery."[11]

There among the English-speaking intelligentsia, Keshub was the hero, though in Mymensingh, the first mofussil town in which Brahmos gained a foothold, it was Bijoy Krishna who won over the youths by effectively communicating with them. Evidently the Hindu fear of Brahmos in a town such as Mymensingh was especially irrational. Because of caste, for example, neither Keshub nor Bijoy was at first invited to anyone's house.[12] According to K. K. Mitra, Keshub lectured in Mymensingh purely in English,[13] although Girish Chandra Sen, also there at the time, claims that he lectured both in English and Bengali. But both agree that it was Bijoy Krishna who had the impact on the local people. He was invited to lecture at the Brahmo Samaj Hall on caste, social reform, and idolatry. At once, many high caste Brahmos, including a newspaper editor, school teachers, and government servants discarded their sacred threads and promised in public to carry out their Brahmo ideals in practice. One clue as to the seriousness of the situation is the fact that, very soon afterwards, leaders of Hindu orthodoxy formed a branch of the Calcutta Dharma Rakhini Sabha (Society to Preserve Hinduism), with the main purpose of persecuting Brahmos and their families.

In both Dacca and Mymensingh, mainly through Bijoy Krishna's efforts, the East Bengali Brahmos prevailed in establishing effective communities. The center of their activities was the mandir, and by

1869 the Dacca community had constructed the largest and most architecturally impressive Brahmo temple in all of South Asia up to that time. Meanwhile, Bijoy Krishna, after his success in Mymensingh, was invited by East Bengalis again and again for speeches, guidance, and inspiration. He was not only interested in towns, but traveled from village to village, "creating everywhere he went an unpredecented agitation and stirring up deep feelings in favor of the movement."[14] According to Girish Chandra Sen, "the people respected him greatly as he carried his own simple belongings and with touching humility traveled on foot from place to place." The success of Bijoy and its implications for the spread of Brahmoism was not lost to Keshub when Bijoy returned to Calcutta in 1867. The fusion of progressive Vaishnava tenets with Brahmoism seemed to appeal to a wide number of people. Would it not be a marvelous thing if the early spirit of Chaitanya could be revived under the banner of the Brahmo Samaj? Keshub himself would attempt what Bijoy had done. He tried, and it worked.

In June 1868, at the East India Railway junction town of Monghyr in Bihar, Keshub publicly assumed the pose of a Brahmo Chaitanya, but with disastrous results. Protap Majumdar has described the event with obvious misgivings. Bengali railway clerks sympathetic to Keshub came to hear him. The congregation was convened weekly to be inspired by the Brahmo leader, who spoke and acted like a Vaishnava saint. "They would often be moved to tears and sobs and ejaculations," wrote Majumdar, "that were well nigh hysterical."[15] Keshub "had the whole town in ferment." Then on June 7, as Sivanath Sastri later wrote with regret: "People prostrated themselves at the feet of Mr. Sen (and each other) and prayers were offered to him for intercession on behalf of sinners."[16] That incident was relayed from Bihar across India from east to west. Keshub's old friend Satyendranath Tagore, now a successful government official in Ahmedabad, wrote that "I see that Keshub has been made an avatar but I doubt whether Keshub himself countenances the folly of his disciples."[17] Protap Majumdar wrote: "Thus began a new apostolic organization. The abnormal excitement of emotions first began at Monghyr and understandably emasculated a good many unripe minds in Keshub's church."[18] The most interesting response was Bijoy Krishna's. The non-Westernized Goswami, whose only extant photograph shows a half nude Sadhu-posed Hindu in what appears to be a trance, pulled Keshub away from "superstition" back to rational Brahmo principles. He was angry with Keshub and those so-called Brahmos "who consider Keshub a savior." In one local Bengali newspaper he lashed out at people who tried to make Keshub "an incarnation of God." Wrote Bijoy: "It is against the principles of the Brahmos to call Keshub Babu the Savior, to pray to him for salvation, to kiss his feet, and to compose sacred songs in his name. It is the duty of Brahmos to revere Keshub as a human being. Brahmoism recognizes only God as the Savior. We request Keshub Babu to dissuade other Brahmos from this dangerous course."[19]

Keshub did precisely that, and by 1869 the rift between himself and Bijoy was healed. From then on, it appears that Keshub took care not to place himself in the position of a divinely inspired prophet of the mass mind. We can only assume that to Bijoy the ideological task was to purify Vaishnavism from abuses through Brahmo rationalism; it was not to derationalize and corrupt Brahmoism through plebeian bhakti. Thus on June 4, 1869, approximately one year after Monghyr, Keshub wrote a piece on the prophet of Nadia in which he tried to vindicate himself from the charges of avatarism and man-worship. "The Brahmo Samaj," he wrote, "will be forever indebted to the spirit of Chaitanya . . . his creed and character." But in "four short centuries," he went on to say, "we have witnessed the rise and decay of that . . . branch of Hinduism which is now in a degenerate condition." What follows, in view of Goswami's influence, is highly significant: "The Vaishnava church which had done wonders in its days will be renewed and reformed, and render valuable services to the course of Indian regeneration. While we sincerely regret that his [Chaitanya's] spirit has so soon passed from the vast majority of his followers . . . we cannot but speak with the utmost reverence and gratitude of him who achieved some of the highest religious and social reforms on effete Hinduism and whose true-hearted disciples are an honor to Hindustan."[20]

In the following years, Bijoy Krishna returned again and again to East Bengal, where the Brahmo Samaj had proliferated enormously since his first visit. Chiefly through his endeavors, the Bengal renaissance, which had been restricted for the most part to urbanized Calcutta, now spread to the municipal settlements of East Bengal. Wherever a Brahmo Samaj was established, there followed an institutional complex dedicated to social and religious reform. Whether in Mymensingh, Barisal, Chittagong, Comilla, or Sylhet, there was invariably the mandir or community prayer hall and meeting place, a girls' school and boys' school on various levels, possibly a college, a Sangat Sabha or discussion society for the youth, a charitable hospital, a library, a printing press for newspapers and tracts, a night school for workers and peasants, and a ladies' society.

The problem, if indeed it was considered such at that early period, was that Bijoy's blending of Vaishnavism and Brahmoism did not in fact awaken the masses—either Hindu or Muslim. There were exceptions, and Bijoy himself worked among low-caste villagers, but Brahmoism continued to appeal to the privileged few who had found elite status under British rule.

In 1878, after his split with Keshub, Bijoy Krishna joined the Sadharan Samaj as a missionary of the East and North Bengal areas, but almost ten years later, in 1886, the Executive Committee of the Sadharan Samaj brought charges against him for backsliding into Hinduism. They accused him of such malpractices as worshiping an image of Radha-Krishna in his Dacca sanctuary,[21] and of having joined the Kartabhaja sect of Vaishnavas which, though it did preach the brotherhood of man, seemed hardly distinguishable from similar groups within popular Hinduism.[22] In September of that year, Bijoy Krishna Goswami resigned his post as a Brahmo missionary.[23]

Bipin Chandra Pal, his most ardent disciple in the later years, has defended Bijoy Krishna as a modernist trying to infuse the Brahmo rational spirit into Vaishnavism. There seems to be no evidence from Bijoy Krishna himself in the last years to support this claim. Possibly as a spiritual guru—which is what he became— he was surrounded by worshipers who saw in him precisely what disciples had seen in Keshub during the Monghyr incident in 1868. Bipin Pal was aware of this, and he even defended the guru by attributing these excesses to the mass hysteria of the crowd, which "blurred the vision of the great and fundamental truths for which he stood."[24]

Perhaps the real fruit of B. K. Goswami's missionizing was a faction of Brahmos who stood by Keshub Sen in the schism of 1878, sustained the Nava Vidhan after Keshub's death in 1884, and constituted a remarkable group of ascetics known as the Durbar. They were among the earliest Vaishnava converts recruited on Brahmo mission tours. Inspired by a saintly ethic of religious reform and social service, it was they, incidentally, who performed the last rites for the famous mystic Ramakrishna, and who had provided Vivekananda and Brahmobandhab Upadhyay with a sense of purpose and direction when the two young men were experiencing the stress of confused identities. They had started as non-Westernized, rural, lower middle-class converts from the hinterland of Bengal, won over to Brahmoism by the neo-Vaishnava zeal of Bijoy Krishna. It was they who spread reformist ideology throughout the eastern Gangetic region in the manner and style of their champion. They originally insisted upon no salary nor any benefits whatever—following Bijoy's example, when Debendranath Tagore offered to pay him a stipend and the missionary angrily refused, treating the gesture as an insult.

Whether a missionary should be paid or not, and whether those in secular professions could do part-time mission work, were critical issues at the time. As early as 1865, when Keshub was still in the Adi Samaj, he had argued that Brahmo missionaries ought not to be paid, so that their life work would remain uncontaminated by worldly concerns. It was not Hindu ascetics whom he had in mind, but the reverse image of the resident Christian missionaries whom he considered to be corrupt, materialistic, and elitist. Keshub even advocated that "the word salary should be excluded altogether from the vocabulary of Brahmo mission work."[25]

After the formation of his own Brahmo organization, Keshub continued to pay verbal homage to the ascetic ideal of the missionary, but for others rather than himself. Neither his affluent style of life in Calcutta as a bhadralok nor his style of mission travel coincided in any way with the stern regime followed by Bijoy Krishna. Whenever he or Protap Majumdar traveled to remote parts of India, they did so in the comfort of the railway; and mingling with counterpart elites from Bombay or elsewhere, they were accommodated luxuriously. Thus, a growing dichotomy developed within Brahmo ranks between worldly ascetic Brahmos who openly employed their rational emancipation to live better materially, and the ascetic Brahmos, no less rational and reformist, but committed to a simple way of life that often denied their families even the barest material comforts.

By 1867, the ascetic group seems to have viewed themselves as the "new saints" of the Samaj, and they began advocating what they called the "Bijoy Krishna way of propagating the faith."[26] This advocacy converged with the Keshubite policy of trying to reach larger numbers of non-Westernized Bengalis who craved a new faith and identity. Not only was Keshub highly successful in proliferating Samajes throughout the eastern Gangetic region, but his very person was becoming popularized among Vaishnavas as the new Chaitanya. It was quite obvious that many of the new recruits into the Brahmo Samaj had not shed their Hinduism so easily to become emancipated Brahmos. And it was this very untutored group of rural Bengalis who formed the most zealous converts to the ascetic faction within the Samaj.

By 1868, practically every one of the sixty-five Samajes in eastern India were in the Keshubite camp.[27] Most of them were located in the mofussil towns of Bihar, East and North Bengal. While this proliferation helped to spread modernizing Calcutta ideas into the more rural areas, at the same time there was the real danger that the Brahmo Samaj would itself become mofussilized. In any event, in 1868 Keshub found himself with twenty-four missionaries, the overwhelming majority of whom were of the ascetic type. He agreed to regularize their duties by defining new functions and by offering "no salary but instead supplying their families with the necessaries of life."[28] In 1870, Keshub further routinized the organization by founding what he termed an "apostolic body of elders and teachers" in the form of Sri Durbar. In this manner, he gave the ascetics a representative body of their own, which in the course of time institutionalized their faction and gave them enormous power in deciding Brahmo policy.

From a Brahmo Mission Report of 1871, it seems fairly certain that Keshub had solved the salary and maintenance issue in a way that satisfied the ascetics. In the first place, the press had been put into the Brahmo Mission Office, and receipts from the sale of literature were used for feeding, clothing, and housing the missionaries and their families. Very important was the appointment of a manager responsible for implementing the new policy. Fortunately, Keshub found a good man named Kanty Chandra Mitra to fill the position. Born in 1838 in Nadia district, he was of the same generation as the Durbar people, and largely sympathetic to them. But he was not a missionary as much as an administrator who made certain the organization was operating smoothly and that mission dependents were content.[29] Mitra came to be known as the "Kaka Babu" of the entire Brahmo family community by looking after everything from marriage to funerals.[30] From 1876 he took care of Keshub's family as well.

The principal figures of the Durbar or ascetic brotherhood were of the generation born in the 1830s and early 1840s (see Table 3). At least half of them were from East Bengal: Girish Chandra and Hari Basu from Dacca district, Kalisankar Das from Mymensingh, and Gour Govinda Roy from Pabna. Of the West Bengalis, Mohendra Bose and Amrita Lal Bose were Calcutta-born, while

TABLE 3

Principal Ascetic Missionaries of the Sri Durbar

Name	Birthdate, birthplace	Caste	Religious orientation	Pre-Brahmo occupation	First exposure to Brahmoism
Girish C. Sen	1834 Dacca, East Bengal	Vaidya	Vaishnava	Clerk in judiciary	Bijoy Krishna lecture while student
Kalisanker Das	1837 Mymensingh, East Bengal	Kayastha	Vaishnava	Physician	Attracted to neo-Vaishnavism
Hari S. Basu	1839 Dacca, East Bengal	Kayastha	Vaishnava	Postal clerk	Attracted to Keshub Sen
Braj G. Niyogi	1857 Pubna, East Bengal	Kayastha	Vaishnava	Unemployed	Influenced by uncle, Hari S. Basu
Gour G. Ray	1841 Pubna, East Bengal	Vaidya	Vaishnava	Sub-inspector of police	Converted by Brahmo preaching
Aghore N. Gupta	1841 Santipur, West Bengal	Vaidya	Vaishnava	Unemployed intellectual in Calcutta	Influenced by Bijoy Krishna
Troilokya N. Sanyal	1840 Nadia, West Bengal	Brahman	Vaishnava	Actor in *jatra* shows	Influenced by Bijoy Krishna
Mohendra N. Bose	1838 Calcutta, West Bengal	Kayastha	Christian	Student at Duff's College	Influenced by Keshub Sen
Amrita L. Bose	1839 Calcutta, West Bengal	Kayastha	Vasihnava	Unknown	Influenced by Bijoy Krishna

SOURCE: Besides individual biographies referred to in footnotes, the principal general source is *The Apostles and the Missionaries of the Naba-bidhan*, compiled by N. Niyogy (Calcutta: The Brotherhood, 1923).

Sanyal and Gupta were from the vicinity of Santipur, the birthplace of Bijoy Krishna Goswami. Information on caste and religious orientation is no less interesting. Of the nine under consideration, five were Kayasthas, three were Vaidyas, and one was a Brahman. If we were to add the names of other members of the Durbar to make the list complete, the result would be a slight preponderance of Vaidyas, the caste into which Keshub himself was born. As for religious orientation, all but one of the eight were Vaishnavas. When we add the fact that virtually all these men were attracted to Brahmoism through contact with Bijoy Krishna, then the intriguing question about Vaishnava influence in the Brahmo Samaj would seem to be significant. Unfortunately, I have only been able to find sufficient early biographical material on five of the nine persons. Nevertheless, a review of the background of these people should establish a pattern that is probably suitable for the other lesser-known figures as well.

We shall begin with Girish Chandra Sen because he was the youngest of the lot, and because his obscurity has been breached somewhat by East Bengali Muslims who were, under Mujib ur Rahman, at the point of resurrecting his name as a cultural hero of Bangladesh. Why a Bengali Hindu should be chosen for this honor will become apparent enough when we treat his scholarly career as a Brahmo. Girish Sen was born in a Dacca village to a family who for generations were Persian-knowing officials in the Muslim administration. Sanskrit, Persian, and Bengali were the three languages Girish mastered as a boy. As for English and Western learning, he was sent to the famous Pagose School in Dacca City, but he proved unresponsive even when beaten on occasion by the headmaster. Indeed throughout his life, as Girish Chandra himself admitted, English made little or no impact on him.

Persian was the language he paid most attention to, and when he went to Mymensingh for his first job in 1853, it was as a Persian letter copyist that he was hired in a criminal court for Rs 16 a month. He evidently wore Persian style clothes to fit the position, and adopted superficial Muslim mannerisms. But he felt lonely and unhappy. Again Girish Chandra tried to learn English in order to advance himself, but again he failed. According to his own account, he became so frustrated that at nineteen years old he attempted suicide at least three times. He finally attended one of the newly created normal schools established by the government, largely through Vidyasagar's efforts, to train teachers in the Bengali medium. Sen wrote later that through "plodding and not intelligence he was able to score well in examinations and win a scholarship." It was in the environment of the school that Girish Chandra finally found some peace of mind by becoming exposed to Brahmoism and turning to social reform, which meant female education and improvement. Thus Girish Chandra imbibed Brahmo "sympathy for women," which led, among other things, to the establishment in his own village of a girls' school, which, he proudly boasted, lasted over forty years.

Some teachers in the school were Brahmos of the Tattvabodhini Sabha variety, and it was they who gave him his first "enlightening literature" to read. This included the work of Akkhoy Kumar Dutt, copies of the *Tattvabodhini Patrika*, and Debendranath's *Brahmo Dharma*. He even joined a reading and discussion club, which seems to have had the effect of introducing him to the excitement and creative achievements of the Calcutta renaissance. He was shocked, however, by the tendency of many Brahmos to violate the ethical norms of Akkhoy Kumar and Debendranath by drinking heavily in private.

Then in 1866 Keshub Sen and Bijoy Goswami arrived in Mymensingh. I have already referred to the excitement generated there among the younger generation by Bijoy Krishna, in particular. His most profound influence was in transferring the allegiance of local Brahmos from the Adi Samaj to Keshub. Girish Chandra joined the newly formed Keshubite group, and found himself promptly outcasted from Hindu society. Yet the experience helped him to find security and psychological well-being. He achieved an identity through the Brahmo Samaj and a modicum of respectability as a teacher in a local school. His new affiliation with the progressive Keshubites provided him with a cause, a clear-cut ideological commitment. Girish Chandra's house then became a refuge for other emancipated young men from East Bengal villages, whose Brahmo sentiments and activities had earned them alienation from family and society. From Sen, the young men could be certain of moral and financial support. To supplement his own meager income of Rs 20 per month as a teacher, Girish would go from door to door selling Brahmo literature.

By 1870, Sen seems to have given up his post as a teacher, and turned to full-time missionary work. Just why he decided to do so is not clear, but it is certain that he was undergoing an ascetic experience and had developed the notion—common in the Samaj at the time—that Brahmoism could only spread by the most dedicated type of saintly devotion. In 1872, he was invited to Calcutta to join the Bharat Ashram, as the new experiment in Brahmo community living was called. His task was to teach in the girls' school, but as a missionary he received no salary for the work, nor for his later job with the Brahmo journal, the *Sulabh Samachar*. For various reasons, including a disagreement with Keshub on female education and a feeling of disappointment with city life in Calcutta, Girish Chandra returned soon after to his native East Bengal.[31]

About the early life of Kalisanker Das, also of East Bengal and Girish Chandra's senior by three years, we know considerably less. Das was born in a Mymensingh village and received a traditional education in the local Sanskrit tol. As with Girish Sen, there is little trace of English educational influence. At an early age he turned to Ayurvedic medicine as a career, and presumably did well. Curiously enough, he was introduced to Brahmoism not by Bijoy Krishna directly but by Bijoy's brother, Srijakta Krishna Gaswami. Kalisankar was an obscure preacher-physician vaguely associated with the establishment of the Brahmo Samaj in Dinajpur. In 1877, a book of his on the *Seeds of Religious Knowledge* in Bengali came to the attention of the Calcutta Keshubites. Though written by a man who did not know English, the book was a sophisticated defense of progress through theism, as against false progress through Comtean positivism. In 1881, Kalisankar Das was invited to Calcutta as a member of the Durbar, and his membership was important for what he represented during the following years. In February 1884, when Protap Majumdar returned from England to find Keshub dead, it was Kalisankar Das who proved one of the "ringleaders" who barred this Westernized "Christian" from occupying the late prophet's pulpit. Not only did Kalisankar and other ascetics bar Majumdar from succeeding Keshub, but they ultimately drove him out of the organization.

A second interesting feature of Kalisankar's role and impact in the Brahmo Samaj was his Vaishnava leanings. Following in the footsteps of Bijoy Krishna, Kalisankar drew closer and closer to the Bengali Chaitanya tradition. The difference between the two men is that Kalisankar never deserted Keshub, nor did he ever resign from the Samaj. Bijoy did both. On the other hand, as the years passed after Keshub's death, members of the brotherhood or Durbar moved separately along paths of their own choosing, and several of them, including Kalisankar, may have become more Vaishnava than Brahmo. Kalisankar's biographer, for instance, refers to his later devotion to "Lord Hari," on whose behalf he would travel widely to join processions and sing songs of praise.[32]

Hari Sundar Basu was another East Bengali Kayastha with strong Vaishnava leanings. Like Girish Sen, he came from Dacca, but unlike either Sen or Kalisankar Das, he did acquire some knowledge of English with family encouragement. It was certainly sufficient to get him admitted into the postal service, at first in a minor position. Then in 1860 the government rewarded him for good working habits by making him Postmaster in Gaya, Bihar. His biographer maintains that Hari Sundar stopped in Calcutta on the way to Bihar, met Keshub Sen, and thirteen years later became a Brahmo in Gaya. He remained there the rest of his life, not always in government service, but always in the service of Brahmo social reform and the Vaishnava religion.

In terms of the questions asked originally, Hari Sundar Basu is important for representing that lower-middle-class type of Bengali who settled outside Bengal and helped build up new communities through a civic spirit generated by Keshubite Brahmoism. These were hardly elitist Bengalis with comfortable jobs in the services, but men with lesser positions in the railway or post office, or in one or another of innumerable clerical positions available to Bengalis with some mastery of English. It was this type—mostly railway clerks, it would appear—who worshiped Keshub in Monghyr and who supported the Durbar ascetics.

These men were often virtual pioneers of new modern communities throughout Bihar: Gaya, Ranchi, Giridih, Bhagalpur, and Hazaribagh. Besides Hari Sundar, the name of Braj Gopal Niyogi stands out as a devout Brahmo Vaishnava who worked tirelessly to build new schools, hospitals, clinics, community centers, cooperatives, libraries, night schools for workers, and orphanages. It is interesting that so many of these men were inclined to Vaishnavism as well as membership in the Durbar. Perhaps they drifted from Brahmoism back to Vaishnavism, or perhaps they merged the two in outbursts of ascetic devotion on behalf of social service. Hari Sundar, by no means atypical, actually began to promote Chaitanya's message in an annual festival dedicated to the medieval Bengali saint.[33]

Braj Gopal Niyogi deserves more than passing reference in this context, though he was born in 1857, thus representing a different generation. He was also born in Dacca, and like almost everyone discussed so far, his background was decidedly Vaishnava. In fact, his mother spent her widowed years in Brindaban and died there in 1882. He was not an exceptional student, nor very intellectual as an adolescent, since he actually failed in his attempt to get an F.A. from the General Assembly's Institution in 1877.

He went back to Gaya, the place where he was destined to find his "true calling." In 1887, "Bhakta" Hari Sundar Basu, the young man's maternal uncle, initiated Braj Gopal into the New Dispensation Church. From then on, Niyogi devoted himself to philanthropic activities of the most strenuous sort, activities that drew on precisely the kind of spirit necessary to pioneer the new Bengali communities in Bihar. Braj Gopal's son, who wrote the most comprehensive biography of his father, attributes this philanthropic spirit to "the sweet Vaishnava piety and fervent mysticism of Hari

Sundar mingling with his own passion for human benevolence. . . .
Deeper experiences of the spirit opened up before him and he
tried to transmit the life around him into reflections of his own
internal goodness. And daily he persisted in his path of sadhan or
service through an arduous discipline."

Niyogi became an active member of the Durbar and spent some
time in Calcutta working on committees and generally advancing
the objectives of the Brotherhood. According to his son, though he
shared his colleagues' view of Protap Majumdar, he was far more
"flexible-minded" than they, and worked hard to reconcile differences with the Unitarian faction for the sake of the church. In
1901, Braj Gopal came close to achieving some unity when he arranged that the two groups congregate to pray together. The attempt was a failure, however, ostensibly because the Brotherhood
objected to Majumdar's growing number of Christian practices. As
noted previously, Majumdar opposed the influence of Vaishnavism
in the Brahmo Samaj, and we may recall that in his published diary
of a world tour, he disparagingly compared Vaishnava practices
with those of the American Negroes. Here was the line on which
the church divided. Braj Gopal, for example, during his mission
tours, dressed in the garb of a Vaishnava, and proclaimed himself
as a "beloved of God" seeking harmony and the brotherhood of
man with the "sweet piety" of Chaitanya.[34]

Another East Bengali, who after Keshub's death became the
most conspicuous member of the Durbar, its "pope," in fact, was
Gour Govinda Ray. From a Vaidya family in a village of Pabna
district, Gour Govinda seems to have been relatively well-educated
in Western learning, even to the point of mastering English at
Rangpur High School. Fitting the pattern already established, Ray
was brought up by an uncle who was a "devoted Vaishnava
scholar," and from whom it is said he acquired two virtues maintained throughout life: an intense love of learning and an intense
belief in the equality of all men under God.

Occupationally, however, like most other Durbar people, Ray
was lower middle-class, having attained for himself the rather
modest position as subinspector of police in a mofussil area. Gour
Govinda was more intellectual than most, and had actually passed
the entrance examination for Calcutta University while at Rangpur
High School. But this young man with a good grasp of English and
the potential for college work neither pursued English for its own
sake nor ever went on to the university. As a Brahmo scholar later
on, he wrote his major works in Sanskrit, which he learned infor-

mally rather than in school. It was in 1866, at the time of the formation of Keshub's Brahmo Samaj, that Gour Govinda Ray officially joined the movement. His conversion is attributed to the preaching of Aghore Nath Gupta in Rangpur and to Keshub's Brahmo tracts. He was twenty-five when he came to Calcutta to join the Sangat Sabha with men younger than himself, and to sit at the feet of Keshub. Keshub remembered him as a good listener with a deep and penetrating look in his eyes, and he felt that Ray had a subtle, intelligent mind.

As anecdotes of those early days intimate, Gour Govinda was a confirmed cultural nationalist. Though from the early days a Brahmo rationalist and reformer, he did not find sympathy with vague universalist sentiments. Once during a discussion on the "Great Prophets" led by Keshub, Jesus was referred to (possibly by Majumdar) as the king of prophets. Gour Govinda promptly rejected the argument and proceeded to show that the message of Christ was an "old conception" found in "our Hindu Sastras." Under Keshub's direction, Ray developed enormous self-discipline which, coupled with his thirst for knowledge and ascetic habits, made his contemporaries acknowledge him the most formidable intellectual personality in the Durbar. It appears likely that from the late 1860s, much of the responsibility for using Sanskrit literature in the service of the Brahmo Samaj was placed on Ray's shoulders. It was he who did the Sanskrit portions for the collection of theistic texts known as the *Sloka Sangraho*, and it was he who for forty years edited the official Bengali newspaper of the Samaj, the *Dharmatattva*. Though after 1872 he lived in the Bharat Ashram with his wife and family, he was generally pictured as the ascetic intellectual who worked on his newspaper, books, and manuscripts fifteen hours a day, saying proudly all the while that he was a "slave to his work." And in the spirit of the Brahmo missionaries, he never accepted a salary for his laborious undertakings.[35]

Unfortunately, our background information on the principal Durbar missionaries of West Bengal is, with one exception, rather sketchy. Aghore Nath Gupta, the exception, was from a Vaidya family. Again, Bijoy Krishna convinced him to become a Brahmo. In fact, similar locality seems to be important in this case, since both he and Goswami came from Santipur, in the heart of the Chaitanya-Vaishnava country. Educationally, Aghore Nath was the product of a neighborhood Sanskrit tol. His youth and adolescence are interesting for typifying the experience of many young men who joined the Brahmo Samaj at about the time Keshub did, and who then supported Keshub's protest and rebellion against the old-guard leadership. In 1853, at twelve years of age, Aghore Nath lost his father, and being a member of a large family of eight children, he watched helplessly as his widowed mother tried to make ends meet. But despite her efforts, the family only sank deeper and deeper into poverty. Evidently his family condition as a youth made him an ascetic in his disciplined habits and simplicity of clothes, food, and general physical demeanor.

In 1859, approximately six years after his father's death, we find Aghore Nath, like Bijoy Krishna before him, a hungry adolescent roaming the streets of north Calcutta in search of food, money, and an identity. Through Bijoy Krishna's help, he met Debendranath Tagore and was given the opportunity to attend classes at Sanskrit College. And like Bijoy, he never got a degree but became a "Brahmo preacher" instead. Again, in the pattern of most other Brahmo recruits of his type and generation who were originally assisted by Debendranath, it was Keshub Sen whom they followed, achieving in the process a new community identity in the Brahmo Samaj. Indeed, in the years of growing disaffection with Debendranath's leadership, Aghore Nath and Bijoy Krishna were the ringleaders, as it were, of the younger progressives.

Gupta and Goswami, though not among the Western-educated, were nevertheless ardent rationalists and supporters of social reform—particulary in matters pertaining to women's rights. It should come as no surprise, therefore, that it was the faction of young ascetic progressives that precipitated the event in 1865 which touched off the final schism. In that year, the Keshubites married off Aghore Nath Gupta, a Vaidya, to a Kayastha girl who happened also to have been a widow. Not only did this marriage spark extreme dissension within Brahmo ranks, but it sparked similar marriages, ultimately compelling Keshub to confront the consequent, troublesome fact that in the eyes of the government neither Brahmo marriages nor the offspring of such marriages were legally recognized.

It was rural Bengal that Aghore Nath visited frequently as a missionary. He and Bijoy Krishna shared east and north Bengal between them for many years. Aghore Nath was evidently effective among the Bengali settlers of Bihar and accompanied Keshub on that ill-fated Vaishnava revivalist tour of Monghyr in 1868. A year later, Aghore Nath went on foot to Assam, where he became the first Brahmo to preach in Gauhati. To indicate the amazing pace and mobility of ascetic preachers like Aghore Nath, he returned in early 1870 to Bengal by way of Mymensingh to reinforce Bijoy Krishna's work there.[36] Then, after a brief stay in Calcutta, he went out again to Bihar.

Of Troilokya Nath Sanyal's early years we know virtually nothing save that he too was born in the Chaitanya country of Nadia, that he was strongly Vaishnava religiously, and that before becoming a Brahmo, he lived as a wandering musician and actor in jatra (folk theater) performances. He was won over to Brahmoism by the dual efforts of Bijoy Krishna and Aghore Nath during one of their tours of North Bengal.[37] Most likely, the event occurred in Dinajpur sometime in 1866.

Keshub made use of Sanyal's talents by appointing him chief musician and composer for the Samaj. The kirtan, sangit, and street processions that we have already noted as an accepted part of the Brahmo devotional pattern in 1867 were largely the work of Sanyal.[38] In 1868, when the foundation stone of the Keshubite mandir was laid, Sanyal composed a sangit for the occasion. It is perhaps the earliest clear document of how the ideals of Vaishnavism were being combined with those of Brahmoism. This was the year, we may recall, when Keshub had moved precariously close to resurrecting Chaitanya in his own image. The song begins with the announcement that because a religious movement has started, "at last the night of sorrow has ended and God's name rises in the city." Wrote Sanyal, "God in His mercy has sent this new gospel, the Brahmo Faith, to save all men." The remainder of the song, which deserves to be quoted in full, contains that blend of Vaishnavism and Brahmoism characterized by an outspoken belief in social equality:

> The gates of salvation are thrown open!
> And each one is called,
> Rich and poor,
> Learned and ignorant;
> All men and women have equal rights,
> For whosoever loves God shall be saved,
> Nor shall caste be a bar.[39]

Through hundreds of such songs, Sanyal created a new art form for Bengal known as the Brahmo sangit. Rabindranath Tagore, also a Brahmo, later brought this musical art to its perfection, and through him and his songs, middle-class Bengali Hindu society accepted it as their own—though by dropping off Brahmo and calling these songs Rabindra sangit. Their importance, which Sanyal realized under Keshub's inspiration, was that they conveyed the ideology of Brahmoism directly and simply through the ears of people accustomed to the Vaishnava kirtan.

Besides Sanyal, of whose early formative years we know comparatively little, there were two other principal types from West Bengal, of whom we know even less. Amrita Lal Bose and Mohendranath Bose were both Kayasthas born in or around Calcutta, just a year apart from one another. But there the similarity ends.

Amrita Lal Bose, when he joined the Brahmo Samaj, placed himself in the faction of Bijoy Krishna, which meant that he was Vaishnava-oriented. Like most others, he appears to have traveled considerably as a missionary. What seemingly distinguished Amrita Lal from the others, and perhaps constituted his most important function in the Samaj, was his practicality and workmanship. For example, in 1868, when the foundation for the new mandir was laid, whereas Keshub conducted the services, Troilokya Nath composed the songs, and most of the others constituted the congregation, Amrita Lal was placed in charge of actually building the mandir, "working on it as a mason." After its completion, Amrita Lal was personally responsible for the church's upkeep and maintenance.

It is noteworthy that the practical few who maintained and managed Brahmo institutions for Keshub were members of the ascetic missionary group. We have already referred to Kanti Chandra Mitra's role in the organization, which included management of the important Brahmo Mission Press. A second figure of the managerial type was Umma Nath Gupta, who among other things administered the Bharat Ashram. Amrita Lal Bose was in charge of the technical department of the Indian Reform Association, and was director of Keshub's hostel for college students known as the Niketan.

Mohendranath Bose, who in his early life was far closer to Protap Majumdar than the men of the Brotherhood, was an intriguing personality who appears to have undergone a radical transformation at a critical time of his life. The little information I have about him suggests someone strikingly different in early background and training from Amrita Lal and most other ascetics. In the first place, he had a fine education along Western lines in Duff's School, with the result that he developed a critical mind and was fluent in English.[40] Second, he came near to Trinitarian Christian conversion, but was apparently dissuaded from taking the plunge by Deben-

dranath Tagore and Keshub Sen. Though he drew away from
Trinitarianism, he retained for some years his sympathy for the
gospel of Christ. His assimilation to Western values and attitudes,
and his knowledge of the Judeo-Christian heritage probably accounts for his sympathy.

Then in the 1870s, as Keshub himself changed, Mohendra Nath
Bose developed a wider and deeper interest in indigenous
prophets of South Asia. His sophisticated Europeanism made him
an excellent choice as missionary to Western India, and he actually
followed in P. C. Majumdar's footsteps in Bombay in 1874 and
1875. He was apparently well received for his progressive views.[41]
As he traveled about, Christ interested him less, whereas a reformer like Guru Nanak, the founder of Sikhism, appealed to him
more.

There were others we have not had the space to mention who
were no less devoted in their task of propagating the message of
theistic reform. Most of them seem to fit this curious blend of
Vaishnava piety and Brahmo progressivism. Someone like Dinanath Majumdar, also a Vaishnava from Nadia, proved an effective
missionary in Bihar.[42] Fakirdas Ray, though of the following
generation (born in 1853),[43] was still another inspired *sankirtan*
type in Keshub's service. In this manner, through the zeal and determination of these inspired ascetic missionaries of Keshub, the
hinterlands of Bengal opened to a trickle of new ideas and possibilities for change.

Though the Sadharan Brahmo Samaj, formed in opposition to
Keshub Sen, appears to have been dominated by Unitarian-like social reformers, political liberals, and neo-Vedantists, the fact is that
Vaishnavism also had its adherents within this association, which
included key members of the Western-educated intelligentsia. One
explanation is that Bijoy Krishna Goswami was among the founders of the Sadharan Samaj. Another factor was the growing
Brahmo "scholasticism," secularism, and politicization discussed
elsewhere, which left a spiritual vacuum for the congregation.
Thus, attempts at a Vaishnava-inspired synthesis in the Sadharan
Samaj were related to the need for piety and devotion as integral
parts of their religious identity.

Perhaps no other Sadharan better represents the multiple identities of political reformer, Unitarian Brahmo, and Vaishnava
bhakto than the fiery "Luther-like missionary," Nagendra Nath
Chatterji. Like Sivanath Sastri, he reconciled religion and politics,

thus appealing to the younger generation who were increasingly disenchanted with the tyranny of British imperial rule. Like Sastri a child of Brahman pandits, he was born in October 1843, in a village of Barisal District, East Bengal. The family moved from there to Hugli District, West Bengal, where the boy was enrolled at the Collegiate School of Chinsura. Nagendra Nath's father was evidently not orthodox, but on the contrary he was sympathetic to Brahmo monotheism through contact with the family of Debendranath Tagore. Indeed, it was Nagendra Nath's uncle (his father's younger brother), Ramanath Saraswati, who was one of the four pandits sent by Debendranath Tagore to Benares in 1845 to ascertain whether or not the Vedanta was a revealed source of the Hindu faith.

In 1850 or 1851, Nagendra was sent to a school in which an uncle of his taught in Tollygunge, then a suburb of Calcutta. His earliest Brahmo contact began a few years afterwards when he and some classmates attended services in nearby Behala. Then in 1858, Nagendra Nath participated in Brahmo activities and actually visited the house of Debendranath Tagore in Jorasanko. Such close involvement with Brahmos evidently did not sit well with the Chatterji family, for his guardian in Calcutta drove the young man from his house. Nagendra turned to Debendranath for help, and Tagore supported him financially. In fact, he was one of the first students enrolled in the experimental theological school established in 1859 by Debendranath and Keshub Sen. In 1861, with a certificate in hand, Nagendra Nath was appointed minister of the Krishnagar Brahmo Samaj. Because of the young man's eagerness to continue his education along Western lines, Nagendra Nath entered Krishnagar College in 1862. At Krishnagar, he moved in the circle of liberal and radical reformers led by the famous Brahmo sympathizer, Ramtanu Lahiri. Sivanath Sastri's friend, Umesh Chandra Dutt, was another conspicuous member of the group. It seems likely that from these progressives at Krishnagar, Nagendra Nath acquired both the rationale and enthusiasm for social activism. To the younger generation of the 1860s, especially among students at Krishnagar and elsewhere, religious change had to be accompanied by social reform. Thus, young Nagendra Nath participated in organizations that were openly antithetical to such malpractices as child marriage and the harsh treatment of widows. Once he arranged a widow marriage in Krishnagar, bringing Keshub Sen from Calcutta to officiate. He also worked as a nurse in the local hospital.

The year 1864 seems to have been a difficult one for Nagendra
Nath. He was twenty-one when he took his F.A. examination and
failed it, ending his student career forever. He underwent some
sort of mental agony as he became more radically involved in social
action. Then, in one of the most important gestures of his life, he
renounced his sacred thread, an act that naturally alienated him
from his family completely. When he returned to Calcutta years
later, as a Keshubite Brahmo, he had become a radical foe of orthodox Hinduism. At the Brahmo Bharat Ashram, where he went
to live in 1872, Nagendra Nath began to side with Sastri's progressive faction against Keshub. His own devout yet rational form of
Brahmoism also endeared him to the neo-Vaishnava leader, Bijoy
Krishna Goswami. Meanwhile, differences with Keshub sharpened
as the latter, obsessed with comparative religion at the expense of
the social gospel, drew closer to the ascetic faction. For a while
Nagendra Nath seems to have left Keshub and Calcutta in 1874 to
live in his native village as a poor recluse.

At this time, when he may have actually given up the Brahmo
Samaj, he seems to have represented a type of Brahmo without a
profession, who offered his intellectual and spiritual knowledge to
Brahmo friends and colleagues willing to subsidize or patronize
him. Like Sivanath Sastri, Nagendra Nath Chatterji was from a
learned Brahman family with a certain religious aura and moral
self-image. Nevertheless, Chatterji no less than Sastri did engage in
secular activities that had to be reconciled with religious devotion
and ministerial duties. When Nagendra Nath reappeared in Calcutta in 1876, his reason was political. In that year, a number of
young Brahmos had formed the Indian Association, a precursor of
the Indian National Congress. Nagendra Nath joined the group,
and in 1877 accompanied Surendra Nath Bannerji on a political
tour of India to win financial and moral support for the association's program.

In 1878, he joined the critics of Keshub Sen and became an enthusiastic founder of the Sadharan Brahmo Samaj. To defend the
Sadharan position as representative of the pure Brahmo faith,
Nagendra Nath brought out a biography of Rammohun Roy,
which portrayed the founder of Brahmoism as a spokesman of rational religion and social reform. Leading Adi Brahmos such as
Debendranath Tagore and Rajnarian Bose supported the project
and the interpretation. It was Nagendra Nath who reinforced the
Sadharan claim to authenticity by establishing a direct link with

pre-Keshubite Brahmo doctrine through a yearly Rammohun Roy memorial meeting. The popular biography, which went through four editions by 1909, was originally financed completely by Debendranath Tagore. From the 1880s to his death in 1913, Nagendra Nath remained the nonprofessional activist and politicized Brahmo missionary. He never accepted a salary for his work, preferring instead to live on charity. He saw himself primarily as a preacher or missionary of the Brahmo faith. Once (between 1881 and 1883), as a favor to Ananda Mohun Bose, he taught in the Brahmo City School. But secular jobs did not interest him. Presumably, his devotion to religion and ascetic style earned him respect from other Brahmos and contributed to his effectiveness as a missionary.[44]

Whether his was a typical and traditional form of Hindu ascetic behavior for a religious cause it is difficult to say. That Chatterji remained a critic of orthodox Hinduism there is little doubt. One has only to refer to his three volumes called *Dharma Jigasa* (Questions of Religion), collected debates against the Hindu revivalists, to appreciate his lifelong adherence to Brahmo precepts. Moreover, like Sastri he was a devoted follower of Theodore Parker's rational Unitarianism. He was one of the organizers of the American's seventieth anniversary celebration at the Sadharan Samaj in 1880.[45] In 1885, he wrote a Bengali biography of Parker in which he accurately captured the social gospel of liberal Unitarianism and strongly identified himself with it.[46]

There is, however, a Vaishnava religious development in Brahmo devotees like Chatterji that seems to run counter to their rationalist posture. Under the influence of Bijoy Krishna Goswami, Nagendra Nath turned to neo-Vaishnavism and flirted openly with a Hindu egalitarian sect known as Kartabhaja. Although Bijoy Krishna and some other Brahmos were initiated into the sect by its guru, Jagat Chandra Sen, as early as 1881, there is no evidence that Nagendra Nath was swept away by the emotional appeal of this charismatic leader or his religious sect. He remained a Brahmo missionary until his death.

Another Sadharan of the intensely religious sort of Brahmo who was also initiated into the Kartabhaja movement was Umesh Chandra Dutt. Born 1840, in the same village as Sivanath Sastri, Dutt's early educational background was partly Bengali in a pathsala, and partly English in a missionary school. While he was at the pathsala, a Brahmo teacher introduced him to Brahmoism through the lectures of Rajnarian Bose, and the works of the rationalist, Akkhoy Kumar Dutt, constituted a second important early Brahmo influence.

Umesh Chandra experienced a great misfortune when his father died early in life leaving the family virtually penniless. When Dutt came to Calcutta in 1859, he was yet another of those poverty-stricken young intellectuals surviving as best they could in the lonely city.[47] In search of an identity, he too joined the Brahmo Samaj and was one of Keshub's young enthusiasts.[48] As with Nagendra Nath Chatterji, Umesh Chandra Dutt could not succeed as a college student. Dutt made the effort at Medical College in 1861, failed, and later blamed the poor results on his eyesight and general physical disability. He met Bijoy Krishna Goswami at Medical College, and in those days they were both Keshub's men. In the decade of the 1860s, Umesh Chandra joined the pro-Vaishnava faction under Bijoy Krishna. Though Umesh Chandra failed in college, he seems to have had the aptitude and the enthusiasm to teach children. From 1867 to 1870, he lived in his native village and taught the rudiments of Western learning in a Brahmo school. This was the time when Brahmo schools and other benevolent institutions were proliferating in the rural areas outside Calcutta. Though not a scholar by any means, Dutt convinced himself and others that he could make his best contribution to the Samaj as a pedagogue. In 1870, after three years of teaching, Dutt was offered a position as headmaster of the Konnagar School for boys by a fellow Brahmo, Shib Chandra Deb. There he labored for the next four years, establishing a reputation for integrity and selflessness.

In the controversy of the 1870s between Keshub and the progressive faction, Umesh Chandra stood with Sastri against Keshub. Here was a case where common locality and friendship reinforced ideological conviction. Not only had Dutt been friendly with Sastri for years because both came from the same village, but he was also very close to Sastri's uncle, Vidyabhusan. Such was Vidyabhusan's fondness for Dutt that when Sastri's family turned against the Brahmo Samaj in 1868, Dutt had come forward as Sastri's intermediary to Vidyabhusan. In this role he ardently defended the Brahmos.

In 1878, at the time of the schism, Dutt was teaching in the Bethune School for girls in Calcutta, a position he very likely owed to the institution's Brahmo secretary, Manomohun Ghose. It was also the only job he ever had outside the Brahmo organization. The next year, when the famous Brahmo nationalist Ananda Mohun

Bose opened the City School, Umesh Chandra was given a teaching post. In 1881, the Brahmos had managed to transform the school into a college, in an effort to reach poorer students in Calcutta who could not afford the tuition of the university. Dutt was appointed professor of English literature, thus beginning a rather peculiar episode in his life, when it is considered that he was never able to speak the language fluently.[49] In 1884, when Calcutta University recognized City College as a respectable affiliate institution of higher learning, Dutt was made its first principal.[50] He served in this administrative position until his retirement in 1900. In interviews with followers of Keshub Sen today, I have been told that Umesh Dutt was a "salaried dependent" of the powerful faction leader, Ananda Mohun Bose. These Brahmos single out Umesh Chandra as an example of a petty bureaucrat, common among Sadharan Samajists, who had abandoned religion in favor of a secular profession. Under Keshub's leadership, so they argue, the secular world was kept outside the sacred world of the Brahmo institution. But with the establishment of the Sadharan Samaj, the floodgates were opened to secular intrusion, because the leading Sadharans with money had allegedly abandoned theism for professionalism and politics. Dependent intellectuals like Umesh Dutt supposedly did the dirty work of secularizing the new church.

In 1878, when the first officers of the Sadharan Samaj were elected, Ananda Mohun Bose became president and Dutt became assistant secretary. Under Shib Chandra Deb's presidency in 1881, 1882, and 1884, Dutt also served as secretary. After two more years of this, 1889 and 1890, under Bose's presidency, Dutt was himself elected president in 1891 and 1892. These facts show that Dutt was a key figure in Bose's faction, and also that he was among the active administrators in Brahmo affairs.

But on closer examination, throughout this period Dutt was hardly what he appeared to be on the surface. Keshubites may be quite right in asserting that a certain degree of religious enthusiasm disappeared from the Brahmo Samaj under the Sadharans, but curiously enough, one of the people searching outside the movement for it was Dutt. Like Nagendra Nath Chatterji, Dutt attended the spiritual meetings of Kartabhaja, which he evidently found satisfying. Sitanath Tattvabhusan, who knew Dutt as a colleague at City College, says of him that he was one of the "most ascetic personalities in the Samaj." For four months of every year, Umesh Chandra would observe a "period of purity" in which he abstained from all indulgences, including sex and rich Bengali food. He would stay at the college, where he shared a room with a mendicant friend of his in austere, ascetic style, and together they would perform yoga.

As for religious performance, Umesh Chandra leaned to Vaishnavism with all its ecstatic emotionalism. It was he who led processional songs within the Samaj during festivals. The rationalism of Unitarian-style Brahmo worship left him unsatisfied emotionally, and according to one source, when kirtans or Vaishnava lyrics were being sung Umesh Chandra would dance in the traditional manner of the sixteenth-century saint, Chaitanya. When one adds Kartabhaja to his religious activities, it would appear that he had more in common with some of the Keshubite ascetics than with the Westernized and secularized Sadharan Samajists. But like Nagendra Nath Chatterji, he was never overwhelmed by the Kartabhaja experience, remaining a "good" Brahmo until his death in 1907. Debendranath Tagore pronounced him a "saintly Brahmo," probably referring to his ascetic way of life. Yet, ironically, however much Umesh Chandra rejected the cold intellectual Unitarian path, he revered the American Unitarian missionary in Calcutta, Charles Dall. Like all Sadharans, Dutt accepted the Unitarian social gospel, supported Dall's social service activities, and worked hard to provide educational facilities for the poor and the handicapped.[51]

Not all Sadharan Brahmos with Vaishnava leanings were as successful as Chatterji and Dutt in accommodating their multiple identities within the larger Brahmo framework. Even Bijoy Krishna, who had led the way in formulating a Vaishnava-inspired synthesis, had himself resigned from Brahmoism to found his own neo-bhakti movement. The life and career of Tara Kishore Chaudhury, founder of the Sadharan Samaj in Sylhet, illustrates vividly how difficult it was for a Western-educated professional with deep piety and devotion to endure the painful process of reconciling conflicting identities as a Brahmo. Born in 1859 of a zamindari family, young Chaudhury was well educated in both Bengali and English. When his parents later sent him to study in Presidency College, Calcutta, Chaudhury lived with two fellow students from Sylhet: Bipin Chandra Pal and Sundari Mohun Das. As it turned out, his two friends were Brahmos, and under their influence young Tara Kishore became one also. As was the pattern, his father immediately cut off his monthly allowance, reducing the young man's style of life to poverty. But again according to the pattern, this act of parental displeasure only reinforced the youth's desire to succeed on his own. With Brahmo help, he moved from expensive Presidency

College to the cheaper Metropolitan College, where he did bril-
liantly in chemistry. It was after receiving his degree in the mid-
1870s that the familiar personality crisis occurred. It was severe
enough in his case to have caused at least one suicide attempt. The
Brahmo leader Ananda Mohun Bose and his Student Association
for East Bengalis saved Tara Kishore's life. Bose, himself from East
Bengal, made Chaudhury a teacher in the Brahmo City School in
1879, and then elevated him to the post of professor at City College
two years later. This form of patronage quite naturally put
Chaudhury in Bose's faction within the Sadharan Samaj, as well as
in Samaj-related organizations dominated by Bose, such as the Indian Association.

In the early 1880s Tara Kishore was a rationalist and a politicized
Sadharan Brahmo of the Bose faction who effectively promoted
this ideal in East Bengal—particularly in his native district of
Sylhet. It was Chaudhury who persuaded Bipin Pal to return to
Sylhet to preach Brahmoism both as a rational religion and as a
movement congenial to political aspirations. As a follower of Bose,
Chaudhury also pursued professional ends, and in 1884 he went to
law school. Four years later, he became an advocate of the Calcutta
High Court. Although it would appear that Chaudhury was very
much the secularized bhadralok Sadharan Brahmo, on further
analysis one finds in him the same ambivalence about secularism
and religious enthusiasm as with other Sadharan Samajists. Tara
Kishore was not only attracted to the Vaishnava faction of Bijoy
Krishna and Umesh Dutt, but actually allowed himself to be initiated into the Kartabhaja sect by their charismatic guru. Unlike his
fellow Brahmos, however, Chaudhury could not reconcile Brahmo
modernism with his need for religious emotion. Again he experienced a crisis that led ultimately to a break with his Brahmo
friends, ideals, and associations. Like Bijoy Krishna, he appears to
have returned to the Hindu fold as a neo-Vaishnava. Indeed, Tara
Kishore Chaudhury, who did so much to spread Sadharan
Brahmoism in Sylhet, was the same man who started the Sylhet
Hindu Sabha, primarily to combat the very influence he himself
had initiated.[52]

Though Chaudhury's case is by no means atypical among the intelligentsia at the turn of the century, when countless younger
bhadralok surrendered their new liberal identity for the security of
Hindu revival, among Brahmos such defections were still rare. In
general, the synthesis between liberal rationalism and the Vaishnava bhakti tradition survived in the reformist mold of

Brahmoism—in spite of Bijoy Krishna's defection. Not only did it survive, but it flourished as a source of inspiration to Brahmo missionaries such as Sivanath Sastri, Bipin Chandra Pal, Hem Chandra Sarkar, and Nilmani Chakrabarti. In fact, as with the Keshubite Durbar years earlier, the progressive spirit of Brahmoism was disseminated beyond Bengal by missionaries concerned essentially with matters of the spirit. As we shall see in the final chapter, it was Brahmo theism modified by a modern perspective—and not the English language—which was crucial to the spread of the Bengal renaissance and reformation to the rest of India.

CHAPTER NINE

World Crisis and the Quest for an Ideology of Salvation: Keshub, Prophet of Harmony

THE name of Keshub Chandra Sen has appeared in almost every chapter of this book. He has appeared as Unitarian Christian, scientist of religion, liberal social reformer, universalist, and one of the earliest exponents of neo-Vaishnavism. Through others who interacted with him at various crucial episodes in his Brahmo career, we have observed him shifting his identity continually. In 1866, he was an ardent champion of constitutionalism against Debendranath, but in 1878 he defended authoritarian rule against the constitutionalists in his own Samaj. In 1870, he started the Indian Reform Association, which was the most radical experiment of its kind up to that time, but several years later he repudiated social reform for quietism and the study of comparative religion. For years he was a tireless champion of women's emancipation, but suddenly he shifted his ground and advocated gradualism along with other conservatives.

The charisma of Keshub seems to have persisted even after the schism of 1878. Debendranath Tagore wrote in 1881 that, "whether it be in praise of him or in blame, men cannot drink their daily drop of water without talking Keshub's name."[1] Of all the obituary notices of prominent Indians known in Western Europe throughout the nineteenth century, probably none gave more extensive coverage than that of Keshub's death on January 8, 1884. The foreign press, representing liberal theologians, orthodox Christians, and secular journalists, could not agree among themselves as to what this stormy controversial figure had aimed to do or what actual impact he had on Hindu religion and society. The English missionary press, which had followed his ideological meanderings over twenty years first with hope and joy, later with consternation and despair, sadly reviewed the reformer's career from one most likely to succeed as the Luther of Hinduism in 1866 to his slow but sure return to the Hindu fold by 1881. Most Unitarians hailed Keshub as one of their own, tracing the influence of Emerson, Parker, Cobbe, and others on his theology, while at the same time they were willing to overlook the embarrassing Cooch Behar marriage and the inconsistencies in his social reform program. The secular press, which recalled his smashing impression on Englishmen during a brief visit to Britain in 1870, remained enamored of his charm and sincerity of purpose, pronouncing him a "Nanak of modern India."[2]

Among Brahmos, since his death, Keshub's image has remained consistently controversial. His own intellectual disciples, whose numbers thinned with each passing decade in the twentieth century, have kept his name and achievements alive in periodic bursts of eulogistic exuberance.[3] His critics, far more numerous and vocal, have been equally enthusiastic in questioning Keshub's sincerity of purpose and intellectual competence.[4] His ideological quest for a universal religion, which his proponents looked upon as the most profound synthesis of East and West yet conceived by any living being, was lampooned by critics as a hodgepodge of culturally discordant religious elements held together by the elastic band of a highly personal mystical vision. Moreover, so his critics have charged, by accepting British rule as providential and by remaining loyal to Queen Victoria, whom he had met in 1870, Keshub committed the unpardonable sin of turning his back on the Indian freedom movement.[5]

In the historiography of the Bengal renaissance, which deals primarily with the Hindu quest for identity during the intercivilizational encounter under British dominance, Keshub's image is again confusing and controversial. His antagonists have reviled him simultaneously as "Jesus-lover," revivalist-follower of Ramakrishna, tool of British imperial bureaucrats, false prophet, and self-seeking hypocrite and opportunist. Among those more sympathetic, such as Rabindranath Tagore in his postnationalist phase, Keshub was seen as a profound scholar of world religions and a sincere believer in universal harmony.[6] Others, such as Bipin Chandra Pal, have found in Keshub's writings the seeds of Indian nationalism.[7]

In fact, the most interesting historiographical feature of the Keshub question is not the controversial aspect, with its immense literature of uncritical acceptance or rejection, but that Keshub has come to mean all things to all men. It is ironic that the real giants of the Bengal renaissance were neither simplistic Westernizers nor traditionalists, but highly sophisticated cosmopolites with subtle, eclectic intellects. The difficulty is that prevailing explanations for the ideological fruits of intercivilizational encounter have been too narrowly confined within the framework of Westernizer-nativist response among the intelligentsia. It is assumed that either a man identified with the West (and was thus rationalist and modernist), or he identified with his own cultural heritage (and was thus traditionalist or orthodox).[8] In this confining conceptual scheme, if a Keshub turned to the New Dispensation or a Rabindranath to universal humanism, both ideological developments were ultimately dismissed as mystical abberrations. Nevertheless, they constitute the most productive side of the Hindu intellectual response to the West. Nor were these responses mystical, unless intuitive genius and inspiration are forms of mysticism. Keshub, Rabindranath, and others who developed universalist philosophies were exceedingly rational men with prodigious and eclectic reading habits. As members of the emancipated Brahmo intelligentsia, they were practical men, engaged in the serious task of constructing ideologies and institutions of salvation for India and the world. Neither their ideas nor the institutions they established to realize those ideas have been taken seriously, because of Western ethnocentricism on the one hand, and dogmatic relativism on the other. Ethnocentric imperialism and relativistic nationalism have tended to negate these universalist philosophies of the intelligentsia as trivia, primarily because such thinkers repudiated the myths of white or Indian supremacy, and aimed instead at finding ways to reconcile sectarian differences by stressing unity over diversity.[9]

In short, the influence of imperialism and nationalism on scholarship has precluded the study of what may be called philosophies of encounter and acculturation, best expressed in the ideologies of comparativism and universalism. Take, for example, Keshub's image, which is confusing not merely because he was controversial but because he was elusive in his multifaceted appeal. The tendency is to try to prove that Keshub was essentially and exclusively Vaishnava, Sakto, Christian, or Unitarian, without considering the possibility that he explored all these avenues of religious endeavor— first, to understand their relationship to one another, and second as part of a larger effort to overcome bigotry and strife through a new dispensation founded on the science (unity) of religion.

Sen's Vaishnavism is a case in point. His own family religious background, his relationship with Bijoy Krishna Goswami, his attempt to update Chaitanya's reformist ideology, and his introduction of Vaishnava kirtan (hymns) into Brahmo services, have all made Keshub appear to some as an indigenous modernizer of the Vaishnava tradition in Bengal. Keshub's tantric leanings and his use of the mother image in the New Dispensation, as well as his continual references to her in his spiritual autobiography, *Jiban Veda*, led the respectable philosopher Hiralal Haldar to conclude that "Keshub's reverence for the Motherhood of God . . . deeply imbued him with the devotional ardor and love of a true Sakto." Indeed, Haldar goes so far as to argue that the unity of the New Dispensation was based primarily on "the worship of God as the great Divine Mother Sakti . . . through which all distinctions and differences in all forms of worship and between all sectarian creeds vanish away in devotional ardour and love."[10]

However, there is also Sati Kumar Chatterji, who has spent a lifetime studying Keshub Sen, and who has ably demonstrated that the reformer's admiration of Buddha was deep enough to arouse considerable public interest in early Buddhism and to influence Dharmapala, a neo-Buddhist from Ceylon, to start the Maha Bodhi Society.[11] Then there is C.H.A. Dall, American Unitarian missionary in Bengal for the last thirty years of his life (1856 to 1886), and the only non-Indian member of the Brahmo Samaj, who claimed both Rammohun Roy and Keshub Sen as creative leaders of the worldwide Unitarian movement.[12] The same Keshub also encouraged Girish Chandra Sen, a Persian scholar of East Bengal and disciple of the New Dispensation, to study Islam from primary sources and to translate its sacred texts into Bengali.[13] Sen was briefly a culture hero of Bangladesh during its secularist period, and the only non-Muslim whose translation of the Koran (1881-1886) has earned unqualified praise from a host of Bengali Muslims.[14] Finally, orthodox Christians today of the Indian National Church variety have appropriated Keshub as one of the pioneers of indigenous Christianity in India. In 1970, M. M. Thomas, Director of the Christian Institute for the Study of Religion and Society, wrote that Keshub's most important role in the "Indian Renaissance" was providing the ideological foundations of "indigenous Christology and ecclesiology" in India.[15]

These tributes to Keshub, when put side by side, which they seldom are, suggest a great adventure of the mind taking place in the Calcutta of the Bengal renaissance. They are as important in understanding the world of the nineteenth century as are the purely European philosophies that were being generated contemporaneously. The philosophies of East-West synthesis in Bengal were strikingly different from both the liberal and nationalist ideologies that we covered earlier in the book. Though Keshub Sen toyed with liberalism from time to time, he was not liberal, primarily because in his ideology of salvation the idea of crisis predominated over the idea of progress. From the mid-seventies, Keshub looked upon the impact of modern civilization with considerable misgivings. Like the nationalists, he saw the West from the perspective of a depressed society at the exploited end of the colonial experience. But Keshub was no nationalist. On the contrary, his ideology of salvation was offered to a sick civilization plagued by national rivalries as well as by materialism, militarism, and imperialism. Keshub finally turned to religion, which he and his followers held to be a providential force arising in history again and again to save civilization from disintegration and impending doom.

Had Keshub remained steadfast in his early liberal stance and British xenophilia, he might have gone through stages of ideological development similar to those experienced by the progressive intelligentsia. But his restless mind and temperament, and his insatiable desire to devour the "truths" about all the major religions, played havoc with his identity. The enormity of his task, the breadth of his vision, and the pretentiousness of his self-chosen role as prophet of a new world religion seem to be outward manifestations of a perennial identity crisis.

The family into which Sen was born on November 19, 1838, was both distinguished and wealthy among the colonialist-engendered Calcutta elite. His grandfather was Ram Comul Sen, a member of the earliest modernized intelligentsia, which originated in the British Orientalist period (1770 to 1830). In fact, Ram Comul Sen owed his rise to fame and fortune as intellectual colleague of his patron, H. H. Wilson, his lifelong friend and "window to the West," but he was no liberal. In 1830, Ram Comul joined the Radhakant Deb faction of the Dharma Sabha in opposition to Bentinck's decree abolishing sati. Sen's last and most lucrative position was chief native manager of the Government Mint of Calcutta, an appointment he owed to Wilson's influence, and which he successfully handed on to his son, Peary Mohun Sen, Keshub's father.[16]

In view of Keshub's lineage, two significant things happened when he decided in favor of Debendranath Tagore's Brahmo Dharma. First, his was the earliest example of a Calcutta elite family that had originally opposed the families of Rammohun Roy and Dwarkanath Tagore, but subsequently shifted their ground as proponents of Brahmoism.[17] Second, Keshub's family and lineal descendants constituted the first important Bengali Vaidya converts to the reformed faith and community. Through Keshub, and in light of the fact that Vaidyas were not so much landowners as they were professionals, and infusion of middle-class types into Brahmo ranks took place, which tended to change the character of the association.

There was a similarity between Keshub and Debendranath in educational background, since both went to Hindu College and both were mediocre students at best. But their differences are significant. Unlike the steady Debendranath, Keshub was a restless intellectual, continually itching with an uncontrollable impulse to embrace new ideas, to form new organizations. In Darjeeling, two years before his death, while already weakened by diabetes, he reminisced about his youth to his disciple, Protap Chandra Majumdar: "To me, the state of being on fire is the state of salvation. . . . It was death to me to awake from my slumber without the consciousness of being baptized anew in fire. . . . From when I was young, I have always kept burning the fire of enthusiasm . . . and to keep up the condition of heat I have always run after what is new, always wished for new achievements, new ideas. What is new is warm, what is old is cold."[18]

According to Protap Majumdar, who knew the reformer more intimately than any other person, the year 1856 was probably the most critical one in Keshub's youth and adolescence. First, Keshub's family arranged a marriage between himself, a student of eighteen, and a girl nine years old. Second, he was caught cheating in a mathematics exam, an experience about which he "felt very sensitive," and which "made him so chronically depressed" that "his whole mental development was affected by it." Third, Keshub turned to acting, which he was rather good at, especially when performing Hamlet. Wrote Majumdar, "he had the constitution of the Danish prince by nature."

At this juncture of Keshub's life, Protap Chandra had depicted him as "morose, sad, and stern," with the result that "few followed and fewer loved him." Keshub tolerated no "gossiping or laughing," but had become "rigorous and truthful in speech." Keshub was then a "youth of so few words" that his neighbors believed him to be "proud, contemptuous and unsociable." The real young man Keshub, concluded Majumdar: "read austere books of philosophy and sermons hating poetry, . . . took long, solitary walks . . . in the darkness of night . . . and wrote secret prayers which he read by himself."

In 1857, Keshub was a student of philosophy and psychology, and was depicted as a "hard reader" of Unitarian theology "from eleven o'clock in the morning to six in the evening." It was at this

time that he started the Goodwill Fraternity. The group represented Keshub's first attempt to organize a religious society, and it
is meaningful that he chose as his source of inspiration the essays of
Theodore Parker. During one of Keshub's sermons, there appeared "a tall, princely man in the full glory of his health and man-
hood." He came "attended by liveried servants," and, as Majumdar
was quick to note, he was surrounded by a "massive stalwart of
Brahmos" who "wore long gold chains and impenetrable countenances." Thus, Keshub met Debendranath Tagore for the first
time. Debendranath had recently returned from a long trip to the
Himalayas, an excursion that has been interpreted generally as an
escape from both property management and the particular turn of
Brahmo affairs. In 1854, with the death of his brother Giren-
dranath, who had been managing the Tagore estates, Debendranath underwent certain financial difficulties which actually led
to his arrest at the instance of a money lender. At this time,
Brahmo affairs were gradually being dominated by humanists and
atheists in the Tattvabodhini Sabha. Debendranath had left for
Simla in 1855, just at the time of Akkhoy Kumar Dutt's mental col-
lapse and Vidyasagar's rise as a popular hero.

The attraction between Keshub and Debendranath, which appears to have been instantaneous, was in part that of a son in search
of a father. Keshub, who was twenty at the time, while Debendranath was forty, had lost his own father when he was ten. There
was also Debendranath's attraction to the young man, who had a
brilliant oratorical gift, was an effective organizer, had Unitarian
theological convictions, and perhaps most important, was a confirmed theist like himself.[19]

Another relationship made at this time, no less important, was
the one between Keshub and Debendranath's son, Satyendranath.
Born in 1842, he was six years Keshub's junior. At the time of their
meeting in 1858, Satyendranath was a brilliant student at Calcutta
University. Of all Debendranath's sons, he was by far the most
Westernized, and ultimately the most successful in carving out for
himself a distinguished career in the upper echelons of the Indian
covenanted service. And of all the sons, Satyendranath was the
most directly influenced by Keshub, whom he revered in the early
years as the true leader of his generation of young Brahmos. Later
in life, in an autobiographical sketch, Satyendranath admitted that
in the mid-fifties "the progress of the Brahmo Samaj was slow."
Then when his father returned from Simla, "an epoch making
event" took place and a "new chapter in the history of the Brahmo

Samaj was opened." It was Keshub's coming into the Samaj that
"created a new life" by giving society a "new image." He recalled
how "I also was swept by the tide of the new enthusiasm."[20]

In September 1859, Keshub did a daring thing on the invitation
of Debendranath and Satyendranath. He left his wife and family
and secretly joined the Tagores on a forty-day cruise to Ceylon.[21]
Keshub's diary of the trip reads too much like the Puritan seeking
to purge himself of his guilt of "idleness," which daily increased its
burden on his conscience and from which he sought release back to
active life.[22] The experience appears to have drawn him closer to
the Tagores, and to have convinced him that he had to make the
break with his family to become a Brahmo.

Figure 1. Keshub Chandra Sen and his wife

Though for the next two years he labored for the Brahmo
Samaj, the actual family rupture did not come until April 13, 1862,
when irate relatives led by his uncle tried to bar Keshub and his
wife from going to Debendranath's home for dinner. Quite possibly, the objection of Keshub's elders may be explained by the fact
that the Tagores, though Brahmans, were Peralis. In the Bengali

Hindu society of the time, this designation meant that they were doomed as impure for all time because one of their ancestors had the misfortune of inhaling the fumes of a dish of *pilau* (rice) prepared by a Muslim.

It appears also that Keshub was excommunicated and physically stopped from reentering the family estate. Thus, the year 1862 was critical for Keshub, who, according to Majumdar, lay bedridden with illness much of the time as a house guest of the Tagores.[23] Satyendranath has recalled the year with considerable nostalgia. "At last Keshub came to live in our house with his wife," he wrote, "and my father accepted him as a son."[24] Keshub's arrival into the Tagore household had enormous religious significance, as well. A special Brahmo ceremony was conducted sometime in 1862 in which two key prayers were offered: one by Debendranath and one by Keshub. They suggest common bonds of filial affection and theism. Debendranath called Keshub a "saintly youth" who "is to me dearer than my son" and who is "religiously of undivided heart with me." At the termination of the prayer, Debendranath's praise of Keshub was uncharacteristically excessive: "Of all who have been associated with me, I declare I have not met with a holier, none more inflexible in purpose, more enlightened, more endowed with spiritual powers as this holy one."[25]

Between 1858 and 1862 Keshub had proved to Debendranath that he was indeed a young man with rare ability. Here was someone more effective even than Rajnarian Bose in debates against missionaries and converts; here was a champion of the young who could compete effectively against the "atheist" Vidyasagar for the sympathies of the young; and here was an unusually imaginative young man who was the continual source for new ideas and projects to help keep the Samaj a vital institution.

In 1860, Keshub brought out his first important tract for the Brahmo Samaj, which he entitled *Young Bengal: This Is for You*. It was a persuasive attempt to win over the college students for the Brahmo idea and community. It was aimed at the liberal youth whose education had freed them "from idolatry and the galling yoke of Brahmanical priesthood," which "for centuries smothered and paralyzed all the nobler sentiments and energies of the people." Keshub expressed sympathy with the young, and realized how desperately India needed social reform and social reformers. Social progress cannot be won by talk, but by "hard work." "There is a lack of moral courage in our country," he proclaimed, and "the sense of duty is dead." In a tone similar to Vivekananda's over four decades later, Keshub asked for self-sacrifice in "the true patriotism of social service." And like Vivekananda, Keshub maintained that social reform in India had to be carried out through religion—but not through the prevailing decadent one. The answer was the active Brahmo religion, which wedded rational religion with "practical work for the social good of the country."[26]

Keshub issued a challenge, quite probably against the Vidyasagar camp, for winning over the unaffiliated, alienated Western-educated. Keshub knew only too well that if the Brahmo Samaj were to appeal to the young, social reform had to be a necessary aspect of its operation. And if the Brahmo Samaj did not appeal to the young it would decline. We can only surmise that Debendranath accepted the challenge as well, at least in principle, during the early years of affiliation with the exuberant Keshub.

A far more important event took place in Krishnagar one year later. Keshub, Satyendranath, and another young Brahmo named Manomohun Ghose decided to carry the new message to students of Krishnagar College. The visit was an enormous success. In the first place, to win over the students, Keshub was compelled to confront an intellectually sharp missionary named Dyson, a task the nimble-tongued Brahmo performer handled admirably well. Second, Keshub had made the trip to prove the value of carrying Brahmoism outside Calcutta—to the rest of Bengal, and possibly to all of India. His success paved the way for the realization of a Brahmo mission. Satyendranath's letters home from Krishnagar were so enthusiastic about the effectiveness of their campaign that it is difficult to doubt their veracity. "We are trying our best to promote the cause of Brahmoism," he wrote in one, and Keshub's lectures have "set Krishnagar aflame." He reported on difficult battles with the missionaries, but in the end "we were clearly the victors in the debates." Satyendranath mentioned also that Ramtanu Lahiri, the Brahmo sympathizer in Akkhoy Kumar Dutt's camp, was completely captivated by Keshub. Moreover, "the local Raja who is a member of Young Bengal" was so impressed that he invited us for dinner and requested Keshub to deliver a lecture at the palace.[27]

Keshub's own letters from Krishnagar were no less jubilant about their "victory," but they also expressed an urgent need for the Brahmo Samaj to change in order to conform to the needs of the younger generation. In a letter of May 12, 1862, to Debendranath, Keshub stressed this idea and went so far as to submit proposals for expanding the functions of the Samaj.[28]

Shortly after returning, Keshub convinced Debendranath that

the Brahmo Samaj needed an English newspaper with wide appeal to the Western-educated. Thus was born the *Indian Mirror*, one of the most influential papers throughout South Asia in the nineteenth century. Its first editor was Monomohun Ghose,[29] who was not exactly a new conquest of the Brahmo Samaj, as his father had already been a close follower of Rammohun Roy.[30]

It was Keshub's great misfortune that in 1863, when he began his crusade to give the Samaj a new reformist image, he was without the support of Satyendranath Tagore and Monomohun Ghose, as both young men had left India in 1862 for England to compete for the Indian Civil Service. Even when Satyendranath returned to India in 1865, he was posted at his own request to Bombay, and it was in West India that he spent most of his official career. His influence on Debendranath was replaced by that of two other sons, Dwijendranath, born in 1840, and Jyotirindranath, born in 1849, both decidedly anti-Keshub and both confirmed Hindu nationalists.

We have seen elsewhere how Keshub and the younger generation of Brahmos broke away from Debendranath Tagore to establish their own Samaj in 1866. We have also noted that Keshub's image between 1866 and 1870 was viewed either as a Westernized social reformer or as a nonsectarian follower of Christ. But, in fact, if we were to collect the various references to Keshub throughout the book for this period, we would find a rather confusing picture of the reformer exploring multiple channels of identity. As a constitutionalist and social reformer, he won the admiration of Ananda Mohun Bose and Sivanath Sastri—both of whom sacrificed a great deal to become his disciples. But at the same time, he came under the influence of Bijoy Krishna Goswami and Vaishnavism. We noted in the last chapter how he experienced a total change of personality in November 1867, singing kirtan in public for the first time as "tears ran down his handsome face." Majumdar has reported how Keshub "was turned into a new man."[31] This was the same Keshub whom the American Unitarian Dall looked upon as his own son, and whose theism in its last "distillation," was the "theism of Jesus."[32]

In September 1866, Keshub gave a lecture in Calcutta which I believe to be important in suggesting that the germ of his new ideology of salvation was already present at the very time of the schism. On the subject of "Great Men," Keshub propounded the idea of prophets who appear in different cultures at different periods of history to save a people from a deepening crisis. The view that history progressed by the emergence of heroes, chosen by Divine Providence to lead men out of chaos to a higher stage of social evolution, was probably as close as Keshub, the future would-be prophet, ever came to a theory of progress.

In what manner does God manifest Himself in history? This was Keshub's central question in the lecture on "Great Men." Extraordinary men arise from time to time to lead mankind. God sends these "geniuses, heroes, redeemers . . . endowed with requisite power and talents . . . to cope with a crisis of a very serious character . . . in order to remodel society on an improved basis." These prophets were "not God putting on a human body—not God made man but God in man." They must struggle against "established errors and prejudices in an effort to revolutionize popular tastes and ideas." Thus concluded Keshub, "a prophet is said to regenerate his people; he infuses new life into them. In him the old generation dies and a new generation is born."

Significantly, Keshub's universalism has in this lecture totally transcended Christ in a wider appreciation of the role of all prophets. Luther, for one, "revived the pulse of Europe" until "society there was altogether reorganized on a new basis and a new life was infused into the organism." Muhammad was another whose "iconoclastic mission" to establish monotheism "amidst the dense mass of ignorance and idolatry" was ultimately crowned with success. We have only to "behold millions owing subjection to the crescent in various parts of the world" to the "Unseen and One Only God," to realize his impact. Perhaps most interesting of all the prophets discussed by Keshub was the one who arose in Bengal hundreds of years before. According to Keshub, "Bengal lay divided then [sixteenth century] between empty ritualism and Vedantic contemplation on the one hand, and the immoral orgies of . . . the *Sakti* worshippers on the other." The bulk of the "Sudra population were almost excluded from the advantages of religious life." Then arose Chaitanya, "great prophet of love and faith," who by "precept and example executed mighty influence to suppress these combined evils." The most pernicious social evil was "the proud head of caste," which "he laid low."[33]

In June 1868, as alluded to in the previous chapter, Keshub assumed the role of nineteenth-century "avatar" of Chaitanya. He was so effective that "people prostrated themselves" at his feet and "prayers were offered to him for intercession on behalf of sinners."[34] He had gone so far as to offend the loyal Bijoy Krishna, who said that "Brahmoism recognized only God as the Savior. . . . We request Keshub Babu to dissuade other Brahmos from this dangerous course."[35] The incident raises some doubt as to whether Keshub wished to infuse Vaishnavism with modern values or whether he had already come to see himself as a prophet.

The Trinitarian missionaries also admired Sen during the years between 1866 and 1870. Though the Reverend Bomwetsch dismissed Keshub Chandra Sen as another fine Bengali talker but "hypothetical doer,"[36] the Reverends Barton, Vaughn, and Long were of a different opinion. Long, for example, who was unique among missionaries for his constructive work among the Hindu masses in Bengal, was at first skeptical as to whether Keshub was "of the people and in sympathy with the people," or whether he was a "baboo type" who "ignores the mass of his own countrymen."[37] But after he met Keshub he was immediately struck by his "more favorable view to social reform than the other Brahmists."[38] He became Keshub's friend and remained so until 1871, when he felt that the Bengali reformer had deserted Christ for the dubious model of Chaitanya's reformation.[39]

In 1870, Keshub went off to England for several months, where he delivered superb and well-received speeches to Unitarians, Trinitarians, teetotallers, academics, and retired Indian government officials. He was even granted an audience with Queen Victoria, with whom some spark of mutual admiration was ignited—an event sadly misused subsequently by critics of Keshub's persisting loyalty to the English crown. One important result of the tour throughout the British Isles was his enormous popularity as a famous Hindu reformer, twenty years before Vivekananda. One lecture of his, while in Britain, deserves particular consideration because of the Adi Brahmo charge that he was a denationalized opportunist. In May 1870, he spoke to a group of prominent British politicians and state officials on "England's Duties to India," a speech which was well publicized in the national press. Keshub referred to the "great work of reformation that has commenced in India," and of the struggle going on "between old institutions and new ideas." It was Providence that had placed his society and culture in the hands of the British nation. "You hold India as trustees," he told his audience, "and you have no right to . . . use its property, its riches, or its resources," or "any of the power God has given you for the purpose of selfish aggrandisement and enjoyment." In the following passage, Keshub sounds very much like Vivekananda decades later: "You are accountable to God for those millions of souls, those millions of bodies, that have been placed in your hands as a sacred trust. You cannot hold India for the welfare of Manchester. . . . If you desire to hold India, you can only do so for the good and welfare of India."

Keshub then proceeded to cite grievances under British rule, a list which compares favorably with more conservative charges prepared by the Indian National Congress fifteen or more years later—especially his plea for British sponsorship of mass education and the Indianization of the civil services. He courageously said that he hoped the British would be able "to raise funds so that 150,000,000 of my fellow-countrymen will not be suffered to remain in ignorance." In a most revealing passage reflecting very much his own dilemma as a reformer in a colonial situation, Keshub made the following acute observation: "The education that you give the upper classes will not uproot idolatry and prejudice, for it is amongst the masses that error and prejudice will always have their power and while you do not uproot those prejudices, a few educated Hindus will never be able successfully to reform the whole country."[40] Needless to say, Keshub never received either moral or financial support from Britishers, who were only beginning at that time to see the value of mass education in their own country.

There can be little doubt that between 1870 and 1872 Keshub worked devotedly in the liberal camp, identifying himself closely with progressive Western values. As demonstrated in the first chapter, his Indian Reform Association was an extension of the Unitarian social gospel to Bengal. He allowed the Reverend Dall to become a member of the Brahmo Samaj of India, and arranged for the distribution of Unitarian literature from the United States to all the branches of the Samaj. He even tried to reach the peasants through his penny newspaper, *Sulabh Samachar*, while at the same time he opened night schools for the working class of Calcutta. The Brahmo Marriage Act of 1872, which was almost entirely his creation, gave legal sanction to most of the social reforms advocated by liberals since the 1850s.

Then, after gaining national fame as India's most successful modernizer, Keshub wrote a series of public letters to the government on education. It was at best a gamble by a reformer riding the crest of his popularity to gain official support for a comprehensive program of national regeneration. In London, he had told the British that no small community of reformers, however well-intentioned or however hard they labored, could possibly change anything without large-scale official support in reaching the masses. Keshub now reiterated his plea for mass education with a practical plan for raising funds. By mass, Keshub meant the ryot or peasant, and in the letters of May 8 and 17 he depicted their deplorable condition under the present zamindari system. On May 21, he asked for a "comprehensive and national system of education for India." "To throw off the yoke of prejudices and corrupt institutions," he wrote, "and to remedy the manifold social and moral evils which have hitherto afflicted her," India requires a system of education that will "bring light to all classes" and "renew her vitality and energy in the path of true reformation." In his letter of July 12, he made an eloquent case for mass education, which was the only way of awakening "the sad and pitiable condition of the dumb millions of India." Compassionately he pointed to their "ignorance, illiteracy, poverty, credulity and helplessness—being at the mercy of gripping priests, rapacious zemindars, cruel planters and a vicious police."

To be sure, as Keshub argued, the British had done much already to spread enlightenment. Were there not 621,342 students in all the Presidencies receiving the blessings of English education? But, he was quick to add, "how small and insignificant is this figure when contrasted with an estimated 151,000,000?"

On August 8, he claimed that all the elite groups would benefit from a "body of honest intelligent ryots." Trade and industry would develop, and "in consequence" there would be "general appreciation for the application of science and the development of the endless "physical resources of the country." Then, with an amazingly rational and modernist spirit for a religious reformer in India a century ago, Keshub said, "The whole history of modern civilization upsets the hypothesis of elitist education. England, Germany and other modern countries have made the greatest progress when their masses have been trained to think and act as rational beings." Keshub's plan was to establish a large network of vernacular schools with "native inspectors." He recommended evening schools for the "agricultural and working classes," who would use them after the day's work was done. The curriculum would include the "useful arts" and the sciences. As for who would pay, Keshub could only recommend "a tax on the wealthier classes of all sections of the country instead of throwing the whole burden on zemindars and landholders alone." The government's function would be to divert much of the current expenditure from training a class "of half-educated, shallow thinking and conceited barbarians" to the more urgent task of uplifting the masses. But the main thrust of his appeal was for new vast expenditures of money by the government in order to carry out the function of a modern state. As Keshub put it, it was "the duty of the State to extend education among the mass of the people."[41]

These letters by Keshub on education suggest that he was an acutely intelligent, sensitive, and sophisticated spokesman of the liberal cause. On the one hand, he found himself between agents of British imperialism, to whom he looked for help, guidance, and acceptance as a human being. On the other, he was situated amid the mass of Hindus and Muslims from whom he was separated by virtue of education and consciousness, and by whom he was treated with indifference.

After 1872, when his plan for compulsory education in India with government assistance was totally ignored, Keshub gradually turned away from a Westernized solution to modernism in India. In so doing, he also appears to have rejected social reform along Western lines. In practice this meant a sudden reversal of his position on female education and emancipation. Immediately upon doing so, he was pounced upon by the nonascetic Westernized faction, or ultra-progressives—the very people who would break with him decisively in 1878. That their hostility to him pained Keshub deeply is obvious from his personal prayers during this period. For him factionalism was the curse of the Bengali and the Brahmo.[42] Later this same faction appeared to him to be sabotaging the community spirit of the Bharat Ashram, ultimately forcing the establishment to close down. Keshub was beside himself with anger, disillusionment, and frustration. Thus, we can understand why he drew closer to the ascetics.

Then in March of 1875, or perhaps earlier, Keshub met Ramakrishna. What transpired between these two men has been buried in a mass of propaganda by both Keshubites and Ramakrishnites principally concerned with whether Keshub or Ramakrishna was the primary influence on the other. Still others, mistakenly convinced that all Brahmos were Westernized and that Keshub in particular was a Christian, have been perennially baffled at Keshub's sudden attraction for the Hindu mystic. The truth is that Keshub was no stranger to ascetics, any more than were devout Vaishnavas, with little English education, strangers to the Brahmo Samaj. And yet Ramakrishna's activities up to 1875 were hardly those of a Brahmo. Still, there were special features of Ramakrishna's mystical equipment and performances that appealed to Keshub and his associates. The attraction was mutual; the influence was mutual.

Ramakrishna was probably born in 1836 in a Hugli village. The first significant fact about him is that he was not susceptible to formal education—either English or indigenous. His anti-bookishness surely separated him from Brahmos of whatever ideological bent. A second aspect of his life that appealed to Keshub was his tantric way of sublimating the sensual desire for woman into the spiritual desire for the holy mother. We have already differentiated between this form of asceticism and that of Bijoy Krishna and most other Brahmo missionaries, who were for the most part husbands and fathers. Third, Ramakrishna claimed to have experienced direct, intuitive contacts with all the major religious leaders of history. In this sense, the Hindu Ramakrishna was perhaps more universalist and Brahmo than most of the Brahmo ascetics, who were narrowly Vaishnava. These three aspects of Ramakrishna's career as a mystic were probably strong influences on Keshub from March 1875, when the two men presumably first met at the Kali temple in Dakshineshwar. Keshub was intrigued by the religious "experiments" performed by Ramakrishna, and wished to adapt them to his own use, especially those elements of the Sakto tradition in Bengal that emphasized the "motherhood of God."

Though Brahmos have argued that Keshub used the term "motherhood of God" thirty-two times before meeting Ramakrishna,"[43] the fact is that the idea of using Saktism for Brahmo ends did not become a part of Brahmo reformist ideology until after 1875. Most Brahmos saw the tantric tradition in Bengal as a horrendous and debased form of religious expression, representing a total and radical departure from the authentic classical Hindu tradition. The idea of differentiating good and bad features within Saktism, then integrating the good into Brahmoism, probably occurred to Keshub after his acquaintance with Ramakrishna. In the early 1860s, Ramakrishna had already performed experiments designed to purify Saktism and tantrism. To achieve a pure state of mind as a Sakto, he believed, required nothing less than a personal transvaluation aiming at the sanctification of women. To sanctify woman properly in her rightful place as a goddess, he had to suppress within himself the "masculine" urge to view woman as an object of sexual gratification. Thus, Ramakrishna stopped intercourse with his wife. Once, while in bed with her, he said to himself: "Oh, my Mind, this is the body of a woman. Men look on it as an object of great enjoyment, something to be highly prized. They devote their lives to enjoy it. . . . Oh, my Mind, don't be one thing in private, and outwardly pretending in another. Be frank. Do you want this body of a woman, or do you want God?" Ramakrishna visited brothels, reenacted sacred myths, underwent trances, and induced states of mystical union with the Mother. As Christopher Isherwood has pointed out, Ramakrishna had started a quest to "find out everything for himself, empirically." He "had no books to instruct him" (naturally, being anti-bookish). He "experienced everything as if for the first time in history." Ramakrishna has described many of these experiments in ecstatic terms:

> Overcome by emotion, I was about to fall at her feet crying Mother, when she passed into my body and became merged in it. As she did so, she told me that she was making me a gift of her smile . . . at another time I'd open my mouth and it would be as if my jaws reached from Heaven to the underworld. "Mother," I'd cry desperately. I felt I had to pull her in, as a fisherman pulls in fish with his dragnet. . . . My hair became matted. Birds perched on my head to peck at the grains of rice. . . . Snakes would crawl over my motionless body.

Between 1861 and 1863, Ramakrishna was deeply involved in tantric experiments while under the tutelage of a guru. Through austerities and visions, he managed to purify and spiritualize Saktism and tantra. A symbol like the "yoni or female organ" now represented the "divine source of all creation." The connotation of such words had become "as sacred to him as the vocabulary of the Scriptures." His experiments with religious behavior dealt ultimately with the same problems of unity and diversity that had plagued Brahmos. When Ramakrishna "tested" most of the major religions of the world to discover the validity of each one's professed uniqueness, Keshub was evidently impressed by the results. Ramakrishna did not approach the problem in the Brahmo way of intellectually dissecting each religion, but in the existential way of experiencing each religion intuitively. In 1865, for example, he practiced the Islamic faith. He would dress like an Arab, repeat the name of Allah, say prayers five times a day, avoid images of Hindu gods and goddesses, and so on. From that experiment he felt the sharp difference that existed between dualistic religion and Vedantic monism. Sometime in the early 1870s, he turned to Christianity and filled his mind with the "love of Jesus." He began to see visions of Christian priests burning incense in their churches, and he "felt the fervor of their prayers." Finally, Christ appeared to him: "This is Jesus Christ, the great yogi, the loving Son of God and the one with his Father, who shed his heart's blood and suffered tortures for the salvation of mankind! We embraced and Jesus passed into my body."

For those who see Ramakrishna only as a Hindu mystic or saint, the true depth of his vision with its meaning and cultural impact are completely missed. From his experience with Christ, for example, he "remained convinced from that day onward, that Jesus was truly a divine incarnation." One day after the Christian experiment, he visited Keshub at the latter's home. The gem of wisdom reportedly offered by Ramakrishna to Keshub was in the form of an analogy between a tadpole and a man. "As long as a tadpole has its tail," Ramakrishna said, "it can live in the water, it can't come on land; but when the tail drops off, it can live on land as well as on water." Then he said, "as long as man wears the tail of ignorance, he can only live in the world; but, when the tail drops off, he can live either in the knowledge of God or in the world, whichever he pleases. Your mind, Keshub, has reached that state now. You can live in the world and still be aware of God."[44]

In 1875, Keshub collected the more scholarly ascetic Brahmos at his home and proposed to them a new intellectual and spiritual quest. He assigned to each a major religion to be studied from the Scriptures as primary sources in the original languages. Keshub was interested in the earliest articulation of the religion by the prophets and reformers. Thus, he began to conduct seminars in which the historical conditions present at the time of each major reformer were reconstructed and each one's leading ideas discussed analytically. Girish Chandra Sen did Islam; Gour Govinda Ray, Hinduism; Protap Chandra Majumdar, Christianity; Mohendra Nath Bose, Sikhism; Aghore Nath Gupta, Buddhism.

That same year he purchased a garden house outside Calcutta which he called Sadhan Kanan, or the forest sanctuary for religious cultivation. Here he met with his Brahmo colleagues and practiced asceticism by "sitting below trees on carpets made of hides of tigers . . . in imitation of Hindu mendicants."[45] In the following year, he constructed a colony of neat little houses near his own Lilly Cottage on Upper Circular Road in Calcutta; and in 1878, Keshub's ascetics and their families moved into the colony. Keshub had traveled a long distance from his original idea of a Bharat Ashram to house the Brahmo community; the idea now was to house together a religious brotherhood in quest of the principles of comparative religion.

To those who remained his devotees after the schism of 1878, Keshub's Naba Vidhan (New Dispensation of God), which he instituted officially in 1881, represented the apex of nineteenth-century Brahmoism. J. K. Koar, for one, who was born in the very year of the inauguration of the New Dispensation and became one of its most ardent defenders, has made a convincing case that the church and ideology were "the result of years of sustained meditation and spiritual striving."[46] To Koar and other devotees, the birth of the New Dispensation was an event of momentous importance not only for Bengal or for India, but for the world, because it illuminated the path from sectarianism, nationalism, and imperialism to a new world order based on religiously inspired universal harmony. Critics of Keshub have seen the new church and its creed as a drift back into Hindu mysticism, as a surrender to idolatry, or as a vehicle for Keshub's exalted paranoia as an inspired prophet. Keshub's defenders have either supported the New Dispensation as true believers, or have pointed to it as the logical culmination of his deepening scholarly interest in comparative religion. His brother, Krishna Bihari Sen, ascribed a scientific motivation to Keshub as a seeker of universal principles underlying all religions. In a book entitled *What Is the New Dispensation?* which Krishna Bihari brought out in 1896, he established a kinship between his brother Keshub and Akkhoy Kumar Dutt, who had dedicated himself to scientific rationalism and the pursuit of natural laws of religion. Koar, writing almost sixty years later and more interested in the psychology of religious symbolism, interpreted Keshub in the light of Jungian psychoanalysis.[47]

Between 1876 and 1878, Keshub Sen changed remarkably. It was not—as many local Christians charged—that he had deserted Christ for Hinduism. His Town Hall lecture for April 1879 on "India Asks—Who Is Christ?" demonstrates that he had not abandoned Jesus as one of the major prophets, but that he had abandoned the missionaries for transforming Christ into a vehicle of imperialism. The real change in Keshub was his total withdrawal from the Unitarian-inspired social gospel of Christ. The Indian Reform Association had died by 1876, as did his Normal School for women.[48] The key to his new position is to be found in a lecture on Christ in which he attributed to the prophet the belief in "self-abnegation." "By his teachings as well as by example," said Keshub, "he declared emphatically that man shall live in God, and not in self." "Complete self-surrender," concluded Keshub, "is the most striking miracle in the world's history."[49]

Keshub's new position alienated the progressives in the Brahmo Samaj, and in 1878 they parted company with him and formed their own organization. Everything Keshub did in those years confused friend and critic alike. Where would Keshub turn now? He had recently led processions loudly "chanting the name of Mother."[50] In 1879, he had given a controversial lecture on "Am I an Inspired Prophet?"[51] The charge of "avatarism" in the press missed the import of the lecture. The reformer was moving toward a momentous decision in his life. Would he choose Christ? Would he reassume the guise of Chaitanya? Or would he, prophet that he implied he was, give the world a new religion?

In February 1880, Keshub conducted a city procession in the Vaishnava style. Krishna Bihari, in the *Indian Mirror*, described the event as a "scene worth beholding." Alongside the usual Vaishnava musical instruments were the Salvation Army trumpets and bugles that "sent forth their piercing deafening notes." Then at Beadon Square in North Calcutta the procession halted and the Minister spoke. As Keshub appealed to the mass for a religious revival of *bhakti*: "the forest of flags reared their heads, before and behind, many were their devices, many their colors, many were their styles. . . . The boys held them, the missionaries held them, the Brahmos who had come from Bombay and Sind held them and the largest which could not be held by anyone were tied to a carriage drawn by two horses. Upon these were inscribed New Dispensation."

What is noteworthy about this particular procession, one of the earliest in the name of New Dispensation, was its emotional and revivalist character, fusing new Salvation Army techniques with Vaishnava appeal. Some 5,000 Hindus showed up, and many of them later prostrated themselves before Keshub, just as enthusiastic devotees had done in Monghyr, Bihar, in 1868. This time none objected to the practice along rationalist lines. Moreover, the kirtan selected for the occasion and written by Sanyal had a traditional quality about it:

> After a long interval the All-loving Hari is dispensing
>   love and *bhakti* from door to door
> Finding carnal indulgence, the pride of knowledge,
>   licentiousness and unbelief in this dark age
> Behold the conspicuous signs of the times

Hari—the savior of the fallen—holding the sinner by
the horns of the head is engaged in saving and giving
him His beautiful feet
(There is then, no cause of apprehension—in this Dark Age).[52]

In 1880, Keshub seemed to envision himself less a religious
prophet in the traditional sense and more as a Newton of religious
science. This was the academic side of his New Dispensation. Probably few scholars in the world knew as much as Keshub about the
major religions of the world. And from Keshub's point of view, he
was in a better position to reason clearly about religion than even
Max Müller because he, Keshub, was free of the biases of the true
believer in a "revealed religion." It was also just at this time that
Ramakrishna had culminated his own experiments with unity and
diversity in the major religions. His conclusion, according to later
disciples, was that each religion was a different path to the same
end. The best course of action—the opposite of Keshub's syncretism—was to stress the unity of purpose but to let the sleeping
dogs of national religious distinction lie without being disturbed.[53]
By the end of that year, Sanyal, who had been composing songs
about Hari for the mass processions, composed a new type of sangit
that began "Victory of Jesus, Moses, . . . and Gour, victory to
Keshub Chandra, Synthesizer of all religions."[54] Keshub was evidently moving away from Ramakrishna's conclusion. He was well
on his way in the direction of pulling together Ramakrishna's many
different paths into one path—the universal religion.

Throughout 1880, Keshub worked feverishly, preparing for the
momentous event. He started the "pilgrimages" to the saints,
elaborately staged devotional seminars designed to trace the history of human crises and the role of ethical and religious reformers
as saviors during these periods of civilizational breakdown and disintegration. In March, for example, Keshub chose Greece at the
time of Socrates. "The age demanded his birth (like Bengal today)," summarized Keshub at the seminar. "Are we not today living
in an age of materialism, shallow refinement, hollow faith, and de-
basing sensuality?" As for Socrates: "It was the grand mission of
Socrates to turn the current of human thought from without to
within . . . he led the Greeks to think of themselves, and by pointing
out the duty of regulating the mind, laid the foundations of that
practical morality. . . . Socrates left two precious legacies—a golden
method and an exemplary life. Living in the midst of corruption,
he was the purest and most self-sufficing of men."[55]

The seminars went on for a week at a time, during which disciples were called upon to "live with Socrates, Moses, Mohammad. . . ." This meant, in effect, lectures, discussions, and quiet meditation on the life of a particular saint. During the concluding Sunday of each pilgrimage, Keshub transformed his home into a "historical site in Palestine, Greece, Arabia, or Navadvip." Someone was chosen for the role of a given prophet, while others engaged him in dialogue on issues relevant during a given period of crisis. Sivanath Sastri, a Sadharan Brahmo critic of the practice because these "saints stood as obstacles to knowing God directly," was nevertheless intrigued by the educational values of the experience. "Each pilgrimage," said he, "brought a different reformer before the assembly, and his utterances of centuries ago were applied more or less skilfully to the difficulties of existing theological speculation."[56] Keshub carried his pilgrimages as far as he believed necessary to achieve greater understanding and rapport with the reformers. Before the pilgrimage to Buddha, Keshub went to Bodh Gaya and meditated under the "Bodhi tree."[57] This kind of existential experience was in its way far more ambitious than similar undertakings by Ramakrishna. Through textual research, meditation, and careful reflection, Keshub sought an empathy with a given reformer that would erase the barriers of temporal and cultural distance.

To Koar, who has studied Keshub intensively during this period of development, the reformer was experimenting on at least two levels—the public intellectual quest for unity, and the more intimate quest for personal transformation through ascetic discipline.[58] Whether, as Sati Chatterji suggests, the influence of Buddha was paramount in Keshub's choice of discipline,[59] or whether yoga was the model, it is difficult to say. In either case, as Koar argues, Keshub operated basically within the Indian tradition, becoming one of a long line of reformers and mystics continually innovating systems of spiritual discipline as a means of salvation.

As Keshub concerned himself more and more with spiritual matters, did he turn his back completely on the social reform aspect of the Brahmo reformation? Critics have argued that by 1881 Keshub was so preoccupied with religion and salvation that he neglected the task of improving the lot of humanity. Both Koar and Chatterji argue otherwise. Keshub had learned from the saints that social improvement was impossible without moral transformation, and morality was useless without spiritual illumination. Each saint taught Keshub his own system or path of moral transformation.

Chatterji has succinctly listed these alternative paths: "Moses represented God's intervention in all of man's worldly concerns—both great and trivial. Socrates represented the path to self-knowledge; Sakhya Muni . . . self-denial; the yogis . . . the power of rapt meditation; Jesus equates the love of man with the will of God; Mohammad . . . the brotherhood of man through rigid monotheism; Chaitanya represented the path of rapturous devotion to God."[60] By 1881, as Koar sees it, Keshub had opted for the monistic path of the Vedanta in a manner similar to Vivekananda's many years later. Koar maintains that Gour Govinda (of Keshub's Durbar) may have influenced Keshub in this respect, helping him to choose the path of unity and oneness so appropriate to Keshub's thinking on the science of religion. The Vedantic ethic seemed to appeal to Keshub then, as he explored the ramifications of the belief that all is in Brahma and Brahma is in all. But Keshub, the theist, did not interpret monism as a sterile abstraction so much as spiritual pantheism. If every human being carries within him the divine spark, then every human being is every other human being's brother.[61]

Conceivably, it was this ethic that inspired Keshub's idea of nava sishu or new child. From Koar's analysis, it appears that this idea was symbolic of a regenerated man imbued with knowledge of, and faith in, the oneness of the spirit, the unity of all creation, and the realization that all men are brothers. According to Koar, Keshub's utilization of the nava sishu is meaningful from the point of view of the psychoanalyst of religion. Koar quotes from Jung, for example, that: "through devotion, through sinking of the libido into unconsciousness, the childhood complex is reactivated." Koar says also that Keshub intended for nava sishu to serve as an alternative to the Judeo-Christian uses of messiah. In any event, Keshub late in the nineteenth century saw salvation in terms of burying nationalist rivalries and other parochialisms by achieving a new spiritual vision. As Koar puts it, "Keshub, himself, by attaining unity through religious synthesis, would make a fresh beginning as a new child."[62]

In March 1881, Keshub's synthesizing process began with the Christian Eucharist. He enculturated the sacrament by exchanging Hindu symbols of rice and water for the Christian bread and wine. The purpose of this experiment, and of others to follow, was to express the universal functional equivalence of most sacramental rituals.

In Keshub's prayer at the eucharist ceremony, he started by imploring Jesus not to ignore "Hindus from the holy eucharist . . .

because we are rice-eaters and teetotalers." Is the sacramental rite "meant only for those nations that are in the habit of taking bread and wine?" "That cannot be," replied Keshub: "Spirit of Jesus! Both into Europe and Asia thou has said, 'eat my flesh and drink my blood.' Therefore the Hindus shall eat thy flesh in rice and drink thy blood in pure water."[63]

Later that year, Keshub led his followers to the Hugly River for a snan jatra, or baptism ceremony. The procession sang all the way to the river to the accompaniment of conch shells and cymbals. The ghat at the river where the baptism took place was decorated with flowers, evergreen branches, and a large flag of the New Dispensation Church. While his followers sat silently under the "torrid sun of midday," Keshub offered a prayer that consisted of a fascinating mixture of cultural symbols to express the universal meaning of baptism as renewal and rebirth. He started by asking his congregation to imagine themselves in the River Jordan eighteen centuries back. The prayer was to Varuna, "Water of Life," whom "we glorify not as God for thou art not God . . . but as having divinity within you." In this prayer, Keshub's Vedantic pantheism was all too apparent. "Each drop," said Keshub, "reveals the Divine Force."

In the ceremonies of the New Dispensation, Keshub was hardly aiming to domesticate Christianity or to Christianize Hinduism. Rather, he was searching for a new synthesis. As the following portion of the prayer should indicate, it was not the trappings of cultural symbols he regarded as essential, but the underlying meaning of baptism wherever practiced: "Oh, Varuna, friend of the human race . . . cleanse our body . . . wash away filth and impurity . . . did you not suggest to Buddha the idea of Nirvana. Oh, extinguisher of the fire of all pain and discomfort. And Jesus too imagined you, and praised you . . . for he found in you new life and salvation."

Then Keshub annointed himself with flower-oil and went into the water saying, "Dear God, convert this water into the water of grace and holiness that I may be immersed in life everlasting." Immersing himself three times, Keshub said, "Glory unto Truth, Glory unto Son, Glory unto the Holy Ghost." Once more he immersed himself and said, "Blessed be Truth, Wisdom and Joy in One!"[64]

Keshub also reinterpreted Vedic rituals such as the fire or hom ceremony in a new light. First performed in June 1881, the ritual was arranged according to orthodox tradition. Then lighting the fire with ghee, Keshub said: "Oh, Blazing Agni, great among forces in creation. . . . You are not God. We do not adore you. But in you dwells the Divine spirit, the Eternal Inextinguishable Flame, the Light of the Universe, the innocent fire, Fire of fire, whom fire reveals and glorifies." This festival, in particular, seems to have rubbed Sadharan Brahmos such as Sivanath Sastri the wrong way. The fire ceremony was condemned as sheer idolatry, but Keshub's defense is significant from the point of view of his comparativist outlook and synthetic intent. This was an experiment to "combine types and symbols, ideas and principles."[65] He wanted to recapture the religious meaning of fire as held universally, using the symbols of fire rituals "in different cultures" interchangeably. He hoped the congregation would understand the symbolic import of the original Vedic ceremony through which the flames engulfed the six enemies of purity: lust, anger, jealousy, infatuation, pride, and envy.

One curious consequence of Keshub's emphasis on sacraments, rites, and symbols was the feeling of some Europeans that the reformer was turning to Roman Catholicism. The Reverend S. W. O'Neill, a friend of Keshub and a devout Catholic missionary, actually gave a public lecture on "Whether the new Brahmoism Were for or against Christianity." O'Neill felt that Keshub was not turning to Catholicism but was playing an intellectual game in a dangerous way. For one thing, the equality of prophets was a false notion because "had they been alive at the time of Christ, they would surely have accepted him as their leader."[66] If Keshub were turning to the Catholic church, he would accept sacraments not as cultural symbols but as manifestation of the Divine Spirit. Though he liked Keshub personally and admired him for his intense spirituality, he was convinced that the reformer's mental gymnastics were paving the way to secularism. Keshub ought to abandon his futile effort and join under the banner of the true revealed religion.

Keshub evidently ignored his opposition, busily engaging himself in the arduous work of constructing a new church. In his yearly lecture at Town Hall, which was always a well-attended community affair in Calcutta, Keshub announced dramatically that "we are disciples of the New Dispensation." He put his own dispensation on the same level with "the Jewish dispensation, the Christian dispensation and the Vaishnava dispensation." Just as "Jesus claimed to be the King of the Jews, so am I ambitious of being crowned as the king of the Indians—of the Bengalis, at any rate."

Why the New Dispensation? "Because of sectarian hatred and bigotry," replied Keshub. "All the old churches exclude and deny one another claiming a monopoly of truth and salvation." But in "the New Temple," said Keshub, "is a catholicity which embraces all space and all time." Keshub hammered away at his familiar theme of unity and synthesis perhaps because few if any of his critics challenged him on this essential ingredient of his new faith. "Gentlemen," said he, "trifle not with unity because in the logic of synthesis is the world's salvation." Was not science unity? "Only science can deliver the world," he continued, "and bring light and order out of the chaos and darkness of multiplied churches." Keshub's church offered unity and love: "In the kingdom of God, there is no invidious distinction and therefore this dispensation gathers all men and nations, all races and tribes, the high and the low, and seeks to establish one vast brotherhood among the children of the great God who hath made of one blood all nations of men. . . . In this anti-caste movement which daily brings Jew and Gentile, Hindu and Christian nearer and nearer in spiritual fellowship, the chief workers are merely spiritual descendants of Moses, Jesus and Paul."

Primarily among the objectives of the dispensation was to bring Asia and Europe together. "We want Europe to enter into the Heart of Asia and Asia to enter into the mind of Europe." "We say to the Pacific," Keshub declared, "pour thy waters into the Atlantic; and we say to the West, roll back to the East." If only "one nation could become another!" "If Asia could eat the flesh and drink the blood of Europe." The following powerful piece of prose by Keshub, on the harmony of nations, should be viewed against the backdrop of the 1880s, when British imperialism had reached its high tide and Indian nationalism had started on its road to aggressive militancy: "Cultivate this communion, my brethren, and continually adore all that is good and noble in each other. Do not hate, do not exclude others, as the sectarians do, but include and absorb all beauty and truth. Let there be no antagonism and exclusion. Let the embankment which each nation has raised be swept away by the flood of cosmopolitan truth, and let all the barriers and partitions which separate man from man be pulled down, so that truth and love and purity may flow freely through millions of hearts and through hundreds of successive generations, from country to country, from age to age." It seems fairly obvious that Keshub sought to demonstrate before the Calcutta intelligentsia that the New Dispensation was neither mysticism nor medieval asceticism, but the prototype for the universal church of the future. In the end of his lecture, he summed up the virtues and aims of the new church: "It gives to history a meaning, to the action of Providence a consistency, to quarreling churches, a common bond, and to successive dispensations a continuity. . . . Before the flag of the New Dispensation, bow ye nations, and proclaim the Fatherhood of God and the Brotherhood of man. In blessed eucharist let us eat and assimilate all the saints and prophets of the world. . . . The Lord Jesus is my will, Socrates my head, Chaitanya my heart, the Hindu rishi my soul."[67]

At the services of the new church, Keshub insisted on displaying the chief symbols of the major religions in a specially arranged banner suggesting the harmonious interaction of all faiths. It contained the Hindu trident, the Christian cross, the crescent of Mohammad, and the om of Hinduism. On the pulpit were five books that the minister would use for his sermons. They were Brahmo editions of works by Buddha, Moses, Christ, Mohammed, and a collection of scriptural utterances by Hindus. The fifth work was the *Sloka sangraho*, or compilation of scriptural fragments from all religions.

In March 1881, Keshub started a newspaper called *New Dispensation*, which, like his lectures, contained sophisticated arguments justifying his new position. Of special interest were his articles on symbols, which he described minutely and explored deeply for religious meaning. On the other hand, his own use of symbols often demonstrated not so much efforts at intellectual synthesis as they did dramatic efforts to simplify ideas visually for popular appeal. Keshub's use of the church flag, for example, seems identical to the way the Salvation Army used their flag at the same time. The flag, wrote Keshub, was to be a "potent symbol of our church militant." The flag was "crimson with the blood of prophets, many of whom were martyrs for the sake of truth. The flag which contained the symbols of all religions in one should be waved high in the air "to suggest the idea of battle and victory." To unfurl the flag, said he, "is to declare war on evil."[68]

On April 14, 1881, the newspaper carried an article on the meaning of the cross, which was typical of Keshub's intellectual groping for insight. What impressed him most of all about the crucifixion was the fact that Jesus "nailed to the cross was incapable of moving in the paths of sin and carnality." Since he was compelled to remain motionless, the crucifixion suggested a "yogic posture" in which one was "dead yet alive." Explained Keshub: "Every man standing alone in the world, whose senses are dead unto the flesh, whose carnal nature has been totally subdued . . . who speaks not, moves not, and is not tempted by temptations, such a man is like a cross." As with Keshub's concurrent experiments with rituals and ceremonies, the object was not to reinforce parochial and national myths, but to understand the human spiritual impulse. Was the cross simply a Christian symbol of the martyrdom of Jesus? "Buddha too is on a cross." Said Keshub: "He is dead, a motionless, statue-like figure representing crucified humanity, slain-self, vanquished senses—Shiva, mahayogi also . . . lying on the ground, dead and senseless with the feet of Shakti, Divine force standing upon him. The whole thing appears like an inverted cross."[69]

That Keshub sought to integrate his thinking on symbols at the same time as he groped for each one's special meaning seems clear also from articles in *New Dispensation*. His acute though often inconsistent mind appeared all-encompassing. On July 22, for example, he discussed "incarnations" as a religious phenomenon that has occurred the world over during periods of crisis, when a culture held down by the "forces of wickedness and darkness evoked the direct assistance of God to save them. Each culture has expressed this human need in its own diverse set of symbols. Unessential cultural trappings ought not to be confused with essential human needs. As the Christian and Hindu cases demonstrate, "the plenitude of redeeming mercy puts on human flesh and comes down to earth as a human being with human passion and feelings." Then "having achieved the work of redemption," he goes "back to the heavens."[70]

Evidently Keshub was moving in various directions simultaneously in his quest to understand and absorb all forms of religious expression. Typical in this regard was his growing fascination with the "Motherhood of God." In his article on March 24, 1881, Keshub went so far as to suggest that perhaps the Mother was a better symbolic representation of God than the Father. In his own words, "the Mother is tender-hearted and indulgent even more so than the father and fondles and caresses and suckles the child day and night with intense affection, inward watchfulness and unitary forebearance . . . so the Lord is sweet and tender, long-suffering and of great mercy. Then why should we hesitate to admit the analogy here? If God is father-like, He is surely mother-like too."[71] Because Keshub referred to God as mother during these later years, some persons assumed he had abandoned Christ and Krishna for Durga or Kali. But on mission tours of Bengal and Bihar, where he sought to reach the masses directly, and reportedly covered 600 miles and spoke to 40,000 people on a single occasion, Krishna and not the Mother was his predominant theme of discourse.[72] What is missed by commentators is that Keshub had given up his faith in sectarian symbols, and now manipulated them to convey ethical and religious principles to people on different social levels who followed various creeds. To be sure, Keshub had prompted Sanyal to begin writing songs on the Mother for the New Dispensation Church. But as one such song suggests, the notion of the Mother in no way contradicts Keshub's neo-Vedantist ethic of the *nava sishu*:

> O Mother make me a lover like yourself
> So I can love all as you love all
> Everyone is your son.
> O Mother you are mine and I am yours
> The Universe rests in your bosom
> As a lover devoted to you,
> I am devoted to all
> And to all shall I give my love.[73]

Another interesting development in Keshub was his public confession of "spiritual madness." In the *New Dispensation* issue of April 14, 1881, Keshub published his first of many essays on the *pagal* or madman. Partly as a brilliant literary device to defend his heterodox position and behavior, and partly as a defense of the God-intoxicated man against secular man, these articles contain highly revealing insights into the mind and heart of a complex human personality obsessed with a mission. In the first *pagal* essay, Keshub confessed that "too much thinking has made me mad, and marred all my prospects in the world." Though Keshub spent so much of his time convincing others about religious reformation, he preferred to be alone because "soliloquy is better than conversation." Did this account for his unpopularity? Why did he prefer to be alone rather than with others? Because "all pagals love themselves and I am no exception." Actually, when alone he was not alone. Keshub admitted to being two personalities in one, and that when "I am walking not I alone but I am two persons walking together." The two persons living within himself who were present in "every act and thought, in every force and energy . . . are the human me and the Divine me closely interwoven."[74]

In June, Keshub wrote his second pagal essay on "the haunted house as his most permanent abode." It is a house filled with ghosts and spirits and the "Captain of the ghosts is called the Holy Ghost." The "Holy Ghost never leaves me . . . because He says He is fond of me . . . and I have grown fond of Him." There are ghosts everywhere in the haunted house: "Here, there and everywhere, in my sanctuary, in my drawing room, in the dining room, all over the garden, under shady trees, hidden in the roses . . . ghosts, ghosts, everywhere. . . . Abraham, Moses, Jesus, Confucius, Hindu Rishis, Buddhist monks, all are in me."[75]

In his third article, Keshub referred to his "pagal ears" which have ceased to hear "human voices." All that he could hear were speakers "that have no tongue" and who "pursue him everywhere and at all times with their talk, talk." Turning skyward, Keshub could hear human sounds articulated in the major languages of the world: "The heavens began to speak in Hebrew, the mountains in Sanskrit, the seas and oceans in English, the winds in French, the birds in German, while the grass and flowers spoke in Bengali."[76]

In the fourth essay, Keshub equated madness with the solitary individual who for the sake of truth moved "contrary to established usage and customs."[77] In this essay, in which Keshub betrayed his loneliness as an unpopular prophet with a superb sense of irony, one is struck by his own awareness of the impossible futility of his scheme. He was also physically ill at the time, as the crippling effects of diabetes gradually inhibited his movements and brought on long periods of despondency.

In 1882, his physical condition made him increasingly unable to participate in church activities. According to Protap Majumdar, who was closest to him among the disciples, "the fatal malady" first incapacitated Keshub during the January anniversary celebrations. "His constitution was exceedingly nervous," reported Majumdar, "and within a few days he began to have fits which greatly alarmed his friends."[78]

By August, from a letter to Max Müller, Keshub had begun to confess to his friends abroad that his disease was chronic and progressive. His "ill-health" had since January made him more and more "irritable, weak and unable to work as hard as usual." This was an agonizing letter for Keshub, but a revealing one about his sense of mission. To Müller, he defended his decision to start the New Dispensation, but bemoaned the bitter fact that he would never be able to complete the "work of construction." What motivated Keshub to establish the new church? Because all his life he had been "torn between sympathy for Europe and Asia," and the New Dispensation was conceived to heal that breach: "If you know the leading principles of my life and character, you will no doubt admit that I am pledged to reconciliation and harmony. If I live for my purpose it is for this, that I will preach the union of Eastern and Western theism, the reconciliation of Europe and Asia. The idea may seem absurd to many in the present age. It may provoke ridicule and angry reviling. But posterity will prove the better judge."[79]

Posterity was obviously on the mind of Keshub in 1882 because, while recuperating in the Himalayan hill station of Darjeeling, he began dictating his autobiography to Protap Majumdar. The title of his spiritual odyssey was *Jiban Veda*, which has considerable symbolic meaning to Koar, who believed that this was Keshub's final testimony to his belief in the Vedantic ethic. The unity of the Spirit made all men brothers under the Fatherhood of God. The meaning of Keshub's title, according to Koar, was that "everyone's life is a Veda written in the blood of all mankind."[80]

There are many passages in the *Jiban Veda* devoted to the Motherhood of God. It was to Mother that he confessed his loneliness because he had been forsaken by his generation. To Mother he prayed that he be given strength never to renounce his pursuit of the truth. And it was Mother who is credited for ending the "austere dry" period of his religious life and bringing the joy of ecstatic love in bhakti. Gradually, said Keshub, "I came to call God Mother." From the autobiography: "Now that I have seen Mother, I feel as if I would be forever maddened with joy. . . . My Mother will visit every house. . . . May my hope and bhakti increase in me day by day! May my insanity further develop! . . . Instead of dryness, I am possessed of bhakti now."[81]

There is probably a relationship between such feelings by Keshub and his decision in 1882 to favor dance as an accepted form of worship in the church. "Nothing excites more powerful emotions of joy in the heart," wrote Keshub in defense of it, "than dancing as a spiritual exercise in which . . . is realized the highest impulses of God." Keshub consistently justified his appeal as a universal religious need in all cultures: "The Yogi Shiva danced on the Himalayas with the dead body of his beloved Parvati on his shoulders. The Bhagavat is full of sentiments on the blessed practise of dancing. In the Bible, David danced before the Lord. The Sufis dance. The Buddhist priests and Lamas of Tibet and Ceylon worship in a weird, quaint dance."[82]

On January 20, 1883, Keshub gave his last annual lecture in Town Hall. In what he called "Asia's Message to Europe," he reiterated most of what he had said and written countless times since the birth of the New Dispensation. Familiar was his rational appeal for his universal religion on the basis of scientific unity and on the need to end sectarian and national strife. To the end of his life he offered harmony to both Indian nationalists and British imperialists. He offered his church and ideology as "a flag of truce and reconciliation" to the "formidable artillery of Europe's aggressive civilization." To the British, Keshub held up the banner of his church and declared that "there shall be no more cruel slaughter of Asia's social institutions and her very industries . . . but henceforth peace and amity, brotherhood and friendliness."[83]

Later in the year, because it was evident that Keshub had become too incapacitated to go to the mandir, a devalaya or private family chapel was built at his Lilly Cottage. The construction of it "was pushed on with all possible haste." On the first day of the new year of 1884, Keshub was carried on his disciples' shoulders from his deathbed to take part in the consecration ceremony of the devalaya.[84]

One of the last functions attended by Keshub was the New Dispensation dance performance, which he and Sanyal presumably wrote together. Community members of all ages started to dance "around the invisible Mother," reported Protap Majumdar, "all in different columns of yellow, white, and brown, moving with hands upraised keeping time to the deep sweet sound of the sacred mridanga."[85]

Sheer physical agony accompanied each waking hour of Keshub's last days. On January 8, with his family, disciples, and the Reverend Dall standing at his bed, Keshub breathed his last. Just before the end, it has been reported that he reached up to embrace Sanyal and asked, "when shall I hear your songs again?"[86]

What happened to Keshub's disciples, each of whom after 1875 studied one major religion from primary sources? Did the seminars on comparative religion and the pilgrimages to the saints produce a new universalist outlook among the members of the Durbar? Aside from religion and ideology, how united were the Keshubites when faced with their leader's untimely death and the need to find an immediate successor? Even if they could rise above ideological conflict could they rise above factional strife?

Girish Chandra Sen, who already knew Persian, had been sent to Lucknow by Keshub to learn Arabic.[87] When he returned he began to read, compile, translate, and then write with a passion. In the next decades, he produced thirty separate works, both original and translated into Bengali, of the scriptures and saints of Islam.[88] As already mentioned, Girish Chandra knew very little English, and never wrote anything in that language. Thus his contribution lay in his faithful translation of the Koran, for example, which took him from 1881 to 1886 to complete, and which has since been praised again and again for representing an Islamic point of view. In the 1936 edition of the work, several leading Muslim scholars of East Bengal pronounced it throughly accurate historically, linguistically, and theologically. This is interesting because in the introduction to the Koran, Girish Chandra wrote candidly that by means of Bengali, he wished to "free the chief scriptural sources of Islam from the imprisonment of Arabic . . . and the monopoly of a few Maulavis."[89]

Interesting also is the fact that in 1905, during the agitation over Curzon's partition of the two Bengals, Girish Chandra, a Hindu-born Vaishnava and Brahmo, supported the move. According to his autobiography, he did so not out of love for "British imperialism," but for love of East Bengal, which had been unable to develop under West Bengal's dominance. "If Dacca be the capital," he wrote, "then it will benefit East Bengalis very much." "No longer will West Bengalis monopolize the land and the jobs," he concluded defiantly. Like a true Brahmo universalist, he warned against the anti-English attitude generated by Swadeshi. "If we close the frontiers to foreign ideas," he prophesied, "then we shall dry up and lose our recent heritage."[90]

Gour Govinda Ray, Keshub's choice for Hinduism, applied himself to arranging and clarifying the various religious traditions by placing them in some historical perspective. In 1876, Keshub dignified his quest by extending to him the scholarly title of "Upadhyay." This was in recognition of the fact that among the ascetic group of comparativists, Gour Govinda was the best Sanskrit scholar.

Like many of Keshub's associates, Gour Govinda seemed most interested in medieval Bengali Vaishnavism, and within that religious movement the Krishna tradition drew much of his critical scholarly attention. By 1900, through countless articles and tracts, he came to the point of pulling together the results of his research on the Krishna tradition in a single volume. From a comparativist point of view, most revealing was his attempt to compare the Hindu Christ (Krishna) with Christ himself. For Gour Govinda, Christ and Krishna were undoubtedly similar as religious and ethical reformers who sought the same end of sanctifying earthly conditions. The original Buddha also could be placed in this category.

"The fact is," wrote Gour Govinda, "that essentially all reformers respond to the same conditions with identical ideas that transcend the particular time and country of birth." Nevertheless, there were differences of custom, language, and historical circumstances. One must understand the pattern of evolution, from the Vedas to the Bhagavad Gita, as against the pattern in West Asia from the Old to the New Testament. We might illustrate with the problem of sin and salvation. Both Krishna and Christ stressed their importance, and for the same human reasons. But Krishna saw sin as a violation of dharma (ethical obligations according to one's station in life), whereas Christ saw himself as apostle of God, interpreting sin as a violation of divine will. Both prophets proscribed severe punishments for sinners, but the systems of retribution differed considerably. Ray also reasoned that both Krishna and Christ were providentially designed for man's salvation. But again, Christ's death on the cross to save mankind was a unique resolution of the problem of evil, "which has no parallel in the Krishna of the Gita."[92]

It should not be thought, however, that the implications of Gour Govinda's scholarship leaned to nationalism. The comparative assessments of the Keshubites loosened the bonds of ideological parochialism and made them value unity over diversity. A good example of this was Gour Govinda's last published work in 1912, shortly before his death. Here he dealt with the philosophy of the Vedanta in a way that resembled the neo-Vedantic lectures of Vivekananda and Brahmobandhab. But if the latter two ended up glorifying its virtues and arguing the superiority of Hindusim, Gour Govinda interpreted monism as "liberal universalism." He argued that Vedantic monism was offered to the world as a universal faith to combat sectarianism and its false loyalty to "partial truths."[93]

Aghore Nath Gupta, who was chosen to rediscover the true path of the Buddha, had what may have been the most difficult task of all. In the first place, Brahmos believed that no true reformer could be devoid of God's grace, and yet Buddha was reputedly an atheist. Second, though devout in faith and comparativist in sentiment, Aghore Nath the Vaishnava found himself compelled to study seriously what amounted to a foreign religion. Unfortunately, also, he died early (1881) in his scholarly quest on a mission tour of the Northwest.[94] He left behind one valuable book, a life of the Buddha, the first of its kind in Bengali or in any other modern South Asian language. Published in 1882, it was a result of a laborious undertaking that included a thorough reading of Orientalist scholarship on the Buddha, consultations with Rajendralal Mitra, the Bengali president of the Asiatic Society, a review of original sources in local libraries, and two years of effort in writing it up. The end product was a convincing case, at least from the Keshubite point of view, that Buddha "though opposed to prevalent notions of God, was himself neither an atheist nor an agnostic." Rather, "he was a religious humanist who did not believe in a creator because to him, the world was false and full of illusion. But as a humanist, he found religion in the notion of infinite knowledge and that man's pursuit of it would grant him salvation."[95]

The evidence suggests that most of Keshub's ascetic followers remained true to their scholarly quest long after their leader's demise, and that ideologically they espoused a universalism characteristic of the New Dispensation Church. But if we see the organization's history during the years after Keshub's death from the point of view of his closest friend, Protap Chandra Majumdar, a very different image emerges. We have shown earlier how Majumdar, the elegant, Westernized, world-traveled Brahmo intellectual, was not only the most unlikely follower of ascetic Keshub but the most avid proponent of Unitarian Christianity. It may be said that after thirty years of missionary activity in Calcutta, the Reverend C. H. Dall's most important convert to Unitarianism was not Keshub, but Protap Majumdar.

On January 10, 1884, P. C. Majumdar had arrived back in Madras from an around-the-world tour, and gone immediately to the telegraph office to send a message reporting the fact to Keshub. There he received what he later recalled as the "shock of his life." "One of the clerks came out," he wrote in his diary, "and said that Keshub was dead." Every organ in his body ached and his "throat and mouth became as dry as dust." His thoughts on the train back to Calcutta: "I know not what will become of me, nor what will become of the Brahmo Samaj. I often thought I would die before him. I was so weak and ill, he so strong and beautiful."

Majumdar had imagined himself to be Keshub's rightful successor to the pulpit. Had he not represented the New Dispensation Church to countless people around the world, and had he not made Keshub's name famous in America as the true successor of Rammohun Roy and as leader of the Brahmo reformation of India? But Majumdar must also have realized that his sympathy for the Unitarian conception of Christ and his intimacy with American Unitarians made him an unsuitable candidate to the ascetic faction. And sure enough, the largely Vaishnava clique barred his attempt

Figure 2. P. C. Majumdar, 1917

to occupy Keshub's pulpit. More disturbing was the fact that the Sen family now looked upon the Brahmo mandir as personal property, and decided to back the ascetics against Protap Chandra.

On February 27, a meeting was supposed to be held at the mandir for the purpose of reconciling differences. But when Majumdar and his supporters arrived at the mandir they found every entrance blocked, the doors locked, and police protecting the property from destruction.[96] So Majumdar led his group to a public square where they gave speeches to enlist sympathy for their misfortune. Majumdar was compelled to form his own congregation, which met separately, prayed separately, conducted its own affairs, and published its own journal. Thus in Keshub Sen's church, which had been founded to give battle to ethnocentricism, nationalism, and parochialism, his followers could not disown their own sectarian passions.

CHAPTER TEN

Rabindranath Tagore as Reformer: Hindu Brahmoism and Universal Humanism

OF all the Brahmos, the one who most captured the imagination of people throughout the world was Rabindranath Tagore. He became famous as the first Asian winner of the Nobel Prize in 1913, and as the founder of an international university at Santineketan. In South Asia, he is revered for having championed the religion of humanity against the forces of parochial creeds. Tagore has been the object of an idolatrous veneration, attested by the staggering number of literary works delineating his achievements in the arts, in education, and in philosophy. It would seem that the enormous body of literature in all the major languages which examines so many facets of his creative genius would discourage the scholar from hoping to say anything new and significant about him. But the fact is that far more than with any other Brahmo discussed in this book, Rabindranath has been subjected to a gurubad (excessive adoration) that has not only dehumanized him, but has dehistoricized him as well. It is unfortunate for historical scholarship, however, that monographs on Rabindranath rarely place the right emphasis on the sociocultural and ideological background of his period and of his own unique personality, which produced that phenomenally versatile creative outburst.[1] Rarely does a writer start from the basic facts that Rabindranath's grandfather was a cofounder of the Brahmo movement with Rammohun Roy, that his father revitalized the movement, and that his brothers were active and dedicated members of the Adi Brahmo Samaj. Rabindranath's life and thought were shaped by a special set of historical circumstances that predisposed him in his choice of life style, and nurtured him in the atmosphere of the most accomplished Brahmo family of the Bengal renaissance. He was intellectually sensitive from adolescence to all the major issues and problems confronted by the Brahmo community, and reacted creatively as a Brahmo to the stresses and strains of traditionalism on the one hand and modernism on the other, or Hindu modernism on the one hand and universalism on the other.

Rabindranath's values, ideals, his very attitudes did not emerge from a vacuum. Though there is a tendency and a temptation to treat a great figure like Tagore as an end in himself, and to become absorbed in the man, it should be obvious that pure aesthetic criticism of a creative thinker such as he was does not absolve the critic from the responsiblity of understanding his historical context. As we shall soon see, his novel *Gora*, which is considered by many to be his greatest, was no mere aesthetic *tour de force*, to be treated as a precious literary gem cut off from history and reality. On the contrary, within the pages of a single book Tagore presented one of the most effective intellectual attempts to capture the dilemmas of Brahmo liberalism under colonial rule on the one hand, and militant Hindu nationalism on the other. I would argue that it is Brahmo history that constitutes the very special milieu that gave rise to the towering genius of Rabindranath Tagore. I would also hypothesize that Tagore's ideology, too often viewed against some vague, East-West encounter model, was really the outcome of his response to the challenge of the unresolved problems that we have explored throughout this book, as part of the legacy of Brahmo social history.

To round out a general hypothesis about Tagore to guide us through the mass of biographical details of a long and richly varied life, I suggest we look closely at his reinterpretation of the Adi Brahmo idea of Hindu modernism, because it may well constitute Tagore's most important ideological contribution to Bengal and to India. Though it is often difficult to find consistency in Tagore's intellectual meanderings, I would recommend that we pay heed to the relationship between Hindu modernist trends and his self-acknowledged adherence to a Hindu Brahmo identity. Hindu Brahmoism, which we have traced in developed form to 1866 as one consequence of Keshub Sen's schism from the Adi Samaj, emerged in the encounter of modernizing alternatives of nationalism and universalism. It was surely no accident that the earliest use of the term Hindu Brahmo was in reference to Adi Samajists such as Rajnarian Bose, Debendranath and Dwijendranath Tagore. To my knowledge, it was in 1890 when Ramananda Chatterji cast off his sacred thread and declared himself a Hindu Brahmo because "Brahmoism was the truest exposition of Hinduism," that the term applied for the first time to a Sadharan Samajist.[2] With the escalation of British imperialism and the consequent rise of militant nationalism about the same time, the underlying problem of modernity became even more acute. Here, in my estimation, is the setting for Rabindranath's role and contribution as a key figure—not merely among poets or litterateurs—but among the reformers and modernizers of the Bengali intelligentsia.

Though the basic biographical data of Rabindranath's life are well known to the general reader of Indian history, the Brahmo side of his life is relatively unknown in print. And, as I have argued, analysis of Rabindranath's life and thought against his sociocultural background is also rare. Stephen Hay, in the most recent monograph on an aspect of Tagore's ideology, states that the earliest formative influence on Rabindranath was Keshub Chandra Sen. That Rabindranath was born in 1861, at the honeymoon period of the relationship between Keshub and Debendranath, is significant to Hay. The fact that Rabindranath's brothers, Satyendranath and Hemendranath, were then very much devoted to the magnetic Keshub is important, as is the fact that Rabindranath was born at the very time that Keshub fled his own house to live in the Tagore *bari*. Indeed, as Rabindranath himself later wrote, "I was fortunate enough to receive his [Keshub's] affectionate caresses at the moment when he was cherishing his dream of a great future spiritual illumination."

No doubt Rabindranath was influenced by Keshub—especially in his ideological development in mature life—since few Brahmos referred to in this book, from Debendranath's time onward, were not at first favorably attracted to the reformer. We may recall Debendranath himself telling Protap Majumdar in the 1880s that it was impossible for any middle-class Bengali to have "a drop of water" without at least once mentioning the name of Keshub. But we should also bear in mind that Rabindranath was five years old when the bitter schism took place that radically transformed the affections of the Tagore family and made them bitter foes of Keshub. For all practical purposes, Satyendranath left the Calcutta scene in 1862, when he went to England and upon his return became a civil servant in West India. We may recall that the family leadership passed into the hands of Dwijendranath and Jyotirindranath, two of Keshub's deadliest enemies ideologically and personally. Indeed, it is Jyotirindranath who became Rabindranath's favorite brother in the years that followed.[3] It was assuredly a strong family commitment to Hindu Brahmoism and cultural nationalism that

Rabindranath experienced during the years of Nabagopal Mitra's nationalist enterprise, the *National Paper* (with its inflammatory articles by Dwijendranath), the Tagore-supported Hindu Mela, and Rajnarian's presidency of the Adi Samaj. As viewed by Keshub and his followers, the Tagores were drifting back into the Hindu fold. If in his youthful years Rabindranath retained some attraction for Keshub's universalism, which is likely but difficult to prove one way or the other, then we may have isolated the origins of that "traditionalist-Westernizer" split in Tagore's personal and ideological makeup which Professor Susobhan Sarkar has interpreted as the two most important currents of thought in the poet's lifetime.

Susobhan, himself of Brahmo background, has written one of the best studies of Tagore in the context of the Bengal renaissance. His Marxist realism and brilliant analytical technique as a historian has cleared away much of the incense-saturated air surrounding the usual iconic approach to the poet. Moreover, his study is a welcome relief from the simplistic "spiritual East" notion that has unfortunately been associated with Tagore. Sarkar has also come as close as anyone to identifying a crucial "dialectic" in Tagore's psychological and ideological development. He has rightly seen the traditionalist-Westernizer split in Tagore's mind as an identity problem similar to, though experienced more intensely than, other members of the intelligentsia. On the other hand, Sarkar may have unnecessarily confused these issues by imposing his own antinationalist value judgment on both extremes of the dialectic. As a result, he seems to have distorted the significance of the polar opposites to which Tagore was alternately attracted. Sarkar's approach to Tagore is analogous to the older concept of the Slavophile-Westernizer schism among the Russian intelligentsia. Thus, he has divided the sentiments of the Bengali intelligentsia into an Orientalist (Slavophile), traditionalist camp and a Westernizer, modernist camp. Traditionalism to Sarkar is tantamount to "worship of past glories," a "consciousness of Hindu superiority," and a "tendency to spiritual mysticism and emotionalism." Westernism equals rationalism and liberalism.

We have demonstrated that Adi Brahmos in the Tagore family camp were not advocating a defense of status-quo traditionalism, but were instead aiming to modernize the Hindu tradition through Brahmoism. Nor were any of the Adi Brahmos given to spiritual emotionalism. On the contrary, we find such religious enthusiasm among the Keshubites, who were more liberal as reformers than Adi Samajists. Often the most Westernized Brahmos were also the most passionate theists, whereas Sanskrit College-trained pundits like Vidyasagar were indifferent to religion. Moreover, Sarkar's stress on the superiority of Hinduism for the Tagores is a reference, quite possibly, to Rajnarian Bose's popular lecture of 1872, which has been greatly misunderstood. Ranjarian was not so much defending the contemporary Hindu faith and society as he was defending the Adi Brahmo interpretation of true Hinduism, which he offered as the crown of tradition. Rammohun Roy had done the same with Vedanta. Actually, in terms of cultural identity, to which Sarkar pays too little heed, nationalism would be a far more accurate description of the Adi Samaj attitude than traditionalism. The challenge by the Keshubites, who were pronounced universalists, only reinforced Adi Samaj loyalty to their own national culture. Thus, when Sarkar quite rightly points out that between 1882 and 1885 Rabindranath was under Rajnarian's influence,[4] this does not imply that the poet was at the time antimodernist. It implies, rather, that he identified strongly with Hindu India against the West. Take, for example, the Tagore family preoccupation with nationalist projects such as the Hindu Mela, or with nationalist societies such as the Secret Society organized in Jorasanko in 1874. Rabindranath, then thirteen years old, was invited to the meetings by Jyotirindranath. Two other conspicuous members were Rajnarian and Dwijendranath. To be sure, the Secret Society identified itself in no uncertain terms with Hindu society. But like the Swadeshi program of the Hindu Mela, the organization promoted among other things the industrial development of India in textiles and jute.[5] Was this position "traditional," "Orientalist," or "reactionary?"

Also in 1884, when Rabindranath was supposedly in one of his dark and reactionary periods as a prisioner of Orientalism, he became secretary of the Adi Brahmo Samaj. According to Ramananda Chatterji, who first met Tagore at this time, Rabindranath was shocked at Bankim Chandra Chatterji's "defense of Hinduism" in the issues of *Prachar* and *Nabajiban*. Ramananda Chatterji was very much taken with Tagore's attitudes as expressed in his lectures. When one considers that Ramananda was then a comparatively radical student socially and politically, it is difficult to believe that he and his peers would have been attracted by the lectures of a "traditionalist-reactionary."

In fact, the young man Rabindranath in the early 1880s was hardly the persevering puritanical type of Brahmo applying himself diligently for some professional career. In comparison with that trio of Satyendranath, Dwijendranath, and Jyotirindranath, Rabindranath was the least formally educated and the least likely to succeed from the standpoint of Brahmo society. Satyendranath was preparing himself for the civil service, Dwijendranath was a self-trained philosopher, and Jyotirindranath an accomplished musician, erudite musicologist, and the author of thirty-two plays. But Rabindranath in 1882, at twenty-one years of age, as Stephen Hay says, "had no worldly responsibilities to concern him," as he "lived off income from tenants of the family's large estates." For a Brahmo to have stopped school at thirteen was most irregular. The 1880s were unsettling for Rabindranath. He evidently suffered a great loss when his sister-in-law, Kadambari Debi, Jyotirindranath's wife, committed suicide. Five months before that, his father had married Rabindranath off to an eleven-year-old girl with little education, the daughter of an employee in the zamindari. This was the period when he moved about in a coarse sheet as a garment and rarely wore shoes, and Hay stresses Rabindranath's feeling as the rootless outsider during this decade.[6]

From Sarkar's point of view, Rabindranath was in a pro-Western phase in the period from 1886 to 1898. Using numerous examples from the poet's writings, Sarkar has made a convincing case for Rabindranath's antipathy to Hindu revivalism. This was the era of *Bangabasi* under the violently anti-Brahmo and generally antiprogressive Jogendra Basu.[7] In this period, the Hari Sabha branches began to proliferate, as did vicious satires against Brahmos in novels and plays by sharp-witted defenders of the status quo, such as Indranath Bannerji.[8] This was the time when Puranic Hinduism and the whole medieval tradition was being defended by such notorious anti-Westernizers as S. Tarkachadamani and K. P. Sen.[9] The ethos of the era was well captured in 1889 when a Sadharan Brahmo missionary named Bipin Chandra Pal lashed out at what he called "the present social reaction": "When education instead of enlarging our minds and making us ready to welcome, and fitted to receive the light of other ages and the truth of other countries, simply helps to envelop us in a mist of narrow and selfish patriotism, that refuses to acknowledge the existence of any virtue beyond the limits of the narrow hole which we call our country, we may shudder to realize how strong this reaction has already become. In fact, the whole atmosphere seems to be literally surcharged with this virulent poison."[10]

Rabindranath also spoke out against the virulent poison of status-quo traditionalism, but not quite in as universalist manner as

Professor Sarkar would have us believe. We must always keep in mind that Tagore was the son of Debendranath, and there is no evidence I have seen that suggests a reaction against the Hindu Brahmo style of the Adi Samaj. Most assuredly, though an-tirevivalist, Rabindranath was no liberal Westernizer. On the one hand, he could and did attack Bankim Chandra Chatterji and Nobin Chandra Sen for their merging of traditionalism and na-tionalism,[11] and here he repudiated the Hindu tradition:

> A lifeless people, stagnant and immobile,
> Its course obstructed by the morass of tradition
> A nation that does not move for its feet are tied
> By scriptural commands and endless incantations.[12]

But, on the other hand, Rabindranath seemed to stay clear of that Sadharan-sponsored alliance between a Westernized Brahmoism and political constitutionalism. His attitude to the Indian Association and the National Congress of Ananda Mohun Bose and Surendra Nath Bannerji is beautifully illustrated in an anecdote by Rabindranath's son, Rathindranath. One night the poet was invited to a dinner of "Anglicized" Congressites for the purpose of enlist-ing his support in the movement. "Father came dressed in a *dhoti* and *chaddur* in the midst of the anglicized diners," wrote Rathin-dranath. He then went on to say that "my father had little faith in their politics," for he "realized the futility of holding meetings and passing pious resolutions."[13] Actually, Rabindranath spent much of his time between 1890 and 1900 in rural East Bengal supervising the zamindari.[14] In sharp contrast to the Brahmo professional in-telligentsia of Calcutta deeply and directly involved in such issues as modernism, revivalism, and nationalism, Rabindranath was the privileged and poetically gifted son of a prominent Brahmo zamindar, who would drift along the rivers of up-country Bengal in a houseboat, cursing "the organized selfishness of Calcutta city life." As a result of this idyll, perhaps no other Bengali poet so cap-tured the natural beauty and simplicity of East Bengal as did Rabindranath.

Between 1898 and 1906, once more Sarkar has placed Tagore in an extreme anti-Westernizer phase. There was deep unrest in the poet, while his work reflected the "shadows of an anguished mind." This was the brief period of Rabindranath's politicized behavior on behalf of the Swadeshi movement. In 1904, at his father's birthday celebration, Rabindranath proudly recalled the Adi Samaj contri-bution to Indian nationalism. He is quoted as having said that the greatness of his father lay in refusing "to dilute our supreme national religion into a vague universalism."[15] This was also the period in Rabindranath's life when, in defiance of Brahmo social reforms, he married off his daughters, aged eleven and fourteen, in the traditional Hindu manner.[16]

One should view this phase of Rabindranath's antiuniversalism against Brahmo defections and the rise of militant nationalism in Bengal. It was probably a kinship of nationalist feelings that prompted Rabindranath in 1901 to invite Brahmobandhab Upadhyay to be headmaster of the new school at Santineketan. Rabindranath's own recorded sentiments during these years resemble those of Brahmobandhab. Even Rabindranath's view that "Brahmanism and not kingship was our country's wealth" in ancient times, uttered in 1904, closely followed Brahmobandhab's own interpretation.[17] Burning with indignation against the abuses of European imperialism, expressed in poems on British intervention in the Boer War or their suppression of the Boxer Rebellion in China, Tagore underwent an experience like Brahmobandhab's, aggressively defying Western racism, militarism, and economic exploitation.[18]

The question may then be asked whether Rabindranath at this point defected from Brahmoism. Certainly, as a militant nationalist, Tagore was never again as suspicious of modernist impulses from the West as during this period in his life. From a Keshubite or Sadharan perspective, Rabindranath's extreme nationalism certainly would make him appear the defector. But in the Adi Brahmo tradition, nationalism was more characteristic than universalism. The question poses a dilemma of a serious nature, which Tagore himself quite possibly sought to resolve in his most powerful novel, *Gora*—first serialized, interestingly enough, in Ramananda Chatterji's *Prabasi* in 1907.[19] We must keep in mind the fact that in 1907 the poet was clearly beginning to retreat from nationalism back to universalism.

Gora, the massively built, fair-complexioned and strong-faced hero of the novel, who is chairman of the Hindu Patriot's Society and detests Anglicized Brahmos, was conceivably a fictionized Brahmobandhab Upadhyay. Just as likely, Gora was Tagore himself during his Brahmobandhab period (1898 to 1906). Written at the end of this phase, the novel can hardly be interpreted as a propaganda piece on behalf of Hindu nationalism and against Brahmo universalism. Instead, it may be seen as a brilliant, soul-searching exploration of the dilemma of Hindu modernism and Hindu modern identity between the polarity of nation and world.

On the surface, the story is about romantic and other entanglements between Gora's Hindu family and friends and those of a
prominent Brahmo family. On another level, the novel is both a
defense and a repudiation of Hindu nationalism and of sectarian
Brahmoism. Only an Adi Brahmo like Tagore could defend Hindu
nationalism with so much fervor through the character of Gora.
Take, for example, Gora's reply to the charge of Hindu social
abuses and cultural decadence: "it matters not whether we are
good or bad, civilized or barbarous so long as we are but ourselves."
There is the dialogue between Gora and his closest friend, Benoy,
in which the former is forced into the position of defending caste,
declaring that "since I owe allegiance to society, I must respect caste
also." "Are we then bound to obey society in all matters?" Benoy
asks. Gora replies that "not to obey society is to destroy it." "What if
it is destroyed," Benoy retorts. Gora's reply: "you might as well ask
what harm there is in cutting off the branch on which one is
seated."

This same theme is pursued later in the book when Benoy sits
with a Brahmo girl, discussing "the defects of our society and the
abuses of our caste system." He explains to her that Gora feels un-
moved by social reformers because he refuses "to regard the broken branches and withered leaves as the ultimate nature of a tree."
Gora regards well-intentioned Brahmo reform as being too often
"simply the result of intellectual impatience." Gora maintains that
he is not a reactionary, because "he does not ask for any praise of
the decaying boughs, but asks us to look at the whole tree and then
try to understand its purpose." The alert Brahmo lady replies that
withered boughs aside, it is the fruits of caste that should be considered; she asks, "what kind of fruits has caste produced in our
country." Benoy, still representing Gora by proxy, gives a significant answer, which again accentuates the need to place the nationalist values of cultural loyalty and self-respect above the
Brahmo propensity to expose Hindu social defects: "What you call
the fruit of caste is not merely that, but the result of the totality of
conditions of our country. If you try to bite with a loose tooth you
suffer pain—for that you don't blame the tooth, but only the loose-
ness of that particular tooth. Because owing to various causes, disease and weakness have attacked us, we have only been able to dis-
tort the idea which India stands for, and not lead it to success. That
is why Gora continually exhorts us to become healthy, become
strong."

But if Rabindranath sympathetically defended the basic tenets of
militant nationalist ideology, he was equally sympathetic to Brahmo

modernism and universalism. The book is as much a repudiation
of the Brahmobandhab thesis that modernism had to be sacrificed
for nationalist goals as it is a defense of the proposition that universalism is not incompatible with the quest for a cultural identity in
the modern world. When Gora, out of compassion for the poor,
travels throughout rural India to arouse the masses to their own
enormous potential for change, he is greatly disillusioned with his
experience:

> This was the first time Gora had seen what the condition of his
> country was like, outside the well-to-do and cultured society of
> Calcutta. How divided, how narrow, how weak was the vast ex-
> panse of rural India—how supremely unconscious as to its own
> welfare. . . . What a host of self-imposed imaginary obstacles pre-
> vented them from taking their place in the grand commerce of
> the world. . . . Without such an opportunity to see it for himself,
> Gora would never have been able to observe how inert were
> their minds, how petty their lives, how feeble their efforts.

That Rabindranath remained faithful to the Adi Brahmo doctrine of nationalistic modernism is quite obvious, even when articulated through the defiant posture of Gora. In one passage, after
Benoy challenges Gora on the validity of Brahmo persistence to reform the society, the reply is the familiar argument Adi Samajists
had been using since the Keshub Sen schism of 1866. Gora says
that he too is for change, but that "it won't do for those changes to
be absolutely crazy ones." In a manner reminiscent of Dwijendranath Tagore, Gora declares that "A child gradually grows up to
be a man but man does not suddenly become a cat or a dog. I want
the changes in India to be along the path of India's development
for if you suddenly begin to follow the path of England's history—
then everything from first to last will be a useless failure. I am sac-
rificing my life to show you that the power and greatness of our
country have been preserved in our country itself."

The crushing blow to Gora in the very end of the novel is Rabindranath's vindication of Brahmo universalism against this extremely narrow national-centered view of change. Throughout the
book, Brahmos continually argue with Gora that effective change
in India is impossible if her cultural frontiers remain shut to the
progressive forces in the West. The persuasiveness of the position
gradually wins over Gora's best friend, Benoy, who becomes a
Brahmo sympathizer. Then, in the final pages, Gora, after burying
himself deeper and deeper in the pit of his Hindu militancy, learns

from the man he had viewed as his father that he is not a Hindu after all, but the son of an Irishman killed in the Indian Mutiny. Both of Gora's parents had been white Europeans. "In a single moment Gora's whole life seemed to him like some extraordinary dream," writes Tagore. In the following narration, Tagore explodes the myth of a narrow confining national loyalty, and places Gora in the limbo of an uncertain identity: "The foundations upon which, from childhood all his life had been raised had suddenly crumbled into dust, and he was unable to understand who he was and where he stood. . . . He felt as though he were like the dew drop on the lotus leaf which comes into existence for a moment only. He had no mother, no father, no country, no nationality, no lineage, no God even. Only one thing was left to him and that was a vast negation." But the book ends positively as Gora begins to accept the wider identity of universal humanism—which Tagore himself was acquiring at this time. Significantly, it is to Paresh Babu, the most sympathetic Brahmo in the book, that Gora discloses, "Today I am free . . . to-day I am really an Indian. In me there is no longer any opposition between Hindu, Muslim, and Christian. To-day every caste in India is my caste, the food of all is my food."

Evidently Tagore, after years of brooding despair among the ranks of the nationalists, now returned to the larger tradition of Brahmo universalism. But it was actually philosophic Brahmoism to which he returned, not to the sectarian community *per se*. The denationalized, professionalized materialist Brahmo cut off from the mass of his own countrymen was as much the object of Rabindranath's wrath as the narrow militant nationalist. Gora's angry denunciation of the Westernized Bengali professional, smoking a cigar like an Englishman on the first-class deck of a Ganges steamer, is one of the most effective testimonies to the fact that Rabindranath was assuredly not a Westernizer in the simple sense of the term. His sympathy lay instead with the Paresh Babu type of Brahmo who was genuinely spiritual, moral, and eclectic. Paresh, a good householder, lived simply, and in his study "on the wall is a colored picture of Christ and a photo of Keshub . . . and in a small bookcase on the upper shelf stood a complete set of Theodore Parker's works arranged in a row."[20]

Gora, in my estimation, represents Tagore's last major reconciliation of opposites leading to a higher synthesis of the nobler features of the Brahmo heritage with the exigencies of contemporary life in Bengal. After 1907, Tagore refined his faith in universal humanism. In a significant essay of 1908, there was still the attack on the injustices of British imperialism, coupled with sympathy for Bengalis who were advocating national self-respect. But there was also this note of warning and hopeful reconciliation: "If we do not come in contact with what is best in the Englishman, seeing in him only a soldier, or merchant or bureaucrat; if he will not stand on the place where man may communicate with man; if, in short, the Indian and the Englishman must stand apart they will simply be objects of mutual repugnance." In this provocative essay, which was, incidentally, delivered to the Sadharan Brahmo Samaj, Tagore has left behind him the negative attitude of militant nationalists against exposure of one's own social defects. The clue in his changing attitude lies precisely in the way Tagore lashed out at those who buried the abuses of the Hindu social order in the patriotic sloganeering of aggressive nationalist ideology. Nowhere earlier did Rabindranath attack the caste system with so much vehemence as a system where "men are looked upon as lower than beasts." Still another clue to his change of heart lay in his conviction that "India today deceives and insults herself because even if we succeeded in pushing out the British by one means or another this pain [social defects] will still be there."[21]

After publishing *Gora*, Tagore reactivated himself as a Brahmo and began giving sermons and lectures from the pulpit. His sermons between 1908 and 1911 are interesting not only for their spiritual insights, but for their expressed purpose of breathing new life into Brahmoism by widening its ideological appeal. His rational theistic approach to classical themes in Hinduism was not only a revival of the spirit of Adi Samaj religiosity, but represents some of his finest prose of the devotional genre. As preceptor of the Santineketan community, he seemed also to have underscored the need of spiritualizing profane matters and issues, continually asserting in the familiar Brahmo style that unless religion accompanies progress, society will ultimately fall apart. The triumph of "universalism over national egoism," that key message of *Gora*, Tagore reiterated again and again in a variety of literary forms.

In 1910, he was invited to give the Keshub Sen anniversary address. For the first time since 1866, the hard feelings between the Adi Samaj and New Dispensation were dissolved. Keshub's recognition of the unity underlying religious diversity was now accepted by Rabindranath as a valuable and courageous defense of the truth. It was not Keshub's spirituality but his universality that won over Rabindranath from enemy to disciple: "Truth is to be sought in all religions—it is to be revealed and then accepted. This was Keshub's burning desire. This is what he achieved [through comparative religion] and then revealed it in the name of the New Dispensation. When I realized this, all my earlier antagonism for him vanished and I came to pay him homage."[22]

In 1911, Rabindranath took over the leadership of the Adi Brahmo Samaj and editorship of its journal, the *Tattvabodhini Patrika*. In the most serious effort to revitalize the ailing organization since Rajnarian Bose became president in 1870, and as part of a larger effort to reconcile the three Brahmo Samajes and to win support from Hindu sympathizers, Rabindranath revived the Tattvabodhini Sabha, with himself as secretary. For some years Rabindranath had been very intimate with Keshubites such as Troylokya Nath Sanyal, who greatly influenced him in the composition of Brahmo religious songs. Kinship with Ramananda Chatterji since 1907 appears in large part to have been derived from the sensible and universalist aspect of the latter's style of creative nationalism. At the same time, Tagore's updated form of Hindu Brahmoism appealed to the younger generation of Sadharan Brahmos, of whom Prasanta Mahalanobis was perhaps the most dedicated disciple.[23]

Tagore's editorials and essays in the *Tattvabodhini Patrika* between 1911 and 1914, as in the case of most of his Brahmo writings, have not been given the attention they deserve either ideologically or aesthetically. Ideologically, they are important in reflecting Rabindranath's intellectual and spiritual outlook at the very time he achieved international fame as recipient of the Nobel Prize in literature. What they reveal in no uncertain terms is that Rabindranath, in his early fifties, was convinced that the Brahmo heritage had to be preserved and elaborated upon as an antidote for what he diagnosed as the disease of contemporary Bengali society and politics. Quite conceivably he was making a bid for charismatic leadership, not only within the Brahmo movement, but outside it among liberal Hindus more attracted to philosophic Brahmoism than to its sectarian aspects.

His *Tattvabodhini* essays fall into four general categories: the true meaning of Brahmoism, the shortcoming of divisiveness within the Brahmo Samaj, Brahmoism and Hinduism, and the application of Brahmo universal humanism to the world of extreme national egoism and rivalry. As for the first question, on the true meaning of Brahmoism, Rabindranath believed it to be essentially "the pervasiveness of rational religion in all our life activities."[24] But like Ramananda Chatterji, Tagore saw an aesthetic side to the uses of icons in religion, thus disclaiming the validity of rigid iconoclasm, on the one hand, and refusing to accept it as fundamental in the Brahmo faith, on the other.[25] According to Rabindranath, most characteristic of the Brahmo is his determination to retain pure theism at the pivot and not at the margin of his existence. He saw Brahmo piety as the ultimate source for that famous Brahmo strength of purpose to accomplish great things. Most significant was Rabindranath's stress on the need to build up this internal vitality through self-discipline and meditation. What was required, in his view, was not a temple for weekly services or a ritual that becomes mechanical, but an "ashram" where religion and "selfless beneficence will result from the beauty of universal nature mingling with the pure heart of men." That he was justifying his Santineketan as the truest form of a Brahmo ashram there can be little doubt, but what he seemed to be defending most against the charge of "monasticism" was the value of such an institution for Brahmos. "They say I am separating the religious life from the world," wrote Rabindranath, "and that this will cripple the human mind." Rabindranath replied that the ashram was designed to impart the necessary education for self-realization under the most favorable natural circumstances. Because the valuable lessons learned could be "applied elsewhere" and for "progressive purposes on a higher plane for all," the charge of life negation was a false one.[26]

For Rabindranath, divisiveness was both the curse of the Brahmo Samaj and its chief reason for decline. Factionalism within the Samaj as well as sectarianism of many Brahmos against Hindus irritated him to no end. He saw this tendency to bifurcate into smaller cliques in endless progression, always involved in petty issues and backbiting, as "an old habit of ours" that was in direct contradiction to Brahmo universalism. On one occasion, when Rabindranath was rebuked by an Adi Samajist for having invited K. K. Mitra, and Kayastha Sadharan Samajist, to sit at the altar, Tagore exploded and exclaimed publicly that he was not sure if in the last analysis Brahmos, "instead of worshipping God, worshipped dol or faction."[27]

On the idea of Brahmoism as the true form of Hinduism, Rabindranath was following the general lines of Adi cultural nationalism. But unlike his brother, Dwijendranath, or Rajnarian Bose, Rabindranath took the whole of Brahmo history as the heritage of a renascent Hinduism. In one essay, dated May 1911, on "The Service of the Brahmo Samaj," Tagore refused to acknowledge the decline of the Brahmo Samaj, though he readily admitted that "a phase of its history has ended." Brahmos should be jubilant, he argued, now that the "Hindu samaj has been awakened." Can we say that the work of the Brahmo Samaj is finished? Hardly. Brahmos should now "help the Hindu samaj follow the right path of reform." If Brahmos remain in "isolation" or in the "self-confinement of sectarianism," warned Rabindranath, then they will not only "place obstacles in the path of reformation," but assure their own extinction. In the very same essay, Rabindranath moved across the lines of Adi Samaj nationalism to the heritage of Keshub Chandra Sen's quest for a universal religion. As Rabindranath rephrased the problem: the world—especially the West—urgently needed the universal humanism of the Brahmo faith. "The problem of Europe," he wrote, "is egocentric nationalism, a disease to be cured only by a universal ideal of humanity." It was the key role of the Brahmo Samaj to help in saving the world from the "madness of nationalism."[28]

In the Brahmo *Maghutsab* festival of January 1912, though Rabindranath was fifty-two years old, he was clearly the most important new leader among the Brahmo community groping for a creative and constructive ideology. At the Adi Samaj hall in Jorosanko, one of the most beautiful of all Brahmo celebrations took place under the spiritual guidance of the Acharya Rabindranath himself. Then, invited by Hiralal Haldar, president of the Sadharan Samaj that year, Rabindranath joined their festivities and made stirring speeches for Hindu Brahmoism, in which he was supported by Ramananda Chatterji and Sitanath Tattvabhusan.[29]

There is another valuable source for ascertaining Rabindranath's ideological development as a Brahmo during this critical period of his life. His correspondence between 1910 and 1915, mostly with fellow Brahmos, has been carefully preserved in the museum of Visva Bharati University at Santineketan. In letters to Promothalal Sen, Ajit Chakrabarti, Ramananda Chatterji, Prasanta Mahalanobis, and other Brahmos of the time, Rabindranath reinforced the four major themes contained in his *Tattvabodhini* essays. Many of these letters were written while on his Nobel Prize tour in Europe and America.

There are many references to Brahmo divisiveness or factionalism in his correspondence; but written as they were for the most part from the West, on the eve of the first World War, the essays inevitably associated this factionalism with the theme of

Brahmo universal humanism. Tagore condemned all forms of factionalism, sectarianism, communalism, and Brahmo nationalism.
In one letter of March 18, 1913, to Chakrabarti, from Urbana, Illinois, where Tagore was visiting his son Rathindranath, the contrast between Brahmo universalism and the varieties of human divisiveness was never sharper. The fact that the letter began with an
agonizing prophecy based on a contradiction between high ideals
and actual practice in the West indicates that Tagore was beginning
to view the problem of doladoli not as unique to Brahmos or Bengalis, but as a human problem. "The West which is about to destroy
the world," wrote Tagore, "has nevertheless produced great men
who have courageously fought against the fashion of placing nationalism above religion."[30] In the same letter, Tagore was extremely perturbed by Brahmo sectarianism. He singled out Rammohun Roy as one of the greatest men produced in modern India.
"But the Brahmo Samaj," wrote Tagore, "is belittling Rammohun
Roy by judging him as a Brahmo minus the Hindu society." To be
sure, because Tagore argued so forcefully for the idea of Hindu
Brahmoism against Brahmo sectarianism, one could easily read
into the letter the familiar Adi Samaj attitude of cultural nationalism. But in the context of the other letters it seems fairly certain that he aimed to integrate a smaller unit into a larger unit of
Hindu society, while at the same time advocating that Hindu society integrate itself into the larger unit of Asian civilizations.

Take, for example, another letter in the same file, which dealt
almost entirely with the theme of Hindu Brahmoism. His argument was that Brahmoism and reformed Hinduism were similar—certainly not an unfamiliar argument among Adi Brahmos.
But at the same time, he made it clear that status-quo Hinduism,
filled with defects and abuses, must be altered in such a way that it
reflected the "inner Hinduism," that is, the true Hinduism. "I cannot separate Brahmoism from inner Hinduism," he said again and
again. There is nothing in the letter to suggest a return to the militancy of *Gora*, but rather one finds the expression of a sagacious
proposition that unless Brahmos identify with Hinduism and attempt to give it progressive leadership, the community would be
committing suicide by allowing the Hindu reformation to drift into
"false directions."

Perhaps the difference between Tagore's Hindu Brahmoism and
the most popular varieties of Hindu reformism can be better ascer-
tained when set against Vivekananda's objectives and influence. As
we have already noted, Vivekananda also adapted the Brahmo her-

itage for the purpose of revitalizing Hinduism, but he had done so by compromising Brahmoism for the sake of mass appeal. In a letter from Tagore to Chakrabarti dated February 15, 1913, Rabindranath attacked the cult of swamis who had visited the West since Vivekananda, who had presented a "false image" of Hinduism and had left nothing behind but "bad taste and grace."[31] When one considers that Tagore was a guest of Unitarians in Boston at the time, and that he was strongly against emotionalism in religion, one is reminded of Protap Majumdar's indictment of Vivekananda at the Parliament of Religions. When one adds the similarity in Rabindranath's and Protap Chandra's low esteem of Bijoy Krishna Goswami's emotionalism, then it is fairly obvious that both identified with the more classically elegant and rational tenets of the Brahmo faith rather than its popularized forms.

Rabindranath's Hindu Brahmoism became more and more of a major issue within the Brahmo community, arousing stormy controversy until 1921, at least. In January 1914, when Rabindranath was invited by Sadharans to explain his position, there was so much opposition to the move that he ended up giving a prayer instead of a speech. His lecture did not take place in the Sadharan Samaj, but in Calcutta Town Hall, with Sivanath Sastri presiding. Meanwhile, Tagore continued to use the *Tattvabodhini Patrika* to air his views on Hindu Brahmoism, Brahmo religiosity, and Brahmo universalism. Again and again he offered the West the "Brahmo religion . . . without dogma" as a potential ideology for "drawing all peoples together."[32]

Tagore's Hindu Brahmoism came to assume different aspects as it came to mean different things to different members of the Brahmo community. An instance of this took place in 1914-1915, when Niranjan Niyogi of the New Dispensation, Ajit Chakrabarti of the Adi Samaj, and Sukumar Ray of the Sadharan Samaj debated the problem of Hindu Brahmoism in the pages of the *Tattvabodhini Patrika*. When Niyogi slighted the Adi Samaj for backsliding into the Hindu fold, Chakrabarti rejoindered by arguing that "unlike Christians and Muslims, Brahmos were not really separate from the Hindu society and race." Then Chakrabarti introduced a new element into the debate, saying that because the Adi Samaj "has kept its link with the highest ideal of the country, it has attained great achievement in the arts, philosophy and literature." Moving onto dangerous ground, Chakrabarti spoke next of the Protestant character of sectarian Brahmoism, which not only accounted for its anti-Hinduism but for its failure to create an art and literature.[33] Niyogi would not be drawn into the argument about aesthetics and Brahmoism, but instead countered by affirming that Brahmos were not Hindus, because of the one vital difference between them—caste exclusiveness. Chakrabarti replied that identifying with the Hindu samaj did not preclude the need for reforming Hindu caste through Brahmo principles. If Chakrabarti were faced with the alternative of alienation from Hindu society to maintain some sort of purity, and identifying with Hindu society in order to reform it from within, he would choose the latter. Besides, by separating himself, the Brahmo had been unable to "construct new ideas in the national life." And again, Chakrabarti returned to the charge of puritanism, which he saw as a crucial factor in denying the creative and aesthetic side of Hinduism.[34]

It was at this point that Sukumar Ray, father of the film director, Satyajit Ray, entered the controversy. Sukumar Ray was both an artist and a writer of children's stories. It was he who reproduced those magnificent paintings which graced the opening page of every issue of Ramananda Chatterji's *Prabasi* and *Modern Review*. He had written poems as a youth, was a brilliant student at City School and Presidency College, and was given a scholarship to learn photography and printing technology in England.[35] Moreover, as a close friend of Rabindranath's, and as a supporter of the ashram at Santineketan,[36] he had accompanied the poet to England in 1913 during the Nobel Prize tour.[37] But Sukumar Ray was also a leader of the younger generation of Sadharan Brahmos, and however partial he was to Rabindranath in 1914, he was equally loyal to the basic tenets of his community. To Ray, Brahmos were neither Hindu nor non-Hindu, but constituted a society of progressive-minded men and women. He could not accept the charge that Brahmos were denationalized, arguing that for generations Brahmos were the only dynamic force actively working to "build the future of the country."

As for Ajit Chakrabarti's charge of puritanism, Sukumar Ray denied that Hindu festivals were all that aesthetic on the one hand, and that Brahmos were all that puritanically antiartistic on the other. What lay behind the Brahmo repudiation of image worship from Rammohun's time to his own was not a deliberate antiaesthetic impulse, but an effort to meet the high requirements of a rational religion. As for Hindu Brahmoism in general, Sukumar Ray warned that the issue could be overemphasized, and that all Brahmos should continue to contribute positively in building up the nation.[38]

In 1914, the great war broke out among the European powers, and Rabindranath held the madness of nationalism responsible for the holocaust. It should come as no surprise that one of the best critiques of aggressive nationalism ever written was penned by the poet during the years of World War I. Tagore's book, *Nationalism*, was also in large part a critique of modernization in the West, where "history has come to a stage when the moral man is more and more giving way . . . to make room for the political and the commercial man, the man of limited purpose." In no other work has Tagore offered such a comprehensive condemnation of every variety of nationalism—including freedom movements. This position did not, however, make him an unwitting apologist of British imperialism. On the contrary, he attacked it with more candor and understanding, perhaps, than any other thinker before him. His most acute insight was a demonstration that aggressive nationalism and imperialism were two faces of the same monster. From the "soil of Europe" arose a virulent poison of "national self-glorification," he wrote, which when politicized, transformed Western civilization into a horrendous monster seeking to devour its neighbors. This "epidemic" of nationalism "is always watchful to keep the aliens at bay or to exterminate them. It is carnivorous and cannibalistic in its tendencies, it feeds upon the resources of other peoples and tries to swallow their whole future. . . . We used to have pillages, changes of monarchies . . . but never such a sight of fearful and hopeless carnage, such wholesale feeding of nation upon nation, such machines for turning great portions of the earth into mince meat, never such terrible jealousies with all their ugly teeth and claws ready for tearing open each other's vitals."

Unlike the later Marxists, Tagore did not place his faith in a simple change of systems or turnover of classes as a means to social salvation. It was the modern politicized and commercialized civilization that he condemned for having "dehumanized man" and destroyed his capacity to "feel the wholeness of humanity." Nor was the solution found in "paying back Europe in her own coin" and "returning contempt for contempt." In Tagore's view, imitating the worst features of modern Western civilization would only extend the virulent poison and ultimately destroy the world. Despite Tagore's indictment of Western civilization, he retained his universalism and interestingly enough, his modernism. While he refused to see only evil in contemporary Western civilization, he also made a perceptive distinction between modernization and Westernization. Said he: "Modernism is not in the dress of the European; or in the hideous structures where their children are interned when they take their lessons; or in the square houses with flat, straight-walled surfaces, pierced with parallel lines of windows where these people are caged in their lifetime; certainly modernism is not in their ladies bonnets carrying on them loads of incongruities. These are not modern but merely European. True modernism is freedom of mind, not slavery of taste. It is independence of thought and action, not tutelage under European schoolmasters."

Neither militant nationalism nor assimilation to Western ways— both of which were to Tagore obvious forms of Westernization— would solve India's problem of modernism. "Our real problem in India is social," he wrote. India, a combination of different peoples and cultures, must acquire a formula for "learning to live together." But he was quick enough to point out that it was not India's problem alone, as much as it was the world's. "Americans criticize our caste distinction," said he, "but have they solved their own problem of relations with the Red Indian or the Negro?" Thus Tagore held out a challenge to the world: "The most important fact of the present age is that all the different races of the world have come close together. And again we are confronted with two alternatives. The problem is whether the different groups of peoples shall go on fighting with one another or find out some true basis of reconciliation and mutual help; whether it will be interminable competition or co-operation."[39]

During World War I, Rabindranath also wrote an antinationalist novel called *The Home and the World* in which he blasted the justification for extremism and terrorism in the Swadeshi period. In this novel, unlike *Gora*, there was no ambivalence about militant Hinduism. In Tagore's portrait of Sandip as a revolutionary there was no sympathy, only repugnance. When the hero, Nikil, refused to condone his wife's act in burning foreign cloth, he justified his position by arguing that to put one's energy into building up a nation constructively was far more helpful than tearing down law and order through "destructive excitement." Must one decide that "you cannot light the home unless you set fire to it?" Nor would Nikil accept the spirit of *Bande Mataram*, because "to worship a country as a god is to bring a curse upon it."[40]

The book is revealing not merely as a critique of nationalism in fictional form, but especially as condemnation of a concrete revolutionary tradition in twentieth-century Bengal. Terrorism inspired by neo-Saktism was the target. It came at the very time of the "Tantric revival" spurred on by K. S. Macdonald, better known as Sir

John Woodruff, who dedicated himself to reevaluating what he termed the "Cinderella" or "Ugly Duckling of the Sanskritic tradition."[41] During the Swadeshi movement, for example, the political affirmations of Kali and Durga had become popular. We can assume that in the following statement by Nikil, Tagore was pronouncing his verdict on this style of Bengali revolutionary nationalism: "Maratha and Sikh turned revolutionary and got statehood but the Bengali contented himself with placing weapons in the hands of his goddess, and muttering incantations to her . . . and as his country did not really happen to be a goddess, the only fruit he got was the lopped off heads of the goats and buffaloes of the sacrifice."[42]

It should be noted that Rabindranath continued to proclaim himself a Hindu Brahmo during these very years of antinationalist sentiment, suggesting no incompatibility in his mind between his Hindu identity and sociopolitical universalism. But his position continued to stir up trouble in the Samajes. In 1917, the younger generation of Sadharan Brahmos under the leadership of Prasanta Mahalanobis, Sukumar Ray, and Kali Das Nag openly revolted against their elders, who opposed admitting Rabindranath as an honorary member of the Samaj.[43] The chief issue appears to have been Tagore's Hindu Brahmoism, and the struggle continued until 1921. In that year, the pro-Rabindranath forces scored a major victory over the so-called "sectarian" party.[44] From a tract written by Mahalanobis in 1921, on "Why We Want Rabindranath," we find nothing new ideologically on the proposition that "Brahmoism represents the new Hinduism."[45] What was new and intriguing was the implication that Rabindranath, then sixty years old, had completely captured the imagination of younger Brahmos like Mahalanobis. One act of youthful courage by Rabindranath, which enhanced his stature among the young, was the dramatic surrender of his knighthood following the Jallianwala Bagh massacre in Punjab on May 30, 1919. Although other Brahmos such as Jessie Bose, Prafulla Chandra Ray, Lord Sinha, and Nilratan Sarkar had been accorded similar honors, only Tagore, the so-called antinationalist, gave it up. And he did so in protest not simply against General Dyer's slaughter of innocent people, but more significantly as a repudiation of British parliamentary indifference to the crime. Amal Home, then a spokesman of the younger Sadharan Brahmos, was among those deeply impressed with Tagore's unique act of heroism.[46]

By 1921, the ever-youthful Rabindranath Tagore was busy

launching the most ambitious institutional project of his career at his beloved ashram, Santineketan. Three years earlier, on December 22, 1918, he had assembled students and faculty of his Vidyalaya (School) to explain to them that a new educational experiment known as Visva Bharati would be founded. His expressed purpose was clearly in the tradition of earlier attempts to implement the ideal of Brahmo universalism, such as Keshub Sen's efforts through his disciples to understand the major religions by means of primary sources in the original languages. It was Tagore's desire to create an "institution which would be a true center for all the existing cultures of the world . . . and where the wealth of past learning which still remained unlost might be brought into living contact with modern influences." The motto taken from a Vedic text was, "Where the whole world forms its one single nest."

By 1919, advanced courses were being offered in the Vedas, Sanskrit, Prakrit, Tibetan, and Chinese.[47] A year later, Tagore had established a library with 7,065 manuscripts and books.[48] In 1920, while he was in Europe, in the midst of war weariness and cultural fatigue, he gained a clear conception of the function of his new university.[49] With the assistance of Kali Das Nag, then a student at the University of Sorbonne, Rabindranath persuaded Professor Sylvain Levi to come to Santineketan and set up a Sino-Indian Department at the cost of 10,000 rupees.[50] In July 1921, Rabindranath returned to Santineketan prepared to announce the main objective of his new institution: "Through the Visva Bharati as a whole we seek to establish a living relationship between East and West, to promote intercultural and international activity and understanding and to fulfill the highest mission of the present age—the unification of mankind."[51] In December of that year, at the meeting called to inaugurate the founding of Visva Bharati, Rabindranath presided, while Brajendranath Seal, Nilratan Sircar, and Sylvain Levi gave eloquent speeches on their varying interpretations of the institution's aims and functions. Rabindranath's own dedication speech neatly summarized his last fourteen years of wrestling with the problems of unity and diversity, universalism and nationalism. Why this university? Tagore answered that "mankind must realize unity." He went on to explain that "the first step towards that realization is revealing the different peoples to one another. . . . We must find some meeting ground where there can be no question of conflicting interest. . . . One of such places is the university where we can work together in a common pursuit of truth, share together our common heritage, and realize that artists in all parts of the world have created forms of beauty, scientists have discovered secrets of the universe, philosophers the problems of existence, saints made the truth of the spiritual organic in their own lives, not merely for some particular race to which they belonged but for all mankind."[52]

In the 1930s, while Tagore was in his seventies, a new generation of Brahmo youth arose to repudiate the Brahmoism of their fathers as an ideology of salvation. There was then no Keshub Sen, no Sivanath Sastri, or Rabindranath Tagore with charisma sufficient to command the respect of the young, nor with a program at all meaningful in a world that had changed so radically for the worse. The great international depression, the rise of fascism, and the outbreak of new imperialist wars made a mockery of Brahmo ideology and buried the ideals of rational religion and universal goodwill in the graveyard of man's disillusionment and despair. Young progressive Brahmos turned elsewhere for ideological comfort and psychological belonging—to Marxism generally, either as communists or as part of a socialist faction within the nationalist movement. Tagore himself was not entirely oblivious to the attraction that the new experiment in the Soviet Union held for the intellectual proletariat of India. His letters from Russia in 1930 suggest the same kind of faith in and hope for the Utopian implications of the Russian revolution as we find in Jawaharlal Nehru's writings. In one letter, for example, Rabindranath compared the dismal record of capitalist England in awakening the Indian masses to the success of the Russian communists in awakening their own European and Asian peoples. About the British record in India, Tagore wrote, "It is not wrong to keep a nation for ever in slavery in order that England may become great and do things for mankind. What does it matter if this nation eats little, wears little—but even so, those others sometimes out of sheer pity help us in slightly improving our condition. But a hundred years have gone by, and we have had neither education nor health, nor wealth."

Only in Russia was "a radical solution to this problem being sought": the "royal road to the solution in education," and "it is astonishing to watch the extraordinary vigour with which education spreads throughout Russia." This was true not merely among the European Russians, but "among the semi-civilized races of Central Asia." Tagore was amazed at theaters crowded with peasants and workers. And "nowhere are they humiliated." In the following passage by Rabindranath, so characteristic of the Russian correspondence, there is contained not only a strong admiration for communist achievement, but more significant the very explanation as to why the Brahmo Samaj had lost its appeal to the young in its abortive attempt to arrest defection and decline: "What we ourselves have been attempting to do at Sriniketan, they are doing on a superior scale all over the land. How splendid it would be if our workers could come here for training. Everyday I compare conditions here with India: what is and what might have been. . . . A few years ago the condition of the masses here was fully comparable with that of the Indian masses: things have rapidly changed in this short period, whereas we are up to the neck in the mud of stagnation."

But unlike the younger generation, Tagore was a product of the Bengal renaissance and Brahmo reformation. He saw the bad in the Russian experiment as well as the good. Because of serious defects in their system, "they will have trouble some day." Thus, the following passage is equally characteristic of the Russian correspondence of Tagore, in which the value of individual freedom is seen in the context of fear for the totalitarian mind: "They have turned their system of education into a mould, but humanity cast in a mould cannot endure. If the theory of education does not correspond with the law of the living mind, either the mould will burst into pieces or man's mind will be paralyzed to death or man will be turned into a mechanical doll."[53]

PART IV

Conclusion

CHAPTER ELEVEN

The Brahmo Reformation Diffused: Bengal's Legacy to Twentieth-Century India

ONE of the chief conclusions of this book is that modern Bengali bhadralok culture was shaped largely in the image of the Brahmo Samaj. No middle-class Bengali Hindu today would deny that much of what he accepts as his normal beliefs and attitudes—from his liberal religious outlook to his appreciation of a certain style of literature, song, and dance—was largely the result of Rabindranath Tagore's Hindu Brahmo synthesis. And it might be added that Rabindranath's influence was considerable among Bengali Muslims, as well. It was Tagore's Brahmo universalism, not simply his Bengali literature, that has made him a revered hero whose ideas serve as a symbolic bridge between Bangladesh and West Bengal. Nor can it be denied that the Brahmo Samaj played a pivotal role in the Bengal renaissance and reformation, and that most of the creative giants of nineteenth-century fame were the liberals, nationalists, and synthesizers of the Brahmo movement. On the other hand, as I have also shown throughout the book, other forces were at work in opposition to the Brahmos, and Brahmos defected to these other movements on occasion. Who would deny that revivalism, nationalism, communalism, and Marxism have not also been important in influencing the configuration of present-day India? Thus, even in Bengal, when Naxalites decapitate statues of Vidyasagar, Brajendranath Seal, and other nineteenth-century bhadralok heroes; when communist or communalist Muslims in Bangladesh attempt to ban Tagore's songs, plays, and essays; or when the Ramakrishna movement attempts to suppress Brahmo history, it becomes quite apparent that memories of the Bengal renaissance and the Brahmo Samaj are not shared by all in the spirit of an unmixed blessing. But is this not obvious? Should it surprise anyone that pluralism exists in Bengal just as it does elsewhere? Nevertheless, if we were to approach the problem in another way and try to understand modern Bengal without an assessment of the Brahmo influence, the result would be ludicrous. It would be like studying the history of social reform legislation in the United States by eliminating the history of the Democratic party, Franklin Roosevelt, and the New Deal.

The same argument applies to Brahmo influence in India as a whole. In 1972, a seminar was organized at the Nehru Museum in New Delhi on "Rammohun Roy as Father of Modern India," as part of the Rammohun bicentenary celebrations. Certainly not all Indians look upon the father of the Brahmo Samaj as the father of modern India. Not all Indians believe in modern India. But for those that do, Brahmo influence has been and continues to be profound. Why has the great Brahmo been accorded this distinction? As the most sophisticated and most articulate member of his generation, his choice of response to the West became the model for subsequent generations of Hindu modernizers. He might have reacted to the West by ardently defending the defects, the abuses, the weaknesses of quotidian Hinduism. He might have taken the opposite course and subscribed totally to a Western culture, either by converting to Christianity or by adopting a secular style of life. But he chose the more difficult middle path through which he sought to wed modernization in the West with Hindu institutions and traditions. Thus, Rammohun turned to the reformation of Hinduism and established the Brahmo Sabha, prototype for the Brahmo Samaj.

What were some of the concrete achievements of Brahmos that they bequeathed to twentieth-century Hindus? The selection of a scriptural source as the holy book of Hindus—Vedas or Vedanta, later appropriated by the Arya Samaj, was a Brahmo innovation. The updating of two traditions as neo-Vaishnavism and neo-Saktism were pioneered by Brahmos. The earliest systematic theology of Hindu religion was Brahmo in inspiration. The symbolic interpretation of Hindu rituals, and the new philosophic-aesthetic reinterpretation of Hindu festival images were the work of Brahmos. The creation of a this-worldly social Hindu ethic parallel to the Protestant or Puritan ethic of the West was originally Brahmo. Hindu dharma as social service and the reevaluation of the Upanishadic ethic for modern use, often attributed to Vivekananda and the Ramkrishna mission, was long before that an established part of the Brahmo missionary program. The crusades to remarry widows, abolish child marriage, encourage intercaste marriage, discourage Kulin polygamy, eliminate prostitution, extend equality of education to women, and support equal professional opportunities for women—these were all begun by Brahmo efforts.

And as we have seen, the earliest night schools for workers and peasants, mass newspapers, savings banks for workers, and missions to improve the lot of the depressed castes and untouchables were all pioneered by Brahmos. In fact, one could argue that the Bill of Rights in the present Indian constitution represents an extension to all Indian citizens of the rights accorded only to members of Keshub Sen's progressive Brahmo community under the Brahmo Marriage Act of 1872.

Especially is the legacy of Brahmoism profoundly felt in the rise and growth of political consciousness and nationalism in India. It was in defense of Brahmoism against missionaries that Rajnarian Bose has earned the title of "Grandfather of Indian Nationalism." It has been demonstrated in this book how and why the Hindu Mela, the *National Paper*, and the various associations of Rajnarian Bose and Nabagopal (National) Mitra were Adi Brahmo Samaj weapons against Keshub Sen and his "universalist" followers. Surendranath Bannerji would have never become the hero of moderate political Hindus if it were not for the support of Ananda Mohun Bose and other Sadharan Brahmos. In fact, the Indian Association, which was precursor of the Indian National Congress, was, as we have seen, founded and dominated by Sadharan Brahmos who had become sufficiently politicized by then to extend themselves beyond their customary socio-religious pursuits. Moreover, Indian Association tours across South Asia to win support for their program from their bhadralok counterparts in north, west, and south India were conducted along the familiar Brahmo missionary routes, which Keshub and his disciples had traveled for the first time in the 1860s. Many of the key members of the Indian National Congress, during the early decades, were a collection of Bengali Brahmos, non-Bengali Brahmos, and Brahmo sympathizers. Finally, the rise of a more aggressive Hindu nationalism in Bengal at the turn of the century was under the leadership of Brahmo defectors such as Brahmobandhab Upadhyay, B. C. Pal, Aurobindo Ghose, and C. R. Das.

The Brahmos also left present-day India a rationalist tradition as characteristic of their movement as were Brahmo piety, morality, achievement, and national devotion. Brahmo rationalism germinated in Rammohun Roy's pronounced iconoclasm, and in his identification with basic Unitarian principles. Denying the efficacy of image worship, a negation that Debendranath later extended to revealed sources, Rammohun shaped Brahmoism into a Judaic, Islamic, and Christian mold in which religious principles were never concretized pictorially (or, especially, in anthropomorphic form), but were raised through analysis and synthesis to an abstract plane to appeal to the intellect. As we have shown repeatedly, Brahmoism became a thinking man's religion, which was one good reason why it could never achieve a mass following—at least under British colonialism, where the goal of mass literacy was never seriously entertained as state policy. Every Brahmo adhered rigorously to Rammohun's model, including the much misunderstood Keshub Chandra Sen, whom critics accused of adjuring Brahmoism in his New Dispensation by returning to ceremonies and images. On the contrary, as we have seen, Keshub's New Dispensation was based on an elaborate ideology of comparative religion whereby he hoped to convince the world that the unity of all religions was essential. It was not the use of images that was important to Keshub, but their symbolic interpretation in terms of his salvation ideology. Rather than constituting a return to popular Hinduism or the adoption of Roman Catholicism in Hindu form, as some critics charged, Keshub's New Dispensation was in fact so thought-provokingly Brahmo that it was one of the great intellectual achievements of the nineteenth century.

To find a true contrast to Brahmo iconoclasm, one has to look to comparable movements, which as a result of compromise with what Rammohun and other Brahmos called "idolatry," were able to win wider mass support for their reform programs. Dayanand Saraswati's use of the Vedas as the book of the Hindus is one case in point, as was Vivekananda's use of the Kali image and other popular Hindu icons. These cases represent a routinization of Brahmoism into modern Hinduism. Though he never compromised with Brahmo rationalism, Rabindranath's defense of Hindu festivals for aesthetic reasons represents the same process of routinization. The same could be said of Ramananda Chatterji, whose liberal attitude to iconoclasm enabled him to communicate Brahmoism to an organization like the Hindu Mahasabha.

Unitarianism was the other germinating influence on Rammohun Roy that seems to account for a nonsecular Brahmo humanism; it also precluded Brahmos from becoming a sect of Hindu Calvinists. Radical Unitarians of the nineteenth century not only repudiated the trinity, as well as most so-called "superstitious" aspects of the popular religions, but they also humanized divine persons such as Jesus, bringing them down to the level of men with a prophetic or reformist mission. This is why Rammohun's *Precepts of Jesus* is important as a piece of Unitarian humanist literature.

Brahmo humanism started with this denial of the divine Christ (or Krishna or Buddha), and the espousal of the ethical Jesus, who was a historic mortal. In addition, the Unitarian social gospel moved Rammohun and Savanath Sastri and many other Brahmos in the nineteenth century to improve the lot of humanity in the kingdom of man. Brahmo social reform was, in fact, rooted in Unitarian religious humanism, which integrated piety with the obligation to help the underprivileged and the oppressed. We may recall that this was the crucial issue between Keshub and the younger progressives in the 1870s. Keshub, now obsessed by religious salvation, turned his back on humanism and social reform.

It was in the intellectual atmosphere of rationalism and humanism that Brahmo scientism was born. As I have tried to demonstrate, the early scientists did not justify their spirit of inquiry in secular terms, but on the contrary they saw themselves and the import of their work in religious terms. We have seen how both Jessie Bose and P. C. Ray were pious men and good Brahmos. Einstein's religiosity comes to mind, as does the great physicist's effort to reconcile "superpersonal values" (religion) with "systematic thought" (science). Nor would any Brahmo scientist have disagreed with Einstein when he said that "science without religion is lame; religion without science is blind."[1]

These are fine suppositions about Brahmo influence on the Indian subcontinent as modernizers of Hindu society and culture, but is there concrete evidence to support such hypotheses? Until I attended an all-Indian Brahmo conference in Hazaribagh in 1970, and met Brahmos from every region of South Asia, the possibility of doing research on Brahmos outside of Bengal never occurred to me. The conference opened up new vistas on what had already become to me a fascinating history of the Brahmo movement. Unfortunately, my ignorance of other South Asian languages and my official responsibilities in Calcutta made it impossible for me to carry on research on Brahmoism as subcontinental. Needless to say, interested scholars from Bombay, Poona, or Madras could do such research which, I believe, would be meaningful in a historical framework similar to that proposed in this book. What I finally did was gather material in Calcutta on the impact of Bengali Brahmos outside of Bengal. Though much of my evidence is from an incomplete file of newspaper clippings in the Sophia Dobson Collet collection in the Sadharan Samaj Library, the pattern of Brahmo expansion in South Asia seems clearly delineated. Certainly no history of the Brahmo Samaj would be complete without reference to the work of the Brahmo missionaries. And the missionary episode seems to belong here in the final section of the concluding chapter, because it suggests that Brahmoism was not so much a parochial movement confined to Bengal as it was Bengal's legacy to modern India.

Back in 1861, as we have already seen, Keshub Sen, Satyendranath Tagore, and Monomohun Ghose started the modern Brahmo mission movement by appealing to progressive students of Krishnagar College who wished to retain and modernize their religion, but without losing their identity as Europeanized Christians. Brahmo mission efforts as such went back earlier, to Debendranath Tagore's method of convincing zamindars to start Brahmo prayer groups, as with the Krishnagar Raja in 1844/45[2] and the Burdwan Raja in 1851.[3] Under Debendranath, Brahmo Samajes were also set up around Calcutta: Kidderpore in 1853, and Behala in 1853.[4] Just before Keshub joined the Brahmo Samaj in 1857, there were already fourteen Samajes associated with the Calcutta parent body.[5] In 1863, a new type of Brahmo missionary appeared—Bijoy Krishna Goswami, during his earliest recorded visit to East Bengal. Though Goswami did ultimately appeal to local elites, he also went to the masses, attempting to bring his message even to the so-called "depressed classes." His work among the Baganchara Mullicks is a case in point. These were former Brahmans outcasted for violation of caste rules and living in the nineteenth century under "miserable economic and social conditions."[6] Bijoy Krishna lived for a time among these two hundred families. He helped them to find dignity by enlisting them as Brahmos, while trying to end their poverty by training the men in craft occupations.[7]

We have seen also that Keshub Chandra accompanied Bijoy Krishna to East Bengal in 1866, and was impressed with how effectively the latter communicated Brahmoism in the garb of indigenous Vaishnavism. But outside Bengal, Keshub used English as his medium of speech and a Westernized form of Brahmoism to appeal to the middle-class counterparts of Calcutta Brahmos. In 1864, for example, while on a mission tour of Madras, Keshub recorded in his diary that the people he met were familiar to him because they were all Anglicized educators and government officials rather like their equivalents in Bengal.[8]

When Keshub found himself the leader of an independent Brahmo society and wished to develop a mission movement to spread the gospel, he felt compelled to do so on two levels. First, to reach the lower middle class of rural East Bengal, he appointed ascetic missionary types like Bijoy Krishna, who moved on foot from village to village or from one mofussil town to another with little money, enjoying minimal comfort. On the second level were Keshub himself and Protap Chandra Majumdar, both of whom traveled about the subcontinent with the utmost convenience of the train along thousands of miles of newly constructed railway lines. Except for rare occasions to the contrary, at the terminal points of their mission journeys there awaited members of the English-speaking regional elites, who greated them warmly and treated them lavishly. As early as 1864, Keshub had traveled between Madras and Bombay, mostly by train, an experience that fired him with enthusiasm about the convenience and potential usefulness of rail travel for the Samaj.[8] Ten years later, Protap Majumdar, in an article summarizing the work of the Brahmo mission, put great stress on the importance of "railway communication between different parts of the country," arguing that Brahmos were using it to their best advantage. By means of the railway, it had been possible to spread Brahmoism to Bihar, U.P., the Punjab, Maharashtra, Tamilnad, and Orissa. Majumdar concluded the report for the 1874 operations by stating that "though we now and then get converts from the extreme sections of society, most of those who become Brahmos belong to the middle and educated classes."[9]

Protap, far more than Keshub himself, soon became the best traveled Brahmo missionary throughout South Asia and the world. Because English had become the *lingua franca* of the new elites from one end of India to the other, there was no need for Majumdar to master Marathi, Urdu, Hindi, Punjabi, Gujarati, or Tamil. Everywhere, Majumdar's flawless English proficiency, his progressive ideas, personal refinement, polish and elegance of manner made him the model for a generation of Indian Western-educated persons who emulated him. Without doubt, of all the early Brahmo missionaries under Keshub, Protap was the most valued emissary of Brahmoism to the non-Bengali intelligentsia. And by means of Brahmoism, the content and ethos of the Bengali renaissance and reformation reached the leading urban centers of the new India.

To clarify Majumdar's role and contribution, it is important to distinguish between the diffusion of Brahmoism among Bengalis and among non-Bengalis. Brahmoism in Greater Bengal (in the nineteenth century it included East and West Bengal, Orissa, Bihar, and Assam) was distinctively Bengali in cultural orientation. The Brahmo mandir, in the leading towns of U.P. and the Punjab, became a community center for Bengali civil servants, judges, railway officials, lawyers, surgeons, educators, and journalists. In the non-Bengali Brahmo communities of West and South India, missionaries like Majumdar only stimulated the diffusion of the faith there, while the actual development of the movement was largely the work of their regional elites adapting the Bengal renaissance and reformation to their own social and cultural needs.

Religious reform movements had existed in Madras and Bombay before Keshub's well-publicized visits there in 1864. All too often, however, these associations, which operated after a fashion during the 1850s, were virtually private clubs with limited membership and with no programs of social action.[10] To argue that Western-educated people in both these cities were instantly stirred up to social reform activities after listening to the magnificent speeches of Keshub Sen would, of course, be clearly an exaggeration. Neither the Vedic Samaj in Madras nor the Prarthana Samaj in Bombay was for many years enthusiastic about the social aspects of Bengali Brahmoism, which they rightly deemed as perilous to their own valued status in the Hindu community. This fear was especially pertinent in Bombay, where Prarthana leaders were virtually all respectable professional Chitpavan Brahmans. Not only were they members of the highest caste in the community, but as Western-created professionals they were notoriously successful as wranglers, judges, medical practitioners, journalists, professors, and civil servants. Dr. Pandurang, leader of the Prarthanas, was a well-known physician, Bal Wagle was a barrister, Janarandan Sakharan was a journalist.[11] The famous elitist Prarthana trio—Sir G. R. Bandavakar, N. Chandavarkar, and Ranade—all responded favorably to Keshub's appeal for social reform, yet curiously enough the only serious reform embraced by the group for almost a decade was a collective decision to renounce idolatry.[12]

In 1871, a Bengali civil servant from Lahore named Navin Chandra Roy came to Bombay to lecture on the virtues of progressive Brahmoism. Roy, a fiery progressive Bengali Brahmo born outside Bengal, has tended to be overshadowed as a missionary by the inflated image of personal appeal attributed to charismatic Calcutta leaders such as Keshub. Roy, who rose to the rather important position of paymaster of the Northwestern Railways in Lahore,[13] was one of many devoted Bengali Brahmos who provide the missing link in the diffusion of the Bengal renaissance from Calcutta to Western India. In 1863, he and six other Bengalis started the first Brahmo Samaj in the Punjab.[14] Sasi Bhusan Bose of the Sindh Punjabi Railway was the earliest secretary.[15]

The history of the Punjabi Brahmo Samaj is important not only for tracing the influence of Bengali ideas throughout West India, but in understanding the Brahmo contribution toward establishing preconditions of reform before the emergence of the Arya Samaj. Under Navin Roy's dynamic leadership, membership was opened to non-Bengalis, while Brahmo literature was translated from English and Bengali into Hindi and Urdu. The Brahmo program of reform was closely modeled after the Calcutta organization, to the point of setting up an Indian Reform Association shortly after the parent organization did so. The Punjabi Brahmos participated in local government educational schemes, and organized relief measures in times of natural calamity. They were also ardent exponents of Vidyasagar's female improvement activities.[16] In December 1871, Roy came to Bombay to help his fellow Brahmos give up their complacency about social action. Speaking in fluent Hindi, he delivered a series of talks that were variations on the theme that "throughout India men's minds are being awakened to a sense of their duty towards God, as well as towards their fellow brethren."[17]

Keshub Sen seems to have provided the initial inspiration for reform among the Prarthana Samajists; Navin Roy prepared their minds for serious action; and Protap Majumdar in 1872 actually provided the catalyst for a concrete program in Bombay. Majumdar's lectures before the Bombay congregation were based on a manifesto he had issued back in 1867 entitled "Brahmos Arise." It was an attack on the debilitating effects of materialism on Indian Western-educated persons and an appeal for the same class to overcome "moral cowardice," to struggle for "social progress" through "reformed religion." What India needed were not the false prophets of atheism but dedicated men of God and social justice: "Brahmos arise! There are periods of human history when the national crisis demands every individual lay down his life as the price of his brother's good. . . . Go as missionaries to all parts of the country and preach noble precepts. . . . Let us carry a fire with us and a thunder-cloud. . . . Brahmos, repent, pray, and arise!"[18]

Evidently, Majumdar electrified his audience and moved his coreligionists to action. V. R. Schinde, a radical Prarthana Samajist of a later era, who compiled a history and directory of the Brahmo movement in 1912, stated unequivocally that every social reform institution started by the Prarthanas in the early 1870s may be traced back "to the influence of P. C. Majumdar." Specifically, Schinde referred to the Arya Mohila Samaj for female improvement, the night schools for workers, the *Subodh Patrika* or Marathi journal of the Samaj, and the creation of branches of the Prarthana Samaj in Poona, Satara, and Ahmednagar.[19] In September 1872, Majumdar and Pandurang went to Poona, where Ranade had moved a year earlier in his assignment as subordinate judge.[20] There with Sukharan Chitnis, also a judge and Prarthana leader, a series of discussions were held on the feasiblity of introducing active social reform programs in Poona. It should be pointed out that Ranade was a warm friend of Majumdar's, and went on record as an advocate of Keshub's progressive form of Brahmoism. On December 17, after a train ride from Bombay to Gujerat, Majumdar arrived in Surat. The Bengali Brahmo was lodged in the house of the local municipal secretary, Mr. Pandurang Balkrish. As was the pattern, the most progressive middle-class citizens constituted the audience for Majumdar's lectures in the local high school, and they were both "aroused to action" and charmed by his two hours of superb English style. As one local journalist put it, "we were deeply impressed with the fluency of his diction and the force of his argument." One of the most popular series of lectures and discussions was the one dealing with the history of the Brahmo Samaj.[21] Majumdar then went on to Baroda and to Amhedabad. In the latter city, he was "enthusiastically welcomed by the prominent citizens." Many of the prominent citizens were local Brahmos who held their devotional meetings in the Government Training College. The principal, himself a Brahmo, offered the hall of the college to Majumdar, who won the hearts of the Gujarati community to become the second "most beloved Bengali" in Amhedabad. The first was another Brahmo named Satyendranath Tagore, who was then a government official there.[22]

Majumdar was equally effective in spreading Brahmoism to the Deccan. On occasion, as in Mangalore, the situation became complicated. Here Majumdar, Amritalal Bose, and Gour Govinda Ray traveled from Bombay by rail as far as they could, then by coastal steamer (a total of four hundred miles), arriving in Mangalore in May 1870.[23] They had a double mission: to salvage some five thousand Sudras who had earlier sought Brahmo spiritual guidance for the Samaj,[24] and to support the morale of a community of Saraswat Brahmans who had sworn their loyalty to Brahmo principles. Majumdar's dress and manner alienated the Sudras, who mistook him for a Christian missionary, but attracted the Saraswats, who became so devoted to Prarthana-style Brahmoism that by 1912 theirs was among the most activist Samajes in all western India.[25]

When, in 1866, Mary Carpenter visited the Madrasi Brahmo organization known as the Vedic Samaj, she spoke of the social gospel of Unitarianism, and urged the gentlemen there to engage themselves in social action as well as religious reform. By 1869, the Vedic Samaj boasted a library; prayer hall and discussion room; a printing press for translating Bengali Brahmo tracts into Tamil and Telegu; and a program advocating female education. But from a report of June 1870, it appears that the Madrasi Brahmos had lost enthusiasm and had virtually collapsed institutionally. The revival of the Samaj in Madras is attributed to P. C. Majumdar, whose first visit to Tamilnad was in August 1870. He seems to have accomplished this task by going directly to the Western-educated students and arousing their interest in progressive Brahmoism. The new leadership revolved around a district magistrate named Visvanath Mundliar, who reportedly organized two generations of "enlightened citizens" and started the Southern India Brahmo Samaj. Mundliar had his own press, which he used for publications and to issue a weekly journal known as *Brahmo Thepika*, which boldly asserted the need for progressive reform of Hindu society. In the Bengali manner, female emancipation became the pivot for an urgent reformation of society, and the articles and editorials stressed the need for educating women, raising the age of consent, and allowing widows to remarry. In one editorial of June 1871, Mundliar went so far as to urge that his fellow Brahmos (at least intellectually) "free themselves from the shakles of Hinduism." Majumdar's influence led to the earliest Brahmo oath or covenant in Madras and to the first Brahmo marriage there in September 1861. Mundliar's untimely death in October of the same year seems to have slowed down activities for a time, but other leaders emerged such as Sridharalu Naidu, who ably filled the gap.[26] As in Western India, branches of the Samaj proliferated not only in Tamilnad but in Mysore and Andhra as well.

In Bangalore, as we have already noted elsewhere, it was not so much Majumdar who influenced events as it was the Reverend Charles Dall, who made yearly visits to the city in the 1870s as dual emissary of the American Unitarian Church and Keshub's Brahmo Samaj of India. In November 1872, Dall urged Keshub to start mission activity in Bangalore, which he viewed as a most fertile ground in the south for the propagation of Brahmoism. "Our brethren must go there with apostolic faith, self-denial and trust," he reportedly told Keshub. Dall's lectures, generally well attended by the middle class, were held at the Bangalore Literary Union. They always combined an attack on Trinitarian Christianity with a declaration of theological unity between Christian Unitarianism and Indian Brahmoism.[27]

By 1872, Keshub Sen's Brahmo Samaj of India had indeed become a national movement. A report of the Brahmo Mission Office for that year suggests several things (see Table 4). In the first place, there were now 101 Brahmo Samajes located throughout the subcontinent. Second, the expansion of Samajes in the rural towns of Bengal was greater than the total expansion of Samajes outside Bengal. Third, even among the Samajes outside Bengal, those in U.P., Bihar and throughout north India were predominantly community centers for the prabasi, or Bengali elite living outside Bengal. Fourth, whereas the Adi Brahmo Samaj was entirely limited to Bengal, the Keshubite Samaj had committed itself to a broad program of expansion. The expansion of the Brahmo Samaj really followed the Bengali bhadralok pattern of diffusion. Most Samajes were located in what, until 1905, was called Greater Bengal, or Bengal, Assam, Orissa, and Bihar. All non-British elitist positions in the services and professions within Greater Bengal were monopolized by the bhadralok. This was true to a lesser extent just outside of Greater Bengal in the towns of Uttar Pradesh, Madhya Pradesh, and so on. But in the cities of Punjab, Western India, and Madras, where local non-Bengali elites had emerged by this period, Bengalis either cooperated with non-Bengalis or were totally absent from the membership.

The year 1872 represents the apex of Keshubite expansion, because up to then the factions within the movement were relatively united behind Sen's leadership. But later in the seventies, as we have seen, the liberals challenged his policies and his authoritarian rule of the Samaj. Then in 1878, the marriage of Keshub's eldest daughter to the prince of Cooch Behar was the straw that broke the camel's back and led to the second major schism in Brahmo history. Before discussing the expansion of Brahmoism under the Sadharan Brahmo Samaj, it may be worth our while to consider the Cooch Behar affair, or rather its aftermath, not from the usual historiographical angle of betrayal and hypocrisy, but from the fresh and relevant perspective of Brahmo diffusion on the subcontinent.

We have already raised the issue of the marriage in various contexts. It has generally been assumed that Keshub sold out to the Hindu raj of Cooch Behar, thereby betraying every reformist prin-

TABLE 4

Report of Brahmo Samajes in India by 1872

Name of samaj	Presidency, province	When established	Sympathy[1]
1. Adi Samaj, Calcutta	Bengal	1830	A.S.
2. Akina	Bengal	1871	N.
3. Allahabad	Northwest	1865	A.S.
4. Allahabad (2)	Northwest	1867	K.
5. Agra	Northwest	1871	K.
6. Ahmedabad	Bombay	1871	K.
7. Brahmo Samaj of India, Calcutta	Bengal	1866	K.
8. Baranagar	Bengal	1865	K.
9. Bhowanipur	Bengal	1852	A.S.
10. Barasat	Bengal	1870	K.
11. Behala	Bengal	1853	A.S.
12. Baruipur	Bengal	1871	K.
13. Boluty	Bengal	1857	A.S.
14. Burdwan	Bengal	1857	A.S.
15. Burdwan (2)	Bengal	1860	K.
16. Bag-anchra	Bengal	1864	K.
17. Bogra	Bengal	1858	K.
18. Beauleah	Bengal	1859	K.
19. Barisal	Bengal	1860	K.
20. Brahmonbariah	Bengal	1863	N.
21. Bareilly	Oudh	1858	K.
22. Bhagalpur	Bengal	1863	K.
23. Bangalore	Madras	1867	K.
24. Berhampore	Bengal	1867	A.S.
25. Blacktown (Madras City)	Madras	1871	N.
26. Bunnoo	Punjab	1866	N.
27. Cachar	Bengal	1864	N.
28. Campoor	Northwest	1865	N.
29. Kalna	Bengal	1868	A.S.
30. Konnaghur	Bengal	1863	N.
31. Coomarkhally	Bengal	1849	K.
32. Utkal (Cuttak)	Orissa	1865	A.S.
33. Cuttak (2)	Orissa	1868	K.
34. Chittagong	Bengal	1853	K.
35. Chinsura	Bengal	1865	K.
36. Choonapooker (Calcutta)	Bengal	1869	K.
37. Chandanagore	Bengal	1860	A.S.
38. Dacca (1)	Bengal	1867	N.
39. Dacca (2)	Bengal	1871	K.
40. Dehradoon	Northwest	1867	K.
41. Dinajpore	Bengal	1867	K.
42. Etwa	Northwest	1871	K.
43. Faridpur	Bengal	1857	K.

TABLE 4 (*cont.*)

Name of samaj	Presidency, province	When established	Sympathy[1]
44. Ghazurpur	Northwest	1871	K.
45. Gaya	Bihar	1866	K.
46. Gournaghore	Bengal	1860	K.
47. Gauhati	Assam	1870	K.
48. Goalpara	Assam	1870	K.
49. Harinavi	Bengal	1868	K.
50. Hazaribagh	Bihar	1869	K.
51. Howrah	Bengal	1864	K.
52. Jamalpur	Bihar	1867	N.
53. Jukbulpur	Central Provinces	1868	K.
54. Kaddalur	Madras	Unknown	Unknown
55. Kalighat	Bengal	1869	K.
56. Kaligutcha	Bengal	1867	K.
57. Karachi	Bombay	1869	K.
58. Kishoregunge	Bengal	1866	K.
59. Krishnagar	Bengal	1844	K.
60. Kusthia	Bengal	1869	N.
61. Lucknow	Oudh	1868	K.
62. Lahore	Punjab	1863	K.
63. Mandarah	Bengal	1871	Unknown
64. Monghyr	Bihar	1867	K.
65. Milapoor (Madras)	Madras	1870	K.
66. Midnapore	Bengal	1846	A.S.
67. Meerut	Bengal	1871	K.
68. Mymensingh	Bengal	1853	K.
69. Malparah	Bengal	1870	A.S.
70. Mangalore	Madras	1870	A.S.
71. Nowgaon	Assam	1870	K.
72. Osmanpoor	Bengal	1870	K.
73. Prarthana Samaj (Bombay)	Bombay	1867	K.
74. Paddapooker (Calcutta)	Bengal	1871	K.
75. Puttokottee	Madras	1865	Unknown
76. Patna	Bihar	1867	N.
77. Poona	Bombay	1870	N.
78. Pratyahik Samaj (Calcutta)	Bengal	1871	N.
79. Rajmehal	Bengal	1868	K.
80. Rawalpindi	Punjab	1867	K.
81. Rutnaghiri	Bombay	1869	K.
82. Rungpore	Bengal	1864	K.
83. Salem	Madras	1866	Unknown
84. Sindh	Bombay	1869	K.
85. Sinduriapatty (Calcutta)	Bengal	1865	K.
86. Serampore	Bengal	1862	N.
87. Santipur	Bengal	1863	K.
88. Shambazar (Calcutta)	Bengal	1864	N.
89. Sultangatcha	Bengal	1863	K.

TABLE 4 *(cont.)*

Name of samaj	Presidency, province	When established	Sympathy[1]
90. Shankaritollah (Calcutta)	Bengal	1868	K.
91. Sylhet	Bengal	1863	K.
92. Sibsagar	Assam	1866	K.
93. Selidah	Assam	1867	K.
94. South India Brahmo Samaj	Madras	1864	K.
95. Serajgunge	Bengal	1870	K.
96. Sat Sungat	Punjab	1871	K.
97. Takee	Bengal	1869	N.
98. Tipperah	Bengal	1862	N.
99. Toondlah	Northwest	1869	K.
100. Tharyetuyo	Burma	1871	Unknown
101. Udunalapiti	Madras	1865	Unknown
102. Vepry	Madras	1870	Unknown

[1] KEY: A.S. Adi Samaj
      K. Keshubite
      N. Neutral
SOURCE: Report of the Brahmo Mission Office, Brahmo Samaj of India, 1873.

ciple he had stood for since 1861. Had not he himself abolished child marriage for the Samaj in the famous Brahmo Marriage Act of 1872? Had not he himself insisted that every Samaj marriage be performed under the Act? But curiously enough, no one has yet explored the interesting possibility that Keshub arranged the marriage not as a hypocritical act of betrayal, but as a missionary act of trying to win over the tribal kingdom to the Brahmo faith. There is only a suggestion of this in Keshub's own defense. No doubt, Keshub at the time had turned his back on social reform, and seemed preoccupied with comparative religion and the New Dispensation. But whatever was in his mind, the facts about the aftermath of the marriage do seem to substantiate the hypothesis that, rather than Keshub selling out to Hinduism in Cooch Behar, it was Cooch Behar that adapted Brahmoism to its own conditions.

The indictment of Keshub Sen for having married off his eldest daughter in violation of every Brahmo precept has generally been accepted in historical surveys, which treat the marriage as a disaster from every point of view and ignore the aftermath of the event. A fact often overlooked, for example, is that the marriage between Prince Nripendra Narayan and Suniti Debi was not consummated until 1880, when he was 18 and she was 16.[28] Second, a study of the facts during the aftermath in Cooch Behar indicates not so much disaster as it does the development of a challenging partnership be-

Figure 3. Maharani Suniti Devi of Cooch Behar
(eldest daughter of Keshub Chandra Sen)
Figure 4. Maharaja Nripendra Narain Bhupa Bahadur of Cooch Behar

tween two people engaged in a rather unusual experiment. It was
an experiment under the guidance of British officials (who arranged the marriage in the first place), ostensibly attempting to in-
troduce modern reform in Cooch Behar, and in fact opening the
remote kingdom to enlightening Bengali influences from Calcutta.
Thus, whether the first marriage in Cooch Behar in 1878 was or
was not performed strictly according to Brahmo rites seems less
significant from a historical perspective than the question about the
subsequent career of the maharaja, whom Keshub sought to inspire as a Brahmo.[29] The answer in large part can be found in the
qualitative difference between the town of Cooch Behar before the
accession of Nripendra Narayan to the throne in 1882, and the
town Brajendranath Seal came to live in 1896 when he was hired at
Victoria College. In those fourteen years alone, through increasing
the annual revenue of state by 300,000 rupees, the king reg-
ularized the administration, established the first railway link to
Bengal,[30] improved communication throughout the kingdom with
the construction of innumerable roads and bridges,[31] created for
the first time a city with a planned sanitation and drainage sys-

tem,[32] constructed the earliest buildings in the country dedicated to the principles of modern justice and administration, started a large fully equipped hospital in the capital and public dispensaries in the countryside,[33] and founded Cooch Behar's first public library,[34] public parks and gardens,[35] a girls' school,[36] college,[37] and a public marketplace.[38] He also abolished polygamy in the royal family[39] and capital punishment throughout the kingdom.[40]

Moreover, some years before Brajendranath's arrival in Cooch Behar, the king and his wife constructed the largest Brahmo mandir in South Asia, primarily with government funds, and they provided an annual grant of 5,000 rupees to help maintain it.[41] In 1888, the king declared Brahmoism of the New Dispensation as the state religion, and though it had no practical effect in spreading the faith beyond the small community of Bengali elite, it did suggest that the promise of the young man to Keshub was fulfilled.[42] Not too well known, either, is that Maharaja Nripendra Narayan, whom critics of Keshub had looked upon as a jungly Hindu raja, left three wishes behind him shortly before his death at forty-nine years of age. The king asked first that he be cremated according to New Dispensation Brahmo rites; second, that his ashes be put in the same garden in Cooch Behar where he had first learned to read and write; and third, he provided that "his casket be placed in a monument of stone similar to the one which had been placed over the ashes of the late Keshub Chandra Sen."[43]

Sivanath Sastri's special, subtle ideological appeal and leadership provide us with precisely the context for understanding the second great period of Brahmo impact on India. No other Sadharan Samajist opposed Keshub and the New Dispensation as effectively as did Sastri. And wherever Sastri went, year after year, on his extensive mission tours of South Asia, he was able to win over a countless number of Indian Brahmos to the proposition that the Sadharan Samaj came into existence to save Brahmoism from Keshub's betrayal. Sastri also proved a good teacher of missionaries, whom he inspired with a love for rational theism, social reform, humanism, and political liberalism. At varying times, Sastri had at his disposal such talented and highly spiritual missionaries as Bijoy Krishna Goswami in East Bengal, S. N. Aghorenotri in the Punjab, Bipin Chandra Pal in the Punjab and South India, Hem Chandra Sarkar in South India, Nagendra Chatterji in West India, Ram Kumar Vidyaratna in East India, and Nilmani Chakrabarti in Assam. The importance of the Sadharan missionary effort under Sastri cannot be stressed enough, since it was this group of religiously inspired devotees who spread the modernistic ideal of the Brahmo Samaj across India. At the same time, they arrested the progress of the New Dispensation in India by convincing most Brahmos that Sadharans were the true believers, and in the process they greatly proliferated Samaj associations everywhere, as they reached out to thousands of their counterparts who had abandoned the tradition of contemporary Hinduism and thirsted for a new, more satisfying identity.

As a result of Sadharan mission work, the Brahmos of South India finally established social reform as a permanent feature of its program.[44] Sivanath Sastri's mission tours of Madras were instrumental in bringing about this change of mentality. The intelligentsia of Bangalore, already exposed to the Unitarian missionary Charles Dall, responded positively to Sadharan missionaries such as Sastri, Hem Chandra Sarkar, and Bipin Chandra Pal. Despite the progress of militant Hindu nationalism and revivalism, the intelligentsia of Bangalore, among other places, welcomed the enlightened Sadharan Brahmos of Calcutta, whose visits were always important social events for the urban elite. In Telegu country, the Sadharan missionaries linked up with Verasalingam's Brahmo movement, and by 1898 their combined efforts had led to the development of active centers in Rajahmundry, Masulipatam, Bapatla, and Guntur.[45] By 1890, Nilmani Chakrabarti had established a Brahmo movement among the Kashis of Assam. His method was largely educational, as he spread literacy among thousands through the medium of Bengali.[46] Single-handedly, Chakrabarti built schools, started newspapers, all the time preaching the Brahmo religion.

The progress of Sadharan mission activity among the intelligentsia of Orissa is a case in which religious modernism held its own against the powerful forces of militant Hinduism. Also important here was Sastri's influence, as well as the leadership of the district Brahmo leader, Madhur Sadhan Rao. Like Bihar, Orissa had been for some time a happy hunting ground for Bengali civil servants and other Western-educated elitists, with the result that Brahmo Samaj branches were already fairly well established in key towns with substantial Bengali minorities. Two well-known Samajes, one in Balasore and one in Cuttack, had been started by Debendranath Tagore.[47] The Keshubite stronghold was the Utkal Samaj founded in 1869. Madhur Sadhan Rao, in the Government Educational Service of Orissa, was originally a follower of Keshub Sen. As with many Bengalis, he grew more and more disenchanted with ordinary Hinduism and sought a new identity in a liberal religious context. Not unfamiliar, too, is the fact that he imbibed his Brahmoism as a student in Cuttack College from classmates. As with other modernizing Indian intellectuals back in the 1870s, Rao looked upon Bengalis favorably as the advance guard of a dynamic, progressive India. In fact, Rao distinguished himself by translating educational texts for schools in Orissa into Oriya, not from English but from Bengali sources.

When the Sadharans split with Keshub in 1878, Rao joined Sastri. No doubt ideological differences were significant, but there was another factor reminiscent of Cooch Behar, which won Orissa to the Sadharan Samaj of Calcutta. Rao's second son married Suklalata, daughter of Upendra Kishore Raychaudhuri, an active Sadharan Samajist of Calcutta and grandfather of Satyjit Ray, the film director. In 1881, Rao's third child married Sivanath Sastri's only son. Subsequently, Rao married off his fourth child to one of Sastri's daughters, and his fifth and eighth children also married into Sadharan Brahmo families from Calcutta.[48]

Sadharan penetration in the Punjab was also effected but fruitless in the sense that, after having achieved much, they watched their accomplishments crumble against the overwhelming success of the Arya Samaj among the masses. Here it was not so much that Brahmo reformism was crushed by Hindu revivalism, but that the Brahmos exposed their flagrant weakness of not being able to share their new identity with the masses. The Arya Samaj was no less reformist or modernist than the Brahmo Samaj, but its members found the key to awaken the general populace. Sadharan Brahmos could only observe from the sidelines how effectively others could democratize their idea of reformed Hinduism. On the eve of Arya Samaj dominance in the region, active Sadharan Samajes were located in Lahore, Rawalpindi, Amritsar, Quetta, and Sialkot.[49] Nor were the Brahmos exclusively Bengalis. Second in importance to Navin Chandra Roy, Bengali founder of the Lahore Brahmo Samaj, was Dayal Singh, who in 1898 established the important Brahmo institution of higher learning in Lahore known as the Dayal Singh College.[50]

In Western India, the Prarthana Samaj continued to expand its organization and community—chiefly in Maharashtra and Gujarat. Here, like-mindedness between Bengali Sadharans and West Indian Prarthanas helped create a united front against the forces of militant Hinduism. Collaboration between the two took place on at least three levels. Brahmo rational religion and religious identity were promoted through an all-India yearly convention known as the theistic conference, which first convened in Allahabad in 1888 with the famous Prarthana leader, Ranade, as its first president.[51] As a principal faction within the National Congress, Prarthana and Sadharan Brahmos worked together to support their own program, electing several of their own members as Congress presidents. In conjunction with the annual meetings of the National Congress, Prarthana and Sadharan Brahmos started the Social Reform Association in 1888, which generally sought to remind delegates that internal Hindu modernism through reform was as important to strive for as were external nationalistic demands for justice against British imperialism.[52]

By the eve of the twentieth century, the Sadharan Brahmo ideology and identity had made an enormous impact on segments of the Hindu community, but numerically that success could not be reflected in the census reports. These census reports were based on straightforward questions as to whether one acknowledged oneself to be a Brahmo, Hindu, Muslim, or Christian. Many considered themselves Hindus, while the sympathizers who were Brahmo in everything but formal conversion and strict practice were, of course, never identified as Brahmos in census reports.[53] On the other hand, the actual number of Brahmos was always comparatively small, since it was restricted to emancipated middle-class professionals and their families.[54] Thus, the expansion was in terms of additional Samaj branches, mostly Sadharan after 1880, established by small elitist communities whose Western education, professional competence, and abstract religious beliefs cut them off sharply from the mass of their own countrymen. In 1884, Sastri claimed that there were 195 Samajes in India, but he refused to disclose the actual number of Brahmos. When the 1891 census reported only 3,051 Brahmos in South Asia, Sastri declared that the figure in no way represented the number of active Brahmos, nor did it include sympathizers. He maintained that the number of Samajes had increased to approximately 200 in seven years. When a Unitarian representative named Sunderland visited Calcutta from America in 1896 to discuss worldwide collaboration efforts, 200 Samajes sent representatives for the occasion. According to Savanath Sastri, the peak of Brahmo expansion was reached before 1912, when 232 Samajes were reportedly active throughout the subcontinent.[55] The Sadharan triumph against the Keshubites can be seen in the comparative congregation figures of Calcutta and

Dacca, the two largest Brahmo centers in Bengal. The Sadharans in
Calcutta numbered 800 in 1912, whereas the New Dispensation
church had 160 in its congregation. As for Dacca, the Sadharan
community could boast 110 anusthanic Brahmos and 70 sympathizers, whereas the New Dispensation church reported 76
members, with no sympathizers.[56]

The fact that Sastri and other Sadharans appeared to the young
as radical religious modernists, social reformers, and political nationalists, whereas Keshubites had lost entirely their revolutionary
image, was undoubtedly a crucial factor in the decline of the New
Dispensation. The Brahmo religious identity of the Sadharan
Samaj seemed to serve as an umbrella attracting both idealistic intellectuals and career-oriented professionals. Younger Kulin
Brahmans from East Bengal, for example, whose new social consciousness made them rebels against the polygamous practices of
their caste, often joined the Sadharan Samaj, which encouraged direct action to alleviate social injustice among Kulin women. In fact,
the daring escapades of young Kulin radicals under Sadharan
sponsorship in East Bengal won for Sastri and the community an
image of champions of the oppressed that persisted well into the
twentieth century. The heroism of young Kulins like Nabakanta
Chatterji and Barada Nath Haldar, who rescued many poor
widows and Kulin girls in trouble, is a case in point.[57] It would be a
mistake, however, to attribute the success of the Sadharans solely to
the missionary zeal of Sastri and his devotees. Nor must it be believed that ideology and religious conviction were the only serious
factors underlying the triumph of the Sadharan Samaj over the
New Dispensation among the Brahmo community. In Bengal, particularly, where the Brahmo community was generations old,
vested interests in political position or property led to vicious legal
struggles for control of Brahmo affairs. In Dacca, which had the
largest Keshubite mandir in South Asia, the ideological struggle
was compounded by a sordid battle over political control and
ownership of vast property assets. Ultimately, the "protesters,"
joined by a legion of young progressives, ousted the Keshubite establishment and transformed the Dacca mandir into a Sadharan
church. As elsewhere in 1882, the Keshubites abandoned their
struggle to regain the Dacca mandir and built their own New Dispensation temple nearby.[58]

The Brahmo movement in its autonomous form is today virtually
dead, though it lives among middle-class Hindus. This, however,

does not explain fully why the independent Brahmo movement ceased to attract progressive young men and women from the 1930s on. It is my contention that neither Hindu revivalism nor nationalism, but Marxism, won the minds of the youth and arrested any continued growth of the Brahmo movement. And to carry the argument further, I believe that it is Marxism that is the most formidable challenge to the Hindu Brahmoism of the present Indian middle class. This should not be too difficult to understand, since it is part of a universal process. In the first place, however liberal or radical socially, Brahmoism was essentially a theistic movement, and religiously oriented movements have been on the defensive in the twentieth century. Second, the Brahmos were the progressive component of the bhadralok elite created in the social atmosphere of British colonialism and imperialism. As we have seen, with few exceptions, Brahmos were middle-class Puritans in their personal habits, their devotion to hard work and achievement, their theory of social change, and, right through the Swadeshi period, in their belief that entrepreneurship and capitalism constituted the panacea for India's socio-economic backwardness.

But the image of Brahmoism is ambivalent, because it is realized that in India it was far more than an ideology of apology for elitism or capitalism. It introduced among the upper castes of Bengal and elsewhere an ethos of heroic self-sacrifice, a sense of justice, a sense of compassion for the underprivileged, a sense of devotion to nation, a sense of accomplishment in creative synthesis, and a sense of individual responsibility and freedom. Brahmos were, for the most part, an idealistic and courageous lot who gave up family and inheritance for an uncertain future, who underwent the mental anguish of an identity crisis, lived in poverty, and suffered humiliation, despair, and persecution for their ideals. The fate of the Indian middle class, and freedom, may well depend on the survival of these nineteenth-century Brahmo values and qualities in the future.

Notes

PREFACE

1. Broomfield, *Elite Conflict in a Plural Society*, p. 322.
2. See, for example, Lavan, "Raja Rammohun Roy and the American Unitarians: New Worlds to Conquer (1821-1834)," *West Bengal and Bangladesh Perspectives from 1972*, pp. 1-16; and by the same author, *Unitarians and India: A Study in Encounter and Response*.
3. Sastri, *History of the Brahmo Samaj*, p. v.

FOUNDATIONS OF MODERNISM

1. L. Carpenter, *A Review of the Labours, Opinions and Character of Rajah Rammohan Roy*, p. 6.
2. L. Carpenter, *Funeral Sermon on the Death of Rajah Rammohan Roy*, pp. 1, 9, 19.
3. Sunderland, "William Ellery Channing," p. 371.
4. *Correspondence of William Ellery Channing and Lucy Aikin (1826-1842)*, pp. 88, 87, 184.
5. Carpenter, *Review*, p. 8.
6. Sunderland, "Channing," p. 731.
7. Edgell, *William Ellery Channing, An Intellectual Portrait*, pp. 5, 130.
8. Ibid., p. 150.
9. Channing, *Religion a Social Principle*, pp. 4, 5, 7.
10. *Dr. Channing's Note Book*, pp. 10, 23.
11. Channing, *Lecture on War*, p. 26.
12. Channing, *On the Elevation of the Labouring Portion of the Community*, p. 2.
13. Channing, *A Discourse on the Life and Character of the Reverend Joseph Tuckerman*, pp. 75, 76.
14. Tuckerman, *Christian Service to the Poor in Cities*, pp. 6-7, 9-11, 19-21, 23.
15. J. E. Carpenter, *The Life and Work of Mary Carpenter*, p. 46.
16. J. E. Carpenter, *Memoir of the Reverend Lant Carpenter*, pp. 65, 71, 194-95, 197.
17. R. L. Carpenter, *On the Importance and Dissemination of the Doctrine of the Proper Unity of God*, pp. 1-5, 6-8, 9.
18. Tuckerman, *A Letter on the Principles of Missionary Enterprise*, p. 37.
19. See evidence of this in P. K. Sen, *Biography of a New Faith*, I, 108-11.
20. Tuckerman, *Letter*, pp. 9, 28.
21. W. E. Channing, *Remarks on Creeds, Intolerance, etc. for American Unitarian Association*, pp. 5, 6, 18.
22. W. E. Channing, *Extracts from His Correspondence*, II, 120.
23. See in particular W. Adam, *The Principles and Objects of the Calcutta Unitarian Committee*.
24. Kopf, *British Orientalism and the Bengal Renaissance*, pp. 196-201, 236-52.
25. Thomas, *The Acknowledged Christ of the Indian Renaissance*, p. 2.
26. See Kopf, *British Orientalism*, p. 202.
27. Thomas, *Acknowledged Christ*, p. 10.
28. Ibid., p. 5.

29. For some of the publications of the press, see Adam, *Principles and Objectives*.

30. *Reprint of a Controversy between Dr. Tytler and Ramdoss*, pp. 2, 4, 6, 17, 21.

31. See R. Roy, *Translation of the Cena Unpanishad*, Vol. CLX of *India Office Library Tracts*, pp. iii-v.

32. "Copy of the Trust Deed of the Brahmo Sabha" (January 23, 1830), KTC.

33. A short but definitive biography appears in *Freedom Movement in Bengal*, ed. N. Sinha, p. 23.

34. "American Unitarian Association."

35. "Reverend Mr. Dall."

36. Dall, *Brahmo Samaj of India Led by Baboo Keshub Chunder Sen with Facts Historical and Personal*, pp. 3, 13.

37. "Mr. Dall and the Brahmo Samaj" (December 27, 1871), SBSL-BSC.

38. "Brahmo Samaj," *Indian Mirror*, XIV, 4.

39. "American Unitarian Association."

40. R. K. Gupta, *Kumari Mary Karpentarer Jiban-Charit*, p. 36.

41. "Annual Report of the Indian Reform Association, 1870-1871," in appendix of P. K. Sen, *Biography of a New Faith*, II, 276.

42. "Behalai Mari Bhoi" (Fear of Epidemic in Behala), *Sulabh Samachar*, I (August 20, 1871), 157.

43. Collier, *The General Next to God*, pp. 44-45.

44. For a descriptive and partly statistical account of intemperance among the Calcutta elite, see "Vice of Intemperance, Spreading among Bengalees," April 6, 1876. See also "Advantages and Disadvantages of the Present Age."

45. "Annual Report," in P. K. Sen, *Biography of a New Faith*, II, 277.

46. Ibid., II, 286.

47. "Sampadoker Nibedan" (Editorial), *Sulabh Samachar*, I (November 15, 1870), 1.

48. "Annual Report," in P. K. Sen, *Biography of a New Faith*, II, 290.

49. C.H.A. Dall, "Missionary Movement, Bangalore" (November 8, 1876), SBSL-SDCC.

50. See for example, Dall, "Progress and Prospects of Brahmoism," ibid; and P. C. Mazoomdar, *Brahmos Arise!* (January, 1867), ibid.

51. Thomas, *Acknowledged Christ*, p. 93.

52. "Mission Work."

53. P. C. Mazoomdar, *Faith and Progress of the Brahmo Samaj*, p. 1.

54. See in particular, letter from J. F. Meyer to P. C. Majumdar, November 25, 1901, reprinted in P. C. Mazoomdar, *Lectures in America and Other Papers*, p. 269.

55. Letter of P. C. Mazoomdar to M. Müller, August 20, 1881, reprinted in F. M. Müller, *Biographical Essays*, pp. 145, 146.

56. P. C. Mazoomdar, *The Oriental Christ*, pp. 18, 42, 43, 44-46.

57. Thomas, *Acknowledged Christ*, pp. 93, 94, 95.

58. "Report of the World's First Parliament of Religions," reprinted in P. C. Mazoomdar, *Lectures in America*, pp. 280, 281.

59. P. C. Mazoomdar, *World's Religious Debt to India*, pp. 6, 8, 11.

60. S. C. Bose, *Life of Protap Chunder Mazoomdar*, II, 187.

61. For example, letter from J. F. Meyer to P. C. Mazoomdar, November 25, 1901, reprinted in P. C. Mazoomdar, *Lectures in America*, p. 269.

62. S. C. Bose, *Life of Mazoomdar*, pp. 261, 253, 295.

63. Ibid., p. 296.

64. Mazoomdar, "What Is Lacking in Liberal Religion?" *Lectures in America*, pp. 192-201.

65. "Max Müllarer Patra, Protap Chandro Majumdar," letter by Max Müller to P. C. Mazoomdar, November 1899, reprinted in B. Ghose, ed. *Samayikpatre Banglar Samaj Chitra*, II, 380.

66. S. C. Bose, *Life of Mazoomdar*, pp. 324-25, 336, 356.

67. Jardine, "Paper on the Brahmo Samaj at the Allahabad Missionary Conference."

68. C.H.A. Dall, "Brahmo Theological School" (February 28, 1873), SBSL-SDCC.

69. "The Brahmo Samaj," *Calcutta Review*, LX, 368.

70. Blumhardt, "On the Schism in the Brahmo Samaj," *Church Missionary Intelligencer*, V (1880), 58.

71. K. C. Sen, "Philosophy and Madness in Religion" (March 3, 1877), SBSL-SDCC.

72. "On Reverend C.H.A. Dall" (April 18, 1877), ibid.

73. K. C. Sen, "The Disease and the Remedy" (February 6, 1877), ibid.

74. C. H. Dall, "Keep a Warm Head [Heart?] and a Cool Head" (February 7, 1877), ibid.

75. "Prayer and Work—A Reply to Mr. Dall" (February 8, 1877), ibid.

76. C. H. Dall, "A Real Issue" (March 4, 1877), ibid.

77. Sunderland, "Theodore Parker: The Great American Reformer."

78. W. H. Channing, *Lessons from the Life of Theodore Parker*, pp. 25-26.

79. Parker, *The Public Education of the People*, pp. 10, 11.

80. Parker, *A False and True Revival of Religion*, p. 11. See also, Parker, *The Revival of Religion Which We Need*.

81. J. E. Carpenter, *The Life and Work of Mary Carpenter*, p. 260.

82. Letter from R. D. Haldar to T. Parker, October 6, 1856, in RBMA, Rakhal Das Haldar Papers.

83. P. C. Mazoomdar, *The Life and Teachings of Keshub Chunder Sen*, pp. 99, 106.

84. S. Sastri, *History of the Brahmo Samaj*, I, 118.

85. B. C. Roy, *The Story of My Humble Life*, p. 21.

86. S. Sastri, *History*, II, 361, 365.

87. D. Datta, *Keshub and the Sadharan Brahmo Samaj*, p. 58.

88. T. Parker, *Prarthana-Mala*, pp. 1, 3, 15, 18, 31-33.

89. S. Sastri, *Maharshi Debendranath O brahmananda Keshub Chandra*, p. 4.

90. B. C. Pal, *Charita-Chitra*, p. 263.

91. S. Sastri, *The Brahmo Samaj of India: A Statement of Its Religious Principles and Brief History*, p. 5.

92. M. Carpenter, *On Ragged Schools*, pp. 5-6.

93. Collier, *General Next to God*, pp. 111-14.

94. M. Carpenter, *Letters on Female Education in India and Prison Discipline*, p. 273.

95. J. E. Carpenter, *Life and Work of Mary Carpenter*, p. 273.

96. "Funeral of Francis Power Cobbe."

97. Beveridge, *India Called Them*, p. 78. See also "Lady's College Established at Oxford."

98. M. Carpenter, *Addresses to the Hindus*, p. 13.

99. S. Chaudhuri, "Victoria Institutioner Ekhso Bachhar" (One Hundred Years of Victoria College), *Victoria Christian College Patrika* (May 1969), p. 63.

100. "Bethune Female School."

101. All references to Akrhoyd's British background are in Beveridge, *India Called Them*, pp. 65, 78-81, 88.

102. It is interesting that the Brahmo Congregation never concerned themselves with whether men would distract women from their spiritual purpose.

103. S. Chaudhuri, "Victoria Institutioner," p. 64. B. N. Bandyopadhyay, *Dwar-kanath Gangopadhyay*, p. 12.

104. S. Chaudhuri, "Victoria Institutioner," pp. 62-63.

105. Miss Akroyd's position and that of Beveridge may be found in Beveridge, *India Called Them*, pp. 89, 96.

106. K. C. Sen, "Native Ladies 'Normal School' " (April 8, 1873), SBSL-SDCC.

107. Beveridge, *India Called Them*, p. 90.

108. K. C. Sen, "Native Ladies 'Normal School.' "

109. B. N. Bandyopadhyay, *Dwarkanath Gangopadhyay*, pp. 12, 13.

110. Beveridge, *India Called Them*, p. 99.

111. S. Sastri, *History*, I, 258, 260-61.

112. S. Debi, *Sivanath*, p. 57; S. Sastri, *History*, I, 252-53.

113. Beveridge, *India Called Them*, p. 100.

114. H. Sarkar, *Life of Ananda Mohan Bose*, p. 99.

115. S. Chaudhuri, "Victoria Institutioner," pp. 66-67.

116. K. C. Sen, "Calcutta Bethune School," *Indian Mirror*, XVII (February 25, 1878), 3.

117. "Banga-Mahila Vidyalaya," pp. 163-64.

118. P. C. Gangopadhyay, *Bangalar Nari Jagaran*, pp. 75, 66-67.

119. *Calcutta Corresponding Committee of the Church Missionary Society*, 63rd Report, 1883, xx, xxii.

120. Gangopadhyay, *Bangalar Nari Jagaran*, p. 77.

BRAHMO SECULARISM

1. See the early history of Hindu College from its inception in Kopf, *British Orientalism*, pp. 178-83.

2. For information on book patronage, presses, libraries, and book dealers, see ibid., pp. 114-21.

3. Hindu College (1816), Sanskrit College (1823), and Serampore College (1817) offered science courses and were equipped with science laboratories.

4. See Kopf, *British Orientalism*, pp. 187-89.

5. For information on the early Bengali newspapers and periodicals, see ibid., pp. 189-92.

6. Ibid., pp. 253-59.

7. For a solid intellectual study on Derozio with an excellent and sympathetic analysis of his teaching influences, see B. Ghose, *Bidrohi Derozio*.

8. Presidency College, Calcutta, *Centenary Volume, 1955*, p. 2.

9. M. N. Ghose, *Sekaler Lok*, p. 157.

10. For a solid study of Duff, see Smith, *Life of Alexander Duff*.

11. L. B. Dey, *Recollections of Alexander Duff and the Mission College*, pp. 3, 120, 124.

12. Wilson, quoted in Lushington, *The History, Design and Present State of the Religious, Benevolent, and Charitable Institutions Founded by the British in Calcutta*, p. 133.

13. Kopf, *British Orientalism*, p. 183.

14. Long, *Brief View of the Past and Present State of Vernacular-Education in Bengal* (1868), reprinted as an Appendix in Adam, *Reports on the State of Education in Bengal, 1835 and 1838*, p. 516.

15. "The Oriental Seminary."

16. B. N. Bandyopadhyay, *Akkhoy Kumar Dutt*, pp. 5-8, 11, 13, 14-17.

17. For an excellent discussion of Dutt's deistic philosophy, see A. K. Bandyopadhyay, *Unabingsha Satabdir Prathamardha o Bangla Sahitya*, p. 292.

18. *Autobiography of Maharshi Debendranath Tagore*, p. 71.

19. Debendranath Tagore, *Atma-Jibane*, p. 4.

20. A. K. Dutt, *Who Is a Brahmo?* (1854), rev. ed., pp. 2, 7, 8, 9-10.

21. P. R. Ghose, *Unabingsha Satabdite Bangalir Manan o Sahitya*, pp. 118, 128.

22. A. K. Dutt, *Dharma Niti*, pp. 3, 4, 9, 14, 30, 31, 34, 35, 60, 65, 67-73.

23. Lethbridge, *Ramtanu Lahiri: Brahmin and Reformer*, p. 198.

24. Letter of testimonial from G. T. Marshall, January 4, 1841, SCAC-GRC.

25. Letter of Navakumar Chakraborti to G. T. Marshall (July 13, 1839), SCAC-GRC.

26. Letter (November 21, 1839), SCAC-GRC.

27. Tripathi, *Vidyasagar: The Traditional Moderniser.* All references to Vidyasagar's modernizing activities in college and reform activities for women are on pp. 1-6, 28-29, 31, 59, 60.

28. M. N. Ghose, *Memoirs of Kali Prosanna Singh*, pp. 13, 17.

29. N. Bose, "Brahmo Vidalaye Debendranath o Keshub Chandra" (Debendranath Keshub and the Theological School), *Prabasi*, xxvii, Part ii (December 1927), 308.

30. Vidyasagar was possibly made editor in August 1858 and secretary in September 1858.

31. S. Sastri, *History*, i, 123.

32. S. Sastri, *Men I Have Seen: Reminiscences of Seven Great Bengalis*, p. 34. See also "Tarkabachaspati," *Freedom Movement in Bengal*, ed. N. Sinha, p. 84; B. B. Majumdar, *History of Political Thought from Rammohun to Dayananda*, i, 21-25.

33. S. Sastri, *Men I Have Seen*, pp. 33, 55, 56; *Atma Charit*, pp. 20, 27.

34. Title and subsequent references taken from Tripathi, "The Lonely Prometheus," pp. 74-99.

35. D. M. Bose, "Acharya Brajendra Nath Seal," p. 513.

36. B. Sarkar, "Acharya Brajendranath Seal: A Life-Sketch," p. 170.

37. D. M. Bose, "Acharya Brajendra Nath Seal," pp. 512-13.

38. Ibid., p. 513.

39. P. C. Ray, "Acharya Brajendra Nath Seal as I Saw Him and Knew Him," *Acharya Brajendra Nath Seal Birth Centenary Celebration*, p. 32.

40. Letter from Brajendranath Seal to the Dewan of State, in DACB, Dewan Office Files (March 22, 1912), 22:474.

41. Letter of Resignation from Dr. Brajendranath Seal to the Superintendent of State, Cooch Behar, DACB (December 20, 1912), 4:1.

42. S. K. Das, "Acharya Brajendranath Seal as Revealed in His Philosophical Remains," manuscript in BI.

43. Seal, "Comparative Studies in Vaishnavism and Christianity," manuscript copy in BI (1912), pp. i, ii, iv, v, vi, vii, x.

44. D. M. Bose, "Acharya Brajendra Nath Seal," p. 515.

45. Lahiri, "Acharya Brajendra Nath Seal," *Acharya Brajendra Nath Seal Birth Centenary Celebration* (Victoria College), p. 23.

46. B. N. Seal, *Rammohun Roy: The Universal Man*, p. 2.

47. B. N. Seal, *The Quest Eternal*, pp. 7, 8, 10, 19, 24, 31, 32, 41, 42, 43, 44, 47, 48, 55, 57, 65, 67, 84.

48. R. Bose, *A Defense of Brahmoism and the Brahmo Samaj*, pp. 5, 6, 14, 17, 22.

49. K. C. Sen, *God Vision in the Nineteenth Century*, p. 80.

50. S. Sastri, *History*, ii, 344-45.

51. Geddes, *The Life and Work of Sir Jagadish Chandra Bose*, pp. 9, 10.

52. Nag, "Sir Jagadish Chandra Bose," p. 698.

53. Geddes, *Life and Work*, p. 25.

54. Ibid., p. 32.

55. *Sir J. C. Bose: His Life and Speeches*, p. 7.

56. Nag, "Sir Jagadish Chandra Bose," p. 700.

57. J. C. Bose, "Address to Presidency College Students," p. 236.

58. D. M. Bose, "Abala Bose: Her Life and Times," *Modern Review*, LXXV (June 1944), 444.

59. *Sir J. C. Bose*, p. 7.

60. Geddes, *Life and Work*, pp. 41, 42.

61. N. C. Nag, "Sir Jagadish Chandra Bose," pp. 698, 700.

62. *Sir J. C. Bose*, p. 19.

63. R. Tagore, "Jagadis Chandra Bose," *Modern Review*, LXII (December 1937), 706.

64. R. Chatterji, "The Hero as Scientist," ibid., p. 705.

65. *Sir J. C. Bose*, p. 26.

66. J. C. Bose, "The Unvoiced Life," p. 718.

67. His career until 1914 is found in *Sir J. C. Bose*, pp. 28, 30, 40-42, 44, 60, 231-34.

68. Geddes, *Life and Work*, pp. 225, 228.

69. *Sir J. C. Bose*, p. 72.

70. D. M. Bose, "Abala Bose," p. 450.

71. J. C. Bose, "The Unvoiced Life," p. 715.

72. D. M. Bose, "Abala Bose," p. 452.

73. J. C. Bose, "Life and Its Mechanism," p. 653.

74. J. C. Bose, "The Unvoiced Life," p. 713.

75. P. C. Ray, *Life and Experiences of a Bengali Chemist*, p. 1. All subsequent references to Ray's educational background and first academic position are on pp. 2, 9, 19, 20, 29-31, 39, 47-49, 53, 80.

76. P. C. Ray, "Memorandum on the Recruitment of the Educational Service of the Bengal Provincial Educational Service," BSP-PCRP, pp. 69, 2-439.

77. Ibid.

78. P. C. Ray, *Life and Experiences*. All subsequent references to his mature life are on pp. 85, 86, 92, 102, 103, 110, 111, 125, 337.

79. P. C. Ray, "Auto-biographical Notes" (December 18, 1920), BSP-PCRP.

80. S. Sastri, *Englander Diary*, p. 180.

81. P. C. Mazoomdar, *Sketches of a Tour around the World*, pp. 173-77.

82. Letter from Rabindranath Tagore to Ajit Chakrabarty (November 27, 1910), in RBMA, Ajit Chakrabarty Papers.

83. H. Sarkar, *Sivanath Sastri*, pp. 66, 68.

84. "A Special Meeting to Honour P. K. Ray" (November 27, 1876), SBSL-SDCC.

85. "Thought Leading in the Brahmo Samaj," *Indian Messenger*, IV (November 14, 1886), 84.

86. B. N. Sen, *Lectures and Essays*, p. 110.

87. B. N. Sen, "The Religious Importance of Mental Philosophy," SBSL-SDCC.

88. G. G. Ray, "Religion and Science" (June 18, 1877), SBSL-SDCC.

89. P. K. Roy, "Philosophy and Theology," *Indian Mirror* (January 14, 1877), SBSL-SDCC.

90. Dall, "A Real Issue," *Indian Mirror* (March 4, 1877), SBSL-SDCC.

91. Tattvabhusan, *Auto-biography*, pp. 21, 24, 37, 49, 51, 52, 59, 114, 124, 125, 126.

92. Tattvabhusan, *Brahmo Jijnasa*, pp. 84, 85, 106, 139-44, 177, 189, 190, 193, 195-202.

93. Tattvabhusan, *Autobiography*, pp. 14, 61, 63, 66, 105, 106.

94. B. N. Sen, *Lectures and Essays*, p. 111.

95. S. N. Dutt, *The Life of Benoyendra Nath Sen*, pp. 107, 109, 179, 180.

96. K. S. Ghose, *The Rise of Scholasticism in the Brahmo Samaj*, pp. 1, 3, 6.

97. S. N. Dutt, *Life of Benoyendra Nath Sen*, pp. 6, 7, 12, 13, 18, 19, 37, 44, 51.

98. *Sadhu Promothalal*, p. 169.

99. *Mohit Chandra Sen: Birth Centenary Publication*, p. 6.

100. B. N. Sen, *Lectures and Essays*, pp. 1-4.

101. B. N. Sen, *The Intellectual Ideal: Three Lectures on the Vedanta*.

THE BHADRALOK REFORMER

1. For a definition of bhadralok as a British-created class who monopolized the land as property owners, the service-related occupations, and the private professions, see P. C. Ray, *Life and Experiences of a Bengali Chemist*, pp. 13-16.

2. For an excellent study done recently on bhadralok, see Broomfield, *Elite Conflict in a Plural Society*.

3. S. Datta, *The World of Twilight*, pp. 55, 82.

4. N. Chaudhuri, *Autobiography of an Unknown Indian*, pp. 203, 211, 226, 438.

5. P. C. Ray, *Bengali Chemist*, pp. 448, 449, 450, 502.

6. Kopf, *British Orientalism and the Bengal Renaissance*, p. 213.

7. One can find ample discussion of this throughout the following sources: Erikson, *Childhood and Society*; *Insight and Responsibility*; *Identity: Youth and Crisis*.

8. Erikson, *Dimensions of a New Identity*, pp. 124-25.

9. For a definition of intelligentsia, see Toynbee, "The Disintegration of Civilizations," *A Study of History*, v, 154-58.

10. Milton Singer, interpreting Redfield, defines the broker as a "new type of professional intellectual . . . who stands astride the boundaries of the cultural encounter, mediating alien cultural influences to the natives and interpreting the indigenous culture to the foreigners." Singer, "The Great Tradition in a Metropolitan Center: Madras," in his *Traditional India: Structure and Change*, p. 141.

11. *Maharshi Debendranath Tagorer Jiban Charit*, p. 65.

12. A. K. Dutt, "Kalikatar Bartaman Durbastha," pp. 97-101.

13. S. Sastri, *Atma Charit*, p. 42.

14. Ibid., p. 57.

15. S. Debi, *Sivanath*, p. 47.

16. S. Sastri, *Atma Charit*, p. 68.

17. Ibid.

18. S. Sastri, *Men I Have Seen: Reminiscences of Seven Great Bengalis*, p. 127.

19. H. C. Sarkar, *Sivanath Sastri*, p. 14.

20. Debi, *Sivanath*, p. 51.

21. H. C. Sarkar, *Sivanath Sastri*, p. 9.

22. Debi, *Sivanath*, p. 52.

23. Niyogi, *Rishi Protap Chandra*, p. 2.

24. P. C. Mazoomdar, *Heart Beats*, pp. xix, xxiv.

25. Niyogi, *Rishi Protap Chandra*, p. 6.

26. P. C. Mazoomdar, *Heart Beats*, p. xxviii.

27. S. C. Bose, *Life of Protap Chunder Mazoomdar*, I, 17, 18.

28. Letter from M. Ghose to G. Tagore (February 9, 1863), RBM-TFP.

29. Letter from M. Ghose to G. Tagore (August 18, 1862), RBM-TFP.

30. Letter from M. Ghose to G. Tagore (May 17, 1862), RBM-TFP.

31. Letter from M. Ghose to G. Tagore (December 2, 1862), RBM-TFP.
32. Tattvabhusan, *Autobiography*, pp. 48, 49, 51, 52, 59.
33. S. Sastri, *Ramtanu Lahiri o Tatkalin Banga Samaj*, p. 278.
34. *Nabakanta Chattopadhyay*, author unknown, pp. 1, 3.
35. B. Ghose, *Amar Jiban Katha*, pp. 2, 5, 9, 11, 12.
36. H. C. Sarkar, *Life of Ananda Mohan Bose*, pp. 16, 22.
37. K. K. Mitra, *Krishna Kumar Mitrer Atma Charit*, pp. 58, 64-65, 103.
38. S. Sastri, *History*, II, 367.
39. Ibid., p. 350.
40. M. Weber, *The Protestant Ethic and the Spirit of Capitalism*.
41. S. Sastri, *History*, II, 352.
42. Debendranath Tagore, *The Brahmo Samaj: Its Position and Prospects*, p. 171.
43. "Brahmo Marriages: Their History and Statistics" (July 1868), SBSL-SDCC.
44. Ibid.
45. P. C. Mazoomdar, "The Relations of the Brahmo Samaj to Hinduism and Christianity" (1873), SBSL-SDCC.
46. P. C. Mazoomdar, *Life and Teachings of Keshub Chunder Sen*, p. 251.
47. S. Sastri, *History*, I, 247.
48. S. Sen, *Jiban Smriti*, p. 81.
49. S. Datta, "Presidential Address," 1916, p. 61, SBSL-ARSBS.
50. M. M. Ali, *The Bengali Reaction to Christian Missionary Activities*, p. 31.
51. Ibid., p. 33.
52. Debendranath Tagore, *Atma Jibane*, p. 377.
53. Debendranath Tagore, *Brahmo Dharma*, pp. 1, 151, 154, 165, 166, 172, 173, 199, 211, 217.
54. K. C. Sen, "Ondha Byabashayi."
55. K. C. Sen, "Somoyer Bhalo Vyabahar."
56. K. C. Sen, "Ucchay Ashay."
57. K. C. Sen, *The New Samhita*, pp. 2, 10, 18, 19.
58. H. C. Sarkar, *Life of Bose*, pp. 4-6, 14.
59. S. Sastri, *Men I Have Seen*, p. 65.
60. H. C. Sarkar, *Life of Bose*, p. 25.
61. P. C. Ray, *Bengali Chemist*, pp. 26, 29, 30.
62. B. Mitter, "Lord Sinha."
63. "Death of Lord Sinha," 1928, p. 2, SBSL-ARSBS.
64. Lord Sinha, "Diary," 1902, 2-480, BSPA.
65. "Obituary—Dr. Mohini Mohun Basu," *Tattva Kaumudi* (September 16, 1901), 127.
66. D. N. Ray, *Atma Katha*, pp. 17, 95-98, 136, 140, 141, 184-96, 214, 233, 236, 265, 307.
67. D. M. Bose, "Nilratan Sircar," in D. M. Bose Collection, Bose Institute, Calcutta, n.d., pp. 1-4.
68. N. Sircar, "British Ban on Indian Medical Degrees."
69. D. M. Bose, "Nilratan Sircar," pp. 6, 8-10.
70. A. Tripathi, *Vidyasagar*, p. 9.
71. A. K. Dutt, "Polligramastha Prajadiger Durabastha," pp. 125-32.
72. A. K. Dutt, "Bangodesher Bartaman Arbastha," p. 181.
73. A. K. Dutt, *Dharma Niti*, pp. 159-62.
74. "Primary Education in Bengal," *National Paper*, v (January 6, 1869), 4-5.
75. J. Long, "The Ryots of Bengal," pp. 132-33.
76. A. Sen, *Notes on the Bengal Renaissance*, p. 381.

77. K. C. Sen, "Doridrer Khed."
78. K. C. Sen, "Projadiger Durobastha."
79. K. C. Sen, "Samanyo Lokdiger Vidyalaya."
80. K. C. Sen, "Modya Pan."
81. K. C. Sen, "Doridrer Khed."
82. "Sarbbo Sadharaner Janya Jelay Jelay Artha Sanchayer Vyabastha."
83. A. R. Bonerji, *An Indian Path-finder: Memoirs of Sevabrata Sasipada Banerji*, pp. 15, 17, 19.
84. S. Sastri, *History*, II, p. 384.
85. A. R. Bonerji, *Indian Path-finder*, pp. 17, 24, 25, 42.
86. "Brahmo Mission Movement: Baranagar" (March 1871), SBSL-SDCC.
87. A. R. Bonerji, *Indian Path-finder*, pp. 77, 75, 84.
88. B. N. Bandyopadhyay, *Dwarakanath Gangopadhyay*, pp. 4, 5, 8, 9, 13.
89. *Krishna Kumar Mitrer Atma Charit*, p. 117.
90. B. Chandra, *The Rise and Growth of Economic Nationalism in India*, p. 450.
91. S. Sarkar, *Bengal Renaissance and Other Essays*, p. 56.
92. Vidyaratna, *Udasin Satyashrobar Assam Bhramon*, p. 96.
93. S. Sarkar, *Bengal Renaissance and Other Essays*, pp. 55, 62.
94. B. N. Bandyopadhyay, *Dwarakanath Gangopadhyay*, p. 17.
95. "Female Education," *Brahmo Public Opinion*, IV (January 6, 1881), 5-6.
96. H. C. Sarkar, *Life of Ananda Mohun Bose*, p. 100.
97. N. Chaudhuri, *Autobiography of an Unknown Indian*, p. 375.
98. "The Bangabasi Case."
99. "Our Opponents" (May 3, 1891), *Indian Messenger*, VIII (July 12, 1891), 267.
100. "The Bangabasi Case," p. 346.
101. "Bio-graphical Sketch of Ramananda Chatterji," *Ramananda Chatterji Centenary Volume*, p. 246.
102. N. S. Bose, *Ramananda Chatterjee*, pp. 80, 81.
103. R. Chatterji, "Frequent Cases of Suicide among Youngmen and Women," *Indian Messenger*, VII (June 8, 1890), 313.
104. "Higher Education for Women: Our View."
105. Sastri, *The Brahmo Samaj of India: A Statement of Its Religious Principles and Brief History*, p. 46.
106. "The Present Situation in the Brahmo Samaj," p. 391.
107. K. N. Tagore "Jon Stuart Mill o Stri Swadhinota," p. 103.
108. S. Debi, *Sivanath*, p. 41.
109. *Brahmo Samaj: The Depressed Classes and Untouchability*, pp. 13-15, 17.

FAMILY, FACTION, POLITICAL REFORM

1. See, for example, N. S. Bose, "Growth of Political Consciousness: The National Movement," in his *Indian Awakening and Bengal*, pp. 235-314.
2. "Renaissance," "Moderate Nationalism," and "Extremism" provides the three-part structure for "Modern Hindu India" in de Bary, *Sources of Indian Tradition*, pp. 603-738.
3. The basis of Gandhi's anti-Western ideology is probably found in *Hindu Samaj*, which he wrote in South Africa in 1921.
4. For among the best studies, see Broomfield, *Elite Conflict in a Plural Society*; Gordon, *Bengal: the Nationalist Movement*; Heimsath, *Indian Nationalism and Hindu Social Reform*; and A. Seal, *The Emergence of Indian Nationalism*.

5. Besides Broomfield and Seal, see D. Chakrabarty, *Sasipada Banerjee: A Study in the Nature of the First Contact of the Bengali Bhadralok with the Working Classes of Bengal.*

6. This is summarized nicely in N. S. Bose, *Indian Awakening and Bengal*, pp. 282-94.

7. For a summary of these reforms, see "Letter from K. C. Sen, U. Gupta, M. Basu et al., to D. Tagore, July 2, 1865, in *Brahmananda Sri Keshub Chandrer Patrabali*, pp. 67-68.

8. Letter by D. Tagore, January 23, 1863, quoted in Sastri, *Jati Bhed*, pp. 67-68.

9. D. Tagore, *Amar Valya Katha o Amar Bombai Prabash*, p. 5.

10. Letter from K. C. Sen to D. Tagore, August 1, 1865, SBSL-SDCC.

11. Letter from D. Tagore to K. C. Sen, August 9, 1865, SBSL-SDCC.

12. S. Sastri, *The New Dispensation and the Sadharan Brahmo Samaj*, p. 9.

13. Requisition by thirty-two Brahmos of Calcutta, March 1, 1865, ibid.

14. Müller, *Biographical Essays*, p. 61.

15. "Letter from K. C. Sen to R. N. Basu, February 6, 1865," *Keshub Patrabali*, pp. 61-62.

16. "General Meeting of the Brahmo Samaj," November 15, 1866, SBSL-SDCC.

17. P. C. Mazoomdar, *The Life and Teachings of Keshub Chunder Sen*, pp. 206-208.

18. For a good discussion of this form of universalism, see S. K. Chattopadhyay, *Samanvay Marga*, pp. 22, 150.

19. "Native Celebrities in Bengal: W. C. Bonnerjee," *Indian Mirror*, XVII (August 3, 1878), 2-3.

20. H. C. Sarkar, *Life of Ananda Mohan Bose*, p. 36.

21. S. N. Banerjee, *A Nation in the Making*, pp. 4, 25, 27, 28, 31, 32.

22. S. Sastri, *The New Dispensation and the Sadharan Brahmo Samaj*, p. 81.

23. S. Sastri, *History*, I, 219, 265, 266.

24. Ibid., pp. 267, 269, 272, 274.

25. "On Legal Proprietorship of the Bharata-varsiya Brahmo Mandir" (June 6, 1878).

26. Ibid. (June 13, 1878).

27. "The Koch Bihar Marriage."

28. Goswami, *The Indian Prophet or a Review of Babu K. C. Sen's 'Am I an Inspired Prophet?'*, p. 9.

29. H. C. Sarkar, *Life of Ananda Mohan Bose*, p. 45.

30. "The Brahmo Dissenters."

31. S. Sastri, *Men I Have Seen*, p. 28.

32. "The Koch Bihar Marriage."

33. "A Few Facts Relating to the Fracas in the Brahmo Mandir," *Brahmo Public Opinion* (April 4, 1878), pp. 18-19.

34. "Babu B. K. Goswami's Suggestion towards the Organization of a New Samaj."

35. "Work Begun Anew" *Brahmo Public Opinion* (May 16, 1878), p. 81.

36. "Town Hall Meeting of the Brahmos."

37. S. Sastri, *Men I Have Seen*, p. 81.

38. S. Sastri, *The New Dispensation and the Sadharan Brahmo Samaj*, pp. 96, 97, 104, 105.

39. S. Sastri, *History*, II, 126, 134, 137.

40. H. C. Sarkar, *Life of Ananda Mohan Bose*, p. 122.

41. D. Datta, *Keshub and the Sadharan Brahmo Samaj*, pp. 257, 261, 263.

42. H. C. Sarkar, *Sivanath Sastri*, p. 96.

43. S. N. Banerjee, *A Nation in the Making*, p. 102.

44. H. C. Sarkar, *Life of Ananda Mohan Bose*, p. 55.

45. S. N. Banerjee, *A Nation in the Making*, p. 50.

46. B. C. Pal, *Charita-Chitra*, p. 97.

47. K. K. Mitra, *Krishna Kumar Mitrer Atma Charit*, p. 125.

48. B. Kar, *Bhakta Nagendra Nath Chattopadhyayer Jiban Brittanta*, pp. 59, 63.

49. S. Sastri, *Men I Have Seen*, p. 86.

50. H. C. Sarkar, *Life of Ananda Mohan Bose*, p. 44.

51. S. Sastri, "The Future of Our Country," *Indian Messenger*, IV (January 2, 1887), 140.

52. S. Sastri, *Englander Diary*, pp. 179, 180, 198, 216-17.

53. S. Sastri, *Jati Bhed*, pp. 39, 50, 52.

54. S. Sastri, "The Duties of the Educated Classes to the Masses," *Modern Review*, VII (January 1910), 70, 71, 73, 74.

55. S. Debi, *Ramananda Chattopadhyay o Ardha Satabdir Bangla*, pp. 5, 7, 13, 17, 19-21.

56. "Heramba Chandra Maitra," p. 238.

57. Nandi, "Ramananda Chatterji: A Bio-graphical Assessment," pp. 41-43.

58. N. S. Bose, *Ramananda Chatterjee*, pp. 29, 31, 80.

59. S. Debi, *Ramananda Chattopadhyay*, pp. 8, 9.

60. Nandi, "Ramananda Chatterji," p. 60.

61. "The New Nationalism and the True Nationalism."

62. "Why Are the Moderates Moderate?" p. 99.

63. N. S. Bose, *Ramananda Chatterjee*, p. 55.

64. S. Debi, *Ramananda Chattopadhyay*, p. 134.

65. Haldar, "Western Civilization."

66. R. Chatterjee, "Nation Building and the Critical Spirit," January 1925, reprinted in *Modern Review: Ramananda Centenary Number*, CXVIII (May 1965).

67. Shinde, *The Theistic Directory and a Review of the Liberal Religious Thought and Work in the Civilized World*, p. 36.

68. *Brahmo Samaj: The Depressed Classes and Untouchability*, p. 13.

69. N. S. Bose, *Ramananda Chatterjee*, p. 84.

70. *Brahmo Samaj: The Depressed Classes and Untouchability*, pp. 10-11.

71. "The Indian Association on Mass Education."

72. B. N. Sen, *The Pilgrim: Experiences in Europe and America*, pp. 16-17.

73. N. S. Bose, *Ramananda Chatterjee*, p. 17.

74. Chatterjee, "Education in Japan and India," *Modern Review*, VII (September 1907), 249, 250.

CONFRONTATION WITH TRINITARIANS

1. See Kopf, *British Orientalism and the Bengal Renaissance*, pp. 236-52.

2. "Macaulayism and the Bengali Intelligentsia," ibid., pp. 253-72.

3. *Freedom Movement in Bengal*, p. 23.

4. See especially Kopf, *British Orientalism and the Bengal Renaissance*, pp. 71-80.

5. Ibid., pp. 259-63.

6. L. B. Dey, *Recollections of Alexander Duff and the Mission College*, pp. 3, 10, 25, 34, 116, 120, 124, 181-210.

7. Letter from M. Ghose to G. Tagore (February 9, 1863), RBM-TFP.

8. K. M. Banerjea, *Review of the Munduck Oopanishad*, pp. iv, v, 46, 9, 10.

9. "Copy of the Trust Deed of the Brahmo Sabha" (January 23, 1830). K. N. Tagore Collection, RBM.

10. For a detailed account of Dwarkanath's entrepreneurial activities, see K. N. Tagore, *Dwarakanath Thakurer Jibani*.

11. S. Tagore, *Amar Valya Katha o Amar Bombai Prabash*, pp. 8, 9, 12.

12. Much material on this side of his life is contained in RBM-TFP.

13. Ali, *Bengali Reaction*, p. 17.

14. Biswas, "Maharshi Devendranath Tagore and the Tattvabodhini Sabha," *Studies on the Bengal Renaissance*, ed. A. C. Gupta, p. 40.

15. Ali, *Bengali Reaction*, pp. 17, 19.

16. D. Datta, *Keshub and the Sadharan Brahmo Samaj*, p. 41.

17. Ali, *Bengali Reaction*, p. 40.

18. Macpherson, *Life of Lal Behari Day*, p. 55.

19. Long, "Letter from Calcutta," *Calcutta Corresponding Committee of the Church Missionary Society: 27th Report, 1846*, p. 9.

20. Letter by De Rozario, ibid., pp. 11-12.

21. For a list of these persons, see Sastri, *Ramtanu Lahiri o Tatkalin Banga Samaj*, p. 17; Leonard, *A History of the Brahmo Samaj*, p. 150.

22. *Brahmo Conference: 76th Annual Report, Patna, 1966*, p. 43.

23. Ali, *Bengali Reaction*, p. 47.

24. *Autobiography of Maharshi Debendranath Tagore*, p. 100.

25. J. Sarkar, "Raj Narian Bose, the Grandfather of Nationalism in India."

26. Bagal, *Rajnarian Basu*, p. 6.

27. R. Bose, pp. 46, 53.

28. J. Sarkar, "Raj Narian Bose," p. 315.

29. *Rajnarian Basur Baktrita*, p. 39.

30. Ibid., pp. 68, 69.

31. Bagal, *Rajnarian Basu*, p. 77.

32. R. Bose, and D. N. Tagore, *Vedantic Doctrines Vindicated*, pp. 7-9.

33. H. Das, "The Reverend Krishna Mohan Banerjea: Brahmin, Christian, Scholar and Patriot," p. 142.

34. Lethbridge, *Ramtanu Lahiri: Brahmin and Reformer*, p. 185.

35. A list of these publications may be found in H. Das, "The Reverend Krishna Mohan Banerjea," n. 50.

36. K. M. Banerjea, *The Arian Witness*, pp. 62, 79, 115, 117, 140, 141, 153-66, 185; Banerjea, *Two Essays as Supplements to the Arian Witness*, pp. 43-61, 64, 72.

37. K. M. Banerjea, *The Relation between Christianity and Hinduism*, pp. 15, 19, 20.

38. K. M. Banerjea, *Arian Witness*, p. 11.

39. K. M. Banerjea, *The Peculiar Responsibility of Educated Natives*, pp. 18, 14, 15.

40. K. M. Banerjea, *Lectures to Educated Young Men on Vedantism*, pp. 13, 25-28.

41. *Encyclopedia Bengalensis in English and Bengali*, VIII, 98-168.

42. K. M. Bannerji, *Upadesh Katha*, pp. 1-23, 64-72, 107-24.

43. Rajnarian quoted in Ali, *Bengali Reaction*, pp. 260-61.

44. R. Bose, *Remarks on Rev. K. M. Banerjea's Lecture on Vedantism*, pp. 15, 16.

45. R. Bose and D. N. Tagore, *Vedantic Doctrines Vindicated*, p. 31.

46. Bose quoted in Ali, *Bengali Reaction*, p. 46.

47. R. Bose, *Atma-Charita*, pp. 61, 110; Bagal, *Raj Narian Bose*, p. 33.

RISE OF CULTURAL NATIONALISM

1. K. C. Sen, *Conscience and Renunciation*, p. 2.

2. For a contemporary missionary account of the talk and of its response in Calcutta, see "The Leader of the Brahmo Samaj, Calcutta, and the Author of Ecce Homo," *Church Missionary Intelligencer*, New Series III (October 1867), pp. 301-308.

3. K. C. Sen, "Jesus Christ: Europe and Asia," May 5, 1866, in *Keshub Chunder Sen: Lectures and Tracts*, pp. 5, 6, 10, 11, 23, 24, 26, 27, 30-32, 34, 37.

4. Letter from R. Bose to G. N. Tagore (January 8, 1869), RBM-TFP.

5. Bagal, *Rajnarian Basu*, p. 47.

6. R. Bose, "Prospectus to Start a Society for the Promotion of National Feeling among the Educated Natives of Bengal, April 1866," pp. 444-47.

7. R. Bose, *The Adi Brahmo Samaj: Its View and Principles*, pp. 2, 3, 6.

8. R. Bose, *Atma Charita*, pp. 88, 89.

9. Bagal, *Hindu Melar Itibritta*, p. 3.

10. D. Tagore, "European Model."

11. Ibid., p. 462.

12. D. Tagore, "Hinduism Is Not Hostile to Brahmoism," p. 448.

13. D. Tagore, "Nationality and Universality," p. 86.

14. D. Tagore, "Nationality Indeed," p. 209.

15. D. Tagore, "Spurious Brahmoism," p. 6.

16. "Babu Keshub Chandra Sen in Lahore."

17. Bagal, *Hindu Melar*, pp. 7, 9, 10, 13, 16.

18. R. Bose, *Atma Charita*, pp. 218-19.

19. Bagal, *Hindu Melar*, pp. 43, 45.

20. Dwijendranath Tagore, *Prabandha Mala*, pp. 4-8, 42, 43, 56, 103-46, 148.

A REVOLUTIONARY NATIONALIST

1. This is beautifully articulated throughout Nehru, *The Discovery of India*.

2. Debendranath Tagore, *Atma Jibani*, pp. 248, 262; S. Sastri, *History*, I, 83.

3. K. N. Tagore, "Manuscript Biography of Debendranath Tagore," p. 10, RBM-KNC; K. N. Tagore, *Dwarakanath Thakurer Jibani*, pp. 71, 74; Debendranath Tagore, *Atma Jibani*, p. 262.

4. Debendranath Tagore, *Atma Jibani*, pp. 249, 250, 259, 269, 270, 276, 277, 295.

5. Letter from Dwarkanath Tagore to Debendranath Tagore, May 19, 1841, quoted in Rathindranath Tagore, *Amar Valya Katha o Amar Bombai Prabash*, p. 7.

6. Letter from Dwarkanath Tagore to Debendranath Tagore, May 22, 1846, quoted in Debendranath Tagore, *Atma Jibani*, p. 310.

7. Letter from Debendranath Tagore to Protap Chandra Mazoomdar, n.d., reprinted in *Calcutta Corresponding Committee of the Church Missionary Society*, 62nd Report, 1881, p. xiv.

8. R. Bose, *Atma Charita*, pp. 6, 7, 9, 12-15, 27, 28, 33, 39, 41, 42, 46, 50, 53.

9. *Rajnarian Basur Bakrita*, p. 104.

10. "The Poverty of India," *Indian Mirror*, XVII (March 7, 1878), 55.

11. "Revival of Indian Arts and Manufactures."

12. A. K. Dutt, "Bangodesher Bartaman Arbastha."

13. "Babu Durga Charan Law," *Indian Mirror*, XVIII (February 12, 1879), 2.

14. "An Average Bengali Middle Class Boy with Education," ibid., XIX (July 15, 1880), 2; "Our Countrymen and the Value of Self-help"; "An Appeal to Our Countrymen and Capitalists on Behalf of Industries and Manufactures"; "Indian Youths and Technical Education."

15. McCully, *English Education and Origins of Indian Nationalism*, p. 215.

16. For a good analysis of this, see Sinha, *Nineteenth Century Bengal: Aspects of Social History*, pp. 40-43.

17. "Higher Education in India."

18. "Distress of the Middle Class Natives."

19. "Practical Closing of the Covenanted Civil Service to the Natives."

20. For a good summary of the results of imperialism as perceived by nationalists, see Rothermund, *The Phases of Indian Nationalism and Other Essays*, pp. 17, 18. See also R. C. Dutt, *Economic History of India in the Victorian Age*, pp. 245, 254, 344, 419.

21. Pal, *Memories of My Life and Times*, I, 408.

22. "The Ilbert Act: A Legislative Patch-Work."

23. "Babu Surendra Nath Banerjee's Release from Jail," *Indian Mirror*, XXIII (July 12, 1883), 2.

24. Greenberger, *British Image of India*, pp. 13, 15, 42.

25. Tripathi, *The Extremist Challenge: India Between 1890-1910*, pp. 48-50.

26. "The Pleadership Examination in Bengal."

27. "Grievances of the Native Engineers of Bengal."

28. "Natives in the Indian Medical Services."

29. "Practical Closing of the Covenanted Civil Service to the Natives."

30. "The Term Babu."

31. S. Datta, *The World of Twilight*, pp. 60, 61.

32. For evidence and discussion of this, see Seal, *The Emergence of Indian Nationalism*, p. 5.

33. Tripathi, *Extremist Challenge*, p. 145.

34. "Bengalis in the North-Western Provinces."

35. "The Bengalis and the Biharis."

36. P. C. Singha, *Upadhyay, Brahmo Bandhab*, pp. 1, 2.

37. "Family Background of Upadhyay," manuscript, 1933, GLA-UC.

38. P. C. Singha, *Upadhyay, Brahmo Bandhab*, p. 4.

39. Bagal, *Hindu Melar*, pp. 70, 71.

40. "Hindu Mela."

41. "Family Background of Upadhyay," p. 149, GLA-UC.

42. Animananda, "An Indian Nation Builder—Brahma-bandhab Upadhyay," 1947, pp. 12, 13, 16, 20, 51, GLA-UC.

43. P. C. Sinha, pp. 20, 22.

44. Animananda, "An Indian Nation Builder," pp. 22, 31, 32, GLA-UC.

45. Isherwood, *Ramakrishna and His Disciples*, pp. 89, 186, 191, 192.

46. Seal, "A Fellow Student's Reminiscence: Swami Vivekananda," n.d., p. 5, BI.

47. Isherwood, *Ramakrishna*, p. 192.

48. K. K. Mitra, *Khrisna Kumar Mitrer Atma Charit*, p. 155.

49. Animananda, "An Indian Nation Builder," pp. 25, 27, GLA-UC.

50. *Cultural Heritage of India*, IV, 697, 703.

51. Animananda, "An Indian Nation Builder," p. 27, GLA-UC.

52. Ibid., pp. 23, 24.

53. See Mallick, "Reminiscences of Ramakrishna and Vivekananda," in G. C. Banerji, *Keshab Chandra and Ramakrishna*, p. 277.

54. Animananda, "An Indian Nation Builder," pp. 31, 34-37, 45, GLA-UC.

55. B. Upadhyay, "Objects," p. 1.

56. B. Upadhyay, "The Hindu Revival."

57. Animananda, "An Indian Nation Builder," pp. 64, 65, 70, GLA-UC.

58. Baago, *Pioneers of Indigenous Christianity*, p. 35.

59. Animananda, "An Indian Nation Builder," pp. 78-80, 82, 83, 104, 105, 108, 109, 112.

60. B. Upadhyay, "Europeanism versus Christianity," pp. 164, 165.

61. B. Upadhyay, "Christianity in India," pp. 66, 67.

62. B. Upadhyay, "Integrity of Hindu Society."

63. B. Upadhyay, "National Memorial."

64. B. Upadhyay, "Imperialism and Christendom"; "Christianity in India"; *Samaj*, p. 28.

65. Rothermund, "Traditionalism and Socialism in Vivekananda's Thought," *The Phases of Indian Nationalism*, pp. 57-64.

66. B. Upadhyay, *Samaj*, pp. 29-31, 35.

67. B. Upadhyay, "Integrity of Hindu Society," p. 4; "Telescopic Nature of Brahmo Endeavours."

68. Animananda, "An Indian Nation Builder," pp. 121-24, 136, 151, GLA-UC.

69. "Family Background of Upadhyay," p. 217, GLA-UC.

70. Animananda, "An Indian Nation Builder," pp. 141, 142, 151, 152, GLA-UC.

71. For a recent, well-documented study of C. R. Das in the nationalist context, see Gordon, *Bengal: The Nationalist Movement, 1876-1940*, pp. 163-88.

72. Tripathi, *Extremist Challenge*, p. 15.

73. Pal, *Charita-Chitra*, p. 210.

BRAHMO EVANGELISM

1. "Life of Bijoy Krishna Goswami," *Tattva Kaumudi* (July 1899), p. 76.

2. Pal, *Saint Bijoy Krishna Goswami*, p. 15.

3. "Life of Bijoy Krishna Goswami," p. 76.

4. Pal, *Goswami*, pp. 21-22.

5. "Life of Bijoy Krishna Goswami," p. 76.

6. Goswami, *Brahmo Samajer Bartaman Abastha Ebong Amar Jibane Brahmo Samajer Parikkhita Bisay*, pp. 4-7, 10, 11.

7. Pal, *Goswami*, pp. 24, 25, 26, 30.

8. Goswami, *Brahmo Samajer*, p. 12.

9. P. C. Mazoomdar, *The Life and Teachings of Keshub Chunder Sen*, pp. 132, 189, 190, 192, 215.

10. P. C. Mazoomdar, *Faith and Progress of the Brahmo Samaj*, p. 224.

11. S. Sastri, *History*, II, 320-21.

12. *The Annual from the East Bengal Brahmo Mission Society: December, 1878*, p. 8.

13. K. K. Mitra, *Krishna Kumar Mitrer Atma Charit*, p. 52.

14. G. C. Sen, *Atma Jiban*, pp. 27-29, 35.

15. P. C. Mazoomdar, *Life and Teachings*, p. 193.

16. S. Sastri, *History*, I, 227.

17. Letter from S. N. Tagore to G. Tagore (January 10, 1868), RBM-TFP.

18. P. C. Mazoomdar, *Life and Teachings*, p. 200.

19. Letter from B. K. Goswami to editor of Somprakash, November 1, 1868, reprinted in *Samayik Patre Banglar Samaj Chitra*, pp. 215, 216.

20. K. C. Sen, "The Prophet of Nuddea," SBSL-SDCC.

21. Pal, *Goswami*, p. 66.

22. D. Datta, *Keshub and the Sadharan Brahmo Samaj*, pp. 237, 238.

23. "On the Defection of Pandit Bijoy Krishna Goswami."

24. Pal, *Goswami*, p. 69.

25. D. Datta, *Keshub and the Sadharan Brahmo Samaj*, pp. 49, 53.

26. "Brahmo Missionaries" (January 15, 1867), SBSL-SDCC.

27. S. Sastri, *History*, I, 216.

28. P. C. Mazoomdar, *Faith and Progress*, pp. 226, 227.

29. D. Datta, *Keshub and the Sadharan Brahmo Samaj*, p. 48.

30. P. C. Mazoomdar, *Life and Teachings*, p. 305.

31. *The Apostles and the Missionaries of the Naba-bidhan*, p. 22.

32. G. C. Sen, *Atma Jiban*, pp. 2, 8, 9, 11, 14-19, 22, 25, 30, 42, 49, 51.

33. *Perita Kalishankar Das Kabiraj*, pp. 5, 7, 8, 10, 15, 16, 18, 36, 68, 91, 191.

34. S. Basu, *Bhakta Harisundar Basu Mahashayer Charita Katha*, pp. 1-5, 13-16.

35. N. Niyogi, *Sadhan o Seba*, pp. 7, 8, 10, 11, 170, 181.

36. S. K. Chattopadhyay, *Upadhyay Gourgovinda Roy*, pp. 1-5, 7, 20, 21.

37. C. Sharma, *Sadhu Aghornather Jiban Charit*, pp. 5-7, 9, 11, 14, 21, 24, 43.

38. *Apostles and Missionaries of Naba-bidhan*, pp. 27-28.

39. P. C. Mazoomdar, *Life and Teachings*, pp. 189-90.

40. *Songs of Tomorrow*, p. 7.

41. *Apostles and Missionaries of Naba-bidhan*, pp. 14-16, 18.

42. S. Sastri, *History*, II, 419.

43. *Apostles and Missionaries of Naba-bidhan*, p. 38.

44. Kar, *Bhakta Nagendra Nath Chattopadhyayer Jiban Brittanta*, pp. 1, 2, 5-11, 20, 26, 27, 29, 48, 49, 52, 53, 56, 57, 59, 60, 67-69, 71, 74-76.

45. "Celebration of Theodore Parker's 70th Anniversary."

46. N. N. Chattopadhyay, *Mahatma Theodore Parker*.

47. *Swargiya Umesh Chandra Dutt: Smriti Sraddhanjali*, pp. 21-23, 25.

48. S. Sastri, *History*, II, 124.

49. *Swargiya Umesh Chandra Dutt*, pp. 24, 53, 55, 56, 158, 177.

50. Sen-Sastri, *Sibchandra Deb o Banglar Unabingsha Satabdi*, p. 62.

51. *Swargiya Umesh Chandra Dutt*, pp. 116, 157, 158, 168, 169, 177, 230, 231.

52. "Life of Tara Kishore Chaudhury," in Pranab Ray Family Collection, Calcutta, pp. 12-14, 17, 18, 30-32, 48, 51, 69, 71-74, 84.

KESHUB, PROPHET OF HARMONY

1. Letter from Debendranath Tagore to Protap Chandra Mazoomdar, n.d., in *Calcutta Corresponding Committee of the Church Missionary Society*, 62nd Report, 1881, p. xiii.

2. A collection of these press notices on Keshub's death can be found in the issues of the Brahmo Samaj newspaper, *The Indian Mirror*, during the week of January 8-15, 1884.

3. The works of Prasanta Kumar Sen and Sati Kumar Chatterji in particular have kept Keshub's name and achievements alive in the twentieth century.

4. The critics of Keshub Sen have been largely Sadharan Brahmos and radical Westernizers who feel that he sold out to Hindu revivalists, even while he supported the British imperial establishment.

5. This position can be traced back to a group of highly politicized Sadharan Brahmos who formed the Indian Association in 1877-1878, which became an effective nationalist organization and the precursor of the Indian National Congress. The leading figure of the movement was Ananda Mohan Bose.

6. According to one scholar of Tagore, the influence of Keshub's universalism on Tagore took place early in the latter's life and remained a profound influence. See Hay, *Asian Ideas of East and West: Tagore and His Critics*, p. 23.

7. See, for example, B. C. Pal, *The Brahmo Samaj and the Battle of Swaraj in India*, pp. 34-67.

8. For an excellent illustration of this position from a Marxist point of view, see S. Sarkar, *Bengal Renaissance and Other Essays*, pp. 148-83.

9. The universalist aspect of Bengal renaissance ideology has generally been ignored in favor of the Westernizing and nationalist aspects. Even the universalist element in nationalist thought has been distorted. Brahmobandhab Upadhyay, for example, carried the baggage of Brahmo universalism into a de-Europeanized form of Roman Catholicism before his final identity crisis and withdrawal into Hindu nationalist fanaticism. Though Sasipada Bannerji's nationalist activities have been depicted, I know of no study of his Debalaya, which aimed at bringing representatives of all castes, religions, and creeds together in order to find ways of ending hatred and strife. Even Vivekananda, alleged cultural nationalist founder of the Ramakrishna Mission, originally offered the world neo-Vedantism as the basis for religious and cultural unity.

10. Haldar, *Tantras: Their Philosophy and Occult Secrets*, pp. 71, 72.

11. For a systematic study of Keshub's contribution to neo-Buddhism in relation to other religious revivals, see S. K. Chattopadhyay, *Samanvay Marga*.

12. Kopf, "The Brahmo Domestication of Unitarianism: Protap Chandra Mazoomdar and the Spread of the Bengal Renaissance in South Asia," *West Bengal and Bangladesh: Perspectives from 1972*, pp. 28-29.

13. G. C. Sen, *Atma Jiban*, pp. 55-56.

14. *Koran Sharif*, p. ix.

15. Thomas, *The Acknowledged Christ of the Indian Renaissance*, p. 58.

16. Kopf, *British Orientalism and the Bengal Renaissance*, pp. 108-26.

17. Ibid., pp. 116-17.

18. K. C. Sen, *Jiban Veda*, pp. 17-18.

19. P. C. Mazoomdar, *The Life and Teachings*, pp. 17, 18, 57, 73, 92, 93, 97, 101-103, 105.

20. S. Tagore, *Amar Valya Katha o Amar Bombai Prabash*, p. 57.

21. P. C. Mazoomdar, *Life and Teachings*, pp. 126, 127.

22. K. C. Sen, *Diary in Ceylon*, p. 52.

23. P. C. Mazoomdar, *Life and Teachings*, p. 115.

24. S. Tagore, *Amar Valya Katha*, p. 57.

25. *Two Documents Reprinted: Maharshi Devendra Nath Tagore and Keshub Chunder*, p. 9.

26. K. C. Sen, *Young Bengal: This Is for You*, pp. 1, 4, 5.

27. Letter from S. Tagore to G. Tagore (January 26, 1861), RBM-TFP.

28. Letter from K.C. Sen to D. Tagore, May 12, 1862, in *Brahmananda Sri Keshub Chandrer Patrabali*, pp. 7-10.

29. *Maharashi Debendranath Tagorerer Jiban Charit*, p. 224.

30. B. N. Ghose, "Lal Lochan Ghose."

31. P. C. Mazoomdar, *Life and Teachings*, p. 189.

32. Dall, *Brahmo Samaj of India Led by Baboo Keshub Chunder Sen with Facts Historical and Personal*, p. 3.

33. K. C. Sen, "Great Men," September 1866, in *Keshub Chunder Sen: Lectures and Tracts*, pp. 57, 62, 65-67, 79-81.

34. S. Sastri, *History*, I, 227.

35. Letter from Goswami to editor of *Somprakash*, November 1, 1868, reprinted in *Samayik Patre Banglar Samaj Chitra*, p. 16.

36. Letter from Reverend Christian Bowetsch to the Church Mission Society in Calcutta Missionary Correspondence, May 3, 1866, o 50/7, Church Mission Society Archives, London.

37. *Calcutta Corresponding Committee of the Church Missionary Society*, 47th Report, 1866, p. 7.

38. "Diary of Reverend James Long," January 17, 1866, *Church Missionary Intelligencer*, New Series, III (1867), 26.

39. "Keshub Chunder Sen," ibid., VIII (November 1871), 341-50.

40. K. C. Sen, "England's Duties to India," pp. 193, 195, 209, 210.

41. *Keshab Chandra Sen's Nine Letters on Educational Measures*, pp. 4, 7, 8, 12, 15, 20, 26, 29-31, 34, 36.

42. K. C. Sen, *Acharyer Prarthana*, p. 7.

43. G. C. Banerji, *Keshab Chandra and Ramakrishna*, p. 7.

44. Isherwood, *Ramakrishna and His Disciples*, pp. 71, 88, 99, 102, 124, 125, 145, 147, 148, 161.

45. Farquhar, *Modern Religious Movements in India*, p. 52.

46. Koar, *Nava Vrindaban*, p. 24.

47. Letter from J. Koar to S. K. Chatterji (May 13, 1954), KL.

48. S. Chaudhuri, "Victoria Institutioner Eksho Bachar," p. 67.

49. K. C. Sen, *India Asks—Who Is Christ?*, p. 8.

50. S. K. Chattopadhyay, *Brahmo Gitapanishader Parichay o Keshub Chandrer Sadhanay Hindu Dharma*, p. 36.

51. Sen, "Am I an Inspired Prophet?" (January 1879).

52. "The Nagar Sankirtan."

53. G. C. Banerji, *Keshab Chandra and Ramakrishna*, p. 42.

54. *Brahmo Sangit o Sankirtan*, p. 9.

55. S. K. Sen, "Socrates."

56. S. Sastri, *The New Dispensation and the Sadharan Brahmo Samaj*, pp. 48, 51.

57. S. K. Chattopadhyay, *Samanvay Marga*, p. 47.

58. Letter from Koar to Chatterji (July 6, 1956), KL.

59. S. K. Chattopadhyay, *Samanvay Marga*, p. 8.

60. Ibid., p. 108.

61. Koar to Chatterji (July 6, 1956), KL.

62. Koar to Chatterji (May 13, 1954), KL.

63. S. K. Sen, "New Sacramental Ceremony."

64. S. K. Sen, "National Form of Our Baptism."

65. "The Meaning of the Fire Ceremony," *The New Dispensation*, I (June 16, 1881), 125.

66. O'Neill, *Brahmoism—Is It for or against Christianity?*, pp. 2-3.

67. K. C. Sen, *We Apostles of the New Dispensation*, pp. 3, 4, 9, 10, 15, 25, 28.

68. K. C. Sen, "The Flag Ceremony," pp. 17-18.

69. K. C. Sen, "The Cross," p. 39.

70. K. C. Sen, "Incarnations."

71. K. C. Sen, "God Our Mother."

72. K. C. Sen, *Book of Pilgrimages: Diaries and Reports of Missionary Expeditions*, p. 201.

73. *Brahmo Sangit o Sankirtan*, p. 235.

74. K. C. Sen, "Pagol I," pp. 77, 78.

75. "Pagol II," p. 106.

76. "Pagol III," p. 150.

77. "Pagol IV," p. 201.

78. P. C. Mazoomdar, *Life and Teachings of Keshub*, p. 454.

79. Letter from K. C. Sen to M. Müller, August 15, 1882, reprinted in M. Müller, *Biographical Essays*, p. 138.

80. Letter from Koar to Chatterji (April 1, 1960), KL.

81. K. C. Sen, *Jiban Veda*, pp. 53, 55, 59.

82. K. C. Sen, "Dance of the New Dispensation," pp. 91, 92.

83. K. C. Sen, *Asia's Message to Europe*, p. 3.

84. S. Sastri, *History*, II, 93.

85. P. C. Mazoomdar, *Life and Teachings of Keshub*, pp. 415-16.

86. *Apostles and Missionaries of the Naba-bidhan*, p. 28.

87. G. C. Sen, *Atma Jiban*, pp. 55-56.

88. *Apostles and Missionaries of the Naba-bidhan*, p. 35.

89. Wrote Mohammad Akram Khan, "There was no want of Muslim scholars well-versed in Arabic and Persian, in those days. Many of the Muslim scholars had command over Bengali literature. But none of them was conscious about the need of translating the Koran. But a Hindu scholar of Bengal, Bhai Girish Chandra Sen came forward to do the job, first on the instruction of Keshub Chandra Sen. This extraordinary and wonderful achievement of Girish Chandra Sen may be called one of the eight wonders of the world." (*Koran Sharif*, p. ii).

90. G. C. Sen, *Atma Jiban*, pp. 119-22.

91. S. K. Chattopadhyay, *Upadhyay Gourgovinda Roy*, p. 11.

92. U. G. Roy, *Srimad Bhagabad Gita: Samavay Bhasya*, pp. iv, xv-xviii.

93. U. G. Roy, *Vedanta Samanvay*, p. 3.

94. C. Sharma, *Sadhu Aghornather Jiban Charit*, p. 39.

95. A. N. Gupta, *Shakyamuni Charit o Nirban Tattva*, pp. 5, 10, 12, 258-60.

96. S. C. Bose, *Life of Protap Chunder Mazoomdar*, I, 174, 176; II, 115, 118, 120, 124.

RABINDRANATH TAGORE

1. For example, there are only three innocuous references to the Brahmo Samaj in Kripalani, *Tagore: A Life*.

2. N. S. Bose, *Ramananda Chatterji*, p. 12.

3. Hay, *Asian Ideas of East and West*, pp. 23, 27.

4. S. Sarkar, *Bengal Renaissance and Other Essays*, pp. 152-57, 161.

5. B. N. Bandyopadhyay, *Jyotirindranath Tagore*, pp. 17, 22-32.

6. Hay, *Asian Ideas of East and West*, pp. 26-28.

7. P. N. Bose, *A 100 Years of Bengali Press*, p. 99.

8. See especially, I. Bandyopadhyay, *Kalpa Taru*.

9. B. C. Pal, *Memories of My Life and Times*, II, 37.

10. B. C. Pal, *The Present Social Reaction: What Does It Mean?*, p. 3.

11. S. K. Chattopadhyay, *Samanvay Marga*, p. 289.

12. S. Sarkar, *Bengal Renaissance and Other Essays*, p. 166.

13. Rathindranath Tagore, *On the Edges of Time*, p. 9.

14. Hay, *Asian Ideas of East and West*, p. 31.

15. S. Sarkar, *Bengal Renaissance and Other Essays*, pp. 168, 173.

16. Hay, *Asian Ideas of East and West*, p. 32.

17. Rabindranath Tagore, *Towards Universal Man*, pp. 49-66.

18. Hay, *Asian Ideas of East and West*, p. 33.

19. P. K. Sen, *Western Influence on the Bengali Novel*, p. 46.

20. Rabindranath Tagore, *Gora*, pp. 6, 24, 32, 38-40, 42, 44-56, 87, 132, 239, 330, 402, 405-406.

21. Rabindranath Tagore, "Purba and Paschim" (East and West), *Towards Universal Man*, pp. 137, 139.

22. Rabindranath Tagore, "Keshub Anniversary Address, January 9, 1910," reprinted in G. C. Banerji, *Keshub as Seen by His Opponents*, pp. 102, 105-106.

23. Mahalanobis, "The Growth of the Visva-Bharati, 1901-1921," p. 89.

24. R. Tagore, "Dharma Siksha," p. 227.

25. R. Tagore, "Adi Brahmo Samajer Vedi," p. 236.

26. R. Tagore, "Dharma Sikkha," p. 230.

27. R. Tagore, "Adi Brahmo Samajer Vedi," p. 263.

28. R. Tagore, "Brahmo Samajer Sarthakata," pp. 6, 7, 10.

29. B. C. Pal, *Memories of My Life and Times*, II, 706.

30. Letter from R. Tagore to A. Chakrabarty (March 18, 1913), in Ajit Charkrabarty Papers, RBMA.

31. Letter from R. Tagore to A. Chakrabarty (February 15, 1913), ibid.

32. S. Debi, *Punya Smriti*, pp. 68, 69.

33. A. Chakrabarty, "Brahmo Samajer Samasya," p. 40.

34. N. Niyogi, "Brahmo o Hindu" (Brahmo and Hindu), *Tattvabodhini Patrika*, xx (June 1914), 45, 46.

35. L. Majumdar, *Sukumar Ray*.

36. S. Debi, *Punya Smriti*, p. 19.

37. L. Mazoomdar, *Sukumar Ray*, p. 29.

38. S. Ray, "Brahmo o Hindu Prabandher Pratibad."

39. Rabindranath Tagore, *Nationalism*, pp. 16, 28, 36, 37, 75, 87, 97, 98, 100, 162.

40. Rabindranath Tagore, *The Home and the World*, pp. 19, 26.

41. Payne, *The Saktas: An Introductory and Comparative Study*, p. 214.

42. Rabindranath Tagore, *The Home and the World*, p. 162.

43. "Letter to the Editor on the Membership of Rabindranath Thakur," *Tattva-Kaumudi* (January 14, 1917), 223.

44. S. Debi, *Punya Smriti*, p. 219.

45. Mahalanobis, *Kaeno Rabindranath ke Cai*, p. 7.

46. Home, *Purushottam Rabindranath*, pp. 47, 57-58, 61.

47. Mahalanobis, "The Growth of Visva-Bharati," pp. 79, 92.

48. Mahalanobis, "Visva-Bharati Annual Report," *Visva Bharati Quarterly*, VI (April 1928), 123.

49. Mahalanobis, "The Growth of Visva-Bharati," p. 92.

50. "Tagore: Pioneer in Asian Relations," p. 110.

51. Rabindranath Tagore, quoted in Mahalanobis, "The Growth of Visva-Bharati," p. 94.

52. Rabindranath Tagore, quoted in *Visva Bharati and Its Institutions*, p. 19.

53. Rabindranath Tagore, *Letters from Russia*, pp. 3, 4.

BENGAL'S LEGACY

1. Einstein, *Out of My Later Years*, p. 30.

2. Lethbridge, *Ramtanu Lahiri: Brahmin and Reformer*, p. 8.

3. M. M. Ali, *The Bengali Reaction to Christian Missionary Activities*, p. 34.

4. Debendranath Tagore, *Atma Jibani*, p. 398.

5. B. Ghose, "Brahmoism and the Bengal Renaissance," pp. 23-24.

6. S. Sastri, *History*, II, 377.

7. "Bijoy Krishna Goswami," *Tattva Kaumudi* (July 30, 1899), p. 76.

8. K. C. Sen, *Diary in Madras and Bombay*, pp. 12-31.

9. P. C. Mazoomdar, "Retrospect," *Theistic Annual, 1874*, pp. 35-36.

10. S. Sastri, *History*, I, 411.

11. Newspaper cuttings on "Brahmo Missionary Movement, Western India" (January 1873), SBSL-SDCC.

12. Ibid., August 14, 1872.

13. N. Ray, "Sraddhiki," unpublished manuscript in private collection of Pronab Ray, Calcutta.

14. Shinde, *The Theistic Directory and a Review of the Liberal Religious Thought and Work in the Civilized World*, p. 24.

15. "Brahmo Missionary Movement, Punjab" (May 28, 1869), SBSL-SDCC.

16. Ibid., July 12, 1871; May 20, 1871; December 12, 1871; July 25, 1871; December 26, 30, 1873.

17. "Missionary Movement, Western India," ibid. (December 26, 1871).

18. P. C. Mazoomdar, "Brahmos Arise" (January 1, 1867), SBSL-SDCC.

19. Shinde, *Theistic Directory*, p. 34.

20. Sastri, *History*, II, 446.

21. "Missionary Movement, Western India" (December 28, 1872), SBSL-SDCC.

22. *Theistic Annual, 1873*, p. 68.

23. "Brahmo Missionary Movement, Southern India" (May 6, 1870), SBSL-SDCC.

24. Ibid. (November 19, 1869).

25. Shinde, *Theistic Directory*, appendix, pp. 106-109.

26. "Missionary Movement, Southern India," November 14, 1869; September 24, 1869; June 10, 1870; January 18, 1871; June 9, 1871; July 22, 1871; September 20, 1871; November 3, 1871, SBSL-SDCC.

27. "Brahmo Missionary Movement, Bangalore" (November 8, 1876), SBSL-SDCC.

28. Devi, *Autobiography of an Indian Princess*, p. 77.

29. *Koch Biharadhipati Sriman Maharaja Sir Nripendra Narayan Bhupa Bahadurer Punya Smriti*, pp. 19, 20.

30. See "Retrospective Sketch of the Government Administration of Cooch Behar during Minority of Maharajah Nripendra Narayan," in *Annual Administrative Report, 1883-1884*, pp. 1-26, DACB.

31. *Proceedings of the Cooch Behar State Council, 1892-1894*, n.p., DACB.

32. "Retrospective Sketch of the Government Administration," p. 25, DACB.

33. DACB, D. C. Duke, "Late Maharaja of Cooch Behar," *Installation of Maharaja Rajendra Narayan Bhupa Bahadur* (November 8, 1911), pp. iv, v.

34. S. Debi, *Swargiya Kumar Gajendra Narayan*, p. 26.

35. *Proceedings of the Cooch Behar State Council*, n.p., DACB.

36. "Suniti College Building Constructed," *Annual Administrative Report, 1889-1890*, pp. 21-29, DACB.

37. "Victoria College Opened," ibid., 1888-1890, pp. 43-44.

38. Hunter, *Imperial Gazetteer of India*, 1886, p. 324.

39. Devi, *Autobiography of an Indian Princess*, p. 78.

40. "Capital Punishment," *Sukatha*, III (July 1893), 70-71.

41. "Brahmo Samaj Building Finished," in *Annual Administrative Report, 1887-1888*, pp. 29-36, DACB.

42. "The New Dispensation Proclaimed as the State Religion of Cooch Behar."

43. "Sradh Ceremony of His Late Highness," in *Proceedings of the State Council* (October 27, 1911), XIX, 97, DACB.

44. Shinde, *Theistic Directory*, appendix, p. 105.

45. S. Sastri, *History*, II, 465, 494.

46. "Some Bengali Brahmos of Shillong."

47. S. Sastri, *History*, II, 527.

48. A. Debi, *Bhakta Kabi Madhusudan Rao o Utkale Nabayug*, pp. 32, 33, 37, 112, 113, 169, 180.

49. Shinde, *Theistic Directory*, p. 24.

50. K. Nag, "The Brahmo Samaj," *Illustrated Weekly of India*, XCII (January 31, 1971), 9, 11.

51. Shinde, *Theistic Directory*, p. 43.

52. "Poona Reactionaries: A Warning."

53. *Report on the Census of British India Taken on 17th February, 1881*, I, 49.

54. Griswold, *Insights into Modern Hinduism*, p. 44.

55. Sastri, *History*, II, 106, 167, 551-57.

56. Shinde, *Theistic Directory*, appendix, p. 42.

57. Sastri, *History*, 253; A. Sen, *Swargiya Dinanath Sener Jibani o Tatkalin Purba Banga*, pp. 154-55.

58. B. C. Roy, *The Story of My Humble Life*, pp. 78, 80.

Bibliography

MANUSCRIPTS

Bangiya Sahitya Parishad, Calcutta
Lord Sinha's Diary, 1902. Ms. 69/2-480.
Prafulla Chandra Ray Papers, Autobiographical Notes, March 1926. Ms. 69/2-452. Diary, December 1927. Ms. 69/2-476.

Bose Institute, Calcutta
D. M. Bose Collection

Church Mission Archives, London
Letter from Blumhardt to the Church Mission Society, December 7, 1879. Calcutta Missionary Correspondence, 0/209/8.
Letters from Reverend Christian Bomwetsch to Church Mission Society, 1866, 0/50/7.
Letters from Reverend John Pratt to Church Mission Society, 1841, 0/231/27.
Letter from Reverend Samuel Dyson to Reverend Vern, November 11, 1877, 0/97/.

Cooch-Behar State Archives, Cooch-Behar, West Bengal
Annual Administration Reports, 1882-1912.
Proceedings of Cooch-Behar State Council, 1882-1898. Vols. I-XVI.

Rabindra Bharati University, Calcutta
Kshitindranath Tagore Collection.

Saint Xavier's College, Calcutta
Brahmobandhab Upadhyay Collection.
Gyanchand Ramachand, Biographical Account of Upadhyay, 1947.

Sanskrit College, Calcutta
General Records and Correspondence, 1829-1855.

Visva Bharati University, Santineketan, West Bengal
Ajit Chakrabarti Correspondence and Papers, 1910-1913.
Amal Home Correspondence and Papers, 1911-1921.
Brajendranath Seal Correspondence and Papers, 1936.
Dwarkanath Tagore Correspondence, 1835-1845.
Gonendra Nath Tagore Correspondence and Papers, 1862-1868.
Dwijendra Nath Tagore Papers.
Rabindranath Tagore Correspondence and Papers, 1901-1941.
Rakhaldas Haldar Diary, 1852-1861; Letters to and from Theodore Parker, 1855-1856.

Ramananda Chatterji Papers.
Sita Debi Correspondence and Papers, 1917.

Sati Kumar Chatterji Collection, Calcutta
J. K. Koar Letters, 1954-1960.

BRAHMO INSTITUTIONAL RECORDS

Annual Reports of the Sadharan Brahmo Samaj, 1903-1948
"Appointment of B. C. Pal as Minister of Bhowanipur Brahmo Samaj,"
    1903.
"Baranagar Workingmen Mission," 1913.
Das, S. "Presidential Address," 1916.
"Death of Annadacharan Sen," 1936.
"Death of Hiralal Haldar," 1942.
"Death of Jyotirindranath Tagore," 1925.
"Death of Lord Sinha," 1928.
"Death of Mrs. A. Bose," 1913.
"Death of P. C. Ray," 1944.
"Death of P. K. Ray," 1932.
"Death of Poetess Kamini Ray," 1934.
"Death of Rabindranath Tagore," 1941.
"Death of Satis Chandra Chakrabarty," 1943.
"Death of Sivanath Shastri," 1919.
"Death of Upendranath Ball," 1947.
"Election of H. C. Sarkar as President," 1929.
"Election of Krishnakumar Mitra as President," 1918.
"Lecture of P. C. Mahanobish on City College," 1918.
"Maitra, Dr. Heramba Chandra: Presidential Address," 1937.
"On Improvement of Finances of the Brahmo Samaj," 1940.
"Presidential Address by Sitanath Tattvabhusan," 1926.
"Report on Brahmo Girls' School," 1904.
"Shastri, Sivanath, Presidential Address," 1907.
"Society for the Improvement of the Backward Classes," 1917.
"Workingman's Mission at Baranagar," 1906.
"Workingman's Mission, Calcutta Discontinued," 1907.

Annual Report of the Indian Reform Association, 1870-1871, in P. K. Sen, *Bi-
    ography of a New Faith*. Calcutta: Thacker Spink & Co., 1933. II, 276-94.

Brahmo Conference: 76th Annual Report, Patna. Calcutta: Brahmo Mission
    Press, 1966.
78th All India Brahmo Report, Bangalore. Calcutta: Brahmo Mission Press,
    1968.
80th Annual Session, Hazaribagh. Calcutta: Brahmo Mission Press, 1970.

*Sophia Dobson Collet Collection of Newspaper Cuttings, Sadharan Brahmo Samaj,
    Calcutta*
"Brahmo Marriages: Their History and Statistics," 1867.

"Brahmo Marriages," January 1876 to July 1877.

"Brahmo Marriages," 1878.

"Brahmo Missionaries," January 15, 1867.

"Brahmo Missionary Movement," Bangalore, November 8, 1876.

"Brahmo Missionary Movement," Bhowanipur, 1877.

"Brahmo Missionary Movement," Bihar, April 8, 1870.

"Brahmo Missionary Movement," Bombay Prarthana Samaj, November 27, 1881.

"Brahmo Missionary Movement," North India, n.c.

"Brahmo Missionary Movement," Punjab, May 28, 1869.

"Brahmo Missionary Movement," Shillong, n.d.

"Brahmo Missionary Movement," Simla, 1879-1882.

"Brahmo Missionary Movement," Sind, 1868-1875.

"Brahmo Missionary Movement," Southern India, January 18, 1871; June 9, 1871; July 22, 1871; September 20, 1871.

"Brahmo Missionary Movement," Western India, August 14, 1872; December 28, 1872; April 11, 1875; February 28, 1875.

Dall, C.H.A. "Brahmo Theological School," February 28, 1873.

———. "The Disease and the Remedy," February 6, 1877.

———. "Keep a Warm Head and a Cool Head," February 7, 1877.

———. "A Real Issue," March 4, 1877.

"General Meeting of the Brahmo Samaj," November 15, 1866.

Mazoomdar, P. C. "Brahmos Arise," January 1, 1872.

"Nabinchandra Ray, Brahmo Missionary," 1872-1876.

"Public Meeting of the Brahmos," May 20, 1877.

"Purba Bangla Sammilani Started by A. M. Bose," September 9, 1877.

Roy, P. K. "Philosophy and Theology in the Brahmo Samaj," January 14, 1877.

Sen, K. C. "Diaries and Reports of Missionary Expeditions," n.d.

———. "Mr. Dall and the Brahmo Samaj," December 27, 1871.

———. "Mr. Dall, Brahmoism and Christianity," January 27, 1871.

———. "Native Ladies' Normal School," April 8, 1873.

———. "On Reverend C.H.A. Dall," April 8, 1877.

———. "Philosophy and Madness in Religion," March 3, 1877.

———. "Prayer and Work: A Reply to Mr. Dall," February 8, 1877.

———. "The Prophet of Nuddea," June 4, 1869.

Tagore, D. N. "Letter to Keshub Chunder Sen," July 8, 1865.

"Theological Class Opens," July 4, 1871.

"Social Movement in India," January 1871.

"Special Meeting to Honour P. K. Ray," November 27, 1876.

Theistic Annual, Brahmo Samaj of India, and New Dispensation, 1872-1885

"General Report of Brahmo Samaj," 1878. Bombay: Indian Printing Press.

"History of the Brahmo Samaj in Dacca," 1881. Dacca: New Press. pp. 40-66.

Mazoomdar, P. C. "The Relation of the Brahmo Samaj to Hinduism and Christianity," 1873. Bombay: Indian Printing Press.

"Theistic Record of the New Dispensation Church in East Bengal," 1885. Dacca: East Bengal Press.
"Punjab Brahmo Activities," 1878. Bombay: Indian Printing Press.
"Retrospect," 1874. Calcutta: Mission Press.
"Statistics and Facts," 1872. Calcutta: Mission Press.

NEWSPAPERS: ENGLISH AND BENGALI

Brahmo Public Opinion, 1878-1881.
Hindu Intelligencer, 1849.
Hindu Patriot, 1856-1858.
Indian Messenger, 1887-1889.
Indian Mirror, 1875-1890.
Indian Social Reformer, 1894-1903.
National Paper, 1867-1869.
Punya, 1897.
Sabuj Patra, 1915-1916.
Sandhya, 1905.
Sanjibani, 1883.
Som Prokash, 1868.
Sulabh Samachar, 1870-1871.
Tattva Bodhini, 1846-1855; 1911-1914.
Tattva Kaumudi, 1880-1922.
Unity and the Minister, 1892.
The World and the New Dispensation, 1881-1904.

PERIODICALS

Bengal Past and Present, 1929.
Calcutta Review, 1845-1928.
Church Missionary Intelligencer, 1851-1890.
Cooch Behar Gazette, 1896.
Modern Review, 1907-1969.
New Age, 1958.
Science and Culture, 1951, 1964.
Sophia, 1894, 1898, 1900.
Twentieth Century, 1901.
Visva Bharati Quarterly, 1920-1960.

ARTICLES

"Acharya Prafulla Chandra Ray and Swaraj and Swadeshi," *Modern Review*, XLVIII (September 1930), 364.
"Advantages and Disadvantages of the Present Age," *Indian Mirror*, XIV (January 3, 1875), 4.
"A Few Facts Relating to the Fracas in the Brahmo Mandir," *Brahmo Public Opinion*, I (April 4, 1878), 18-19.

"Age of Consent," *Indian Messenger*, VIII (September 14, 1890), 100.

"Agitation against Child Marriage," *Modern Review*, XLIV (August 1928), 242-43.

"American Unitarian Association," *Indian Mirror*, XIV (November 7, 1875), 1.

"Annual Prize Exhibition Meeting of Sylhet Union at Albert Hall," *Unity and the Minister*, III (January 31, 1892), 4.

"An Appeal to Our Countrymen and Capitalists on Behalf of Industries and Manufactures," *Indian Mirror*, XXI (June 9, 1882), 2.

"An Appeal to Young Brahmos," *The World and the New Dispensation*, XII (May 18, 1902), 6.

"Appointment of Brajendranath Seal as Principal of Coochbehar Victoria College," *The Cooch Behar Gazette*, VI (March 16, 1896), 54-55.

"Are We Brahmos Exclusive?" *The World and the New Dispensation*, XII (May 18, 1892), 15.

"A Report of the Brahmo Niketan from Its Foundation," *Indian Mirror*, XIV (September 26, 1875), 2.

"Babu Akshoy Coomar Dutt," *Church Missionary Intelligencer*, New Series, III (1878), 38.

"Babu B. K. Goswami's Suggestions towards the Organization of a New Samaj," *Brahmo Public Opinion*, I (May 9, 1878), 70.

Banerji, P. "The Remarriage of Hindu Widows," *Calcutta Review*, CXV (1902), 101-110.

"The Bangabasi Case," *Indian Messenger*, VIII (July 12, 1891), 346-47.

"Banga-Mahila Vidyalaya" (Bengali School for Women), *Brahmo Public Opinion*, I (July 4, 1878), 162-64.

"The Bengalis and the Beharis," *Indian Mirror*, XXII (October 6, 1882), 2.

"Bengalis in the North-Western Provinces," *Indian Mirror*, XIX (March 2, 1880), 3.

"Bethune Female School," *National Paper*, IV (May 13, 1868), 241-43.

"Bijoy Krishna Goswami," *Tattva Kaumudi* (July 30, 1899), p. 76.

Blumhardt, Rev. E. K. "On the Schism in the Brahmo Samaj," *Church Missionary Intelligencer*, V (February 1880), 56-62.

Bose, D. M. "Abala Bose: Her Life and Times," *Modern Review*, LXXV (June 1944), 441-56.

―――. "Acharya Brajendra Nath Seal," *Science and Culture*, XXX (November 1964), 507-18.

―――. "Visva Bharati," *Science and Culture*, XVII (November 1951), 185-92.

Bose, J. C. "Address to Presidency College Students," *Modern Review*, XXXVII (February 1925), 236-38.

―――. "Life and Its Mechanism," *Modern Review*, XXXVI (December 1924), 653-58.

―――. "The Unvoiced Life," *Modern Review*, XXXVIII (December 1925), 713-22.

Bose, Lady. "The Present State of Primary Education," *Modern Review*, XLI (February 1927), 353-55.

Bose, R. "Prospectus to Start a Society for the Promotion of National Feel-
ing among the Educated Natives of Bengal, April 1866," reprinted in
Modern Review, LXXV (June 1944), 444-47.
"Brahmo Balika Sikshalaya" (Brahmo Girls' Academy), *Indian Messenger*,
VII (July 20, 1890), 364.
"The Brahmo Dissenters," *Indian Mirror*, XVII (February 22, 1878), 3.
"Brahmo Girls' School," *Indian Messenger*, VII (June 1, 1890), 308.
"Brahmo Mandir" (Brahmo Temple), *Brahmo Public Opinion*, I (June 6,
1878), 117-18.
"Brahmo Samaj," *Indian Mirror*, XIV (April 25, 1875), 4.
"The Brahmo Samaj," *Calcutta Review*, LX (1875), 365-74.
"Brahmoism: Its History and Literature," *Calcutta Review*, VIII (1871),
102-27.
"Brahmo Samaj Anniversay in Calcutta," *Modern Review*, XLI (February
1927), 264-65.
"Brahmo Samaj, the Depressed Classes and Untouchability," *Modern Re-
view*, LIII (June 1933), 731.
"Calcutta Bethune School," *Indian Mirror*, XVII (February 25, 1878), 2.
"Calcutta in 1860," *Calcutta Review*, XXXIV (January-June 1860), 280-312.
"Celebration of Theodore Parker's 70th Anniversary," *Indian Mirror*, XX
(October 17, 1880), 1.
"The Census and the Decline of Bengal," *Calcutta Review*, CVII (1893),
308-25.
Chakrabarti, S. "Humanism and the Brahmo Samaj," *Modern Review*, CXX
(1967), 414-20.
Chakrabarty, A. "Brahmo o Hindu" (Brahmo and Hindu), *Tattvabodhini
Patrika*, XVIII (July 1914), 97-98.
———. "Brahmo Samajer Samasya" (Problems of the Brahmo Samaj),
Tattvabodhini Patrika, XX (May-June 1914), 40-42.
Chaman, L. "Champion of India's Freedom," *Modern Review*, LX (October
1936), 369-70.
Chatterji, N. "Kulinism amongst the Brahmins of Bengal," *Calcutta Review*,
XCIII (1891), 127-33.
Chatterji, R. "Brahmo Samajer Sahitya" (The Literature of the Brahmo
Samaj), *Tattva Kaumudi* (April 29, 1914), pp. 20-21.
———. "Foundation of a Key Industry in India," *Modern Review*, LXIV (Au-
gust 1938), 2.
———. "Keshubchandra Sen and Nation Building," *Modern Review*, LXIV
(November 1938), 602-606.
———. "Nation Building and Critical Spirit," *Modern Review*, CXVIII (May
1965), 118-23.
———. "Nationality: Past, Present and Future," *Modern Review*, VII (Janu-
ary 1910), 1-3.
———. "The Hero as Scientist," *Modern Review*, LXII (December 1937),
704-705.
Chatterji, S. C. "Acharya B. N. Seal: His Contribution to Philosophical
Studies," *Modern Review*, CXIII (January 1963), 22-29.

Chattopadhyay, A. "Rabindranath o Sadharan Brahmo Samaj" (Rabindranath and the Sadharan Brahmo Samaj), *Tattva Kaumudi* (January 14, 1921), pp. 257-62.

Chaudhuri, N. "The Ideology of the Indian Renaissance," in his *The Intellectual in India*. New Delhi: Associated Publishing House, 1967. Pp. 13-26.

Chaudhuri, S. "Victoria Institutioner Eksho Bachar" (A Hundred Years of Victoria College for Women), *Victoria Institution College Patrika*, May 1969, 57-124.

"Christian Convert in India," *Church Missionary Intelligencer*, II (December 1851), 266-99.

Das, H. "The Reverend Krishna Mohan Banerjea: Brahmin, Christian, Scholar, and Patriot," *Bengal Past and Present*, XXXVII (January-June 1929), 133-44.

Das, R. "Homage to Reverend Dr. Sunderland," *Modern Review*, LX (October 1936), 367-68.

Das, R. K. "Sir J. Bose in Europe," *Modern Review*, XL (October 1926), 409-10.

"Death Anniversary of Rajnarian Bose," *Modern Review*, LXVIII (October 1940), 380.

"Death of Sivachandra Dev," *Indian Messenger*, VII (November 16, 1890), 83-84.

"Distress of the Middle Class Natives," *Indian Mirror*, XIX (May 21, 1879), 2.

Dutt, A. K. "Bangodesher Bartaman Arbastha" (Present Condition of Bengal), *Tattvabodhini Patrika*, XIII (July 1855), 179-87.

———. "Kalikatar Bartaman Durbastha" (The Present Degeneration of Calcutta), *Tattvabodhini Patrika*, IV (July 14, 1846), 96-104.

———. "Polligramastha Prajadiger Durabastha" (Distressing Conditions of the Tenants), *Tattvabodhini Patrika*, VIII (November 1850), 125-32.

"Duty of Self-help and the Privilege of Self-government," *Indian Mirror*, XII (June 23, 1882), 3.

"Education in Japan and India," *Modern Review*, VII (September 1907), 249-64.

"Encouragement of Indian Industry," *The World and the New Dispensation*, XII (May 18, 1902), 3-5.

"English Education in India from a Native Point of View," *Calcutta Review*, LXXVIII (1884), 327-44.

"Frequent Cases of Suicide among Youngmen and Women," *Indian Messenger*, VII (June 8, 1890), 313.

"Funeral of Francis Power Cobbe," *The World and the New Dispensation*, XIV (June 19, 1904), 46.

Gangopadhyay, J. "Brahmo Samajer Samajik Adarsha" (Social Ideals of the Brahmo Samaj), *Tattvakaumudi* (April 29, 1922), pp. 17-18.

Ghose, B. "Brahmoism and the Bengal Renaissance," *New Age* (September 1958), pp. 22-34.

Ghose, B. N. "Lal Lochan Ghose," *Bharat Barsha*, I (September 1932), 613-14.

"Grievances of the Native Engineers of Bengal," *Indian Mirror*, xxiv (January 30, 1884), 2.

Guha, A. C. "The Agonies of Bengal," *Modern Review*, lv (March 1934), 346-98.

Haldar, H. "Realistic Idealism," in *Contemporary Indian Philosophy*. Edited by S. Radhakrishnan. London: George Allen & Unwin, 1936. Pp. 215-32.

————. "Western Civilization," *Modern Review*, vii (January 1910), 96-97.

"Heramba Chandra Maitra," *Modern Review*, lxiii (February 1938), 236-38.

"Higher Education for Women: Our View," *Indian Messenger*, iv (October 21, 1886), 58-59.

"Higher Education in India," *Indian Mirror*, xvii (February 13, 1878), 2.

"Hindu Mela," *Indian Mirror*, xvii (February 13, 1878), 3.

"The Ilbert Act: A Legislative Patch-Work," *Indian Mirror*, xxiv (January 31, 1884), 2.

"The Indian Association on Mass Education," *Brahmo Public Opinion*, ii (August 7, 1879), 232.

"Indian Youths and Technical Education," *Indian Mirror*, xxiv (March 1, 1884), 2.

"Internal Workings of the Hindu Widows' Home in Bengal," *Indian Social Reformer*, v (November 17, 1894), 90-91.

Jardine, Rev. R. "Paper on the Brahmo Samaj at the Allahabad Missionary Conference," *Christian Missionary Intelligencer*, x (January 1874), 18-23.

"Keshub Chunder Sen's Admiration of Chaitanya," *Church Missionary Intelligencer*, First New Series, viii (1878), 341-50.

Khastagir, A. "Keshub Chandrer Samanvaya Marga o Koekti Samasya" (Some Problems and Keshub's Path to Synthesis), *Tattvakaumudi* (April 14, 29; May 15, 30; June 15, 30; July 16, 30, 1970).

"The Koch Behar Marriage," *Brahmo Public Opinion*, i (March 21, 1878), 8.

"Lady's College Established at Oxford," *Brahmo Public Opinion*, ii (May 8, 1879), 73.

"Law Durga Charan: Native Celebrities of Bengal," *Indian Mirror*, xix (February 12, 1879), 2-3.

"Letter by Devendranath Tagore to Protap Chandra Mazoomdar quoted in 62nd Report of Calcutta Corresponding Committee of the Church Missionary Society," *Christian Missionary Intelligencer*, First New Series, xi (1881), xiii-xiv.

Long, Rev. James, "The Ryots of Bengal," *Church Missionary Intelligencer*, ix (June 1858), 132-37.

Macdonald, K. S. "Tantra Literature," *Calcutta Review*, cxiii (1901), 100-11.

Mahalanobis, P. "First Annual Report of Visva-Bharati," *Visva Bharati Quarterly*, i (April 1923), 409-24.

————. "The Growth of the Visva-Bharati, 1901-1921," *Visva Bharati Quarterly*, vi (April 1928), 79-94.

Maitra, H. "How To Be Profitably Ideal," *Modern Review*, XI (August 1914), 137-40.

Mazoomdar, P. C. "The Emancipation of Women in Bengal," *Calcutta Review*, CXVIII (1904), 125-31.

"Mission Work," *Indian Mirror*, XIV (January 31, 1875), 4.

Mitra, K. K. "Amadiger Sankat" (Our Crisis), *Sanjibani*, I (April 14, 1883), 2.

Mitter, Sir B. "Lord Sinha," *Calcutta Review*, XLIII (April 1928), 454-57.

"Mohini Mohun Bose," *Tattvakaumudi* (September 16, 1901), p. 127.

Mukherjee, S. "Social Reform in Bengal," *Calcutta Review*, CXXX (1910), 145-63.

"Muller, Max, O Protap Mazumdar," *Tattvabodhini Patrika*, DCLXXV (November 1899), 380.

Nag, N. C. "Sir Jagadish Chandra Bose," *Modern Review*, LXII (December 1937), 698-703.

"The Nagar Sankirtan," *Indian Mirror*, XX (February 1, 1880), 3.

Naidu, P. O. "Hindu Reform and Reformers," *Calcutta Review*, CXIV (1902), 282-88.

Nandi, K. K. "Ranananda Chatterji: A Bio-graphical Assessment," *Modern Review*, CXVIII (Centenary Number, May 1965), 36-75.

"National Celebrities in Bengal," *Indian Mirror*, XVII (August 3, 1878), 2-3.

"Natives in the Indian Medical Service," *Indian Mirror*, XXIV (July 13, 1884), 2.

"The New Nationalism and the True Nationalism," *Indian Social Reformer*, XVII (September 15, 1906), 27-28.

"On Average Bengali Middle Class Boy with Education," *Indian Mirror*, XIX (July 15, 1880), 2.

"On Legal Proprietorship of the Bharat-varsiya Brahmo Mandir," *Brahmo Public Opinion*, I (June 6, 1878), 117-18; (June 13, 1878), 130-31.

"On the Death of Reverend C.H.A. Dall," *Indian Messenger*, IV (September 19, 1886), 17.

"On the Defection of Pandit Bijoy Krishna Goswami," *Indian Messenger*, IV (September 26, 1886), 26.

"The Oriental Seminary," *Indian Mirror*, XVII (February 12, 1878), 3.

"Our Countrymen and the Value of Self-help," *Indian Mirror*, XXI (September 22, 1881), 2.

Patvardhan, V. B. "Hindu Widows' Home—Poona," *Modern Review*, I (January 1907), 35-42.

"People Proposed for Brahmo Samaj Membership," *Brahmo Public Opinion*, IV (September 1, 1881), 415.

"The Pleadership Examination in Bengal," *Indian Mirror*, XXIV (February 27, 1884), 2.

"Poona Reactionaries: A Warning," *Indian Social Reformer*, V (July 27, 1895), 371-72.

"Practical Closing of the Covenanted Civil Service to the Natives," *Indian Mirror*, XXIV (May 21, 1884), 2.

"The Present Situation in the Brahmo Samaj," *Calcutta Review*, CIX (October 1895), 391-401.

"Present Struggle for Existence . . . Our Youngmen Should Learn Arts and Manufactures," *Indian Mirror*, XIX (May 14, 1879), 2.

Ray, P. C. "The Problem of Scientific Education in India," *Calcutta Review*, CVIII (1899), 347-55.

————. "The Tantras, the Rosicrucians and the Seekers after Truth," *Modern Review*, I (March 1907), 237-39.

Ray, P. K. "Thought Leading in Brahmo Samaj," *Indian Messenger*, IV (November 14, 1886), 83-84.

Ray, S. "Brahmo o Hindu Prabandher Pratibad" (Rejoinder to the Essay on Brahmo and Hindu), *Tattvabodhini Patrika*, XVIII (July-August 1914), 97-98.

"The Religion of the Brahmo Samaj," *Calcutta Review*, LXIV (1877), 332-50.

"Reverend J. Long's Diary," January 17, 1867, *Church Missionary Intelligencer*, First New Series, III (1867), 26.

"Reverend Mr. Dall," *Hindu Patriot*, IV (October 23, 1856), 338.

"Revival of Indian Arts and Manufactures," *Indian Mirror*, XXII (September 2, 1882), 3.

Sarkar, B. "Acharyya Brajendranath Seal: A Life-Sketch," *Acharyya Brajendranath Seal Birth Centenary Commemoration Volume*. Cooch Behar, West Bengal: Victoria College, 1965. Pp. 168-85.

Sarkar, J. "Raj Narian Bose, Grandfather of Nationalism in India," *Modern Review*, V (April 1909), 311-19.

Seal, B. "Shiksha Bistar" (Spread of Education), *Sabuj Patra*, II (April 1915), 607-14.

Sen, J. "The Philosophic Background of Eastern and Western Cultures," *Visva Bharati Quarterly*, V (1927), 350-56.

Sen, K. C. "Am I an Inspired Prophet?" *Keshub Chunder Sen's Lectures in India*. Vol. I. London: Cassel, 1901. Pp. 327-58.

————. "Behalai Mari Bhoi" (Fear of Epidemic in Behala), *Sulabh Samachar*, I (July 29, 1871), 145.

————. "The Cross," *The New Dispensation*, I (April 14, 1881), 39-40.

————. "Dance of the New Dispensation," *The New Dispensation*, II (August 20, 1882), 90-92.

————. "Doridrer Khed" (Grievances of the Poor), *Sulabh Samachar*, I (December 28, 1870), 25.

————. "England's Duties to India," in *Keshub Chunder Sen's English Visits*. Edited by S. D. Collet. London: Straham, 1871. Pp. 193-226.

————. "The Flag Ceremony," *The New Dispensation*, I (March 23, 1881), 17-20.

————. "God Our Mother," *The New Dispensation*, I (March 24, 1881), 3-4.

————. "Great Men," in *Keshub Chunder Sen: Lectures and Tracts*. Edited by S. D. Collet. London: Straham, 1870. Pp. 49-93.

————. "Incarnations," *The New Dispensation*, I (July 22, 1881), 174.

————. "Jesus Christ: Europe and Asia," *Keshub Chunder Sen: Lectures and Tracts*. Calcutta: Indian Mirror Press, 1879. Pp. 3-46.

———. "Modya Pan," Intemperance, *Sulabh Samachar* (December 21, 1870), p. 21.

———. "Ondha Byabashayi" (Blind Businessman), *Sulabh Samachar*, 1 (November 15, 1870), 1.

———. "The Pagol I-V," *The New Dispensation*, 1 (April 14, June 2, July 29, August 12, 1881), 77-78, 106-107, 149-51, 186-87, 201-203.

———. "Projadiger Durobastha" (Deplorable Condition of the Tenants), *Sulabh Samachar*, 1 (November 23, 1870), 5.

———. "Samanyo Lokdiger Vidyalaya" (School for the Poor), *Sulabh Samachar*, 1 (November 30, 1870), 9.

———. "Sampadoker Nibedan" (Editorial), *Sulabh Samachar*, 1 (November 15, 1870), 1.

———. "Somoyer Bhalo Vyabahar" (Proper Use of Time), *Sulabh Samachar*, 1 (February 18, 1871), 55.

———. "Sarbbo Sadharaner Janya Jelay Jelay Artha Sanchayer Vyabastha" (Arrangements for Saving Money in Banks for the General Public), *Sulabh Samachar*, 1 (April 8, 1870), 82.

———. "Ucchay Ashay" (High Hopes), *Sulabh Samachar*, 1 (March 18, 1871), 70.

Sen, S. K. "National Form of Our Baptism," *Indian Mirror* XXI (June 26, 1881), 6.

———. "New Sacramental Ceremony," *Indian Mirror*, XII (March 27, 1881), 3.

———. "Socrates," *Indian Mirror*, XX (March 7, 1880), 3.

Shastri, S. "Bipin Chandra Pal as Missionary to the Punjab," *Indian Messenger*, V (February 19, 1888), 177.

———. "The Duties of the Educated Classes to the Masses," *Modern Review*, VII (January 1910), 70-75.

———. "Five Hundred Widows Married Since Vidyasagar's Movement," *Indian Messenger* (December 22, 1888), p. 129.

———. "The Future of Our Country," *Indian Messenger*, IV (January 2, 1887), 140.

———. "The New Dispensation Proclaimed as the State Religion of Cooch Behar," *Indian Messenger*, V (May 27, 1888). 297.

———. "Some Causes of the Weakness of Our Organization," *Indian Messenger*, VI (September 1, 1889), 4.

Sircar, N. "British Ban on Indian Medical Degrees," *Modern Review*, XLVII (April 1930), 503-504.

"Slurs against the Brahmos," *Indian Messenger*, VIII (May 3, 1891), 266-67.

"Social Science in India," *Calcutta Review*, XLIV (1866), 424-42.

"Some Bengali Brahmos of Shillong," *Modern Review*, XVII (March 1915), 300-12.

"The Study of Science," *Unity and the Minister*, III (April 3, 1892), 9.

Sunderlund, J. T. "Principal Heramba Chandra Maitra in America," *Modern Review*, LX (February 1911), 151-56.

———. "Theodore Parker: The Great American Reformer," *Modern Review*, LXII (July 1937), 2-12.

Sunderlund, J. T. "William Ellery Chaning," *Modern Review*, LIII (April 1933), 377-84.

Tagore, D. (Dwijendranath). "Babu Keshub Chandra Sen in Lahore," *National Paper*, III (March 27, 1867), 150.

──────. "European Model," *National Paper*, III (September 25, 1867), pp. 462-63.

──────. "Hinduism Is Not Hostile to Brahmoism," *National Paper*, III (September 18, 1867), pp. 448-49.

──────. "Nationality Indeed," *National Paper*, v (May 5, 1869), 207-209.

──────. "Nationality and Universality," *National Paper*, v (February 24, 1869), 86-87.

──────. "Primary Education," *National Paper*, v (January 6, 1869), pp. 4-5.

──────. "Spurious Brahmoism," *National Paper*, III (January 2, 1867), 5-7.

Tagore, K. N. "Jobane Vibaha Shastra Siddha ki Na?" (Is Marriage Sanctioned in Youth?), *Punya*, I (1897), 174-83.

──────. "Jon Stuart Mill o Stri Swadhinata" (John Stuart Mill and Women's Emancipation), *Punya*, II (1898), 97-106.

──────. "Ramoner Brahmocharay ó Potisheba" (Chastity and Service to Women), *Punya*, I (1897), 65-74.

──────. "Shastre Ramoner Uccha Shikshar Vidhi" (Provisions of Higher Education for Women in the Scriptures), *Punya*, I (1897), 339-54.

──────. "Tagorer Poribare Stri Shiksha" (Education of Women in the Tagore Family), *Punya*, III (1898), 458-71.

Tagore, R. "Adi Brahmo Samajer Vedi" (Altar of the Adi Brahmo Samaj), *Tattvabodhini Patrika*, XVIII (February-March 1912), 263-64.

──────. "Antorer Naba Varsha" (New Year of the Soul), *Tattvabodhini Patrika*, XVII (May 1911), 31-34.

──────. "Brahmo Samajer Sarthakata" (Significance of the Brahmo Samaj), *Tattvabodhini Patrika*, XVII (May 1911), 6-10.

──────. "Dharma Siksha" (Religious Education), *Tattvabodhini Patrika*, XVIII (January 1912), 227-38.

──────. "The Future of India," *Modern Review*, IX (March 1911), 238-44.

──────. "The Impact of Europe on India," *Modern Review*, IX (July 1911), 498-502.

──────. "Message to the Parliament of Religions," *Visva Bharati Quarterly*, VII (April 1929), 1-4.

──────. "The Problem of India," *Modern Review*, IX (February 1911), 184-87.

──────. "Stri Shiksha," (Female Education), *Sabuj Patra*, III (April 1915), 377-84.

"Tagore: Pioneer in Asian Relations," *Modern Review*, CXIX (February 1966), 109-12.

Tattvabhusan, S. "Hindu and Christian Ideals of Worship," *Modern Review*, XVI (November 1914), 512-16.

──────. "Social Reform: A Forward Look," *Indian Social Reformer*, XIII (January 18, 1903), 188-89.

"Temperance in Bengal," *Hindu Patriot*, IV (May 8, 1856), 115.

"The Term Babu," *Indian Mirror*, XXIV (May 22, 1884), 2.

"Town Hall Meeting of the Brahmos," *Brahmo Public Opinion*, I (May 23, 1878), 101.

Upadhyay, B. "Debendranath Tagore," *Sandhya*, I (January 22, 1905), 2.

———. "An Exposition of Catholic Belief as Compared with the Vedanta," *Sophia*, V (January 1898), 10-14.

———. "Christianity in India," *Twentieth Century*, I (March 30, 1901), 65-68.

———. "Europeanism versus Christianity," *Twentieth Century*, I (July 31, 1901), 164-66.

———. "The Hindu Revival," *Sophia*, I (June 1894), 1-2.

———. "Imperialism and Christendom," *Sophia*, I, New Series (October 20, 1900), 4.

———. "Integrity of Hindu Society," *Sophia*, I, New Series (November 10, 1900), 4.

———. "Modern Education and Hindu Thought," *Sophia,* I, New Series (June 30, 1900), 4-5.

———. "National Memorial," *Twentieth Century*, I (February 28, 1901), 34.

———. "Objects," *Sophia*, I (January 1894), 1-2.

———. "Telescopic Nature of Brahmo Endeavours," *Sophia*, I, New Series (November 17, 1900), 7-9.

"Vernacular Literature," *Calcutta Review*, L (1870), 231-44.

"Vice of Intemperance, Spreading among Bengalees," *Church Missionary Intelligencer*, III, Second New Series (January 1878), 37.

"Why Are the Moderates Moderate?" *Indian Social Reformer*, XVII (October 28, 1906), 99-100.

TRACTS AND BOOKS

Adam, W. *The Principles and Objects of the Calcutta Unitarian Committee.* Calcutta: Unitarian Press, 1827.

———. *Reports on the State of Education in Bengal, 1835 and 1838.* Edited by A. Basu. Calcutta: University of Calcutta, 1941.

Adi Brahmo Samjer Sabalata o Durbolata (Strength and Weakness of the Adi Brahmo Samaj). Calcutta: Adi Brahmo Samaji Press, 1917.

Ali, M. M. *The Bengali Reaction to Christian Missionary Activities.* Chittagong: Mehrub Publications, 1965.

Amragari Brahmo Samajer Itibritta (History of the Amragari Brahmo Samaj). Calcutta: Bengal Press, 1900.

Andrews, C. F. *The Renaissance in India: Its Missionary Aspect.* London: Church Missionary Society, 1912.

The Apostles and the Missionaries of the Naba-bidhan. Compiled by N. Niyogy. Calcutta: The Brotherhood, 1923.

Aurobindo. *The Renaissance in India.* Pondicherry: Ashram, 1966.

Baago, K. *Pioneers of Indigenous Christianity*. Bangalore: Christian Institute for the Study of Religion and Society, 1969.

Bagal, J. C. *Hindu Melar Itibritta* (History of Hindu Mela). Calcutta: Maitri, 1968.

———. *Rajnarian Basu*. 3rd ed. Sahitya Sadhak Charitmala Series. Calcutta: Bangiya Sahitya Parishat, 1955.

Bandyopadhyay, A. K. *Unabingsha Satabdir Prathamardha o Bangla Sahitya* (The First Half of the Nineteenth Century and Bengali Literature). Calcutta: Book Land Private, 1965.

Bandyopadhyay, B. N. *Akkhoy Kumar Dutt*. 5th ed. Sahitya Sadhak Charitmala Series, 1959.

———. *Dwarkanath Gangopadhyay*. Sahitya Sadhak Charitmala Series, 1964.

———. *Dwarka Nath Vidyabhusan*. 5th ed. Sahitya Sadhak Charitmala Series, 1956.

———. *Iswar Chandra Vidyasagar*. 5th ed. Sahitya Sadhak Charitmala Series, 1955.

———. *Jyotirindranath Tagore*. 2nd ed. Sahitya Sadhak Charitmala Series, 1956.

———. *Madhusudan Dutt*. 4th ed. Sahitya Sadhak Charitmala Series, 1955.

Bandyopadhyay, I. *Indranath Granthabali* (Indranath's Collected Works). Calcutta: Bangabashi-Elektro-Mashin-Jantra, 1925.

———. *Kalpa Taru* (Wishing Tree). Calcutta: Canning Library, 1875.

Banerjea, K. M. *The Arian Witness*. Calcutta: Thacker, Spink & Co., 1875.

———. *Dialogue on the Hindu Philosophy Comprising Nyaya, Sankhya, the Vedanta*. Calcutta: Thacker, Spink & Co., 1861.

———. *Lectures to Educated Native Young Men on Vedantism*. Calcutta: Star Press, n.d.

———. *On the Death of Baboo Mohesh Chunder Ghose*. Calcutta: Bishop's College Press, 1837.

———. *The Peculiar Responsibility of Educated Natives*. Calcutta: Bishop's College Press, 1865.

———., ed. *Purana Samgraha*. Collection of Medieval Texts. Calcutta: Encyclopedia Press, 1851.

———. *The Relation between Christianity and Hinduism*. Calcutta: Oxford Mission Press, 1882.

———. *Review of the Manduck Oopanishad by Ram Mohan Roy*. Calcutta: Enquirer Press, 1833.

———. *Rig Veda Samhita*. Calcutta: Thacker, Spink & Co., 1875.

———. *A Sermon Preached at St. John's Cathedral, Calcutta*. Calcutta: Ostell & Lepage, 1847.

———. *Two Essays as Supplements to the Arian Witness*. Calcutta: Thacker, Spink & Co., 1880.

———. *Upadesh Katha* (Sermons). Calcutta: Bishop's College Press, 1840.

Banerjee, A. C. *Brahmo Samaj and Freedom Movement*. Calcutta: Nababidhan Press, 1957.

Banerjee, H. *Iswar Chandra Vidyasagar*. New Delhi: Sahitya Akademi, 1968.

———. *The House of the Tagores*. Calcutta: Rabindra Bharati, 1963.

Banerjee, S. N. *A Nation in the Making*. London: Oxford University Press, 1925.

Banerji, G. C. *Keshub as Seen by His Opponents*. Allahabad: Indian Press, 1930.

———. *Keshub Chandra and Ramakrishna*. 2nd ed. Calcutta: Naba-bidhan Publication Committee, 1942.

Basu, I. C. *Brahmo Samajer Sadhya o Sadhana* (Resources and Accomplishments of the Brahmo Samaj). Calcutta: Adi Brahmo Samaj Jantra, 1914.

Basu, S. *Bhakta Harisundar Basu Mahashayer Charita Katha* (Life Story of Devotee Harisundar Bose). Calcutta: Maitreyi Bose, 1954.

Beveridge, Lord W. H. *India Called Them*. London: George Allen & Unwin, 1947.

Biswas, D. K. "Maharshi Debendranath Tagore and the Tattvabodhini Sabha," *Studies on the Bengal Renaissance*. Edited by A. C. Gupta. Jadavpur: National Council of Education, 1958.

Bonerji, Sir A. R. *An Indian Pathfinder: Memoirs of Sevabrata Sasipada Banerji*. Oxford: Kemp Hall Press, n.d.

Bose, D. M. *Life Sketch of Ajit Mohan Bose*. Calcutta: Prabashi Press, 1945.

Bose, J. C. *Sir J. C. Bose: Life and Speeches*. Madras: Ganesh, n.d.

Bose, N. S. *The Indian Awakening and Bengal*. 3rd ed. Calcutta: Firma K. L. Mukhopadhyay, 1969.

———. *Ramananda Chatterjee*. New Delhi: Ministry of Information and Broadcasting, 1974.

Bose, P. N. *A Hundred Years of Bengali Press*. Calcutta: Central Press, 1920.

———. *History of Hindu Civilization during British Rule*. 2 vols. London: Kegan Paul, Trench Trubner, 1894.

Bose, R. *The Adi Brahmo Samaj: Its Views and Principles*. Calcutta: Adi Brahmo Samaj Press, 1870.

———. *Atma Charita* (Autobiography). Calcutta: Kuntaline Press, 1909.

———. *Brahmo Samaj as a Church*. Calcutta: Adi Brahmo Samaj, n.d.

———. *A Defense of Brahmoism and the Brahmo Samaj*. 2nd ed. Calcutta: Brahmo Samaj Press, 1870.

———. *The Hindu Theist's Brotherly Gift to English Theists*. Calcutta: Adi Brahmo Samaj Press, 1881.

———. *Hints Shewing the Feasibility of Constructing a Science of Religion*. Harinabi (Bengal): East India Press, 1878.

———. *Remarks on Reverend K. M. Banerjea's Lecture on Vedantism*. Calcutta, 1851.

———. *Theistic Toleration and Diffusion of Theism*. Calcutta: G. P. Roy & Co.; 1872.

——— and D. Tagore. *Vedantic Doctrines Vindicated*. Calcutta: Tattva Bodhini Press, 1845.

Bose, S. C. *Life of Protap Chunder Mazoomdar*. 2 vols. 2nd ed. Calcutta: Naba-bidhan Trust, 1940.

Brahmananda Keshub Chunder Sen: Testimonies in Memorium. Compiled by G. C. Banerji. Allahabad: Naba-bidhan, 1934.

Brahmananda Sri Keshub Chandrer Patrabali (Correspondence of Keshub

Sen). Compiled by M. Mahalanobis. Calcutta: Bharatvarshiya Brahmo Mandir, 1941.

The Brahmo Samaj and Other Modern Eclectic Systems of Religion in India. Madras: Christian Literature Society, 1893.

Brahmo Samaj: The Depressed Classes and Untouchability. Compiled by S. C. Chakrabarti and S. N. Ray. Calcutta: Sadharan Brahmo Samaj, 1933.

Brahmo Samaj o Akkhoy Kumar Dutta (Brahmo Samaj and Akkhoy Kumar Dutta). Calcutta: Adi Brahmo Samaj Jantra, 1886.

Brahmo Sangit o Sankirtan (Brahmo Songs and Vaishnava Processional Music). Compiled by S. K. Chattopadhyay. Calcutta: Naba-bidhan Publication Committee, 1958.

Broomfield, J. H. *Elite Conflict in a Plural Society: Twentieth Century Bengal*. Bombay: Oxford University Press, 1968.

Carpenter, J. E. *The Life and Work of Mary Carpenter*. London: Macmillan, 1879.

Carpenter, L. *An Examination of the Charges Made against Unitarians and Unitarianism*. Bristol: T. J. Manchee, 1820.

————. *Funeral Sermon on the Death of Rajah Rammohan Roy*. Calcutta: Military Orphan Press, 1857.

————. *On the Importance and Dissemination of the Doctrine of the Proper Unity of God*. London: C. Stover, 1810.

————. *A Review of the Labours, Opinions and Character of Rajah Rammohan Roy*. Bristol: Brome & Reid, 1833.

Carpenter, M. *Addresses to the Hindus*. Calcutta: Newman, 1867.

————. *The Last Days in England of Raja Rammohan Ray*. London: Trubner, 1866.

————. *Letters on Female Education in India and Prison Discipline*. Bristol: I. Arrowsmith, 1877.

————. *On Ragged Schools*. Birmingham: Benjamin Hall, 1861.

————. *Six Months in India*. 2 vols. London: Longmans Green, n.d.

Carpenter, R. L. *Memoir of the Reverend Lant Carpenter*. London: E. T. Whitfield, 1875.

Chakrabarti, S. C. *Brahmo Samajer Ar Proyojan Acche ki Na* (Is the Brahmo Samaj Necessary?). Calcutta: Brahmo Mission Press, 1922.

Chakrabarty, D. *Sasipada Banerjee: A Study in the Nature of the First Contact of the Bengali Bhadralok with the Working Classes of Bengal*. Calcutta: Centre for Studies in Social Sciences, 1975.

Chandra, B. *The Rise and Growth of Economic Nationalism in India*. New Dehli: Peoples' Publishing House, 1966.

————. *Travels of a Hindu*. London: Trubner, 1869.

Chandra, B. L. *The Unreasonableness of Brahmoism*. Calcutta: Baptist Mission Press, 1878.

Chandravarkar, G. L. *The Brahmo Samaj*. Bombay: N. H. Talvar, n.d.

Channing, W. E. *A Discourse on the Life and Character of the Reverend Joseph Tuckerman*. Boston: William Crosby & Co., 1841.

Dr. Channing's Note Book. Compiled by G. E. Channing. New York: Houghton, Mifflin, 1887.

———. *Extracts from His Correspondence*. Boston: William Crosby & H. R. Nichols, 1848.

———. *The Importance and Means of a National Literature*. London: Edmund Rainford, 1830.

———. *Lecture on War*. Boston: Dutton & Wentworth, 1837.

———. *On the Elevation of the Labouring Portion of the Community*. Boston: William D. Ticknor, 1840.

———. *Religion a Social Principle*. Boston: Russell & Gardner, 1820.

———. *Remarks on Creeds, Intolerance, etc. for American Unitarian Association*. Boston: James Munroe & Co., 1837.

Channing, W. H. *Lessons from the Life of Theodore Parker*. London: Edward T. Whitfield, 1860.

Chattopadhyay, N. N. *Mahatma Theodore Parker*. Calcutta: Brahmo Mission Press, 1885.

Chattopadhyay, S. K. *Brahmo Gitapanishader Parichay o Keshub Chandrer Sadhanay Hindu Dharma* (Introduction to the Brahmo Gita and Upanishads and Keshub Chandra's Interpretation of Hindu Religion). Calcutta: Naba-bidhan Publication Committee, 1967.

———. *Niti Vidyalaya Katha* (Anecdotes about the Youth Academy). Calcutta: Naba-bidhan Publishing House, 1964.

———. *Samanvay Marga* (Paths to Synthesis). Calcutta: M. C. Sarkar & Sons, 1961.

———. *Upadhyay Gourgovinda Roy*. Calcutta: Bharatabarshiya Brahmo Samaj, 1951.

Chaudhuri, N. *Autobiography of an Unknown Indian*. Bombay: Jaico Publishing House, 1969.

———. *Mahim Chandra Chaudhurir Jiban Charita*. Calcutta: n.p., n.d.

Collet, S. D. *Outlines and Episodes of Brahmic History*, London: W. Speaght, 1884.

Collier, R. *The General Next to God: Booth and the Salvation Army*. London: Fontana Paper Back, 1968.

Correspondence of William Ellery Channing & Lucy Aiken (1826-1842). Edited by A. L. Breton. London: Williams & Norgate, 1874.

Cultural Heritage of India. 4 vols. 2nd ed. rev. Edited by H. Bhattacharyya. Calcutta: Ramakrishna Mission Institute of Culture, 1953-1962.

Dall, C.H.A. *Brahmo Samaj of India Led by Baboo Keshub Chunder Sen with Facts Historical and Personal*. Calcutta: Central Press, 1874.

———. *Lecture on Raja Rammohan Roy*. Calcutta: Central Press, 1871.

———. *The Theistic Creed*. Calcutta: Central Press, 1872.

Das, C. R. *Way to Swaraj*. Madras: Tamilnadu Swarajya Party, 1923.

Das, J. *Bangalar Jatiya Itihasher Mul Bhumika Va Rammohan o Brahmo Andolan* (The Roots of Bengal National History, Rammohun and the Brahmo Movement). Calcutta: Sadharan Brahmo Samaj, 1946.

Das, S. *Desha-bandhu Chittaranjan Das* (C. R. Das: Friend of the Nation). Calcutta: Baraga Agency, 1936.

Datta, D. *Keshub and the Sadharan Brahmo Samaj*. Calcutta: Naba-bidhan Press, 1930.

Datta, N. K. *A Lecture on the True Idea of Salvation*. Calcutta: I. C. Brothers, 1879.

Datta, S. *The World of Twilight*. Calcutta: Oxford University Press, 1970.

Debendranather Patrabali (Correspondence of Debendranath). Edited by P. Shastri. Calcutta: Hitabadi Press, n.d.

Debi, A. *Bhakta Kabi Madhusudan Rao o Utkale Nabayug* (Devotee Madhusudan Rao and the Utkale Renaissance). Calcutta: Amarnath Bhattacharya, 1963.

Debi, S. *Punya Smriti* (Pious Memories). 2nd ed. Calcutta: Moitree, 1964.

———. *Ramananda Chattopadhyay o Ardha Satabdir Bangla* (Ramananda Chatterji and Bengal in the First Half of the Century). Calcutta: Prabashi Press, n.d.

———. *Sivanath*. Calcutta: Sadharan Brahmo Samaj, 1966.

———. *Swargiya Kumar Gajendra Narayan* (The Late Kumar Gajendra Narayan). Calcutta: Lakshmibilas Press, 1928.

Dev, H. *A Short Life-Sketch of Bipin Chandra Pal*. Calcutta: New India Publishing, 1957.

Devdas, N. *Swami Vivekananda*. Bangalore: Institute for the Study of Religion and Society, 1968.

Devi, Maharani S. *Autobiography of an Indian Princess*. London: John Murray, 1921.

Dey, Reverend L. B. *Recollections of Alexander Duff and the Mission College*. London: T. Nelson & Sons, 1879.

Dey, R. *Charita Madhuri* (Beauty of Character). Calcutta: Kuntalin Press, 1919.

Discourses Delivered at the Meetings of the Society for the Acquisition of General Knowledge. Vol. 1. Calcutta: Sangbad Purno Chundrodoya Press, 1840.

Dutt, A. K. *Dharma Niti* (Ethical Philosophy), 8th reprint. Calcutta: New Sanskrit Press, 1930.

———. *Who is a Brahmo?* Simla: Himalaya Brahmo Samaj, 1966.

Dutt, R. C. *Economic History of India in the Victorian Age*. London: Routledge & Kegan Paul, 1903.

Dutt, S. N. *The Life of Benoyendra Nath Sen*. Calcutta: Naba-bidhan Trust, 1928.

Dyer, Reverend S. *Lal Behari Dey*. Calcutta: n.p., 1900.

Edgell, D. P. *William Ellery Channing, an Intellectual Portrait*. Boston: Beacon Press, n.d.

Einstein, A. *Out of My Later Years*. New York: Philosophical Library, 1950.

Encyclopedia Bengalensis in English and Bengali. Edited by K. M. Banerjea. 8 vols. Calcutta: P. S. D'Rozario, 1848.

Erikson, E. *Childhood and Society*. New York: W. W. Norton Paperback, 1963.

———. *Dimensions of a New Identity*. Indian Reprint. New Delhi: Light and Life Publishers, 1975.

———. *Identity: Youth and Crisis*. New York: W. W. Norton, 1968.

———. *Insight and Responsibility*. New York: W. W. Norton, 1964.

———. *Young Man Luther*. New York: W. W. Norton, 1958.

Farquhar, J. N. *The Crown of Hinduism*. London: Oxford University Press, 1913.

———. *Modern Religious Movements in India*. New York: Macmillan, 1917.

———. *The Future of Christianity in India*. Madras: Christian Literature Society, 1904.

Freedom Movement in Bengal. Compiled and edited by N. Sinha. Calcutta: Government of West Bengal, 1968.

Furrel, J. W. *Tagore Family—A Memoir*. Calcutta: Thacker, Spink & Co., 1892.

Gangopadhyay, D. *Sisur Sadachar* (Good Behavior of Children). Calcutta: Sadharan Brahmo Samaj, 1964.

Gangopadhyay, P. C. *Bangalar Nari Jagaran* (The Awakening of Bengal Women). Calcutta: Sadharan Brahmo Samaj, 1946.

Geddes, P. *The Life and Work of Sir Jagadish Chandra Bose*. Calcutta: Longmans, Green, 1920.

Ghose, B. *Amar Jiban Katha* (Autobiography). Calcutta: Narendra Nath Mukherji, 1923.

———. *Bangalar Samajik Itihasher Dhara* (The Course of Bengali Social History). Calcutta: the author, 1969.

———. *Bidrohi Derozio (The Rebel Derozio)*. Calcutta: Book Sahitya, 1961.

Ghose, K. S. *K. C. Sen and the New Reformation*. Allahabad: G. C. Banerji, 1938.

———. *The Rise of Scholasticism in the Brahmo Samaj*. Calcutta: Naba-bidhan Publication Committee, 1940.

Ghose, M. N. *Memoirs of Kali Prosanna Singh*. Calcutta: Barendra Library, 1920.

———. *Sekaler Lok* (The People of Those Days). Calcutta: Gurudas Chatterji & Sons, 1939.

Ghose, P. R. *Unabingsha Satabdite Bangalir Manan o Sahitya* (Nineteenth-Century Bengali Mind and Literature). Calcutta: Paran Press, 1968.

Gordon, L. A. *Bengal: the Nationalist Movement, 1876-1940*. New York: Columbia University Press, 1974.

Goswami, B. K. *Brahmo Samajer Bartaman Abastha Ebong Amar Jibane Brahmo Samajer Parikkhita Bisay* (The Present Condition of the Brahmo Samaj and Brahmo Experiments in My Life). Calcutta: Sadharan Brahmo Samaj, 1882.

———. *The Indian Prophet or a Review of Babu K. C. Sen's 'Am I an Inspired Prophet?'* Dacca: New Press, 1879.

Greenberger, A. J. *British Image of India: A Study in the Literature of Imperialism, 1880-1960*. London: Oxford University Press, 1969.

Griswold, H. D. *Insights into Modern Hinduism*. New York: Henry Holt, 1934.

Guha-Thakurta, P. *The Bengali Drama: Its Origin and Development*. London: Kegan Paul, Trench, Trubner, 1930.

Gupta, A. N. *Shakyamuni Charit o Nirban Tattva* (The Life of Buddha and the Truth of Nirvana). 4th ed. Calcutta: Naba-bidhan Publications, 1957.

Gupta, B. B. *Puraton Prasanga* (Old Reminiscences). 2nd ed. Calcutta: Bidya Bharati, 1968.

Gupta, N. *Reflection and Reminiscences*. Patna: Hindi Kitab, 1947.

Gupta, R. K. *Kumari Mary Karpentarer Jiban-Charit* (Miss Mary Carpenter's Biography). Calcutta: Sadharan Brahmo Samaj, 1882.

Haldar, H. *Essays in Philosophy*. Calcutta: Calcutta University Press, 1920.

———. *Hegelianism and Human Personality*. Calcutta: Calcutta University Press, 1910.

———. *Tantras: Their Philosophy and Occult Secrets*. 3rd ed. Calcutta: Oriental Publishing, 1956.

———. *Two Essays on General Philosophy and Ethics*. 2nd ed. Calcutta: S. C. Gupta, 1910.

Hamlet, Reverend G. *The Contribution of Keshab Chunder to Modern Christian Thought*. n.p., 1919.

Hay, S. N. *Asian Ideas of East and West: Tagore and His Critics*. Cambridge: Harvard University Press, 1970.

Heimsath, C. H. *Indian Nationalism and Hindu Social Reform*. Princeton: Princeton University Press, 1964.

Home, A. *Purushottam Rabindranath* (The Great Rabindranath). Calcutta: M. C. Sarkar & Sons, n.d.

Hunter, W. W. *Imperial Gazetteer of India*. London: Trubner, 1886.

In Memorium—Karmayogi Nandalal Sen. Karachi: Naba-bidhan Brahmo Mandir, 1926.

Isherwood, C. *Ramakrishna and His Disciples*. Calcutta: Advaita Ashram, 1965.

Jones, K. W. *Arya Dharm: Hindu Consciousness in 19th Century Punjab*. Berkeley and Los Angeles: University of California Press, 1976.

Kar, B. *Ambica Charan Sener Jiban Brittanta* (Biography of Ambica Charan Sen). Calcutta: Bengal Printing Works, 1921.

———. *Bhakta Nagendra Nath Chattopadhyayer Jiban Brittanta* (Biography of Devotee Nagendra Nath Chatterji). Dacca: Purba Bangal Brahmo Samaj, 1932.

Kathia Babaji, Das Dhananjay Maharaj. *Sri Santadas Kathia Babaji Maharajer Jiban-Charit* (Biography of Santadas Kathia Babaji). 2 vols. Brindaban: Kathia Babaka Sthan, 1963.

Keshub Chandra Sen's Nine Letters on Educational Measures to Rt. Hon'ble Lord Northbrook, 1872. Calcutta: Naba-bidhan, 1872.

Keshub Chandra o Sekaler Samaj (Keshub Chandra and the Society of the Time). Vol. 2. Edited by J. Gupta. Calcutta: the editor, 1949.

Keshub Chunder Sen: Lectures & Tracts. Edited by S. D. Collet. London: Straham & Co, 1870.

Kling, B. B. *Partner in Empire: Dwarkanath Tagore and the Age of Enterprise in Eastern India*. Berkeley and Los Angeles: University of California Press, 1976.

Koar, J. *Naba Vrindaban* (New Brindaban, in the sense of New Jerusalem). Sind Naba-bidhan Mission, n.d.

Koch Beharadhipati Shriman Maharaja Sir Nripendra Narayan Bhupa Baha-

durer Punya Smriti (In Fond Memory of Cooch Behar King Sir Nripendra Bhupa Bahadur). Cooch Behar, 1930.

Kopf, D. *British Orientalism and the Bengal Renaissance.* Berkeley and Los Angeles: University of California Press, 1969.

Koran Sharif (Holy Koran). 4th ed. Translated into Bengali by G. C. Sen. Calcutta: Naba-bidhan Publication Committee, 1936.

Kripalani, K. *Tagore. A Life.* New Delhi: the author, 1971.

Lavan, S. *Unitarians and India: A Study in Encounter and Response.* Boston: Beacon Press, 1977.

Leonard, G. S. *A History of the Brahmo Samaj.* Calcutta: Haripada Mukherjee, 1879.

Letters of Swami Vivekananda. 2nd ed. Calcutta: Advaita Ashram, 1964.

Lethbridge, R. *Ramtanu Lahiri: Brahmin and Reformer.* Calcutta: S. K. Lahiri & Co., 1927.

Life and Teachings of Pandit Sitanath Tattva-bhusan. Calcutta: Sitanath Birth Centenary, 1960.

Life of Girish Chunder Ghose. Edited by M. N. Ghose. Calcutta: R. Cambray, 1911.

Lillinyston, F. *The Brahmo Samaj and the Arya Samaj.* London: Macmillan, 1901.

Longbridge, G. *A History of the Oxford Mission in Calcutta.* Oxford: A. R. Moulray, 1910.

Lushington, C. *The History, Design and Present State of the Religious, Benevolent, and Charitable Institutions Founded by the British in Calcutta.* Calcutta: Hindoostanee Press, 1824.

Macpherson, G. *Life of Lal Behari Day.* Edinburgh: T & T Clark, 1900.

Mahalanobis, P. *Keno Rabindra Nath ke Cai* (Why We Want Rabindranath; for private circulation only) N.p.: the author, n.d.

Maharshi Debendranath Tagorerer Jiban Charit (Debendranath Tagore's Autobiography). Edited by B. Dutt. Calcutta: Brahmo Mission Press, 1915.

Majumdar, B. B. *History of Political Thought from Rammohan to Dayananda.* Vol. 1. Calcutta: University of Calcutta Press, 1934.

———. *Militant Nationalism in India and Its Socio-Religious Background.* Calcutta: General Printers and Publishers, 1966.

Majumdar, L. *Ar Konokhane* (And Elsewhere). 4th reprint. Calcutta: Mitra & Ghose, 1969.

———. *Sukumar Ray.* Calcutta: Mitra & Ghosh, 1969.

Majumdar, M. *Bangalar Nabayug* (Bengali Renaissance). New ed. Calcutta: Indian Association Publishing, 1957.

Majumdar, R. C.; A. K. Majumdar; and D. K. Ghosh. *British Paramountcy and Indian Renaissance.* Bombay: Bharatiya Vidya Bhavan, 1965.

Martinieu, J. *The Three Stages of Unitarian Theology.* London: Essex Hall, 1869.

Mazoomdar, P. C. *Aids to Moral Character.* 2nd ed. Calcutta: S. K. Lahiri, 1900.

———. *Faith and Progress of the Brahmo Samaj.* Calcutta: Central Press, 1882.

Mazoomdar, P. C. *Heart Beats*. Calcutta: Naba-bidhan Publication Committee, 1935.

———. *The Improvement of Women*. Bombay: Asiatic Press, 1877.

———. *Lectures in America and Other Papers*. Calcutta: Naba-bidhan Publication Committee, 1955.

———. *The Life and Teachings of Keshub Chunder Sen*. Calcutta: Baptist Mission Press, 1887.

———. *Protestantism in India*. Boston: George H. Ellis, 1888.

———. *The Oriental Christ*. Boston: George H. Ellis, 1883.

———. *Simple Religion*. Manchester: Johnson & Rawson, 1874.

———. *Sketches of a Tour around the World*. Calcutta: S. K. Lahiri, 1884.

———. *The Spirit of God*. Boston: George H. Ellis, 1894.

———. *Stri Charita* (Biographies of Women). 3rd ed. Calcutta: Naba-bidhan Publication Committee, 1936.

———. *Will the Brahmo Samaj Last?* Calcutta: Indian Mirror Press, 1880.

———. *World's Religious Debt to India*. Lahore: Punjab Brahmo Samaj, 1894.

McCully, B. T. *English Education and the Origins of Indian Nationalism*. New York: Columbia University Press, 1940.

Mindoch, J. *The Influence of Vedantism in India*. Madras: Christian Literature Society for India, 1903.

Mitchell, M. V. *Hinduism Past and Present*. London: Religious Tract Society, 1897.

Mitra, K. K. *Krishna Kumar Mitrer Atma Charita* (Krishna Kumar Mitra's Autobiography). Calcutta: Bashanti Chakraborty, 1937.

Mohit Chandra Sen: Birth Centenary Publication. Edited by S. K. Chatterji. Calcutta: Naba-bidhan Trust, 1969.

Mukherjee, A. *Reform and Regeneration in Bengal*. Calcutta: Rabindra Bharati University, 1968.

Mukhopadhyay, H. *Shrijukta Nishikanta Chattopadhyay Samkhipto Jibani* (Brief Biography of Nishikanta Chatterji). Dacca: Ganderia Press, 1902.

Müller, F. M. *Auld Lang Syne and My Indian Friends*. 2 vols. London: Longmans, Green, 1899.

———. *Biographical Essays*. New York: Charles Scribner's Sons, 1884.

Mullick, P. *History of the Vaisyas of Bengal*. Calcutta: n.p., 1902.

Nabakanta Chattopadhyay. Calcutta: Nalinikanta Chattopadhyay, 1922.

Nehru, J. *The Discovery of India*. Edited by R. I. Crane. New York: Anchor Books, 1960.

Niyogi, N. *Rishi Protap Chandra* (The Wise P. C. Mazumdar). Calcutta: Art Press, 1936.

———. *Sadhan o Seba* (Meditation and Service). Calcutta: the author, 1963.

———. *Smritir Gaurab—Smritir Saurab* (Proud Reminiscences—Fragrance of Memories). Calcutta: Dibyanjan Niyogy, 1969.

O'Neill, S. W. *Brahmoism—Is It for or against Christianity?* Calcutta: Oxford Mission Press, 1881.

Pal, B. C. *The Brahmo Samaj and the Battle of Swaraj in India*. Calcutta: Brahmo Mission Press, 1926.

———. *Brahmo Samaj: Hindu Church of the Divine Unity*. Calcutta: Brahmo Mission Press, 1956.

———. *An Introduction to the Study of Hinduism: A Study in Comparative Religion*. Calcutta: S. C. Ghose, 1908.

———. *Bengal Baishnavism*. Calcutta: Yugayatri Prakashak, 1962.

———. *Charita-Chitra* (Character Sketches). Calcutta: Yugayatri Prokashak, 1958.

———. *Markine Chari-Mash* (Four Months in America). Calcutta: Yugayatri Prokashak, 1955.

———. *Memories of My Life and Times*. 2 vols. Calcutta: Modern Book Agency, 1932.

———. *Naba Yugar Bangla* (Bengal Renaissance). Calcutta: Bipin Chandra Pal Institute, 1964.

———. *The New Spirit*. Calcutta: Sinha, Sarvadhikari & Co., 1907.

———. *The Present Social Reaction: What Does It Mean?* Calcutta: Brahmo Samaj Press, 1889.

———. *Saint Bijoy Krishna Goswami*. Calcutta: Bipin Chandra Pal Institute, 1964.

———. *Soul of India: A Constructive Study of Indian Thoughts and Ideals*. Calcutta: Choudhury & Choudhury, 1911.

Parker, T. *A False and True Revival of Religion*. Boston: William L. Kent, 1858.

———. *Prarthana Mala* (Garland of Prayers). Translated into Bengali by G. C. Majumdar. 1st ed., 1866. Calcutta: Premanjan Majumdar, 1913.

———. *The Public Education of the People*. Boston: William Crosby & H. P. Nichols, 1850.

———. *The Revival of Religion Which We Need*. Boston: William L. Kent, 1858.

———. *Views of Religion*. Boston: American Unitarian Association, 1885.

Pathak, S. M. *American Missionaries and Hinduism*. Delhi: Munshiram Monoharlal, 1967.

Payne, E. A. *The Saktas: An Introductory and Comparative Study*. Calcutta: YMCA Publishing House, 1933.

Perita Kalishankar Das Kabiraj (The Ordained Kalishankar Das). Calcutta: Naba-bidhan Prachar Karyyalaya, 1903.

Pioneer Zenana Missionary of 1856: A Brief Reminiscence of Keshab Chunder Sen. Calcutta: Bidhan Press, 1910.

Poddar, A. *Unabingsha Satabdir Pathik* (Pathfinder of the Nineteenth Century). Calcutta: Indiana, 1955.

Presidency College, Calcutta. *Centenary Volume, 1955*. Alipore, West Bengal: West Bengal Government Press, 1956.

Ramananda Chatterji Birth Centenary Volume. Edited by A. Chatterji. Calcutta: Prabasi Press Private Limited, 1965.

Rajnarian Basur Baktrita (Rajnarian Bose's Lectures). Calcutta: Valmiki Press, 1872.

Ray, P. C. *Life and Experiences of a Bengali Chemist*. Calcutta: Chukervertty, Chatterjee & Co., 1932.

Raychaudhuri, S. *The Religious Life of Sevabrata Brahmarshi Sasipada Bannerjee*. Calcutta: Develaya Association, 1920.

Reminiscences & Anecdotes of Great Men of India. Edited by R. Sanyal. Calcutta: Woomachurn Chukerbutty, 1894.

Reprint of a Controversy between Dr. Tytler and Ram Doss. Calcutta: Tattvabodhini Press, 1845.

Rothermund, D. *The Phases of Indian Nationalism and Other Essays*. Bombay: Nachiketa Publications, 1970.

Roy, B. C. *The Story of My Humble Life*. Dacca: East Bengal Press, 1913.

Roy, D. N. *Atma Katha* (Autobiography). Calcutta: A. Ray, n.d.

Roy, D. S. *The Story of Religious Progress in India*. Calcutta: Naba-bidhan Publication Committee, 1940.

Roy, P. C. *Life and Times of C. R. Das*. Calcutta: Oxford University Press, 1927.

Roy, U. G. *Dharmatattva* (The Truth of Religion). Calcutta: Mangalgunge Mission Press, 1914.

———. *Keshab's Religion of Inspiration*. Translated by J. K. Koar. Bombay: Sind Naba-bidhan Mission Trust, n.d.

———. *Srimad Bhagabad Gita: Samanvay Bhasya* (Interpretive Synthesis of the Bhagabad Gita). Calcutta: Mangalgunge Mission Press, 1900.

———. *Vedanta Samanvay* (Synthesis of Vedanta). Calcutta: Mangalgunge Mission Press, 1912.

Sadhu Promothalal (The Venerable Promothalal Sen). Edited by S. K. Ray. Calcutta: Naba-bidhan Ashram, 1933.

Samayik Patre Banglar Samaj Chitra (Pictures of Bengali Society in the Bengali Press). Edited by B. Ghose, Calcutta: Bikshan Grantha Bhavan, 1963.

Sarala Ray Birth Centenary Volume. Calcutta: Sarala Ray Birth Centenary Committee, 1961.

Sarkar, H. C. *Brahmo Prayer Book*. Calcutta: Sadharan Brahmo Samaj Press, 1922.

———. *Life of Ananda Mohan Bose*. Calcutta: A. C. Sarkar, 1910.

———. *Sivanath Sastri*. Calcutta: Ram Mohan Roy Publication Society, 1929.

———. *Swargiya Braja Sundar Mitra* (Late Braja Sundar Mitra). Dacca: n.p., 1915.

———. *The Religion of the Brahmo Samaj*. 3rd ed. Calcutta: Classic Press, 1931.

Sarkar, S. *Bengal Renaissance and Other Essays*. New Delhi: Peoples' Publishing House, 1970.

Sastri, S. *Atma Charit* (Autobiography). Calcutta: Signet Press, 1952.

———. *Englander Dayeri* (England Diary). Calcutta: Bengal Publishers Private, 1957.

———. *The Brahmo Samaj of India: A Statement of Its Religious Principles and Brief History*. Lahore: Upper India Brahmo Mission, 1915.

————. *Jati Bhed* (Caste Distinction). Reprint. Edited by D. K. Biswas. Calcutta: Sadharan Brahmo Samaj, 1963.

————. *History of the Brahmo Samaj*. 2 vols. Calcutta: R. Chatterjee, 1911.

————. *Maharshi Debendranath o Brahmananda Keshub Chandra* (Debendranath Tagore and Keshub Chandra Sen). Calcutta: Sadhan Ashram, 1910.

————. *Men I Have Seen: Reminiscences of Seven Great Bengalis*. Calcutta: Modern Review Office, 1919.

————. *The New Dispensation and the Sadharan Brahmo Samaj*. Madras: Viyavharatharunjinee Press, 1881.

————. *Ramtanu Lahiri o Tatkalin Banga Samaj* (Ramtanu Lahiri and Contemporary Bengali Society). 2nd ed. Calcutta: New Age Publishers, 1957.

————. *Self-examination*. Calcutta: Sadharan Brahmo Samaj, 1953.

Seal, A. *The Emergence of Indian Nationalism*. Cambridge: At the University Press, 1968.

Seal, B. N. *Comparative Studies in Vaishnavism and Christianity*. Calcutta: Hare Press, n.d.

————. *The Quest Eternal*. Calcutta: Oxford University Press, 1936.

————. *Rammohun Roy: The Universal Man*. Calcutta: Sadharan Brahmo Samaj, 1924.

Sehanabis, C. *Tagore and the World*. Calcutta: Mukund Publishers, 1961.

Selections from the Writings of Grish Chunder Ghosh. Edited by M. Ghosh. Calcutta: Indian Daily News Press, 1922.

Sen, A. *The Brahmo Samaj and National Integration*. Calcutta: Calcutta Brahmo Mission Press, 1962.

————. *Notes on the Bengal Renaissance*. Calcutta: National Book Agency, 1957.

————. *Swargiya Dinanath Sener Jibani o Tatkalin Purba Banga* (The Late Dinanath Sen: His Life Story and Contemporary East Bengal). Calcutta: Brindaban Dhur & Sons, 1948.

Sen, B. *Gita Odhyaon* (Study of the Gita). Calcutta: Naba-bidhan Publication Committee, 1934.

————. *Jibane Brahmo Kripa* (Blessings of Brahmoism in My Life). Calcutta: Premier Works, 1923.

Sen, B. N. *The Intellectual Ideal: Three Lectures on the Vedanta*. 2nd ed. Calcutta: Art Press, 1934.

————. *Lectures and Essays*. Calcutta: Naba-bidhan Trust, 1927.

————. *The Pilgrim: Experiences in Europe and America*. 3rd ed. Calcutta: Naba-bidhan Publication Committee, 1940.

————. *The Problem of Religion in Modern India*. Simla: Himalaya Brahmo Samaj, 1967.

Sen, G. C. *Atma Jiban* (Autobiography). Calcutta: Gupta, Mukherji & Co., 1904.

————. *Mahaparush Mohammed o Tatprobartita Islam Dharma* (The Prophet Mohammed and the Preaching of Islam). Calcutta: Mangalgunge Mission Press, 1917.

Sen, K. C. *Acharyer Prarthana* (Prayers of the Preceptor). Calcutta: Bharatabarsha Brahmo Mandir, 1939.

————. *Book of Pilgrimages: Diaries and Reports of Missionary Expeditions.* Calcutta: Naba-bidhan Publication Committee, 1940.

————. *The Brahmo Samaj: Essays Theological and Ethical.* 2nd ed. Calcutta: Keshub Mission Society, 1885.

————. *The Brahmo Samaj—God Vision in the Nineteenth Century.* Calcutta: Indian Mirror Press, 1880.

————. *The Brahmo Samaj: A Missionary Expedition.* Calcutta: Brahmo Tract Society, 1881.

————. *Conscience and Renunciation.* Calcutta: Naba-bidhan Publication Committee, n.d.

————. *Diary in Ceylon.* Calcutta: Brahmo Society, 1888.

————. *Diary in Madras and Bombay.* Calcutta: Brahmo Society, 1887.

————. *Discourses and Writings.* 2nd ed. Calcutta: Brahmo Society, 1917.

————. *God Vision in the Nineteenth Century.* Vol. 492. *India Office Library Tracts.* Calcutta: Indian Mirror Press, 1880.

————. *India Asks—Who Is Christ?* Calcutta: Indian Mirror Press, 1879.

————. *Jiban Veda* (Life Inspiration). Calcutta: Keshub Mission Society, 1915.

————. *The Liquor Traffic in India.* London: United Kingdom Alliance, 1870.

————. *The New Dispensation.* Calcutta: Brahmo Tract Society 1884.

————. *The New Samhita.* Calcutta: Keshub Mission Society, 1884.

————. *Religion of Love: Love Every Man as Thy Brother.* Calcutta: Brahmo Samaj Press, 1860.

————. *The Reverend S. Dyson's Questions on Brahmoism Answered.* Calcutta: Brahmo Samaj Press, 1861.

————. *We Apostles of the New Dispensation.* Calcutta: Bidhan Press, 1881.

————. *Young Bengal: This Is for You.* Calcutta: Brahmo Samaj Press, 1860.

Sen, P. K. *Biography of a New Faith.* 2 vols. Calcutta: Thacker, Spink, & Co., 1933.

————. *Western Influence on the Bengali Novel.* Calcutta: Calcutta University Press, 1922.

Sen, S. *Jiban Smriti* (Life Memories). Calcutta: Dakhina Sen, 1933.

Sen-Shastri, A. T. *Sib Chandra Deb o Bengalar Unabingsha Satabdi* (Shib Chandra Deb and Nineteenth-Century Bengal). Calcutta: Sadharan Brahmo Samaj, 1970.

Sharma, C. *Naba Vrindaban Orthat Dharma Samanvay Natak* (New Brindaban Play on Religious Synthesis). Calcutta: Bidhan Press, 1884.

————. *Sadhu Aghornather Jiban Charit* (The Holy Aghore Nath's Biography). 3rd reprint. Calcutta: Mangalgunge Mission Press, 1912.

Shastri, S. *Theism as Practical Religion.* Allahabad: Theistic Conference, 1911.

Shinde, V. R. *The Theistic Directory and a Review of the Liberal Religious Thought and Work in the Civilized World.* Bombay: Prarthana Samaj, 1912.

Shri Shriman Maharaja Nripendra Narayan Bhur Bahadur: Swargarohan Dine Shradhanjali (Prince Pripendra Narayan Bhup-Bahadur: Obituary on the Day He Died). N.p., n.d.

Singer, M. *Traditional India: Structure and Change*. Philadelphia: American Folklore Society, 1959.

Singha, P. C. *Upadhyay, Brahmo Bandhab*. Uttapara, West Bengal: Amarendra Nath Chatterji, n.d.

Sinha, P. *Nineteenth Century Bengal: Aspects of Social History*. Calcutta: Firma K. L. Mukhopadhyay, 1965.

Sircar, M. N. *The Life of Peary Churn Sircar*. Calcutta: Cotton Press, 1914.

Slater, T. E. *Keshub Chunder Sen and the Brahmo Samaj*. Madras: Society for Promoting Christian Knowledge, 1884.

Smith, G. *Life of Alexander Duff*. 2 vols. New York: A. C. Armstrong and Son, 1879.

Songs of Tomorrow. Compiled by L. M. Chatterji. Calcutta: Naba-bidhan, 1933.

Sources of Indian Tradition. Edited by T. de Bary. New York: Columbia University Press, 1959.

Studies in the Bengal Renaissance. Edited by A. C. Gupta. Jadvapur, West Bengal: National Council of Education, 1958.

Swami Vivekananda and His Guru with Letters from Prominent Americans. Madras: Christian Literature Society for India, 1897.

Swargiya Umesh Chandra Dutt: Smriti Shraddhanjali (The Late Umesh Chandra Dutt: Memorial Service). Calcutta: A.I.C. Press, 1941.

Tagore, Debendranath. *Acharyer Upadesh* (Sermons of the Preceptor). Calcutta: Adi Brahmo Samaj, 1899.

———. *Atma Jibani* (Autobiography). 4th ed. Edited by S. C. Chakrabarty. Calcutta: Visva Bharati Granthalaya, 1962.

———. *Autobiography of Maharshi Debendranath Tagore*. Translated by S. N. Tagore and I. Devi. London: Macmillan, 1914.

———. *Brahmo Dharma*. Translated by H. C. Sarkar. Calcutta: Brahmo Mission Press, 1928.

———. *Brahmo Dharmer Byakhyan* (Explanation of the Brahmo Religion and Ethics). Calcutta: Adi Brahmo Samaj Press, 1910.

———. *The Brahmo Samaj: Its Position and Prospects*. Bhowanipore: Satyajnan Sancharini Press, 1855.

———. *Kalikata Brahmo Samajer Baktrita* (Lectures of the Calcutta Brahmo Samaj). Calcutta: Presidency Press, 1858.

Tagore, Dwijendranath. *Probandha Mala* (Garland of Essays). Shantineketan: Dinendra Nath Tagore, 1920.

———. *Tattva-Vidya* (Philosophical Learning). Calcutta: Nutan Sonskrita Jantra, 1914.

Tagore, K. N. *Alap* (Dialogue). Calcutta: Harishankar Mukhopadhyay, 1910.

———. *Brahmo Dharma o Swadhinata* (Brahmoism and the Independence Movement). Calcutta: Brahmo Samaj Press, 1926.

Tagore, K. N. *Brahmo Samaj ke Raksha Koritei Hobe* (The Brahmo Samaj Must Be Preserved). Calcutta: Adi Brahmo Samaj Press, 1931.

———. *Dwarkanath Thakurer Jibani* (Biography of Dwarkanath Tagore). Calcutta: Rabindra Bharati Bisha Bidyalaya, 1969.

———. *Kheyal* (Whims). Calcutta: Adi Brahmo Samaj Press, 1929.

———. *The New Dispensation—Is It Brahmoism?* Calcutta: Adi Brahmo Samaj Press, n.d.

———. *Swarbojonin Brahmotswave Shabhapotir Abhibashan* (Address of the President to the All-Brahmo Conference). Calcutta: Adi Brahmo Samaj, 1929.

Tagore, Rabindranath. *Gitanjali*. London: Macmillan, 1967.

———. *Gora*. London: Macmillan, 1924.

———. *The Home and the World*. Translated by S. N. Tagore. London: Macmillan, 1967.

———. *Letters from Russia*. Translated by S. Sinha. Calcutta: Visva-Bharati, 1960.

———. *Nationalism*. London: Macmillan, 1950.

———. *Rachanabali* (Collected Works of Rabindranath). Centenary Edition. Calcutta: Paschim Banga Sarkar, 1961.

———. *Religion of Man*. London: George Allen & Unwin, 1958.

———. *Towards Universal Man*. Calcutta: Asia Publishing House, 1967.

Tagore, Rathindranath. *On the Edges of Time*. Calcutta: Orient Longmans, 1958.

Tagore, S. *Bharater Shilpa Biplab o Rammohan* (Industrial Revolution and Rammohun). Calcutta: Rupa, 1963.

———. *Amar Valya Katha o Amar Bombai Prabash* (My Youth and My Stay in Bombay). Calcutta: Indian Publishing House, 1915.

———. *Rabindranath Tagore and Universal Humanism*. N.p., 1961.

Tattvabhusan, S. *Autobiography*. Calcutta: Brahmo Samaj Press, n.d.

———. *Brahmo Jijnasa* (Inquiry into the Philosophical Basis of Theism). Calcutta: Kuntaline Press, 1916.

———. *Brahmoism: Principles and Practice*. Calcutta: Sadharan Brahmo Samaj, n.d.

———. *Krishna and the Gita*. Calcutta: Brahmo Samaj Mission Press, n.d.

———. *The Philosophy of Brahmoism*. Madras: Higginbotham, 1909.

Thomas, M. M. *The Acknowledged Christ of the Indian Renaissance*. Bangalore: Christian Institute for the Study of Religion and Society, 1970.

Toynbee, A. J. *A Study of History*. Vol. 5. New York: Oxford University Press, 1962.

Tripathi, A. *The Extremist Challenge: India Between 1890-1910*. Calcutta: Orient Longmans, 1967.

———. *Vidyasagar: The Traditional Moderniser*. Calcutta: Orient Longmans, 1974.

Tuckerman, J. *Christian Service to the Poor in Cities*. Boston: Phillip & Evans, 1839.

———. *A Discourse Preached before the Society for Propagating the Gospel*. Cambridge: Hilliard & Metcalfe, 1821.

———. *A Letter on the Principles of Missionary Enterprise*. Boston: Isaac R. Bitts, 1826.

Two Documents Reprinted: Maharshi Devendra Nath Tagore and Keshub Chunder. Edited by J. K. Koar. Calcutta: Peach Cottage, 1935.

Utsab (Festival). *Proceedings of the Brahmo Youth Conference, 1917*. Calcutta: Nirmal Chandra Bandyopadhyay, n.d.

Upadhay, B. *Samaj* (Society). Calcutta: Burman Publishing House, n.d.

Vedantabagish, A. C. *Brahmo Bivaha Dharmashastranushare ki Na* (Are Brahmo Marriages Sanctioned by Religious Scriptures?). Calcutta: Adi Brahmo Samaj Press, 1872.

Vidyaratna, R. *Udasin Shatyashrobar Assam Bhramon* (Travel through Assam by a Wondering Monk). N.p., 1880.

Visva-Bharati and Its Institutions. Santiniketan, West Bengal: Visva-Bharati Press, 1961.

Wadud, K. A. *Bangalar Jagaron* (Bengal Renaissance). Calcutta: Visva-Bharati, 1957.

Woodroffe, J. *Sakti and Sakto*. 2nd ed. London: Luzac, 1920.

Weber, M. *The Protestant Ethic and the Spirit of Capitalism*. Translated by T. Parsons. New York: Charles Scribner's Sons, 1958.

West Bengal and Bangladesh Perspectives from 1972. Edited by S. Lavan and B. Thomas. East Lansing: Michigan State University, 1973.

Index

Adam, William, as Unitarian convert, 12

Adi Brahmo Samaj: opposes Brahmo Marriage Act, 103, 104; indigenous modernization of, 218

Age of Consent controversy, Brahmo support of, 126-127

Aiken, Lucy, on Rammohun Roy and American Unitarians, 4

Akroyd, Annette: Unitarian background of, 34-35; predisposed to Brahmo ideals on women, 35; meets Keshub in London, 35; arrival in Calcutta, 35; breaks with Keshub on women's education, 36; disappointed with Keshub's wife, 37; marries Lord Beveridge, 38

alcoholism in London and Calcutta, 17

Amhedabad, Brahmo Samaj in, 322

Andhra Pradesh, Brahmo Samaj in, 330

Anglicist-Orientalist controversy, 10

Arya Samaj, 218; Brahmo Samaj and origins of, 321; overshadows Brahmo Samaj in Punjab, 331

Assam, Brahmo Samaj in, 329, 330

avatar issue, Keshub and, 225-226

babu: applied to Monomohun Ghose, 97; held in low esteem by British imperialists, 198-200

Ballantyne, J. R., on the juxtaposition of Western and Eastern learning, 56

Banerji, Surendra Nath: background and British education of, 137; dismissed from service, 137; emerges as a nationalist, 138; as a spokesman of Indian Association, 145; despised as a moderate, 203

Bangal, as term of derision for rustic youth of East Bengal, 101

Bangalore, Brahmo Samaj in, 322-324, 330

Banga Mohila Vidalay, first women's liberal arts college in India, 38-39

Bannerji, Kali Charan, Christian uncle of Brahmobandhab Upadhyay, 201

Bannerji, Krishna Mohun: as major convert of Alexander Duff, 160; attacks Rammohun's interpretation of Upanishads, 161; Christian background of, 170; Christian ideology of, 170-172; accuses Brahmos of being denationalized, 172; partial to the West in the scholarship of, 172-173

Bannerji, Sasipada: identity crisis of, 120; works among industrial proletariat, 120; early life and Brahmo conversion of, 120-121; establishes Brahmo structure for jute workers, 120-123; takes wife to England, 121; explains moral rationale for work among poor, 121; starts earliest journal devoted to industrial worker, 122-123; universalist ideology of, 381 n 9

Barrows, John Henry, visits Protap Chandra Majumdar in Calcutta, 23

Basu, Hari Sundar: life and career of, 233; as a Brahmo in Bihar, 234

Bedford College, Unitarian institution in England awarding degrees to women, 35

Bengal Chemical and Pharmaceutical Works, as a Brahmo business, 75. *See also* Ray, Prafulla Chandra

Bengal renaissance: theory on termination of, 88; politicized, 129

Bengali character: viewed as all talk and no action, 36; viewed as deficient in entrepreneurial spirit, 88-89; assailed by puritanical Brahmos for lack of morality and discipline, 193-194

Bengali intelligentsia: as humanists, 44; as modernizers, 46-47; and British colonialism, 86; and British liberalism, 86; as intellectual proletariat, 89. *See also* Brahmo intelligentsia

Bengali language, Rajnarian Bose's apology for, 180

Bengalis outside Bengal (*prabasi*): challenged by non-Bengali elites, 200-201; reached by Brahmo mission, 319-320

Bentinck, Lord, supports Macaulay, 158

Bethune College: merged with Brahmo women's college, 39; awards B.A. degrees to its women graduates, 40-41; Brahmo women are majority of students in, 127. *See also* Banga Mohila Vidyalay

Bethune School, as early experiment in educating Bengali girls, 34

Beveridge, W. H. (Lord): on Bengali character, 36; on Keshub, 38

bhadralok: in the Brahmo Samaj, xiv; defined, 87; as Bengali Brahmans, Vaidyas, and Kayasthas, 87, 89; spirit along modernist and nationalist lines, 187; educated unemployed among, 200. *See also* Brahmo elite

bhadralok frustration, 95; and revolutionary nationalism, 188; cases of, 195-196; in achieving qualification and recognition in professions, 198-199; in covenanted civil service, 200

bhakti: Brahmo appropriation of, 218; introduced into Brahmo songs, 223. *See also* Goswami, Bijoy Krishna; Sanyal sangit

Bharat Ashram: liberal Brahmo family expelled from, 38; as refuge for persecuted, 96; established by Keshub, 105

Bihar, Brahmo Samaj in, 234

Bombay, Brahmo Samaj in, 321-322

Bonnerji, W. C., 137

Bose, Amrita Lal, in charge of building and maintaining Keshubite mandir, 239

Bose, Ananda Mohun: persecuted for becoming Brahmo, 100; early background and education of, 108-109; puritanism of, 109; as brilliant student in Presidency College and Cambridge, 109, 137; as Brahmo politician, 130; starts career as barrister, 137; seeks representative government in Brahmo Samaj, 137-138, 140-142; as most powerful leader in Sadharan Brahmo Samaj, 142-144; final assessment of, 145-146; is held in low esteem by revolutionaries, 203

Bose, Bhagaban Chandra: professional career of, 69; Jessie Bose's father, 69, 70

Bose, Jessie Chandra (Jagadish): first impulse to become scientist, 69; early life and education of, 69, 70; at Cambridge University, 70; joins faculty at Presidency College, 70; discriminated against for his race, 70; marries Abala Das, 70; scientific career and inventions of, 70-73

Bose, Kasambini: first to receive B.A. degree from Bethune College, 40; education and career of Brahmo woman physician, 125; becomes Mrs. Dwarkanath Ganguli, 125; defamed by orthodox Hindu man for being Brahmo woman, 126

Bose, Mohendranath: Christian leanings and Brahmo conversion of, 239, 240; studies Guru Nanak for Keshub, 240; as Brahmo missionary in West India, 240

Bose, Mohin Mohun, 109

Bose, Mukhi, first Christian woman to receive B.A. degree from Bethune College, 40

Bose, Nanda Kishore, father of Rajnarian, 167

Bose, Rajnarian: on the science of religion, 67-68; opposes Brahmo Marriage Act, 104; as grandfather of Indian nationalism, 167; early background of, 167; Anglicized education of, 167; antithetical to Westernized Bengalis, 167; earliest nationalist sermon by, 167-168; in defense of Bengali language, 168; collaborates with Debendranath Tagore in defense of Vedanta, 169-170; as a devastating critic of Christianity, 173-175; unhappy when Vedanta abandoned as Brahmo revealed source, 175; leaves Calcutta for Midnapur, 175; succeeds Debendranath as president of Adi

Brahmo Samaj, 179; issues prospectus to start nationalist society, 179-180; on the superiority of Hinduism, 181-182; recollects harsh discipline at Hare School, 191-192; and Young Bengal background, 192; addicted to alcohol, 192; identity crisis of, 192; becomes a Brahmo, 192-193; repudiates his Young Bengal past, 193; stresses physical strength in nation building, 202

Brahmans, as part of bhadralok, 87

Brahmo asceticism, 211

Brahmo Bhasa, as ghetto of the emancipated in Bengali towns, 102

Brahmo constitutionalists: importance and legacy of, 131; English legal training and, 136-137; revolt against Keshub's paternalistic rule, 138-141. See also Sadharan Brahmo Sumaj

Brahmo elitism, defined, 87. See also bhadralok

Brahmo ethic: decline of, 88, 105; makes heroes of bhadralok progressives, 102; first codified by Debendranath Tagore, 105-107; journalistic evidence of, 107-108; as work ethic, 108; codified by Keshub for New Dispensation, 108; deeply motivates P. C. Ray, 110; illustrated by Lord Sinha's life and career, 110-111; and compassion for underpriviledged, 114-117; modified to reach peasants and workers, 118-119, 121. See also Brahmo puritan

Brahmo factionalism: and formation of Samadarshi group against Keshub, 38; in Tattvabodhini Sabha, 57-58; in opposition to Brahmo ideals, 131; deplored by Keshub, 264; in New Dispensation, 284-286; contributes to birth of Sadharan Brahmo Samaj, 138-142; attacked by Rabindranath, 300, 302; in Dacca, 333. See also Brahmo schism

Brahmo Girls' School, high rating of, 127

Brahmo intelligentsia: identity crisis of, xiii-xiv; non-Western educated among, xvi; choose Vedanta as Bible of Hindu reform, 157. See also Bengali intelligentsia

Brahmo Marriage Act, 103-105

Brahmo medical practitioners, 111-114

Brahmo mission: in East Bengal, 99, 100, 224-227, 318-319; and saintly ethic of Durbar, 228; question of salaries for, 228, 229; reaches out among non-Western educated, 228, 229; under Debendranath, 318; and Keshub, 318-320; utilizes railway system, 319; and P. C. Mazumdar, 319-323; and Bengalis outside Bengal, 319-320; in Lahore, 320, 331; in Bombay, 320; in Punjab, 320-321, 331; in Madras, 320, 323; in Poona, 322; in Gujarat, 322; in Surat, 322; in Amhedabad, 322; in Mangalore, 322-323; in Bangalore, 322-324, 330; and interregional marital alliances, 324, 327-329, 331; in Cooch Behar, 328, 329; in Assam, 329, 330; and Sadharan Samaj, 329-333; in Andhra Pradesh, 330; in Orissa, 330-331

Brahmo Mission Office, 229

Brahmo Niketan, as a refuge for Brahmo youth, 80, 98

Brahmo philosophers: characteristics of, 76; and the Vedantic tradition, 78

Brahmo Protestantism, as viewed by Nirad Chaudhuri, 88. See also Brahmo ethic

Brahmo puritan: Heramba Maitra as model of, 149-150; and lack of entrepreneurial spirit in Bengal, 193-195. See also Brahmo ethic

Brahmos: and Indian modernization, xiii; political consciousness of, xv; persecuted in East Bengal, 97-101; adult personality of, 114; Calcutta and Dacca congregations of, 333

Brahmo Sabha: origins of, 15; Trust Deed of, 15; responds to Westernization, 158

Brahmo Samaj: as modernizers, xiii; as bhadralok, xiv; and schism of 1866, xv, 132-136; important events in history of, xxi-xxiii; origins and early principles of, 15, 163-164; as movement for workers and peasants, 18;

Brahmo Samaj (*cont.*)
  and divisive issue of female emancipation, 31-41; schools in Calcutta, 45; opposed by Dharma Rakhini Sabha, 99; appeals to persecuted youth, 107; universalist aspects of, 136; defends reformed Hinduism against Christians, 157-158; expansion of, 164-165, 229, 324, 332-333; early zemindar support for, 165; depicted as eclectic religion, 207-208; in Bihar, 234; role of Vaidyas in, 253-254; legacy of, 313-317, 334; displaced by Arya Samaj in Punjab, 331; and Prarthana Samaj, 331-332; and origins of Arya Samaj, 321; final assessment of, 334; and Marxist challenge, 334
Brahmo schism: of 1866, 132-136; of 1878, 138-141. *See also* Brahmo factionalism
Brahmo scholasticism, 48, 83, 240. *See also* Brahmo philosophers
Brahmo scientists: and religion, 44; general characteristics of, 69; and Jessie Bose, 72, 73; and P. C. Ray, 76
Brahmo social reformers, 114, 117-128
Brahmo theology: and religious inspiration among Brahmos, 79; attempts at sythesizing, 79-80; Sitanath Tattvabhusan's contribution to, 80-83
Brahmo universalism, 136, 176-177, 180-181. *See also* New Dispensation; Sen, Keshub Chandra
Brahmo women: as first women delegates to Indian National Congress, 125; defamation of, 125-126; constitute majority of students at Bethune College, 127; educated in the Sadharan Samaj, 127
British imperialism: analysis of, 197-198
British Orientalism: as alternative form of modernization, 10; and the modern Bengali mind, 47. *See also* modernization
Buddhism: and Keshub Chandra Sen, 252; Aghore Nath Gupta's study of, 283-284

Calcutta: as laboratory of intercivilizational encounter, 42-43; viewed as metropolis of sin and corruption, 91-93; violent attack on Bengalis living in, 92; number of Brahmos in, 333
Calcutta Medical College, 49
Calcutta Unitarian Committee, xiii, 7, 12
Carpenter, Lant: and Rammohun Roy, 3, 4; on Rammohun's Unitarian credo, 4; as radical social activist, 6-7; on the new Unitarian theology, 7
Carpenter, Mary: turns to social work as career, 6; visits Calcutta, 16; and Theodore Parker, 29-30; as a social activist, 32-33; and female emancipation in England, 32-33; professionally discriminated against, 33; comes to India to advance women's emancipation, 33-34; recommends women's school for Brahmos, 34; advocates higher education for Brahmo women, 38; last visit to Calcutta, 38; advocates penny banks for Indian workers, 119-120
caste in India: deplored by Sivanath Sastri, 148; attacked by Rabindranath, 298
Chaitanya: reinterpreted by Keshub for Brahmo Samaj, 226; as Bengali savior, 260
Chakrabarti, Ajit: discusses Hindu Brahmoism, 303, 304
Chakrabarti, Nilmani: as Brahmo missionary in Assam, 329, 330
Channing, William Ellery: as Rammohun Roy of America, 4; radical Unitarian ideas of, 5; Christian Unitarianism of, 8-9; known in Bengal, 16
Chatterji, Nagendra Nath: as Brahmo in Indian Association, 145; at Krishnagar, 241; Brahmo conversion of, 241; enrolled in Brahmo Theological school, 241; family background and early education of, 241; Brahmo activities of, 241, 242-243; joins Indian Association, 242; writes popular biography of Rammohun, 243; writes biography of Theodore Parker, 243; as Brahmo missionary, 243; Vaishnava leanings of, 243

Chatterji, Ramananda: converts Braille into Bengali system, 126; as social reformer, 126, 127; early background and education of, 149; identity crisis of, 159; journalistic career of, 150, 151; as Hindu Brahmo, 150-151; develops idea of creative nationalism, 151-152, 153-154; Swadeshi idea of, 152; advocates mass education, 154; and Rabindranath, 291

Chattopadhyay, Kali Kanta: founds Dharma Rakhini Sabha against Brahmos, 99

Chattopadhyay, Naba Kanta: as Brahmo convert, 99

Chaudhuri, Nirad: on Brahmo Protestantism, 88

Chaudhury, Tara Kishore: background and education of, 246-247; at City College, 247; identity crisis of, 247; as politicized Brahmo, 247; as advocate of Calcutta High Court, 247; defects from Brahmoism, 247; converted to Kartabhaja sect, 247

Chitpavan Brahmans, 320-322

Christ: Rammohun's ethical image of, 12, 14; P. C. Majumdar on, 18, 19-21; Keshub's view of, 177-179, 268-269; Gour Govinda Ray on, 236; and Ramakrishna, 266-267; Keshub on the crucifixion of, 276-277; compared with Krishna, 282-283

Christianity in India: krishna Mohun Bannerji's idea of, 170-172; critiqued by Rajnarian Bose, 173-175; Keshub's contribution to the domestication of, 252

Christian mission in India: identify Brahmos as Unitarians, 23-24; critiqued by Keshub, 177-179, 261; dismal record of, 210

City College, 143, 244-245

Cobbe, Frances, 33

colonialism in India, negative features of, 86

compradore, in Bengali context, 87

Cooch Behar: Brahmo Samaj in, 328, 329; marriage controversy, 324, 327

Croft, Alfred, 70

cultural encounter, India and the West:

historical context of, 9-10; Brahmo ideology of, 250-251, 381 n 9; Keshub Chandra Sen's harmonizing ideology of, 274-276, 279-281; Rabindranath on, 298, 308, 309

Dacca: number of Brahmos in, 333; Brahmo factionalism in, 333

Dacca Brahmo Samaj, mandir of , 224-225

Dall, Charles (Reverend): arrives in Calcutta, 15; as social reformer, 16; first meeting between Debendranath and, 16; sees Keshub as Rammohun's successor, 16, 252; admitted into Brahmo Samaj by Keshub, 16; influences P. C. Majumdar, 19; assists Brahmos with theological school, 24; rebukes Keshub for abandoning social reform, 25-26; on the need for Brahmo theology, 79-80; as missionary in Bangalore, 323-324

Das Ashram, 126

Das, Durga Mohun: breaks with Keshub on purdah issue, 35-36; persecuted as a Brahmo, 101; and Sadharan Brahmo Samaj, 143, 144

Das Kalisankar: early life and career of, 232-233; leans to Vaishnavism, 233; as a Brahmo in Durbar, 233

Datta, Sasibhusan, 105

Datta, Sudhindranath: on achievement-oriented Brahmos, 87-88; on British contempt for Bengalis, 199-200

Dayal Singh College, 331

De, Lal Behari: refused admission in Hare School, 44; as convert of Alexander Duff, 160; on Brahmoism and Christianity, 164

Deb Radhakant, 166

Deb, Sib Chandra, 27

Debi, Suniti, married to Cooch Behar raja, 324, 327

Derozio, Henry, 43

Dharma Rakhini Sabha, 99

Dharma Sabha, 158

Doss, Ram, 12

Duff, Alexander: as a teacher, 45-46; greeted in Calcutta by Rammohun,

Duff, Alexander (*cont.*)
46; background of, 159; as a Christian
missionary in Calcutta, 159-160; Bengali converts of, 160; launches attack
on vedanta, 164

Duff's School, 45

Durbar: established by Keshub in New
Dispensation, 227, 228; saintly ethic
and social service of, 227, 228;
Keshub's reasons for founding, 229;
general description of, 229-231. *See
also* New Dispensation

Dutt, Akkhoy Kumar: education of, 49;
as pioneer of science and rationalism
in Bengal, 49; joins Tattvabodhini
Sabha, 49; Brahmo activities of, 49; as
a leading Bengali journalist, 49-50;
deistic philosophy of, 50; convinces
Debendranath to abandon Vedanta as
revealed source, 50-51; and the science of religion, 51; social thought of,
51-54; on the Bengali family, 52-54;
on the need to emancipate women in
Bengal, 53-54, 117; thirst for knowledge by, 54; and his dismal view of
Calcutta, 91-92; and his compassion
for peasantry, 117-118

Dutt, Michael Madhusudan, 160

Dutt, Umesh Chandra: background and
early education of, 254; Brahmo conversion of, 243-244; Brahmo activities
of, 244, 245; as principal of City College, 245; as Brahmo official, 245;
Vaishnava leanings of, 245, 246; as a
Unitarian, 246

Dyson, Christopher, 24, 175, 258

Emerson, Ralph Waldo, known in Bengal, 16

English language, important in Bengal,
158-159

Erikson, Eric: and idea of human development, xv; on identity crisis, 89-90;
as a psychohistorian, 90-91; and idea
of adult personality applied to Bengali Brahmos, 114

Franklin, Benjamin: Keshub's
puritanism and, 108; as model for
young P. C. Ray, 110

Gandhi, nationalist role of, 129

Ganguli, Dwarkanath: headmaster of
Hindu Mahila Vidyalay, 38; early life,
erratic education of, 123; becomes a
Brahmo, 123-124; joins Samadarshi,
124; as radical on behalf of women's
education, 124; as champion of peasants and coolies, 124, 125; radical
posture in Indian National Congress,
125; wins libel case in defense of his
wife, 126

General Assembly's Institution, 159

Ghose, Buikunthanath, persecuted in
East Bengal, 99-100

Ghose, Monomohun: and Mary Carpenter, 16, 34; and Annette Akroyd,
35; expatriate letters of, 96-97; as
Anglicized Bengali, 97; leaves for
England, 259

Goodwill Fraternity, 255

Gora: as fictional hero by Rabindranath
to depict problem of Hindu identity,
294-297

Goswami, Bijoy Krishna: as source of
Vaishnava influence on Keshub, 94;
compiles eclectic text of prayers for
Keshub, 135-136; saintly ethic of,
219; early life and education of, 219;
Brahmo conversion of, 219-220; and
Debendranath, 220; abandons sacred
thread, 220-221; family relations of,
220-221; Vaishnava-Brahmo synthesis of, 221-222; never writes in English, 222; as follower of Keshub, 222;
as a householder, 222; critical of
Keshub's avatar role, 225-226; as missionary in East Bengal, 225-227; as
founder of Brahmo samaj, 227; resigns from Sadharan Samaj, 227

Goswami, Srijakta, 233

Gupta, Aghore Nath: as Brahmo missionary, 224, 232, 238; early background and education of, 236-237;
Brahmo conversion of, 237; inter-
caste marriage of, 237; writes life of
the Buddha, 283

Gupta, Umma Nath, 239

Haldar, Hiralal: opposes xenophobic
side of nationalism, 152-153; on
Keshub's Saktism, 252

Haldar, Rakhal Das, 30
Hare, David, 44
Hare School: promotes secular rationalism in Calcutta, 44-45; harsh instructional methods at, 191-192; Sivanath Sastri in, 92
Hind Mela, as Tagore-sponsored precursor of Swadeshi movement, 184-185
Hindu Brahmoism (Brahmo Hinduism); Rabindranath's idea of, xii, 299-303; controversy on, 303-304
Hindu Charitable Association, 166
Hindu College, 42, 44
Hindu Mahila Vidalay, 38
Hindu reformation: Rammohun and, 14; social aspect of, 14-15; Vedanta as Bible of, 157
Hindu revivalism, 88, 292
humanism: defined, 43; in Bengal, xv, 43-44

identity crisis: among Brahmos, xiii-xvi, 90-91, 101, 103-105; Erik Erikson's idea of, xiii; in life of Sivanath Sastri, 93, 94; in life of P. C. Majumdar, 95; in life of Sitanath Tattvabhusan, 98; in life of Sasipada Bannerji, 120; in life of Ramananda Chatterji, 149; differs between nationalists and modernists, 187, 188; in life of Debendranath, 190; in life of Rajnarian, 192; in life of Brahmobandhab Upadhyay, 206, 207; in life of Tara Kishore Chaudhury, 247; in life of Keshub, 254
identity problem: among progressive Brahmos, 188-190; in the life of Rabindranath, 290-294; explored in Rabindranath's fictional hero, Gora, 294-297
Indian National Congress, xv, 129
Indian Reform Association, 17, 18, 118, 268
Indigo Rebellion, 117-118
Institute of Brahmo Theology, 80
International Council of Unitarians and Other Liberal Religions, 23
Islam: Keshub's interest in, 252; Girish Chandra Sen as scholar of, 252, 383 n

89; Ramakrishna experiments with, 266

Jesus, see Christ
jute workers of Baranagar, and Brahmo ethic, 120-123

Kartabhaja sect: attracts Brahmo Vaishnava, 227; and Nagendra Nath Chatterji, 243; and Umesh Chandra Dutt, 245; Tara Kishore Chaudhury converted to, 247
Kayasthas, as part of bhadralok, 87
Kulin Brahmans, and Brahmo social reform, 99; and the oppression of women, 123-124

Lahiri, Ramtanu, 241
Lahore: Brahmo Samaj in, 320, 331
Levi, Sylvain, 308
liberalism in Bengal, xv, 147-148
Lilly Cottage, 267-268
Long, James (Reverend), 117

Macaulayism, 158-160. See also modernization; Westernization
Macaulay, Thomas Babington, 158
Madras, Brahmo Samaj in, 320, 323
Mahalanobis, Prasanta, 307
Maine, Henry, 105
Maitra, Heramba Chandra, 149-150
Majumdar, Dinanath, 240
Majumdar, Protap Chandra: influenced by Charles Dall, 18-19; on Rommohun, 19; travels to England and America first time, 19; on the ethical Jesus, 19; defends Brahmoism in letter to Müller, 19-20; on the Oriental Christ, 19-21; and the Parliament of Religions, 21-22; in America, 21-22, 23; well received by American Unitarians, 22-23; Christian leanings of, 23; reflects on world tour, 77; compares Vaishnavas with American blacks, 77; difficult early years of, 94-95; identity crisis of, 95; becomes a Brahmo, 95; on problem of Brahmo identity, 104; ambivalent about Vaishnavism in Brahmo Samaj, 223, 235; on Keshub's identity crisis, 254; on death of Keshub, 284; claims to be Keshub's

Majumdar, Protap Chandra (*cont.*)
successor, 284-285; as a Brahmo missionary, 319-323
Mangalore, Brahmo Samaj in, 322-323
Marshman, Joshua, 11-12
Marx, Karl, possibly influences Keshub,
18
Marxism: and Unitarianism in Bengal,
9; and decline of Brahmo Samaj, 309,
334
mass education for India: championed
by James Long, 117; Brahmo support
of, 119; advocated by Ramananda
Chatterji, 154; dismal British record
of, 154; Keshub's appeal for, 262-
264; compared unfavorably with
Societ example, 310
Mitra, Kanty Chandra, 229
Mitra, Krishna Kumar: education and
early Brahmo career of, 100-101;
member of Indian Association, 145
Mitra Nabagopal: defends Adi Brahmo
samaj, 136; as a journalist, 182
modernization: in the nineteenth-
century world, 9-10; in India, 10, 40,
158-159, 218, 221-222, 252-253,
313-317, 328-329. *See also* British
Orientalism; Westernization
Monghyr, Keshub proclaimed avatar at,
225
Müller, Max, 19, 135
Myminsingh, Brahmo activities in,
99-101

Nag, Kali Das, 307, 308
Narayan, Nipendra, 327-329
National Mitra. *See* Mitra, Nabagopal
nationalism in India: historiography of,
129-130; differentiated from modernization, 131-132; accelerates in response to British imperialism, 149;
Ramananda Chatterji's idea of, 151-
154; Hiralal Haldar's attack on excesses of, 152-153; Rajnarian as
grandfather of, 167; and the Brahmo
schism of 1866, 176; Rajnarian's idea
of, 179-180; Dwijendranath Tagore's
ideological contribution to, 182-186;
Hindu Mela and, 184-185; identity
crisis associated with, 187, 188; and

virtues of physical strength and
sports, 202; Brahmobandhab Upadhyay's ideological contribution to,
212-213; Rabindranath's critique of,
305-307. *See also* identity crisis
nava sishu, as idea of salvation by
Keshub, 272
New Dispensation (Nava Vidhan): origins of, 268; as synthesis of great religious teachings, 271-272; synthesizes
idea of Christian Eucharist, 272-273;
synthesizes idea of baptism, 273;
modifies idea of Vedic rituals, 273-
274; Roman Catholic view of, 274;
Keshub's justification of, 270, 274-
276; church flag as symbol of, 276;
importance of Motherhood of God in,
277-278; rejects P. C. Majumdar as
Keshub's successor, 284-285. *See also*
Sen, Keshub Chandra
Niyogi, Braj Gopal: early life and education of, 234; as Brahmo in Bihar,
234-235; Vaishnava leanings of,
234-235; as member of Durbar, 235;
tries to heal breach with P. C. Majumdar, 235
Niyogi, Niranjan, 303, 304

Oriental Seminary, 49
Orissa, Brahmo Samaj in, 330-331

Pal, Bipin Chandra: on Theodore
Parker, 31; as disciple of Bijoy
Krishna, 227; as Brahmo missionary,
330
Parker, Theodore: widely read and
deeply appreciated by Bengali
Brahmos, 27, 30-31; Unitarian background of, 27; attacks British elitism,
27-29; as an American radical
thinker, 29; and Mary Carpenter,
29-30; translated into Bengali, 31; as
subject of biography in Bengali, 243
parliamentary process in India, traced
back to Brahmo constitutionalists,
131. *See also* Brahmo constitutionalists
Parliament of Religions, sponsored by
American Unitarians, 20
peasantry in Bengal, 117-119, 124
Penny Banks, 119-120

Piggot, Miss, 34
pilgrimages to the saints, as staged seminars to study world religions, 270-271. *See also* New Dispensation; Sen, Keshub Chandra
Poona, Brahmo Samaj in, 322
Positivism in Bengal, 46
Prarthana Samaj, 320-323, 331-332
Punjab, Brahmo Samaj in, 320-321, 331
Purba Bangla Sabha, 100
purdah, 15, 35-36
Puritan ethic, in Bengal, xv, xvi, 102

Rabindra sangit, Brahmo influence on, 238. *See also* Sanyal sangit
Ramakrishna: uses prostitutes to suppress desire for sex, 222; Brahmos conduct last rites for, 227; and Keshub, 264-265, 267; early background of, 265; starts experiments with religion, 265; tantric experiments of, 265-266; experiments with Islam, 266; experiments with Christianity, 266-267
Ramakrishna Mission, 168, 218
Rao, Madhur, 330-331
rationalism in Bengal, xv, 48
Ray, Fakirdas, 240
Ray, Gour Govinda: on Jesus Christ, 236; life and career of, 235-236; becomes a Brahmo, 236; as Sanskrit scholar, 236; compares Christ with Krishna, 282-283; studies Hinduism for Keshub, 282-283
Ray, Prafulla Chandra: early background of, 74; reveres Theodore Parker, 74; earliest interest in chemistry by, 74; receives doctorate from Edinburgh, 75; discriminated against professionally, 75; as entrepreneur, 75; on the history of Indian chemistry, 75-76; as a Brahmo scientist, 76; on Bengali lack of entrepreneurial spirit, 88-89; as a puritan, 110
Ray, Sarat Chandra, 102
Ray, Sukumar: background and career of, 304; discusses Hindu Brahmoism, 304; as follower of Rabindranath, 307
Roy, Dwarkanath, 112
Roy, Navin Chandra, as Brahmo missionary in Punjab, 320, 321, 331
Roy, Prosanna Kumar: educational background of, 78; distinguished career of, 78; Brahmo philosophy of, 79. *See also* Brahmo philosophers
Roy, Rammohun: charismatic image of, xiii; death of, 3; funeral oration on, 3, 4; in correspondence with American Unitarians, 7-8; and Bengali modification of Western Unitarianism, 11; debates Marshman on Christianity, 12; and William Adam, 12; on the ethical Jesus, 12, 14; in defense of Vedanta, 12-13; on popular religion, 13; influenced by British Orientalism, 10, 14; attacks idolatry, 14; and the oppression of Hindu women, 14-15; establishes Brahmo Sabha, 15; befriends Alexander Duff, 46; updated by Brahmos to combat Christians, 161

Sadharan Brahmo Samaj: origins of, 39, 141-143; defends Bethune College for women, 39-40; constitutional structure of, 142-144; officials of, 143, 144; mission activities of, 329-333; appeals to younger generation, 333. *See also* Brahmo constitutionalists
saintly ethic among Brahmos, xvi, 211, 219, 228
Saktism in Brahmo Samaj, xiv, 251-252, 265-266, 277-278
Samadarshi party, 38
sankirtan becomes standard part of Brahmo service, 223
Sanskrit College, 47, 48
Sanyal sangit: infused with Vaishnava sentiments, 94; as blend of Vaishnavism and Brahmoism, 238-239; for New Dispensation, 269, 270
Sanyal, Troilokya Nath: a musician and actor by profession, 238; Vaishnava leanings of, 238; Brahmo conversion of, 238; as composer of Brahmo songs, 238
Sarkar, Hem Chandra, 330
Sastri, Sivanath: deeply influenced by American Unitarians, 26-27; and his role in Brahmo history, 26-27; progressive views of, 31; imbibes

Sastri, Sivanath (*cont.*)
  liberalism from pundits, 59; and his
  youth in Calcutta, 92-93; educational
  background of, 92-94; compelled to
  marry against his will, 93; identity
  crisis of, 93-94; converted to
  Brahmoism, 93, 94; breaks with
  father, 94; Saktism of, 94; founder of
  Sadharan Samaj, 141, 142; as
  spokesman of English liberalism,
  147-148; travels to England, 148; on
  the evils of caste, 148; as a Brahmo
  missionary, 329, 330, 333
sati, 15
science of religion, 67
scientism in Bengal, xv, 48. *See also* Dutt,
  Akkhay Kumar; Vidyasagar
Scottish Church College, 46, 159
Seal, Brajendranath: educational background of, 60; compared with Vidyasagar, 60; and Vivekananda, 60; as
  principal of Victoria College, Cooch
  Behar, 61; attends international conferences, 61; compares Vaishnavism
  with Christianity, 62-63; and task of
  comparative historian, 63; on Rommohun Roy, 63; scientism of, 63;
  career of, 63-64; poeticizes human
  quest for meaning of existence,
  64-66; final statement on science and
  religion by, 66
Seal, Mohendranath, 60
secularism: in Bengal, 44; in the West,
  46
Sen, Benoyendra Nath: as Keshubite
  philosopher of Vedanta, 83; early life
  and education of, 83-84; seeks to wed
  Vedantism with religious inspiration,
  84-85. *See also* Brahmo philosophers
Sen, Girish Chandra: early background
  and education of, 231; fails to learn
  English, 231; on oppression of
  women, 231; early Brahmo influences
  on, 231-232; converted to
  Brahmoism, 232; in Calcutta, 232; as
  Islamic scholar, 252, 281-282, 383 n
  89; looks at Partition of Bengal
  through East Bengali eyes, 282
Sen, Keshub Chandra: pivotal importance of, xvi; meets Mary Carpenter,
  16; befriends Charles Dall, 16; admits

Dall into Brahmo Samaj, 16; founds
Indian Reform Association, 17, 18;
tries to reach workers and peasants,
18; abandons Unitarian social gospel,
24-26; breaks with Dall, 24-26; defends purdah in services, 35-36; debates Annette Akroyd on education
of Begali women, 37; opposes
Bethune College merger, 39; on the
science of religion, 68-69; and
Brahmo Marriage Act, 103-105;
codifies Brahmo ethic for New Dispensation, 108; introduces cheap literature for Bengali masses, 118-119;
as leader of 1866 schism, 132-135; as
target for Brahmo constitutionalists,
138-141; and controversy about marriage of his eldest daughter, 139, 141,
324, 327; accused of building empire
through his family, 139-140; final Adi
Samaj sermon by, 176-177; on Jesus
Christ, 177-179; belittles achievements of Christian missionaries in India, 177-179; on human nature, 178;
influenced by Bijoy Krishna Goswami's Vaishnavism, 222-224;
changes personality as a result of Vaishnavism, 223; as Brahmo missionary
in East Bengal, 224; proclaims himself avatar in Monghyr, 225-226; ap-
propriates Chaitanya as prophet of
Brahmoism, 226, 260; and proliferation of Brahmo Branches, 229;
charismatic image of, 249; Western
views of, 249-250; as viewed by
twentieth-century Brahmos, 250; in
Indian historiography, 250; as all
things to all men, 251-252; influenced
by Buddhism, 252; contributes to Indian Christology, 252; ambivalent
about modern civilization, 252-253;
perennial identity problem of, 253,
254; family background of, 253; as a
college student, 254; first meets Debendranath, 255; and Satyendranath Tagore, 255-256; lives at Tagore household, 257; greatly admired
by Debendranath, 257; as opponent
of Vidyasagar, 257; strives to win over
Young Bengal, 257-258; at
Krishnagar, 258; on Brahmo expan-

sion, 258-259; on the importance of
great men in history, 259-260; on
prophets as saviors of civilization,
260; as viewed by Christian missionaries, 261; in England, 261; on
England's duties to India, 261-262; as
a progressive, 262; on mass education
for India, 262-264; and Ramakrishna,
264-265; conducts seminars on world
religions, 267; purchases Lilly Cottage, 267-268; and origins of New
Dispensation, 268, 270; on Christ as a
prophet, 268-269; and pilgrimages to
the saints, 270-271; on nava sishu,
272; on Vedanta, 272; as a religious
synthesizer, 272-277, 279-280; on the
meaning of the crucifixion, 276-277;
on the Motherhood of God, 277-278;
confesses his spiritual madness, 278-
279; final episodes in the life of, 279-
281; final lecture on East and West,
280-281; influences Rabindranath,
289; as a Brahmo missionary, 318-
320. *See also* New Dispensation

Sen, Mohit Chandra, 84

Sen, Promothalal, 84

Shinde, V. R., 154

Singh, Dayal, 331

Singh, Kali Prosanna: and Brahmo factionalism, 57-58; as a liberal zemindar, 58; influenced by Vidyasagar and
A. K. Dutt, 58

Sinha, Satyendra Prosanna (Lord), as
Brahmo over-achiever, 110-111

Sircar, Hilratan: as colleague of P. C.
Ray, 75; education of, 112-113;
Brahmo ethic of, 113; medical career
of, 113; as entrepreneur, 113

slavery in Assam, 124, 125

Social Reform Association, 147, 332

social reform in Bengal, 114, 117-128

Society for the Improvement of Backward Classes, 128

society for the promotion of national
feeling among educated natives of
Bengal, 179-180

Surat, Brahmo Samaj in, 322

Swadeshi, 89, 113, 152

Swaraj, 149

Tagore, Debendranath: establishes
Brahmo Samaj, 15, 16; suspicious of
Charles Dall, 16; fears influence of
Theodore Parker among Brahmos,
31; befriends A. K. Dutt, 49; abandons Vedanta as Brahmo revealed
source, 50-51; on Brahmo problem of
identity, 103; codifies first official
Brahmo ethic, 105-107; defends conservatives in Adi Samaj against
Keshub, 132, 134, 135; starts
Tattvabodhini Sabha, 161-162; offers
reasons for starting Tattvabodhini
Sabha, 163; praised for organizing
ability, 165-166; collaborates with
Rajnarian in defense of Vedanta,
169-170; early background and education of, 189; identity crisis of, 190;
differs with father on Brahmo concerns, 190-191; and lifetime problem
of identity, 191; befriends Bijoy
Krishna, 220; befriends Aghore Nath
Gupta, 237; befriends Nagendra
Nath Catterji, 241; on importance of
Keshub in Calcutta, 249; first meets
Keshub, 255; viewed as father by
Keshub, 255; welcomes Keshub into
household, 257; Brahmo mission
under, 318

Tagore, Dwarkanath, 12, 162, 190-191

Tagore, Dwijendranath: nationalist
ideology of, 182-186; as nationalist
opponent of Keshub, 259

Tagore, Ganendra Mohun, 160

Tagore, Jyotirindranath, 259, 289, 291

Tagore, Prosanna Kumar, 160

Tagore, Rabindranath: on Hindu
Brahmoism, xiii, xvi, 299-303; on
universal humanism, xvi; deplores
Vaishnava emotionalism, 77-78; and
Brahmobandhab Upadhyay, 212,
294; charismatic image of, 287; meaningful Brahmo background of, 287-
291; Keshub's influences on, 289;
identity problem of, 290-294;
Jyotirindranath Tagore's influences
on, 289, 291; uses fictional hero,
Gora, to explore Hindu identity,
294-297; resolves identity problem
through universal humanism, 298; as
a critic of caste system, 298; and
East-West confrontation, 298;

Tagore, Rabindranath (*cont.*)
Brahmo activities and writings by,
298-303; reactivates Tattvabodhini
Sabha, 299; attacks Brahmo factionalism, 300, 302; importance of
Rammohun to, 302; on Vivekananda,
302-303; critical of emotionalism in
Hinduism, 302-303; as a critic of nationalism, 305-307; surrenders
knighthood, 307; establishes Visva
Bharati, 308-309; and harmonizing
purpose of Visva Bharati, 308, 309; in
Russia, 309-310; enthusiastic about
mass education in Soviet Union, 309,
310; on Soviet totalitarianism, 310;
importance of, 313
Tagore, Satyendranath: leaves for London, 96, 259; background and education of, 255; admires Keshub, 255-
256
Tattvabhusan, Sitanath: Brahmo conversion of, 80; persecuted for being
Brahmo, 80, 98; philosophic development of, 80, 98-99; as Brahmo philosopher and theologian, 80-83; attacks Vaishnavism, 81-82; identity
crisis of, 98. *See also* Brahmo philosophers
Tattvabodhini Sabha: theist-atheist split
within, 58-59; establishment of, 161-
162; early history of, 162-163; reasons for establishment of, 163; success
of, 165-166; Rabindranath reactivates, 299
Trinitarian Christianity, xv, 11-12, 19,
157
Tuckerman, Joseph: meets Rammohun,
4; biographical account of, 6; on the
misery of the industrial poor, 6; advocates Unitarian mission in Calcutta,
7-8

Unitarianism: in Bengal, xv, 9, 11; in
Great Britain, xv, 3, 9; in the United
States, xv, 5-6, 9, 21-23
Unitarian mission in Bengal, 7-8, 15, 16
Universal humanism, 298
Untouchability, Brahmo opposition to,
153, 154
Untouchability Conference, 154

Upadhyay, Brahmobandhab: and desanctification of the West, xiii; family
background and early life of, 201;
early education of, 201-202; stress on
physical strength by, 202; and dismal
view of Brahmo constitutionalists,
203; emphasizes chastity, 203; as a
mediocre student, 203; joins New
Dispensation, 204; admires Keshub,
205-206; as a Brahmo missionary,
206; identity crisis of, 206, 207, 218;
converts to Protestantism, 206; converts to Roman Catholicism, 207; on
the Brahmo Samaj, 207-208; on Vedanta, 208, 209; domesticates Roman
Catholicism, 208, 209; in trouble with
Catholic authorities, 209; analyzes
imperialism, 209, 210-211; on failure
of Christianity in India, 210; returns
to Hindu fold, 210; saintly ethic of,
211; on evils of capitalism, 211; in defense of Brahman caste, 211, 212; on
decline of Hindu golden age, 212;
reaches peak as militant nationalist,
212, 213; at Santineketan, 212-213;
depicted as Hitlerean type, 212-213;
martyred death of, 213; final assessment of, 213-214; and Rabindranath,
294; universalist ideology of, 381 n 9

Vaidyas: as part of bhadralok, 87; im-
portance of in Brahmo Samaj, 253-
254
Vaishnavism in Brahmo Samaj, xiv, 77,
78, 81-82, 94, 218-219, 222-224, 227,
234, 235, 238-240, 251
Vedanta in Brahmo history, 161, 162,
169-170, 272
Vedantic Academy, 167
Vedic Samaj, 320, 322
Victoria College for Women, 127
Vidyabagish: as Rammohun's successor,
15; administers first oath in Brahmo
Samaj, 163
Vidyabhusan, 59, 92, 93
Vidyaratna, Ram Kumar, 124-125
Vidyasagar: and Mary Carpenter, 16;
supports Bethune School, 34; as secu-
lar rationalist, 47; as a student in
Sanskrit College, 48, 54-55; as an in-

digenous modernizer, 55-57; reforms Sanskrit College, 55; favors modern learning from the West in curriculum, 56; educational philosophy of, 56; and the emancipation of Hindu women, 56-57; and Widow Remarriage Act, 57; in the Tattvabodhini Sabha, 57; forced out of Tattvabodhini Sabha, 58-59; liberal puneit circle around, 59; final years of, 59; as opponent of Keshub, 257

Visva Bharati, 308-309

Vivekanananda: and Brajendranath Seal, 60; early background and education of, 204; and Brahmobandhab Upadhyay, 204; emphasizes physical development and chastity, 204, 205; as a Brahmo, 204, 205; meets Ramakrishna, 205; post-Brahmo career of, 205; a contemporary Brahmo's assessment of, 206; saintly ethic of, 211; Rabindranath's evaluation of, 302-303; universalist ideology of, 381 n 9

Ware, Henry, 8

Weber, Max, and Puritan ethic in Bengali context, 102

Westernization in India, 10, 40. *See also* Macaulayism; modernization

Western philosophers read by Young Bengal, 43

Widow Remarriage Act, 57

Wilson, Horace H., 47

women in Bengal: oppression of, 14-15, 123-124; educational progress of, 36-41; A. K. Dutt on the emancipation of, 53-54; Vidyasagar on the emancipation of, 56-57; prostitution among, 92

women in England, oppression of, 32-33

workers in Bengal, 120, 122-123

Young Bengal, 43, 158-160, 165, 166, 257-258

zemindars and Brahmo Samaj, 165

Library of Congress Cataloging in Publication Data

Kopf, David.
   The Brahmo Samaj and the shaping of the
modern Indian mind.

   Bibliography: p.
   Includes index.
   1. India—Intellectual life.   2. Intellectuals—
Bengal.   3. Bengal—Intellectual life.   4. Brahma-
samaj.   I. Title.
DS428.K66   954.03   78-70303
ISBN 0-691-03125-8